That Knock at the Door

at the

The History of Gold Star Mothers in America

by Holly S. Fenelon

iUniverse, Inc.
Bloomington

" *To be killed in a war is not the worst that can happen.*

To be lost is not the worst.

To be forgotten is the worst."

—Pierre Claeyssens

Table of Contents

That Knock at the Door

DOZENS OF GOLD STAR MOTHERS across the nation shared their stories and memories with me as I researched this book. During those interviews, I heard one phrase so often that I began to anticipate hearing it from each mother with whom I spoke. That phrase was "until I got that knock at the door."

It was not the knock of a military attaché bringing news of a loved one's death that these mothers remembered so clearly. Instead, it was a gold star mother's knock at the door, a member of American Gold Star Mothers, Inc., and most often a stranger, who came to offer support and understanding to a family experiencing what hers had already known. The mothers' recollections often sounded like this:

> I didn't even know what gold star mothers were until I got that knock at the door. She came in and spoke with us. She understood what we were going through. I cried on her shoulder for hours, but we laughed together too after those first few horrible days were over. I don't know how I would have made it without her. She is my dearest friend now.

Variations on this theme were repeated time and time again in the interviews. That knock at the door is symbolic of all the doors that the members of American Gold Star Mothers, Inc., have knocked upon over the years as they devoted themselves to service in the memory of those they lost. They have knocked at the doors of other gold star mothers; of veterans in need and their families; of Congress and the White House; of veterans' hospitals and care facilities; and at the door of American history. In each of these places, they entered and made a difference.

—Holly S. Fenelon, 2012

Dedicated to
America's Gold Star Mothers—
They gave that which was
most dear to them
to keep our nation free.
—— and ——
Rear Admiral
John J. Higginson, U.S.N. (Ret.)
(October 24, 1932–January 12, 2010)
A patriot and an
ever-faithful friend
to
American Gold Star Mothers, Inc.

American Gold Star Mothers, Inc.

National Headquarters
2128 Leroy Place, NW
Washington, DC 2008
202-265-0991

National President

Ruth Stonesifer

Organized June 4, 1928
Incorporated January 5, 1929
Chartered by Congress June 12, 1984
Founded by Grace Darling Seibold

June 25, 2010

It has been an honor to serve as National President as the first comprehensive history of the American Gold Star Mothers is being published after so many years of hard work and research. It must have been serendipity since I have such a reverence for preserving this type of "family" history.

That personal reverence is rooted in the twelve years I devoted to researching my own family tree. I became obsessed with finding the farms they worked, took hundreds of pictures, and discovered the inner workings of historical archives to glean all the tidbits about my heritage.

By all accounts that is just what Holly S. Fenelon has done for this Gold Star Mother's history. I doubt there is a library in the country that escaped being asked for every picture or newspaper article about Gold Star Mothers. Her work was relentless and thorough.

Her wealth of knowledge about our organization has been a great resource for answering the questions posed by the public, the media, and the descendants of our membership researching long lost Gold Star relatives. She has delved into each question with the same enthusiasm she did on day one of this project.

As I learned what it means to be a Gold Star mother after my son Kristofor's death at the onset of Operation Enduring Freedom in 2001, I came to appreciate the legacy left by the women who traveled this path before me. They have bestowed a gift that none of us take lightly. The lessons learned and passed on by the example of lives lived with grace and dignity volunteering for our veterans is both humbling and inspiring.

I thank Holly for this gift of knowledge.

Ruth Stonesifer
Proud Gold Star Mother of
Kristofor T. Stonesifer (KIA 19 Oct. 2001)

Fig. 1-1. A postcard designed for soldiers to send to their loved ones reminded the recipient of the reasons young Americans were serving in the Great War. *(Fenelon Collection)*

CHAPTER 1

The World War and the Gold Star

*Adopt as the national symbol of mourning...
a small gold star of a certain size. What could
be more appropriate or expressive than a Gold
Star, representing as it would earth's most
precious treasure?*

—ALLEN NICHOLSON

FEW AMERICANS RECOGNIZED WHAT THE effect might be on the United States as Europe went to war in 1914. As the editor of a book called *Fulton County in the World War* recalled in 1920, the seemingly distant events in Sarajevo in June 1914 ultimately impacted every aspect of American life:

"That the assassination of Archduke Ferdinand... was an event which would vitally affect the daily life of every citizen of Fulton County [Indiana] would have seemed preposterous had such a prediction been made when the news was flashed around the world on that memorable day.

"That the fanatical youth who slew the royal pair should involve the whole world in war and bring death to over five million men; that his act should have to do with the peace and prosperity of Fulton County; that it should take the best of our young men from the fields, the stores, the factories, and send them beyond the seas to fight and die, if need be; that it should have to do with the food we ate, the clothes we wore, the money we spent or saved; that it should mobilize the thought and energy of practically every mind in Fulton County and bring us to stand united in a single purpose, was wholly unbelievable when the newspapers carried the story of his crime."[1]

President Woodrow Wilson immediately declared a policy of American neutrality regarding the war in Europe. Many young Americans, however, rushed to join the fight. Privileged young men who had studied and traveled abroad joined the Allies, eager to help preserve the cultures they knew so well. Other well-to-do young Americans joined assistance groups such as the Ambulance Corps and Red Cross, where their experience in driving automobiles, not yet commonplace in the nation, was of significant value. Many German immigrants and sons of German immigrant families chose to return and support their fatherland in the war.

Some believed that America could not maintain neutrality for long and would eventually be forced to enter the war. In April 1917, they were proven right when President Wilson asked Congress for a declaration of war.

The Service Flag: A New Symbol of Support for the Military

In 1917, R. L. Queissner of Cleveland, Ohio, wanted to publicly acknowledge the pride he felt for his family members serving in the United States armed forces. A veteran himself—retired captain of a machine gun company of the 5th Ohio Infantry—Mr. Queissner designed and patented what he called a "service flag."

Also known as a "blue star flag" or "service banner," it was constructed of red, white, and blue fabric

Fig. 1-2. The service flag of World War I.

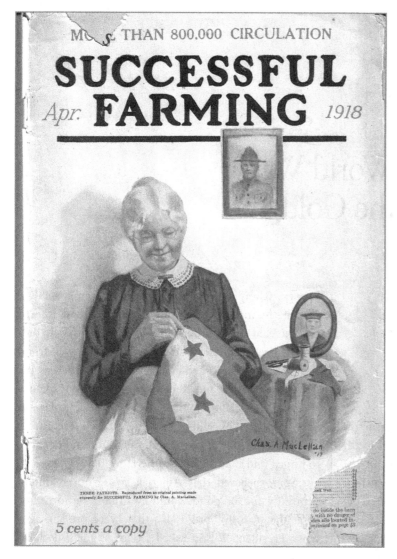

MORE THAN 800,000 CIRCULATION

SUCCESSFUL FARMING

Apr. 1918

THREE PATRIOTS. Reproduced from an original painting made expressly for SUCCESSFUL FARMING by Chas. A. MacLellan.

5 cents a copy

Chas. A. MacLellan

continued on page 43

Fig. 1-3: This 1917 illustration by Charles A. McLellan was used in a variety of formats throughout the war. The title of the painting, "Three Patriots" refers to the photos of the two servicemen and the mother herself. The service or blue star flag she is sewing is typical of those displayed during World War I. *(Fenelon Collection)*

wounded or killed, they should continue to be represented by the blue service star.

"The width of the outer blue margin was to be in proportion to the size of the stars used and of such size as to be visible from the beholder's usual distance, if possible; and hence, should be more than a mere thin edge, if possible. [2]

In the 1919 *World Almanac,* the Army codified the use of the flag as it had been used in the war, although, as the first line of the article explained:

"The service flag is not an official flag of the United States. It has, however, taken such firm root in popular sentiment and been of such beneficial influence that it is officially recognized and everyone who is entitled to fly it is encouraged and urged to do so." [3]

The article carefully and specifically defined who was entitled to be represented on a service flag. For example, members of state militias, reserves, or other similar entities were not entitled to representation until called to active duty. Non-combatants on active duty could be represented since it was "in the best interest of the service" that their contribution to the war effort not be made at the front. Citizens who served in other forms of "patriotic service" such as the YMCA, Selective Service boards, and Red Cross were not eligible although their work was "most necessary and helpful":

"There should be no desire anywhere to minimize its importance and value or to detract in any wise from the credit they should be given…

"Undoubtedly such persons are performing a splendid service, for which they should receive full recognition and appreciation, but such representation would be contrary to the spirit and purpose of the service flag, which was designed to be, and has been accepted by the people of this country as a means of showing our hom-

in a simple rectangle roughly eight by fourteen inches. Made to be displayed in a window, a blue star was sewn in the white center of the flag for each family member serving in the armed services. If the soldier died, either on the battlefield or subsequently as a result of injuries received in the line of duty, a gold star was sewn over the blue star:

"The idea of the gold star is that of the honor and glory accorded the person for his supreme sacrifice in offering up for his country his last full measure of devotion and the pride of the family in it, rather than the sense of personal loss, which would be represented by a mourning symbol, even though white were to be used instead of black.

"[If a soldier was reported as missing,] the presumption is that they have been taken prisoner, unless the circumstances clearly indicate the contrary, and unless authentic information is received that they have been

age to those who have entered the military and naval service in this crisis, our appreciation of the sacrifice they are making and the pride taken therein by members of their families and organizations with which they are affiliated, and a visible token to them and to us that while away in their country's service they are not forgotten by their loved ones at home." [4]

Businesses, clubs, and schools could display service flags under specific circumstances:

"When flown by a business concern, it should represent only members of the firm and employees going directly to the service from such place of business with some continuous relation existing and where there is an expectation of a return to employment. Since the stars should represent only those who are an integral part of the business or organization which flies the flag, the service flag of a building should not contain stars to represent tenants who have gone into service from such building any more than the service flag of a mercantile concern should represent its customers, of a professional concern its clients, or of a hotel its guests. Schools and colleges may properly represent trustees, members of the faculty, graduates and undergraduates." [5]

Homeowners were advised that "domestic servants, roomers, or boarders should not be represented" on the family's service flag, although a husband, father, son, or brother may be properly represented even if he did not reside in the house when he entered the service.

Families with members serving in the Allied forces prior to America's declaration of war were also entitled to display the service flag:

"The use of the service flag is customarily limited to those in the military or naval service of the United States, but no objection is seen to extending the honor of representation thereon to those in the service of our allies, at least where they enlisted before our entrance into the war or were so situated that they could not enter the military service of their own country." [6]

Considering that the women's suffrage movement had not yet succeeded in procuring the right for women to vote, one additional directive regarding the use of the service flag seems particularly enlightened:

"As will be noted, all persons included in the several military forces... enumerated are, without regard to their sex, deemed to be persons in military service, and no good reason is perceived why a woman performing active service in any of the foregoing branches should not be accorded the honor of representation on

the service flag." [7]

In September 1918, the city of New Haven, Connecticut, held a Commemoration Day Parade to mark the anniversary of the departure of a local regiment for duty "over there." Part of the day's festivities included the raising of a service flag with more than 8,000 stars representing the men and women of New Haven who were serving in the armed forces. [8] A month later, another organization raised a service flag that represented 30,000 union members serving in the armed services:

"A service flag for American hoboes will be raised in the Bowery near Manhattan Bridge with appropriate ceremonies,... according to Jeff Davis, known as the king of the hoboes. Davis claims that out of a membership of 507,546 in the Itinerant Workers' union, 30,000 hoboes are with the American army and navy. A single gold star will appear in the center of the flag, Davis announced." [9]

The Congressional Record, referring to the displaying of service flags, stated in 1917:

"The world should know of those who give so much for liberty. The dearest thing in all the world to a mother and father—their children.'[10]

Fig. 1-4: A proud World War I war mother displays her unusual service flag with two blue stars representing her sons.
(Fenelon Collection)

Fig. 1-5: This image of a mother holding a service flag was used for advertising everything from Liberty Bonds to sheet music; the star on the service flag would show as either blue or gold, depending on the intent of the image. *(Fenelon Collection)*

A National Symbol

The practice of displaying a service flag was immediately and overwhelmingly embraced by the American public on a national scale. Manufactured versions of the flags and stars could be purchased in local stores, particularly those of the five and dime variety. In many stores, as a sensitive gesture of respect, the flags and blue stars were displayed with the regular merchandise, but the gold stars were often kept in a drawer, out of sight, and available only on request. Despite the ready availability of the manufactured flags, many families chose to make their own. Although the flags' sizes, colors and workmanship varied, the pride with which they were hung in windows was universal.

The image of service flags quickly began to appear in Liberty Bond advertisements, on magazine covers, in product ads, on jewelry, and in popular music of the day. One Liberty Bond advertisement sponsored by the United States Treasury Department in *Ladies' Home Journal* showed a sweet-faced older woman holding to her cheek a service flag on which one gold star is shown. The heading in a boxed caption reads, "Her Boy":

"My star in my flag, put there for my boy. Love him? Yes, more than I love my own life! Miss him? Why, my heart seems empty save for the ache in it. He finished his great fight—his fight to make his mother safe and to make other mothers of the world safe for all time.

"Yes, my star in my flag, my boy who fought for me. He rests now under the poppies of Flanders' fields, but God gives me strength to look at this gold star and say, 'Not my will, but thine, O God, be done.'"[11]

The same image of a mother holding the service flag was used in many other formats including sheet music. The star on the service flag she held was alternately blue

Fig. 1-7: A brooch incorporating a service flag with a gold star. *(Fenelon Collection)*

Fig. 1-6: Jewelry incorporating an image of a service flag was known as "sweetheart jewelry". This pendant shows a blue star flag. *(Fenelon Collection)*

Mother
Hurrah for the Army man!
Hurrah for the Navy man!
Hurrah for the Mothers
who gave them to win in the name of FREEDOM

Fig. 1-8: A World War I postcard honoring the mothers of the men at war.
(Uncredited; Fenelon Collection)

Fig. 1-9: Citizens of Geneva, New York gather for a ceremony to dedicate a service flag with stars representing every resident of Geneva serving in World War I.
(Postcard: Palmer Publishing, NY, 1918: Fenelon Collection)

or gold, depending on the intent of the image. It was, in every case, a powerful evocation of the spirit of the American mother.

On November 17, 1917, the front cover of *Leslie's Illustrated Weekly Newspaper* pictured a service flag under a headline that read, "Hang Out This Flag." Designed to be cut out and used by the public, it was printed with a single blue star in the center field of white but additional stars were included to be cut out and added, as required.

The service flag image was used to sell products of all types. Known as sweetheart jewelry and intended for both family members and sweethearts, enameled rings, pins, and bracelets based on the service flag design were manufactured and available with any combination of blue and gold stars. For mothers whose sons were serving with the Allies, the flags of Great Britain, France, and the United States could be incorporated in the design with the service flag. Small, embroidered service flag patches were sold to sew on clothing or

Fig. 1-11: Proud parents pose before the family service flag with one of their soldier sons. *(Fenelon Collection)*

Fig. 1-10: A World War I hand-crocheted service flag. *(Fenelon Collection)*

wear as pins. Some came on a printed card with the verse: "If I know I'm not forgotten I'll have less cause to grieve; Won't you wear this little Service Flag on hat, coat or sleeve." Postcards printed with service flag motifs also carried little homilies such as "Faithful to our Country's call, The home where the Service Flag waves. Let's honor it!" and "I'm proud to sign myself a friend to one who displays this flag!"

Popular music of the day described both the image and the spirit of the service flags. In "The Service Flag," a portion of the lyrics are attributed to the flag itself:

> *"Dear little flag in the window there,*
> *Hung with a tear and a woman's prayer...*
> *And now you've come, in this frenzied day,*
> *To speak from a window—to speak and say:*
> *'I am the voice of a soldier son,*
> *Gone, to be gone till the victory's won.*

"DON'T WORRY ABOUT ME"

Fig. 1-12: Postmarked November 7, 1917, a post-card sent to Mrs. Sarah Derbaum, New Kensington, PA from her son: "Dear Mother, Am in Petersburg YMCA tonight. Put my uniform on for the first time today...Will write soon. Am well and hope you and the rest are also. (Fenelon Collection)

"'I am the flag of The Service, sir;
The Flag of his mother—I speak for her
Who stands by my window and waits and fears,
But hides from others her unwept tears...
I am the flag of a mother's son,
And won't come down till the victory's won!'" [12]

A mother's voice was heard in "There's a Little Blue Star in the Window and It Means All the World to Me:"

"There are stars in the high heavens shining,
With a promise of Hope in their light;
There are stars in the field of Old Glory,
The emblem of honor and right.

"But no star ever shone with more brightness
I know,
Than the one for my boy o'er the sea;
There's a little blue star in the window,
And it means all the world to me." [13]

In January 1918, the Cleveland Advocate published an article that described the emotional impact of a service flag hanging in the window:

"When one passes a home in whose window hangs a service flag—that little bit of muslin with a red border and a background of white in which appears one or more blue stars—involuntarily, the heart throbs. That little service flag, dumb though it may be, speaks volumes. It is like a wreath of JOY tied with 'black MOURNING.' JOY, in some instances, that the mother and father within the home were blessed with a son, or sons, they could send forth to fight for our country and fires... MOURNING, in many instances, because those little blue stars [stand] for one who may never return to caress mother, to imprint upon those sweet lips a kiss; to be a staff for father when age has whitened his head and made halting his step." [14]

A service flag in a window imbued the displaying family with a patriotic status that was both public and desirable. As an editorial in the Chicago Tribune stated:

"It is with a feeling of respect and admiration that one passes a house from which a man has gone to join the fighting ranks. The service flag in the window is a symbol of sacrifice that is noble and inspiring. It is at once a challenge of and a rebuke to disloyalty. It is an eloquent lesson in patriotism." [15]

As the war progressed, some families began to feel that their patriotism was questioned because they did not have a member of the family serving in the war—a message publicly proclaimed by the lack of a service flag.

Elia W. Peattie wrote about service flags for the Chicago Tribune in December 1917. She observed another aspect of the service flags—they were a symbol of unification for the nation:

"The little flags are democratic things. You see them in the windows of beautiful and scrupulously kept homes, and in little cottages on grimy streets and high, high up in the apartment houses. When I was in New York the other day, I was thrilled to see the flags by the fifties, glowing out from the tenement windows above the dingy bed clothing that is forever hanging from the sills and triumphing over the high swung lines of ill washed clothes. All the sordid confusion of that crowded life was transformed by the little flags. And on Fifth Avenue, the Vanderbilt mansion was made human and kind by its flag, precisely like the others, with its two stars."[16]

With the advent of the service flag and its gold stars to signify the greatest sacrifice a parent could make, a new term began to enter the American lexicon—gold star mother—an honorific to describe a mother who had lost a child in the nation's wartime service.

The Bond Between Mother and Son

Americans were a sentimental people in the pre-war period and this tendency carried into the war years as well. Heartfelt ballads about loving mothers who sacrificed for their families were popular, such as the famous "M-O-T-H-E-R," which described a mother's saintly attributes with words that spelled "mother," or "The Little Grey Haired Mother Who Waits All Alone."[17]

Mothers were the emotional and spiritual center of the home and family; no familial relationship was thought closer than the bond between a mother and a son. When war was declared and young American men began to enter the service through enlistment or the draft, the mother/son relationship came sharply into focus.

A 1918 YMCA Mother's Day publication prepared for soldiers reminded the fighting men of their mothers:

"There is nobody just like her. For tenderness and patience, for long suffering and understanding, for sure remembrance or, if need be, for quick forgetfulness, there's 'only one Mother the whole world over.' Every good woman reminds us of her. Every dimpled baby is a text for thoughts of her. Violets and cello tones, pretty trinkets and soft colors, gentle deeds and the silence of the House of Worship, all are messengers of God whispering: 'MOTHER! MOTHER!'

"Far, far away we said good-bye to her; but she would not be left behind; she is with us, always with us. 'God could not be everywhere so he gave us Mother.' We had boasted to ourselves that we were men, no longer held by apron-strings; and now we find it true, for the strings are become chains, and we are proud of our shackles. Who would have guessed from knowing us that Mother sits throned in our hearts? But there she is,

Fig. 1-13: A smiling World War I mother bravely sends her son to war. *(Postcard: Fenelon Collection)*

the one who knows us best, the one who counts upon us most, and by her very expectations makes us men such as we had not dreamed to be. Aye, God did a good thing when He gave us MOTHER."[18]

A publication prepared by the YMCA for the "Fathers and Mothers who live in homes with the Service Flags" credited the success of the American forces to the "tradition of the American Mother."

John Mott, General Secretary of the YMCA, told of an experience he had while accompanying an AEF general in France. The general had just been advised that an AEF company had been pinned down between "the enemy's barrage and the fire of their own artillery" and had been "terribly punished":

"He led me across the room to a great map of the front lines and pointed out where the awful punishment had taken place.

"'It was their first baptism of fire,' he said sorrowfully, 'Their first exposure to the fearful destruction of modern warfare.'

"I looked from the map to him and said: 'General, how do you explain it? How is it possible for these boys to come from their peaceful homes right into the teeth of such a terrible experience, and to stand up before it like veterans?'

"And turning to me very impressively, he gave this splendid answer:

"'If you want my explanation, Mr. Mott,' he said, 'It is very simple. I give all the credit to the tradition of the American mother.'

"The tradition of the American mother—among all the priceless treasures we are risking in this battle for democracy, there is none more precious than this. We should be cheated indeed, were we to win this war and lose one particle of the power of that tradition. Whatever comes—that tradition must be kept bright in the hearts of the men who are to rule America after this war."[19]

The mothers of America were asked to do what history has always asked of its mothers—teach their precious children right from wrong and instill them with patriotic ideals, but be willing to sacrifice those children on the altar of those ideals.

Mary Roberts Rinehart, a popular mystery writer and playwright who would herself become a gold star mother in the World War, wrote about the role of mothers in a book titled *The Altar of Freedom*. Published in April 1917, the same month America entered the war, Mrs. Rinehart wrote of the patriotism of mothers:

"We are virtually at war. By the time this is published, perhaps the declaration will have been made.

"Even now, all over the country, on this bright spring day, there are mothers who are waiting to know what they must do. Mothers who are facing the day with heads up and shoulders back, ready to stand steady when the blow falls; mothers who shrink and tremble, but ready, too; and other mothers, who cannot find the strength to give up to the service of their country the boys who will always be little boys to them.

"I love my country. There is nothing she can ask that I will not do. I am ready to live for her or die for her… Because I am a woman, I cannot die for my country, but I am doing a far harder thing.

"I am giving a son to the service of his country, the land he loves…

"Men fight wars, but it is the mothers of a nation who raise the Army. They are the silent patriots. Given

Fig. 1-14: Gold star father Joseph McCaskey, president of the Gold Star Fathers organization in Chicago. *(Used by permission: DN-0079625, Chicago Daily News negatives collection, Chicago History Museum.)*

her will, every mother in this great land would go to war, if by so doing she could keep her sons in safety. It is easier to go than to send a boy."[20]

Many of the songs from the early days of the war were upbeat and cheery melodies about sons leaving for war while the mothers, and occasionally the fathers, bravely waved goodbye. Songs such as "That's a Mother's Liberty Loan"; "America, He's For You!"; "So Long, Mother"; "America, Here's My Boy (The Sentiment of Every American Mother)"; and "When A Boy Says Goodbye to His Mother and She Gives Him to Uncle Sam" were heard in homes, theaters and gatherings.[21]

A mother's ability to bravely and lovingly send her son to war without tears or histrionics was considered a gift to the young man that enabled him to do his duty without undue emotional encumbrance. While no one was fooled by this cheery facade, the mothers of the nation were expected to indulge their fears privately, not publicly. Yet no one doubted that they sorrowed over their sons who had gone to war. Songs such as "A Mother's Prayer For Her Boy Out There"; "Each Stitch a Thought of You, Dear"; and "There's A Battlefield in Every Mother's Heart" disclosed the thoughts of the mothers while they waited for word of their soldier sons.[22]

This worry was not one-sided. Many songs of the day were written from the soldiers' perspective and described their concern for their mother should the worst

To the "Real" Men of America

THE GREATEST STORY EVER TOLD
(WHEN THE BLUES ARE CHANGED TO GOLD)

by W. R. WILLIAMS

Writer of "IT'S HARD TO SAY GOOD-BYE."
"WE DON'T KNOW WHERE WE'RE GOING
BUT WE'RE ON OUR WAY" &c

Published by
WILL ROSSITER THE CHICAGO PUBLISHER
71 W RANDOLPH ST. CHICAGO, ILL.

Fig. 1-15: Sheet music from 1918 shows the image of Columbia, symbolizing the spirit of America, changing a blue star to gold on a service flag. "The Greatest Story Ever Told (When the Blues are changed to Gold)." Music and Lyrics by W. R. Williams. Published by Will Rossiter Publishing, Chicago, Illinois, 1918. *(Fenelon Collection)*

men in uniform, working outside the home in many cases to release a male worker for military service, and volunteering in hospitals and bond drives, the mothers of America were also morale managers for both those at home and overseas. The soldiers cherished the memories of those mothers who reacted calmly to the news of their sons' enlistment or draft call and were able to send their sons to war with a smile rather than tears.

The mothers' efforts to keep up their sons' morale didn't end when they waved goodbye at the train station. Mothers were usually the main correspondents with their sons and most tried to send only good news, cheerfully told, rather than burden the fighting man with the difficulties and sadness of those at home.

befall the warrior. "Break the News to Mother" had been written in 1897 during the Spanish-American War and was reintroduced to great popularity. Songs that described the worries of the sons for their mothers included "In The Gloaming, Mother Darling, When The Message Comes to You"; "Mother, I'm Dreaming of You"; and "If I'm Not At The Roll Call, Kiss Mother Good-bye for Me."[23]

In addition to sending her sons off to war, planting a war garden, caring for the family at home, scrimping and saving to free up more money and goods for the

The Fathers of the Soldiers

With the relationship between mothers and sons the focus of so much attention, the role of the fathers in sending their sons to war was largely overlooked. Fathers were often portrayed in illustrations and text as stoically sending their sons off with a handshake and a pat on the back to wish him farewell and good luck. A poem titled "I Have a Son" appeared in the *Saturday Evening Post* and provides insight into what a father's more pri-

22 | THAT KNOCK AT THE DOOR

vate reveries over his son's departure might have been:

I have a son who goes to France
Tomorrow.
I have clasped his hand—
Most men will understand—
And wished him, smiling, lucky chance
In France.
My son!...

He said, one day: "I've got to go
To France—Dad, you know how I feel!"
I knew. Like sun and steel
And morning. "Yes," I said; "I know
You'll go."

I'd waited just to hear him speak
Like that.
God, what if I had had
Another sort of lad,
Something too soft, too meek and weak
To speak!

And yet—
He could not guess the blow
He'd struck.
Why, he's my only son!
And we had just begun
To be dear friends. But I dared not show
The blow.

But now—tonight—

No, no, it's right,
I never had a righter thing
To bear. And men must fling
Themselves away in the grieving sight
Of right.

A handsome boy—but I, who know
His spirit—well, they cannot mar
The cleanness of a star
That'll shine on me, always and true,
Who knew.

I've given him.
Yes; and had I more
I'd give them too—for there's a love
That asking asks above
The human measure of our store—
And more.

Yes; it hurts!
Here in the dark, alone—
No one to see my wet old eyes—
I'll watch the morning rise—
And only God shall hear my groan
Alone.

I have a son who goes to France
Tomorrow.
I have clasped his hand—
Most men will understand—
And wished him, smiling, lucky chance
In France.[24]

Fig. 1-16: "A Letter from the Front." From the painting by Harry. F. Roseland. *(Pictorial Review.* August 1918, p17. *Fenelon Collection)*

Fig. 1-17: Gold star parents of the Great War. *(Fenelon Collection)*

YOUR Boy and MY Boy

She thinks of her boy most of the time—homesick for a sight of his face, the sound of his voice. She sees him, first as a little tot among the flowers; then standing in front of her with his first school prize; then, for an unforgettable moment he is there in his new uniform, straight as an arrow, proud beyond words.

She holds in her hand his letter. She is very happy and yet tears make it hard for old eyes to follow the lines, as she reads: "I am all right, sweetest mother in all the world. I am where I ought to be and I am going to make you proud of me. Don't worry—I'll come back. We have got to win and we are going to win. You are always near me, dearest mother; I will be very near you when you read this letter. Think of me as having my arms about you, as in the old days."

And beside that spirit that is going to win must be your spirit, just as bound to win and just as willing to sacrifice. Buy Liberty Bonds—all you have the cash to pay for and all you can possibly carry on installments.

This space contributed by patriotic business firms of Philadelphia

LIBERTY LOAN COMMITTEE, 3d FEDERAL RESERVE DIST., LINCOLN BLDG., PHILADELPHIA

Fig. 1-18: Liberty Bond advertisement. *(Fenelon Collection)*

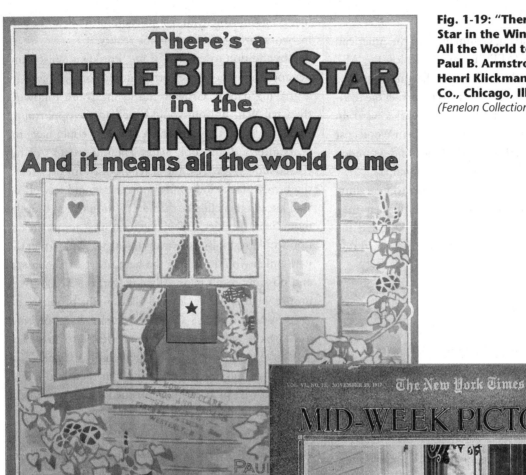

Fig. 1-19: "There's a Little Blue Star in the Window and It Means All the World to Me." Lyrics by Paul B. Armstrong; Music by F. Henri Klickman. Frank K. Root & Co., Chicago, Illinois, 1918. *(Fenelon Collection)*

Fig. 1-20: A mother bids her sons farewell as they leave for military service—one to the Army and the other to the Navy. *(The New York Times Mid-Week Pictorial.* November 29, 1917, cover: *Fenelon Collection)*

The World War and the Gold Star | 25

Casualties Mount

As General John Pershing, Commander of the American Expeditionary Force (AEF), began to deploy the AEF troops, casualty lists changed from reflecting in-service deaths due to illness and accidents to reporting the terrible front-line casualties resulting from actual combat. In May, 1918, for example, the Battle of Belleau Wood cost the AEF more than 9,500 soldiers killed and wounded with another 1,600 taken as prisoners of war.

Service flags across the nation began to bear stars of gold as families reflected the deaths of their men in the service. Again, the popular music reflected the psyche of the nation in songs such as "There's a Little Gold Star in the Service Flag":

CHORUS
There's a little Gold Star in the Service Flag,
For a soldier who fought and fell,
'Twas blue as the sky when we kissed
*   him good-bye,*
And he answered his last farewell. [25]

The nation mourned deeply for the men who sacrificed their lives for liberty.

An Alternative to Mourning

Woodrow Wilson had known from the beginning that the war would be unbearably costly in terms of human

Fig. 1-21: Chicago gold star mothers wearing the gold star armband endorsed by President Wilson as an alternative to traditional mourning clothes. Two of the mothers have simply added the armband to their dark-hued mourning outfits.
(Used by permission: DN-0070373, Chicago Daily News negatives collection, Chicago History Museum.)

life. As more American troops took to the field, he saw his worst premonitions become reality.

In addition to the loss of life, President Wilson understood how the war effort could be compromised by a grieving nation. Growing up in the South following the Civil War, Wilson would have had the opportunity to see the effect that mourning and grief could have for years after a death took place. The sad specters of bereaved mothers, wives, and sisters dressed for decades in the heavy black clothes of mourning would have been well known to a child of that era. Wilson feared that the mounting casualties and related mourning across the nation would result in Americans losing the will to win the war which would prolong the fight, increase the losses, and possibly result in an Allied defeat. But Wilson was unsure what could be done to alleviate the problem.

On May 3, 1918 Caroline Seaman Read of New York wrote a brave and poignant letter to President Wilson on a matter that was intensely personal for her, and of interest to all mothers in the nation. The widowed wife of William Augustus Read, a prominent New York banker, Mrs. Read wrote:

"My dear Mr. President,

"Mrs. Henry P. Davison tells me that you fear this is not the right moment to open the discussion as [to] whether the women of America are to meet the inevitable death roll of our heroic defenders of Liberty as a matter of glory, honor and pride, or as a matter of prostrating grief and mourning.

"One of my four Naval Aviator sons has recently been killed on active service at Dunkirk, so I know the costliness of such supreme glory and sacrifice, and weighing both the selfish temptation to hide our pain behind a mourning that would hold off intrusion, and the inspiration and stimulation of keeping up to my gallant son's expectation that I should regard his death as a happy promotion to higher service, I must urgently beg of you, Mr. President, to speak now to the tense American motherhood your personal message of courage and understanding that patriotism means such exalted living that dying is not the harder part.

"Could we have awarded by our President, Commander-in-Chief of our men in Army, Navy, Air and all services, a badge of honor to wear, showing only the gold star with the rank and branch of service of our man gladly dedicated to his country's service in this Great Cause, we should not dare to mourn, lest those seeing our insignia and knowing of that supreme sacrifice, might think we felt it a precious life thrown away.

Fig. 1-22: Ensign Curtis Seaman Read—U.S. Naval Reserve Flying Corps—"Killed flying in the line of duty near Dunkirk, France on February 26, 1918." *(Photo from:* The "World War"—History of the Village of Rye, New York: *Fenelon Collection.)*

"Not one of us who have been in touch with the magnificent spirit which takes these finest of our country's young manhood unfalteringly to face the New Death, renouncing without complaint or bitterness life at its most beautiful moment, can feel that we are rightly bearing the glory they bestow upon their families unless we keep the flame of their high devotion clear burning until the accomplishment of the Victory they died to hasten, and not one of us could fail with such an emblem of our country's gratitude and trust in our unfaltering patriotism.

"In every home in this wide land is now a service flag, or explanations for the embarrassing lack of one, and nothing could so unite our nation now as the President's word of understanding that our forces are composed of individuals, each the central object of in-

tense love, pride, high hope and costly sacrifice.

"The sublime loyalty to you, Mr. President, of all these magnificent men, in spite of the heartbreaking delays and wastage of officialdom, is a possession I long to make known to you as you are the only one who never hears their fine voices, excluded from official reports.

"With high respect, Faithfully yours,
Caroline Seaman Read"[26]

Just four days after Mrs. Read wrote to President Wilson, a similar sentiment appeared in an editorial printed in the *Union Progress,* a small newspaper in Union, South Carolina:

"What could be more appropriate or expressive than a Gold Star, representing as it would earth's most precious treasure, the purest of substances from which all the dross of the world had been refined, the symbol of fame and immortality 'as the stars that shine forever and ever?'... The wearing of a small gold star, or stars, as the case might be, would be a far more beautiful reminder of the life that has been given as a sacrifice in the struggle to maintain Liberty, Justice and Truth throughout the world."[27]

Fig. 1-23: Uncle Sam contemplates the stars in the heavens—God's service flag. *(Fenelon Collection)*

The World War and the Gold Star | 27

The letter from Mrs. Read offered the president an idea for a new symbol of mourning. Such a decision, however, was not one that Wilson felt he should make on his own. Instead, he turned to Dr. Anna Howard Shaw, a prominent suffragette and the chairwoman of the Woman's Committee of the Council of National Defense. On May 16, 1918, President Wilson forwarded Mrs. Read's letter to Dr. Shaw with the following note:

"My dear Doctor Shaw:

"The enclosed beautiful and touching letter will speak for itself. My present judgment is that it would not be wise for me to make any public utterance in this delicate matter, because I would inevitably seem to be conveying a warning that mourning might presently become universal amongst us. It has occurred to me, therefore, that your own committee might think it timely and wise to give some advice to the women of the country with regard to mourning...

"It may be that service badges, upon which the white stars might upon the occurrence of a death be changed into stars of gold, would be a very beautiful and significant substitute for mourning. What do you think? Can your committee wisely act in this matter?"[28]

Dr. Shaw and her committee acted promptly and she responded to President Wilson on May 21:

"Upon my return to Washington on Monday morning, I found your letter ...concerning a badge of loyalty and remembrance as a substitute for mourning for those who have given up their lives in the service of their country...

"I submitted the matter at yesterday's conference, with the result that the Committee voted to recommend a three-inch black band, upon which a gilt star may be placed for each member of the family whose life is lost in the service, and that the band shall be worn on the left arm.

"We have had numerous letters and discussions on this subject, and it is quite evident that the time has come for some definite understanding..."[29]

President Wilson immediately indicated his pleasure at the action taken by the Committee:

"I do entirely approve of the action taken by the Woman's Committee in executive session, namely, that instead of the usual mourning a three-inch black band should be worn upon which a gilt star may be placed for each member of the family whose life is lost in the service, and that the band shall be worn on the left arm. I hope and believe that thoughtful people everywhere will approve of this action, and I hope that you will be kind enough to make the suggestion of the Committee public with the statement that it has my cordial endorsement."[30]

Wilson's endorsement was an indication that he thought the idea a good one, but it carried no legal weight nor was it a requirement—it was just a suggestion. And despite the efforts of the Women's Committee to communicate the suggestion, the armband idea was met with little enthusiasm by the public. It did, however, reinforce the gold star as the symbol of a parent's ultimate loss. The concept of the gold star mother had firmly taken root in the nation's consciousness.

The Cost of War

General Pershing's planning and restraint meant that American troops were prepared and supported when he committed them to action.

Faced with continuous unrelenting pressure from the Allies, and experiencing civil discontent at home, the Germans finally entered negotiations for an armistice. Agreement was reached, and on November 11, 1918 at the eleventh hour of the eleventh day of the eleventh month, the Great War ended.

Some numbers are easy to calculate but impossible to comprehend; the loss of life during the Great War is such a number. In simple terms, at least eight million died in combat while another two million died of disease and malnutrition, twenty-one million were wounded, and another eight million were taken prisoner or declared missing.[31]

From a worldwide perspective, the American war casualties of more than 81,000 dead and 200,000 wounded were relatively light. In fact, more Americans died during the 1918 influenza epidemic (668,000) than were lost or injured in the war. But for families, friends and the nation, these losses were a tragedy that would never be forgotten and would only be eclipsed by another war in which even more American lives would be lost.

America had won the war, but surrendered its innocence for evermore. From the viewpoint of humanity, there were no winners of the Great War.

Fig. 1-24: "There's a Service Flag Flying at Our House." Lyrics by Thomas Hoier
& Bernie Grossmn; Music by A. W. Brown. Joe Morris Music Co., New York,
1917. Images from this publication continue on the next three pages.
(Fenelon Collection)

There's A Service Flag Flying At Our House

Words by
THOMAS P. HOIER and
BERNIE GROSSMAN
Authors of:
"Don't Bite The Hand That's Feeding You"
"Say A Prayer For The Boys Out There."

Music by
AL. W. BROWN

Marcia moderato

Piano

See the peo-ple run-ning, Hear the rum-tum-tum-ing . Mil-i-ta-ry
There be-side old glo-ry, Tell-ing all our sto-ry, Un-til the end, that

mu-sic fills the air. Ev-'ry one is wait-ing, Hearts are pal-pi-tat-ing,
flag is going to fly. We are proud to show it, Want the world to know it,

Flags are fly-ing ev-'ry-where. Of ev-'ry al-lied na-tion, from near-ly all cre-g-
We will do or we will die. There's a mil-lion oth-ers giv-ing sons and

a-tion, Their ban-ners wave from ev-'ry staff and Dome, But the one I love to
broth-ers, And proud-ly watch them as they march a-way, And Al-though their hearts may

J. M. Co. 603-2
Copyright 1917 by The Joe Morris Music Co., 145 W. 45th St., New York, N.Y.
The Publishers reserve the right to the use of this Music or Melody for any Mechanical Instruments
International Copyright Secured   All Rights Reserved   *Albert & Son, Australian Agents, Sidney*

see, That means so much to me, Is the flag that's fly-ing at home._____
ache, Al-though their hearts may break, There's a mil-lion glad they can say._____

Chorus

There's a ser-vice flag fly-ing at our house,_____ A blue star in a field of red and

white_____ Fa-ther is so proud of what his boy has done, There's a tear in moth-er's

smile and she mur-murs "my son" Per-haps he may re-turn with fame and glo-ry_____ But

if by chance we lose him in the fight,_____ There'll be a ser-vice flag fly-ing at

1
our house_____ And a new star in Heav-en that night,_____ There's a
2
night._____

J. M. Co. 603-2

F. J. LAWSON CO. N.Y.

Fig 1-25: "If I Had a Son for Each Star in Old Glory (Uncle Sam, I'd Give Them All to You)". Lyrics by J. E. Dempsey; Music by Joseph A. Burke. Leo Feist Inc., New York, 1917. *(Fenelon Collection)*

Fig. 1-26. "When a Blue Service Star Turns to Gold." Lyrics by Casper Nathan; Music by Theodore Morse. Leo. Feist Inc., New York, 1918. Images from this publication continue on the next three pages. *(Fenelon Collection)*

When A Blue Service Star Turns To Gold

Words by
CASPER NATHAN

Music by
THEODORE MORSE
Composer of "Mother" "Dear Old Girl"
"Sing Me Love's Lullaby" etc.

Moderato with expression

Pic-ture a win-dow at sun - rise, With a blue serv-ice star on dis - play, __ Then
Pic-ture the great field of hon - or, While the strug-gle for coun-try holds sway, __ The

pic-ture that win-dow at sun - set, When a soul that was brave passed a - way. __
young life that's giv-en in bat - tle, Forms a part of war's re - cord each day. __

Pic-ture a moth-er or sweet - heart, Proud, tho' the worst has been told, __
Pic-ture a sol-dier on dut - y, Vig-or-ous, youth-ful and bold, __

Pic-ture that scene, what it must mean, When a blue ser-vice star turns to gold. __
Glad that he may, serve in the fray, Tho' a blue ser-vice star turns to gold. __

3976- 2

Also published for
Band................25¢
Orchestra.........25¢
Male Quartette 10¢

Suggestion:– This chorus can be played as a Reverie
on the style of "Star Of The Sea."

CHORUS *Slowly and tenderly*

When a blue ser-vice star turns to gold,_____ What a tale of af-fec-tion is

told!_____ Dut-y to coun-try has cost one his all, While oth-ers, at

home, are bowed down with the call. In their sor-row, the ones left be-hind,_____ Voice a

pray'r that is e'er borne in mind:_____ Till souls meet on high, they must whis-per "Good-

bye" When a blue ser-vice star turns to gold._____ When a gold.

a poco *rit.* *tempo* *dim.* *p*

3976-2

Fig. 1-27: "Each Stitch Is a Thought of You, Dear." Lyrics by Al Sweet;
Music by Billy Baskette. Leo. Feist, Inc., New York, 1918. Images from
this publication continue on the next three pages. *(Fenelon Collection)*

With ev-'ry stitch that is fash-ioned, She breathes a gen-tle pray'r:
And tho' the cra-dle stopped rock-ing For my four big brave men:

CHORUS

"Each stitch is a thought of you, dear, Wov-en with lov-ing care, I'm

knit-ting my heart in each gar-ment, dear, To send to you some-where; My

hands are old and worn, dear, The stitch-es may not be true; But there's love in each

one, a moth-er's love for her son, Each stitch is a thought of you." "Each you."

3788-2

40 | THAT KNOCK AT THE DOOR

Fig. 1-27A: Advertising page from "Each Stitch Is a Thought of You, Dear."
Lyrics by Al Sweet; Music by Billy Baskette. Leo. Feist, Inc., New York, 1918.
(Fenelon Collection)

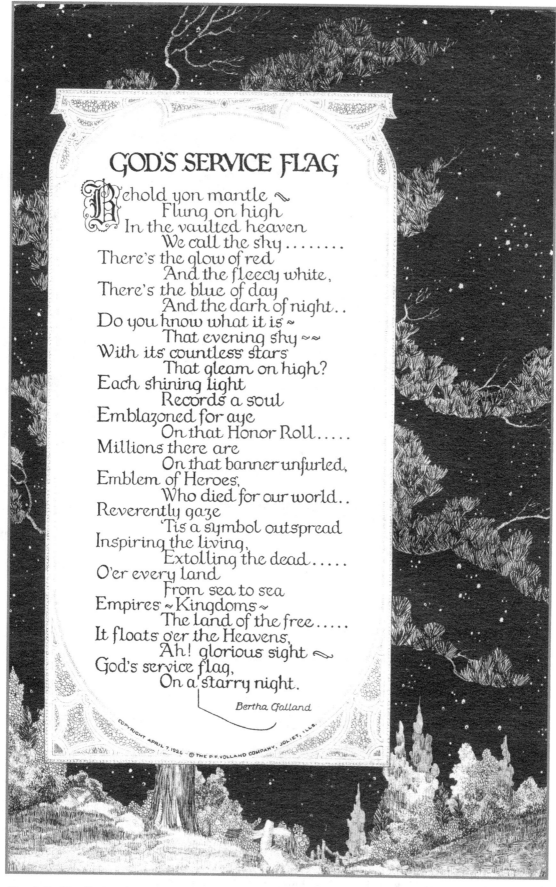

Fig. 2-1: "God's Service Flag" by Bertha Gallard.
(Copyright April 7, 1926 by the P.F. Volland Company, Joliet, Illinois: Fenelon Collection)

CHAPTER 2

The Post-War Period: Shaping the Memory of the War

War never leaves a nation as it found it.
—Edmond Burke

For the people of America, once the war ended there was one important question to be answered: How best to commemorate and honor the Americans who had fought to save the world? It is human nature to shape the memory of an event after it occurs; the way in which a nation remembers an event can shape the history of the event itself. Were America's soldiers heroes who saved the world or governmental pawns caught up in an event that really didn't concern America? Had Wilson waited too long to become involved or had he rightly saved tens of thousands of American lives by advocating neutrality for three years while Europe sacrificed a generation of its own young men? For historians, these were questions that time would answer, if indeed, answers could ever be found. Much energy and emotion were expended in the 1920s to form the national memory of the Great War.

Perpetuating the War Connections

For the soldiers of the AEF, the connection to their military comrades did not end when they were demobilized. A generation of men now found that their military service had become the defining experience of their lives. They were part of a huge national culture that shared a common history and experience, a culture that was not influenced by who they had been before the war or what they became afterward, whether they were rich or poor, became educated or remained illiterate, or hailed from the north or south. To their service buddies, for better or worse, they would always be who they had been in the military.

Feeling the need for an organization that would speak for the men of the AEF after they returned home—and become a voice for their comrades who did not survive—a group of serving and demobilized soldiers met in Paris, France, in March 1919 to discuss the need for and purpose of such an organization. Before their informal and raucous meeting ended, they had agreed on a name, the American Legion, and worked out the draft of a preamble to describe their purpose:

"We, the members of the Military and Naval Services of the United States of America in the Great War, desiring to perpetuate the principles of Justice, Freedom, and Democracy for which we have fought; to inculcate the duty and obligations of the citizen to the State; to preserve the history and incidents of our participation in the war; and to cement the ties of comradeship formed in service, do propose to found and establish an Association for the furtherance of the foregoing purposes."[1]

From this simple beginning, the nation's largest, most enduring, and most influential veterans' organization would grow, expanding its membership time and again to enfold new members whose military experience came in later wars. No other organization would influence the national memory of the Great War as strongly as the American Legion, and no organization would do so much for the nation, the soldiers of the AEF, and the families of veterans.

The American Legion was not the first such

group dedicated to veterans in the nation's history. Organizations such as the Grand Army of the Republic celebrated and commemorated the soldiers of the Civil War. Soldiers from a later war had founded the Spanish-American War Veterans Association. In 1899, the American Veterans of Foreign Service was formed. In 1913, they merged with another veterans' organization, the Army of the Philippines, to form the Veterans of Foreign Wars of the United States.

It was not only the soldiers who felt the need to continue with the relationships that had been initiated by the war. In August 1918, a national organization, the American War Mothers, was formed. The organization had grown out of a desperate effort by the National Council of Defense to convince the nation that huge efforts must be made to preserve and conserve food so that neither the fighting men nor the nation went hungry as the war continued. At one meeting, a young man from the Indiana State Office of Food Conservation said to the Council, "If the Mothers of men in service could be made to know the necessity staring the world in the face, the food conservation program would be solved."[2]

The criticality of the food preservation program was made known and Alice M. French, an Indiana mother, took responsibility for planning how the need could be communicated. The women of the nation responded, just as the young man had anticipated, and a huge, successful food program was launched.

From that initial effort, the need for and value of an organization to represent the war mothers of the nation became apparent. The national American War Mothers (AWM) organization was formed in 1918 with Mrs. French serving at its head as the National War Mother with seventy-two charter members. The organization's purpose was simple:

"To keep alive and develop the spirit that prompted world service; to maintain the ties of fellowship born of that service and to assist and further any patriotic work; to inculcate a sense of individual obligation to the community, State and Nation; to work for the welfare of the Army and Navy; to assist in any way in [our] power [the] men and women who served and were wounded or incapacitated in the World War; to foster and promote friendship and understanding between America and its Allies of the World War."[3]

In 1925, Mrs. French wrote a letter of greeting to the membership of the American War Mothers in which she articulated her fervent hope for the organization's legacy:

"If we mothers forget the promise made to our boys—that they were to fight in the last war—then who will remember to keep faith with them? I expect the War Mothers to go down in history as an organized body of mothers who put an end to war, and if I have gone on to the great adventure before the last surviving member of the American War Mothers receives her reward of a World's Peace, I shall be happy to have done something worthwhile in founding and organizing the mothers of men who fought the last war."[4]

Remembering the Gold Star Mothers

Both the American Legion and the VFW added auxiliaries to their organizations that included the wives, daughters, and sisters of veterans. These auxiliaries and the American War Mothers offered a special place and status in their membership to gold star mothers in recognition of their special sacrifices. But small groups of gold star mothers organized locally during the war remained together after the war ended, united by their common loss and experience. A gold star mother could choose to belong to one or more organizations—or not affiliate herself with any group—without affecting the gold star status accorded by the loss of a child in wartime.

One group of gold star mothers who formed an independent organization typifies the activities of many post-war groups at the local level. The impetus for

Fig. 2-2: World War I gold star mothers of Salt Lake City, Utah participate in a post-war Victory Parade. *(Fenelon Collection)*

Fig. 2-3: A gold star badge was given to each of the "The Mothers of the Defenders of Liberty" in Rochester, New York.
(Fenelon Collection)

forming this group was the death of an orphaned serviceman they hardly knew:

"The Gold Star Mothers of America, Corps No. 1, was promoted at Rochester, New York, March, 1919 ... At that time funds were collected for the purpose of erecting a memorial headstone in Riverside Cemetery at the grave of Jewell Howard Edwards, a young soldier who died of pneumonia while in Rochester assisting as a speaker during the Fourth Liberty Loan campaign. Private Edwards was an orphan, and his case appealed strongly to the Rochester Mothers. Through the efforts of Mrs. Evans and others, the memorial was obtained, and dedicated with fitting ceremonies on the Sunday before Decoration Day, 1919. This enterprise brought many of the Gold Star Mothers together and led to the organization of Corps No. 1, on June 9, 1919, by Mrs. Ida Evans and 87 Charter members..."[5]

The objectives of this new organization were clearly stated:

"The joining together in a body those who suffered loss by death of the noble patriots who made the su-

preme sacrifices in the service of their Country during the World War, for the purpose of mutual sympathy. To visit the sick; to give comfort; to bring cheer into the lives of the ex-service boys in hospitals; and to perpetuate the deeds of our noble dead who could do no more than die for their country."[6]

Where Should the Fallen Rest?

Following the war, one of the earliest and most difficult decisions for many gold star families was whether to bury their slain soldier in Europe or have the remains brought back to America for interment. The government had made the promise that all bodies would be returned to America at the end of the war. But the magnitude of the casualties and condition of the bodies made this promise difficult to keep; the first bodies of the war dead were not returned to the United States until March 1920.[7]

During World War I, health requirements necessitated the immediate burial of casualties in order to avoid the spread of disease among the troops. However, as battles were fought back and forth across the same landscape for months on end, many of the temporary markers and landmarks noted by their buddies to identify a grave's location had ceased to exist. The government's Graves Registration Service's initial task was to locate and identify the remains of more than 76,000 soldiers.

Once located, the bodies were transported from their temporary resting places to the closest of the locations that had been selected for American war cemeteries in Europe. While this sad and arduous duty was

Fig. 2-4 The temporary burial place of the first Americans killed in France.
(Fenelon Collection)

THE FIRST AMERICAN GRAVES IN FRANCE.

The Post-War Period: Shaping the Memory of the War | 45

Fig. 2-5: A temporary cemetery near the Belleau Wood battle site in France. *(Fenelon Collection)*

underway, the government asked gold star families to decide where they wanted their loved one to be permanently interred.

For most families, there were two choices: burial with the soldier's comrades at an American military cemetery near the European battlefield where he had died, or repatriate the body to America and inter the remains in a location chosen by the family. In either case, basic expenses related to the transportation and reburial were paid by the government.

For some families, there was a third option. A few of the war's casualties had been buried in what were referred to as isolated graves. These were individual graves where local residents or, in some cases, German troops, had buried an American soldier and marked the grave. A famous example of an isolated grave was that of Quentin Roosevelt, the twenty-year-old aviator son of Theodore Roosevelt, who died in a plane crash near Chamery, France, in 1918. Recognizing who he was from the identification he carried, German soldiers buried Quentin with full military honors in an open field near where his plane had crashed following aerial combat. His grave was marked with a cross of boughs, a sign identifying him, and parts from his demolished plane. Following the war, at the request of Roosevelt's parents who said "We feel that where the tree falls, there let it lie," Quentin's grave was not disturbed.

Other isolated graves were located along roadsides and in village cemeteries; the families of these soldiers had the option to leave them where they had been initially buried.

In America, controversy soon arose over the issue of burial for the war's casualties. While the media described the plans in place for the creation of beautiful American military cemeteries in Europe and many publications spoke out against disturbing the dead, public pressure was applied by special interest groups, such as mortuary owners, to encourage gold star families to bring home their dead.

In February 1920, *The Outlook* magazine published a letter that the editors felt "expresses so effectively a message to mothers and fathers that we desire to make it our own message":

Fig. 2-6: A photo of the original grave of aviator 1st Lt. Quentin Roosevelt, son of Theodore and Edith Roosevelt, who died at the age of 20 in World War I aerial combat. Lt. Roosevelt was buried by German soldiers who witnessed the crash of his airplane. *(Fenelon Collection)*

Fig. 2-7: Gold star mothers gather to honor World War I casualties as their coffins arrive on the dock in Hoboken, New Jersey.
(Uncredited news photo: Fenelon Collection)

"As I have read recently of the many bodies which may be brought back to this side …the ghastliness of it grows on me. I have watched the papers and magazines in eager hope that someone of influence will try to change the mistaken conception of death which so many who have lost their sons in the war seem to have.

"I was a canteen worker at Romagne, where the Argonne Cemetery is located, during those days when a thousand bodies a day were being brought in from isolated graves and small cemeteries all over the Meuse-Argonne front. Many of the bodies were badly decomposed and some, of course, were mutilated at the time of death. There were ten thousand American soldiers who worked faithfully in locating those graves… bringing the bodies in for reburial. The heat of those June days, the long hours on the road during transportation, the inspecting of the bodies and the burying, which often lasted well into the night, took heroism as great and real, I believe, as during the war—for there was no adventure and conquest in that work.

"And they left our dead buried in a beautiful cemetery—a cemetery which lies on a gradually sloping hill. Thousands of straight, straight rows of white crosses follow up that hill and disappear over its crest. Why can't we honor those dead bodies by letting them remain together in that beautiful spot in the heart of the American battlefront? Why should they be dug up, loaded into box cars, packed into the steerage of an ocean liner and inspected in their present state when they reach this side? For how can such a procedure bring comfort to any parent or friend?

"I wish every one might remember that, wherever they lie, they are in God's keeping."[8]

The magazine's editors added their own words to the plea of the writer:

"Is there no better way of keeping alive the sacred memory of our soldier boys than by freighting the moldering bodies to America and following the procession of our living soldiers with a gruesome procession of our coffined dead? Wholly righteous is the desire to do them honor, to keep alive their memories, to hand down to future generations their names and some memorial of their services… Individual graves of individual soldiers will by the next generation be forgotten…"

Fig. 2-8: A stateside funeral for a World War I casualty. *(Fenelon Collection)*

In January, 1920, Mrs. O. L. Gordon, a gold star mother from Robinson, Illinois, wrote a troubling letter to the *Chicago Tribune* urging families to leave their dead in Europe:

"I am a 'Gold Star' mother, and the agitation to desecrate the poor shell-torn bodies of our beloved dead impels me to write to the other grief stricken parents who, like us, bridge the distance and in spirit look down upon the little white cross that marks the resting place of one we hold so dear. But we know it is his grave, and whatever that mound of dirt holds, it is one of our own dead.

"A gang of laborers, working against time, shovels something into a box, fastens it up, and with thousands of other boxes, it is loaded into the hold of a ship. Do you know anything of the awfulness of the hold of a ship, the evil smells, the rolling and slipping and bumping? These poor bodies will not be treated tenderly, re-

Fig. 2-9: A memorial postcard for Stanley W. Kulas, Battery A, 332nd Field Artillery, American Expeditionary Force. *(Fenelon Collection)*

member. Most of the identification tags are gone, but your name is down for a box and so one is sent to you. It may not contain even the bone that one poor mother wanted; a black mammy in Alabama or Georgia may be weeping over the box that contains all that is mortal of your dead, thinking it her own. In many cases several were buried in one grave; there could be no care in burying them, there will be even less in taking them up.

"Keep their names and the memory of their bravery alive in this country, but let our blessed dead rest where they fell in France."[11]

On the third anniversary of the end of the war, the American Legion reported on the burial controversy and the result:

"On the question of the return of the overseas dead there has been a marked difference of feeling, even among the next of kin. Public opinion, while inclining to the view that it would be a beautiful and gracious thing to leave the men where they fell, has always freely acknowledged that it was a matter for the loved ones of the dead to decide. And their decision, while it has resulted in the return of 42,098 bodies, has also left 31,749 American dead forever overseas."[12]

By 1924, the Graves Registration Service reported that the number of identified dead in the cemeteries abroad had been further reduced to 30,216 with the number of unidentified dead at 1,624. More than 46,000 bodies had been brought back to the United States, and the bodies of more than 500 American soldiers who were born under other flags had been sent to their native lands for burial. In addition to the graves in the cemeteries, 89 isolated graves had been left untouched at the request of the families of the dead. [13]

For those soldiers who were brought back home for burial, it was not only their families who attended their final ceremonies. Across the nation, American Legion posts sponsored and participated in tens of thousands of military funerals to assist the families and honor their comrades in arms. The veterans who had returned

Fig. 2-10: A bronze plaque serves as witness to one family's contribution to World War I. *(Fenelon Collection)*

alive from the war demanded continued respect for their buddies who had made the final sacrifice:

"I want to relate an incident that I saw in Los Angeles, California, recently when I was waiting for a train. On a truck alongside the track was a casket covered with the flag. As I looked a sailor wearing a Croix de Guerre and Victory Medal passed it and saluted sharply. A civilian smoking with his hat on the back of his head lifted up one corner of the flag, evidently to see what was there. The sailor saw this mark of disrespect for the dead and without a word walked up and knocked the civilian flat on his back, saluted the casket, about faced and continued on his way."[14]

Memorials to Honor Those Who Fought and Those Who Died

Even before the war ended, people began to consider appropriate ways to memorialize those who fought and those who died. Almost every city and hamlet in the nation eventually built a war memorial of some type. Some were simply painted signs with the names of those from the town who had gone to war and a star next to the names of those who did not return. Pedestals, columns, arches, fountains, and carved figures in classical styles graced town squares across the nation. Memorial groves and forests were planted in many cities by American Legion posts. Victory Highways were endorsed by *The Outlook* magazine as a practical yet powerful type of memorial:

"We may study to obtain the most magnificent effects in stone and bronze and marble; we may plan to erect shafts to the very clouds; we may hope to dwarf anything that has been done in colossal architecture. But nowhere can we find a better way to appropriate the memorial offerings of a grateful Nation than in the construction of permanent roads which in their completion will form a great system of Victory Highways."[15]

The American Legion funded and built thousands of memorial parks, pools, gymnasiums and even schools. American Legion halls were often named in honor of specific gold star veterans and frequently served double duty as community social halls and a meeting place for other organizations.

On a grander scale, communities endorsed and funded huge permanent edifices such as the Liberty Memorial in Kansas City, Missouri. Within two weeks of the Armistice, an idea had been born among the people of Kansas City for a memorial to honor and memorialize all those who fought and died in the Great War. Once the idea was launched, more than $2,500,000 was raised by public subscription in just two weeks. Prominent architects were asked to submit designs for the memorial and groundbreaking ceremonies were held on November 1, 1921, before a crowd of nearly 200,000. On Armistice Day, November 11, 1926, the Liberty Memorial was opened to the public with a dedication speech by President Calvin Coolidge followed by a speech from Queen Marie of Romania. Massive by any measure, the complex consists of several structures, including a Memorial Tower, two museum buildings in which the names of Kansas City's gold star veterans were inscribed on bronze tablets, and a Great Frieze that depicts progress from war to peace.

Gold Star Highways

In Missouri, a commemorative organization started during the Great War took on a new purpose after the war ended. The Adjutant General of the State of Missouri had begun an effort to collect and compile the military and family records of Missouri's fighting men for inclusion in the *Blue Book of Missouri War Veterans.* To compile the *Blue Book,* a group of women volunteers was recruited and became known as the Associate Registrars. Following the end of the war, the efforts of the Associate Registrars continued, supported by a new Adjutant General who encouraged the completion of the records and supported the publication of "a true history of the Missouri Veterans who served so nobly."[16]

In August 1920, a group of twelve Associate Registrars with a wider vision met to form a new group—the National Society of 1917 World War Registrars. In the words of their founder, Mrs. Frank DeGarmo, they were "women who… saw a vision [of] making immortal records for our country's gallant knights and brave women who went forth to make the world safe for democracy and to secure future generations' peace, enduring peace, with right triumphant and freedom for the world, while their history is still in the making."[17]

The goal of the new organization was to assume responsibility for creating on a national level the same type of records that Missouri was creating at the state level. The group saw their mandate clearly:

"No national organization has undertaken to apply the purposes of patriotic Societies, which are historical, fraternal and memorial, in a way to make each individual relative of every World War Veteran contribute his part to honor the men and women who served, as well as to secure to those relatives who suffered most, the Gold and Silver Star Mothers, a monument and a tribute to their service which would be useful as well as beautiful and comforting to all people, for all time."[18]

The primary goal of the organization was the collection of service records and family information for all the nation's veterans. This information would be used to create a clear, permanent and incontrovertible biography for each veteran and those records would be presented to the War Department in Washington, D.C. for safekeeping.

The Registrars' secondary goal, however, was probably more exciting to the citizens of the nation—the establishment of a system of Gold Star Highways. Starting as a local project in Missouri, the Gold Star Highway concept soon spread to adjoining counties, adjacent states, and eventually the nation.

The vision of a Gold Star National Highway system was perfect for its time and place. In the years following the war, the nation resumed work on its infrastructure, an effort that had become secondary to the war effort. Missouri had recently passed a $60 million highway building bond, and other states were looking at their transportation needs in an era where the automobile was no longer just a toy for the rich.

The Registrars' vision was huge, but not unattainable. Their plan was to connect Gold Star State Highways in every state to create a system of transcontinental Gold Star Routes that would intersect in the central part of the nation. At the hub of this intersection, a National Gold Star Crossroads Center was planned that would be highlighted by a "magnificent Gold Star Perpetual Light Monument" erected through contributions by all the states. This was to be the "National Monument to the Gold Star Mothers of fallen veterans, the Taj Mahal of America for its martyred sons and daughters."[19]

A resolution regarding the establishment of Gold Star Highways in Missouri was sent to the governor and each member of the state legislature in the winter of 1920. Governor Hyde responded that he would "proclaim all roads built by the funds from the [current] bond issue [to be] Gold Star Highways of Missouri" as soon as the roads had been selected and improvements begun by the State Highway Commission.

With this initial victory in hand, the Registrars then broadened their efforts with an eye on the national system of highways. In 1921, letters asking for support of the effort were sent to President Hoover, the commanding general of the United States, and leading citizens. Governors of all the states and territories were asked to designate a cross-state highway leading to St. Louis as a Gold Star Route.

In 1922, the state highway from Kansas City to St. Louis was named the Gold Star Route of Missouri. Before the end of 1922, thirty-eight governors and their Highway Commissions had either identified a Gold Star Highway in their state or confirmed their willingness to do so when roads had been selected in adjacent states so they could ensure that their route connected seamlessly.

Then a bureaucratic pothole rattled the effort. It was found that, under the law, state roads named by the governors as a Gold Star State Crossroad (a national designation) could not be improved at the expense of the state in places where it passed through incorporated cities. This meant that roads named as a Gold Star Highways were not eligible for future improvements by the states through which they ran. Refusing to be thwarted, the Registrars refocused their efforts at the community level and created a new objective:

"[To] create a sentiment of patriotism in the minds of relatives of all the veterans and citizens in all the communities to honor their dead heroes of the World War by improving a connecting link thoroughfare and planting trees along the roadside—Gold Star Memorial Trees—one for each Gold Star Veteran, thus constructing a Gold Star Memorial Boulevard Court of Honor through every town and city."[20]

"The Court of Honor Memorial met with unanimous approval and the idea... spread rapidly. In Missouri, the City of Trenton, the home of Governor Hyde... established a Gold Star Court of Honor as a memorial to veterans who had died from Grundy County. At the entrance to [the] Court of Honor, a Gold Star Arch of Freedom was erected... large enough to allow all kinds of vehicles to pass beneath."[21]

St. Louis, Missouri also moved quickly to create its Court of Honor. At a cost of "many thousands of dollars," the city redesigned a section of Kingshighway Boulevard to be two lanes in each direction and designated that stretch of road as the Gold Star Court of Honor of St. Louis. When completed, the Court of Honor contained 1,103 oak trees, each dedicated to a specific gold star veteran from Missouri and marked by a star-shaped bronze tablet engraved with the veteran's name and service record. Each bronze star cost six dollars and the cost was paid through donations from groups and individuals:

"[When it was completed in 1924, the] Gold Star Court of Honor.... became the Mecca and shrine of the Gold Star Mothers of Missouri. Visitors from all parts of the United States and Canada have been attracted by the long line of trees decorated with flags and flowers along both sides of this beautiful parkway."[22]

Efforts by the Registrars in other states also began to bear fruit. A California-based group, formed in 1928, took on the task to ensure that California's 600-mile long Pacific Coast Highway would be marked with bronze star markers for the gold star veterans of California, although the state would not allow trees to be planted. The Alabama Highway Commission designated a Gold Star Highway that ran from the state line at Snowfawn, Georgia, across the state to the Mississippi border. The Registrars made a plea before the U.S. Route 66 Highway Association and, at their request, the Association agreed that Route 66 would be named the Transcontinental Gold Star Highway.[23] The vision of the future was clear to Mrs. DeGarmo:

"[Thus] we may look forward through the vista of years and visualize the monuments of the Gold Star Highways marked by the Gold Star Route Markers as a nation's tribute to the Gold Star Mothers and a monument to their sons and daughters."[24]

The *Book of Gold*

A unique form of memorial was presented to the people of San Francisco by philanthropists Adolph and Alma Spreckles. The California Palace of the Legion of Honor in San Francisco was designed as "an exact replica and sister institution of the Palais de la Legion d'Honneur in Paris which Napoleon used to honor French soldiers." In November 1924, the couple presented the Palace to the people of San Francisco as a monument in honor of the California men who had died in the World War:

"In 1923, one year before the completion of the Legion of Honor, the American Legion held its annual convention in San Francisco. Alma Spreckles asked the Legion to hold a special ceremony in the Legion of Honor's outer courtyard —the Court of Honor. Among the invited guests was a group of Gold Star Mothers, who had lost sons in France. Seated with them were disabled veterans—amputees, blind, shell-shocked...

"It was this event that probably inspired Alma to create the *Book of Gold* and dedicate it to the Gold Star Mothers. Alma Spreckles had military records painstakingly searched for the names and hometowns of California men who died in World War I. The men were mostly army, but also included navy and marines. A calligrapher then inscribed approximately 3,600 names in the *Book of Gold*. The project took eight years to complete.

"When the *Book of Gold* was finished, Alma

Spreckles took it to Paris. There at the Palais de la Legion d'Honneur, Marshals Foche, Joffre and Petain signed the book. In addition, other distinguished people of France added their signatures and personal messages. General John J. Pershing, Commander of the American Forces in France, signed the title page under the single word "Mothers!" written in Old English type.

"The *Book of Gold* is a large, leather bound volume with ivory-colored crosses attached to the front and back covers with gold stitching. The front cover is stitched with the title, "Our Sons 1914–1918." The pages are made of parchment and the quotes and names on each page are handwritten in black ink. The *Book of Gold* was on display in the [Palace] vestibule until 1941 when it was put away for safe keeping."[25]

The *Book of Gold* is still periodically displayed for the public at the Palace.

The American Battle Monuments Commission

The American Battle Monuments Commission was created by an Act of Congress in 1923 and given the mandate "to secure designs for and erect suitable memorials to commemorate the services of the American forces in Europe during the World War." General John J. Pershing was named as the Commission's chairman. The Commission's members included "foremost American landscape gardeners, artists and engineers."[26]

According to the *American Legion Monthly* magazine, "General Pershing always regarded his duties as Chairman of the Battle Monuments Commission as the most sacred undertaking of his peacetime years, and... devoted himself loyally and ceaselessly to the prosecution of the task assigned him."[27]

In 1927, General Pershing reported on the activities and accomplishments of the Commission in an *American Legion Monthly* magazine article titled "Forever America":

"Since it came into being, the Commission has carefully prepared plans which involve three distinct parts: first the development of the eight American military cemeteries themselves into fitting memorials; second, the erection of suitable monuments in honor of the services and sacrifices of our troops; and third, the publication of a guidebook which will present in condensed form a true picture of the American effort.

"Our cemeteries are in [the] charge of the War

Department, under whose direction they have been well arranged and carefully maintained. It is the purpose of the Commission to carry out further development from the architectural and landscape viewpoint in order to express as fully as possible the appreciation and affection our people feel for the men who gave up their lives and who now rest over there."[28]

While each cemetery was necessarily designed in part for the specific site it occupied, the Commission required that there be certain architectural and aesthetic uniformities shared between the cemeteries that would mark them as American cemeteries. These included the style and material of the headstones marking the graves, the manner in which the graves were arranged, the landscaping (no plantings on the individual graves) and other points such as the chapels, visitor facilities and access:

"The central feature in each cemetery will be a beautiful memorial chapel, non-denominational in character... Each chapel will contain a tablet bearing the names of the missing in battles fought in the vicinity. Each cemetery will be enclosed by a masonry wall to give the necessary protection."[29]

When the Commission was formed, the Graves Registration Service of the Army had been at work since the end of the war locating and identifying the dead and gathering the remains in the eight American cemeteries that had been established. The cemeteries were placed near those battlefields or locations that had claimed large numbers of America's soldiers.

In 1925, the Commission's annual report included statistics for the graves at each cemetery. A portion of the graves at each location were those of unknown soldiers who could not be identified. Those numbers would change as additional bodies were located in the French and Belgian countryside and moved to the appropriate cemeteries.[30]

Each cemetery was dedicated in solemn ceremonies that included the American military, representatives of the allied forces and the public. In July 1923, Major General James G. Harbord of the United States Army, himself a veteran of the military operations in the area, gave a moving dedication speech at the Aisne-Marne Cemetery (often referred to as Belleau Wood Cemetery):

"It is very appropriate that this shell-torn wood and blood-soaked soil should, with the consent of our great sister republic, pass forever to American owner-ship. It is too precious in its associations, too hallowed with the haunting memories of that fateful June of five years ago to be permanently sheltered under any flag, no matter how much beloved, other than our own, and now in the quiet sunshine of a happier summer it has become a tiny American Island, surrounded by lovely France. I cannot conceive that in all time to come our country will ever permit the pollution of this consecrated ground by the foot of an invader marching on that Paris which Americans have died to defend...

"This melancholy spot with its tangle of wildwood, its giant boulders, its mangled trees, with here and there the wreckage of war, a helmet, a rusty canteen, or perhaps in some lonely forest aisle, the still tangled evidence of deadly hand-to-hand struggle, will for all time be a Mecca for pilgrims from beyond the western ocean. Mothers will consecrate this ground with their tears; Fathers, with grief tempered with pride, will tell its story to their younger generations. Now and then a veteran, for the brief span that we still survive, will come here again to relive those brave days of that distant June. Here will be raised the altars of patriotism; here will be renewed the vows of sacrifice and consecration to country. Hither will come our countrymen in hours of depression and even of failure and take new courage from this shrine of great deeds."[31]

Major General Harbord's prophecy that the American cemeteries in Europe would become Meccas for gold star families and veterans of the war quickly proved true. In May 1924, the *American Legion Weekly* reported that "more Americans will travel to Europe this year than in any preceding year in history, according to those who ought to know—the tourist agencies and the steamship lines." The magazine attributed the travel to the fact that the American war cemeteries were now essentially completed.

Time was yet another factor that contributed to the increase in war-related pilgrimages by Americans at this time. More than six years had passed since the war. The loss, now more distant, was probably more bearable for many gold star family members. The opportunity to grieve at the graveside of a lost son or husband in the place where he would lie for all time, surrounded by his comrades who had also made the final sacrifice, offered more comfort at this point than it might have when the loss was new.

Fig. 2-11: Gold star mothers pay tribute at the Tomb of the Unknown Soldier on Armistice Day, November 11, 1925.
(National Photo Company Collection (Library of Congress); Ref: LC-DIG-npcc-15075)

The Tomb of the Unknown Soldier

Following the lead of many of the Allied countries, on March 4, 1921, Congress approved a resolution providing for the burial of an unidentified American soldier of the World War in Arlington National Cemetery Memorial Amphitheater on Armistice Day 1921. The American Graves Registration Service in Europe was charged with the selection of the remains of four soldiers from among America's unknown dead who had died in combat areas; one of those four would be selected for burial as the nation's Unknown Soldier:

"No one will ever know whether the unknown American soldier buried in Arlington Cemetery came from Maine or California, whether he died on the Somme, in Belleau Wood, in the Argonne or at St. Mihiel. His body was chosen from the graves of all the unknown American dead in France so that these questions can never be answered."[32]

On November 9, 1921, the flag-draped casket of the nation's unknown was escorted to the Rotunda of the nation's Capitol. The body lay in state under a guard of honor composed of selected men of the Army, Navy and Marine Corps. During the next day, more than 90,000 individuals filed past the casket, including the highest officials of the government, members of the diplomatic corps, gold star mothers, and private citizens, to pay homage to the Unknown Soldier who symbolized all the nation's unknowns.

On the morning of November 11, 1921 Armistice Day, the casket left the Rotunda of the Capitol and was taken to the Memorial Amphitheater in Arlington National Cemetery under a military escort. There a simple, solemn funeral ceremony was conducted and then the coffin was borne to the sarcophagus where a brief committal service was held. With three salvos of artillery, the sounding of taps, and the national salute, the ceremonies ended for "an unknown American soldier who gave his life in the Great War."[33]

Gold Star Mothers as a Continuing Symbol

A decade after the war ended, General Pershing called upon the nation's gold star mothers to steadfastly continue to serve the nation as a symbol of strength:

"The bugles are not blowing, the drums of war are not throbbing. Yet a grateful nation needs the Gold Star Mother just as much today as it did then. She cannot be less fearless, less brave, nor less unswerving in devotion to her country than she was ten years ago. We reach out for her support, her patriotism, her moral grandeur, just as we did in those troublous days…

"The millions America rushed to arms were not professional soldiers. They were mothers' boys, with the upbringing and the splendid spirit of the dauntless, enlightened women, whose blood coursed through their veins. They were as great as any soldiers ever assembled under any flag."[34]

Of all the monuments and memorials raised by the nation following the Great War, none would equal the power, the piety, and the strength of the image of the gold star mother. No other symbol would continue to embody both the glory and the true cost of war as the memory of the Great War grew more distant.

Fig. 3-1: Surrounding the initials "SL", the words on this gold star pin read: Died in France, Age 23, Dec. 20, 1918.

CHAPTER 3

Creating the American Gold Star Mothers, Inc.

Gold Star Mothers have learned that only in an organization that is exclusively Gold Star can they find their best opportunity for service.
—GRACE D. SEIBOLD

THE CIRCUMSTANCES THAT LED TO the creation of the American Gold Star Mothers, Inc. (AGSM) were similar to those that occurred in tens of thousands of American homes during the Great War—a child gone to war; worry and fear for his safety; the dreaded message that the soldier had made the final sacrifice; and, for those left behind, a lifetime of sadness and loss. The difference was Mrs. George Gordon Seibold, a formidable and determined woman who believed that she could best honor her fallen son's contribution and sacrifice by aiding the young men who had returned from their nation's military service with injuries to their minds, bodies or souls.

Grace Darling Whitaker Seibold

Grace Darling Whitaker was born in Hartford, Connecticut, in 1869. When she was three, her family relocated to Washington, D.C. Her father, General Edward Washburn Whitaker, had been Chief of Staff to General George A. Custer during the Civil War. Under a flag of truce, General Whitaker had traveled behind Confederate lines to arrange the discussions between Generals Ulysses S. Grant and Robert E. Lee that eventually culminated in the surrender of the Confederate forces. General Whitaker kept the flag of truce under which he had traveled and later cut it apart, giving the larger portion of it to General Custer's widow who donated it to the National Museum in Washington, D.C.

The General willed the smaller portion of the flag to his daughter, Grace.[1]

On January 16, 1893, Grace married George Gordon Seibold at the Calvary Baptist Church at 8th and H Streets NW in Washington, D.C. Grace was twenty-three years old and George turned twenty-eight on their wedding day. Born in Washington, D.C., in 1865, George was the second of five children. George's first job was selling *The Star* newspaper as a newsboy; his relationship with *The Star* would last his entire life. In 1889, he joined the Columbia Typographical Union and remained a member for more than seventy years.[2] At the turn of the century, he worked at the *Times Herald* for three years. In 1904, he left that position to become the secretary of Columbia Typographical Union, a position he held from 1904 to 1926. He joined *The Star* again in 1926 on a part-time basis as a printer.

Fig. 3-2: Grace Darling Whitaker Seibold, Founder of American Gold Star Mothers, Inc.
(AGSM Collection)

George and Grace's first child, George Vaughn Seibold, was born in 1894. He was followed in 1895 by a sister, Theodosia, and in 1903 by a brother, Louis Edward. The family lived in Washington, D.C., at 756 Rock Creek Church Road NW. Mrs. Seibold became well known in the community for her church, civic, and patriotic work. She was a member of the North Star Union, the Women's Christian Temperance Union, the Daughters of the American Revolution, and Ladies' Auxiliary of the International Typographical Union.[3]

Oldest Son Becomes an Aviator

We know little of Grace and George's oldest son's childhood, but as a young man, he began preparing for military service before America entered the war in Europe. In 1916, he attended Officers' Training Camp in

Fig. 3-3: The Seibold home at 756 Rock Creek Church Road NW in Washington D.C.
(Photo by Ruth Stonesifer)

Fig. 3-4: George Vaughn Seibold, son of Grace Darling Seibold.
(AGSM Collection)

Plattsburgh, New York and, at the conclusion of that training, received his commission as a Lieutenant at the age of twenty-two.[4]

In 1917, George Seibold was called to Fort Sheridan, Illinois. He volunteered for the Aviation Corps early in July of that year, passing the examinations and being ordered to Canada on July 22, 1917, for training. The previous day he was married to Miss Kathryn Benson of Lake Forest, Illinois.[5]

In 1917, America was ill-prepared to train pilots and crews for war in Europe and certainly not in the numbers that would be required. Consequently, the majority of Aviation Corps trainees were sent to locations where they could be trained by British, Canadian, French and Italian pilots. An agreement was made between the British and American flying corps that one group of flyers would be given instruction in flying, repair and maintenance by the British in Canada in exchange for British use of Texas airfields during the winter. George was among the group of 300 university

cadets sent to Camp Bordon, near Toronto, for training; they became known as the Toronto Group:[6]

"He was the first member of this Fort Sheridan unit to do solo flying as flying alone is called. After attending the ground aerial photographic, machine gunnery and other schools in different parts of Canada, he was ordered to Fort Worth, Texas early in October as [an] instructor of cadets, having been commissioned First Lieutenant."[7]

"With the advent of winter, the entire flight training facility had transferred to Texas where the training continued at Taliaferro Fields 1 and 2. The training was risky and many aspiring pilots lost their lives in accidents in the air and on the ground. George narrowly escaped death in November 1917 when, 'while testing a new machine, he had a fall of 1,500 feet.'"[8]

Once the cadets had "earned their wings" they were formed into units for overseas duty. Ten squadrons were formed from the Toronto Group and eight were eventually sent to France for combat.[9] Early in 1918, George's unit was ordered overseas. He wrote home of traveling on the transport just behind the *Tuscania,* which was torpedoed by a German submarine on January 24 with a loss of 230 soldiers and crew members. On July 3, 1918, in France, George was assigned to the U.S. 148th Pursuit Squadron, which had been placed under British direction while the squadron adjusted to the combat environment.

His Sister Relates the Family's Experience

George's sister, Theodosia, later explained that from June to August, the family heard from George regularly.[10] He was cited by the British government for distinguished service for flying over German lines and "accounting for a number of enemy planes, three on one occasion."[11]

Then a month passed with no word. Mr. Seibold contacted the War Department but was told that the United States did not "keep tabs" on the aviators who were under British authority and control. Three months passed and still no word was received from either George or the War Department. A premature Armistice celebration was followed by the real Armistice on November 11, 1918. But while the nation deliriously celebrated the end of the war, the Seibold family feared to celebrate for there was still no letter or word from George, and no information from the War Department.

On Christmas Eve 1918, the postman delivered a small package addressed to Mr. Seibold. The package was marked "Effects of Deceased Officer, First Lieutenant George Vaughn Seibold, attached to the 148th Squadron, British Royal Flying Corps." No other notation or explanation was included.

Continuing inquiries at the War Department failed to provide further information. Theodosia recalled that it was not until some months later that the Seibolds received word from a former school friend of George's who had served in the same combat area. He had heard a report that George had been identified as "missing in action." Subsequently, the family received official notice that George had been killed in aerial combat during the heavy fighting over Baupaume, France, on August 26, 1918, four months before the family received his effects. They were also told that George's remains could not be identified and he had been listed as an "unknown" in the cemetery at Bony, France.

Another Version of the Story

Other sources offer a different story about what the family knew and when. On Sunday, December 15, 1918, nine days before Christmas Eve, the following obituary appeared in the *Washington Star:*

> *"Lieut. G. V. Seibold Killed in Action*
> *Battling Aviator, Recently Cited for*
> *Bravery in France, is War Victim*
>
> "Lieut. George Vaughn Seibold, battling aviator, cited for bravery in action some time ago, lost his life in a fight in the air August 26, last. His father, George G. Seibold... has been officially notified of his son's death by the War Department.
>
> "Lieut. Seibold was a member of the 148th U. S. Aero Squadron. He was first reported missing in action, though a number of circumstances led to the fear that he had been killed. Hope was sustained until now, however, by the failure to receive definite word.
>
> "On October 11, last, Lieut. Seibold's wife, who lives in Chicago, received a package of effects from a commercial agency in London marked 'Effects of a Deceased Officer.' As they were belongings of her husband, she was nonplussed, no word having been received from the War Department that anything had happened to him.
>
> "Wiring her father-in-law in this city to make inquiry, it developed that the War Department officials had received word that Lieut. Seibold was 'missing in action' on 'August 26.' Efforts to secure further information proved unavailing for a long time, [with] the War Department, under date of November 30, stating that it had received word that 'Lieut. Seibold was last seen flying east of Bapaume' and that they had no information upon which to change the status of the original report of 'missing in action.'
>
> "The father of Lieut. Seibold, however, had received a statement from a nephew in Paris that reports confirmed the death of his cousin, forwarding, under date of November 4, an account of the aerial battle in which Lieut. Seibold was killed, made by a British lieutenant, as follows:
>
> "On the 26th of August, 1918, at 5:10, I saw a flight of [Sopwith] 'Camels' attacked by a Hun formation of Fokkers. After a short but sharp scrap, one 'Camel' came down out of control, followed by the Hun, who was firing the whole time. The 'Camel' eventually crashed about 200 yards from me, being absolutely wrecked. I rushed out to see if I could aid

FIRST LIEUTENANT GEORGE V. SEIBOLD

148th Aero Squadron, attached to B. E. F.   Killed in action near Baupaume, France, on August 21, 1918.

Lieutenant Seibold was born in Washington, D. C., on February 6, 1894. He was educated in the public schools of that city, and then moved to Chicago, where he was employed by the real estate firm of Aldis & Co. He attended the first Plattsburg Camp for civilians, and was admitted to the First Training Camp at Fort Sheridan, which course he did not finish, as he was transferred to the Aviation Service, taking up training in Canada and Texas, and being commissioned in that branch as a pilot. While flying at an altitude of 2,500 feet over Talipera Field, Tex., Lieutenant Seibold fell to earth, but recovered from his injuries. On January 31, 1918, he sailed for France with the 22nd Aero Squadron. Upon arrival overseas, he was assigned to the 148th Squadron, operating in conjunction with the British. On August 21, 1918, while on duty near Baupaume, Lieutenant Seibold was shot down, dying instantly. He was cited three times by the British. He was unmarried. His parents, Mr. and Mrs. George G. Seibold, one sister and one brother, of 756 Rock Creek Church road, Washington, D. C., survive.

1st Lt. GEORGE V. SEIBOLD

BORN FEBRUARY 6, 1894
DIED AUGUST 21, 1918

Fig. 3-5: A somewhat inaccurate official summary of George V. Seibold's military career.
(Provided by Pat McGovern)

the pilot in any way, but unfortunately he was dead. I believe he was killed before he hit the ground, as he was stone cold when I touched him. I looked to see if he had any valuables on his person, but the only thing I could find was a ring inscribed thus: 'From ? to G. V. S., July 1917.' I cannot remember the other person's initials. I could not look into his pockets because the machine was on its back and he was doubled up inside, and also on account of the shell fire, which was extremely heavy.

"The ring I gave to an American pilot of the 148th Squadron, who recognized my description of the squadron's distinguishing marks. He said he would forward it on. This was done on or about the 22nd of October, 1918. The reason I kept the ring for so long was because I couldn't find anyone who knew of the above mentioned squadron..."

"Lieut. Seibold, in his last letter to his wife, dated August 24 [two days before his death], wrote that if by giving his life he could help only just a little, he would be glad to do so."[12]

Another description of the battle in which George was killed is found in *Wings of Honor* by James J. Sloan, Jr.:

"At 4:30 in the afternoon, the Colonel rang up and said there were a lot of Huns about on the lines and some of our 'low strafers' [were] in trouble on the Bapaume-Cambrai road. Tipton got the patrol away in good style and they disappeared—11 of them—over the trees...

"The Squadron Record Book for August 26th showed: On crossing the lines, 5 Fokkers [German planes] were seen climbing... Immediately afterward, one Camel was seen being attacked by the [five] Fokkers at about 1000 feet. The patrol at once went down to the assistance of this Camel. Several other flights of Fokkers were seen coming down from 6000 [feet]. A general engagement occurred in which two other separate flights of Fokkers came down from higher up.

"The Camel first seen, which Tipton and his flight rushed to aid, was flown by George Seibold of the 148th, out with his patrol shooting up the enemy ground troops along the road to Cambrai. As the melee raged from 1000 feet down to the deck and lasted but fifteen minutes, Tipton, Todd, Bittinger, Roberts, Jackson and Frost were shot down. Tipton and Frost were wounded and [taken as] prisoners of war. The others [including Seibold] crashed, KIA..."[13]

There is no way to reconcile the discrepancies between Theodosia's remembered version of the events and the information provided in the obituary that contradicts her memories. The legend of the Christmas Eve delivery of George's effects is a powerful one and has been part of the AGSM mythos for decades. Perhaps the holiday exacerbated the family's sense of loss and that memory remained strongest for Theodosia sixty years later. Regardless, although the family's loss was shattering, it would prove to be the impetus from which American Gold Star Mothers, Inc. was formed.

Turning Grief to Service

Like so many women across the nation, Mrs. Seibold had volunteered in various organizations and capacities throughout the war. When the letters from George ceased to arrive and the family began to fear the worst, she continued to visit and aid hospitalized veterans in the Washington, D.C., area. She sustained the hope that George might have been badly injured and returned to the United States without identification, as had so many others. She found that her own sorrow eased as she cared for the returning servicemen, although many were so emotionally, mentally, and/or physically damaged that there was little hope of them ever being restored to normalcy.

Once the family knew of George's fate, they grieved for their lost son and brother. But Mrs. Seibold believed that "grief, if self-contained, is self-destructive."[14] She continued to devote her time and efforts not only to working in the veterans' hospitals but also to extending the hand of friendship and consolation to other mothers who had lost their children in military service. She eventually organized a small group of mothers in the Washington, D.C., area with the "purpose of continuing not only their friendship, but also the loving care for the hospitalized veterans confined in government hospitals far from home."

Fig. 3-6: Wounded World War I soldiers arrive in New York on the SS Leviathan. (International News Photo; Fenelon Collection)

Needing a Special Place

During the post-war years, organizations such as the American War Mothers, the American Legion, the VFW and the World War 1917 Registrars had made a special place for gold star mothers within their membership. Special privileges were accorded the gold star mothers in many cases. In 1918, the American War Mothers passed a resolution that gave gold star mothers life memberships without paying dues, although gold star mothers who were interested in holding office or voting in elections were required to pay dues.

However, in 1927, the American War Mothers officially revoked automatic life membership for gold star mothers. For many gold star mothers across the nation, this was a catalyst that resulted in their complete withdrawal from that organization. As Mrs. Seibold, herself a founding member of the American War Mothers, later wrote:

"Had these Mothers felt the injustice was against them personally, they might have submitted for the good of the organization that they had labored so hard to build up, but in memory of their dead, they saw but one course to pursue and that was to withdraw from an organization that would make a gesture of giving life memberships in the sacred name of the Dead and then revoke such action. Hundreds of Gold Star Mothers therefore severed their connection then and there with the American War Mothers and formed exclusively Gold Star Organizations throughout the United States."[15]

Many of these mothers continued to be interested in being part of a national organization through which they could contribute in some way. Mrs. Seibold felt that she heard a clear call to provide an alternative for these gold star mothers:

"The World War had come to be known as the Boys' War and this was particularly true of the American participation therein. The bulk of our forces was composed of youths still too immature to have taken unto themselves lifemates. The nearest and dearest thing on earth to them (as evidenced by the insurance files of the Veterans' Bureau) was Mother. Who then should carry on to see that his deeds are recorded, his valor recognized, [and] his patriotism memorialized except that Mother?

"Many patriotic organizations were formed following the close of the War, some of which have grown into Noble American Institutions. Gold Star Mothers were thoughtfully admitted to membership in most of these orders, but just as the Blind Veterans have demonstrated that they function better in Chapters for the exclusively Blind, so Gold Star Mothers have learned that only in an organization that is exclusively Gold Star can they find their best opportunity for service.

"In other orders, the Mothers of the Living so vastly outnumber the Mothers of the Dead (and for this let God be praised) that the interests of the minority are rarely considered and their motives are often misunderstood.

"Thus came the need for this organization composed exclusively of the Mothers of the Dead."[16]

Creating an Exclusive Organization

Mrs. Seibold was willing and able to put together this new "distinctive body of exclusively gold star mothers."[17] She recruited other interested mothers from among her friends and acquaintances and, on June 4, 1928, "at the request of some 35 Gold Star Mothers," the first meeting of the American Gold Star Mothers, Inc., was held at the Hotel Hamilton in Washington, D.C. To test the broader interest in such an organization, the twenty-five gold star mothers in attendance voted to keep the charter membership rolls open until September.

The constitution of the new organization was a simple one that clearly stated the members' common connection and purpose. The following version was prepared and presented by Mrs. Seibold for discussion at the initial meeting:

Preamble:
Whereas, we, the mothers of heroes who made the supreme sacrifice in the cause of humanity while in the service of the United States or who died as a result of such service, unite to establish a permanent organization for loyal and patriotic purposes.

Constitution:
Article I—Name
This organization shall be known as the American Gold Star Mothers.

Article II—Objects
    Section 1: To unite with loyalty, sympathy and love for each other, mothers whose sons or daughters have made the supreme sacrifice while in the service of the United States of America or died as a result of such service.

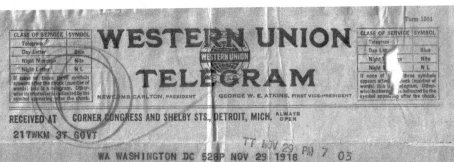

WESTERN UNION TELEGRAM

Form 1201

NEWCOMB CARLTON, PRESIDENT   GEORGE W. E. ATKINS, FIRST VICE-PRESIDENT

RECEIVED AT   CORNER CONGRESS AND SHELBY STS., DETROIT, MICH. ALWAYS OPEN

21 TWKM 37 GOVT

TT NOV 29 PM 7 03

WA WASHINGTON DC 528P NOV 29 1918

MRS OLIVE CARPENTER   1535   230

212 FORT ST CARE BOSTON HOTEL DETROIT MICH

DEEPLY REGRET TO INFORM YOU THAT LIEUT DICK D SMITH INFANTRY

IS OFFICIALLY REPORTED AS KILLED IN ACTION OCTOBER SEVENTEENTH

HARRIS THE ADJUTANT GENL

623P

FIG. 3-6: DICK DEWITT SMITH, son of AGSM charter member Olive Smith Carpenter, was the acting commander of Company A, 108th Infantry Regiment, 27th Division (formerly New York National Guard) when he was killed during the last phase of the Selle River crossing. He had survived the September 29 bloodbath at the St. Quentin Canal on the Hindenburg Line only to die less than a month later in the last combat action in which his unit participated. He was cited for gallantry and Mrs. Carpenter received the silver citation star for his Victory Medal from the War Department in 1923.

In his last letter home, Dick had written that while he didn't mind the poisonous gas so much, the machine guns were frightening. Nearly blind from a gas attack when he led his company over the top on the day of his death, Dick died instantly from a machine gun burst.

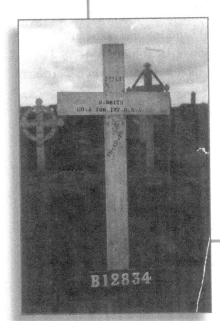

His sweetheart in Rochester, New York, refused to believe he was dead until she met with another officer, Harry Farmer, who was wounded in the action in which Dick died. Harry told the young woman that he had witnessed Dick's death and there was no hope that he had survived.

(Illustrations and information courtesy of Pat McGovern.)

Section 2: To preserve the records and perpetuate the memory of those whose lives were sacrificed.

Section 3: To maintain true allegiance to the United States of America; to inculcate lessons of patriotism and love of country in the communities in which we live; to inspire reverence for the Stars and Stripes in the youth of the Nation.

Section 4: To extend needful assistance to veterans and mothers when possible.

Attached to the draft of the constitution was a list of attendees at the June 4 meeting and others who received copies on June 6 and 7 (apparently there were not enough copies for everyone on June 4 and some mothers had to wait for a copy).

It was voted that the membership of the AGSM would be left open for a period of time to enable other mothers to join and be considered charter members. The charter members of the American Gold Star Mothers, Inc., would make significant contributions to the history of the organization in the years to come. Among these women were:

1. Alexandra Kocsis Anderson
2. Catherine Barrack
3. Pearl D. Berger
4. Ida Mae Blue
5. Alida Talbot Bruce
6. Olive Smith Carpenter
7. Matilda Clark
8. Mary Costello
9. Annie Clark DeArkland
10. Elizabeth A. DeGaw
11. Mrs. Ben H. Fuller
12. Catherine Taylor Geddes
13. Mary E. Greene
14. Mary Ellen Greenwell
15. Ella Montague Hammond Guedry
16. Frances E. Hibbs
17. Ella Coulter Holmes
18. Hattie Lee Hurley
19. Roberta Estelle Jacobs
20. Mary K. Killeen
21. Margaret E. Loveless
22. Fannie F. Meeks
23. Anna Moore
24. Ettie M. Nash
25. Carrie Jane Searl
26. Alice Clarke Seelye
27. Grace Darling Seibold

28. Mrs. John Spengler
29. Lena Biggs Thornton
30. Lillie F. Tibbits
31. Modesta Wolfe
32. Mrs. Thomas W. Woltz

Original membership applications still exist for many of the charter members. Taken from their applications, the following tells of the losses that made these women gold star mothers:

Alexandra K. Anderson (Mrs. John Townsend Anderson)—Mother of Alexander Kocsis Anderson who died of pneumonia just two months after reporting for duty:

> "His Commission was given for First Lieutenant although his professional credentials entitled him to Major. He had to fight to get in as he was over-age (33) and employed in an important engineering business. So [he] was glad to accept the lieutenancy to enter service. He sailed in September 1918 on the SS Calamares, one of the FLU SHIPS, and he died in Brest [Belgium]."

Pearl D. Berger (Mrs. Louis W. Berger)—Mother of Roy Joseph Schaefer:

> Joseph was killed in action on October 18, 1918, just two months after his twentieth birthday, in the Champagne Offensive. Mrs. Berger was a resident of the Canal Zone in Panama when she joined AGSM.

Alida Talbot Bruce (Mrs. Eugene Sewell Bruce)—Mother of Thomas Grant Bruce:

> Thomas Bruce was "killed while at the head of a combat patrol enroute... to fight against the rebel forces of General Sandrine" in Nicaragua. Mrs. Bruce's application is dated June 24, 1928. Her son died just six months before the first meeting of the AGSM.

Olive Smith Carpenter (Mrs. William C. Smith)—Mother of Dick Dewitt Smith:

> Mrs. Carpenter wrote "Lieutenant Dick Dewitt Smith was killed on the morning of October 17, 1918, while leading his men in making a charge on a German machine gun nest. He was cited for valor and meritorious conduct at this time." Dick served with Company A, 108th Infantry and was thirty-two at the time of his death. [Fig. 3-6]

Matilda Clark (Mrs. J. Wilson Clark)—Mother of Stafford Clark:

A 2nd Lieutenant in the Aviation Section and Signal Reserve Corps, Stafford was assigned to Taylor Field in Alabama where he was killed at the age of twenty-three in an airplane accident on June 20, 1918.

Elizabeth A. DeGaw (Mrs. Harvey S. DeGaw)—Mother of Edward H. DeGaw:

Edward DeGaw reported for federal service on July 25, 1917, and died at Camp McClellan, Alabama in October 1918 of "lobar pneumonia" (probably related to the influenza epidemic that was raging at the time). Having already served six months on the Mexican border, Edward was twenty-three at the time of his death.

Mrs. Ben H. Fuller—Mother of Edward Canfield Fuller:

Marine Captain Edward Fuller was awarded the Army's Distinguished Service Cross and the Navy Cross for bravery. A graduate of the 1917 class of the Naval Academy, Edward was sent to France in 1918. He died on June 12, 1918, when he "exposed himself fearlessly to a stunning barrage [of artillery fire by the Germans] to superintend personally the assurance of shelter to his men. The boy did not know the meaning of fear; he died a glorious death, killed by shell fire."

Ella Montague Hammond Guedry—Mother of Holman Montague Hammond: Mrs. Guedry wrote:

"The organization to which the boy was attached was known as the Washington Artillery of New Orleans, a famous command that had participated in every American War for over 100 years. When a cadet at Rugby Academy, New Orleans, Louisiana, this boy joined the Washington Artillery by misstating his age so he could go with them to the Mexican Border, and served as a bugler until the return of the Regiment in February 1917. He volunteered for Federal Service in the World War in April 1917, as a private, was promoted to Corporal in August 1918 when barely 18 years old, and died two months later en route to France.

"The blood of American Patriots flowed in his veins… [his] grandfather was a United States Navy Commissioned Officer; his paternal grandfather a lieutenant in the CSA [Confederate States of America]. The boy took pride in saying that he was 50% Rebel, 50% Yankee and 100% American."

Ella Coulter Holmes (Mrs. Winfield Scott Holmes)—Mother of Oliver Wendell Holmes:

Oliver had been promoted to Headquarters but his transfer had not yet taken place when his company was ordered to the front a second time. He died in action at St. Mihiel on September 12, 1918. He was posthumously awarded the Distinguished Service Cross for "extraordinary heroism in action" on the day of his death. Oliver was a private in Company G, 353rd Infantry.

Hattie Lee Hurley (Mrs. Harry Leonard Hurley)—Mother of James William Hurley:

James drowned "during field operations in the Dominican Republic when he and the rest of the company of Marines were commanded to ford a mountain stream." A Pharmacist's Mate 3rd Class attached to the Marines, James was serving at the Field Hospital in Santiago, Dominican Republic. He was twenty-one when he died in August 1918.

Mary K. Killeen (Mrs. John F. Killeen)—Mother of George Emmett Killeen:

George died September 18, 1918, in the military hospital in Ravenna, Italy from burns sustained in an accidental explosion of a gasoline torch. George was twenty-six as the time of his death.

Anna Moore (Mrs. James Moore)—Mother of William Frederick Moore:

William died in the battle of Belleau Wood on June 7, 1918. A twenty-year-old Marine Corps private at the time of his death, he had already served in two of the war's fiercest battle zones: the Toulon sector of Verdun and in the Chateau Thierry Sector during the Aisne defensive.

Carrie Jane Searl (Mrs. Edward Lewis Searl Sr.)—Mother of Edward Lewis Searl Jr.:

A 1st Lieutenant, Air Service, Edward died in an airplane crash at Brooks Field, Texas in June 1925 at the age of thirty-five.

Alice Clarke Seelye (Mrs. William James Seelye)—Mother of Julius Franklin Seelye:

On her application, Mrs. Seelye wrote, "Hoping to sooner reach [the fighting], Julius enlisted in the regular army but fell a victim of "malignant pneumonia." Corporal Seeyle died on May 26, 1918, eleven months after enlisting.

APPLICATION FOR MEMBERSHIP
American Gold Star Mothers
(Organized June 4, 1928, Washington, D. C.)
(Incorporated Jan. 5, 1929, Washington, D. C.)

Mothers of Sons and Daughters who served in the Army, Navy or Marine Corps of the United States in any war or in any Military or Naval Service of the United States, having made the supreme sacrifice in the service or as the result of the service.

Date *June 4, 1928*

Name of Applicant *Grace Darling Whitaker Seibold*

Name of Husband *George Gordon Seibold*

Married at *Washington, D. C.* Month *January 16* 18 *93*
          Town   County   State

Parents of *George Vaughn Seibold*
                    Son or Daughter

Facts concerning Son or Daughter whose Mother is the applicant:

Born at *Washington, D. C.* Birthday *February 6, 189*
        Town   County   State   Month   Year

Branch of Service *Army Aviation*

First Lieutenant, 148th United States Aero Squadron

Company *Attached to Royal* Regiment *Air Force*

Stationed at *France*

Date of Death *August 26, 1918* Cause of Death *Killed in action*

Remarks: *near Baupaume, France*

Brief data of record attached to this application

_____ ited States, and certify that the above statements are true.

_____ me of Applicant *Grace Darling Whitaker Seibold*

Street *756 Rock Creek Church Road N.W.*

City *Washington, D.C.* State _____

Fig. 3-7: **Grace Darling Seibold's original membership application.** *(AGSM Collection)*

Fig. 3-8: Grace Darling Seibold (at left) and First Lady Grace Coolidge (accompanied by James Haley) return to the White House following a National War Mothers tree planting ceremony at the Lincoln Memorial on October 13, 1924. *(National Photo Company Collection (Library of Congress); Ref. LC-DIG-npcc-12429)*

Applying for Membership

The AGSM membership application was a simple form with "American Gold Star Mothers" printed at the top followed by the dates of organization and incorporation. The original version of the form started with the following statement:

"Mothers of Sons and Daughters who served in the Army, Navy or Marine Corps of the United States in any war or in any Military or Naval Service of the United States, having made the supreme sacrifice in the service or as a result of the service."

Information required on the form included:

- Date of application
- Name of natural mother of veteran
- Name of natural father of veteran
- Location and date of marriage
- Veteran's name
- Location and date of veteran's birth
- Branch of service
- Military company
- Regiment
- Date of discharge
- Date of death
- Cause of death

The signature at the bottom of the page indicated "I am a citizen of the United States and certify that the above statements are true."

When an application was received, an inquiry was sent by AGSM's custodian of records to the appropriate branch of the service to verify the service record of the named veteran. The Adjutant General's Office normally responded for Army inquiries; the Adjutant and Inspector's Office for the Marines; and the Chief of the Bureau of Navigation's for the Navy.

The Army responses were usually tersely worded confirmations of service with the date of induction, date of departure for foreign service, if appropriate, the date of death or discharge, and the serviceman's rank. The Marine and Navy responses were far more informative and usually included the date of birth, dates of transfer, battles participated in, cause of death, and a character rating, most often noted as "Excellent."

Once the service record was verified, and if all the other concerns had been met, such as blood relationship between mother and serviceman, and dues paid (application fee—50¢; first year dues—$1), applicants' names were brought before the membership for consideration at a monthly meeting. Once voted upon and approved by the membership, the recording secretary affixed a gold star seal to the lower left corner of the application. Membership records were then amended to include the new mothers.

Mrs. Seibold's handwritten application is dated June 4, 1928, although the organization's incorporation date is shown as January 5, 1929. Evidently a decision was made to have each charter member complete an original application form for record-keeping purposes. Mrs. Seibold dated hers to match the first meeting of the organization.[Fig. 3-7]

AGSM Finds Its Way

No internal records of the organization's early days have been located. However, *Leatherneck* magazine, a Marine publication, reported on AGSM's founding and subsequent meetings and encouraged gold star mothers of Marines to become part of the fledgling organization. The level of detail included in the reports seems to indicate that a *Leatherneck* reporter was in attendance at the meetings rather than relying on secondhand reports.

Leatherneck reported the details of the first meeting of the American Gold Star Mothers advising that the charter roll has been left open until the next meeting. The officers who would guide the organization in its first year were:

President: Mrs. George Gordon Seibold
1st VP: Mrs. John F. Killeen
2nd VP: Margaret E. Warfield

3rd VP: Mrs. John Spengler
Flag Custodian/Press Correspondent:
Mrs. E. M. H. Guedry

The second meeting of the AGSM was held on September 18, 1928, and again *Leatherneck* covered the event:

"The mothers were deeply touched by the unsolicited offer of a high ranking officer of one of the branches of the service in Washington tendering legal aid and offering to personally assume all costs connected with the incorporation of the order. The gentleman's name cannot, of course, be mentioned without his permission, but it is safe to say that no document will be more highly treasured than the gracious letter bearing this message of esteem and good will...

"After a very active business session the mothers were entertained delightfully by Miss Hoch and Mrs. Minnie Hoch Smith... Miss Hoch's lovely voice harmonizing perfectly with the soft tones of accompaniment produced by Mrs. Smith on the trombone...

"At the request of a number of applicants, the time for admission of charter members was extended from September 18 to September 30, and under this ruling, the names of six additional mothers were added to the Charter Roll."[18]

The December meeting of the AGSM included both business and merriment, according to *Leatherneck*:

"A donation of one hundred comfort pillows was made to be used by the boys in Walter Reed [Hospital]. Two slips were provided with each pillow...

"A musical program had been arranged to follow the business session and the artists had arrived when it was found that there was no piano in the room. Mrs. Seelye, exemplifying the spirit of the sons these Mothers gave to their country, was not to be thwarted by such a trifle, and in a jiffy had commandeered a piano and crew to install it, and the program went on."

The next meeting was held in February, 1929:

"Mrs. Catherine Barrack, chairman of St. Elizabeth Hospital committee, rendered an interesting report of several visits to that institution, when, aided by her assistants, refreshments and entertainment were supplied to ex-servicemen who gathered in the Red Cross hut. An interesting report was given of the part taken by the American Gold Star Mothers, who were well represented at the Women's Patriotic Conference on National Defense... The organization sent five delegates...

"The president presented the certified copy of the articles of incorporation…

"A comprehensive report of the activities of the legislative chairman was read by Mrs. E. M. H. Guedry, who has acted in that capacity since the formation of the organization. The jurisdictions of the Pension Office and the Veterans' Bureau were outlined, the different forms of compensation explained and some corrective legislation proposed. The cooperation of the Veterans' Bureau in adjusting a number of claims was extolled by Mrs. Guedry."[19]

A Thriving Organization

By the end of the 1920s, AGSM had firmly established itself as a growing and significant organization. The small group quickly expanded as gold star mothers across the nation joined with their sisters in other states to care for and act on the behalf of veterans who had returned from the war in need of care.

There were obstacles ahead for the fledgling organization. The Depression would challenge the first half of the coming decade and war in Europe would define the decade's final years. But the AGSM women were made of stern stuff and the organization moved into the new decade with plans, dreams, and the will to make them happen.

Fig. 4-1: Chicago gold star mothers of the Great War gather for a post-war event. *(Used by permission: DN-0070373, Chicago Daily News negatives collection, Chicago History Museum.)*

CHAPTER 4

The Gold Star Mothers
of the Great War

Having made the supreme sacrifice, I hope and
pray that my darling son was not killed in vain
and that the world will be at peace before long.
 —BESSIE HARRIS, *World War I*
 Gold Star Mother (1938)

WORD OF THE NEW ORGANIZATION and its offer of open membership quickly spread across the nation. Women learned of it by letter, in newspapers, and over their back fences. It was a topic of discussion in churches, diners, and markets. Soon, membership applications began to arrive at the AGSM headquarters for consideration. The Washington, D.C., mothers now devoted a portion of every business meeting to reading the names of the applicants whose eligibility had been verified and voting to admit them to full membership.

Who were the new members? Truly a cross-section of America, these mothers had one thing in common— each had lost a child in the defense of freedom and American ideals. Beyond that connection, these women were as diverse as the nation itself. They came from big cities, small towns, and isolated farms. Some were well educated while others could only sign their marks on applications filled out by another's hand. Many were still hale and hearty in the 1930s, but the less lucky told of the illnesses, fear, and despair that were their constant companions in age. Many were foreign-born while others lived on the same American farms that their ancestors had homesteaded a century before. Some wrote in detail of their son's accomplishments, bravery, and military citations while others, with no less pride, simply noted that their child had done his duty.

Many applicants enclosed photographs of proud, uniformed, smiling young men with an arm around their mothers, while others looked serious against dramatic backgrounds in photographic studios or struck a brave, stalwart pose with comrades in military camps and barracks. The applications covered every branch of the American armed services and many of the Allied forces, including the Canadian and British Expeditionary Forces. A few applications told of long military careers; far too many noted a service experience that had lasted less than a month. Every application, regardless of the details, depicted a terrible, grievous loss that had been borne but not forgotten, and represented a mother whose heart had been broken but continued to beat.

World War I Gold Star Mothers
AGSM archives at the Library of Congress contain 1,597 original membership applications from gold star mothers and fathers of the Great War. These applications were received between 1928 and 1944, reaching a count of 1,000 by 1937. Although they do not represent the full World War I AGSM membership, they do offer touching insight into the membership of that era as a group. The applications introduce the mothers who forged the organization in its earliest days and tell the stories of the children they lost. These applications also reflect the experiences of the nation as a whole during the period known then as the Great War or the "war to end all wars." In sad hindsight, we know it today as World War I.

Unless otherwise noted, information in this chapter is taken from the named gold star
mother's membership application.

Where the Mothers Lived

The World War I membership applications represent forty-four of that era's forty-eight states and Panama. The applications' points of origin reveal an unexpected and unexplained concentration in some states. In 1930, federal census estimates reported a national population of 123 million. While it could easily be assumed that the membership in the organization would proportionally follow the same trends as the national population, the applications tell another story.

More than twenty percent of the mothers applying for membership lived in California at the time they applied, although only about five percent of the nation's population resided there. Michigan and California together account for 38 percent of World War I mothers' applications, but only nine percent of the population.

This unexpected distribution cannot be explained as the result of the mothers moving to a new state following the end of the war. In 1930, the *American Legion Monthly* magazine reported that two-thirds of Americans lived in the states in which they were born, and at least half of the nation's citizens spent their lives in the county of their birth.[1] In most cases, the veteran's point of induction noted on the War Department letters still matched the state of residence of his gold star mother at the time the AGSM application was completed.

Some states may have been more active in establishing small, independent groups of gold star mothers during the 1920s, or perhaps the news of the new organization was more effectively disseminated in some states than others. Whatever the explanation, one fact was apparent—from California to Washington, D.C., and from Maine to Louisiana, American Gold Star Mothers, Inc., had begun to establish a national identity.

Membership Growth

The existing World War I mothers' applications were submitted over a period of seventeen years starting in 1928—predating the stock market crash and the Depression—and continuing through 1944 at the height of World War II. Membership growth during this period can be verified using the meeting minutes of the Washington, D.C., chapter meetings where applicants were voted into membership. Membership grew slowly at first, but in 1931, new members accounted for twice the number of members accepted from 1928–1930.

The impact of the Depression was one factor that probably limited membership in the early years. During the Depression, many Americans struggled to feed their families from day to day, and the modest AGSM membership dues of $1 per year and 50 cents to join may simply have been beyond the reach of many mothers' finances. New membership applications dropped off in 1932, but picked up again strongly in 1933 and 1934. As the political situation heated up in Europe in the mid-to-late 1930s and Hitler became a household name in American homes, membership began to climb again; perhaps the news of war in other nations reminded gold star mothers of their own losses.

Many mothers waited to join AGSM until a chapter formed or became active in their area. Some told of caring for an ailing husband or family member and being unable to join sooner due to these constraints on their time. In a few cases, a veteran injured in the Great War did not die until the 1930s, at which time his mother became a gold star mother if the cause of death was determined to be service-related. Once she became a gold star mother through the service-connected death of a child, she could then apply for AGSM membership.

Ages and Origins

Although the applications did not ask for the age or birthdate of the mother, some told their years with pride. Alice Croghan's application noted she was the widow of a Civil War veteran while Lillie T. Rivenbark shared that she was the daughter of a Civil War veteran, as were a large percentage of these mothers. A 1929 government report stated that the average age of gold star mothers across the nation at that time was sixty-five. It can be assumed that the mothers sending applications for AGSM membership were of a similar age, most having been born during the Civil War or within a few years of that war's end. Early versions of the applications asked for the date of marriage between the veteran's parents; the majority of the marriage dates fell between 1866 and 1895.

The applications required the name of the father of the veteran. Although it was not requested, many mothers noted that the father of the veteran was deceased. Most fathers had died subsequent to their child's death in war, but some had been taken from their family when their child was still young. A note on the application of Christine Olson of Tacoma, Washington indicated that she had been widowed when her son was one year old and she had never remarried. Her son, Eric

Olson, was killed in action in 1918, two days past his twenty-first birthday. Mrs. Mary E. Fagan of Westport, Connecticut, wrote, "I was left a widow very young and my boy was all I had. I have never been well since but God is good to me to leave me able to keep [getting] around." Her son, John Joseph Fagan, died of pneumonia on Christmas Day 1918 at the age of twenty-nine.

Among the applications are fifty-three for gold star fathers. Gold star fathers could join the organization as associate members, but as such, they could neither vote nor hold office. Membership allowed them to participate in certain activities and recognized them for their relationship to the lost veteran.

Many of the gold star parents were of foreign birth. Among the countries identified as lands of origin were Russia, Ireland, Germany, Sweden, and Italy. Many of the couples had been married in their native land before coming to America, and some families had older children born in their homeland as well as younger children born in America. Since American citizenship was a requirement for membership in the AGSM, it is clear that these mothers had embraced their new land with enthusiasm and become citizens. For those who hadn't, it was never too late. Sevilla Mary Stewart, a Canadian by birth, became a U.S. citizen on January 31, 1939, and sent her membership application on March 23, 1939. A note on the application for the mother of Frances Perry Goulart of New Bedford, Massachusetts, advised that she had received her citizenship papers after filling out the application, but before she mailed it.

Elderly and Ailing

The passage of time between the Great War and the 1930s had been neither easy nor kind for some mothers and fathers. Included in the applications are pleas from family members and friends for AGSM to help the gold star parents in some way—securing government compensation, sending money, or having someone come to visit them.

A friend completed the application for Beulah A. Keeling Gates of Jackson, Michigan. Her son, William Arthur Keeling, died at sixteen of spinal meningitis in a hospital in France, having misrepresented his age in order to enlist in the Navy. He had enlisted at fifteen and served five months before he died. The application states that "this Mother is a cripple, unable to use her hand to write, confined to her bed most of the time."

The 1934 application for Adrienne Aubin of Willamette, Connecticut, was completed by her husband, Stanislas:

"You notice this application is signed by the father, a conservator for the Mother. After the death of our son, she became ill and has been seven years in Norwich State Hospital. She is home now but mentally unable to sign any papers, so if this paper is OK, I will send you the money for the membership."

Their son, Joseph Orner Aubin, died in the Army at the age of 19 in July 1918.

Susan Ann Wells of Boston, Massachusetts, had lost her son in the war, but his widow was still a part of her life in 1940. Chester Alexander Wells was killed in action in September 1918 at the age of twenty-seven and, unlike many of his counterparts in the service, he left behind both a mother and a widow. "My only child was married," his mother wrote. "His widow [Serena] married again—a man named Wells, no relation to me. She stands by me."

The Mothers of New Castle

An unidentified sympathizer was looking out for the ailing gold star mothers of New Castle, Pennsylvania. Five applications written in the same hand were submitted for the ill, elderly and needy gold star mothers of the town.

The February 1939 application for Mary Phillips of New Castle contained this note at the bottom: "P.S. Her hand shakes, she cannot write." Mrs. Phillips signed her application with an "X." Her son, James Phillips, had served in the Army and been killed in action:

Mrs. Phillips will be 80 years old next birthday; is totally disabled; under a doctor's care all the time and receives no compensation since her insurance ceased. [She] lives with a widowed daughter who works in a small store. Her husband [William], 82 years old, is also disabled. Their condition is pitiful as well as serious. She sure deserves the $45/month [government compensation to gold star parents] so please give this your immediate attention. She is deserving—having [had] two sons [serve] overseas. They are in bad shape.

Another New Castle gold star mother in poor circumstances was Maud Lena Lamm. On her 1931 application was written "receives no pension, suffers from foot trouble making it impossible at times for her to walk. Please see about her pension." Mrs. Lamm's son,

Raymond LeRoy Lamm, died in action in September 1918 at the age of 32.

Inez Bryson Custer, mother of Reed C. Bryson, was another gold star mother whose application was completed by the concerned friend in New Castle. The comment in the Remarks section tells a sad story:

Mrs. Custer receives no pension. She was not living with the boy's father at the time he enlisted at the age of 16. [Reed] said he was 18 and ran away because his mother would not consent [to give her son permission to enlist although underage]. [Reed] got angry and left his insurance to his father [and died in action at the age of 17]. The father then died, leaving a balance of $1,200 [out of the $10,000 government insurance policy] and she only received $700. The lawyer in New Castle kept $500. What a shame on him! Her second husband hurt his back and cannot work. [They] have a 1 acre farm and she sells a few eggs. They can't pay taxes. She has chronic bowel troubles. Please help her.

P.S. The above mother's condition is serious, [she] passes blood all the time and has not enough to pay the doctor what she owes. Please write her.

The same hand wrote the 1939 application for Alice Good:

The above boy [Harry David Good] died in the service [of pneumonia] on October 14, 1918 at Post Hospital, Fort Oglethorpe. The mother receives no pension. The father is 80 years old, totally disabled, an invalid. The mother's health is so bad it keeps her under a doctor's care all the time. Please see about her pension.

We can only hope that the guardian of New Castle was successful in his or her efforts to find compensation and assistance for this group of gold star parents who seemed to represent the worst of the scenarios reported on the membership applications.

Gold Star Daughters

Who were the children whose loss made these women gold star mothers? Collectively, the World War I gold star mothers' applications reflect the experiences of all the soldiers and sailors who fell in the Great War. Among the 1,597 applications, five of the mothers had lost daughters in the conflict. During this era, American women were assigned only to non-combatant positions—secretaries, nurses and communication workers—and, with the exception of nurses, their service was usually stateside.

Two of the daughters served with the Army Nursing Corps in France. On October 19, 1918, Army Nurse Gladys Watkins died of influenza in Allery, France at the age of twenty-seven, just six weeks after leaving the United States. Katie Geyer Moeschen's daughter, Frances, died of lobar pneumonia (probably the result of influenza) at the age of twenty-eight in a Red Cross hospital in France. Frances, an Army nurse and native of New York City, died in September 1918, less than two months after assuming her post in France.

Mary Pickard's daughter, Lena Mary Sylvester, also died of pneumonia. A U.S. Navy yeoman, she reported for active duty in June 1918 and, just three months later, she died at the age of twenty-one. She was assigned to the First Naval District in Cambridge, Massachusetts, not far from her hometown of Medford.

Mother Maude Quin of San Francisco, California, offered little information about her daughter, Jessie Jean Mackintosh, beyond the facts that she died in the base hospital at the Army's Camp Eustis in Virginia in October 1918 at the age of thirty-four.

Elizabeth Knox Wagner, a "Navy yeomanette," died on September 29, 1923, nearly three years after her honorable discharge from the Navy. Her mother, Emma Wagner of Poughkeepsie, New York, said her daughter "never recovered from [the] nervous shock received in the Wall Street explosion." The September 1920 explosion, thought to be the work of anarchists, killed dozens of people and injured more than 200. No information was provided as to whether Miss Wagner was a victim of the explosion or a traumatized observer. The cause of death was listed as "cerebral hemorrhage" and Miss Wagner's death at the age of thirty was considered to be service-related.

Gold Star Sons

The other gold star mothers applying for membership were created by the loss of sons serving in the U.S. armed services and the forces of the Allies. The length of their sons' service experience varied from eighteen years to just two weeks. They died in combat, in accidents, from disease, and a few died by their own hands. Most died during the war, but some returned home, broken in body and spirit, and survived many more arduous years before succumbing to their war wounds. Despite their grievous and acknowledged losses, not all the gold star mothers who applied for AGSM membership were eligible.

Early Service in the Allied Forces

In the opinion of many Americans, the nation came late to the Great War. Europe had been gripped in horrific combat since 1914. Stirred by curiosity, patriotism, or family ties to the land of their own or their parents' birth, some Americans had chosen early to join the military service of nations already fighting. The deaths reported by the gold star mothers prior to America's entry into the war came in the service of nations with which we would become allies in 1917. Britain's Royal Air Force, the Canadian Expeditionary Force, the French Aviation Corps, the Irish Guard, and the British Expeditionary Force were all represented among the World War I AGSM applications.

While these sons joined the forces of the Allies, other sons joined and fought on the side of Germany and its allies. Many American families found that they had family members fighting on both sides of the Hindenburg Line. And, sadly, some mothers' sons waged war against their brothers, for they had chosen different sides on which to serve.

For many young men eager to join the fight, Canada was their gateway to the conflict. Charles Joseph Kelly, son of Cecilia Kelly of Riverton, New Jersey, went to Canada seeking military service and misrepresented his birthdate. Born August 14, 1900, in Philadelphia, Charles advised the enlisting officer that he had been born in Nottingham, England on August 14, 1899. Enlisting in Ottawa at the real age of eighteen, Charles served only six weeks before he died in Canada's Camp Niagara of influenza and pneumonia.

An associate application submitted by William Seymour Brewer, a gold star father, tells of his son's eagerness to be part of a military force. Cedric Seymour Brewer enlisted in the Canadian Service in May 1913. He was sent to France in October 1915 but was returned to England in December of that year suffering from "illness and nervous breakdown" and was honorably discharged in 1916, "having been found no longer fit for War Service." Cedric subsequently joined the London Scottish Regiment in November 1917. He returned to France with this regiment and was killed in action ten months later at the age of twenty-seven.

Young Soldiers

Under President Wilson's military draft plan, men "in their twenties" were required to register for the national draft. On June 5, 1917, the day designated for the na-

tional registration, more than 9.6 million eligible men duly entered their names into the record. The first draft number was drawn on July 20, 1917, and America began to build its forces for war.

Enlistees had to be at least eighteen years of age, but many younger men refused to let their age prevent them from doing their duty as they saw it. In order to enlist, George Thomas Willis, son of Florence Willis of Philadelphia, Pennsylvania, reported his birthday as January 23, 1899, rather than December 20, 1899. On her membership application, Mrs. Willis wrote, "I am proud of my son who enlisted at the age of seventeen years... 10 days after the war was declared." A Marine, George quickly became a seasoned veteran who was repeatedly posted in the worst fighting at locations recognized today as turning points of World War I: the Toulon Sector, the Aisne Defensive sector and the Chateau-Thierry Sector (Belleau Wood). It was at Belleau Wood that he received his fatal wounds. Having served fourteen months that almost covered the entire length of the American involvement in the war, George was just eighteen when he died.

Marguerite Stricklen reported that her son Irving Alexander Slicklen enlisted in March 1918, just two months past his fifteenth birthday. Lost in foreign waters with the sinking of the *Tampa* in September 1918, he died three months prior to his sixteenth birthday after six months of service.

Although World War I has often been referred to as "The Boys' War," it was not only young men who fought. AGSM membership applications tell of sons whose ages ranged from fifteen to thirty-eight years at the time of their deaths. Among those who died of injuries after returning home, the oldest was fifty-nine at the time of his death in 1934. Based on the ages reported on the applications:

- 3% died at ages between fifteen and seventeen;
- 18% between eighteen and twenty;
- 51% between twenty-one and twenty-five;
- 19% between twenty-six and twenty-nine; and
- 9% died at the age of thirty or older.

Refusing to be Left Behind

Once America joined the war, the public and personal pressure on young men to serve their nation became stronger. Many who were judged unfit for service in the American forces refused to accept that decision and the public humiliation that could accompany it. Canada became their gateway to service—just as it had been for those who enlisted before America joined the fighting.

Jane Berry of Portland, Oregon, explained that her son, Carl, was "rejected by our [United States] examining physicians [due to] throat trouble. But [he] immediately enlisted with the Canadian Forces. [He] contracted TB and was gradually declining [when he was involved in an] air crash in Ontario." Discharged in December 1918 after nine months of service, Carl died in March 1919 at the age of thirty, due to service-related injuries.

Sergeant John H. Neilson was another American eager to join the fighting. His mother, Margaret McConaugley Neilson of Peoria, Illinois, explained that her son enlisted four times, but was rejected because of "defective eyesight. But he had memorized the eye test and finally passed the fourth time." His July 1918 death in France at the age of twenty-nine was attributed to eusphymia (infection). He had served seven months.

Veterans Answer the Call

Thousands of veterans chose to re-enlist when America entered the war. Their experience and maturity were invaluable to the armed services faced with the task of training hundreds of thousands of raw young recruits and draftees. Corporal George Gurney Christensen of Tustin, California, had served four years in the Marines, which included three years in Asia. He had been discharged from service in July 1916, but enlisted again just three days after war was declared. His mother, Emma Gurney Christensen, indicated simply that he died of "wounds received in action somewhere in France." Marine Corps records indicate that Corporal Christensen saw combat in the Toulon-Toyon Sector from March 19 to May 13, 1918, and at Aisne from June 1 to June 5. Severely gassed in action at Chateau-Thierry on June 15, he died the following day at a Paris hospital at the age of twenty-five.

How the Soldiers Died

The gold star mothers' applications tell a frightening tale of the hazards facing World War I soldiers. While every soldier mentally accepted that death might come on the battlefield, few could have anticipated the other hazards that jeopardized their survival in this modern war. Among the applications, only 53 percent indicate that the soldier was killed in action or subsequently died of wounds received in action. Fully 22 percent of the deaths were attributed to Spanish influenza, the unstoppable and untreatable pandemic scourge that took the lives of more than 21 million people worldwide between 1918 and 1919, killing "more Americans in a single year than died in battle in World War I, World War II, the Korean Conflict and the Vietnam War."[2]

Pneumonia, usually this influenza's final symptomatic manifestation, was often used synonymously with flu as the cause of death in military records. The flu swept through military camps, hospitals, and cities around the world. Ships transporting soldiers to Europe would leave the dock with apparently healthy crew members and passengers and, often within twenty-four hours, illness would begin to manifest itself, leaving hundreds dead in the few days it took to cross the Atlantic Ocean. These ships began to be referred to as flu ships. Influenza victims often felt fine in the morning but died by nightfall.

Attacking the body's immune system, this flu took an unparalleled toll among the young and healthy whose immune systems were strong, rather than striking the ill, elderly, and very young as other strains of influenza usually do. Physicians and nurses were helpless to cure the disease or even mitigate its symptoms, and often fell victim to it as well. One in four Americans contracted the flu during this period, and more than half a million died from the disease in the United States.[3]

With no respect for gender, age, education, trade or responsibilities, the influenza epidemic was a terrifying and brutally swift counterpoint to the horrors of war. Cora Maze's son, Frank, and daughter-in-law, Constance, both died of the flu while Frank trained in the Student's Army Training Corps at the University of Utah in Salt Lake City. Frank's death came just two months after he reported for service and he died at twenty, a married man whose young widow soon followed him in death. Student Army Training Corps camps had been set up across the nation, and the toll taken by influenza among the young men gathered in those compounds was enormous.

The swiftness of the flu's onset and the speed with which it killed its victims meant that few parents were able to see their sons for a last good-bye. Mrs. May Hart (Gabb) Smith of Ontario, California wrote about her desperate journey to the bedside of her son, George Percival Gabb:

"I received a telegram from Fort Stevens [Oregon] that my boy was seriously ill and left at once to go to him. A message reached me en route with the word—he had passed away. I left the train at the last station, which was Ashland, Oregon, and waited there for the remains and attendant."

What else faced the World War I soldier? Among the causes of death listed on the membership applications are the common diseases and injuries of mankind at any time in any land: measles, infections, appendicitis, diphtheria, tetanus, anthrax, meningitis, and accidents and injuries related to physical exertion and handling livestock. There were also those sources of death provided only through the invention and intervention of humankind: poison gas (first used in 1915), explosions, air crashes, transport accidents, shrapnel, bullets, and ships sunk by torpedoes. One mother wrote that her son survived the shelling and sinking of his ship only to die of a heart attack after being rescued at sea. Another died of exposure after being adrift in a lifeboat for many days. Others did not survive shipboard surgeries for appendicitis and bowel obstructions.

Aerial warfare and transport were in their early stages during World War I; many of the airplanes of the time appeared to be no sturdier than the fragile balsa wood and paper models built by children. Among AGSM applicants, airplane crashes claimed twenty-three of their sons, including the son of founder Grace Seibold. Drowning claimed twenty-two others, although not all drownings were ship-related. One young man on leave lost his life in an unsuccessful attempt to rescue two comrades caught in a riptide off the coast of Southern California.

Some soldiers neither died of their battle wounds nor recovered from them. Many of the mothers' sons returned home from the war with physical, mental, and emotional damage that would never heal. Their release from the military was often categorized as "honorably discharged for the convenience of the service." Some came home as amputees, paraplegics, quadriplegics, or shell-shocked mutes. Others were blind or in severe respiratory distress due to the effects of poison gas. Many were profoundly depressed and suffering from diseases and injuries for which there was no cure at the time. For some, there was a merciful release through death within weeks of returning home; others would live for years at home or move from hospital to hospital with little hope or relief from pain.

The horrors of poison gas were vividly recounted by Elizabeth Millard of East Rochester, New York when she described her son's last few years:

"[Army Sergeant Murray M. Millard died of] lobar pneumonia, caused by being so badly gassed ... in France. [He was also] blinded badly. [He was] sent to England to several hospitals before being returned home. Never recovered from that dreadful gas cough. Doctors said his lungs were eaten out by gas."

Honorably discharged in January 1919, Sgt. Millard suffered until March 1921 when he died at the age of thirty-three. (Mrs. Millard would later succeed Grace Darling Seibold as national president of AGSM from 1932 to 1934.)

Tuberculosis (TB) was listed as the cause of death for forty-five of the servicemen named in the available World War I applications, but only four died of TB during active service. By 1925, thirty-seven of the remaining forty-one had died. One of them was Chester B. Spencer, son of Agnes B. Spencer of Los Angeles, California. She wrote that Chester was injured while on "special duty":

"A trench mortar exploded causing an explosion of a [munitions] magazine. Chester was thrown against the walls, crushing his side, breaking four ribs, puncturing his lung, causing hemorrhages and bursting his eardrums... [as a result of his injuries, he] became infected with TB."

Released from duty in January 1918 "by reason of physical disability," Private Spencer died of his service-related injuries in January 1919 at the age of twenty-seven.

More than thirty of the soldiers named in the available World War I applications died of a non-specified "disease"—possibly unknown or unrecognized diseases resulting from the horrible conditions, injuries, and stress to which the soldiers were subjected. Looking at the dates of death, it is possible that in many cases, the causes were influenza and pneumonia that some harried and desperate doctor, surrounded by dead and dying soldiers, had simply noted as "disease."

For some soldiers, even the Armistice brought no safety. Anna Mary Roth of Portland, Oregon, lost her son, Peter B. Roth, in November 1920, two years after the war ended. Peter was a member of the Army's Provisional Guard when he died "of a gunshot wound—shot by a German officer in the Army of Occupation, Coblenz, Germany." Peter, age eighteen, had served seven months when he died.

Choosing Suicide

For some soldiers, the experience of war was so horrifying they were emotionally and psychologically unable to deal with it. Many returned home from the service and struggled desperately with their memories and fears at a time in which the science and use of psychology were in their infancy. What would today be classified as post-traumatic stress syndrome was simply referred to as bad nerves or malingering for these stricken soldiers.

Susie Bishop of Detroit, Michigan, wrote that her son, Benjamin, had committed "suicide [while] mentally deranged" in 1936. Benjamin "was not able to work much of the time [after his discharge in August 1919 and] drove taxis when he was able to work." Repeatedly hospitalized before and after his discharge, Benjamin apparently found no peace and committed suicide in 1936 at the age of forty-four. Mrs. Bishop wrote "he was my only help as my husband is dead." Her application for AGSM membership was rejected as "ineligible due to the lapse of time" from Benjamin's military service to his death and the lack of confirmation that the death was service-related. AGSM membership at this time was never granted to a mother whose child had died by suicide while serving in the military.

Mary Ellen Wheeler of Portland, Oregon, was denied membership when she wrote that her son, William, died of "the effects of inhaling illuminating gas" five years after his discharge from the Army. This application was marked by the AGSM as ineligible, citing "suicide" as the reason, although an accompanying letter from the Veterans Administration indicated that William's death was "a result of a disability incurred during his service."

Edgar Fay Stahl, son of Leona Parmalee Stahl of Los Angeles, California, enlisted in the Army in May 1914. A musician, he rose steadily through the ranks and accepted a commission as a second lieutenant band leader in July 1918. Until then, his various postings had all been stateside. In August 1918, he left for service in Revingy, France, in the Meuse-Argonne Sector. On November 7, 1918, just four days before the signing of the Armistice, he died as a "result of [a] gunshot wound, self-inflicted, not in the line of duty" according to the War Department's adjutant general's letter. Mrs. Stahl's application listed Edgar's service in some detail, but for "cause of death" she simply noted "illness." While we will never know with certainty, it is not difficult to image the shock that Edgar must have experienced when he was assigned to that corridor of carnage in the midst of the war's worst fighting. His service experience prior to that time had been filled with performing at military ceremonies, entertaining troops, and representing the military at public events far from real combat and the horror of war. Regardless of his reasons, at the age of twenty-seven, Edgar could no longer cope and took his own life.

Acknowledging the Possibility of Death

Susie Elizabeth Mabry of Marietta, Georgia, shared letters from her son, Lawrence G. Mabry, with a local newspaper reporter and they were reprinted in an article under the headline of "Cobb County Boy Writes of Being under Fire in a Recent Battle with Germans":

"Somewhere in France, June 15, 1918

"Dear Mother: After three weeks I write again to let you know I am still alive and well. Since writing the last time, I have been through a real "nerve-tester" which was a siege with the Germans. Never got a scratch during the whole time, which I can say was very lucky according to what some of the fellows got. The Germans are a hard lot, but, believe me, the Americans are just as hard. We were subjected to artillery fire, gas and machine gun fire. Of course, some were killed and wounded but not a man lost his nerve or showed a yellow streak.

"I always had doubts about the hospital corps, but now I see there are no braver men anywhere than they are. They go out in the midst of a heavy barrage and face death every second to care for the wounded. Germany will never whip the United States as long as they fight like they did this time.

"We are back in the lines now in a nice town for a little rest. It sure seems good to sleep without shrapnel flying around."

The newspaper reported that Mabry's "nerve-tester" was "no doubt the now famous battle of Chateau Thierry in which the Marines made such a wonderful drive against overwhelming odds and won. His letters indicate that this is correct as he names his commander and the commander is the same as the one that led the charge."

A later, undated letter was also printed in which Mabry shared with his mother that he knew his luck might not last:

"We are in a nice little town situated on a river, which makes it very handy for bathing and swimming,

Fig. 4-3: A World War I soldier's rifle and helmet mark his temporary burial place. (Fenelon Collection)

Fig. 4-2: Marine Glenn Shotwell Loomis died at the age of twenty-three during the fight for the Belleau Wood. (AGSM Collection)

which you can imagine is appreciated, after going so long without even a face wash.

"Now I will tell you something, but don't think that I am superstitious or scared, for that is not it, but a fellow can never tell when he will get knocked off. If such should happen, I turn everything over to you to do as you see fit. Don't worry a minute about me for I realize to a great extent the times I am now passing through, and am fully prepared for anything that comes my way. I still believe as I always did, that a fellow don't die until his time comes. When I think of some of the narrow escapes some of us had, I begin to think I bear a charmed life. Six men around me were hit and I didn't get a scratch. Six of us were behind a bank and one was killed and one wounded on each side of me and I wasn't hurt."

Lawrence Mabry's premonition came true on September 15, 1918, when he was shot and killed while on duty near Harcourt, France. Lawrence's death at age 26 must have created a hard future for his mother. A handwritten note at the bottom of her September 1931 membership application states "dues exempt until ability to pay."

Knowing How Their Sons Died

For some mothers, there was little information avail-able about the circumstances surrounding their son's death. Official military telegrams gave few details; often, for security reasons, not even the date or location in which the death occurred was disclosed. Luckier parents subsequently received letters from their son's commanding officers, comrades, and friends or, in some cases, from a nurse, doctor, or ambulance driver who had cared for the soldier in his last days or moments.

Myra Buckman of New York wrote about her son, Jewell, who was killed in a night attack in France: "We have much to be thankful for, even in our irreparable loss. His comrades took off his broken body [a] pocket diary… and in it were the names and addresses of his comrades. And, through them, we have learned every detail of his heroic death."

Kate Shotwell Loomis, mother of Glenn Shotwell Loomis, learned from eyewitnesses about the details of her son's death at age twenty-three. Her hometown newspaper published the following account of his death: [Fig. 4-2]

"This was the beginning of the fight for the Belleau Wood in the course of which the Brigade of Marines engaged, in fifteen days, five German Divisions and part of a sixth. On the night of June 7, Glenn was assigned to an advanced listening post. During the night, the Germans counter attacked. Lt. Gissel, in charge of the platoon of which Glenn was a member, in a letter to his parents, wrote: 'His last deed was to give us warning and then as a good Marine, [he] went one better and went after the Boche. I do not doubt but that he saved many a life in my platoon. The boy died game.'

"First Lt. Robert Blake [his commanding officer]… wrote concerning him: 'Your son, as long as I knew him, was a clean, quiet, able, courteous soldier and a credit to the service. No one regrets his taking more than we with whom he served and under whom he served. He died in the front line, in the midst of battle, facing the enemy as only a brave man can.'"

For others, sadly, little information ever came back to them. Anna Popp of Norwood, Ohio, was able to report only that her son, Albert Popp, was killed in action with the Army "somewhere in France." Of Albert, who died at twenty-five, she wrote:

"He was a good, hard-working boy, never idle and always did the hardest kind of labor. [He] was always my companion. He enlisted to keep from being drafted. He said he did not want a "D" [for "draftee"] with his name."

Of her son, Roy Daniel Gardinier, Myrtle Gardinier of Cannonsville, New York, wrote, "from all I have been able to find out, he was struck by a shell. It happened during the Battle in the Argonne. His father passed away soon after, leaving me alone."

Martha H. Martin of Sullivan, Indiana, had conflicting information about the death of her son, Corporal Charles A. Martin, a Marine serving in France, who she said died of "shell fire/weak heart" at the age of twenty-five. On her 1930 application, she wrote:

"Some said he died on the battlefield. A comrade said he was taken to the hospital and if it had not been for his heart, he would have pulled through. His death was reported the 8th of June. I never got the notice until the 8th of July. I have been an invalid since I heard—the shock was too much for me."

The Pain of an Unmarked Grave

For many mothers, another type of sorrow had to be borne. In the midst of battle, proper identification and marked burial of the dead were often impossible. Soldiers who died were buried quickly as a health pre-

caution. Too often, the bodies were not carefully identified when buried and, in many cases, the temporary gravesites were forgotten or lost. Some mothers learned not only that their son had died, but that his place of burial was unknown. The Army Quartermaster Corps, responsible for the burial and transport of the remains of American soldiers, worked assiduously after the war to locate, identify, and honorably inter the body of every American soldier, but the task was tremendous, given the numbers of soldiers who died and the manner in which the battlegrounds had shifted back and forth across the same territory. Etha May Jackson of Philadelphia, Pennsylvania, wrote that the body of her son, Winfield A. Jackson who was killed in action in France, had been buried and exhumed three times and then lost.

An amazing story was told on the application of Elizabeth West Stevenson, mother of George West Stevenson of Price, Utah. According to his military record, George, a twenty-year old Marine private, had survived some of the worst fighting of the war in 1918:

- Toulon Sector, March 18 to May 13
- Ainse Defensive, June 1 to June 5
- Chateau Thierry Sector (Belleau Wood), June 6 to July 16
- Marne-Marne Offensive, July 18 to July 20
- Marchone Sector, August 6 to 16

His luck ran out on the fourth day of the St. Mihiel Offensive when he was killed in battle. Mother Stevenson wrote that George was buried by the Germans, and for nine years the notation "no record of a burial and no record of a grave" stood in the government records. Then one of the Germans who had buried him wrote the *Epworth Herald*'s editor providing details about the burial. After investigation, George's body was identified by the Marine insignia on the collar and dental records. For many years, stories like this one kept other gold star mothers' hopes alive that their children, who also lay in an unknown and unmarked place, might yet be found.

Two-Star Mothers

Among the World War I gold star membership applicants whose records still exist, there were twenty-two mothers who lost two sons in the military service. One, Mrs. Florence L. Denn of Clarke Summit,

Pennsylvania, was a stepmother who had raised her deceased husband's two sons, Alexander and Richard, both of whom were killed in the war. Despite a poignant plea for membership and her statement that she had raised the boys from young children and they considered her to be their mother, as evidenced by making her the beneficiary of their military insurance coverage, her relationship of stepmother to the young men made her ineligible for AGSM membership. The other twenty-one two-star mothers met the requirements and were admitted to membership.

Every Son a Hero

In many ways, every soldier who serves his country is a hero—willing to forego personal safety to ensure the safety of others or to fight for a cause in which he truly believes. Heroes rise from every rank and service, in everyday action and in horrific combat, and from every background and age. Many gold star applicants wrote proudly of their sons' bravery, service accomplishments, and the recognition and honors they had received.

In action worthy of a thrilling Hollywood movie, Mary Talbot reported how her son, Ralph Talbot, a Congressional Medal of Honor recipient, risked his life to save an injured crew member aboard his airplane:

"On October 14, 1918, while on an air raid over Pittham, Belgium, Lt. Talbot and one other plane became detached from the formation due to loss of power by motor, and were attacked by twelve enemy scouts. During the severe fight that followed, his plane shot down one of the enemy scouts. His observer was shot through the elbow and his gun jammed. [The observer] cleared the jam with one hand while Lt. Talbot maneuvered to gain time, and then returned to fight. The observer fought on until shot twice in the stomach and once in the hip. When he collapsed, Lt. Talbot attacked the nearest enemy scout with his front guns and shot him down. With his observer unconscious and his motor failing, he dived to escape the balance of the enemy and crossed the German trenches at an altitude of 50 feet, landing at the nearest hospital, left his observer and returned alone to his aerodrome."

A member of the First Marine Aviation Force, Ralph lost his own life at age 21 in an air crash just two weeks after his heroic effort to save his crewman.

Regardless of citations and medals, one Cleveland, Ohio, mother, Lillie T. Rivenbark, clearly understood her son's contribution to ending the war. She explained, "My son was killed in that famous battle that first broke through the German lines in Meuse-Argonne under the leadership of General Douglas McArthur that finally brought in the signing of the Armistice."

Ineligible for Membership

Not all of the mothers who applied for AGSM membership were accepted. Death by suicide was not considered service-related by AGSM even if the suicide had occurred while the soldier was on active duty. Mothers of suicides were therefore ineligible for membership.

Stepmothers were not eligible for membership in the early days of AGSM, although they were recognized as gold star mothers by the government and public.

A lack of confirmation from the government that the death was service-related prevented acceptance of Nellie E. Gillett's application. Her son, Sergeant Arthur Briggs Gillett, had been demobilized in July 1919. He died in early October 1919 at the age of twenty-eight from "tubercular meningitis brought about by exposure, hardships and supposed serum treatments while on active duty in France," according to his mother. Able to verify only that Arthur had been honorably discharged, but not that his death was service-related, the AGSM custodian of records marked the application, "Ineligible for lack of proof."

Ellen Gately of Arlington, Massachusetts, lost her son, John Edward Gately, to influenza at the age of nineteen in September 1918. Assigned to meet the transport ships returning with the wounded and ill, John contracted influenza while on duty in Boston. A reply to the AGSM inquiry for service confirmation, signed by the Chief of the Navy Department Bureau of Navigation, bluntly explained a harsh fact: "enlisted men of the Merchant Marine during the World War were not in the same status as enlisted men of the U.S. Navy." The note at the top of Mrs. Gately's application reads: "Not a gold star mother—Ineligible."

The membership application for Sarah E. Pulver of Seattle, Washington, was also determined to be ineligible as the death of her son, Ralph K. Pulver, was not considered service-connected. Ralph, twenty-seven, was "given his discharge at Fort Liscum, Alaska on the 18th day of January. On his way home to Anchorage, Alaska, he was killed in a snowslide" on January 22, 1919. Technically, since Ralph had been discharged, the death was not considered service-related although he was returning home from military duty.

Remarks on the Applications

Personal notes were added to the applications of many mothers. Some were sad, others proud, and a few simply provided more detail. Anna Gorst completed an application for Anna Dubravsky of Lawrence County, Pennsylvania, who signed with an "X." Although Mrs. Dubravsky's son, Mick, had died at age seventeen of wounds received in action in the October 1918 Meuse-Argonne Offensive, she did not send in a membership application until April 21, 1939. There was some urgency at that point though—the note under Remarks read, "Please send her [membership] card so she can go with all the other gold star mothers [to the] Mother's Day Banquet given by the Service Star Legion." Actually, Mrs. Dubravsky's status as a gold star mother was not dependent upon membership in AGSM since she became a gold star mother when her son died in military service. This public confusion about gold star mothers' status versus membership in AGSM would continue for many decades.

The note on Mary E. Salsbery's application told of the comfort she took in hearing the purported last words of her son. The Dunmore, Pennsylvania, mother wrote that her son, Sergeant Duane Sherwood Salsbery, had been "hit by machine gun [and his] jugular vein severed. He died as he was being carried to the hospital, but said, 'Tell Mother I died happy for my country.'" Duane died at Fisme, France at the age of twenty-one.

For Hannah Westberg Olson, the date of her son's death was particularly significant. She wrote that Fred Carl William Olson, a Marine, was "wounded in ac-tion on October 3, 1918; rejoined his division and was killed in action on his twenty-first birthday, November 4, 1918."

Anne Elizabeth G. Shea of Philadelphia, Pennsylvania, had to bear double grief:

"[My husband] was stricken October 15th, 1918 on parting with an older son. Frank, my sailor son, died in the Naval Hospital in Philadelphia [of influenza and pneumonia] on October 20th. His father (my husband) died October 22nd. I buried them both on the same day (October 25th)."

Mrs. Margaret C. Ransom of Rochester, New York, wrote at the bottom of her application, "For the Stars and Stripes and the good old USA which we all so dearly love." Her son, Private Raymond R. Ransom, was killed in action in September 1918. Amelia S. Heckert of Bakerstown, Pennsylvania wrote of her son, Seaman 2nd Class William Paul Heckert, and his attitude toward the war. "Dear Paul was a fine business fellow," she wrote, "and said he would go and have a hand in it." Paul died of pneumonia at the age of twenty-nine while serving on board a receiving ship in Boston Harbor.

Their Fondest Hope

The gold star mothers and fathers of the Great War would undoubtedly have agreed with the sentiment of Bessie Harris, mother of Corporal Harry Harris, when she wrote on her 1938 application, "Having made the supreme sacrifice, I hope and pray that my darling son was not killed in vain and that the world will be at peace before long." Albert E. Forker's mother, Josephine, wrote in 1931, "I pray there will never be another war." Sadly, in the decades that followed, neither mother's wish would be granted.

Fig. 5-1: Gold star mother Hanna Snidow of Willamette, Oregon at the grave of her son, Private George Milner Snidow, at the St. Mihiel Cemetery in 1930. Mrs. Snidow was sixty-six years old when she traveled to France. *(Fenelon Collection)*

CHAPTER 5

The Gold Star Pilgrimage

By far the most representative American pilgrimage that ever left our shores. There goes your real "good will" delegation. No diplomacy, no schemes to put over, just mothers, the same the whole world over.

—WILL ROGERS

FROM THE BEGINNING OF AMERICA'S involvement in the Great War, much attention had been given by the nation, the government, and the military to methods of demonstrating the respect and homage due the mothers and widows of the fallen. Following the Armistice and continuing through the 1920s, the American Legion, Veterans of Foreign Wars, American War Mothers and other organizations held the gold star survivors in special esteem and diligently worked to honor the loss of their loved ones and assist them wherever possible. For many of the survivors, however, neither their dearest wish nor their greatest need would be satisfied until they stood beside the graves of their lost sons and husbands to say farewell.

The majority of gold star families had elected to bring home their veterans' remains for burial in a family plot, church graveyard, or veterans' cemetery. The panoply of a military funeral and the support of family and friends helped the majority of these survivors deal with their loss and move forward. But for many of the more than 30,000 families who chose to bury their dead near the European battlefields where they had fought and died, the process of grief was still unfinished. The vast majority of these families had no hope of traveling to Europe to grieve and say their final goodbyes at the graves of their lost soldiers. Most were constrained and daunted by the cost and magnitude of such a trip or by the language barriers—and, in the case of many gold star mothers, limited by age and illness.

Post-war Pilgrimages Begin

As soon as the war ended, some well-to-do families began to make trips to the European battlegrounds to see where their sons or husbands were buried. Until the work of the American Battle Monuments Commission was completed, these families often found only a crude marker in an isolated copse or a cross wavering in ground still upturned from the battles that had been waged across it.

As early as 1919, war veterans who had been elected to or returned to Congress, such as Fiorello LaGuardia, began to call for a government program that would enable gold star mothers to visit the European graves of America's soldiers. But the government was still in the process of bringing the last remnants of the AEF's Army of Occupation back to the United States and, knowing the chaos of the temporary burial sites and the numbers of soldiers whose remains had not yet been found or identified, little attention was given to encouraging travel by the families, especially at government expense.

As time passed and the vision of the American Battle Monuments Commission was brought to fruition, non-governmental organizations began to sponsor pilgrimages to the American military cemeteries in Europe. In May 1925, a party of more than 900 gold star pilgrims traveled to France under the auspices of the Gold Star Association of America. The pilgrimage was organized and led by Effie Vedders, a New York gold star mother who had lost both her sons in France. While this group

Fig. 5-2: On a private pilgrimage in 1919, relatives of naval veteran Fredrick W. Van Horne gather at his gravesite in a temporary cemetery in Europe.
(Fenelon Collection)

of travelers only visited American cemeteries in France, their trip included the sights of Paris and many meetings with American and French diplomats.

May W. Reynolds, a gold star mother from St. Louis, Missouri, spoke publicly of her pilgrimage experience after her return from that trip. As the day neared on which they would finally stand beside their loved ones' burial places, all the sights and fetes in Paris were quickly forgotten by these mothers:

"All this had been preliminary to the one great object and desire of the gold star mothers since their arrival in France—that is, to visit the cemeteries containing the last resting place of their beloved dead. So... the mothers were taken by train and auto cars to the cemeteries they wished to visit—Bony, Thiancourt, Romaine, Belleau Wood, [and] Chateau Thierry.

"My heart went out in sympathy to the mothers as they sought the crosses that bore the names of their loved ones, but at last I was going to my boy—to Leland—to his cross in Belleau Wood, alone with my grief, my memories, my longings for hopes unfulfilled, all the yearnings of the bereaved mother for her only son! What did I expect—a neglected, nameless grave? I hardly know, but what I saw was the most beautifully kept spot that one can picture! The snowy cross bearing the proud inscription:

Leland M. Reynolds
Private
Co. K-5, Marines"

Her appreciation of the work done by the American Battlefield Monument Commission was evident as she continued:

"I came away comforted and at peace. I am glad my boy is there, in that sacred spot, which he earned in his loyal service to France and the Allies. I shall want to go back again, I think, but there is a feeling that I shall always have now, that whether I go back or not, 'all is well' over there. His comrades in life who made the supreme sacrifice are "resting" nearby. They are all there together.

"I was greatly impressed by the beauty and perpetual care of our cemeteries, and more touched by the sympathy and kindness of even the children of France as they placed flowers upon the graves of our American Dead."[1]

Despite the satisfaction and comfort the visit had brought to her, Mrs. Reynolds found it difficult to leave France:

"As we left the shores of France, perhaps for the last time, no doubt a feeling of longing and agony of parting welled up in the hearts of the mothers; but to be quickly subdued by the memory of the white crosses in their perfect and peaceful settings, and the assurance that America will preserve and care for these sacred dead in their 'God's Acre' in France through the coming generations."[2]

The Government Considers Pilgrimages

In the decade following the war, repeated efforts were made by many groups and individuals to convince the government to organize and fund trips to the American military cemeteries in Europe for gold star mothers. Repeated hearings were held but for many years the proposed legisaltion simply died without action. The testimony of the gold star mothers on behalf of the pilgrimages was emotional, personal, and difficult to ignore. Effie Vedders, who lost two sons in the war, started her testimony by telling the committee that, as men, they could never really understand the issues involved for the mothers of these soldiers:

"I want to begin by telling you that you are all men and you have not and cannot feel the way a mother does. It is a part of her body that is lying over there. She spent 20 years… in bringing up that boy; she gave her time, both day and night, and none of you can realize what a mother's loss is. Several of my mothers [members of the Gold Star Association of America] have their only sons over there, and when the shock came, it looked as if there was nothing in the world left for them and their minds wandered off—where was he; what is the country like; what had he done; where had he been?

"They do not want his body desecrated by being moved around; they want it left where his companions put it. That is why the majority of them did not want them brought back. I have any number of letters from mothers wailing—where? What is the country like? Where is he? Could I only see it? And these little pictures of the cross [photographs of the headstones provided by the YMCA] do not mean anything."[3]

The statement of Mrs. M. Steinkant of New York exposed the agony and insecurity that many mothers still experienced despite the six years that had passed since the war ended:

"Now, I give two sons for this country, and my oldest boy, he was not born in this country; he was born in Germany, and they both enlist when they wanted the boys [at the time of the draft], and both not come back. The little one I know for sure he is killed, but the other, I am in doubt, because there were plenty of boys who said my son is alive, and I cannot find him, and I now ask you men folks to help me to find that boy, who shall be shell-shocked, who shall be known as the unknown man in this country, and I do not know where. I am looking for him for five years, and I cannot get him. All I ask is please help me—to carry me to Paris—and I will go through anything. That is all I want; that is all I ask."[4]

Jennie Walsh of New York was identified as a representative of the American Gold Star Mothers' Association. She spoke of losing her only child in France when he was just eighteen years old. Her final comments brought a round of applause from the audience at the hearing:

"It is not a question of money with your Government; they have plenty of money. They have money for everything else—they had money for the war; they had money for guns; they had money to kill them, and then why have they not the money to help these poor mothers, whose hearts are just breaking for the sight of the grave of their boy?"[5]

Despite these pleas, more than ten years passed following the war with no pilgrimage legislation.

In early 1929, pilgrimage hearings were once again held by the Committee on Military Affairs in the House of Representatives. Presented by Representative Thomas Butler of Pennsylvania, H.R. Bill 5494 proposed sending gold star mothers to the European war cemeteries. Under his proposal, the planning and coordination of the trip would be handled by the American Red Cross. Representative Butler stressed the urgency of acting on the proposal this time:

"This movement has been talked about for 10 years and I now ask you gentlemen to dispose of it for all time. If the women described are ever going to go as the guests of the Government, if they are ever to go at all, now is the time for them to go. Many who might have been included died in the last year. In my own Congressional District… six have gone during that period."[6]

Several members of Congress spoke before the Committee urging the immediate passage of the Bill, stating that the time had come for such legislation and that action must be taken before it was too late for the majority of the gold star mothers to make the journey. Many speakers cited letters from their constituents urging the passage of H.R. Bill 5494.

There were also some who spoke against the proposed legislation. Many mothers and wives of servicemen who had returned with horrific permanent physical and mental injuries felt the government funds should be spent on the living. Some citizens felt the pilgrimages should be funded by public contributions rather than using federal funds. And others felt that, having received insurance compensation following the death of the servicemen, the survivors of the gold star veterans had been recompensed enough.

Gold Star Pilgrimages Become Law

On March 2, 1929, President Calvin Coolidge signed an Act of Congress that approved and funded the Gold Star Pilgrimage of Mothers and Widows. In its final form, the law provided more than $5.8 million to enable gold star mothers and widows to travel to the gravesites of their World War dead at government expense on government-organized pilgrimages. Travel would begin in 1930 and continue through 1933 during the spring and summer of each year to take advantage of optimal weather.

The legislation placed the Army Quartermaster Corps in charge of the pilgrimages. An inspired choice, the Quartermaster Corps was the logistics and supply arm of the armed services and its burial and registration services had worked unceasingly for years to find, identify, and properly inter the war dead. Perhaps better than any other military division, the Quartermaster Corps knew the true cost of the war in terms of lives and horror, for they had been responsible for assuring dignity in death for those who had fought and died. Following the war, the Corps had corresponded with the families of the war dead to determine their wishes regarding the interment of sons and husbands, and they knew first hand the anguish these families had experienced.

The first task was to determine the number of gold star pilgrims eligible for and interested in making a pilgrimage. Gold star mothers "of deceased soldiers, sailors, and marines of the American Forces now interred in the cemeteries of Europe" were automatically eligible. Gold star widows were eligible only if they had not remarried in the period between the war and the pilgrimages, a restriction that eliminated many. The legislation was amended to include mothers and widows of Americans who had died in the service of the Allies if they had joined the Allies prior to America's entrance into the war. (From this point forward, for the sake of simplicity, any reference to gold star mothers on the pilgrimages will include gold star widows as well.) The task of determining the number of eligible participants, who they were and where they lived, was assigned to the War Department under the supervision of Acting Secretary of War Patrick J. Hurley. The Department used Army records, pension records, the Veterans Bureau files, and local veterans groups in an effort to identify and contact every eligible gold star mother. What they found reinforced the position of those who said that such a pilgrimage could no longer be postponed. The *New York Times* quantified the effort and findings for its readers:

"There are more than 30,000 graves of American soldiers in France, Belgium and England, mostly in France, with names on the headstones. There are 1,643 graves which cradle the bodies of men whose identities are unknown.

"It was no easy task to search out the mothers of these 30,000 who are known. There has been no occasion for locating these mothers until the present legislation was passed. The Quartermaster Corps started with the name of the next of kin which was given by each man when he went into the army. It wrote 30,000 letters to the addresses given. [Another source from the same period indicates that more than 35,000 letters were sent.[7]] Out of every 100 sent, forty came back unclaimed. Those who had been set down as the next of kin had died, or moved away, or otherwise faded from the picture during the twelve or thirteen years that had passed.

"But 60 per cent of these next-of-kin letters brought answers. Of mothers… less than half were still alive. Of wives… there were many who had married again and so become ineligible for the trip. [Although the search for missing relatives continued,] there has been found only one mother or widow to about three men buried abroad—11,630 out of 30,792."[8]

In December 1929, the War Department published the official findings:

- 11,440: Total number of mothers and widows entitled to make the Pilgrimage
- 6,730: Number of such mothers and widows who desire to make the Pilgrimage
- 5,323: Number of such mothers and widows who desire to make the Pilgrimage during the calendar year 1930
- $5,653,000: Probable cost of the Pilgrimages ($870 per pilgrim)[9]

The decision was made to group the pilgrims by state to simplify transportation to New York where the sailing portion of the pilgrimages would begin. To maintain fairness, President Hoover's wife, Lou Henry Hoover, in the presence of General Pershing, the Secretary of War and selected Army officers, drew the names of states and U.S. Protectorates from a goldfish bowl (the same one used for the draft in 1917). The gold star mothers of Nebraska became the first group to be scheduled for their pilgrimages.

As the planning progressed, there were still those who felt the money could be better spent. Even some gold star mothers who were eligible to participate in the pilgrimages took exception to the plan. Clara Dubois of New York City wrote to President Hoover in March 1930:

"I am a gold star mother. I received an invitation from the government to visit my son's grave. I am opposed to this way for the Government to spend money for free excursions for relatives to go to graves when our reconstruction work goes so slowly with our shattered men who suffer so desperately still… I wish this Government would spend the money on the reconstruction of all those men who were almost killed in the war instead of sending mothers and wives abroad to see the graves and be harrowed by that unhealthy new touch with the Past. Norman was my only son and if international conditions have been right I should never have had to suffer that Eternal Separation. Take my travelling expenses to help one of his suffering comrades."[10]

A response drafted for President Hoover's signature read:

"I am deeply touched by your letter, its brave acceptance of sorrow and its unselfish thought of others, whose sufferings can yet be ameliorated. Not many have your wisdom and generosity. It is impossible now to withdraw the Government's offer, but be assured that I deeply appreciate what you have done. And I do pray that you may ever be comforted."[11]

The Quartermasters' Preparations

From the very beginning, Major General J. L. Dewitt, the Quartermaster General, understood and anticipated the huge scope and magnitude of the Pilgrimage effort. Every detail of each pilgrim's trip was planned down to the smallest detail. From the moment the mother stepped onto the transportation that would bring her from her home to New York City, she was under the observation and care of either a military aide or someone designated by the military to ensure that she remained safe and comfortable and was never out of contact with someone connected with the Pilgrimage.

Train conductors, bus drivers, and station masters across the nation helped escort the women to their des-

Fig. 5-3: A name badge was provided by the government for each participant in the Gold Star Pilgrimage of Mothers and Widows.
(Fenelon Collection)

tinations and worked closely with the War Department to assure every possible comfort. In some locations where stopovers were required, the railroad lines offered local tours to the pilgrims as their contribution to the success of the pilgrimages. The travelers appreciated this careful attention and one woman from a western state remarked upon her arrival in New York that "I could have made the trip blindfolded." Another said, "My only chance to go astray was to try to think by myself."

In April 1930, just prior to commencing the first round of pilgrimage trips, General DeWitt spoke to the Army officers who would be escorting the gold star pilgrims in New York City, on board the ships, and in France, Belgium, and England. He traveled to New York specifically to address the group and required that a roll of the attendees be called and absentees noted so he could later find out why they had not been in attendance.

He spoke plainly and bluntly to the escort officers of their responsibilities, and challenged them to speak up if they felt for any reason that they could not discharge their duties appropriately. He advised them that they would be removed immediately from their assignment if they failed at any time or for any reason to meet his standards of conduct for the Pilgrimage. In simple terms, nothing was more important than the care and safety of the gold star mothers and nothing would be spared in terms of time, commitment, or funds to make sure that the gold star travelers had the best possible experience. Ensuring that outcome was the responsibility and duty of the escort officers. DeWitt understood the heroic scope of the task and that this was not a homogeneous group of women for whom the trip would be a casual experience:

"You must remember that these women will be from all classes of society and will be just as true a cross section of the country as was the draft during the war. Some of them will be highly refined, educated women. Some of them will be illiterate. Some of them will not be able to speak English. Some of them will be absolutely poverty stricken and will be dependent upon you and the Government and the organization to pay all their expenses. [That] many of them cannot read or write, I know from the correspondence we have received. Many of them will be invalids. The average age is over 65. One is 88 and one is 91...

"We must expect deaths and a great deal of sickness...

"If you could see some of the correspondence, some of the letters that we have received in the Quartermaster General's office from mothers and widows making this pilgrimage, you would realize the conditions under which many of them are making the trip. Some of them are so poor that they have been unable to buy even the suitcases that they are supposed to have, and we limit them to two. Some have been provided for by subscriptions raised in their communities. I have no doubt that many of these women, when they land in New York, will not have a nickel over and above the money we gave them to make the trip here. Many of them will be very easy to handle and [to] meet their requirements. Many of them will be very difficult. You have got to be very careful how you deal with them."[12]

He emphasized the intentions of Congress and the Secretary of War so there would be no confusion among the officers regarding their mission or duty:

"I want to say that [there is] probably no case in history where such thoughtful and human recognition has ever been given by any government of the sacrifice of its women in war. I want you to bear that in mind during the entire period you are on this duty. I want you to perform your duties in the spirit in which that law was conceived. Bear that in mind. I am emphasizing it because I want no doubt to exist in your minds as to what Congress intended and as to what the Secretary of War expects."[13]

He reminded them that planning and logistics could only go so far, and that they would be called upon frequently to personally take action to ensure the success of the pilgrimages stating, "If you are not diplomats now, you will probably be diplomats by the time you get back."[14]

Controversy Over Treatment of African-American Mothers and Widows

Almost as soon as the Pilgrimage was approved, a bitter controversy arose regarding the proposed segregation of more than 600 eligible African-American gold star mothers and widows. While the War Department and White House insisted that the experience and accommodations provided for these mothers would be equivalent to those provided for the white mothers, there were, in fact, significant differences.

The pilgrimage experience of the African-American mothers reflected the societal mores of the time that placed minorities in a subordinate position. Even in their war-time service, African-American soldiers had usually been formed into segregated military units that were assigned to labor/support positions behind the front lines. And now, while the white mothers traveled on luxury liners, the African-American mothers were assigned to commercial steamers. While the white mothers stayed at the main-line luxury hotels in Paris, the African-American mothers stayed in smaller, second-class boarding house accommodations off the fashionable main avenues of Paris.

There were protests from the fledgling National Association for the Advancement of Colored People (NAACP), the National Equal Rights League and Race Congress, and other organizations. Individuals of all colors raised their voices against the decision. It was clear, however, that the nation was divided on the issue. In a letter that chills the heart of the modern reader, Catherine B. Daniels, president of the Chatham Unit of the American Legion Auxiliary in Savannah, Georgia, wrote a letter of appreciation to President Hoover for not backing down on the issue of segregated pilgrimages:

"[Wish] to thank the President for his action in upholding the War Department in its arrangements for the voyages of several groups of gold star mothers to France in spite of the attitude taken by the Negro gold star mothers in this matter."[15]

A differing opinion was expressed by Tom Canty of Chicago who wrote to George Akerson, personal secretary to President Hoover:

"George—We all make mistakes. We will all agree to that. But the person who discriminated against the colored gold star mothers pulled the worst boner contributing to the ever increasing unpopularity of your administration… You may rest assured, George, that it will take some hokus pokus, raised to the nth power, to repopularize Mr. Hoover with our people in the middle west."[16]

In July 1930, *The Nation* published a scathing editorial denouncing the planned segregation of the Pilgrimage, stating "There is no record, as far as we know, that any officer in the late war refused a Negro soldier the inestimable privilege of dying for his country because of his color.[17]

The editorial called the plans an "incredibly stupid and ungracious gesture… Their black sons died as white men die."[18]

The outcry proved fruitless. The War Department hinted that there had been pressure applied by officials of the shipping lines who worried about losing the business of white passengers if African-American travelers were provided with first-class accommodations. The shipping lines implied that the hotels in New York and France were worried about having these guests mixing with their regular clientele.

No organization or individual took responsibility for having made the decision regarding segregation until Major General B. Franklin Cheatham, who had been called out of retirement to oversee the pilgrimages, stepped forward on the eve of the first African-American pilgrimage sailing:

"It was General Cheatham's proposal to segregate the white women from the Negroes, and in explaining this action today, he disavowed all motives of race, prejudice and personal feelings.

"'The motive behind this plan,' he said, 'was that I thought they would be happier going over by themselves than with white women. I was not influenced by any sort of race prejudice. I was born and raised among these people and I like them.'"[19]

General Cheatham and Colonel Benjamin O. Davis, the highest ranking African-American officer in the United States Army, accompanied the first segregated group of gold star pilgrims on their trip to France.

Acting Secretary of War Frederick Trubee Davison continued to maintain that "the Negro gold star mothers were grouped separately after the most careful consideration of the interests of the pilgrims themselves," and that "no discrimination whatever will be made as between the various groups. Each group will receive equal accommodations, care and consideration."[20]

The African-American gold star mothers were encouraged by the NAACP to decline their pilgrimage opportunity as a protest against the unequal treatment. No less anxious to see the final resting places of their loved ones than their white sisters, the majority of the African-American mothers graciously accepted the opportunity as it was offered. As one of these gold star mothers commented to a reporter for a New York newspaper:

"Ever since I lost my son in 1918, I have been wanting to come. I would have come over on a cattle boat. I love my race as strongly as any other, but when I heard the United States was going to send us over, I could not refuse."[21]

Once in France, these gold star mothers experienced an outpouring of support and friendship that they could never have received in their own country. The people of France recognized no color line and they accepted the African-American mothers with open arms. The large expatriate community in Paris included many trend-setting African-American musicians, artists, dancers, writers, and chefs who offered these mothers opportunities to experience the richness of Paris that went far beyond the normally planned pilgrimage activities. Concerts, dances, exhibits, and dining experiences were planned specifically for these mothers and they enjoyed special performances by some of the premier African-American performers of the age, including dancer Josephine Baker and bandleader Noble Sissle, who had once served with the American Expeditionary Force.

Fig. 5-3: A tribute to the gold star mothers and widows who were participating in the first gold star pilgrimages in 1930.

(Magazine section of The Times-Piucayune, *May 25, 1930: Fenelon Collection)*

Making the Pilgrimage

Each mother and widow who indicated interest in participating in the Pilgrimage was scheduled for a specific trip, and complete travel arrangements were made for her. As the date for their pilgrimage drew near, the mothers received frequent correspondence from the Quartermasters' Pilgrimage offices in New York and Washington, D.C., containing advice, instructions, itineraries, reservations, tickets, and checks to cover incidental travel expenses, such as meals and tips, on their journey to New York to rendezvous with other gold star travelers.

The first pilgrimages began in the spring of 1930, just six months after the October 1929 stock market crash that resulted in the collapse of the nation's financial systems. The pilgrimages continued through 1933—a four-year period that corresponded with the worst years of the Great Depression. Without the money provided in advance to the travelers for their incidental expenses, many would never have been able to make the trip.

As the gold star pilgrims traveled to their first rendezvous with the Army escorts in New York City, their expenses for food and incidentals were generously covered. In 1930, the *New York Times* reported approvingly that "When employees of the government travel, if they are of modest rank, they get $4 a day to cover... expenses. First-class officials get $6 a day. But when Gold Star Mothers travel under the auspices of their government, they have $10 a day expense money."[22]

For many of the mothers, ten dollars may have represented more cash than they had held in their hands for many years. The government's generosity was not taken for granted—more than one mother attempted to return the unused funds from her expense allocations after she returned home. These attempts resulted in a kind note from a Quartermaster official with the money enclosed and assurances to the mother that the unused funds were hers to keep.

In an article titled "The War Mother Goes Over There" in the May–June 1930 issue of the *Quartermaster Review,* Major Louis C. Wilson of the Quartermaster Corps described what the pilgrims could expect and outlined the arrangements that were being made for each participant:

"Let us, for the purpose of illustrating the extent of such plans, take a concrete example of a mother who is eligible for the pilgrimage and who has accepted the

S.S. "GEORGE WASHINGTON"
U.S.L.

Fig. 5-4: The SS *George Washington*—a ship of the United States Lines used to transport participants in the Gold Star Pilgrimages of Mothers and Widows. *(Fenelon Collection)*

Fig. 5-5: Ohio gold star pilgrims aboard the SS *America* in May 1930.
(Sarah J. Russ pilgrimage memorabilia: Fenelon Collection)

invitation extended by our government. Her name is Mrs. Brown and she lives next door to us in the little western town of Smithville. We have known her for many years and we knew her boy, too.

"All the 5,000 or more mothers and widows making the pilgrimage this year will travel on boats of the fleet owned and operated by the United States Lines, an American corporation. Mrs. Brown is going on the S.S. George Washington because that sailing fits in with the system adopted so that mothers and widows from the same State could travel together in the same group.

"So, in ample time before she is to leave Smithville, Mrs. Brown will receive personally from the local ticket agent, a railroad ticket to New York, including a Pullman sleeping car (lower berth) reservation together with advice as to the train she is to take. About the same time, the postman will bring her registered mail containing a check to cover her meals and incidental expenses while traveling to New York.

"When Mrs. Brown (and all that follows applies equally to her companion, the widow) arrives in New York, she will be met by an officer of the Regular Army,

in uniform, who will provide transportation and escort her to her hotel, where a room, meals, and high class accommodations for every convenience, have been arranged for her in advance by her host...

"[Rejoining] Mrs. Brown, now comfortably in her hotel where she will have time, during two days, to rest up from the journey from her home town, we find that she has already met other mothers, and also some war widows, who form part of her group and whose common bond has started friendships that will continue throughout the pilgrimage and perhaps throughout her life...

"[When they board the ship,] Mrs. Brown is delighted to find she has cabin class accommodation, that her baggage is in her room when she arrives and that her stateroom companion is also a fellow traveler and guest of the American nation bound for the same destination. The seasickness that Mrs. Brown had somewhat timidly feared did not materialize. While she noticed that a few of the others were somewhat indisposed for a day or so, she also saw such solicitous care of them taken by those delegated by the War Department to attend, that she will probably laughingly remark that she believes she has missed some attention by not having a touch of seasickness."[23]

The narrative continues with a description of the week-long voyage and the mid-ocean ceremonies held for those who had been lost at sea. The pilgrims arrive in France and travel by train to Paris where they rest for a few days prior to traveling to the cemeteries which were the true purpose of their visit:

"One of the outstanding events of the trip, upon which Mrs. Brown will undoubtedly love to dwell when she relates her experiences to her friends and neighbors when she gets back home, will be her surprise and pleasure when she saw the beauty and peacefulness of the war cemeteries. She has learned that, with the exception of one, that at Suresnes just outside of Paris where lie men who died in Paris hospitals, all the cemeteries in France where American troops are interred are on ground captured by American troops so that in the main, our boys 'over there' now lie where, or near where, they fought and fell.

"Mrs. Brown will be greatly impressed by the trees, the shrubbery, and the flowers and by the white marble headstone in the form of a cross, over three feet high, which marks her son's resting place, and which has inscribed upon it her soldier boy's name, his rank, his organization, the name of his State and the date of his death. While her mother pride and love will naturally be cen-

Fig. 5-6 (left): Gold star mother Nettie C. Newman stands at the grave of her son, Corporal William H. Newman, at the Meuse-Argonne Cemetery in France. *(Fenelon Collection)*

Fig. 5-7 (below): Ohio gold star mother Anna C. Kaupp kneels for a moment longer at the gravesite of her son, Carl C. Kaupp, at the Meuse-Argonne Cemetery in 1930. *(Uncredited news photo dated May 24, 1930: Fenelon Collection)*

Fig. 5-7: An unidentified mother embraces her son's headstone in France in 1930.
(*Russ memorabilia: Fenelon Collection*)

tered on this one, she will note with general pride that all her boy's comrades who lie there, if of the Christian faith, have similar markers, while those of the Jewish faith have a Star of David instead of a cross.

"She notes, too, that at intervals there is a headstone with no name upon it, which indicates that it marks the grave of one who is unknown, and she reverently reads the inscription "Here rests in honored glory an American soldier known but to God." And as she looks around to drink in the beauty of the scene as a whole, Mrs. Brown sees the unfurled Stars and Stripes of Old Glory, floating on the breeze and symbolizing our Nation's tender and protective care for this bivouac of its soldier dead, an interest that will continue in its zeal through all the coming years.[24]

After describing the touring and entertainment opportunities provided to the pilgrims and their return to Paris, the homeward voyage to New York, and their journeys back to their hometowns, the writer describes the lasting memories that Mrs. Brown will share with her friends and neighbors:

"Back in our home town we are looking forward to Mrs. Brown's trip with keen pleasure, and how interesting it will be to hear her tell us all about it when she returns! We know how enthusiastic she will be in detailing all the many kindnesses that our nation, as her host,

extended to her and the others; how outside of a few purchases she made from a purely personal viewpoint, the wonderful trip meant no outlays of funds by her, for did not her host provide customs fees, tips for bell-boys and maids at hotels and on the boat, tips for porters, waiters, stewards on the steamer, baths and laundry, steamer chairs and rugs, drugs and medicines, to say nothing of interpreters and guides, all the railroad and steamer fares, all automobile and bus transportation, and many other incidentals too numerous to mention? But, above all these essential evidences of a Nation's solicitude for these mothers and widows who will be able to participate in these pilgrimages, there will be the outstanding fact that each was afforded an opportunity to visit and see the last resting place of one who to her was the greatest hero of them all. What a golden field of memories in reflecting upon the loved one who served and fell in serving."[25]

While the proud tone of Major Wilson's article may bring a smile to the reader, the experience of the pilgrims ran by and large in accordance with his narrative of what they might expect. The careful and meticulous planning done by the Quartermaster Corps, the scrupulous attention to detail by the escorts and aides on both sides of the Atlantic, the overwhelming support and friendship of the French people and their government for the pilgrims, and the cheerful participation of the travelers themselves resulted in a nearly flawless series of pilgrimages between 1930 and 1933.

Mrs. Seibold's Pilgrimage

Grace Darling Seibold, the founder and first national president of AGSM, was one of those mothers who participated in a pilgrimage voyage in 1931. Initially, the mothers of the soldiers whose burial places were unknown were not included in the Pilgrimage planning. However, the act was amended in 1930 to include mothers of the unknowns, and Mrs. Seibold became eligible. Following her trip, she wrote a narrative of her experiences that was probably presented at an AGSM meeting or convention for the benefit of those mothers who had not yet made their pilgrimages or were not eligible, having had the bodies of their sons returned to the United States for burial.

In many ways, Mrs. Seibold's narrative is similar in tone and content to other surviving journals kept by gold star pilgrims. One aspect of Mrs. Seibold's pilgrimage experience that differed from the majority of travelers was that her husband traveled with her. Pilgrims were allowed to travel with guests, but no portion of the guests' expenses were paid by the government and often the additional guests had to make their own arrangements for transportation and meals.

Following their arrival in Paris and a few day's rest, it was soon time for the pilgrims to accomplish the purpose of their pilgrimage. Mrs. Seibold's pilgrimage took her to the Somme Cemetery where the sons and husbands of her fellow pilgrims were buried. Since the final resting place of Mrs. Seibold's son was unknown, another spot claimed her attention as the pilgrims move on:

"Of all places in France, an unknown spot somewhere near Baupame was to me the most sacred for it was there, fighting 5,000 feet above the earth, for you and me and all humanity, that my brave boy gave his all. I stopped for a brief period as close to the location of the fight in which he was killed as possible."[26]

Paris Presents an Extravagant Tribute

In her pilgrimage journal, gold star mother Belle M. Harner described a visual exhibition that was presented by the city of Paris for the benefit of the gold star pilgrims:

"The Eiffel Tower was illuminated several years ago. The lower part of the Tower needed repairing, but the City of Paris was not financially able to do so. One of the great auto companies said they would do it if the City would allow them to use it in advertising. The large electric C is shown on all four sides. Then the figure 4 followed by the company name, Citroen, reading from the top down. Next, sharp, jagged streaks strike near the base of the tower illustrating lightning. Once the tower is "fired" myriads of small colored lights work their way up to the top, then a stream of yellow light strikes the top—water; and the fires gradually die out from the top down. Then the whole round is repeated. It is so expensive that it is only shown once a week, but for the benefit of the Gold Star visitors, it was shown oftener. I saw it at least three times. It is a most beautiful and wonderful display."[27]

One of the most famous Parisian entertainments proved a little too European for gold star mother Nora G. Weld of Canaan, New Hampshire. Her journal entry for September 15, 1930, noted that they were going to the Follies that night and all the gold star mothers from the various hotels would be together for the show. Her next notation read, "Got home at 12:30 a.m. I do not think the U.S. would allow the actors or actresses to go so bare. It was all right to see once."[28]

Ceremonies At Sea

Each pilgrimage group participated in a special ceremony during the crossing to Europe. At a point in mid-ocean, each ship's engines would be brought to a full stop and a somber memorial gathering would pay tribute to those soldiers who were lost or buried at sea during the Great War:

"To honor the memory of American soldiers, sailors, marines and coast guardsmen who lost their lives at sea during the World War, California gold star mothers on their way to France to visit the graves of their sons cast four wreaths into the Atlantic from the *S.S. America* today.

While a bugler sounded 'Taps' and flags flew at half mast… wreaths were dropped overboard by Mrs. Ettie M. Brown of Hollywood and Mrs. Emily Andrews, Mrs. May Brucker and Mrs. Ellen Kelly of San Francisco. [Note: All four women were or later became members of AGSM.]

The Rev. Francis P. Duffy, chaplain of New York's famous 'Fighting Sixty-Ninth'… and Rev. E. Bertram Runnall of Calvary Church, Syracuse, were speakers.

'Personally,' Father Duffy said, 'I feel it would have been a lesser sacrifice to have been buried with the sons than to view the sorrows of the mothers.'"[1X]

Gifts of Remembrance

Many of the gold star pilgrims carried mementoes of home to the gravesites of their children. In the first group of pilgrims, "a few of the band clasped small boxes filled with a couple of handfuls of black dirt—soil from the homeland they intended to bury in the fields of Flanders where the American boys now lies."

Mrs. William H. Sidells of North Carolina carried a rose from the bridal bouquet of her son's wife. "I'm going to place it on Jimmy's grave," she explained. Kate Mike brought a wreath fashioned from the boughs of a tree that her son had played beneath as a boy. A widow brought bottle of water from her husband's favorite swimming hole. The offerings were as varied as the pilgrims themselves:

"A little lady from Florida, with gray hair and young eyes, is carrying a box of sand from the beach her son loved so well. A war mother from Nebraska has a baby shoe. Many of them are carrying pressed flowers from their gardens."[2X]

The significance of these gifts was not in their value but in their meaning. Sharing simple, personal reminders of the lifetime shared by the mothers and sons and, for the young widows, the memories of perhaps a few bright days or weeks, reconnected the mourners with the happier days when they had shared their lives with the loved ones. For the vast majority of these women, the few days spent at their loved one's final resting place would be their last and only opportunity to commune with the spirit of their lost one.

Assessing the Pilgrimage

In November 1933, an article written by a pilgrimage escort appeared in the *American Legion Monthly*. Summarizing the pilgrimage experience from the perspective of both pilgrims and escorts, the article proved the accuracy of General DeWitt's initial assessment of the pilgrims' diversity and the challenges this would present to the Quartermaster's escorts and planners:

"There were some women who several times had girdled the globe and others who, despite our modern facilities of transportation, never before had left their cottage and their farm. There were mothers of means, though seldom of affluence, who packed a fairly complete wardrobe in the two suit cases which the Army had suggested as the limit and others who had no dress but the one on their back. There were college-trained mothers and widows who often helped their conducting officers translate a rapid flow of French words from the mouth of a harassed traffic officer, and others who had difficulty comprehending even the simplest English.

"In practically every one of the forty-nine groups there were some women who not only could not speak English but who understood very little… They read and wrote Norwegian, Italian, Yiddish, Czech, Portuguese, Finnish, Greek and other languages…

"There were women who carried plenty of extra money to buy souvenirs and the latest Parisian gowns and others who arrived in Paris with no money at all.[29]

The *Legion* article noted that these differences proved of little importance to the pilgrims themselves:

"Despite the striking difference in experience, education and training among its members, each group of Gold Star Pilgrims soon developed into a cohesive unit, only equaled in the outfits of their own sons and husbands. The younger gave deference to the elder. Those of more worldly goods often freely gave of their wardrobe to the less fortunate. Patronizing airs toward the poorer, the less literate of the foreign members seldom manifested themselves. Women of the South whose memories still vividly recalled Fort Donelson and Fort Sumter shared rooms with New England Yankees, and often they grew quite fond of each other."[30]

Pilgrimage statistics were also noted in the article and the Quartermaster Corps was shown to have acquitted itself in an exemplary manner. The pilgrimage busses in France had covered more than 217,152 miles during the four pilgrimage seasons. Each pilgrim had traveled more than 500 miles while in France, "yet only one accident occurred and that through no fault of the driver."[31] Overall, including the ocean voyages, the pilgrimages covered 3,283,828 passenger miles, and "in the four years, the Army handled thousands of pieces of baggage and did not lose one."[32]

The job of making the pilgrimages a success didn't fall exclusively on the shoulders of the Quartermaster officers in France. By the time the pilgrimage parties arrived in France, substantial groundwork had been laid stateside in preparation for their journey. Hometown physicians who cared for the mothers had been queried and railroad agents had provided additional information so, by the time "the Pilgrim arrived in New York, the Army had a complete record of her physical condition."[33]

The bond that developed between the escorts and the pilgrims was a strong one. If a mother wanted to talk about her loved one, the Army escort was often the person to whom she turned:

"For this sympathetic role, the army officer was especially prepared. He had the military record of the fallen soldier, knew where he came from, to what outfit he belonged, where he served, where he fought, where and when he died, and usually where he was buried. His thorough knowledge of the soldier's career immediately won him a friend and an admirer in the mother… and a complete and sympathetic understanding followed."[34]

Often the trusting relationship between a mother and her Quartermaster escort resulted in an unexpected revelation of personal circumstances. The following exchange was reported in the *American Legion Monthly* article:

"'You don't hate Germans, do you?' pathetically asked one mother.

"'No, I certainly do not,' answered the conducting officer.

"'Oh, I am so glad to hear you say that. After I visit my boy's grave in the American Cemetery, I want to go at my own expense to Cologne. I had another boy in the army. He died fighting for Germany and I want to visit his grave, too.'"[35]

Whenever possible, such requests were quickly and sensitively acted upon.

It was not only the Quartermaster escorts that the pilgrims turned to with questions. One mother sought out a military nurse who was traveling with the group:

"One of the pilgrims addressed the nurse, asking her first name. On being informed it was Mary, she inquired if she had been at a certain hospital in France at a given time. The nurse replied that she had and it developed that this was the identical nurse who had cared for the pilgrim's son, whose grave she was now to visit. She had with her a number of letters received from the nurse during the time she was nursing her son, and one received after his death."[36]

In some cases, the Quartermaster Corps and War Department found themselves cutting through government regulations to assure that an eligible pilgrim could take advantage of the opportunity to which she was entitled. On May 19, 1930, the *Washington Star* reported on the efforts underway on behalf of Thora Holt of Hackensack, New Jersey:

"The War Department cut reams of red tape quickly today in order that Mrs. Thora Holt… might visit her son's grave in France. Because her citizenship papers were burned with her home… Mrs. Holt faced the prospect of remaining behind when 12 other Gold Star Mothers in her home county left for France. Their pilgrimage is planned for July 23.

"Advised of Mrs. Holt's predicament, the Quartermaster General of the Army today began an investigation and indicated that the State Department will be asked to instruct the proper New Jersey courts to make the necessary arrangements for Mrs. Holt to make the trip… War Department officials said today that similar cases had been considered favorably, and that if Mrs. Holt's case is as represented, she undoubtedly will be able to sail with the delegation in July."[37]

As General DeWitt had so carefully explained, no effort was to be spared to make the pilgrims happy. The pilgrimage officers took their duties seriously and continuously performed their work in a manner that amazed even their supporters back home.

Few expressed their appreciation of the women better than Major General Benjamin Franklin Cheatham. To ensure that all had been done to the standards he and General DeWitt had established, Cheatham personally traveled with pilgrimage groups on occasion, including one voyage of African-American gold star mothers. He wrote to General DeWitt after accompanying a pilgrimage party that sailed in May 1930:

"I should like to bear witness to the extraordinarily high type of women who made up the pilgrimage; they come from every walk of life, but they all seem imbued with the loftiest ideals of patriotism, and conducted themselves with high courage and self-control when brought face to face with the crosses which mark the resting places of their loved ones. The more one sees of them, the more one appreciates how really big this pilgrimage is, how far reaching in its effect and how wise Congress was in enacting the legislation."[38]

The Pilgrims' Responses

Were the pilgrimages meaningful for the mothers and widows? The pilgrims were overwhelmingly generous and emotional in their praise for the experience they had been given, and for the people who made it possible.

A typical letter of appreciation was sent to the Adjutant General of the War Department on September 9, 1931, by the mothers and widows of Party Q and signed by Minnie Wilkinson, Party Q Chairman. It was addressed to all the officers, aides and medical staff members associated with their pilgrimage:

"We, the Gold Star Mothers and Widows of Party Q, wish to express to you our sincere appreciation for the many thoughtful courtesies and kindly care bestowed upon us on this memorable Pilgrimage.

"You have been our guide, counselor and friend, ever mindful for our welfare, health and comfort. To the feeble and ill mothers you have ministered untiringly with gentle, tender solicitude and so you have all endeared yourselves to each of us Gold Star Mothers and Widows...

"To our U.S. Government we are indebted for this opportunity to make this Pilgrimage and are most appreciative of the honor they have conferred upon us for we feel that in honoring us, they are also honoring our beloved boys who made the "Supreme Sacrifice." No other nation has ever given a more gracious and generous tribute than this..."

Another mother wrote:

"I wish that I could find words to express my appreciation for the most wonderful thing the government has done in arranging for our Gold Star Pilgrimage to the cemeteries of Europe. It was a wonderful trip, and my heart has known more peace than I ever thought it would. I am perfectly satisfied with everything now."[39]

In addition to the respect and homage shown to the gold star mothers, the pilgrimages conveyed another important message to the women and the nation, according to the writer of an *American Legion Monthly* magazine article:

"To most of these women by this time, death had become a frequent visitor. By 1933, most of the Gold Star Mothers had become widows; some had lost other children. Alone among the lost ones, their soldier son's life had counted in the affairs of the world and still seemed to count in the eyes of his Government. Otherwise, why the Pilgrimages at all? they reasoned...

"The Pilgrimage did convince these women that [the] nation still shares their loss. Their boys' graves had become national shrines. Their own sacrifices were remembered. They traveled in Europe as representatives of a great Government, truly as its ambassadors and ministers. They counted. Their sons' lives counted. A generation may have grown up to whom the World War has become an impersonal chapter of past history. But a nation that lives from one generation to another has not forgotten. It still recalls with pride the services of its soldiers and sailors of 1917–18 and, despite any present day skepticism, still recognizes the fact that these men died to save their country. It was such thoughts, not often made articulate, and such emotions, that surged in the minds and hearts of the American gold star mothers and widows."[40]

One gold star mother who had visited her son's grave at Romagne stated it simply and eloquently: "My country has kept faith."

Altruism or Propaganda

In many ways, the gold star pilgrimages may have been the most altruistic act ever sponsored or performed by the United States government. Yet some argue that the pilgrimages were a carefully orchestrated propaganda attempt to continue to mold the national memory of the Great War as a valiant and successful effort to save the world.

For the gold star mothers and widows, however, the pilgrimages met a desperate longing that could be assuaged in no other way—the need to say goodbye to their loved ones and know that they were at peace in a place worthy of their sacrifice. Surrounded by other women who had shared a similar loss, escorted and supported by brothers-in-arms who might have fought alongside their lost boys, and embraced by the people of France for whom their sons and husbands had fought and died, the nation gave these gold star pilgrims the opportunity to finally experience a personal resolution to the loss of their loved ones.

Fig. 6-1: Gold star mothers and other notables attended the dedication of a memorial to Illinois' gold star mothers on January 2, 1931. The bronze statue by Leon Hermant was installed at the Centennial Building in Springfield, Illinois. Gold star mother Mrs. J. E. De Lacey (holding bouquet) accepted the memorial on behalf of the state's gold star mothers. Illinois Governor L. L. Emmerson gave the dedicatory speech (he is on Mrs. De Lacey's right).
(International Newsreel Photo 558697: Fenelon Collection)

CHAPTER 6

The 1930s: Remembrance, Respect, and Recognition

The Gold Star Mothers of America have already given the most positive proof of their devotion to their country, both in war and in peace, and we as a nation are honored by their very active presence.
— MAYBELLE HINTON

AMERICA EXPERIENCED GREAT ECONOMIC, SOCIAL and political change during the 1930s. This decade that started with a fast slide into a worldwide economic depression ended with Europe once again at war. Although the United States made every attempt to stay out of the war that engulfed Europe, as the decade drew to a close, few believed that America could long remain uninvolved.

Yet it was not all a dark decade. Movies went from black and white to Technicolor; Shirley Temple danced and sang to lift the hearts of the nation; and Franklin and Eleanor Roosevelt, the nation's surrogate parents, put America back on the road to hope.

During this period, the American Gold Star Mothers, Inc., faced great changes as well. The fledgling organization was just finding its way as it entered the 1930s. By the end of the decade, the organization had grown in both presence and prestige, weathered some battles of its own, and come out strongly as a voice for peace.

The AGSM Mission
In August 1936, AGSM national president Della Towne Blake was interviewed on radio station WIXBS in Waterbury, Connecticut. Her description of AGSM's organizational goals captured the essence of the AGSM's activities during this decade. Before she spoke, program hostess Maybelle Hinton introduced president Blake to the listening audience:

"We have the privilege of welcoming the National President of the most beloved group of women in America—the Gold Star Mothers. Mrs. Blake carries on the work so nobly inaugurated by Mrs. George Gordon Seibold of Washington, D.C., Mrs. Elizabeth Millard of Rochester, deceased, and Mrs. William Bates of Jackson, Michigan, former presidents of the organization."[1]

She then asked Mrs. Blake about the growth of the organization. Mrs. Blake responded:

"We are now represented in forty-three states out of forty-eight, by active chapters in several and members-at-large in others... The state of Michigan leads in number of chapters. California is second and Pennsylvania leads in size of Chapters, with the Philadelphia chapter having the largest enrolled membership."[2]

Mrs. Blake then detailed the work of AGSM:

"We divide our work into four main channels, with Committees overseeing each phase of the work. We concentrate on Hospitalization, Americanization, Legislation, and Welfare among our own Gold Star Mothers and dependents of the ex-serviceman, the latter being done through the local chapters.

"We expect to do a great deal of hospital work during the coming two years among the veterans in hospitals, especially among the blind and mental cases.

"The Americanization Committee is scattered over the country to enable us to contact many who are sadly in need of help to become good American citizens. In some cities, we endeavor to cooperate with the missions and settlement houses in the work they are doing in teaching the principles of Americanism, the love of Country and the respect for the flag of our country and our established institutions... We would also like to as-

Fig. 6-2: Elizabeth I. Millard, AGSM National President 1932–1934
(AGSM Collection)

Fig. 6-3: Mary Jane Bates, AGSM National President 1934–1936
(AGSM Collection)

Fig. 6-4: Della Towne Blake, AGSM National President 1936–1938
(AGSM Collection)

Fig. 6-5 : Bess Duncan Wells, AGSM National President 1938–1939
(AGSM Collection)

sist in teaching the fundamentals of good government. [In the area of legislation,] we stress justice in Veteran legislation. We are concerned with fair compensation for dependent parents whose source of income was removed when their sons gave more than the full measure of duty to their country. We wish to establish a monetary compensation that shall be stable, and not subject to the whims of individuals or groups of individuals having no interest in the class termed 'veteran dependents'...

"We support every cause that is for the betterment of American Living. We campaign against child labor and the sweatshops of Industry. We uphold the Bill of Rights for Women, and we are greatly interested in any project to insure the future of the youth of America, and give them opportunities for honest self-support now and in the years to come. We support the better housing movement and stand for slum clearance. We protest the spreading of Communistic propaganda and subversive teaching in our schools, colleges and universities, and the irreligious tendencies often found in the personnel of the schools of our country."[3]

When asked by Miss Hinton about what AGSM was doing to prevent war, President Blake clearly outlined the organization's position on national defense and war:

"We, as Mothers and good citizens, are, of course, opposed to war. Anyone knowing our background could scarcely doubt that fact. However, we are not pacifists. We as individuals and as a group are subscribed to National Defense. We desire an adequate Army and Navy comparable to those of other first power nations, for defense only. In the event of a justifiable war, such as a war of invasion, etc., we should be the first to lend our support."[4]

Miss Hinton closed the interview with a heartfelt tribute to gold star mothers across the nation:

"The Gold Star Mothers of America have already given the most positive proof of their devotion to their country, both in war and in peace, and we as a nation are honored by their very active presence. At the risk of seeming sentimental, I just want to express my admiration for you and every Gold Star Mother who turned a great sorrow into a great triumph. Anyone who says we have lost the sturdy spirit of the American Pioneer Woman, who could endure hardship and still press on to new achievements, need only consider your organization to see that all our World War Heroes did not serve in France."[5]

AGSM Leaders of the 1930s

From the initial meeting of the organization in June 1928, Grace Darling Seibold led the organization as founder, president, and visionary. Notes from the early 1930s indicate that she missed numerous organizational events during that time due to serious and continuing ill health. Other officers and members had carried on in her absence and her term as president officially lasted until the first national convention, which was held in November 1932. Then, in accordance with the organizational policy that allowed an individual only one term as national president, she relinquished her office.

Elizabeth I. Millard [Fig.6-2]
National President, 1932–1934
At the first national convention, Elizabeth I. Millard of East Rochester, New York, was elected national presi-

Fig. 6-6: M. Jennie Williams, AGSM National President 1939–1940
(AGSM Collection)

dent for the two-year term beginning in 1932. With a membership of more than 550 mothers, Mrs. Millard's role was truly national in scope. Reflecting the growth of the membership in the first four years, the members of the national executive board elected with Mrs. Millard hailed from across the nation— New York, Michigan, Pennsylvania, Louisiana, California and Washington, D.C. An AGSM scrapbook clipping stated that the "loss of a son in the World War never dimmed the cheery smile of the kindly old lady who served as the [second] National President of the American Gold Star Mothers."[6]

Mrs. Millard joined AGSM just one year before she was elected national president. Although relatively new to AGSM, Mother Millard was well known and much respected in her home state of New York for her long years of work on behalf of gold star mothers and injured veterans.

Mary Jane Bates [Fig. 6-3]
National President, 1934–1936
Elected national president at AGSM's third national convention in Washington, D.C., Mary Jane Bates had been a member of AGSM since June 1929. Her son, Robert Ferdinand, had died at the age of twenty-four as the result of an accident in France while serving in the Army. Long active in gold star activities in her home community of Jackson, Michigan, Mrs. Bates' efforts had resulted in the Jackson chapter being the first chapter in the nation to be issued an AGSM charter. Mrs. Bates proposed holding the national convention at a location other than Washington, D.C., suggesting that it was time to recognize the growth of the organization and give members in other states an opportunity to attend.

Della Town Blake [Fig. 6-4]
National President, 1936–1938
Della Towne Goodridge Blake (Mrs. Horace B. Blake) joined AGSM in September 1934. It was Mrs. Blake who started the tradition of each national president's term having an associated theme. Influenced by the

harbingers of war in Europe, Mrs. Blake chose "Let there be peace—and fewer Gold Star Mothers" as her theme.

Born in Woodbury, Vermont, Mrs. Blake was a graduate of Women's College in Montpelier. Moving to Philadelphia when she married, she had two children. Her son, Phillip Roy, had been killed in action in France at the age of nineteen. Phillip had been buried in France and Mrs. Blake had participated in the gold star pilgrimages. In a clipping from an unidentified Baltimore newspaper in 1938, a reporter described Mrs. Blake as "modest, charming, youthful in action and outlook. Mrs. Della T. Blake is the sort of woman you'd classify as a likable, everyday housewife with, perhaps, an unusually large share of generosity."

Mrs. Blake was a frequent radio speaker, artfully using that medium and newspapers to reach gold star mothers and the nation at large. Her messages most often focused on the Communist threat to America and the need for peace. In 1936, president Blake issued a warning against what she saw as a growing Communist threat: the distribution of subversive literature to schoolchildren. She said she was "amazed and frightened" at what was occuring in the nation's schools.

"I don't know much about the distribution of literature of Communists in Washington but I do know that in schools in Philadelphia, subversive literature that gives the young people the wrong idea of our country has been widespread. It has always been the aim of my organization to support everything that assures future American happiness and with communistic literature creeping into the schools and homes, an irreparable harm can be done."[7]

Perhaps more loudly than any other group whose genesis came from the World War, AGSM advocated convincingly and resoundingly for peace at every opportunity during the mid-to-late 1930s:

"Every mother whose son gave his life to his country should feel that hers is the greatest honor a woman can have. We must accept the responsibility that wearing the gold star, the emblem of our honor, confers upon us, and take up the fight for peace that will prevent any other mother's son from giving his life for his country. Our organization is pledged to national defense. But this doesn't indicate a militaristic attitude. Our numbers may be diminished but let us not diminish our efforts toward peace."[8]

By the late 1930s, the membership of the AGSM

was aging. Twenty years after the war, those mothers whose sons had been lost were now facing challenges of age, illness and, in some cases, destitution, despite the nation's improving economic status. In June 1937, Mrs. Blake encouraged the mothers to not flag in their efforts to make the world a better place:

"We hear some of our members saying, 'We are getting too old to work.' That is not so. We may not all work in the same degree, but we can all do something to make life a little easier, a little brighter for someone. There never has been a time in our national life when the opportunity to serve has been greater. In our own individual lives, we find on every hand opportunities to serve our fellow-man, and to take on that grace and poise that is the result of enjoyment of doing something for the betterment of someone…"[9]

Bess Duncan Wells [Fig. 6-5]
National President, 1938–1939
A member of AGSM since 1933, Bess Duncan Wells was a widow whose son, Thomas Emerson, was killed in action in France in August 1918 at the age of nineteen. When she came to office, Europe was poised for war. In the April 1939 AGSM *Bulletin*, Mrs. Wells offered her prayer for peace:

"May we, as the glad Easter season approaches, awaken… with new and renewed hope in the peace of the World and the understanding of nations! Words seem… futile, giving helpless expression to our bewildered conscience in awestricken realization of the probable repetition of 1914… You say I anticipate the improbable or the millennium—well, be that as it may—we could and would live at peace with all men and nations if hearts would change, [and] greed would give place to sharing."

M. Jennie Williams [Fig. 6-6]
National President, 1939–1940
Margaret Jennie Williams (Mrs. Gerlynn Walter Williams) joined AGSM in December 1932. Her son, Ralph Gunter Williams, had enlisted in the U.S. Naval Reserve Force just one month after President Wilson declared war. An Electrician 3rd Class (Radio), Ralph reported for active duty in August 1917 at Newport, Rhode Island. He died of pneumonia on January 30, 1918, at the age of twenty-one.

National Conventions

First National Convention—1932
Washington, D.C.
The first national AGSM convention was held in November 1932 at the Hotel Hamilton in Washington, D.C. Founder and national president for the past four years, Grace D. Seibold's continuing serious illness prohibited her appearing at the convention. Her speech was read to the delegates, recapping the origins of the group and its accomplishments:

"It is with great regret, as I approach the task of giving a brief account of my stewardship, that I am unable to be present with you at this gathering. However, my thoughts and prayers are with you and I am confident that your deliberations will be marked with great consideration for those who are among the membership of the organization, as well as those who are working along the lines of activity in the interest of ex-servicemen.

"Organized by reason of conditions with which you are all familiar, it was the desire of those who assisted in the foundation of the American Gold Star Mothers that we should have a distinctive body, as there was no other organization of exclusively Gold Star Mothers in existence… It is with a great deal of satisfaction that we can now show a membership represented by chapters and affiliates in 42 States of the Union and the Isthmus of Panama…

"In addition to the organization work undertaken by the body, we have been able to contribute largely to the relief of veterans and their wives and families…

"I cannot refrain from reference to the splendid co-operation of all those who have contributed to the upbuilding of the organization. I shall not endeavor to name them personally, as you no doubt will have them in mind when I refer to the splendid membership work of many, as well as the great assistance and relief of Gold Star Mothers through our connection with the Veterans' Administration. This work has been characterized by great success in assisting Gold Star Mothers to secure relief through the adjusted service compensation, as well as death compensation, in some cases the amount reaching thousands of dollars.

"And now, as the time has arrived when I must relinquish official position, I do so with the realization that those who are entrusted with the duties of national officers will devote their efforts to perpetuating an organization that has just cause to be proud of its entire history. May our Heavenly Father crown your efforts with success and bless you all."[10]

A new board of officers was elected, to be led by Elizabeth I. Millard. Activities for the delegates extended past the official closing of the convention on November 10 and included Armistice Day ceremonies around the Capitol.

Probably the most significant event related to the first national convention occurred after hours on November 9 when Washington, D.C., gold star mothers who were members of the national chapter met to form a new chapter, the Grace Darling Seibold Chapter. For the first time, there was separation between the national executive board and the founding chapter of the organization. The new chapter met every other Tuesday night at 8:00 p.m. at the Hotel Hamilton in Washington, D.C. Since there was an overlap between the chapter members and the members of the national board, board meetings were usually held following the chapter meetings. Traditionally, each meeting ended with the mitzpah blessing ("God be with you 'til we meet again") and a reading of the American's Creed:

"I believe in the United States of America as a Government of the people, by the people, for the people; whose just powers are derived from the consent of the governed, a democracy in a republic, a sovereign nation of many sovereign States; a perfect union, one and inseparable, established upon those principles of freedom, equality, justice, and humanity for which American patriots sacrificed their lives and fortunes.

"I therefore believe it is my duty to my Country to love it; to support its Constitution; to obey its laws; to respect its Flag; and to defend it against all enemies."

At the chapter's first meeting, a committee was appointed to draft a constitution and bylaws for the new chapter which would be submitted for comment and review at the second meeting. There was already agreement on one policy that they would pursue:

"The chapter will sponsor a movement to discourage the costly custom of promiscuous placing of wreaths on the Tomb of the Unknown on Armistice Day, advocating that one tribute be placed by the 'President of the United States' and one from 'A grateful people.'

"The organizations known as 'The Seven,' comprising the welfare organization that served the boys of the AEF and those on this side during the war, already observes this custom. Only one emblem is placed for the seven organizations and each in turn is nominated to take charge of the program for that day. This year the YWCA had that honor."[11]

The establishment of a Washington, D.C., chapter freed a large group of mothers from being involved in decisions that affected the organization on a national level, giving them instead an opportunity to focus on local issues as did other chapters. With the election of Elizabeth Millard, the national executive board was now headed by a president who was not able to attend the majority of meetings due to distance and cost. This election of a national president who did not live in the nation's capital set a precedent that would stand for decades and required that the national board learn new ways of managing the business of AGSM.

Second National Convention—1934
Washington, D.C.

AGSM's second national convention was held in May 1934 at the Hotel Hamilton. There were forty-seven registered delegates in attendance.

National president Elizabeth Millard led the convention ceremonies. President Franklin D. Roosevelt extended greetings to the delegates by telegram, which read, in part, "You, whose sons and daughters made the supreme sacrifice, are creating through this national organization a monument to those that gave their lives to make possible our present state of peace and well-being. I hope this message will denote in part the sincere gratitude of our nation for the fine spirit of patriotism and self-sacrifice you have evidenced."[12]

The report on membership statistics indicated that AGSM now had 525 members. Since the 1932 convention, 172 new members had been admitted. The membership roster recorded 353 chapter members, 162 members-at-large, and 36 members whose death had been reported since the last convention.[13]

A resolution, introduced by the Long Beach Chapter in California, was adopted by the membership. The goal outlined in the resolution would be pursued by the AGSM for many decades:

"Be it resolved that all American Gold Star Mothers be given Government Hospitalization or Medical treatment as the case may demand, giving them the same privilege to which their sons would have been entitled. The membership of the AGSM is small and therefore would not create hardship on the government."[14]

The question of whether future conventions would always be held in Washington, D.C., was scheduled for debate at the convention. The decision was made that conventions would be held in a city selected by the serving national president. Some of the states where large chapters were located were "already in the field for selection as the next meeting place" for the convention in 1936.[15]

Third National Convention—1936
Detroit, Michigan

The third AGSM national convention was held in June 1936 at the Book-Cadillac Hotel in Detroit, Michigan, the home state of AGSM national president Mary J. Bates. A *Detroit Free Press* article printed on the opening day of the convention lovingly described the delegates:

"Their average age is 62 years. Upon their silvery heads white flannel overseas caps, marked with a gold-thread star, sit in jaunty incongruity. Arms that once, in years long gone, cradled baby sons now pull about their shoulders long white flannel capes lined in pale gold satin.

"They are valiant, these American Gold Star Mothers who have gathered at the Book-Cadillac Hotel for their third national convention. Approximately 100 are expected to attend from California, Massachusetts, Pennsylvania, and other states, including Michigan, which has five chapters.

"Each one of these mothers represents a son who died in service during the World War. Each of them proves that, in spite of the casualty lists which struck at their hearts in 1917 and 1918, one does not die of a broken heart.

"'No other person is stronger for peace than a Gold Star Mother, for she knows what it means. But we believe in keeping peace by being prepared at all times,' said Mrs. William Bates, National President.

"Oldest of the Gold Star mothers is Mrs. Margaret Byrne [of Detroit] who celebrated her eighty-second birthday June 8. To the other mothers she is "Ma" Byrne… Six years ago this month, Mrs. Byrne left with other Gold Star Mothers to visit the battlefield cemeteries of France. [Her son] Sergeant Charles Leo Byrne is buried in the Oise-Aisne Cemetery. 'I feel more contented since I made that trip,' Mrs. Byrne said. 'It is a beautiful place where my boy is buried.'"

Della Towne Blake of Philadelphia was elected AGSM national president for the 1936–1938 term.

Fourth National Convention—1938
Philadelphia, Pennsylvania

Hosted by the Philadelphia Chapter, the fourth AGSM national convention was held in May 1938 at the Hotel Walton, located at Broad Street and Locust, in Philadelphia. The convention registration fee for each of the 119 delegates was 50 cents.

In her opening remarks, national president Della Towne Blake said:

"I am happy to be able to report at this time that in every department of the work of the Organization there is a stimulus for growth and progress, in the minds of our members generally, that has not been equaled or exceeded in the past… Marked and judged by past achievements, as well as well-laid plans for the future, it is my pleasure to report to you that the Organization is progressive and wholly devoted to the purpose of and for which we were organized and incorporated…

"Let us make this the happiest, most interesting and constructive Convention we have ever held and meet in love and loyalty of purpose, with a compelling desire to carry the torch left in our hands, inspired by the love we bore for those in whose honor we wear the Star of Gold."[17]

Among the highlights of her administration, President Blake listed the following:

- Seven new chapters and two new departments formed since June 1936 in addition to one chapter being reinstated.
- Many new members-at-large and "almost no resignations. Surely this is Progress!"
- Presentation of a "beautiful Founder's Pin—the gift of the entire national organization" to Mrs. Seibold.
- AGSM was being "recognized more and more as a potent factor among other organizations."[18]

A long business agenda was scheduled for the convention with numerous resolutions and constitutional amendments proposed for consideration. Resolutions adopted by unanimous vote included the following:

1. AGSM reaffirmed "its stand against Communism, Fascism, Nazism, and all other "isms" and/or organizations that seek to weaken or destroy the free institutions of our Constitutional system—and we join with other veteran groups in their campaign against these forces… We pledge our assistance in the enactment of the Universal Service Act, taking [the] profits out of war."

2. AGSM "wishes the United States to remain at peace with all nations of the world... We urge the United States Government to maintain a strict policy of NEUTRALITY regarding foreign affairs, and further urge the United States be kept from any alliances which draw this country into war."

3. AGSM expressed its "support of legislation designed to preserve American institutions, ideals, customs and methods of living, from subversive and foreign influence."

4. "Being vitally interested in preserving America for Americans, and in preservation of the fundamentals of our great Government, for which our sons fought and died, [we] endorse any proposed legislation pertaining to restricted immigration, mandatory deportation and the prohibiting of the employing of aliens in the Federal Government, or any branch thereof, and we urge the enactment of such legislation."

5. "There are dependent Gold Star Mothers who are in need of hospitalization and are without the funds necessary to provide themselves with such hospitalization ... [Therefore we support] the granting to Mothers of the dead, who died in the line of duty in the Military or Naval forces of the United States, the same privileges as to hospitalization and treatment in hospitals owned or controlled by the United States, as is given the veterans so qualified."[19]

As the clouds of war gathered again across the sea, a Philadelphia newspaper reported on the AGSM convention and detected a note of bitterness and disillusionment among the membership that affected even the newly elected national president:

"The majority of the 150 Gold Star Mothers gathered here for their fourth biennial convention agreed today that the sons they gave to 'save democracy' twenty years ago died in vain. The women, who became Gold Star Mothers by the sacrifice of a son on the World War battlefields, are ardent exponents of peace.

"'We are working for peace—and fewer Gold Star Mothers,' said Mrs. Horace B. Blake of Philadelphia, National President of the Gold Star Mothers Inc. recognized by the War Department in 1929. 'We must maintain our national defense system at its highest possible peak as the best method of retaining friendly relations with the rest of the world.'

"Delegates at the Hotel Walton from every section of the country and from nearly every State in the Union concurred in a single slogan—'let there be peace.'

"[Newly elected National President] Bess Duncan Wells... is one of the many mothers who feel that their sons died in vain. 'The present outlook for world peace is very dreary,' said Mrs. Wells. 'My 18-year-old son was killed in France and to me he wrote, "It is better to live for your country than to die for it." And he was a Volunteer.'

"Mrs. G. Walter Williams said, 'For defense, I would give my children and grandchildren. If by our sacrifice we have sown the seed of world peace, it would have been all worthwhile. Any of the Gold Star Mothers would give her life to save America from another war.'"[20]

Fifth National Convention—1939
Portland, Oregon

As decided at the 1938 convention, the fifth national convention was held just one year after the fourth national convention. Held in Portland, Oregon, known as the City of Roses, delegates met at the Portland Hotel.

The convention committee started advertising the convention early in the year in the AGSM *Bulletin* in hopes of encouraging many mothers to attend:

"We do expect you and believe you will feel more than glad of a real sacrifice upon your part to share in the delightful features the week of June 6–10 holds for Delegates and Guests of our 1939 Convention. 'For you, a rose in Portland grows!'"

An amendment recommended for consideration at this convention suggested returning to the biennial convention schedule due to the cost of the conventions and the amount of work required by the hosting chapters.

On May 31, President Franklin D. Roosevelt responded to a request for a message to be read at the opening of the convention, "This country, which has no imperial designs and which seeks no territorial aggrandizement, desires peace and will work to promote peace among all peoples. This is the pledge I desire to give to the Fifth National Convention of the American Gold Star Mothers, with best wishes for the health and happiness of all the members of the organization."[21]

The Organization's Growth

Across the nation, individual gold star mothers as well as existing independent gold star groups were invited and encouraged to join the national group. For some groups, the decision to become part of AGSM was a simple one; for others, often the larger groups, issues of autonomy were a concern. One by one throughout the 1930s, groups across the nation became AGSM chapters, greatly extending the scope and influence of the organization. In California, one group of gold star parents came together specifically to create an AGSM chapter:

"Bonded together through an understanding which broadens as the years pass by, Gold Star Mothers of Santa Ana, following in the footsteps of mothers in other localities, have formed a chapter (number 4) to 'American Gold Star Mothers,' a national organization. Nine noble parents met in the American Legion Hall Saturday, eager to add their names to the list of the nation's members, and to share in the close associations which such a chapter can bring. The local group, however, has not yet obtained a charter, as rules for granting charters determine that there must be at least 10 members. Interest in this first meeting indicates that there are other mothers in the city who will want to join."[22]

In Detroit, Michigan, many city-based gold star mothers' groups had formed in the years since the war ended. Gold star mother Mary J. Bates, who would later become AGSM's national president, was the catalyst that brought many of these groups together under the AGSM banner. In New York, Dr. Emma Balcom served as state organizer and brought numerous independent groups into the AGSM fold.

In May 1931, it was reported that "the petitions of four California chapters of AGSM for admission to the national organization were unanimously granted—Los Angeles, San Diego, Long Beach and Santa Ana. They [are] being allowed to retain their present names. The Gold Star Mothers of San Francisco have also signified their desire for admission to the national organization and will be accepted."

As word of the organization spread, the work required of the national executive board increased exponentially. In 1931, a list of the correspondence received in a single two-week period reflected the exposure the organization was receiving across the nation; letters inquiring about membership and chapter requirements were received from Cleveland, Ohio; Elgin, Oregon; San Francisco and Los Angeles, California; Polkville, Iowa; and St. Louis, Missouri.

One of the oldest, best known and largest (150 members) groups to join (and quite a feather in the white garrison caps of the AGSM) was the Philadelphia-based Gold Star Mothers of the World War:

"In line with a program to combat legislation and other Government action disadvantageous to the mothers of soldiers who died in the World War, the Gold Star Mothers of the World War, a Philadelphia organization, has joined the American Gold Star Mothers." In an undated press release, AGSM legislative liaison Ella Guedry explained why the Philadelphia group was so important to the AGSM:

"The national [AGSM] has long desired such a union for the Philadelphia Mothers have earned for themselves an enviable reputation through their activities in behalf of veterans and their dependents ever since the close of the war. The AGSM is putting on a strong campaign to unite the countless groups of Gold Stars now operating throughout the United States, independently of each other."[23]

The installation of the Portland Chapter [Oregon] in June 1933 was more dramatic than most. The ceremonies were conducted on the battleship *Oregon*. The new chapter brought fifty new members into the organization.

In September 1930, the decision to admit gold star fathers as honorary members of AGSM was approved. The first honorary member was gold star father Albers S. Buckman of New York. Within three months, fourteen other gold star fathers had joined the organization including George Gordon Seibold and Henry Leonard Hurley of the District of Columbia, and William Bates of Jackson, Michigan.

Establishing Departments

In states where several chapters had formed, attention was soon given to the organization of state departments. Originally, five chartered chapters in a state were required in order to form a department; in 1937, that requirement was reduced to three chapters. The benefits to forming a department were many—more political clout at the state and national levels, more opportunities for publicity thereby capturing the attention of new members, and a stronger say in AGSM issues.

In July 1937, the application for a department charter in the state of New York was approved. Department organizers were ready to move forward immediately; the first annual New York State AGSM convention was held in September 1937 at the Hotel George Washington in New York City.[24] Shortly thereafter, in October 1937, several chapters in Michigan petitioned to form a Michigan department.

Finding Their Way

As the new organization grew, questions and situations frequently arose for which there were no established precedents. Achieving agreement on the right answers was not always a smooth process for the board members.

In March 1933, the newly elected officers of the national executive board were invited to dinner at the home of AGSM past national president and founder Grace Seibold. At one point, the meeting took a turn for the worse as the discussion of a Past President's pin for Mrs. Seibold exposed strong feelings among the executive board:

"After a very lovely dinner was served, an impromptu meeting was held with the National President Mrs. Millard, presiding. Mrs. Seibold was invited to join us. The minutes of the Executive Meeting of November 12, 1932, were read by Mrs. Bruce, the Recording Secretary. The minutes were not approved as read, as it was stated by Mrs. Guedry and Mrs. Hood that the minutes had entries that were not true. Much discussion arose to the great embarrassment of our hostess, Mrs. Seibold, as the discussion pertained to her Past President's pin. Discussed Past President pin for Mrs. Seibold; Mrs. Gallagher moved that Mrs. Seibold should have pin.

"Mrs. Guedry moved to put old gold into melting pot to make the pin. Mrs. Seelye and Mrs. Guedry suggest that we do not make pin at this time, as funds are so low. Mrs. Guedry moved that we lay the matter of

Fig. 6-7: Singer/actress Jeanette MacDonald was the hostess for 250 gold star mothers at an afternoon tea held at Metro-Goldwyn-Mayer Studios in September 1939. Sharing the receiving line with Miss MacDonald were her husband, actor Gene Raymond, and the mothers of many of Hollywood's biggest film stars. Seated at the table in the photo are Mrs. Elizabeth H. Harrison, Los Angeles Chapter No. 1 president (age fifty-six), and Anna Mary Barnbrock of Waterbury, Connecticut (age ninety-two).

(Uncredited publicity photo: Fenelon Collection)

pin over until the next convention, or [until] a decision was made to rescind the action."

That same month a question arose concerning AGSM President Millard's expenses to attend the inauguration of Franklin D. Roosevelt. One mother, Catherine J. Loomis Hood, objected on the grounds that the AGSM had no official part in the Inauguration. The Inaugural Committee had assigned a place for the AGSM flag in the parade but the mothers had declined an invitation to march in the parade, preferring to occupy seats along the parade's route. Mrs. Hood was overruled, however, and it was voted to reimburse President Millard for her transportation to and from New York which amounted to $15.60.

It was decided in 1933 that all new admissions would be classed as chapters. A chapter would require at least ten members to be eligible for formation. Prior to this, the individual groups were interchangeably referred to as units or chapters.

In 1933, a proposal was put before the national executive board to have a cap designed specifically for the national president. Mrs. Seibold, past national president, lobbied strongly instead for a sash or ribbon with the gold star insignia to be worn across the breast. After extended discussion, it was voted that a cap with a gold star insignia would be procured and presented to president Millard.

The executive board in June 1934 faced a new issue when the Detroit Chapter advised them that a Gold Star Sisters Auxiliary group in Detroit had asked permission to affiliate with the Detroit Chapter. Although the AGSM constitution did not prohibit such an affiliation, there were no provisions to take such a step. While the "sentiment of the national executive board was favorable to the formation of such groups of sisters of deceased veterans" the board elected to propose amendments at the next national convention that would permit the forming of auxiliaries.[25] (No record has been found of this issue coming to vote at any subsequent convention.)

The issue of a salary for certain board positions was raised in 1936. It was proposed that a $25 annual salary be paid to the national corresponding secretary per a resolution passed at prior convention. An objection by Mrs. Seibold was overruled. It was then voted that the national treasurer would also receive a $25 annual salary.

In June 1936, after eight years of association with the Hotel Hamilton, the board named the New Colonial Hotel as the organization's headquarters site. AGSM rented office space in these hotels. No reason was given for the change.

A charter approved in November 1937 for a Rochester, New York, chapter raised a difficult question for the national board. Some original members of the Rochester group were the stepmothers of deceased veterans and therefore not eligible for membership in AGSM. "Not wanting to disrupt the Rochester Mother's organization by dropping these mothers who were either a step- or foster-mother," the board voted to leave the Rochester Chapter "intact" but only the birth mothers of the deceased veterans could join AGSM. This decision gave tacit approval to other chapters that had quietly allowed long-time members to participate in AGSM activities although they remained ineligible for AGSM membership.

By a vote of 4-1, the executive board in March 1937 authorized amending the original Articles of Incorporation. The action resulted in limiting recognition for membership to "no Service other than [the] World War." This created a difficult situation for at least one charter member, Alida Talbot Bruce, mother of Thomas Grant Bruce, who had been killed in 1928 while serving with the Marines in Nicaragua. The organization's records do not indicate whether any action was taken concerning Bruce's eligibility and it is possible that, as a long-time member, she was grandfathered into the membership despite this change.

Changes in September 1938 at the Veterans' Administration necessitated the addition of a new organizational advisor. Due to newly enacted privacy laws, the Veteran's Administration was no longer permitted to give out information from a veteran's file. In order to ascertain eligibility for membership, it became necessary to engage a pension attorney vested with power of attorney to act for AGSM. Pauline B. Werner was engaged to act for AGSM. In view of this change, Roberta Jacobs relinquished the office of national membership chairman but continued in her capacity as custodian of records.[26]

A Growing National Presence

As the decade progressed, AGSM found itself increasingly in the public eye. National presidents were questioned by the media on world events and national policies, and opportunities to speak on radio programs

Fig. 6-8: In October 1936, gold star mothers of the AGSM Los Angeles Chapter #1 attending a Mother's Peace Night celebration at Patriotic Hall in Los Angeles met eight-year-old movie star, Shirley Temple. Acting as hostess for 20th Century-Fox Studios, where she was filming in "The Stowaway," Miss Temple was presented with a scroll by Elizabeth Hurst Harrison, president of Los Angeles Chapter #1. Miss Temple had been designated "America's Child of Peace" in anticipation of World Peace events scheduled for the summer of 1937. *(Uncredited press photo; Fenelon Collection)*

offered open access to the nation at large. As new chapters were added and the mothers took part in local activities as a group, the visible presence of the mothers dressed in white at memorial events was a grave reminder of the cost of war.

In Washington, D.C., the AGSM calendar of activities was never empty. Gold star mothers were guests of honor at many events, including Armistice Day, Mother's Day, Memorial Day, and Gold Star Mother's Day, as well as ceremonies at the Tomb of the Unknown Soldier. AGSM's close relationship with other patriotic organizations such as the American Legion, Veterans of Foreign Wars, and disabled veterans groups led to their frequent participation in events sponsored by those groups. Civic, educational, and religious projects also consumed their energies.

In May 1930, AGSM participated in Mother's Day ceremonies at Arlington National Cemetery. Retired Major-General Amos A. Fries spoke there of the nation's connection to its mothers, stating "So long and in exact proportion as we revere mothers, so long and in that exact proportion, shall we continue to grow and prosper."[27]

On Armistice Day 1932, an AGSM delegation was part of the crowd of 5,000 onlookers attending services to rededicate the Tomb of the Unknown Soldier and its surrounding grounds, which had been reworked since the original dedication in 1921.[28]

In 1939, gold star mothers were feted on both coasts as the Golden Gate International Exposition and the New York World's Fair designated specific dates as Gold Star Mothers' Days. The Golden Gate Exposition called their event a "tribute to Mothers all over the United States who wear the gold star."

The 1930s: Remembrance, Respect, and Recognition | 113

Chapter Activities

The independent gold star mothers' groups that became AGSM chapters in the 1930s often already had a long history of activities and service benefiting the veterans who had returned from the war, especially those who had not come back whole in body or mind. In addition, they did what they could for the many gold star mothers in need.

Their fundraising activities were often inventive and amusing—such as the $18 added to the coffers of the Detroit Chapter one year by holding bunco parties following the monthly meetings. Fundraising efforts were not always successful, however. In 1935, having planned a dinner party to raise money for the national treasury, Delia Barber reported a profit of only $1.16 from the dinner. To those who had contributed freely of time and money, this dinner was "a sore disappointment." [29]

Despite the overwhelming financial constraints felt by the people of the nation during the Depression, the gold star mothers somehow managed to make their meager funds accomplish much for many. And they were establishing a notable national presence as they appeared at various events:

"Before the long line of paraders entered the [Los Angeles Memorial] Coliseum, a group of 25 Gold Star Mothers, smartly attired in white capes and white overseas caps, which bore the traditional gold stars, marched to their seats in a body... The mothers, all of them gray now, joined in the cheering as the various units went by, but now and then a tear dropped as they recalled the holocaust of 16 years ago."

Throughout the 1930s, one of the largest and most active groups was Los Angeles Chapter No.1 (sixty-six members in 1931). In her report for 1933, chapter president Alice Davis reported the following activities:

"Visited the Rural Rest Home in Azusa where we have some Gold Star Mothers, and the County Farm; Our chapter gave $49 in cash to the Purple Heart Auxiliary as our share in providing needy [veterans'] families with Christmas cheer;

"In March, through contact with Fox Studios, was able to secure five days [work] for eleven mothers and one day for twenty mothers to assist in making the motion picture 'Pilgrimage.' While at the studio, Lucile LaVerne, working in the same picture, presented our Chapter with passes to the theater to see her in one of her famous plays;

"[Following the catastrophic 1933 Long Beach, California earthquake in which 120 people died,] the Chapter provided $75 in relief work in clothes, food and such;

"Able to secure homes for three Mothers and one for a veteran's sister;

"For the Chapter, in honor of my son, Arthur, I gave the library at Sawtelle [Veterans' Hospital] one set of George Eliot's works; and,

"Paid a month's rent for a Gold Star Mother who was a Ward of Long Beach Chapter #2."

Gold star mothers were often guests and honorees of other organizations such as the American Legion and the Veterans of Foreign Wars. Participation in these activities was open to all gold star mothers, not just AGSM members:

"As guests of Clyde M. Spencer [American Legion] Post No. 1... thirty Gold Star Mothers and five blind veterans from Sawtelle were entertained at dinner yesterday at the Hotel Robinson. Seventy-five were seated at the U-shaped table... Following the dinner, the guests were taken to Municipal Airport for a ride over the city and ocean, two Gold Star Mothers going up with each of the blind veterans." [30]

Detroit Chapter No. 3 seemed to have a flair for raising funds in unusual ways:

"Following one meeting, $69.68 was added to the coffers as proceeds from a sauerkraut supper and raffle of a quilt donated and created by Mrs. Dora Merrow. At a prior meeting, the Chapter had approved spending three dollars to purchase backing for the quilt so it could be completed. Raffles featuring two pillows made by Gold Star Mothers brought in $3.25 and $6.05 respectively." [32]

Charitable Acts

Despite the hardships of the economic situation, the chapters did what they could for gold star mothers in need, regardless of whether they were members of AGSM. By the 1930s, the financial situation faced by many gold star mothers was dire. Often widowed with no income from pensions or Social Security to fall back on, the child lost during the war might have been their only hope for security in old age.

Long Beach Chapter No. 2 took on a particularly difficult case in 1933 that required the efforts of the Navy and the Legislature to resolve:

"Because of the efforts of Long Beach Gold Star

It was Christmas Eve of 1933. A little boy of seven who lived in a small Kansas border town approached the door with leaden steps. The question had been on his mind all day: 'Would Santa come tonight?' He knew that his dad, uncle and grandpa had not been able to find work for quite a while. He had heard the words 'Depression' and 'layoffs' but didn't quite understand what they meant.

After church, Dad opened the door and the little boy's eyes lit up, for there before him was a fully decorated Christmas tree with candles glowing in the branches and presents around it. There was the largest tricycle he had ever seen, with a tag: 'To Johnny from Santa.' Sure, it wasn't new and had been repainted, but to his eyes it was the grandest ever. Many years later, the little boy learned that it was the Gold Star Mothers who, having lost their sons in the Great War, kept a seven-year-old boy's hope and faith alive by providing his Christmas."

~John Darby, Hemet, CA—*Press Enterprise* (Riverside, CA) December 24, 1998

Mothers, a broken home has been reunited and peace has been brought to the heart of a lonely mother who gave a son in the World War.

"Due to a turn in the wheel of fate, the mother, Mrs. Nancy Drake... has been brought from the County Farm, where she was placed through adverse circumstances, and reunited with a 15-year-old grandson whose father was a World War veteran. That her newly found good fortune seems assured is forecast by a bill, H.R. 5178, introduced April 22 by Congressman John H. Burke before the House of Representatives providing for relief of the Gold Star Mother and her grandson. The bill has been referred to the Committee on Naval Affairs and efforts are being made for immediate and favorable action on the measure.

"An involved story is behind the twisted skeins of fate that fifteen years ago separated the grandmother and a five-weeks-old infant boy, whose mother had just died and whose father was in the U. S. Navy. The child's father, son of Mrs. Nancy Drake, left his ship on a leave of absence on May 28, 1919, in New York, never to be heard of thereafter. On the day of his departure, he sent his mother, then in Los Angeles, $30; left $80 with the quartermaster and left a month's pay, due that day, uncollected. Time has disclosed no trace of the sailor, who left a record of four years' in the Naval service without a blot against his name. The Naval Department feels that the sailor met with foul play.

"According to Mrs. Taylor [Mrs. Jane E. Taylor, President, Long Beach Chapter No. 2], the local Gold Star Mothers have worked faithfully and diligently providing for the unfortunate woman and boy.

"'We are happy to be able to provide Mrs. Drake and the boy with a home,' she stated, 'And are hoping that permanent relief will be offered to this worthy Gold Star Mother.'

"Congressman Burke of California introduced a Congressional bill to aid the family that declared Vernald Drake to have been 'honorably discharged' as of the date he was last seen, thereby enabling his mother and son to draw survivor benefits."[33]

As the Drake Bill made its way through Congress, AGSM legislative chairman Ella Guedry wrote to Mrs. Taylor:

"Enclosed you will find some papers that will be of much interest to you and to Mrs. Drake and the Mothers of your Chapter. I am sending copies to the Los Angeles Chapter too so that these Mothers may know that in the Congress of today, a Gold Star Mother has a friend in the person of Representative John H. Burke.

"Certainly it was not because Mrs. Drake occupied a position of prominence in the community that Mr. Burke essays to help her. His offer of assistance must have been prompted solely by a sincere desire to help one, who, though not entitled to the term 'Gold Star' (until such time as her boy's records have been cleared), yet has suffered just as Gold Stars have."[34]

In her 1933 annual report, Mrs. Taylor outlined the funds expended by the chapter on other charitable causes and the types of succor the mothers provided:

- Altar cloth for blind boys [disabled veterans]—$11.50
- Food and clothes for Mrs. Drake and grandson—$50.00
- Sawtelle [Veterans' Hospital] Christmas—$5.00
- Donation to *Press Telegram* for Xmas baskets—$5.00
- Baskets for Christmas—$15.00
- Visited 25 sick mothers; sent flowers for 44 mothers; helped 22 poor families; gave seven comforters.
- At Sawtelle Veterans Hospital, thirty bags of candy, nuts, cookies, cigarettes and fruit were distributed among the boys and each was given a stamped Christmas card to send home. A visit was also paid to the blind veterans where the Gold Star Mothers distributed lap robes and caps among wheelchair patients.

The chapter spent $275.73 in 1933 for various charitable activities.[35]

Chapters across the nation responded similarly to the need for charity in their own areas. Much of the energy of the organization was given to efforts to improve the lives of injured veterans and their families.

The Comfort of Shared Loss

The chapter meetings offered a social opportunity for these women who had suffered a common loss, and served as a place and time in which work, in addition to the business of the chapter, was accomplished:

"Banded together in deep friendship by that common bond of each having surrendered a son to her country's need, the Gold Star Mothers find their monthly meetings in the Santa Ana Legion clubhouse of unusual interest as time is given over to working for the benefit of [veterans] and their organizations. Monday's all day session provided the usual friendly gathering and morning hours were given over to quilting and other needlework."[36]

Visits between the chapters were common and enabled the chapters to support each other in their various endeavors. Meetings also provided an opportunity to hear news from the national organization.

Despite their busy schedules, the Chapters remained in close contact with gold star mothers in the community who had not joined the organization:

"Mrs. Jane Taylor and other members of the Gold Star Mothers of Long Beach were hostesses at a luncheon yesterday… to honor Gold Star Mothers who will make the pilgrimage to France to visit the graves of sons who lost their lives in the World War.

"Several of the members are contemplating the trip abroad this summer to visit the "Little green tents where the solders rest," and will have their plans pretty well arranged by the time of the April meetings. The larger number of the local organization are debarred from making this trip by the fact that the bodies of their hero sons were returned home for burial, so the mothers are denied the mournful satisfaction of seeing the land where they fell."[37]

Finances

Throughout the decade, funds to support the work of the chapters were in short supply. Chapter meetings often offered impromptu opportunities to add to the treasury. Information was often shared between chapters about methods of making money.

The Grace Darling Seibold Chapter seemed to have a flair for turning every opportunity into a fundraising event. When the chapter received a box of candy as a gift from a gold star mother who made and sold candy, Mrs. Killeen proposed the box of candy be raffled off for ten cents a chance in order to add a small sum to the treasury. Another impromptu fundraiser occurred when a bag of groceries donated by a local firm was raffled off at a meeting. A card party at the Cairo Hotel in 1932 netted $10 while the receipts from a bingo party at Edna Boardman's home added $12.15 to the treasury ($13 taken in, less eighty-five cents for punch ingredients).

Roberta Jacobs introduced a drawing for the meeting attendees that she called "a pig in the bag." It was a nice gift wrapped so that no one could tell what was contained. Chances were sold at ten cents each. Alida Bruce won the first drawing and $1.70 was added to the funds. The pig in the bag drawing continued for several meetings with a new "pig" being raffled each time. At one meeting, a motion was made to discontinue the "pig in a bag" activity, but the motion was not carried.

Questions of finance consumed much of the time of the executive board and, at times, board meetings grew rancorous over the issue of expenditures. In particular, issues arose between the national presidents and their boards over the fact that the national presidents were often expected to pay their own way to attend AGSM-related events. In October, national president Mary J. Bates wrote:

"I have received invitations from the National VFW, and the National Departments of Michigan's and the District of Columbia's American Legion to attend their conventions, all of which I had to decline with thanks. I do hope the time will come when our organization... will be able to contribute to expenses so that our President will feel able to represent our organization in the proper manner in person."

A suggestion was made to the board in 1934 that the chapters should contribute financially to the operation of the executive board.

In 1935, a request from President Bates asked that "in view of there being no fare required for her to attend the coming national convention [to be held in her home state of Michigan], she be allowed the fare one-way for attending the National Defense Council meeting." The expense was approved by the board.

A letter from national president Bess Duncan Wells in 1937 was read at a meeting of the executive board:

"[It offered] a short resume of her recent trip into nearby States in the interest of trying to organize chapters in these several States. The President requested the cooperation of the National Board by allowing her a refund for money spent for gas for her car while on this trip. The amount of $15 was requested. The request was met with disapproval by a majority of those present. A letter was to be sent to Mrs. Wells apprising her of the reason for refusal of her request."

The Pursuit of a Congressional Charter

Throughout the decade of the 1930s, as time and resources allowed, AGSM pursued the goal of receiving a congressional charter. A law passed by Congress, a congressional charter states the "mission, authority and activities of a group." Similar to being incorporated at the federal level and largely honorific, these charters are most often presented to veterans' and fraternal organizations whose activities are unique and "clearly in the public interest".[38]

While obtaining a congressional charter would have added to AGSM's prestige and recognition, the national board repeatedly reminded the membership that failure to obtain a national charter would not hinder their goals or activities.

In an August 1930 letter to Colonel J. Miller Kenyon (AGSM's legal advisor), Mrs. Seibold admitted that she "had not given the [charter] proposition serious consideration until I had heard your view... [now] I find it imperative that we take some action in preparation for desired legislation during the next session of Congress. I am calling an executive session for Tuesday evening to consider the importance of protection of our rights."

On January 3, the first executive meeting of 1931 was called by Mrs. Seibold and held at her home. The main purpose of the meeting was to review and approve the proposed charter prepared by Colonel Kenyon. The charter was approved by the board for presentation to the 72nd Congress, then in session, for ratification.

In 1931, Bills S. 459 and H.R. 9 were introduced in the 72nd Congress calling for AGSM to be granted a congressional charter. AGSM had one request of the Judiciary Committee concerning the legislation:

"Of this Committee we would ask just this one thing. That it fail not to report the bill out of Committee. We are of the firm conviction that the membership of Congress is too magnanimous to deny us this Honor. Like good soldiers we will accept the verdict if it be approval or disapproval rather than that the bill should die in Committee."[39]

To support the charter legislation, AGSM provided information on the significance of a national charter as well as the history of the organization:

"The Charter that these Mothers plead for will cost the Government nothing but it will say to the World that there is nothing the Congress of the United States will not do in recognition of the sacrifice which cost the Gold Star Mothers their sons. Medals are conferred upon heroes and monuments and statues are erected at enormous cost to memorialize their deeds and we trust that Congress will not deny to the Mothers of these heroes a comparably small honor of granting them a Charter."

The American War Mothers (AWM) organization quickly lodged a protest against the granting of a charter to AGSM, although AWM itself had received a Congressional charter in 1925. Despite the bills having made progress and being "reported favorably," the AWM protest blocked the bills' passage out of committee.

AGSM submitted a Supplemental Statement in Defense of Bills S. 459 and H.R. 9 stating that they had hoped to "close our appeal without criticizing in any way the protest to said Bill filed by the American War Mothers." In the statement, they strove to clearly delineate the difference between the AGSM and AWM organizations and membership, advising "The American War Mothers is not a Gold Star Organization though it admits Gold Star Mothers to membership."

They told of the AWM first offering and then rescinding the offer of lifetime memberships to gold star mothers, an act which prompted the establishment of AGSM:

"Hundreds of Gold Star Mothers therefore severed their connection then and there with the American War Mothers and formed exclusively Gold Star organizations throughout the United States.[40]

"The only such organization with headquarters in the City of Washington, D.C. is the American Gold Star Mothers, whose bill for a Congressional Charter is now before the Congress of the United States. This is the motive for the unwarranted protest filed by the War Mothers against the granting of an honor to the Mothers of the Dead by the Congress of the United States when they, the Mothers of the Living, have already been paid such an honor.

"Hundreds of these Gold Star Mothers who withdrew from the American War Mothers have already united with this organization and hundreds more have voted to unite with us providing this Charter is granted us.

"The uniting of dozens of Gold Star Organizations under one banner, that of the American Gold Star Mothers, would clarify the Gold Star movement throughout the United States and relieve Congress of passing upon the merits of various bills seeking honors for these Mothers. We can submit the names of hundreds of such Mothers who stand ready to join us if the Charter be granted."

AGSM's efforts were unsuccessful and the bills failed to be passed out of committee by the 72nd Congress. Year after year, AGSM continued to pursue a Congressional charter without success. In 1937, the national board voted to rescind the charter effort in favor of more important legislation.

In 1938, Ella Guedry discussed the pursuit of the national charter in her report on legislative activities for the AGSM Convention:

"As to a Congressional Charter, if we have to perjure ourselves as to the volume of our membership, and the state of our treasury, I hope we may never have one. It is not my observation that the membership in organizations which have been granted a National Charter has increased by leaps and bounds. We are experiencing a very healthful growth and expansion without one, and while we do not underestimate the honor attached to such a grant from the Congress of the United States, it must come as a Testimonial to Mothers of the Dead of the World War that our sacrifices have earned for us. My personal views are that Congress should tender such an honor to the rightful organization of Gold Star Mothers if it can be done without precipitating another Civil War to determine just which of the many groups is the rightful one.

"I desire to correct an impression that it is necessary to secure a charter from Congress in order to be a national organization. I need only call your attention to the fact that neither the Democratic nor Republican National Committee have a charter from Congress. This is true of innumerable organizations and industries, and yet they are national, just the same as the American Gold Star Mothers.

"Let our best boast be that we have ever put the needs of our Mothers ahead of any honor or glory that might be sought."

Five decades would pass before the AGSM was honored with a Congressional charter in 1984.

Legislation

From its inception, AGSM worked diligently to encourage and influence legislation to benefit veterans and their families and to protect AGSM's interests. Charter member Ella Montague Hammond Guedry served throughout the decade as the legislative liaison for the organization. In 1932, a newspaper article discussed Mrs. Guedry's efforts and successes:

"Mrs. Guedry is making her tour to contact mothers whose claims for pensions seem to hang fire. She helps assemble evidence for the Veterans' Bureau. Through her own case, Mrs. Guedry became interested in a study of the work, which she began fifteen years ago. Her son, who was killed in the war, was her only child. The American Gold Star Mothers have helped obtain more than $200,000 for mothers who didn't know how to present claims, according to Mrs. Guedry."[41]

Despite frantic action by President Roosevelt and the new administration, the nation continued to suffer deeply from the effects of the Depression during the early 1930s. As more businesses closed, the loss of a family breadwinner's occupation often led to homelessness. Many families were broken up in an effort to stave off starvation, and elderly couples who had once lived with their children's families found themselves relegated to "poor farms" where they lived on county charity. In 1933, the Grace Darling Seibold Chapter adopted a resolution endorsing a movement to secure Congressional help so that destitute aged couples would not be separated in their declining years, but "be provided for so they can live together and be with each other when the end comes."

In March 1937, national president Della Towne Blake was one of three gold star mothers who testified before the Congressional Committee on World War Veterans Legislation that was considering legislation to provide extended death benefits to parents of soldiers killed in the World War. The other women called to testify were Ethel Nock, representing the Gold Star Auxiliary of American War Mothers, and Matilda Burling, national president of the American Gold Star Mothers of the World War. One of Mrs. Nock's statements was a warning to the legislators of the dire condition many of these parents now faced, explaining "The Gold Star Mother is dying more rapidly than the insurance life-expectancy tables would indicate. We realize the reason for that is that she has not the incentive to live that she would have, had her son lived."[42]

Two days later, a newspaper article reported on the effect of the gold star mothers' testimony on the listeners:

"Committee members, many of whom had been hardened by actual wartime service, failed to conceal their emotions when they were faced by the mothers, all of whom lost their sons in the World War."[43]

A bill proposed in 1936 and known as the Rankin Bill (H.R. 6384) brought hope to those concerned with the welfare of the nation's gold star parents. If passed by Congress, the bill would increase the mothers' death compensation from $20 per month to $45 per month and when the father and mother are both living, the increase would be from $30 per month to $50 per month. The bill was introduced in anticipation of the World War death benefit insurance payments expiring in 1938. The AGSM membership responded with a letter-writing effort that resulted in more than 600 letters supporting the bill being sent to legislators while mothers in the Capitol labored tirelessly in support of the legislation.

Late in 1937, the AGSM board rejoiced over what they termed "three legislative triumphs" that included the passage of the Rankin Bill, blocking the passage of the Army Recreation Fund dispersal, and preventing a rival organization, American Gold Star Mothers of the World War, from being granted a Congressional charter.

The Rankin Bill or Gold Star Mothers' Bill was passed by Congress and became law. The pen used by President Roosevelt to sign this act was presented to the AGSM national president Della Towne Blake.

Senate Bill 1516 proposed that the unexpended balance left in the Army Recreation Fund (also known as the Stars and Stripes Fund) after the World War be divided between the American War Mothers and other patriotic organizations. The bill passed both houses of Congress but was vetoed by the President. Ella Guedry explained the national board's stance against this bill in response to member queries:

"Many of our members have written to inquire why we have not petitioned Congress for a share in the distribution of this fund... It is the opinion of the National Executive Board that these funds should remain just where they are in the United States Treasury for availability in the emergency of another war since that is what Congress has ordered; that certainly no organization without a Congressional Charter would presume to claim any of this money; that only one with an enormous treasury and stupendous membership and

Fig. 6-9: Missouri gold star mothers with General John J. Pershing at the Tomb of the Unknown Soldier in Arlington National Cemetery, September 21, 1930.
(Panoramic photographs (Library of Congress); Ref. LOT 8838 no. 2)

a large staff of salaried officers to administer the law could honestly qualify to handle such a business since the cost of administering the law must be borne by the organizations. These funds must be used to aid and assist disabled, destitute or unemployed veterans and their dependents.[44]

"We were not in accord with such distribution and so wrote the President calling his attention to the fact that while some of the petitioners would have to account annually for expenditures, others would not be so bound. Mrs. Burling's organization, American Gold Star Mothers of the World War, was specifically pointed out to the President as an organization without a Congressional Charter that, as a potential recipient, would not be required to account annually for their share of the Fund.[45]

Bill H.R. 2514 sought a Congressional Charter for Mathilda Burling's American Gold Star Mothers of the World War. However, the bill was never acted upon in Congress, due in part to pressure applied by AGSM:

"We placed before the Judiciary Committee facts showing that the organization named in said Bill was organized two years after our incorporation and Congress adjourned with the Bill still in committee."

In May 1938, national president Della Towne Blake reported to the membership that there had been a change in the government's stance on the eligibility of stepparents for death benefit compensation:

"By a ruling of the Attorney-General, stepparents of the World War Dead are restored to eligibility for death compensation, from which they were cut off in March 1933, providing the marriage took place during the life of the veteran. This order does not make stepparents eligible for membership in our Organization [AGSM], but does provide benefits for them just as in the case of blood parents. We have had to deny membership to many of these stepmothers, but are glad to pass this good word along to them."

In 1938, Ella Guedry made it clear what the primary focus of future legislation would be for AGSM:

"Hospitalization of indigent Gold Star Mothers in Government facilities is undoubtedly the most important legislation looming before us. With the Veterans Administration records to prove that these Mothers are slipping away at an amazing rate each day, it should not prove burdensome for the Government to give hospital care to any Gold Star Mother who will swear that she is without income other than her compensation."[46]

The *AGSM Bulletin*

In September, 1936, the first issue of the *AGSM Bulletin* was published. Distributed every other month, the typeset newsletter would prove a reliable way to keep chapters and members advised of activities, issues and concerns at both the national and chapter levels. In the first issue, national president Della Town Blake explained the origins of the *Bulletin:*

"[It was] decided at the Detroit Convention in June 1936 that a bulletin be issued by the National President bi-monthly in which there should be such information as would be helpful and informative for all Chapters and members-at-large pertaining to matters of interest concerning plans for work as laid down by the President. This is the first of such bulletins."

The *Bulletin* was an immediate success. One hundred copies of the first issue were printed; sixteen months later, each printing produced 1,100 copies.[47] The *AGSM Bulletin*, in one form or another, has been the organization's method of sharing information for more than seventy years.

National Gold Star Mother's Day

When legislation was proposed in 1936 to establish a national gold star mother's day, AGSM took a surprising stand against the proposal. They relayed their opinion to the White House in a telegram that cost ninety cents to send:

"[AGSM believes] there is no justifiable reason for the passage of a law creating a 'Gold Star Mother's Day' since all mothers have sufficient honored recognition enacted in the Bill for 'Mothers Day' annually observed on the second Sunday in May. Therefore, we object to the passage of the proposed Gold Star Mothers Bill with all its undesirable requirements."

Despite their protest, the bill was passed and the last Sunday in September officially became a national day of recognition for gold star mothers across the nation, calling for "All government officials to display the United States flag on all Government buildings, and the people of the United States to display the flag and to hold appropriate meetings at their homes, churches and other suitable places, on the last Sunday in September, as a public expression of the love, sorrow and reverence of the people of the United States for the American Gold Star Mothers."

In November, President Blake reported on the recognition she had received on the first national Gold Star Mother's Day in the form of letters, telegrams, and beautiful flowers. She also told of having sent a lovely telegram and letter to the founder, Grace Seibold, on Gold Star Mother's Day, which "was ignored."

The Franklin D. Roosevelt presidential papers collection contains letters of appreciation concerning Gold Star Mother's Day from the AGSM National Board and the Grace Darling Seibold Chapter in Washington, D.C. —as well as AGSM Chapters in Philadelphia, Spokane, Saginaw (Michigan), Jackson, Kalamazoo, and New Bedford.

One gold star mother would later ask a question about the new legislation that troubled many across the nation. On September 18, 1939, Mrs. William H. Henning, a Montevideo, Minnesota, gold star mother, wrote to First Lady Eleanor Roosevelt:

"Our beloved son Walter was killed in action on the battlefields of France on November 11, 1918. I'm a Gold Star Mother and fully appreciate the honor bestowed on all Gold Star Mothers.

"What about the Fathers? Aren't their sons just as dear to them as they are to the Mothers? Why not share the honors with the Gold Star Fathers—they are the forgotten fathers and simply ignored. I have been thinking about it for years but do not know what to do about it. Then the thought came to me, 'Why not write to Mrs. Roosevelt? She will know what to do.'

"When I read the enclosed clipping [announcing plans for Gold Star Mother's Day to be held on September 24] I could not rest until I had written this letter. Dear Lady, can't you do something about this? These dear old fathers won't be with us much longer. Can't we share the honors with them while we are here. May I humbly suggest a Gold Star Parents Day?"[48]

Eleanor Roosevelt wrote back that she agreed with Mrs. Henning and would give her letter to the President.

Memorials

While the urgency to memorialize the World War in stone, concrete, metal, paint, and living trees had lessened by the 1930s, there was still a strong desire in many hearts to honor the memory of those who fought, those who died, and those who lost a child in the conflict. Memorial Day and Armistice Day ceremonies were major events in most towns and cities, and gold star mothers were traditionally guests of honor at these events. Throughout the nation, cities and organizations continued to find ways to honor the war's gold star mothers as well as their sons who had died.

Originally dedicated in 1921, the Tomb of the Unknowns and its adjoining areas had been remod-

eled in a project that wasn't completed until 1932. At the rededication of the Tomb, on Armistice Day 1932, an event at which AGSM was represented, American Legion National Commander Louis Johnson spoke of the mother of the Unknown Soldier:

"We know not whether he was our friend lost in battle, nor the manner of his going. All we know is that he was born of a mother and that he had love before he had breath. We know he loved and was loved in his mother's arms, and, as a boy enjoyed life, stepping forth to meet manhood, the fruition of a mother's dreams. We know he lived for peace, died for peace, and dying, found that peace that passeth understanding."[49]

By the 1930s, many of the memorial highway and bridge-building projects started in the 1920s were being completed. In May 1933, the mayor of St. Louis, Missouri invited President Roosevelt to attend the ceremonies for the dedication of the Kingshighway Memorial Gold Star Tree Court of Honor.[50] On August 23, 1933, more than 5,000 people marched from downtown Sidney, Ohio to the new Gold Star Bridge for a dedication ceremony. The town paid tribute "to a group that always pays the ultimate sacrifice in wartime but is now largely forgotten: the Gold Star Mothers."[51]

In Greenwood, Wisconsin, a Gold Star Mothers' Memorial was unveiled on October 3, 1937. Created by noted Washington, D.C., sculptor Professor Ernest Durig, the memorial represented a warrior-like gold star mother holding in one arm a fallen soldier and the other the American flag.

As in the decade past, trees of all types were planted as living memorials to the war dead. Planted singly, in groves, or in rows, bronze plaques were often imbedded at the base of the trees to dedicate each tree to a specific fallen serviceman.

In 1923, the white birch tree had been designated as the Mother's Tree. In 1924, one planted on the White House lawn was dedicated to the mothers of the presidents of the United States. In 1928, a birch tree was planted at the grave of George Washington's mother. In 1932, the gold star mothers planted a white birch tree in Arlington Cemetery for the mother of the Unknown Soldier. Gold star mother Madame Ernestine Schumann-Heink sang at the planting ceremony as soil from each of the forty-eight states and other locations around the world was added as the tree was planted:

"The soil, carried in small cups, was placed at the roots of the tree by little children dressed to represent the different states and territories and the tree itself was dedicated to the Mother of the Unknown Soldier. No matter from what state the hero came, the soil of his native state nurtures the living tree."[52]

The Bonus Army

In May, 1932, Washington, D.C., was "invaded" by an army of men who had fought for the nation in the Great War. Calling themselves the Bonus Expeditionary Force, but usually referred to as the Bonus Army, the nation's capital became the temporary home of some 25,000 unemployed and desperate veterans and their wives and children. The veterans wanted only what had been promised to them, but they wanted it early—a bonus for World War I military service that had been promised for 1945.

The bonuses took on new urgency in the midst of the Depression as veterans struggled to find work and to feed their families.

The veterans arrived in Washington, D.C., to support legislation introduced that would allow immediate payment of their veterans' bonuses. A gathering that had started spontaneously soon grew to a city within a city. The makeshift village formed by the always increasing but peaceable Bonus Army was regarded sympathetically by most of the District's residents, including the police. Agencies, individuals, and organizations, including the AGSM, donated all they could in terms of food, clothing, funding, shelter, and medical care.

When the Bonus legislation was defeated in June, the protesters refused to leave. The Administration and Congress would not negotiate with the protesters and the situation grew increasingly tense on both sides:

"[On July 28] General [Douglas] MacArthur led his secretly trained riot troops into the makeshift city, pressing protesters and on-lookers ahead of his cavalry troops who were followed by tanks and 300 armed infantrymen. Tear gas grenades tossed into the crowds ignited the makeshift shacks that the protestors had built. The protesters at a second camp were given one hour to evacuate and the camp was burned to the ground.[53]

President Herbert Hoover, who had ordered the troops to clear out the protesters, was severely criticized for his action by the press and public; his actions, in part, kept him from being elected for a second term.

Veterans of Future Wars

While the Bonus Army was as serious as life and death to those who made their way to Washington, D.C., it was mocked by many privileged young academics of the time. In 1934, a student prank started on the East Coast quickly spread across the nation, but few individuals other than the perpetrators found it amusing.

In his book about famous pranks and hoaxes, Neil Steinberg refers to the Veterans of Future Wars (VFW) as "the most controversial political prank of the prank-laden 1930s":

"The VFW was organized as a put-down of the Bonus Bill (thousands of World War I veterans, caught in the grip of the depression were demanding their pensions). Reasoning that they would certainly someday be sacrificed in a future war, they argued that it was only natural that, when prematurely doling out pension money, that the future vets be remembered as well. The most deserving, the group noted, would be killed or severely wounded in the pending war, and thus would not enjoy the full benefit of their country's gratitude unless it was bestowed before the fact.

"Coming from an enclave of privilege, such as Princeton, the Future Veterans perhaps can be seen as a mean-spirited effort, which may explain why it was quickly embraced by more than 50 campuses across the country. Many professors joined the organization, and women's colleges formed Gold Star Mothers of Veterans of Future Wars, demanding to be sent to France at government expense (as actual Gold Star Mothers had been) to see the future graves of their as-yet-unconceived sons."

Before long, the Veterans of Future Wars had over 6,000 members, drawing the livid, sputtering rage of real veterans' organizations.[54] The public also found it difficult to be amused by the VFW's rhetoric:

"Students of Princeton must have a perverted sense of humor. A group has organized 'The Veterans of Future Wars' and some young women at Vassar have been persuaded to form 'The Association of Gold Star Mothers of Veterans of Future Wars.'

"The object, of course, is to lampoon the Veterans of Foreign Wars, one of the most progressive of ex-service men organizations, and the Gold Star Mothers, made up of women who lost sons in the World War.

"These students will discover they are engaging in a highly hazardous business. The American people are not likely to applaud the spectacle of a group of rich young upstarts ridiculing mothers who gave their sons to their country and men who fought for the flag on foreign soil."

A letter to the editor of *People's Forum* took exception to the ill-mannered prank, not on behalf of the World War veterans who he said had taken worse abuse already, but on behalf of the gold star mothers:

"In reference to a news item that appeared in your paper a few days ago. The item concerned told of the formation, at Princeton University, of a society for the collection of soldier bonuses for future wars. Also an auxiliary society of future Gold Star Mothers and a prosecution of their claims to visit their sons' graves at Government expense. It has become the fashion, in some quarters, to ridicule the veteran and his attempts to obtain a small measure of justice. However, I am not writing in his defense. The veteran can 'take it on the chin' and come up for more. If his hide were not thick he could not have survived the last few years of calumny, ridicule and vilification. But these detractors, in their efforts to belittle the veteran, have overstepped the bounds of common decency. They have attacked that noble band of mothers whom we all revere. That band whose gold star is a symbol of sacrifice; of sacrifice so great it is not comparable to any other.

"When the Federal Government sent the Gold Star Mothers to France to visit the graves of their sons, it was the finest gesture ever made by any Government in the history of the world. To ridicule this act is contemptible, to say the least.

"This writer, believing that he voices the sentiment of all veterans, calls upon the authorities of Princeton University to censure the guilty parties and demand from them a sincere apology to the Gold Star Mothers. If there is an iota of manhood and patriotism among these young men, their apology will be full and complete. Their sin can only be excused on the grounds of youth and thoughtlessness."

It is ironic that these outrageous pranksters of the mid-thirties would be called upon in just a few years to serve in their nation's cause during World War II. They would perform bravely and come to be called "The Greatest Generation."

Gold Star Mother Zinnias

In May 1937 the Long Beach Chapter sent President Roosevelt an unusual gift—seeds for a new variety of zinnia named the Gold Star Mother Zinnia. Developed by Major Harry L. Bateson, an internationally known horticulturist and disabled veteran, the bright gold zinnias developed in a Long Beach experimental garden would become the national flower of the gold star mothers. The seeds were presented by president Blake and custodian of records Roberta Jacobs at a private reception with President Roosevelt. Plans were made to send the seeds abroad to become the flowers of other sorrowing war mothers. Major Bateson vowed that the zinnias would never be put on the market commercially.

President Roosevelt set aside a half acre of land adjacent to the field of Flanders poppies in Washington, D.C., to plant the seeds, and declared them "one of the nicest gifts I ever received."[55]

The Battle of Burling

One of the most difficult and public problems faced by the AGSM during the 1930s was created by one of their own members—gold star mother Mathilda H. Burling. Mrs. Burling was one of the earliest applicants for membership in the newly formed AGSM. Approval of her application proved to be an act that the organization came to rue. As Grace Seibold wrote in 1939:

"Mrs. Burling's enrollment for membership in our organization... was the greatest farce we have ever experienced as evidenced by her harmful perpetrations against us. Her... one dollar fee was the most disastrous ever received. By the unanimous vote of our organization she was dropped from our Membership for disloyalty on December 1, 1931, then also in arrears for two years."[56]

More specifically, the executive board's meeting minutes state that she was "dropped from the rolls because of unfaithfulness, opposition, lack of interest and disloyalty to our organization."[57] But long before she was dropped from AGSM membership, Mrs. Burling had gone her own separate way. In 1930, Mrs. Burling formed an independent gold star mother organization—American Gold Star Mothers of the World War, Inc. Her title was National Gold Star President.

The similarity in the groups' names created endless confusion in the mind of the public between Mrs. Siebold's American Gold Star Mothers, Inc. (AGSM), and Mrs. Burling's American Gold Star Mothers of the World War, Inc. (AGSM-WW). This confusion was increased by Mrs. Burling's indefatigable talent for self-promotion and her willingness to muddy the waters whenever possible.

Married to George B. Burling Sr., a New York City policeman, Mathilda H. Burling was the stepmother of Private George B. Burling Jr., who was killed in France in 1918. The fact that she was the stepmother of a gold star veteran rather than the birth mother should have prevented her from being granted membership in AGSM. Her membership application has not been found so it is unclear whether this was an oversight on the part of AGSM or the result of false information being provided.

Mrs. Burling had been very active as a gold star mother in the 1920s. A member of an American Legion gold star group called Gold Star Mothers of America, she rose to the position of vice president. She testified before Congress in 1927 regarding legislation to fund a gold star pilgrimage and corresponded with General John Pershing in 1928 seeking his support for the pilgrimage. Her stepson had been buried in the American Cemetery in St. Mihiel, France, and Mrs. Burling sailed with a gold star pilgrimage group in 1930. She later claimed to have been the "sponsor" of the Pilgrimage in Congress.

During the summer months of 1930, more than 300 gold star mothers left New York each week to begin their pilgrimage journey. Mrs. Burling was often found at the dock from which the travelers departed where she handed out her cards to the gold star mothers about to sail and invited them to join her organization.

As early as December 1932, AGSM looked for legal advice on the issue of Mrs. Burling's organization and the difficulties it was creating for their Washington, D.C.–based group as well as gold star mothers interested in joining with them. In a letter from Ella Guedry to Colonel J. Miller Kenyon, a legal adviser to the group, she asked:

"Will you be good enough to advise us if we have a legal right to complain of the action of one of our members in forming an organization and calling it American Gold Star Mothers of the World War? Is this similarity of the title not an infringement upon our rights since we were organized and incorporated long before her order came into existence?

"Not only does the similarity of name cause confusion but they copy our membership cards and other literature and, more than once, Mothers have joined that order thinking they were uniting with us. Can we

Fig. 6-6: Mathilda H. Burling, President of American Gold Star Mothers of the World War. *(Fenelon Collection)*

enjoin them from using this name on the ground that we are injured through the confusion occasioned by their adopting a name so nearly like ours after we had been entitled to such name for a period of two years or more before they organized?"[58]

Mrs. Guedry did not exaggerate about Burling's group copying the materials of the AGSM. Comparing letterhead, membership cards, and other documents, such as the constitution and by-laws, Burling's group's documents match AGSM's materials almost word for word, and the format and fonts are identical.

Even the White House had trouble differentiating between the two groups. As early as 1933, the following file memo began to be circulated with documents and requests received from or pertaining to either group:

American Gold Star Mothers
American Gold Star Mothers
of the World War, Inc.

When this file is withdrawn, attention should be invited to the fact that there are two organizations of Gold Star Mothers, one, the older, the American Gold Star Mothers organized June 4, 1928, and incorporated January 5, 1929; and the other, The American Gold Star Mothers of the World War, Inc., organized March 5, 1930 and incorporated February 24, 1931.[59]

Mrs. Burling continually worked to bring new members into her organization and her frequent radio addresses gave her national exposure. While some new members may have wandered in thinking they were joining the Seibold organization, as the AGSM alleged, others were actively recruited to join the AGSM-WW, based largely upon the reputation that Mrs. Burling had created for herself.

From the perspective of the AGSM in Washington, D.C., Mrs. Burling's encroachment continued despite their continuous efforts to clarify and contradict the misinformation that her efforts engendered. In 1938, an unsigned handwritten document was prepared outlining the "transgressions" of Mrs. Matilda Burling. They included:

- "Appearing at patriotic Gatherings in uniform with 'National President Gold Star Mothers' on her white cape.
- Masquerading as the National President of the American Gold Star Mothers.
- Mrs. Matilda Burling presented a diamond-studded star to Attorney General John J. Bennett, a couple of weeks ago, having her photograph in the Daily News with a caption, "Mrs. Matilda Burling, National President of the American Gold Star Mothers, pins a diamond-studded star on the lapel of the coat of Attorney General John J. Bennett in recognition of his services and assistance."
- At the World's Fair Preview, she paraded around the entire fairgrounds in uniform as the National President, so much so that when we arrived, the real New York Department President, Mrs. Emma L. Balcom, was greeted with the news "that the National President was already there." It is most embarrassing to the Department President to meet her at civic and patriotic ceremonies.
- Mrs. Burling has been and still is sowing seeds of distrust and disloyalty around the cities she visits and especially in the northern end of New York State."[60]

As Mrs. Burling's activities expanded and became more public, AGSM consulted again with legal advisors to determine what could be done. But their efforts were hampered by the potential cost of a legal proceeding, the members' unfamiliarity with the legal process, and the possibility that they would not be successful in their case, thereby drawing even more attention to Mrs. Burling's efforts.

Their first efforts to understand what could be accomplished through the legal system, the potential cost, and the actual possibility of success were directed to J. Miller Kenyon, a long-time advisor to the organization. One of his suggestions must have been met with horror when received at the AGSM headquarters in Washington:

"Possibly you could induce the New York organization... to become a Chapter of our corporation, then reincorporate and adopt the name, 'American Gold Star Mothers of the World War.' It would be much better to have all join with the corporation that exists in the national capital rather than to have a conflict involving all who might choose to incorporate using the name, and in several jurisdictions... This seems to me to be a solution of the whole matter if it could be brought about."[61]

AGSM continued to look for a legal solution to the problem for several years. In January 1938, responding to a report on the Burling situation from Ella Guedry, founder and past national president Grace Seibold made perfectly clear what she felt the organization's stance should be on the issue of Mathilda Burling and also intimated her frustration with not having been asked for an opinion earlier:

"I am glad to offer... suggestions in reply to the first official request received by me for my views in connection with the attempt to have our legal rights granted in NY State...

"As you have stated, I do realize that the dearth of legal minds in our (elderly) organization, in which class I evidently belong since I have not had the advantage of a college career which some of our officials claim they have experienced; however, my limited intelligence enables me to believe that we should seek our just recognition only through the NY state lawful legal procedure. I, for one, have never approved of our organization becoming involved in any court procedure... Some of the legal advice has been disappointing and some is worth considering especially that advice to refrain from any controversy that would result in undesirable legal action for our organization.

"Mrs. Burling will get sufficient adverse judgment from her own followers in due time.

"Our only objective should be to have an error by the State Department corrected in justice to us, if possible. If the NY State Department has or does decide that they are not for any reason going to correct their error, then I am of the opinion that the incident should be considered closed in the interest of peace and contentment for the few years in store for any of us...

"In answer to your questions submitted for considering:

"No. 1: I would not authorize or advise our legal advisor to file an injunction against the Burling group for reasons already given;

"No. 2: I would advise the Executive Board members to instruct the legal advisor of this organization to abandon the intentions of filing an injunction suit;

"No. 3: I do not approve of submitting a list of Burling offenses to the Post Office Department."

Based in part on Grace Seibold's comments and the cautious approach counseled by the organization's new lawyer, the group's insistence on legal recourse diminished. However, their efforts to rein in Mathilda Burling and set the truth before the public did not end. Mathilda Burling survived the decade of the 1930s without changing her tactics. She led her group of gold star mothers through World War II and into the period of peace that followed.

Gold Star Mothers in the News

Newspapers were always interested in news, good or bad, as it related to gold star mothers. In April 1930, a Detroit gold star mother was charged with bootlegging just prior to sailing to France on the gold star pilgrimage:

"Mrs. Elizabeth White, 50, Gold Star mother who is scheduled to sail for France June 14 with other pilgrims to the graves of world war heroes, appeared before Judge Henry S. Sweeney in Recorder's court today as an alleged prohibition law violator.

"Patrolman Hugh Cavill of Trumbull station charges he bought a pint of whiskey from her for twenty-five cents.

"Learning Mrs. White's son was killed in France in 1918 and she was to make the overseas pilgrimage Judge Sweeny reduced her bail from $1,000 to $500 personal bond. An effort will be made to hold Mrs. White's trial before the sailing date."[62]

In June 1930, charges of bootlegging were brought against a gold star mother who had lost four children in the world war:

"Friends of Mrs. Ada Tenney, 60-year-old gold star mother of San Diego County, are formulating plans to defend her against liquor charges in the Federal court.

"Mrs. Tenney was four times bereaved by the world war. She lost two daughters, who served as nurses, and two sons.

"Prohibition officers stopped her at the Mexican border with her nephew, Frank L. McManus. She is charged with having ten pints of liquor in her possession."[63]

A March 1931 scrapbook clipping titled "In a Flash! Bolt Gives Blind Mother Sight" told the unusual story of a Burlington, Iowa woman:

"Mrs. Mary Richardson, 72, a Gold Star Mother who has been totally blind for nine years, regained her eyesight for a few moments when a bolt of lightning went through her house. Momentarily, she saw her housekeeper, the radio and other objects in the room. She feels she may regain her sight again."

In 1937, three new Staten Island ferries were commissioned, replacing boats that had been in service since 1905. *The Gold Star Mother* was named to commemorate the mothers of sons who were killed in the World War and many gold star mothers participated in her launching ceremony. *The Gold Star Mother* sailed in New York Harbor until the late 1960s when she was retired.[64]

On the Brink of War

As the decade of the 1930s drew to a close, the nation was once again watching the world erupt into war. Despite AGSM's decade-long effort to remind the nation of the true costs of war, America's military involvement once again seemed inevitable. The next decade would challenge the organization in many ways as the nation again fought a world war and gold star mothers from a new conflict looked to the World War I mothers of AGSM for guidance and comfort.

Fig. 7-1: A World War I gold star mother mourns over her dead son's belongings.
*(Los Angeles Herald Examiner—*Pictorial Review; *July 15, 1941; Fenelon Collection)*

CHAPTER 7

The 1940s: Growth, Recognition, and Discord

Your organization stands in the minds and hearts of your countrymen and women as a thing apart. You wield an influence out of all proportion to your numbers.

—MRS. ARTHUR WOODS,
Consultant to Secretary of
War Patterson (1947)

AT THE START OF THE new decade, war was raging in Europe. In America, many began to see the United States' involvement as inevitable. Others, however, responded by increasing their efforts to counsel the nation toward peace. No group spoke more meaningfully and fervently for peace than gold star mothers of the first World War.

Gold Star Pleas for Peace

Mae Cushman spoke strongly for peace to the *Los Angeles Times* shortly after her election as national president of AGSM in 1940. The headline for the article read "Gold Star Mothers Unalterably Opposed to Fighting on Alien Soil, Declares New Leader: Their sons died in the last war:"

"They don't want any more of America's youth to perish on foreign battlefields.

"But if the fight is carried to the soil of this nation then they will be in favor of an 'all out' combat.

"This, according to Mrs. Mae Cushman, newly elected national president of the Gold Star Mothers, is the sentiment of the organization she heads.

"'We know what it is,' she reported on returning yesterday from the Boston convention of the group, 'to lose our boys in war. We don't want any other American

mothers to experience the same loss unless it becomes a matter of defending this nation against an attack on our own land.'

"As president of the gold star movement, Mrs. Cushman... will direct a nation-wide campaign to keep this nation out of war.

"'We're going to talk peace until the last breath,' she said.

"Beneath the pride she felt in being elected head of the mothers' organization, Mrs. Cushman reported she experienced great sadness because her election fell on the 21st anniversary of the death in France during the World War of her only son, Clifford Cushman.

"The gold star group, Mrs. Cushman reported, is more concerned with the communistic menace to the nation than the war danger because it believes the former is the greater peril. 'The women of America have to stand squarely behind their menfolk in combating all subversive activities,' she emphasized."[1]

At the New York World's Fair in May 1940, the National Legion of Mothers of America presented their goals to fair visitors. Speakers included "Emma L. Balcom, national second vice president of the American Gold Star Mothers, Inc., who prayed for the maintenance of peace by the United States." While praying for peace, the group also took practical action with the formation of a women's rifle corps to shoot down parachutists who might invade American soil.[2]

In February 1941, the *Chicago Tribune* reported the formation of a new "national committee of patriotic mothers in opposition to President Roosevelt's war dictatorship bill and involvement in foreign wars." The bill to which the mothers referred was H.R. 1776, which formalized the type of aid the United States could give to its allies, culminating in the Lend Lease program. The new organization, called We, the Mothers, Mobilize for America, was headed by Ethel S. Nock, a prominent gold star mother and past national gold star chairman of the American War Mothers. According to Mrs. Nock:

"The dictator bill is not only a threat of involvement in war, but a menace to free institutions in America... Any senator who votes to send an American boy abroad to die for a foreign empire should go to Europe or Asia and not remain in the supreme legislative body of the American people."[3]

Another spokesman for the group stated:

"No sacrifice is too great for the mothers of America to make to join in this great mobilization... Little will matter if we lose our republic and our sons. Participation in this war will mean 1,000,000 Gold Star mothers for America, and millions more will see their sons return maimed."[4]

A poignant reminder of war's cost appeared in the July 15, 1941, "Pictorial Review" section of the *Los Angeles Examiner*. A full-page illustration of a gray-haired World War I gold star mother mourning over memorabilia of her dead soldier son was accompanied by a poem, "Gold Star Mother," by Nick Kenny:

They took her bright-eyed son away
To die on fields afar.
And so they took her sky away
And left her with a star.
The patter of his baby feet
With daylight used to start
His baby shoes are empty now
As empty as her heart.
And there's his helmet, worn while he
Was fighting for the cause
Fighting out on foreign soil
A war to end all wars.
Her boy who loved the goldenrod
That flamed on hills of home,
Was killed on some unfriendly shore
Across the bitter foam.
One day a year her grateful land
Bedizens her with praise.
One day a year she tries to smile,
But oh... the other days...

Fig. 7-2: World War II service flag-themed music. "There's a Blue Star Shining Bright (in a Window Tonight)." By Jack Foy, John Ravencroft, Ira Bastow and George Howard. ABC Music Corporation, New York, 1943. *(Fenelon Collection)*

America Goes to War

The nation became a participant in World War II when Japanese forces attacked the U.S. Pacific Fleet at Pearl Harbor, Hawaii on December 7, 1941.

Some eighteen months before, the Fleet had been transferred to Pearl Harbor to establish a presence that would hopefully deter Japanese aggression throughout the Pacific. Just before 8 a.m. on Sunday, December 7, the Japanese fleet struck Pearl Harbor, simultaneously attacking both the anchored fleet and nearby military airfields in an attempt to ground any aircraft that might be able to take off and counter the attack. In less than two hours, 21 ships of the Pacific Fleet were sunk or damaged, 188 aircraft were destroyed with damage to another 159, and more than 2,400 Americans were dead.[5]

On Monday, December 8, the United States and Britain declared war on Japan. President Roosevelt referred to December 7 as "a date which will live in infamy." On Thursday, December 11, Germany and Italy declared war on the United States. World War II had suddenly become a global conflict and America had become a major combatant. The horror of the attack at Pearl Harbor rallied the nation behind the President and essentially silenced the isolationists.

The Service Flag Tradition Continues

The return of the service flag (blue star flag) was almost immediate following the attack at Pearl Harbor. Within a week of the attack, Mathilda Burling publicly presented a gold star flag to a mother whose son had died at Pearl Harbor. Patriotic groups, such as the American Legion, did their best to ensure that every family of a fighting American had a service flag to display.

In most cases, the service flags were identical to those used in the Great War—simple fabric rectangles bordered in red around a white center. But as the war progressed, more elaborate service flags became available. The United Veterans Emblem Agency of Los Angeles designed a new service flag, copyrighted in 1942, and explained its use: [Fig. 7-4]

"This flag is to be hung in your window or in your home. This is the current official service flag for World War No. 2. It is not to be confused with the service flag that was used during World War No. 1.

"As you look at the picture, you will see the flag of our nation. Beneath the flag you will see the emblem of what we are striving for—VICTORY, and in or about the V you will see stars representing men who are fighting for their country.

Fig. 7-3: "Dorothy Pearl & Jericho the pup" play in front a window with a service flag on June 28, 1943. *(Fenelon Collection)*

Fig. 7-4: A World War II version of a service flag produced by the the United Veterans Emblem Agency of Los Angeles.
(Fenelon Collection)

Fig. 7-5: An alternative style of World War II service flag. *(Fenelon Collection)*

"Everyone who has a right to possess this flag should be very proud and we are proud to know you are entitled to display this flag in your home. (Our prayers and every good wish go out to you, and to the boys who are serving so gallantly, and, by the grace of God and by his divine help and assistance, may the millions of blue stars ever remain blue!)"[6]

For those handy with crochet needles, the *Chicago Tribune* ran an advertisement on August 22, 1943, offering instructions for crocheting a service flag using four-ply knitting and crochet cotton. The patterns were available through the *Tribune* for just twelve cents, including postage.[7]

As in World War I, the omnipresent service flag appeared in every World War II venue, from churches to businesses and family homes to ballparks.

World War I Gold Star Mothers Offer Comfort

The gold star mothers of the Great War had never forgotten their lost children. Now, more than two decades after the war in which their children had died, groups of mothers still met to offer comfort to one another and to reassure themselves that their children's sacrifices were not forgotten. They reached out to the gold star mothers of this new war, offering a level of comfort and sympathy that could only come from those who had experienced a similar loss.

A year after Pearl Harbor, gold star mothers from the Great War worried about the boys who were now "over there" experiencing what their own sons had gone through:

"Gold star mothers of the World War turned their thoughts to the new boys yesterday. Still misty-eyed with memories of the morning pause for facing east [in honor of their soldier sons of the Great War], a band of 55 gathered... to hold their 23rd annual Armistice Day dinner and worry, mother-like, about the lad next door, the boy from across the street.

"Are the boys in Africa getting enough sleep? Are the boys really happy?

"Of course the troops in Africa are rested. Mrs. Anna Bruckner... remembered how well her son, Charles, 19, who was killed in the Argonne forest, was trained.

"'They have lots of pep,' she said. "They could go for three days at a time without sleeping. The boys aren't lie-in-beds like they are when they are home...'

"And Mrs. Bruckner's daughter-in-law, Charles' widow Esther... smiled. She knew how lively the new boys are. Her son, John Charles, was trained at the same camp as his dad...

"All cast admiring glances at the Distinguished Service Cross awarded posthumously to Bugler Frank B. Swift, who was killed in the [World War I] Chipilly Ridge battle. His mother, Mrs. Mabel Swift,... took it to the dinner with her. Also present were two gold star mothers of this war.

"They are Mrs. Ella Dreesbach... and Mrs. Lucille Novack whose sons Herbert, 23, and Donald E. Hamel, 19, both went down on the *Arizona* at Pearl Harbor. Mrs. Dreesback and Mrs. Novak didn't know each other until the casualty lists came out."[8]

For some mothers, this was the second war in which a son had fought for America. A 1942 Mother's Day article in the *Chicago Tribune* told of one woman's loss in the Great War and her younger son's service in the second World War:

"Today Mrs. O. James Vogl is experiencing her second wartime Mother's Day. It's marked with hope and prayer and confidence, unlike another Mother's Day in World War I. That was a day filled with prayer, too, but it was overshadowed by sorrow and despair.

"Her son, Corp. Homer Grossman, who stretched his age so he could fight for his country, was a World War I fatality. He was killed in action at the age of 19 in a battlefield in France. He was a Marine enlistee.

"In World War II, another son, Capt. O. James Vogl Jr., is seeing action. He's stationed now at Camp Custer, Michigan and he remembered Mother's Day with a message for Mrs. Vogl. He's in this war for a double reason: to avenge his brother's death and the attack on United States' possessions.

"Mrs. Vogl's grandson, another Homer Grossman, 19, expects to be in the service soon. All that stands between him and an enlistment in the air corps is 15 pounds. A student now at the Wright Aeronautical School, he'll be eligible with the additional poundage. He was named for his late uncle.

"Facing another Mother's Day with another son's fate in the balance, Mrs. Vogl retains hope and philosophy. 'All we can do,' she said, 'is hope and pray that they'll return as they left; but that they will return, in any event.'"[9]

An unidentified August 1942 newspaper clipping told the story of Mary Susan Myers, a sixty-six year

old widow of Browning, Missouri, who had lost a son in both wars and believed a daughter had lost her life in war service during World War I:

"Youngest son, Gernie T. Myers, was killed in action on the first day of the present war. A U.S. Navy man of 14 years, he was on the battleship Arizona, which was sunk in the Japanese attack on Pearl Harbor. Another son, Claude H. Myers, was killed at Coulemells, France, June 9, 1918. The American Legion Post in Browning [Missouri] was named after him. Another son, Berney Myers, was 15 years old in 1914 when he was struck by lightning on the family farm.

"One of Mrs. Myers' five daughters, Ruth, was lost shortly before World War I. She had studied in Kansas City to become a nurse and it is believed that she lost her life on the way to a post of duty overseas."[10]

Mrs. Myers shared her memories of her children and how she had learned to cope with their deaths:

"When my boys left home, I felt that I would never see them again. I gave them up, but in my heart I always remember them as babies. I suppose a boy, however old he grows or how long away from home, is always a baby to his mother.

"I had bad luck with all my boys. But there'll be other mothers who must lose two sons, or more. They'll just have to learn to accept their losses and take it on the chin, as I have had to do."[11]

In World War I, Mary McCoy lost four sons and was named the nation's Gold Star Mother of 1920. Her sons, John, James, Leo and Thomas, died in France and their bodies were returned home for burial in November 1920. Mrs. McCoy received condolences from President Wilson and the governors of several states when her sons were buried. When World War II began, one of her three remaining sons, William, was inducted into the Army but after ten months of service was honorably discharged before being sent overseas. Despite her losses in World War I, Mrs. McCoy was not disheartened when William was called to duty, stating "I am willing to give another son if it will stop Hitler."

Mrs. McCoy, who had come to America from France in 1864 with her parents, had also lost a daughter during the influenza pandemic of 1918. Mrs. McCoy died at age seventy-nine, one month after William was released from the Army. She was survived by three sons and a daughter.[12]

As the war progressed, gold star mothers of the two world wars turned to each other for comfort:

"Gold star mothers of two wars reached across the years separating them in age to share a common grief in attending a program given in their honor yesterday by the Cook County [Chicago] Council of the American Legion auxiliary…

"The sentiment of the older women was expressed by Mrs. Mary Longshaw, 74… who lost her son, John, in France. She said, looking at the younger women: 'When our sons died, they told us there would never be another war. I never thought I'd meet another group of gold star mothers here.'

"The council invited the 385 gold star mothers among the membership of its units. Nearly 200 attended… The program is held in November, because Armistice Day falls in this month.

"The youngest mother at the meeting was Mrs. Ada Smith, 42… Her son, Lt. Frank Smith of the Army Air Forces was killed at Las Vegas, Nevada 16 months ago. He was 23. Some of the younger mothers, whose grief was newer and therefore keener, brought pictures, letters and other mementoes of the sons they had lost. The older women were content with renewing friendships. One said: 'I love this meeting because some of the women who never come to any of the others do come here.'"[13]

In 1944, the *Chicago Tribune* reported on a group of mothers whose children served in the same branch of the military and how that connection had brought the mothers together in friendship:

"A group of women who bring hope and encouragement to each other met yesterday... They are the Chicago mothers of army officers in the air forces, and they meet once each month to give each other moral support.

"Yesterday it was necessary for them to remove two blue stars from their service flag and replace them with gold stars. One star was draped which signified another mother had been notified that her son was missing. There are now 21 gold star mothers among the 180 members and 16 have been notified that their son is missing. Fifteen of their sons are listed as prisoners of war and of this number all except three are German prisoners...

"Christmas boxes for overseas were packed yesterday, but you couldn't tell which of the mothers carefully placing articles in the boxes had been notified their sons were killed in action. Each seemed to find comfort and solace in putting idle hands to work.

"'That's the way it is,' said Mrs. Vera Ruth Clark, widow, whose son has been missing in the South Pacific for more than a year. 'We find consolation in helping each other. Being together seems to sustain us in our sorrow and it certainly reduces our worries.'

"The mothers seem reluctant to talk about the possibility of the war's ending shortly. They read the headlines and listen to the radio, but seem to hold themselves aloof from optimistic views.

"'It means so much to them that they are afraid to believe it,' she explained. 'Their silence is a shield.'"[14]

Multiple Gold Stars for Some
In May 1942, official casualty lists confirmed what Mrs. Peter Barber had known in her heart since the Japanese attack at Pearl Harbor:

"Three of her sons were killed when a warship was bombed and sunk at Pearl Harbor. So far as is disclosed by casualty lists, this is the largest loss inflicted on a single family in the United States in this war... Mrs. Barber lost [her three sons] all at once. She is the mother of five sons. The survivors are Clayton, 16 years old,

and Robert, 9. Her husband is a veteran of the first World War...

"There was a phone call at 2:30 a.m. on December 21 which brought the family the news that the three inseparable Barber boys were dead.

"The brothers were Malcolm (23), Leroy (21), and Randolph (19), all firemen aboard a warship. Leroy was the first to enlist, his mother said today, and received preliminary training at Great Lakes. He was so impressed with the ship to which he was assigned that he wrote his brothers, advising them to enlist and to request a similar assignment. The Navy made an exception in the case of the three brothers to its rule against permitting more than one member of a family to serve on the same ship.

"Their father wrote the navy two weeks before their deaths asking that they be transferred to separate ships so they would not be subject to the possibility of being lost in one disaster.

"'I remember how grand they thought it was that they could all be on one ship,' Mrs. Barber said. 'While in Hawaii they met Gene Autry, the movie star, and last fall they were his guests for a week at his ranch in California.'

"'We are not bitter,' the father said, 'but there is one thing neither of us can forgive. We were at peace when the attack started. Our boys didn't even know about it. They must have been caught below decks without any chance to fight back. If they had known—if we had been on guard—they would have returned the fire and they might not all have died.'

"'We have no choice, we must go on despite what has happened,' Mrs. Barber added, glancing at 16-year-old Clayton. He is a [high school] student and for him going on means getting old enough to avenge the deaths of his older brothers."[15]

The horror of the loss of the three Barber boys shook the nation but it was eclipsed just a few months later when news of the Sullivan brothers became known. Although tragic, the story of the five Sullivan brothers became one of the most inspiring war stories of World War II.

Raised with a strong commitment to family and faith, the five Sullivan brothers—George Thomas, Francis Henry, Joseph Eugene, Madison Abel and Albert Leo—were well known to friends and neighbors in Waterloo, Iowa, and had a reputation of watching out for each other. After the attack on Pearl Harbor, the

Hitler's Deadliest Enemy

That day she saw her first born march away... Hitler made his deadliest enemy.

She's still the same sweet-faced mother her son kissed good-bye... but now there's steel in her heart and a fierce determination to back up her boy with every ounce of strength and courage she's got.

The letters she writes are like a drink of fresh spring water to a homesick lad... thirsty for all the little details, the homey, newsy details that link him to a dear familiar life.

And if she's cut expenses to the bone to buy War Bonds, if she's put up the car, if meat is scarce, if she's taxing her strength to the utmost at the Red Cross... no hint of it creeps through to him. He knows only that she's backing him to the limit, and working in her own quiet way to bring him home again, soon.

She's somebody Hitler didn't reckon with when he told his people, "Americans are too soft to fight." He didn't know our women.

— From "Dear Mom, Courage and Comfort for War Mothers"
Submitted by the Eureka Vacuum Cleaner Co.,
Copyright by William O. Rogers, Denver 1942

brothers enlisted in the Navy, where two had previously served in peacetime; they insisted on serving together on the same ship or there was "no deal." Their motto had always been "we stick together."

Despite the loss of the three Barber brothers at Pearl Harbor and a naval policy to separate family members, all five Sullivan brothers were assigned in February 1942 to the USS *Juneau,* a newly commissioned cruiser bound for the Pacific. Their assignment soon led to celebrity status for them in the press since they were the nation's only group of five family members serving on the same ship.

During the Battle of Guadalcanal in November 1942 the *Juneau* was sunk. Initially reported as missing, subsequent eyewitness reports stated that four of the brothers died in the initial explosion aboard the *Juneau;* George Thomas was wounded, but made it to a life raft. He died after five days at sea, possibly the result of "wounds and exhaustion or a shark attack."[16]

The Sullivan brothers were survived by their parents, Thomas and Aleta Sullivan; a sister, Genevieve; Albert Leo's wife, Katherine Mary, and their 22-month-old son, James Thomas.

On February 2, 1943, President Roosevelt wrote on behalf of the nation when he sent condolences to Mrs. Sullivan:

"Dear Mrs. Sullivan:
The knowledge that your five gallant sons are missing in action, against the enemy, inspired me to write you this personal message. I realize full well there is little I can say to assuage your grief.

"As the Commander in Chief of the Army and the Navy, I want you to know that the entire nation shares your sorrow. I offer you the condolences and gratitude of our country. We, who remain to carry on the fight, must maintain the spirit in the knowledge that such sacrifice is not in vain. The Navy Department has informed me of the expressed desire of your sons... to serve on the same ship. I am sure that we all take pride in the knowledge that they fought side-by-side. As one of your sons wrote, "We will make a team together that can't be beat." It is this spirit which in the end must triumph.

"Last March, you, Mrs. Sullivan, were designated to sponsor a ship of the Navy in recognition of your patriotism and that of your sons. I am to understand

Fig. 7-7: The five Sullivan brothers who died in 1942 when their ship, the USS *Juneau*, was torpedoed in the Pacific. *(Fenelon Collection)*

that you are, now, even more determined to carry on as sponsor. This evidence of unselfishness and courage serves as a real inspiration for me, as I am sure it will for all Americans. Such acts of fate and fortitude in the face of tragedy convince me of the indomitable spirit and will of our people.

"I send you my deepest sympathy in your hour of trial and pray that in Almighty God you will find a comfort and help that only He can bring."[17]

In honor of the Sullivans, President Roosevelt ordered the Navy to name the next ship to be commissioned after the brothers. On September 30, 1943, a destroyer, *The Sullivans,* was christened by the boys' mother. In service from 1943 to 1965, the ship earned nine Battle Stars during World War II and two more during the Korean conflict.

Following the death of their sons, the Sullivan family did not retire from the scene as others might have done. Mr. and Mrs. Sullivan worked tirelessly on behalf of the war effort, appearing at bond rallies, war plants, and shipyards across the nation. Their daughter, Genevieve, often accompanied them until joining the WAVES in June 1943. They hoped their efforts would keep other families from losing their sons.

In 1948, Mrs. Sullivan became a member of American Gold Star Mothers, Inc. Her membership added immense prestige to the organization. Her contributions and conduct were acknowledged and honored by others who knew the pain of loss as she did—other gold star mothers. In May 1943, she was named the "Most Courageous Mother in America":

"Selection of Mrs. Thomas F. Sullivan, whose five sons lost their lives last November in the Battle of Guadalcanal, as the 'most courageous mother in America' was made yesterday by the Los Angeles chapter of the Gold Star Mothers.

"'Never in all the history of our nation,' said Mrs. Margaret J. Benapfl, chapter president, 'has any mother been dealt such a terrible, shocking blow as the loss of all her sons—five fine boys—in a single engagement. We who have suffered similarly, though in a lesser degree, can appreciate the awful anguish of such a bereavement.

"'Instead of giving way to grief, burying herself in sorrow when she got the news that her boys had died in action, this noble woman went to Washington and volunteered to serve her country, just as did her boys after Pearl Harbor.'"[18]

Reverend Amos W. Ligon of Chicago had served as a chaplain in World War I. He was the father of five sons, all of whom had followed his example and joined the ministry. At the time the war began, four of the young men had their own pastorates. One after another, they each left their families, churches, and congregations to enter military service:

"The eldest, Lt. Amos Jr., chaplain of the Infantry in Italy, was reported killed November 7, 1942. Then in almost breath-taking succession, Lt. Raymond, chaplain aboard a transport in the Pacific was killed March 4, 1944; Chaplain James was killed aboard a transport on March 16, 1944; then Lt. William, a chaplain in Italy, was killed May 15, 1944; and finally Lt. John, the youngest, was killed with the infantry in England May 21, 1944.

"Unable to locate the service flag with five gold stars that he would like to have, the 59-year old father was able to philosophize: 'It's a good sign when I can't find one though. It shows they aren't needed often.'"[19]

Mr. and Mrs. Albon Borgstrom of Tremonton, Utah, had already lost three sons and had another son listed as missing when they appealed to the Marines to allow their fifth son to return home from military service. Their son Clyde, twenty-eight, had died in the Solomon Islands in March 1944. His brother LeRoy, thirty, died in Italy in May 1944. Rolon, nineteen, died in the crash of a bomber in August 1944; his twin brother Rulon was reported missing in September 1944.

Private Boyd C. Borgstrom, twenty-three, spent eighteen months in the South Pacific before coming home on a month's furlough in September 1944. He was then assigned to Camp LeJeune in North Carolina for further training:

"I do hope they will give Boyd a release and let him come home," said his mother. "We need him here at the farm. And he wants to come, if it can be worked out without any reflection on him."[20]

The Borgstroms were later informed that their missing son, Rulon, had been declared dead. The Borgstroms became members of AGSM.

Just as some families seemed to pay a greater price to the war effort, certain neighborhoods also saw their young men swept away to war, never to return again. In Boston, a neighborhood hard hit by the war was given special recognition:

"Nine gold stars shine among two score blue on Yorktown Street—a dead-end street on the Cambridge and Somerville line.

"The nine gold stars tell a story of neighborhood kids who played ball and 'soldiers' together in their boyhood days and died as real soldiers so that the 'kids' of this and future generations may play in peace.

"Personal messages from President Truman, the late President Roosevelt, General MacArthur and General Arnold praising the heroes of Yorktown Street have followed the messengers who brought the tragic news so many times. On May 19, 1947, Yorktown Street and Yorktown Court in Cambridge were officially changed to Gold Star Road and Gold Star Court, respectively; on May 26, 1947, Yorktown Place was changed to Gold Star Place."

World War II Gold Star Organizations Form

While American Gold Star Mothers, Inc., held a preeminent place in the nation's roster of patriotic organizations, World War II saw a proliferation of new organizations for war mothers and gold star mothers. Mothers of World War No. 2, Inc., was founded in 1942 by Gretta Roush. Headquartered in Indianapolis, the organization's purpose was to "unite fraternally all Mothers who have sons or daughters in the service of the Military Forces of the United States of America." The organization focused on helping maintain the morale and courage of those serving in the military and work in any way they could to "HELP WIN THIS WAR!" Their motto was:

*While our sons fight
We war mothers unite*

*Soldiers, today;
Statesmen tomorrow.*

The organization included gold star mothers within their membership. They were differentiated from the rest of the membership at their gatherings by their blue caps; white caps were worn by the president and past presidents and red caps were worn by the general membership.[21]

One of the earliest World War II groups to be established was the Blue Star Mothers of America:

"Army Captain George H. Maines conceived the idea for the Blue Star Mothers in 1941. He ran a newspaper article in Flint, Michigan on January 22, 1942 requesting information about children serving in the armed forces. More than 1,000 mothers responded.

"By March 8, 1942 more than 600 mothers organized the Blue Star Mothers of America, Inc.… Chapters quickly formed in Michigan, Ohio, Wisconsin, Oregon, Iowa, Washington, Hawaii, Pennsylvania and New York."[22]

Blue star mothers were women who had children serving in the American military. Like the gold star mothers, their name derived from the stars on service flags hung in homes in World Wars I and II to denote family members on active service in the military. Membership in Blue Star Mothers would have drawn from the same base as the American War Mothers, which was established in 1918 and had expanded its membership to include mothers from World War II (and subsequent wars).

The Gold Star Mothers of Kansas City formed in 1945 when Myra Willock brought together a group of ten gold star mothers. Initially meeting to provide comfort and encouragement to each other, they continued to volunteer their time after the war to serve the needs of veterans, especially in hospitals.[23]

Despite the huge growth of the membership of American Gold Star Mothers, Inc., during and following World War II, the organization had still not incorporated many of the nation's independent gold star groups. Among correspondence received by President Truman in the late 1940s are letters from the Gold Star Mothers of Wisconsin, Missouri State Gold Star Mothers, Inc., and Gold Star Mothers of Illinois. Sadly though, with nearly 300,000 World War II casualties in the nation's armed services, there were more than enough gold star mothers in the nation to support all these organizations and more.

Fig. 7-8: M. Jennie Williams, AGSM National President 1939–1940 *(AGSM Collection)*

Fig. 7-9: Maretta Mae Cushman, AGSM National President, 1940–1941 *(AGSM Collection)*

Fig. 7-10: Dr. Emma Balcom, AGSM National President, 1941–1942 *(AGSM Collection)*

Fig. 7-11: Mary F. Hill, AGSM National President 1942–January 1946 *(AGSM Collection)*

AGSM leaders of the 1940s

Seven women led AGSM during the decade of the 1940s: M. Jennie Williams, Dr. Emma Balcom, Maretta Mae Cushman, Mary F. Hill, Emily M. Cunningham, Eleanor D. Boyd and Anna Hagerty. Of those, six would influence the organization for their terms as national presidents, but the decisions and actions of one leader who served five terms as national president—Eleanor D. Boyd—would influence the organization for more than sixty years. For other than Mrs. Boyd, very little personal information remains about the women who led the organization through World War II and the remaining years of the 1940s.

Fig. 7-12: Emily M. Cunningham, AGSM National President Pro Tem, January 1946–June 1946 *(AGSM Collection)*

Fig. 7-13: Eleanor Boyd, AGSM National President, 1946–1947, 1948–1952 *(AGSM Collection)*

M. Jennie Williams [Fig. 7-8]
National President, 1939–1940

The last six months of Jennie Williams' term as president covered the first half of 1940, making her the first AGSM president of the new decade. While little is known about her background or the major issues of her time in office, a *New York Times* article reported that her legislative activities did not end when she left office. In August 1940 she lent her personal support to a bill that was being debated in Congress:

"Nine American mothers who, dressed in mourning clothes, have been holding a 'death watch' in a Senate reception room for more than a week as a protest against the Conscription Bill had competition today. Mrs. W. Walter Williams, 70... past president of the National Gold Star Mothers [actually AGSM], women who lost sons in the World War, has started a one-woman campaign for the bill.

"Asked whether she planned to confer with the 'mourning' mothers, who hanged Senator [Claude] Pepper, an advocate of conscription, in effigy in a maple tree last week, Mrs. Williams replied:

"'Well, I do not know. Why are they wearing mourning? Do any of them have sons that fought in the last World War?'

"Mrs. Rose Farber of Detroit, leader of the group of nine, said:

"'Our group will not ask Mrs. Williams for a conference. If she wants to see us, she will have to initiate the move. We were here first.'"[24]

Maretta Mae Cushman [Fig. 7-9]
National President, 1940–1941
Mae Cushman joined AGSM in November 1931. She and her husband, Jesse Willard Cushman, lost their son Clifford Snider at the age of nineteen when he was killed in action in France. Mae had long been active in the Los Angeles Chapter No. 1 and had served as chapter president prior to taking the helm of AGSM at the convention in Boston.

Emma L. Balcom, MD [Fig. 7-10]
National President, 1941–1942
Emma Balcom (Mrs. William H. Balcom) joined AGSM in October 1936. Already active in her native New York in other gold star organizations, she was quickly appointed state organizer for New York and was instrumental in bringing many new chapters together as well as organizing one of the first state departments.

Her son, Willard A. Balcom, had been killed in action in France at the age of nineteen, just one month before the war ended. He was buried in the Meuse-Argonne cemetery, and Dr. Balcom took part in the gold star pilgrimages. The Willard A. Balcom Post of the American Legion in the Bronx was named for her son.

One of the last official acts of Mrs. Balcom's presidency was the decision in convention to admit World War II gold star mothers to AGSM membership.

Fig. 7-14: A World War II service flag.
(Fenelon Collection)

Mary F. Hill [Fig. 7-11]
National President, 1942– January 1946
A member of AGSM since October 1934, Mrs. David Franklin Hill's son, Richard Franklin Hill, MD, was a member of the Navy Medical Corps. He died in July 1918 at age thirty of spinal meningitis contracted while treating sailors with the disease. Two of her other three sons also served in World War I.

Much of her time was spent sponsoring and organizing national support for veterans' legislation in Congress. She made trips to Washington to discuss this with committees studying veterans' legislation and had been consulted by President Roosevelt and President Truman on features of the G.I. Bill of Rights. Mother Hill was active in many service-related organizations including the auxiliaries of the Jewish War Veterans, the Veterans of Foreign Wars, the American Legion; the Military Order of the Purple Heart and the Society of the 28th Division, AEF.[25]

Mrs. Hill was elected for the 1941–1942 term as national president. When the United States entered World War II in December 1941, war conditions made it impossible to hold another AGSM convention until 1946.

Very little information survives concerning AGSM activities during those four years when restricted travel and gatherings affected how the organization could operate and communicate. At the 1946 convention, one national officer stated that "we realize that it is only since the war is over that we are actually becoming organized."[26]

Mrs. Hill's term as president continued through the war years and until her death in February 1946, a period of four years.

Emily M. Cunningham
[Fig. 7-12]
National President Pro Tem,
January 1946–June 5, 1946
When it became clear that Mrs. Hill would not be able to carry on her duties as national president following a stroke, first vice president Emily M. Cunningham (Mrs. John S. Cunningham) of Milton, Massachusetts, was named national president pro tem in January 1946 for the remainder of Mrs. Hill's term in office. A member of AGSM since 1940, Mrs. Cunningham's son Clarence B. Cunningham had died of "disease" in August 1917 at the age of twenty-one while serving in the Army. Mrs. Cunningham was not elected to the national presidency after she fulfilled what remained of Mrs. Hill's term in office.

Anna G. Hagerty
Eleventh National President, 1947–1948

No membership application survives for Anna G. Hagerty of New Jersey although it is known that she was the daughter of Elizabeth I. Millard, the second national president of AGSM.

The two primary foci of Mrs. Hagerty's term appear to have been managing the rapid post-World War II growth of the organization and trying to deal with her predecessor's unexpected and, according to AGSM, unauthorized activities related to the national gold star home. (The history of the Memorial National Home Foundation is contained in Chapter 9.)

The Iron Fist in the Velvet Glove

At the 1946–1947 national convention in Philadelphia, Eleanor D. Boyd (Mrs. Walter Harrington Boyd) of Long Beach, California, was elected as the eleventh national president of American Gold Star Mothers, Inc. [Fig. 7-13]

Easily the most controversial figure in the organization's history, Eleanor Boyd would come to be considered an angel by some and a scourge visited upon AGSM by others. She was inspirational and dictatorial; she professed humility but remained patrician in her outlook and lifestyle; mercurial in temperament she was always conscious of her image; and although frequently sympathetic, she could be brutally dismissive of others' opinions. Despite her myriad flaws, during the multiple terms in which she served, a foundation was laid that enabled American Gold Star Mothers, Inc., to continue and prosper as a strong, effective organization for the next sixty years, even as the membership declined to a fraction of its former numbers.

Mrs. Boyd stood out among the members of the organization. She was a woman of vision and considerable personal force, confident and dynamic, a prominent socialite, and the wife of a respected medical doctor. Active in numerous organizations ranging from the

Fig. 7-15: A World War II service flag with a 1944 calendar. "This year there is but one word of greeting: "VICTORY" *(Fenelon Collection)*

Council of Religious Education to the Camp Fire Girls and the PTA, Eleanor had been recognized in 1944 as an Outstanding Woman of Long Beach.[27] She also headed the Women's Division of the War Savings Committee, a group that led a successful fundraising campaign that enabled the City of Long Beach to buy a bomber for combat. The first gold star mother of World War II in Long Beach and in California, she was selected to christen a frigate, the USS *Long Beach*.[28]

Mrs. Boyd lost two sons, her only children, in World War II. Her oldest son, Air Force First Lieutenant Walter H. Boyd Jr., died in 1941 at the age of twenty-four in a plane crash while serving as a war-mission observer in Marshall, Texas. Her younger son, Truman O. Boyd III, twenty-three, was called to the military from his pre-med studies at Stanford University and died in action with a tank unit in Tunisia in 1943.[29]

Three months prior to his death, Lt. Truman Boyd had been interviewed by an Associated Press reporter following an encounter with a superior German force. The resulting article was published around the world.[30]

Outmanned and outgunned, Boyd and his men were forced to abandon and burn their tanks to prevent them from falling into German hands. Leading his troop on a thirty-five-mile trek to safety through enemy lines, Boyd had been cited by his commanding officers for not losing a single man (in fact, the troop sustained only one injury). As they headed back to their own lines, Boyd also rescued a contingent of Allied soldiers thought to have been lost and released many British officers and men who had been taken prisoner by the Germans. He had become well known to radio audiences across the nation when he led a retaliatory tank blitz against a German outpost and that action was dramatized in a worldwide radio broadcast.

Truman's strong belief in what he was doing and his understanding of the dangers faced by the fighting men were made clear in a letter he wrote to his parents that arrived less than a week before they received news of his death. He wrote, "Many of my friends here I will not see again for a long, long time. They have gone to serve with Walt's [his deceased brother] men, who like Walt, have added another page to man's history and man's fight for the right."[31]

He was posthumously awarded a Silver Star medal for gallantry and bravery in the action that took his life.

Even among gold star mothers, the loss of two children accorded Mrs. Boyd special respect and status. When elected national AGSM president, she was serving her second term as president of the Long Beach Chapter, one of the organization's largest with more than 130 members. She was the first World War II gold star mother to serve as AGSM national president. Already known as a mover and shaker in national political circles, she had lobbied successfully to have a government-built wartime housing project in Long Beach named in honor of her younger son—the Truman Boyd Manor. Clearly understanding the potential power of the AGSM, Mrs. Boyd always identified herself as a gold star mother of two sons when meeting with legislators, politicians and other policymakers. Her loss opened many doors and increased her success in accomplishing her goals. Her style was brisk, efficient and business-like, a good combination for an organization that had essentially just been holding on during the war years. Mrs. Boyd's energetic leadership and focus revitalized the organization and provided a vision to the membership of what AGSM could become if its resources, talents and power were dedicated to appropriate causes. Bolstered by an expanding membership and loyal support from the nation and government, AGSM wielded a strong emotional appeal in the aftermath of the second world war. They began looking for new, broader issues to which they could lend their support.

For the gold star mothers of World War I, aging and now greatly outnumbered in the organization by World War II members, the new energy and direction of the organization must have been bewildering. The new generation of gold star mothers had been empowered by World War II as they moved into the workplace and military to take over non-traditional work that freed men for military service. The World War II gold star mothers were young, more independent and ready to establish their place in the post-war society. Mrs. Boyd was recognized as having the perfect combination of

Fig. 7-16: A World War II grandmother and grandson pose before the family's service flag in the window. *(Fenelon Collection)*

experience, leadership, and style to lead the revitalized gold star mothers organization.

Following her election, Mrs. Boyd communicated frequently and in detail with the membership about issues from the mundane to the significant. In *Bulletin No. I* (June 30, 1946), Mrs. Boyd set a cordial, concerned tone that invited members to communicate with her on any topic:

"First your national president wishes you to know that she is your servant for service this year. Never feel that you are troubling her or in any way a nuisance. That is what she is here for, to hear from you with both your joys and sorrows, so feel free at any or all times to drop that note, knowing that it will be appreciated and answered."

Within weeks of her election, she had already begun to create order and accountability at the top levels of the organization:

"All National officers handling money have been bonded and the work has been delegated to a greater number, making it easier on the individual and, if possible, to be business-like and efficient at the same time. Let us spread the responsibility and work this year."[32]

She recommended that each chapter appoint a publicity officer so the organization's activities at all levels would receive the broadest possible public exposure. She also counseled kindness and care in dealing with gold star mothers who were not eligible for AGSM membership:

"When you are having membership application forms filled, have the exact wording the War Department sent in the telegram or letter, remembering that the son must have been killed in the line of duty, in combat or the wound therefrom. The mother must have borne him and be an American citizen. Be very careful that we do not hurt more deeply some mother who is not eligible. You who are eligible can belong with honor. It is with sadness that the Veterans Department tells us some mothers are not eligible. Again I warn you to take care, kindness is so important."[33]

In *Bulletin* No. II (July 31, 1946) Eleanor offered guidelines and interpretations on various rituals, by-laws, and protocols for color bearers. Such guidance would become common topics for her as she tried to recharge an organization that had idled administratively while growing dramatically during the war years. During those years, many of the traditions practiced by the organization for various events had lapsed and been forgotten as war restrictions prohibited travel and made it difficult to hold large gatherings. The confusion at the 1946 AGSM convention over procedures, protocols, and points of order was to be expected at the first convention to be held in four years. The department and chapter levels had suffered similar losses and confusion.

It was now critical that AGSM re-establish itself traditionally and, at the same time, recreate itself as a meaningful organization for the new members, the gold star mothers of World War II, as well as the gold star mothers of World War I. In the same *Bulletin* No. II, Mrs. Boyd again set the tone of a letter between friends:

"[It's] so nice to be able to drop in and chat with you, at least once a month. So many letters have come in from officers and members throughout the Nation that your president feels very humble and proud to hear from so many of you. One wrote, 'I believe you truly love us as you said in your bulletin.' I want you all to know that I really do, and it is in that spirit that I chat with you today."

She suggested bonding chapter treasurers "not because you think she is going to be dishonest, but because it is the business-like way to proceed, and we should set the example for the Nation in being straightforward, and business-like in things we do... and we should set an example in the Nation of kindliness, justice and mercy."

She created a new national board position—national musician. Hadavig McFaddin of Cedar Rapids, Iowa, was named to the post and Mrs. Boyd advised the membership that "she is working out a very lovely musical program that will fit into your chapter's ritualistic work."

In *Bulletin* No. III (August 31, 1946), she touched on issues including deceased members, payment of per capita dues, and repatriation of remains of World War II dead. She encouraged members to move between offices in their chapters to gain experience and new ideas, saying "it is not a disgrace to lose an elective office but it is to accept an office and do nothing worthwhile for the members of the Chapter."

Finances were always an issue of concern for the chapters—how could they finance their community activities? Mrs. Boyd had suggestions for the chapters as well as individual members who were hoping to earn money to attend the next convention:

"Rummage sales are always profitable; bazaars usually pay well. Whenever a Chapter has an affair to make money, be sure it is high class...

"Now, how can the individual member make money? It would please me to be able to honor a large number of women at the National Convention next June in Long Beach, California who have made every dollar of their expenses to the Convention by their own effort in service to their community—by being a sitter and relieving a mother to properly care for her teeth at the dentist, to shop for her family's welfare or to have recreation with her husband. You in turn have had experience in bringing up children. The best is not good enough for a child. Its future is guided by the companionship, training and love it obtains in early childhood. You should be able to give superior service.

"I firmly believe if the Gold Star Mothers of America would give of themselves to the young children of America by being sitters of service, we would be able to solve many problems in the homes of America and save many a child from the delinquency rolls of the community. I feel sure your sons would want you to do real service of such permanency. You cannot even count it, and yet you would be able to collect money rightfully earned and honestly begotten that would bring you to the National Convention. Your National President will be proud of you when you arrive."

Mrs. Boyd encouraged each chapter to purchase a past president pin when their president left office. She described the pin as "very beautiful" and quite reasonable at only $18.75. In addition to being a gift from the chapter, the pin "continues to carry responsibility by the person wearing it to the Chapter, to the National organization, and to the community. It states not only that the mother has given her son, but that she should be a citizen above reproach. May all Chapters pay honor to such an officer."

Bulletin No. V (October 22, 1946) addressed the responsibilities of various positions within the organization including color bearers, corresponding secretaries, historians, and custodians of records. *Bulletin* No. VI (November 30, 1946) focused more on housekeeping issues such as ordering past presidents pins before it was too late, ordering chapter membership cards, distributing *Bulletins* to chapters, and the procedures for holding elections. In it, Mrs. Boyd encouraged every AGSM member to serve as an inspiring example for her community and the nation:

"Unless the American Gold Star Mothers set the example of making democracy work, we cannot expect other organizations or nations to make it work. As I have traveled throughout this nation, I feel a greater responsibility on the shoulders of the American Gold Star Mothers. We definitely are obligated to honor our sons' ideals by living so carefully in each community that others will want to live like us. Our organization should carry good will and understanding, with justice so definite that others may look to us to settle their misunderstandings in the manner in which we should solve ours. There is plenty of responsibility for each of us, and if we take care of it, there will be no time to say unkind things. Let us share all the good things of life with each other and our communities. There is so little time to do the good things; let us not forfeit any of that time with undesirable words or actions."

The American Gold Star Mothers, Inc. thrived under Mrs. Boyd's leadership in 1946 and 1947. She used her considerable organizational and personal skills to help energize and guide the group into a post-war form.

It was said by members that, under Mrs. Boyd's leadership, the organization accomplished more than in any previous twelve-month period.[34]

At the national convention in 1947, after declaring herself not interested in serving another term as national president, Mrs. Boyd told the delegates of a dream and a vision that she had. She wanted to build a home for members of AGSM where they could live out their lives in comfort; if their means were limited, it would be a place where they could live with grace and dignity on what funds they did have. The convention attendees enthusiastically endorsed her plan, gave her the mandate she requested to pursue the idea further, and contributed more than $400 in seed money for the venture, which was to be called the Memorial National Home Foundation. (The story of the Home is told in Chapter 9.)

Anna G. Hagerty succeeded Eleanor Boyd as national president for the 1947–1948 term, but Eleanor did not step very far from the limelight when she stepped down from the presidency.

Re-elected as national president for the 1948–1949 term, Eleanor wasted no time in communicating with the membership. Her *Bulletins* continued to be full of recommendations concerning organizational procedures and policies interlaced with helpful hints for the home, such as how to match plaids when sewing and how to store cheese so it won't dry out. She advised the mothers of the occasions on which their uniform caps were and were not to be worn:

- When riding in a parade
- At the funeral of a mother
- In the veterans hospital when working on behalf of the Chapter
- Not in the meeting room for regular meetings nor at installations (should be bareheaded)
- Not on the street, in street cars or busses, not to luncheons given in your honor
- "You do not wear them promiscuously at any time. Why? Because we want to keep the dignity and reverence due our sons and daughters who were gallant, honorable and true to all of us."[35]

When re-elected to a third term (1949–1950), Eleanor's newsletters began to contain reports on more serious issues. In the October 1949 editorial, she wrote:

"There are those among us who would destroy us. Their names are known...

Specifically, our organization of American Gold

Star Mothers, Inc., at both the chapter and national levels, is being undermined by members who would destroy the ideals of those mothers who have through the years built up the organization to the high place it now holds in the public mind. Some officers and members of our organization have combined to form a new group known as National Gold Star Mothers, and are withholding membership applications to our organization and even side-tracking entire chapter applications for our organization to their new group, all the while giving members and groups the impression they are joining the American Gold Star Mothers, Inc.

"With the foregoing in mind, it may be necessary to make public the reports of private investigators, giving names and other facts, in the November issue of the Gold Star Mother."

It was also noted elsewhere in the newsletter that:

"In a very recent broadcast from the east, Kate Smith, well known and loved radio personality, complimented the American Gold Star Mothers, Inc., and its national president, Mrs. Eleanor Boyd, on the splendid work the organization is doing in cleaning up the Fifth Column influence that attempted to invade its ranks.

"Miss Smith warned her listeners to check carefully on anyone soliciting funds for the American Gold Star Mothers, Inc. She stated that donations should be given only to those who can show credentials authorizing them to accept money in the name of American Gold Star Mothers, Inc."

What Eleanor failed to disclose was that the reason these women had broken with AGSM was over her handling of the Memorial National Home Foundation. Repeated requests for documentation had been ignored and a number of members found that their eligibility for AGSM membership was closely examined after they challenged Mrs. Boyd on any aspect of the Home.

In the November issue, the names were made public of AGSM members alleged to have been diverting funds and gold star mothers to a new organization called National Gold Star Mothers:

"To keep the membership informed of the activities of those engaged in the endeavor to form a group in competition with the American Gold Star Mothers, Inc., we report from the records of the State of Pennsylvania on the names of the following mothers who signed an application to charter a new organization: Evangeline Trenchard, Anna Greenblatt, Margaret Cooney, Ruth Barnes, E. Maria Reeves, Clare J. McCoy.

"Many other names have been mentioned as participating in the above activity. Where these names have been of State or Chapter officers, these officers have been removed from office.

"Some of the individuals whose names have been given us have denied any connection with the proposed new organization and have written us to that effect. A few of these letters are being published. It is requested that any member who receives a communication or literature soliciting her support of a new organization report the same to National Headquarters so that we may protect those mothers who are loyal."

In the late 1940s, loyalty became a national issue in response to concerns that foreign organizations, such as the communists, were infiltrating the government in positions of trust. In 1947, President Truman instituted a Loyalty Program that required loyalty oaths and background investigations on suspect persons employed by the federal government.[36] Despite cautions by many public leaders that such a program was more suited to a police state and that it suppressed the civil liberties of the public, the idea of loyalty ignited the media and the minds of the public.[37] In the controversy surrounding the formation of the National Gold Star Mothers by members of AGSM, several members of AGSM felt it necessary to publicly reassert their loyalty to the organization. Their comments were printed in the November 1949 newsletter under the headline "Loyalty Affirmed." In the same newsletter, a new resolution limiting members' participation in other organizations was announced:

"The National Executive Board passed a resolution November 12, 1949 that prohibits any member of the American Gold Star Mothers, Inc., from holding an office or serving on any committee at Chapter, Department or National level if that member belongs to any other Gold Star Mother organization.

One month later, in *The Gold Star Mother* newsletter, Eleanor's editorial justified the resolution: "We have received many communications regarding the justifiableness of the limiting of office holding to members who do not belong to other organizations of Gold Star Mothers.

"Unfortunately we have mothers who are not above using the name of the American Gold Star Mothers, Inc. to raise funds to be used for programs which are not in accord with the policies of the National Executive Board or of the National Convention. There are also mothers who are not above using the American Gold Star Mothers, Inc. for their personal advantage. Their actions have jeopardized the personal freedom of action we have always enjoyed in the American Gold Star Mothers, Inc.

"Events have proved that if we were to continue to enjoy our comradeship and unity of purpose, we would have to place certain restrictions on our officers and others in a position of trust. We must all suffer for the actions of a few.

"Let us remember that while our membership is made up of women of all faiths and of all political philosophies, we are all members of American Gold Star Mothers, Inc. by virtue of one single fact. We all lost a son or daughter as a result of service in the Armed Forces of our country in time of war. We also are bound together by one purpose: to do our best to preserve those things for which our sons and daughters died."

While serious issues such as the new organization being formed and loyalty oaths occupied the minds of many, Eleanor still managed to make the newsletter an inviting and entertaining source of information for the membership.

Eleanor Boyd would be elected for a total of five terms as national president. Her actions as president in the early 1950s involved AGSM in lawsuits that threatened to bankrupt the group and caused such divisiveness among its members that it would take years for the wounds to heal.

Growth of AGSM

Once the war ended, AGSM membership started to grow at a meteoric pace. In the first newsletter following her election as national president, Anna G. Hagerty stated that, as of July 8, 1947, the organization had expanded to 145 chapters and added 3,000 new members in the last year. But she also advised that with "280,000 Gold Star Mothers in the country, we are hopeful that all members will apply themselves during the coming year to get in as new members as many of these mothers as possible.[38] Between 1944 and 1947, the organization doubled its membership and added 106 new chapters.

In the period between the 1947 national convention in June and Mrs. Hagerty's *Bulletin* No. 2 (August 20, 1947), she was "happy to report that 563 new members have come in since I returned from the Convention as well as seven new chapters."

Just five months later, in January 1948, Mrs.

Hagerty reported that sixty new chapters had been established since June 1947 and there had been an increase of 2,074 new members with 952 additional membership applications in process. With these additions, membership at the beginning of 1948 would have been more than 7,500 mothers in more than 212 chapters plus members-at-large. By 1948, the group's gold star mothers of World War II significantly outnumbered the mothers of World War I.

In an effort to better manage the business of the organization, the AGSM national executive board voted in January 1948 to "create state Departments in every state in the Union which has five or more chapters." Every chapter was required to join their state's department. The fee for the state charter was $10. Some states had already taken the step of forming departments and now the remainder of the states followed suit. At least one department president, Stella G. Duncan of New York, believed the funding allotted to the departments from membership dues was inadequate for the activities expected of the departments:

"Some of the things we planned for and hoped to do may have to be abandoned owing to lack of finance. You cannot run a Department on 25¢ annual dues [per member]. It takes more than that to bring in one new member."[39]

National Conventions in the 1940s
[Unless otherwise noted, the source for information on the annual AGSM conventions is the published convention minutes/report for that year.]

Sixth National Convention—1940
Boston, Massachusetts
The sixth national convention of the American Gold Star Mothers, Inc. was held June 4–7, 1940, at the Parker House Hotel in Boston, Massachusetts. The convention program contained enthusiastic greetings from state and city officials. The message from Governor Leverett Saltonstall included a photograph of his family showing the Governor, Mrs. Saltonstall, their five children and their pet beagle:

"To the American Gold Star Mothers: We cordially welcome you to Massachusetts. The people of Massachusetts honor the mothers of this, and of every state, who made a sacrifice which can never be repaid. This year, when the world is again filled with violence and dread, the gathering of the gold star mothers is an occasion of deeper meaning than ever before. May we all face these critical times with the strength which you have already shown."

Boston's Mayor Maurice J. Tobin also welcomed the mothers and offered his hope for peace:

"At this particular time, when the whole world across the seas seems bent on destruction, deep and tender memories of your loved ones must be surging strongly within you. May we, with the help of Divine Providence, never again sacrifice the lives of our youth in order to bring peace to a part of the world that, seemingly, wants no peace. It is indeed fitting that your organization meet at this time, and declare most convincingly of our opposition to America's entry into the holocaust across the seas."

In reporting the election of a new AGSM president, the *Chicago Tribune* misnamed the organization, an error that would occur time and again throughout the decade as various events were reported: "Mrs. Mae Cushman [Mrs. Jesse W. Cushman] of Los Angeles, California recently was elected president of the Gold Star Mothers of America at the organization's sixth annual convention in Boston, Massachusetts."[40]

Seventh National Convention—1941
Los Angeles, California
AGSM's seventh national convention was held at the Biltmore Hotel in Los Angeles, California from June 10–13, 1941. The program was so packed with activities, honors, guests, and topics for discussion that it is amazing they were able to complete all the official business in just four days. According to Mrs. Cushman, some aspects of the event had been in planning for a year. Mrs. Cushman also introduced a special guest:

"We have, the first thing this afternoon, a rare treat for us. The Los Angeles Chapter No. 1 has a mother [Anna M. Barnbrock] who is ninety-four years old and has been an invalid. Through our Mr. Eugene Biscailuz, the Sheriff, she will be here. He is sending his private conveyance to bring this gold star mother down, so she may look in for about thirty minutes of this convention. She is a lovely mother. Her daughter will be with her. We all feel proud of her, though she has not been able to be with us for more than a year."

The report by the credentials committee advised that twenty of the current twenty-nine chapters were represented and there were 145 members registered for the convention.[41] A current balance of $377.82 was reported in the AGSM treasury. Reports were heard from eighteen chapters and the Departments of Michigan and New York.

A discussion relating to the formation of State Departments quickly went out of control. Some felt that forming departments took money away from the chapters that the chapters could not afford to lose. In the convention minutes it was noted that "discussion against forming departments [was] frequently interrupted by applause from the delegates."

Dr. Emma Balcom of New York was named national president for 1941–1942.

Eighth National Convention—1942
New York, New York
The eighth national convention was held June 10–12, 1942 at the New Yorker Hotel in New York. Marie V. Koeneke, chairwoman of the Distinguished Guests Committee, wrote to President Roosevelt prior to the event asking for a message on his behalf to bring to the mothers:

"We are planning to make this one of the happiest they have ever enjoyed. A message from their beloved President would make this convention long remembered by the mothers of the boys who made the supreme sacrifice in World War I."[42]

Despite other pressing matters in these early months of war, President Roosevelt responded to Mrs. Koeneke's plea:

"It is a great privilege for me to extend greetings to the participants in the Eighth National Convention of the American Gold Star Mothers. On behalf of our nation I pay to you a tribute which belongs only to you, the mothers of those who rendered the noblest and most glorious service for their country. Through that service you have been granted an eternal place in American history and the right to the stars of gold which are your symbol. I wish for you a successful Convention as you renew the ties that bind you closely together in a mutual interest."[43]

In the open sessions of the convention, President Balcom introduced a number of visitors to the delegates —World War II gold star parents who had lost children in the first few months of the war:

"We have on the platform today to hear this resolution, pro and con, the dear little mother whose son passed away at Pearl Harbor... I met this little lady and this is a very trying hour for her, but she is as brave as her son who gave his life. She is Mrs. Rita Wilson. Her boy, Bernard, was a radio man and sank with the USS *Arizona* on December 7 and he was buried at sea…

"We have in this audience a little mother whose mother in 1918 was a gold star mother too, giving four sons; one of them, a fifth, was ready to go. Her daughter now is repeating history—Mrs. Gertrude Kram. This little mother's son's body was found floating in the ocean and he was given a military funeral. We admire her for her courage and she has made application for membership to this organization…

"Mr. Isreal Schwartzberg, who lost his son three weeks ago, is with us today to get an application for his wife so she may join us."

One of the first issues brought before the delegates was opening the membership of AGSM to the gold star mothers of the new war. The issue had been addressed at a January 1942 executive board meeting and it had been agreed to allow gold star mothers of World War II to join the organization. In the interim before the convention, however, a number of chapters had protested the decision. President Balcom introduced the topic and explained how the decision had been made:

"December 7, 1941 there was a war declared. This nation was attacked. We are not asleep. We must act wisely and well for our best interests and for the best interests of the organization. We took action at our board meeting in January to amend our constitution to admit to membership the mothers of today, feeling that they, as we, suffered that same sacrifice. Why should we close our doors to them and why should we have another organization? How would they carry on against us?

"We are only 15 years old. We are a young organization and there are many things for us to do. Isn't it wonderful that since there is this privilege of asking these mothers who have gone through what we suffered a few years ago to help us and carry on with us under this same name and all [building together]. I believe there is strength in union. A divided house can never stand. And now, Mothers, if you feel that there is anything wrong with having these members ratified, you will have a chance to speak."

Mae Cushman, past national president, explained that one concern was procedural—applications for World War II mothers had been printed prior to the decision being ratified by the membership in convention.

Mary Hill, first national vice president, responded to Mrs. Cushman's concerns:

"We did not go over our chapters' heads. We simply worked on it in our Executive Board Meeting and asked that it be voted on in our chapters and then brought to the convention for debate and questions on it. We are getting older every day and these mothers are young and our founder agreed that our places should soon be filled with younger women in the organization or it shall die in a very few years if we do not fill it up. We must perpetuate the names of our men who gave their lives for this country and perpetuate in this organization this wonderful gold star mothers' trust."

The discussion continued and finally Mrs. Balcom called for a vote:

"Now on to the question, remember this is to amend your constitution to admit mothers of the World War No. 2. We can say that because we are of World War No. 1, and this is World War No. 2 and all wars to follow. Then there need never be another amendment when it is put in that form.

"Now does anyone feel in doubt? If there is any question, would you like to ask it now? Speak now and then you will all understand. Hearing no questions, I ask all those that are in favor of this motion to accept these dear little mothers to our hearts and open your constitution to admit to membership mothers of World War No. 2 and the wars to come. All those in favor, stand. The majority rules and the resolution is passed."

Mary Frances Hill (Mrs. D. Franklin Hill) was elected national AGSM president for the 1942-1943 term, the first full war-time term to be served by an AGSM president. In her acceptance speech she told the mothers:

"We are again going through a dreadful conflict; need I say we must help our new mothers by getting as many as possible to join our organization in order to help keep alive that for which we have strived so long to do. In doing this, we will perpetuate those who have left us gold star mothers."

Wartime restrictions on travel made it impossible for the mothers to hold a convention again until 1946. Mrs. Hill held the office of national president until her death in February 1946.

Ninth National Convention—1946
Philadelphia, PA

The ninth national convention was held June 3–5,

1946 in Philadelphia, Pennsylvania, at the Hotel Philadelphian. The convention was opened by Emily M. Cunningham, national president pro tem:

"We welcome you again to a national convention of the gold star mothers. What a thrilling experience it is to stand here before you and say those simple words: 'We welcome you again!' For these words have not been spoken before a national convention of gold star mothers since June of 1942, and but for the noble sacrifice of our sons and daughters, they may never have been spoken again. But today we are able to assemble as free Americans, to speak our minds without fear; to greet each other as equals, no matter what our race, creed or color; to clasp each other's hands in the friendship of a common bond, the motherhood of those who gave their all that this—our way of life—might continue.

"I shall not attempt to tell you at this time all the happenings within our organization during the past war years, but I do want to mention the name of one under whose able leadership we were able to carry on, our beloved president, Mother Hill, whose recent death saddened all of us. The example of her generosity, her patriotism and her love of the gold star mothers which led her to working for us even while she was ill shall always be before us. Her name will go down in the history of our organization as one of our most honored presidents."

In the absence of Mrs. Hill, Mae E. Cushman, past national president, was selected as national chairman of the convention. It was noted that the treasurer's report was incomplete due to death of Josephine Talks. Agnes O'Loughlan cautioned the assemblage stating "as your parliamentarian, I would like to comment that any irregularity in the procedure of this convention is due to the fact that it is the first convention since the war, and there may have been some important duties overlooked … we realize that it is only since the war is over that we are actually becoming organized."

Emma Balcom, past national president, reported that 450 delegates had registered for the convention and that sixteen states plus the District of Columbia were represented.[44] The total registration would rise to 512 by the end of the convention. She proudly announced that eighty-five new chapters had been added to the organization since June 1942.

Two honored guests among the mothers were introduced: Mrs. Albon Borgstrom of Utah who had lost four sons in the war, and Ellen Dobermeier of Philadelphia, who had lost three sons.

A slate of eighteen resolutions was proposed for action but the minutes of the convention offer very little detail on their content:

• Resolution No. 5, proposed by Battle Creek Chapter No. 7, recommended admitting mothers of Merchant Marines who died as a result of military service in World War II. It was approved.

• Resolution No. 9, proposed by Manhattan Chapter No. 9, called for the establishment of an AGSM national bulletin. This resolution was approved. Of all of the proposals brought forward at this convention, Resolution No. 9 would have the most significant and long-term effect on the organization.

When it was time to elect new officers for the next year, Mrs. Cushman announced a deviation from past procedure, explaining "We do not have a nominating committee. This is the first time, to my knowledge, that we have not had. Since our convention call does not otherwise provide, nominations will have to be made from the floor."

Immediately the delegates began shouting questions. There was tremendous confusion about calculating the voting strength of chapters at the convention, which was to have been based on chapter membership. Many delegates claimed they had been misinformed by the board about the number of voting delegates they could bring to the convention and were therefore deprived of their full voting strength. The issue of whether past national and chapter presidents voted independently from their chapter's delegation or as part of it generated much confusion. The board members on the dais were unable to control the discussion, and the parliamentarian threatened to quit her post if the delegates did not allow a reasonable discussion to take place.

Once the board members were able to speak and be heard, it became apparent that they too were confused regarding the calculation of chapter voting strength and the issue of past officers voting. They were unable to explain it to the satisfaction of the membership. Finally, the issue of past national and chapter presidents voting with or separately from their chapters was decided by a vote of the convention delegates—they would vote separately. Procedures were quickly established to calculate the voting strength of the chapters and the elections finally took place.

Nominations for the various offices were made

and, when the votes were counted, it was apparent that no chapter had been disadvantaged by the confusion surrounding the voting. The new national president, Eleanor D. Boyd of Long Beach, California, garnered four times as many votes as her closest contender.

As if the day had not been trying enough, when the delegates reconvened for the reading of the election results, certain key individuals, including several of the candidates themselves, were missing. National convention chairman Mae Cushman explained to the audience, "We wondered why our candidates were not here. It seems as though they were caught in the elevator. I wondered where they were hiding out."

Tenth National Convention—1947
Long Beach, California

The tenth national convention was held from June 3–8, 1947. It was the longest and largest convention yet held. The citizens of Long Beach were proud to host the gold star mothers. Local civic groups, veterans associations and the gold star mothers carefully coordinated myriad events. From opening day, every activity was filled to overflowing by nearly a thousand delegates. Members of the Long Beach Chapter hosted a Spanish Fiesta welcome and buffet for the delegates and dressed in Spanish costumes to add a bit of regional dash to the proceedings.

Eager to document conference activities, reporters trailed the gold star mothers to various events. Mrs. Albon Borgstrom of Utah, a gold star mother who had lost four sons within six months in 1944, was especially honored by the gold star mothers and people of Long Beach. Her husband moved on the outskirts of the activities offering pithy comments to reporters on the "idleness" of the young men he saw lounging about the streets and beaches. He did, however, offer one comment with which few could disagree when he said, "If the fathers who have lost sons could lay down the peace, there wouldn't be any more wars."[45]

Numerous memorial services were held in conjunction with armed forces personnel. The city organized a huge parade dedicated to the gold star mothers that included thirty-four bands and bugle corps, more than 400 horses, numerous veterans groups, and delegations from the city's government, schools, and churches. The people of Long Beach embraced the gold star mothers with love and affection, as reported in a local newspaper on June 6:

"Mrs. Etta Ingersoll, 74, of Sparta, Michigan, who

Fig. 7-17: Estelle Hendel, a guard at the Bendix Aviation Plant in Brooklyn, stands before the company service flag in March 1943.
(Farm Security Administration—Office of War Information Photograph Collection (Library of Congress); Ref: LC-USE6-D-009757)

lost her son, William Austin, in the first World War was deeply touched and mystified yesterday afternoon over an incident in the lobby at the Hilton. As Mrs. Ingersoll lounged in a lobby chair, a tall, well-dressed, blond-headed young man observed her. He went to the flower shop, had a corsage made up, took it to her and presented it with a bow and no more words than: 'Please accept this, Madam!' As the happy gold star mother accepted the corsage, the young man went his way."[46]

Throughout her year in office, Eleanor Boyd had encouraged the membership to lead the nation by example. She continued to emphasize that message to convention attendees:

"We are mothers of men who died for their country. As your national president, I would like the American Gold Star Mothers to compliment Motherhood by their conduct in their home communities. I want your leadership to be so fine and strong that the young women of this Nation will want to be like you! This will take self-discipline on your part for you must always radiate good-will, courage, love, kindness and fair play. Our sons gave their lives that this Nation might live. We must devote our lives to the ideals they would have wanted carried to completion in their community. This is a big order, but you and I together can keep the Faith."

In the general business portion of the meetings, it became apparent that AGSM was thriving under Eleanor's leadership. Second vice president Martha Davies reported that membership had increased 50 percent in the year since the last convention. There were 3,668 new members, including 48 members-at-large who were not affiliated with a specific chapter, and 145 chapters. The treasury held a healthy $710.27 in funds. According to convention minutes, there were 696 delegates and alternates registered for the convention plus 209 registered guests, twice the number at the prior year's convention in Philadelphia. The *New York Times,* however, tallied the delegates at "nearly 1,500" in a June 2 report of the proceedings.[47]

Death had not been a friend to the gold star mothers in the past year; 146 deaths among the membership were reported. The majority of the losses were among the aging World War I gold star mothers whose children had died for their country some thirty years before.

Entertainment included a recitation by William Farnham of the poem "Abraham Lincoln Walks at Midnight" and a performance by Marion Darlington, a noted bird singer. Congressional Medal of Honor recipients Audie Murphy and George B. Turner also made appearances.

Probably the most difficult topic for the attendees was presented by Major Pederson of the Graves Registration Service who spoke about the planned repatriation of the World War II dead. At his suggestion, questions were taken from the floor. One delegate asked:

"Would it be possible to make arrangements with the government to have the casket opened?

"Major Pederson: The government has advised not opening any casket for any reason. It will be sealed; it will be possible to seal it again only with a certain gadget provided by the government.

"Mrs. Boyd: I have seen the bodies of our war dead. Will you please remember your sons as you saw them last? Remember, these lads and lassies are not dead until you let them die. It is by your conduct, whether you are a good mother, a good woman and a good citizen; that is what counts."

On Sunday, June 8, a memorial service was held in Stark Center at the Enlisted Men's Center on Terminal Island, California. In the national broadcast of the service over the CBS network, it was announced that "gold star mothers, over a thousand strong, have gathered from all over the nation." The program included Helen McClure, contralto, who sang Schubert's "Ave Maria" and "The Lord's Prayer." The announcer said that Miss McClure "has sung wherever the boys of the services were stationed overseas. In two and a half years, she has traveled over a 175,000 miles to give over 3,000 concerts."

Commander Carl Sitler, Staff Chaplain of the Naval Base, spoke to the mothers and the nation:

"It is a great honor to have you gold star mothers aboard this Naval station for this memorial service. A mother's love for her children is the greatest human influence in the world; it is transcended only by the love of God. There is no sacrifice too great for a mother to make for the sake of her children. Her only reward for her sacrifice is the hope and anticipated joy of seeing them grow up into strong, successful manhood and womanhood.

"The American Gold Star Mothers are no exception to this kind of sacrificing and understanding love. They loved their sons and daughters too as only a true mother can love. But an all-wise providence ruled that their sons and daughters had to be sacrificed in the fields of battle. They fought and gave up their lives for the high and holy principles of equality, freedom, justice, liberty, and peace—the principles which have made our country so great and powerful."[48]

On the second day of the convention, Mrs. Boyd challenged the delegates to support a project that was very important to her—establishing a national home for needy and destitute gold star mothers:

"While working in the hospitals and generally looking for ways to solve the needs of our returned veterans, your national president found, among the American Gold Star Mothers, many who were forced to live on a meager subsistence level. Some did not have adequate shoes or clothes for wear on the street. Some were existing—not living—in basements without windows. Many badly needed what they were not getting. Someone who really cares for them in every sense of the word is a necessity. These are mothers whose sons died for their country but today are forgotten except for too few dollars received monthly."[49]

Four resolutions were approved by the membership

in convention: exploring the possibility of establishing a national home for AGSM members (see Chapter 9); support of universal military training; equal rights for gold star mothers in civil service employment; and support of a government commission to distribute proper relief in money and food.

The tenth national convention closed with the election of new officers and Anna G. Hagerty of New Jersey was named as the new national president.

Eleventh National Convention—1948
Atlantic City, New Jersey

The 1948 convention was held in Atlantic City, New Jersey from June 1–6 at the Chelsea Hotel (corner of Boardwalk and Morris). At the convention, the press wasted no time in cornering gold star mothers and asking for their opinions on issues of the day such as the draft and universal military training. The gold star mothers were never reticent about sharing their opinions:

"Three American Gold Star mothers [in Atlantic City] for their 11th national convention said today they favored a draft and universal military training. Mrs. Ruth Singer of Los Angeles said her son was killed in North Africa.

"'I am satisfied he would be alive today if he had received more training,' Mrs. Singer said.

"Mrs. Elizabeth Benson of North Hollywood, California, Third National Vice President, said, 'We feel that the best way to keep our country from becoming involved in another war is through proper preparedness for peace.'

"Mrs. Margaret Luce, President of the San Bernardino (California) chapter, said, 'If our youths are properly trained, other countries won't get any wild ideas about us.'"[50]

Eleanor Boyd was re-elected for a second term as national president. While not specifically prohibited in the organization's by-laws, it was the first time that a national president had been elected to serve more than one term. The following day she advised the *New York Times* that one of her goals for the new year was improving the lives of handicapped veterans.[51]

Twelfth National Convention—1949
Chicago, Illinois

Early in 1949, the twelfth national convention planned for Chicago was already under discussion in the newsletter. Some of the issues expected to be decided included:

"Whether we amend our articles to include foster mothers and stepmothers. The United States Government legalized [pensions for] foster and stepmothers if they were the legal guardian in a law passed two years ago last November. It is time that we consider and bring our organization up to date.

"Another question will be whether to bring the fathers in as associate members. As I have traveled about the country I find this seems to be the wish of most of the fathers. Have your husband at the convention so he may express himself; and vote intelligently upon all matters that come before us at the National Convention.

"[We also need to reaffirm] that the eligibility of a mother be that she is an American citizen and that her son or daughter died as part of the Armed Forces of the United States or the Allies. The Armed Forces means the Navy and its component parts, the Army and its component parts, the Coast Guard and the Marines and their component parts. Any other groups are recognized as civilians according to our government and therefore the mother of said men and women are not eligible for membership in our organization."

The Twelfth National Convention met in Chicago from June 4–9, 1949, at the Hotel Sherman. More than 1,500 delegates from 400 chapters were in attendance and all forty-eight states in the union were represented.

Among the events planned for the convention were a memorial ceremony at the University of Chicago's Rockefeller Memorial Chapel; a tour of Swift and Company's Chicago meat-packing plant followed by a luncheon for gold star fathers; a fashion show at the Marshall Field department store, as well as tea and tour at the Chicago Art Institute. The Chicago Bible Society, which presented a gold Bible to Mrs. Boyd for the organization's use, encouraged the delegates to assist in their effort to compile "the largest handwritten Bible in the world." Each gold star mother was offered the opportunity to write a verse in the Bible in Higgins Eternal Ink "so that it will last."

Re-elected for an unprecedented third term, Mrs. Boyd described the convention events and decisions in a *Bulletin* for those who had been unable to attend. She noted that "we have grown to such a number that it takes a very large auditorium to even commence to accommodate us." Regarding the resolutions, she reported:

"The proposed change in by-laws to admit fathers as associate members with the right to voice and serve on committees was changed from the original to state that fathers were welcome at chapter and national meetings without voice and without the right to serve on an official committee. The fathers spoke to this and seemed satisfied in that they wish to be welcome and feel that they can participate in the activities of their wives and did not particularly care to have a voice. So all ended happily on that change.

"The proposed amendment to admit foster mothers and step-mothers did not carry. Since the government recognizes, under certain circumstances, these mothers, the amendment no doubt will be proposed with specific changes at the next national convention."

Convention attendees heard presentations by the Deputy Chairman, Veterans Administration Voluntary Service, who discussed the volunteer program at the veterans hospitals, and by Mr. Hylton of the Veterans Administration who assisted mothers who were eligible to prepare their pension applications.

One convention controversy not discussed in Mrs. Boyd's subsequent *Bulletins* was extensively covered by the press. A gold star mother who had been part of the organization for several years and who had become an outspoken critic of Mrs. Boyd was advised by the national board that her eligibility had been reviewed and she had been found ineligible for membership. She was then forced to resign. Unwilling to accept the decision of the national executive board, she demanded a hearing at the convention. The *Chicago Tribune* ran the article on June 7 under the headline "Ousted Mother Seeks Gold Star":

"The question of whether the mother of a young man killed nearly two months before Pearl Harbor while a member of the British civilian corps is eligible for membership in the American Gold Star Mothers was brought before delegates to the organization's 12th annual convention in the Sherman Hotel yesterday. It kept the meeting in an uproar for an hour and a half.

"The issue was touched off by Mrs. Ethel Godfrey of Providence, R.I., former president of the Rhode Island chapter, whose resignation was demanded in February when national officers of the gold star mothers ruled she was ineligible for membership. She is asking reinstatement. She and a group of supporters were admitted at the afternoon session to state her case.

"Mrs. Godfrey's son, Reginald, 22, had enlisted in the British civilian technical corps and was on his way to England as a radio technician when his ship was sunk by a German submarine on October 12, 1941. Mrs. Godfrey maintains that the corps was a part of the armed forces and that her son is considered a victim of World War II, altho war was not officially declared by President Roosevelt until December 8. She presented an opinion from the British counsel general in Chicago that 'civilian' in the title of the corps is a misnomer and that it was considered part of the British armed forces. She also said her son was deferred by his draft board when he joined the corps and pointed out that he was in uniform.

"She said Mrs. Walter H. Boyd, national president, 'told me when I showed her his picture that the British put anything in uniform!'

"Mrs. Boyd denied this, and said her statement had been that "the British put everything in uniform.'

"The president explained that the national committee held a three hour hearing for Mrs. Godfrey and ruled she was ineligible because her son was serving in a civilian capacity and was killed before the United States' official entry into the war.

"Mrs. Godfrey, also the mother of Capt. John T. Godfrey, an air force pilot who shot down 37 German planes and who was found alive after being missing eight months, pleaded over the loud speaker for 'the gold star to which I am entitled.'

"Excited women all over the auditorium jumped up to speak for or against her. Mrs. Boyd put an end to the discussion, however, by entertaining a motion to adjourn, which was carried. The Godfrey forces hope to force a vote on the issue today."

On June 8, the *Chicago Tribune*'s headline read "Ousted Mother Renews Fight for Gold Star at Convention Today:"

"Mrs. Ethel Godfrey of Providence, R.I., made plans yesterday for another plea for reinstatement into the American Gold Star Mothers today, the final day of the organization's national convention in the Sherman Hotel. She awaited the arrival of more documents to prove that her son, Reginald, was considered a member of the armed forces when he went down with his ship, sunk en route to England October 12, 1941.

"Meanwhile she was made an honorary member of the Chicago Council of Gold Star Mothers of World War I, at the invitation of Mrs. Anna Bruckner, president. Many of its members are attending the convention, altho it is not affiliated with the national organization. In a letter to Mrs. Walter H. Boyd of Long

Fig. 7-18: "A Family Affair—Mr. & Mrs. James Fere of Watervliet, New York for Navy Day buy two Victory Bonds for their two sons in the service from two Gold Star Mothers who are, left to right, Mrs. Alice M. Conlon... and Mrs. Stella G. Duncan. The booth is in Woolworth's at 40th St. & Fifth Avenue."
(Uncredited press photo; Fenelon Collection)

Beach, California, president of the national group, Mrs. Bruckner termed Mrs. Godfrey 'a gold star mother even as you and I.'

"When Mrs. Boyd was re-elected as AGSM president at the convention that night, Mrs. Godfrey was said to be 'shocked' by the vote. Re-election of Mrs. Boyd was termed 'a continuance of a dictatorship' by Mrs. Ethel Godfrey:

"'It was a shock to hear that Mrs. Boyd had been re-elected,' Mrs. Godfrey said last night. 'I think it is most unfortunate because she rules the organization with an iron hand.'

"Mrs. Godfrey said, however, that she will continue her battle for reinstatement. She said she was working on plans to bring her case before the national officers again in the near future."

Failing to reach a resolution at the convention, Mrs. Godfrey took her suit to the courts and, in December 1949, a decision was handed down:

"Mrs. Ethel A. Godfrey... has won a superior court order in her fight to retain membership in the Gold Star Mothers, Inc.

"A preliminary injunction was granted... against national and local officers of the organization. [The court] ruled that Mrs. Godfrey should be restored to active membership through the Providence chapter with the right to attend meetings... Judge Curran rebuked officers of the Gold Star mothers for the manner in which they had tried to expel Mrs. Godfrey."[52]

Chapter/Department Activities

In the period before World War II, members of American Gold Star Mothers across the nation had continued much as they had since the Great War. They volunteered in veterans hospitals, doing what they could to make less bleak the lives of those veterans, some of whom had been hospitalized more than twenty years. They worked on behalf of veterans, their families, and other gold star mothers. Their voices were constantly heard promoting peace and preparedness. They attended memorials, were feted in parades, planted gardens of memory, and dedicated statues to the war dead and motherhood. Whether massed at events in their formal white outfits or appearing singly, the gold star mothers were a constant reminder to a nation that might otherwise have forgotten the true cost of war as time passed.

With the advent of World War II, they added new tasks to their list of duties. They were active in Victory Bond sales across the nation. Frequently appearing in the newspapers, they were photographed selling bonds to celebrities of the era as well as commonplace folks. [Fig. 7-18] The mothers continued their dedicated work at veterans' hospitals and facilities across the nation as the number of patients grew with casualties from the current war. The headline for a 1944 article about the forty-five members of the Long Beach Chapter No. 2 proclaimed proudly "City's Gold Star Mothers Doing a Remarkable Job."

According to the article, since the chapter's inception the gold star mothers had gone about their many tasks "with little or no recognition. Time was a great healer to many, but these women never forget";[53]

"At Christmas time they provide an old-fashioned celebration for at least two wards at Sawtelle [Veterans Hospital] and are making preparations to do the same at our Naval Hospital. During their year-round work, they knit hot water bottle covers, fashion house slippers, supply cigarettes, candy and razor blades and are on hand to provide a personal touch here and there so deeply appreciated by bed-ridden patients.

"The gold star mothers of Chapter No. 2 are themselves comforted by what they were accomplishing among their adopted sons at Sawtelle VA Hospital and the U.S. Naval Hospital in Long Beach [the predecessor to today's Long Beach Veterans Hospital]."[54]

As they continued their work at the now overcrowded veterans hospitals, the mothers made suggestions for changes they saw as necessary. In 1945, at the state convention, the Department of New York went on record urging the government to provide separate hospital facilities for women veterans. Past national and department president, Dr. Emma L. Balcom, explained to the press, "We have learned veterans hospitals now in existence are primarily for men, resulting in women patients being restricted from activities and freedom of the hospital."[55]

In October 1947, the Bronx County Chapter made headlines when it approved a resolution calling for the State of New York to "provide free medical, surgical and hospital care for gold star mothers."[56]

On occasion, the AGSM national board would embark on projects to be supported by the national membership. In January 1948, Evangeline Trenchard, AGSM national hospital chairman, advised the membership of the National Hospital Project for 1948:

"[The goal was] to raise, through the Chapters, a fund of at least $7,000 to purchase three iron lungs and one hundred collapsible wheel chairs to be used in and distributed to various Veterans Hospitals. While iron lungs would be property of VA, they would be available to all 'suffering humanity' who may have need of their use."

Many of the chapters seemed to hit their stride in 1948 and the news of chapter activities filled the AGSM newsletters:

"Iowa Chapter No. 1 (Cedar Rapids, Iowa): Mothers spent about 2000 hours making 400 baskets. These were filled with homemade cookies and candies, cigarettes, candy bars, popcorn balls and Christmas candies, with each tied in gaily colored paper napkins."

"Chester No. 1 Chapter (Pennsylvania): [The chapter] gave a fine television set to Ward 8 at the Valley Forge General Hospital. The mothers of the Chapter felt amply repaid for their gift when Major Adams of the hospital staff wrote as follows: 'If you could see the boys relaxing, chuckling and forgetting their ills, you would be very happy.'"

"Indianapolis Chapter: Our main project has been the care of hospitalized tuberculosis patients at Billings V. A. Hospital where we have held parties on each Wednesday afternoon. Besides the regular prizes for the games, cigarettes, gum and matches have been furnished. We have held special parties on Washington's Birthday, Easter, Father's Day, Halloween and Thanksgiving. We are planning big things for the boys at Christmas. Some of the members have made it possible for us to supply the boys with books, records, candy bars and special cash prizes for the puzzles they solve, decks of cards and homemade cookies."

In 1949, "knowing what the boys enjoyed," the Lancaster [Pennsylvania] Chapter "gave $35.00 so that

Fig. 7-19: Gold star mothers were among 2,500 friends and relatives who assembled at Pier 3 in New York City to honor the World War II dead who were returned by ship in 1947. *(Culver Pictures, New York; Fenelon Collection)*

the patients at the Coatesville Veterans Hospital could take a bus trip to attend a ball game in Philadelphia."

In October 1947, *The Gold Star Mother* newsletter reported on another chapter-supported activity:

"Many chapters throughout the Country are now holding Americanization Classes for non-citizens. Gold Star Mothers are teaching them the things necessary to become citizens, such as the history of our Country, how to read and write, etc. These classes are usually held in the home of one of the Mothers since they are reluctant to attend regular classes held in school rooms. They soon get over any shyness when they find that only Gold Star Mothers are present. This is a recommended project [because] after completing the course [and becoming American citizens], these Mothers may join our Organization."[57]

Citizenship and Other Eligibility Issues

United States citizenship had been a requirement for AGSM membership from the very first version of the organization's constitution. No records indicate that this requirement was questioned or challenged by the World War I gold star mothers. In fact, several World War I membership applications indicate that the mother had become a citizen specifically so she could join the organization. But in World War II, the citizenship requirement became a public issue with many faulting AGSM for its intractable stand.

In December 1947, the *Chicago Tribune* told of a triple gold star mother who had been unable to join the American Gold Star Mothers, Inc., because she was not a U. S. citizen:

"The widowed mother of three sons who lost their

lives in the war fighting for the United States has been assured of citizenship. Because she lacked American citizenship, membership in the Gold Star Mothers has not been open to her.

"She is Mrs. Stella Lewandowski of Lyndhurst, N.J. For many years she had presumed herself an American citizen by virtue of her husband's gaining citizenship in 1923. Under a law of 1922, however, it is necessary for husband and wife to obtain citizenship independently. Action now seems imminent, following an almost unanimous clamor in Lyndhurst for her speedy naturalization. It was announced she will be called shortly before County Court in Hackensack for a preliminary hearing, and after 30 days, will be sworn in as a citizen. The two year period ordinarily required between the hearing and the swearing ceremony in this case will be waived."[58]

In January 1948, Mrs. Lewandowski became an American citizen:

"After the ceremony, by permission of Judge A. Demorest Dalmar, Mrs. Lewandowski was the center of a special induction ritual that made her a member of the Gold Star Mothers. This was the last of honors that included the naming of a street in the Borough of Lyndhurst 'Lewandowski Street.'

Fig. 7-20: A graduate of Woodrow Wilson High School in Washington, D.C. stands before the school's service flag in October 1943. *(Farm Security Administration - Office of War Information Photograph Collection (Library of Congress); Ref. LC-USW3-038446-E)*

"As the widow became a citizen, the judge did not bother with the usual instructions about citizenship. Nor did he bother to try to explain to her the meaning of the citizenship certificate.

"'I think,' he said, 'that in your heart you became a citizen long before you complied with the law governing such matters. I believe that the suffering and heartaches which have been your lot in life make it unnecessary for me to give you any instructions on your newly assumed duties. I hope that the future will be more kind to you than the past.'"

A similar case became news when Mrs. Katie Nemeth, another triple gold star mother, applied for AGSM membership and was determined to be ineligible because she was not a citizen of the United States. A Hungarian immigrant, Katie had lost three sons in the American military during World War II—two in combat and the third in a service-related accident. The outbreak of the Korean War would see another fourth Nemeth son, Stephen, head to war. In 1954, Mrs. Nemeth became an American citizen and was admitted to membership in AGSM.

The public was aware of these situations and many spoke out to government officials to right what they saw as an inequity for mothers of the war dead.

At the national board meeting in January 1948, discussion took place relative to changes in the group's constitution and by-laws in reference to "citizenship as a requirement for membership in our organization." It was decided that the by-laws would be examined and brought up to date; outmoded parts were to be deleted and necessary additions and improvements made. The revisions would be "referred to delegates in Convention at Atlantic City, New Jersey, June 1948."[59] However, no change was made to the citizenship requirement at the 1948 convention.

During the same period, national president Anna G. Hagerty tried to clarify the issue of foster and step-mothers who wanted to join AGSM but were ineligible because they were not the birth mother of the dead soldier:

"Letters have come to me complaining of step-mothers and foster mothers coming to Chapter meetings. In some cases, they are considered Members.

"I would like to quote... our Constitution and Bylaws states that ONLY Mothers of Sons or Daughters who served and died in the Allied Cause in World War I and World War II, or who died as a result of said service or Mothers who are citizens of the United States whose sons served and died in the United States Merchant Marines of World War 2, or who died as a result of said service are eligible for membership in the American Gold Star Mothers, Inc.

"This is what we must abide by. I would, therefore, suggest that you do not accept any more dues from any step-mother. Be careful not to hurt her feelings, explain kindly but firmly about our By-laws. Then she will understand it is not your fault but a National Law."[60]

Legislation

Throughout the decade of the 1940s, AGSM continued to influence legislation at the national level. Focusing on issues relating to veterans, their families, and gold star parents, they were often a significant factor in the passage or failure of congressional efforts.

In 1940, the House of Representatives' Committee on World War Veterans' Legislation conducted hearings on the issue of pensions for world war widows and orphans. M. Jennie Williams, national president of the American Gold Star Mothers, spoke strongly and poignantly before the committee on behalf of the many gold star mothers of World War I who were in dire financial need:

"At the end of the war, a great many mothers had the insurance and, at the end of 20 years, that insurance has disappeared. [The insurance benefits had been fully paid out to the beneficiaries.] It not only stopped, but the money disappeared. During that time that money not only took care of the gold star mothers, but it was in the time of Great Depression, and that mother, of course, having any money, helped to take care of her son's and daughter's family and children. So at the end of the insurance time there was nothing left to be saved, and nothing could have been saved out of that because she had to use it.

"Then there was a bill [that] came up, which was a splendid thing, that the mothers should receive $45 [monthly] or the father and mother receive $25. They have been living on that since, and they are most grateful. That money today covers everything many of the women have.

"Probably you do not realize how these mothers are living. They have had a larger income with their insurance. It means that they have to let down on their idea of the old mode of living that they have had for 20 years. And these mothers are all 20–21 years older than at the end of the war when they had insurance. Today they are living on the $45, many of them… Many of them are 79, 80 and 81. It means that they have many expenses, they are sick, a great many of them cannot go out, cannot walk up steps, and have to have a taxi, have to be taken care of and have no hospitalization, have no money for it, and if the doctor is there they are continually wondering how they are going to pay the bill."[61]

The day before Gold Star Mothers' Day in 1944, the *Chicago Tribune* interviewed several national officers including Grace Seibold, the AGSM founder, about plans under discussion in the government to eventually authorize World War II gold star pilgrimages to the overseas gravesites of World War II casualties, as had been done in the 1930s for World War I gold star mothers. The mothers, many of whom had been part of the original pilgrimage, were fiercely opposed to any such plan:

"Tomorrow is Gold Star Mother's Day and the mothers are up in arms.

"To a woman, the national officers here of the American Gold Star mothers are united in registering 'vehement protest' against President Roosevelt's recommendation of legislation permitting not only mothers but families to visit the graves of service men throughout the world, at public expense, after the war.

"Some bitterly recalled the squabbling which dampened the government-sponsored pilgrimages to French cemeteries in 1930–32. Others dub the present plan a "vote-getting scheme" but every one interviewed was agreed that the gigantic proportions of such a plan make it unfeasible after this war.

"'I know I speak for our 5,000 members,' Mrs. Roberta Jacobs, national secretary, declared, 'when I say we are unalterably opposed to such an impractical undertaking. Why, eligible relatives of this war's dead might run into the millions. Besides, many of those who made the other pilgrimage regretted it. The conduct of a few was disgraceful. It was a scandal the way some stepmothers who had never laid eyes on their heroic stepsons took advantage of the government bounty for a joy ride to Europe.'"

"Mrs. Franklin P. Nash, national chaplain, fervently agreed; 'This is obviously just a bid for votes,' she said. 'I'm too practical to believe that such a thing could be carried thru and I shall take the matter up at our board meeting.'

"Mrs. Fanny Meeks, a national vice president, who was among those making the last pilgrimage, said she considered such excursions after this war 'out of the question, with our terrific national debt.'

"'We all lived like millionaires for a month,' she

recalled. 'But if we have any extra money to spend next time, let's use it for mothers on this side of the ocean. Many are distressingly poor.'

"Mrs. Grace Darling Seibold, founder of the Gold Star organization, remembered: 'Some mothers didn't go in the right spirit, and there was entirely too much pleasure involved. Our country is too depleted financially to send whole families abroad.'

"Pointing out that trips for 6,674 mothers and widows after the last war cost the government $5,386,267, an army officer remarked: 'If only 800,000 relatives were declared eligible under the present plan, [and it would probably be much higher], 6,000 ships would be required to transport the groups half way around the world. Estimating the cost at $1,500 each, over a billion dollars would be involved.'

"Mrs. Anna Bruckner, president of the Chicago Council of Gold Star Mothers, and one of its incorporators, said last night she believes some provision should be made for mothers and fathers to visit graves of their sons killed in the war, but was uncertain whether the plan should include other members of bereaved families.

"Mrs. Bertha Fish, vice president of the council, said she did not go to France after the last war, but that she talked with several mothers who did and they did not view the expedition as a success."[62]

It was not always just on gold star issues that AGSM's voice was heard. In February 1949, national president Eleanor Boyd took a stand on a conservation issue:

"American Gold Star Mothers have added their strength to the movement of State-wide women's organizations to save the giant sugar pines and sequoias of Tuolomne County [California]. Making a memorial park of the big tree area, dedicating it to those who lost their lives in World Wars I and II is proposed.

"Mrs. Walter H. Boyd of Long Beach, National President of the Gold Star Mothers, was informed that in a recent caucus of California Congressmen in Washington, D.C., it was disclosed that under a federal statute the Secretary of Agriculture has discretion in the matter of safeguarding trees from commercial logging. Mrs. Boyd immediately wired Secretary Charles F. Brannan regarding the Gold Star Mothers' support in the conservation proposal and asked that the forest be made a memorial."[63]

In September 1940, by Executive Proclamation, President Roosevelt proclaimed that "the last Sunday in September of this and each succeeding year" would be Gold Star Mother's Day. Since 1936, when President Roosevelt had named that day as Gold Star Mother's Day, a presidential proclamation had been issued each year to officially designate the day. The 1940 Executive Proclamation, however, had "been drafted in such a way as to make it unnecessary to proclaim Gold Star Mother's Day in 1941 and succeeding years."[64]

Public Honor and Recognition

In 1918, gold star mother Caroline Seaman Read of New York wrote to President Wilson to ask for one small thing on behalf of all gold star mothers, stating "Could we have awarded by our President ... a badge of honor to wear, showing only the gold star with the rank and branch of service of our man gladly dedicated to his country's service in this Great Cause, we should not dare to mourn..."[65]

In May 1945, Hazel I. Curry of North Haven, Connecticut wrote to President Truman and, among other requests, asked:

"Also that every Gold Star Mother be given a gold bar with a gold star attached to it... On this bar, I believe it should read 'In honor of my son' with his name on the bar. If a mother has given more than one son, there should be a star with their names attached to the bar for each one. The Mothers of World War I and their sons are among the forgotten ones. Mothers and their sons of World War II are the almost forgotten ones and this war is only half over. Won't you please try to make our request come true? Our boys died for Liberty, Freedom, and 'Old Glory.' Please give them thanks and their mothers too."[66]

The President's staff sent a cordial acknowledgement of Mrs. Curry's letter but promised nothing in response to her request for a gold star emblem.

Just a month later, a request from John E. Kerrigan, Mayor of Boston, Massachusetts, was acknowledged by William Hassett, secretary to President Truman:

"[Regarding your communication] recommending that steps be taken for the erection of a national monument by the federal government in honor of the Gold Star Mothers of the Nation and that the Gold Star Mothers be further honored through the bestowal of individual medals. This, of course, would require authorization by the Congress, and the initiative could be taken by either member of the House of Representatives or of the Senate

Fig. 7-23: The parents of World War II casualty Kenneth P. Hamlin decorate his grave on Memorial Day. *(Fenelon Collection)*

or both. I am glad to assure you that your recommendation will be given very careful consideration."[67]

On July 4, 1945, Kerrigan again broached the subject in a telegram to President Truman:

"May I respectfully recommend for your consideration the erection of a national monument by the federal government in honor of the Gold Star Mothers of the Nation.

"On Mother's Day of each year we pay tribute to these mothers, but I feel that something more fitting and permanent than words is needed. In addition to the erection of a monument, may I respectfully recommend that consideration be given to the honoring of these mothers individually, the honor to be in the form of a suitable medal under an act of Congress."

While the war continued, little attention could be given to these requests. But the suggestions were not forgotten.

In August 1947, Congress approved two methods to recognize and honor the sacrifices of American soldiers—an accolade and a gold star pin:

"As a token of appreciation and in recognition of services rendered by those who died in the service of their country, an Accolade signed by the President is issued to the next of kin of record of all military personnel whose death occurred in the line of duty during World War II, December 7, 1941, to July 25, 1947, both dates inclusive... The Accolade is also issued to the next of kin of civilians who died overseas or as a result of injury or disease contracted while serving in a civilian capacity with the Armed Forces of the United States...

"The Accolade reads as follows:

In grateful memory of _____who died in the service of his (her) country at_____. He (she) stands in the unbroken line of patriots

The 1940s: Growth, Recognition, and Discord | 159

Fig. 7-21 (left): A Gold Star Lapel Button (often called a "gold star mother's pin") was created by an Act of Congress on August 1, 1947. The button shows a gold star on a purple circular background, bordered in gold and surrounded by golden laurel leaves. On the reverse of the original issue is the inscription "United States of America, Act of Congress, August 1947." *(Fenelon Collection)*

Fig. 7-22 (right): The newswire photo of the Gold Star Mothers stamp issued on September 21, 1948.
(Wide World Photo; Fenelon Collection)

who have dared to die that freedom might live and grow, and increase its blessings. Freedom lives, and through it he (she) lives on in a way that humbles the undertakings of most men.

President of the United States"[68]

A more public honor was designed to honor the dead of World War I as well as World War II [Fig. 7-21]:

"In order to provide an appropriate identification for widows, parents, and certain next of kin of members of the Armed Forces of the United States who lost their lives in World War I, April 6, 1917 to March 3, 1921; World War II, September 8, 1939 to July 25, 1947… a Gold Star Lapel Button was established by an Act of Congress on August 1, 1947.

"The Gold Star lapel button consists of a gold star on a purple circular background, bordered in gold and surrounded by gold laurel leaves. On the reverse is the inscription 'United States of America, Act of Congress, August 1947' with space for engraving the initials of the recipient. (The button is approximately 16mm in diameter.)

"One Gold Star lapel button will be furnished without cost to the widow or widower and to each of the parents of a member of the Armed Forces who lost his or her life while in the active military service during the periods indicated above…

"One Gold Star lapel button will be furnished at cost price to each child, step-child, child through adoption, brother, half brother, sister, and half sister of a member of the Armed Forces who lost his or her life during any period indicated herein."[69]

The War Department's estimate of cost to enact the gold star pin legislation was $65,000.

In 1947 another form of public recognition of gold star mothers was set into motion when Congress ap-

proved an Act to authorize a special series of commemorative stamps in honor of gold star mothers. Public Law 259 authorizing the Gold Star Mothers stamp was passed in the Senate on July 3, 1947. [Fig. 7-22]

The Gold Star Mothers stamp was identified by the postal service as Commemorative Stamp #969:

"The Gold Star Mothers memorial [stamp], to receive first-day sale at Washington on September 21, pictures a five-pointed star superimposed on a palm branch, with 'Gold Star Mothers' inscribed in dark modified Roman. 'United States' is at the top and '3¢ Postage 3¢' at the bottom, each in white Roman with uncial characteristics. The design is arranged vertically. The stamps will be in sheets of fifty and the initial printing order is 75,000,000 subjects."[70]

On September 21, 1948, there was much fanfare in Waterloo, Iowa, and across the nation as Robert E. Fellers, United States Superintendent of Stamps, presented an album containing the first sheet of Gold Star Mothers stamps to Aleta Sullivan, mother of the five Sullivan brothers who died together in the sinking of the USS *Juneau* in 1942.[71]

Anticipating the selection of the unknown soldier of the Second World War, in January 1948 AGSM's national board wrote to President Truman, the Speaker of the House, and the President of the Senate requesting that AGSM's national president be given the honor of selecting the unknown soldier. No record of a response to this request has been found. It was not until 1958 that an unknown soldier of World War II was selected for interment at Arlington National Cemetery.

When World War II ended in September 1945, the American Gold Star Mothers, Inc., found itself firmly established as a strong advocate for veterans and their families. The organization was recognized and respected by the government, the press, and the public. In fact, it was among the most revered institutions in the nation, according to G. Kurt Piehler, Director of the Rutgers University Oral History Archive of World War II.[72]

Despite that recognition and respect, however, there were some people who still didn't understand the "membership fee" that was paid to become a gold star mother. In a 1945 letter to President Truman, Julia McAuley asked a favor for a friend:

"[Her letter] tells of constant service of an American Restaurateur, Mary Elizabeth Jackson, who served boys in service without charge and now makes the kind of pies they like; wants her to have a Gold Star so she too can be a Gold Star Mother."[73]

Loss of the Founder

On June 12, 1947, the organization suffered the loss of its founder, Grace Darling Seibold. Following a long battle with cancer, she died at home at the age of seventy-eight, just five days after the death of her sister, Theodosia. Her obituary in the *Washington Post* referred to her as "the founder and first national president of American Gold Star Mothers, Inc." and listed the many organizations to which she had belonged.[74]

In the May 1949 *Gold Star Mother* newsletter, national president Eleanor Boyd wrote a tribute to the organization's founder:

"Grace Darling Seibold was a cultured woman whose ideas and ideals were to educate others to realize that kindliness and understanding would bridge the cavern of tragedy, and that service to others was an honorable way to honor the dead. Let us honor the dead by serving the living. When Mrs. Seibold was working to found our organization it was with an unselfish thought in mind and a hope that others might benefit and learn to live in peace with one another, whether it be in our own chapters, community, nation or internationally. A husband, son and daughter remain to show the genteel living gained from the fellowship and companionship of our first National Leader. They are simple folk, genuinely gracious, courteous and an honor to the home life created by Grace Darling Seibold."

In 1949, four gold star mothers who had witnessed and influenced the history of the organization died: past national president Della Towne Blake; national custodian of records emeritus Roberta Jacobs; Anna Brown, national chaplain, and Emily M. Cunningham, past national president pro-tem.[75]

Changes to *The Gold Star Mother* Newsletter

In March 1949, *The Gold Star Mother* newsletter took on a new look. No longer free to the membership, the newsletter was offered on a subscription basis at 50 cents per year. A managing editor "experienced in newspaper work," Mabel Patton, was hired to work under the direction of national president Eleanor Boyd.

To help underwrite the cost of the publication, starting in March 1949 a different city sponsored each issue. The inaugural sponsor was Redlands, California. Advertisements from local merchants in the sponsoring city were also solicited. The March 1949 issue listed seventeen Redlands merchants offering a variety of services that included a "Washateria" (do-it-yourself laundry), a liquor store, a bakery, multiple plumbers, and a "fountain-grill" among others. Sponsors of subsequent issues included Laguna Beach ("mountains, surf and strand"), and Bakersfield ("the throbbing heart of Kern County").[76]

Expanded to eight pages, the newsletters now contained filler materials from other sources—Red Cross advertisements, household hints, a short story titled "Ocean Romance," and cartoons, as well as reports on the activities of the organization. And, in September 1949, it contained a cautionary note under the headline "Warning to All Gold Star Mothers":

"There is no such thing as a Gold Star Mother Memorial in any State, and you should not contribute to any who say that there is. You have one National Memorial for Gold Star Mothers. It is known as the Memorial National Home Foundation, which will be used exclusively for the Gold Star Mothers and fathers. Anyone else soliciting funds from you is illegal and undesirable.

"Those of you who have heard from Cheyenne, Wyoming soliciting funds from you are hereby notified that the Cheyenne, Wyoming project is not an official Gold Star Mother project. It is a local Memorial to the men who gave their lives from the State of Wyoming. Therefore, it should be financed by the people of Cheyenne and the State of Wyoming."

In response to members' requests for official dresses rather than a uniform, national president Eleanor Boyd had contracted with a manufacturer in Los Angeles who agreed to provide:

"[Both] a white costume street-length for our mothers and also a white costume, floor-length for institutions and installations, chorus work and for formal dinner or banquet wear. It is of especially good quality crepe and is made so that it flatters an older woman or a larger woman as well as the smaller figure. The price of the street length is $13.75 plus 50 cents postage... the long dress is $14.75 plus 50 cents postage."

The Battle of Burling Continues

As they entered the decade of the 1940s, gold star mother Mathilda Burling continued to garner newsprint for herself and her organization. Apparently having decided to let her carry on without challenge, AGSM records from this period contain little information about her. In newspapers, however, she was the subject of frequent headlines, often self-perpetuated; their frequency was far out of proportion to the size of her membership, which at its peak numbered less than a thousand mothers.

In the late 1940s, Mrs. Burling ran afoul of her own organization, just as Mrs. Seibold had foreseen a decade before, and was taken to court by the membership. In February 1948, headlines read "Gold Star Mothers Sue Group's Founder":

"The American Gold Star Mothers of the World War, Inc. charged yesterday in an action filed in the Supreme Court that Mrs. Mathilda Burling, a former president of the organization, was representing herself illegally as the 'national president of an alleged corporation known as the American Gold Star Mothers of the World Wars, Inc.'

"The plaintiff group, which is a New York corporation, seeks an injunction to restrain Mrs. Burling from using the corporate title 'American Gold Star Mothers of the World Wars' ["Wars" in the plural]. Alleging that this is a 'non-existent' corporation, the New York body's petition says that Mrs. Burling has 'collected money or attempted to collect money for the benefit of such pretended benevolent organization.' The papers assert that Mrs. Burling ceased to be a member of the suing group in February 1947 and in March of that year 'wrongfully and fraudulently' took 'flags, banners and other insignia.'

"Mrs. Burling said last night at her home... that she had founded the gold star movement in September 1918 and was elected national president of the American Gold Star Mothers of the World War, Inc., in Staunton, Virginia in 1936. She said she was re-elected for a two-year term at a convention last July at which a new charter changing the name of the organization was framed. This charter, she said, was recorded at Albany. She declared that she was 'legally and lawfully' the national president of the organization and that her attorney would file her answer in a few days."[77]

Within a few days, Mrs. Burling had countersued the organization and again made the headlines as the *New York Times* announced "New Inning Starts in Gold Star Fight." By March 12, the courts had ruled in favor of the gold star mothers' organization.

A Gold Star Mother Goes to Jail

In 1949, a Salt Lake City court case that had gone on for five years suddenly became national news when the judge jailed a gold star mother for contempt of court. He also threatened to leave her in jail for the rest of her life if she did not comply with his ruling.

Nettie W. Capps, fifty-seven, of Bountiful, Utah, was the mother of Jacob L. Capps, who died in the Battle of the Bulge. At the time of his death, he was the father of three young children but had separated from his wife, Maureen, the mother of his children. When he entered the service, he listed his wife as his beneficiary for the $10,000 veterans life insurance policy. When they formally separated, he made his mother, Nettie Capps, the beneficiary of the policy:

"[Following Jacob Capp's death in 1944,] Capps' widow, Mrs. Maureen Stamm of Monterey, California who has since twice remarried, brought suit to obtain proceeds of the policy for the couple's three children. She won a District Court judgment, later affirmed by the State Supreme Court. It directed Mrs. Capps to transfer proceeds of the policy to a trust fund for the children."[78]

Once the monthly $53 checks were endorsed to the trust fund, Mrs. Stamm alone would have access to the funds. But Mrs. Capps steadfastly refused to sign over the allotments, asserting that she feared her grandchildren would not receive the money. The Veterans Administration sided with Mrs. Capps, indicating that she was the sole beneficiary per the soldier's direction. They would not, even under court order, change the beneficiary from Mrs. Capps to her former daughter-in-law, Mrs. Stamm. They did, however, comply with Mrs. Capps' request to hold up payment of any further benefits until the issue was resolved:

"Utah District Judge Ray Van Cott Jr. ordered Mrs. Capps to accept the $53 monthly checks from the Veterans Administration and endorse them to the First Security Trust Company, which is designated as trustee for the three children of Jacob Capps and his former wife. This Mrs. Capps refused to do, saying she feared the money would not all go to the benefit of her grandchildren.[79]

"[On the court record,] Judge Cott advised Mrs. Capps that 'any word of comfort that you receive from the Veterans Bureau to the effect that you are the one who is to be benefited by this money you must disregard... because while we haven't jurisdiction [over] them, can't compel them to do anything different than what the federal law and their administration requires them, we can compel you and if necessary I can and will incarcerate you in the county jail until you do comply with these orders.'

"Last June 30 [when she refused to accede to the court's direction], she was sentenced to 30 days in jail or pay a fine of $200 and was given a stay of execution to comply. [On August 2,] she appeared in court again... repeating her refusal."[80]

The judge immediately ordered Mrs. Capps jailed on a charge of contempt of court:

"Judge Van Cott and the determined woman are at loggerheads, the jurist reportedly having said that he will keep her in jail for the rest of her life—one 30-day sentence after another—on the contempt charge and she having said steadfastly that she will not surrender the insurance payments which she has been receiving from the Veterans Administration until she is certain they will go for the support of her dead son's children."[81]

"Widely publicized, the case has caused a wave of controversy throughout the country and especially in Utah. Gov. J. Bracken Lee's office asked the Utah Attorney General for an opinion as to the Governor's authority to intervene in the five-year-old case...

"And in Monterey, California, Mrs. Maureen Stamm, former daughter-in-law of the woman, commented that Mrs. Capps got what was coming to her when she went to jail."[82]

Readers across the nation followed the story eagerly while headlines such as "Jailed Gold Star Mother Crochets as Row Boils" and "Mother of Dead GI Takes Jail to Avoid 'Unjust' Court Order" created sympathy for Mrs. Capps.

While Mrs. Capps crocheted, fellow gold star mothers in Utah made a decision to get help for her and turned to another gold star mother:

"Mrs. Walter H. Boyd of Long Beach, national president of the Gold Star Mothers of America, flew... to Salt Lake City, Utah yesterday to mediate unofficially in the case of a Utah mother who's in jail for failure to turn over her dead war hero son's GI insurance to the son's thrice married widow.

"'The people of Utah have called me to look into this matter,' said Mrs. Boyd as she prepared to leave here yesterday.

"'I am taking nothing for granted,' said Mrs. Boyd. 'I want to get the facts about these trust funds.'

"She went on to say with some feeling, however, that if she fails to straighten out the situation and get Mrs. Capps out of jail in a 'sensible way,' there are 'other steps I can take.' These, she said, would be in the form of legal action rather than a reliance upon pressure from public sentiment.

"Mrs. Boyd said that, as she understands it, Jacob Capps, the jailed mother's son, named his mother as beneficiary of his GI insurance shortly before he left for overseas where he was killed.

"'A man's signature which he made in life,' declared the gold star mothers' president yesterday, 'should hold after death. Otherwise no insurance policies would be valid.'

"'Mrs. Capps,' said the president of the gold star mothers, 'is not a member of our organization. But we feel we should help her.'"

Consultation between the judge, Mrs. Boyd, Mrs. Capps and her attorney, and attorneys brought in by Mrs. Boyd, finally bore fruit:

"After 11 days of defiance, Mrs. Nettie W. Capps, gold star mother, submitted to a District court order and was freed from jail ... In an order directing her release, District Judge Ray Van Cott said Mrs. Capps had turned over to the court $1,200 she had received from the policy."[83]

In her August 1949 newsletter, Mrs. Boyd detailed what had been done on Mrs. Capps' behalf:

"To all the nation, I would like to report upon my trip to the State of Utah to assist a gold star mother who had gone to jail rather than break faith with her dead son... The people from the State of Utah phoned and wrote, asking would I please come and see what could be done. Upon arrival at Salt Lake, I went over all court evidence and reviewed it before contacting the Judge who had tried the case. I then visited the mother in jail for a few minutes before going to see the Judge. I conferenced with the Judge in the details of the case; he refused to assist in working it out. Upon the refusal of the Judge to assist, I engaged top attorneys in the city of Salt Lake. However, further meetings were held ... and the Judge promised that he would consider a proposal that would work within the law he had made as binding and on which the statute of limitations had run out so there could be no appeal.

"The attorneys and your national president presented to the Judge a very fine workable plan. Fair to the children and the grandmother and staying true to the sacred wishes of the dead soldier; on Saturday morning, the Judge... refused. The only course left open after full investigation was to get her out of jail and have a few statements written into the action of the court which would give Mrs. Capps a chance for assistance from the Veterans Administration at Washington, D.C. Mrs. Capps is a small, very sweet-appearing woman and I found her gracious and easy to work with.

"It is our duty as gold star mothers of this nation to see that the wishes of our dead sons are carried out in a lawful manner. The fact that they signed who they wished as beneficiaries and can no longer state their wishes in words, [means] we as mothers and the other citizens must see that the sacredness of a dead man's signature and his desire to try to give a bit of security to his beneficiary will not become a mockery. We must protect the faith in the country they fought and died for.

"Mrs. Capps refused to disburse any further sums to the trust account until she could be assured that it would not all go for attorney fees ... Up until this date, under the guise of helping the children, the court had issued checks to the opposing attorney for $1,396.00, which is all the money that Mrs. Capps had received to that time.

"Before she was interfered with by the court, she had been buying clothes, bonds, and necessary furniture for the welfare of the three children. She was being a good grandmother and was accepting the responsibility and challenge of watching out for her son's children that he had expected of her in leaving her the sole beneficiary of his insurance.

"This case is most important and, if at any time in the near future, someone tries to question your rights, before you get into local difficulties at all, please get in touch with me. Poor advice will make the case much more difficult to handle and it must be thoroughly reviewed or no one's insurance in the United States is secure. The Veterans Administration in Washington has

put their top men on to investigate the situation.

"A government insurance policy is a sacred contract between a man who may die and his government. He can and should state whom he wishes as his beneficiary and we, the people, should honor his signature after death. The Judge most decidedly ruled exactly opposite from what Jacob Capps wanted done. We must bring justice and faith back to our servicemen who have government insurance... I have tried to be unbiased and factual and fair in spite of pressure and unfair practices by others. We must keep faith with dignity and honor, both for the dead and the living."

In the September 1949 newsletter, the gold star mothers of the Utah Chapter expressed their thanks to Mrs. Boyd:

"Utah Chapter is greatly indebted to our national president, Mrs. Eleanor Boyd, for the excellent assistance she rendered in behalf of Mrs. Nettie Capps. It was through her tireless efforts that Mrs. Capps was released from jail."

Mrs. Capps died in Bountiful, Utah, in 1983.

Gold Star Mothers in the News

More so than in World War I, newspapers in the 1940s began identifying women as gold star mothers in the headlines of articles. And, sadly, not all the stories contributed to the respect normally granted gold star mothers.

In 1948, gold star mother Veronica Elliot was accused of murdering her husband of eleven years, Cecil Elliot. Various headlines blared "Gold Star Mother Convicted of Murdering Husband"; "Gold Star Mother Calm as She Hears Sentence for Murder"; and "Gold Star Mother Convicted of Murder to Seek New Trial":

"Mrs. Elliott, who is a grandmother, testified during the trial that she married Elliott, a watchman, in... 1937. She said he also was known as 'Pug' because he was a former prize fighter. She said Elliott [56] was good to her for a year, then began beating her.

"Mrs. Elliott [48] also testified that her husband beat her on the day of the killing and tried to choke her to death with a pillow when he caught her looking at a picture of her dead son. She said he took $21 from her purse and went upstairs. She testified that she obtained a revolver, followed him to the bedroom and shot him when he again beat her...

"In her trial before a jury, she pleaded self-defense,

testifying that he had beaten her often. Her son by a previous marriage testified that "he had seen Elliott beat and threaten his mother "so many times I can't remember them all." Another son, Bernard, was killed in the war."[84]

Her attorney said "the beatings, together with her constant thoughts of her dead son, were enough to make a person do 'queer things'." Jurors, however, believed that the evidence of the bullet's path showed that Elliott had been shot while asleep in bed and no evidence indicated that a struggle had taken place. After just four hours of deliberation and two ballots, they found Mrs. Elliott guilty and sentenced her to fourteen years in prison—the minimum for murder:

"[She fainted when the verdict was read, and] after being revived, Mrs. Elliott fainted again and was removed to the county jail hospital where she was unconscious for some time. A physician found her pulse rate had dropped to 48, but he reported her in good physical condition, although suffering from shock."[85]

Her plea for a new trial was overruled by the presiding judge.

Chicago gold star mother Amy Weiland won the respect of the public and the police department for her actions when her home was burglarized in February 1949. An article titled "Gold Star Mother Helps Capture Parolee in Her Home" told the story of her bravery:

"A 60-year-old widow and gold star mother last night caused the capture of a paroled burglar who had broken into her home, by locking herself in her bedroom and telephoning police. After they arrived, she ran to the front door, despite the intruder's shouted threats to kill her, and admitted them. The ex-convict was caught in the house.

"Mrs. Weiland… was alone in the house when the convict entered by scaling a drain pipe and breaking a second story bathroom window… Uneasy because of repeated knocking at the front door, which she declined to answer, Mrs. Weiland said she was 'very frightened' when she heard blows on the bathroom window. She was in a second floor hall when she heard them and close to a telephone.

"Mrs. Weiland seized the telephone, took it to the nearby door of her own bedroom, and shut the door on the cord. She locked the door and called police… A squad car… pulled up in a little more than a minute. Meanwhile, the bathroom window had shattered noisily and Mrs. Weiland knew that the intruder had entered.

"She leaned from her window and shouted her predicament to police, but they called back that they had no way to enter the house. Despite sounds from the man showing that he was in the hall, Mrs. Weiland unlocked her door and fled down the stairs.

"'Stop or I'll blow your head off,' the man shouted. Mrs. Weiland stumbled twice but kept going. She opened the door to the waiting detectives, who rushed in with drawn guns.

"The ex-convict surrendered. He said that he had returned to crime because he did not make enough money to support his wife… and two young daughters."[86]

Many gold star mothers refused to believe that their sons had died in the war. In Connecticut, a mother dismissed the Army's claim that the remains identified as her son were actually his. Her concern led to two exhumations and examinations of the remains, but she still refused to accept the opinion of the military experts:

"The Army said today that on the basis of tooth charts alone, there was but one chance in 24,000,000 0,000,000,000,000,000,000,000 (octillion) that some other soldier with almost identical dental work lay in the grave it has marked as that of Pvt. Stephan C. Lautenbach over his mother's objections.

"The War Department's report was advanced in the case of disputed identification after the mother, Mrs. Udya C. Podoloff, said through her lawyer that she is convinced that the body is not that of her son and that he may be alive.

"The grave in question is No. 123 in the Army military cemetery hear Hochfelden, France. Mrs. Podoloff of New Haven, Connecticut says the body is someone buried in her son's clothing, possibly a German soldier. Late in December 1944 the War Department notified Mrs. Podoloff that her son had been killed charging an enemy machine-gun nest near Naguenau, France.

"Four months later, American prisoners of war were liberated from a camp at Limbur-on-Lahn, Germany. [A photo of the liberated prisoners was taken] which Mrs. Podoloff saw in the *New York Times*. The mother thought one of the prisoners was her son and began a search for him.

"Acting on slim leads supplied by [the photographer], the Army went into an elaborate manhunt which eventually turned up [the soldier identified by Mrs. Podoloff as her son in the photograph].

"When the body was exhumed it permitted comparisons of physical characteristics with those of Lautenbach when he entered the Army. As a result, the Army says: 'Exhumation of the body buried as Lautenbach at Hochfelden and comparison of bodily features and dental characteristics of the body with known features of Lautenbach have reaffirmed beyond doubt the Army's original identification of the remains.'

"Besides, it said, the search that led to Woolf also led to three former buddies of Lautenbach 'who saw him die.'

"[Mrs. Podoloff's attorney] said soldiers killed in action are buried as they fall, but Lautenbach's clothes showed no tears, bullet holes or blood, although the War Department said death was caused by severe chest flesh wounds from shell fragments.

"That indicates, he said, that Lautenbach's clothes were placed on the body of someone else.

"Furthermore… there is a discrepancy in height, color of hair, scars and dental work between Lautenbach and the body in the grave. He said one dental inlay was of a foreign kind, that two wisdom teeth apparently had been pulled only a few weeks before, whereas Lautenbach lost his years earlier. But the Army cited what it said were 24 octillion odds on the dental [records] and said this was 'beyond the possibility of coincidence.'"[87]

In June 1947, a story was published that brought fresh hope to many gold star mothers who, like Mrs. Podoloff, refused to believe the news brought by the military that their son had died:

"The telegram from the War Department in August 1944 said her son, Martin, was missing in action. Later he was listed as dead, but Mrs. Hanna Papula [of Plymouth, Pennsylvania] refused to believe it. So sure, in fact, that she told the parish priest not to put a gold star after her son's name on the honor roll. For three years she prayed that her boy would be found safe. And today, her prayers were answered.

"A newspaper reporter told her Martin was alive and well; that he was working as a blacksmith in the little Normandy village of Airel.

"'Thank God, he's alive,' the mother said. 'I have prayed always that my son would be found safe and was sure that God would someday answer my prayers.'

"Authorities said the soldier told them in halting English—a tongue he seemed almost to have forgotten—that he suffered a temporary loss of memory after a brain concussion in heavy fighting at St. Lo in the summer of 1944. After brief hospitalization, he returned to his unit at Montabot, near Villedoux, and his platoon was cut off by the Germans.

"Papula, a veteran of the D-Day landing on Omaha Beach… said he did not recall leaving his unit. When he regained his memory he found himself in Airel and remained there for fear he would be tried as a deserter."[88]

In 1947, public sympathy came to the aid of a blind gold star mother, Mollie Sampson. Mr. and Mrs. Sampson had learned that they were to be evicted from a home they rented with two other family members in Secaucus, New Jersey. They spent their life savings to purchase a small house, only to find that the house was occupied by a woman with eight children who had nowhere to go:

"When Mayor [John J.] Kane heard of the Sampsons' plight yesterday, he offered them the use of a three-room apartment [in] the Municipal Building, formerly occupied by a caretaker."[89]

The apartment was provided rent-free.

The loss of precious mementoes prompted many gold star mothers to ask the press for help in their recovery. In 1945, Mrs. Thomas Vincent asked "the thief who stole her purse in the Loeser Department Store [in Brooklyn] to "keep the $110, but please return the picture and the letter":

"The picture was of the crew of the submarine *Bonefish,* which was lost in the Bay of Tayoma, near Tokyo, about July 27 [1945]. Seventy-five members of the crew, including Mrs. Vincent's 19-year old son, Thomas, were reported missing.

"Mrs. Vincent was shopping in the store prior to meeting Mrs. Grace Johnston… mother of Lieut. (j.g.) Russell Mackaye Johnston, another missing member of the crew, to whom she had promised a copy of the photograph if Mrs. Johnston could identify her son in it."[90]

Gold star mother Mrs. John Drennan of Cincinnati turned to the *Chicago Tribune* to express her thanks to an anonymous gift that she received:

"[She] asked the *Tribune* to convey her gratitude to the anonymous Chicagoan who last week mailed her the prayer book of her son, Robert H. Drennan, who was killed November 3, 1944 while serving in the Army. The prayer book arrived, she wrote, in a package with no return address. The mother begged that whoever sent it contact her so that she could thank him herself.

Gold Star Mothers in Chicago

In 1941, an individual signing as "A Gold Star Mother" was a frequent correspondent in the letters to the editor section of the *Chicago Tribune* called "The Voice of the People." The correspondence began before the U.S. entered World War II so if the correspondent was indeed a gold star mother, her child would most probably have been lost in the Great War. Her letters were usually poignant and sympathetic. But neither public figures nor the newspaper itself were exempt when she felt a wrong had been done:

January 20, 1946: "Last week I read Mayor Kelly's pledge to support the national clothing collection. His concluding remark was 'Under no circumstance will a single item in any category be given to nationals of former enemy nations.' Somehow I feel these sentiments are very unfitting to a victorious nation and to a Christian city executive.

"When my son enlisted, no one objected that his parents came from a land that had suddenly become an enemy. These parents were proud to give their boy to fight for the United States, a country they had adopted and loved. When I became a gold star mother, I hoped that my son had given his life so that tolerance and the four freedoms would survive. Obviously, our mayor advocates quite the contrary. Also I wonder if the 125 organizations connected with this drive condone such prejudice.

"Don't misunderstand. I realize a vanquished country is not to be glutted with kindness, but surely the words 'love thine enemy' could be observed and not overdone where food and clothing are concerned."[91]

June 27, 1948: "Last Friday, you [the *Chicago Tribune*] reported that a Jap officer was sentenced to 15 years in prison for ordering his men to torture and kill an American soldier. The article told just how they tortured him and gave his name and address. How do you think his poor mother feels reading that terrible article? I lost my boy in the war and those things are hard to take."[92]

In 1947, a gold star mother who signed her letter as Mrs. G.B.C. wrote to the *Tribune* to express her grief at how neglectfully parents of a dead soldier were treated by the military if the soldier had left a widow behind:

"On behalf of all mothers whose sons gave their lives for their country, I would like to voice a grievance.

"My son married a lovely girl—she was 19 and he was 20—but because of that, when word came of his death, I had to hear of it from her mother, which must have been a difficult task for her at best. All letters of condolence were sent to his wife. All citations and medals were given to her. I cannot forget the scornful look on the good major's face when he awarded the Silver Star posthumously. I was only the mother, you see, and my grief was at that time more poignant than it is now. I would have loved some small token sent to me personally, to hug to my heart; something to show for all the years that I loved him and took care of him. He was to me the dearest son a mother could have had. But 'A son is a son 'til he gets him a wife' is never truer than when he gives his life for his country. The mother ceases to exist. One little word written to me personally by one of the many men in high standing in this country, from whom my daughter-in-law received letters, would have done much to assuage my grief."[93]

A gold star mother of World War II responded the same day to Mrs. G.B.C.'s letter, signing herself "Another Gold Star Mother":

"The letter by 'Gold Star Mother' in today's *Tribune* expresses for many gold star mothers the things we feel and would like to say. As in Mrs. G. B. C.'s experience, our only son (a young medical student) married in November, shipped overseas in June 1944 and was killed the following August. It has now been three years of waiting for us. No correspondence pertaining to our son comes to us. We can't even get a report from the government of any details or the name of someone in his company who might have known him or been there. All requests are answered by the form letter that he was killed in action August 10, battle of San Lo, and is buried in France. The plot and grave numbers are also given.

"How many mothers and fathers would give much to share the letters concerning their sons; yet we who raised them must be grateful for the crumbs if the daughter-in-law sees fit to toss us a few.

"As to bringing our son home, we were not asked. The daughter-in-law may have remarried or will soon. Do you not think we parents should be given the chance to choose whether the body shall be returned or shall remain undisturbed?"[94]

The End of the War for Some

When the war ended, the nation went wild. People poured into the streets and celebrated with laughter, music and hope for a new world in which war did not exist. But for some, the end of the war did not mean their loved ones would be coming home. Robert Gaskill shared his memories of the end of the war:

"After hearing the war was over, I made my way up our street to join everyone who was outside, celebrating. Everyone was stopping to shake hands or wish each other well on this wonderful day.

"Then I noticed Mrs. Dorman, one of our neighbors, standing alone on her front porch. She cried uncontrollably, tears streaming down her face, as she watched the happy scene before her. To those of us who knew the Dorman family, no explanation was necessary. Mrs. Dorman had just learned she was a Gold Star Mother.

"Imagine the feelings she must have been experiencing. The war was finally over, but her son would not be coming home. He was killed while trying to land his crippled bomber, but only after having his crew bail out first. It was a hero's death.

"My feelings of jubilation were immediately replaced by guilt and remorse. I pushed through the crowd and went up on the porch. Mrs. Dorman met me on the top step, put her arms around me and wept in convulsive sobs that seemed to last an eternity.

"She finally pushed herself back from me, hands on my shoulders and said, 'Thank you for coming up, Bob. I feel better now.'

"With that, she turned, opened the door with the gold star on it, and disappeared inside.

"I stood there for a long time, reflecting what had just taken place. When I reached up to wipe the tears from my face, I realized they weren't Mrs. Dorman's. They were my own."[95]

Bringing Home the War Dead

As in World War I, it took many years for the remains of the American war dead to be returned to their final resting places on American soil:

"During World War II, the U.S. Government called to service approximately 15,000,000 men and women. The number of American war dead totaled around 359,000, of which 281,000 were recovered and given burial in more than 250 temporary military cemeteries around the globe…

"It took almost another six years after the war (until the close of 1951) for final disposition to be accomplished. In all, some 171,000 casketed remains were delivered to next of kin in the United States. At the same time, approximately 97,000 dead were, according to wishes of the next of kin, buried abroad in permanent U. S. military cemeteries. Another 10,000 'unknowns' likewise found their final resting place on foreign soil."[96]

The nation waited patiently for its dead to return home. To honor the dead and represent the mothers who could not be there, gold star mothers on both coasts met the transport ships carrying military coffins as they arrived in port:

"Six hundred men and women mourned over their war dead on Pier 3 at the Army Base in Brooklyn yesterday [November 27, 1947]… There were 4,212 coffins aboard, 411 for [New York State]. All were from Henri Chapelle Cemetery near Bayeux in Belgium.

"The American Gold Star Mothers of World Wars were represented by women from both state and national units. They and others looked down on the transport's open holds, where the caskets lay in flag-draped rows."[97]

In this case, it would take five days to unload the sad cargo. From Brooklyn, the caskets were dispatched across the nation to cemeteries and family plots near the families they left behind.

Public memorial services were often held to honor the dead and console the living. One such service, held in Chicago on October 20, 1947, was described by Robert Cromie for the *Chicago Tribune*:

"Admirals and generals and opera singers, a governor and a mayor and a movie star. All these were in Soldiers' Field last night and thousands of Chicagoans heard them talk and saw them move across a flood-lit stage. Bands played, too, and there were choruses singing.

"But it was not for these things that the thousands of Chicagoans came and sat quietly—except for a little weeping—on the hard seats of Soldiers' Field beneath the stars, looking out across the green football field, aglow with light.

"They came because this was the only way they knew to pay tribute to the 10 unseeing and unhearing men who lay in flag-draped coffins before a backdrop of yellow and white chrysanthemums. And in paying tribute to the 10 brought home at last from Pearl Harbor and Wake [Island] and Iwo Jima, the crowd offered homage also to the other dead of World War II—those who have been brought home for burial, those who will be brought home, and those who will lie in lonely lands throughout the world until Judgment Day.

"[A cantor] sang... the ancient Hebrew memorial hymn of repose for the souls of the departed. And as the cantor sang the strange, sobbing words, two women in the section reserved for Gold Star mothers stood, weeping, in the front row... Then Anna Kaskas, Metropolitan Opera star, sang 'The Rosary' and others in the Gold Star section began weeping.

"Mayor Kennelly said: '... I bring the sympathy of the city of Chicago to all Gold Star mothers.'

"Then came taps, the time-honored call to rest, and the ceremony was ended. But there was no rush for exits, such as follows other Soldiers' Field events. Most of the throng rose respectfully and then waited patiently, the young and the old, until the 10 coffins were trundled slowly by once more and off the lighted field into the darkness beneath the stands."[98]

In 1947, as the flow of the war dead returning to the states increased, AGSM national president Anna G. Hagerty responded to questions about the role of the AGSM in the funerals that were taking place:

"Many letters have been received asking what action has been or will be taken by our Organization concerning the return of our War Dead. As we are all Mothers of Heroes, who have given their lives for our Great Country, we can well understand the proud but sad hours the Mother will experience, when the body of her son or daughter is returned to her.

"We, as an Organization, have no set ritual or procedure to follow, as the Service Organizations are taking care of this function. However, we can share and help to bear the Mother's heartache. Many of our Chapters send a spray of flowers to the funeral home if the body lies in state. If there is no funeral, they are sending a dozen roses to the Mother at her home. We can most certainly help at a time like this and it would be a nice thought and most gracious on the part of Chapter members to call on the Mothers; ask if you can assist her in any way; do a few errands for her; mind the younger children; answer the phone and in fact anything to help her in this time and surely the flowers your chapter sends will speak volumes. Many of our Mothers will attend the funeral rites wherever they are held. It will be hard, but a Mother's lot is always hard or at least never easy."[99]

At funerals where there would be no mother due to illness or death, AGSM members would attend whenever possible, to honor both the lost child and the mother who bore him, their sister in sorrow.

Fig. 7-24. The U.S. Air Force Military Cemetery in Ipswich, Queensland, Australia where Rose Manson cared for the graves of more than 1,400 American servicemen and servicewomen during World War II. *(Photo dated November 1945: Courtesy of Peter Dunn's "Australia @ War" website at www.ozatwar.com.)*

In Australia, A Friend to the Gold Star Mothers

In April 1949 *Coronet* magazine told the story of an Australian woman, Rose Manson, whose efforts brought solace and comfort during World War II to more than 1,400 gold star families in the United States.[100]

The story began in 1942 in the small Australian town of Ipswich. Ipswich didn't provide much entertainment for the young American men and women assigned to nearby airfields such as Eagle Farm, Archerfield and Amberely. But word-of-mouth at the USO canteens soon directed the young people to the home of Rose Manson, a home away from home where the soldiers were treated like family by Mrs. Manson, Mr. Manson, a disabled veteran, and the eight Manson children ranging in age from five years to three older daughters and a son serving in Australia's military.

The Manson house overlooked a cemetery where Australian war dead had been buried. One day in 1942, Private Peter Strange, a young American airman, commented to Mrs. Manson, "Mom, what a stark, cold place that cemetery is. I'd hate to be buried there." The next week, Peter's body was brought back from a military mission and buried in the cemetery.

Rose had previously cared for the graves of ninety-eight Australian soldiers buried there, and later said "it seemed quite natural that I do the same for the Americans."[101]

From the very first day, Mrs. Manson kept on Peter's grave a bower of flowers. One day her daughter

Judy said to her, "Mother, if Peter could see his grave, I think he would tell you to 'spread them out'—give everybody a chance."

Rose Manson began to spread them out. Although the cemetery was kept immaculate by personnel of the American Graves Registration, every day she made a special trip to place flowers to honor the sons of Americans buried in that peaceful spot.[102]

A mother herself, Rose realized what it would mean to the mothers of the American soldiers buried there to have any word about their sons' and daughters' resting places. She began to write to the family of each American soldier buried in the cemetery:

Dear Mrs. Wheeler
I thought you would like to know, that someone as far away as Australia is caring for your loved one's grave. Our garden overlooks the little Cemetery, and in appreciation for all your Boys have done for us—the token of flowers is the least I can give to express my own personal gratitude. If you would care to write and ask anything—please do so. I would count it a privilege to be of service to you.[103]

In response, Rose was inundated by letters from grateful parents. Some "begged for more information; offered money for the care of the graves; wanted to know what they could do for Mrs. Manson." She wrote back to each saying, "Just send some flower seeds to plant and, if you like, some small American flags."[104]

Seeds began to arrive from all parts of the United States; Rose planted them all and "soon morning glories and California poppies began to push Australian flowers over the fence."[105] The sacks of mail from America continued to arrive—there were hundreds of American boys buried in the cemetery—and she was only one woman. "But I had got hold of something and couldn't let go," she said simply. "I couldn't bear to think of an American mother waiting in vain for an answer to her letter."[106]

The Mansons had little money and the postage associated with her letters soon became more than they could manage. Rose took a job cleaning the local post office at night, dedicating her earnings to continue the correspondence with the American gold star parents. She attended every funeral for the 1,409 American soldiers laid to rest in "her" cemetery and "sent to each mother all the information she could find about the boy:"[107]

"Every one of the 1,400 next of kin have received a photo of the cemetery and, on Memorial Day of 1946, I sent 1,800 newspapers with various accounts of the service and the Legion poppies from the grave.

"When Mother's Day came, I mailed 800 cards and on Christmas 1,000 letters. My incoming mail was equally as heavy. On Memorial Day I sent invitations to all parts of Australia and over 3,000 people came to that service. The hymns sung were chosen by the mothers of boys of every nationality resident there—Indians, and Negroes, too."[108]

Following the end of the war, unbeknownst to Mrs. Manson, gold star parents with whom she had corresponded were hard at work on her behalf. In Wichita, Kansas, Mrs. David Moretz, whose son lay at rest in the Ipswich cemetery, wrote to 1,408 gold star families with whom Mrs. Manson had corresponded asking if they would contribute to a fund to pay for Mrs. Manson to travel to the United States. The response was enormous and in August 1947 Mrs. Manson was on her way to America for a trip that would last nearly a year.[109]

For ten months, she toured America from coast to coast. She visited every state in the Union, traveling by train, car and bus—and even hitchhiking. Funds were not available for her to travel in royal style, but to her, half the fun lay in "making things meet and enjoying the adventure."

She talked to hundreds of mothers, visited in the homes of Chinese, African-Americans, and even a few Native American tepees on the Navajo Reservation; she stayed at homes where servants did her every bidding—and slept on the floors of mountain cabins.[110]

What did the visits mean to the gold star families? Mrs. Eugene Wheeler of Kansas said that without Rose, she would never have known the details of her son Robert's funeral service, the cemetery, and his gravesite. As Mrs. Samuel Redmond said, hugging Rose when meeting her in Rapid City, South Dakota, "It's the next best thing to having John home again."[111] Gold star parents often drove 500 miles or more to meet with Mrs. Manson, asking countless questions. And Rose had answers in a ledger she had meticulously kept with the record of each American buried in the cemetery and all the information available to her about their deaths.

Following the war, the remains of the American dead were removed from the Ipswich cemetery and returned home for burial or reinterred at the national cemetery in Hawaii. The Ipswich cemetery was subsequently named Manson Park in tribute to Rose Manson and her tender care of the servicemen and women who rested there until their nation could bring them home. [Fig. 7-24]

Fig. 8-1: Pontiac (Michigan) Chapter No. 9 gathers for Memorial Day services in 1957. *(Fenelon Collection)*

CHAPTER 8

The 1950s: Dissension and Challenges

America is as great as she is because she always has been blessed with great-hearted women like yourselves, women of unconquerable valor.
— RALPH STONE, *Veterans Administration*

FOR MYRIAD REASONS, THE 1950S proved to be the most difficult decade AGSM had yet faced. Continued rapid growth in membership created administrative confusion; traditional guidelines were questioned, and often deviated from, by the new, younger members. The group struggled to maintain organizational neutrality about the nation's involvement in an unpopular and costly foreign conflict in Korea that was never actually declared a war.

Eleanor Boyd's iron hand continued at the AGSM tiller for the first two years of the decade, effectively silencing questions about the propriety of her actions. For the first time, memberships were punitively rescinded if a member ran afoul of Mrs. Boyd. At her direction, multiple lawsuits were initiated by AGSM against members who resigned in protest of her actions and formed another organization for gold star mothers.

Lawsuits were also initiated against AGSM by members who felt they were slandered by Mrs. Boyd. And overshadowing all of these difficulties was the continuing controversy over the Memorial National Home Foundation; the lawsuits related to the Home would embroil the AGSM in costly litigation throughout the decade. Despite the internal chaos, the organization's commitment to service and the nation never faltered. From the public perspective it continued to be "the most honored, most respected and most worthy of any organization in our country."[1]

The War in Korea

Occurring between World War II and the Vietnam War, the Korean War is often referred to as "the Forgotten War" although it was one of the most destructive conflicts of the century. Nearly four million Koreans died in the fighting (two-thirds of them civilians) and China lost as many as one million soldiers. Untold economic damage was done to the Korean peninsula, especially in the north where three years of bombing left few buildings standing. The cultural and social aspects of the war still have repercussions in the divided Koreas today. Ultimately, little was gained from the fighting—an armistice was established rather than a permanent peace; a heavily fortified demilitarized zone still exists between North and South Korea; and there was no clear victor or loser. Most historians agree that the Korean War marked the beginning of the Cold War.

From the perspective of most Americans, the Korean War developed quickly. On June 25, 1950, North Korea declared war and invaded South Korea. Under pressure from the United States, the UN Security Council quickly passed a resolution calling for the immediate cessation of hostilities and withdrawal of North Korean forces to north of the 38th Parallel. On June 26, President Truman authorized General Douglas MacArthur to send ammunition and equipment (using Air Force fighters and Navy ships) to prevent the loss of Seoul; to provide ships and aircraft to protect the evacuation of American citizens; and to send a group to Korea to determine how best to help the South Korean government and military.

That same day, Truman ordered General MacArthur to deploy Air Force aircraft and Navy ships against North Korean military forces south of the 38th Parallel.

General MacArthur issued an alert order telling all combat units in the Far East to prepare for possible deployment to Korea.

On June 27, the UN Security Council passed a resolution calling for member nations to give military aid to South Korea. That day, three North Korean fighter planes were shot down by UN forces. Two days later, the first American ground troops arrived in Korea from Japan.

The United States committed fully to the conflict on June 30 when MacArthur received permission to deploy U.S. ground support forces. He was ordered to carry the war into North Korea and the waters offshore, although he was warned to stay well clear of the Manchurian and Soviet borders. The UN Security Council repeatedly called for the United States to name a commander of the UN troops. On July 8, Truman named MacArthur as Commanding General of United Nations Military Forces, directing him to use the United Nations flag concurrently with the flags of the sixteen nations participating in the course of operations against North Korean forces.

The war continued for three years. On July 27, 1953, the UN, North Korea, and China signed an armistice agreement to end the fighting. South Korea refused to sign the agreement. By then, nearly 40,000 American soldiers had died, more than 103,000 had been wounded, and more than 7,000 had been taken as prisoners of war.

Service Flags Revived for Korean Conflict

While there was little dissent initially from the American public about the actions taken in Korea, the government eventually began to worry about the possible consequences of public indifference to the war.

KOREA

Today I silently shed a tear
Not for my son, who isn't here,
But for another mother's son now gone
Who laid down his life
In a far off land—
Just as my son died in Baatan.

His buddies leave him there and mourn
And another mother's heart is torn.
They sadly miss him,
And for his voice they yearned
As neath the sod he lies
In sleep and peace he earned.

~Submitted by Margaret Weiser
The Gold Star Mother February 1951

In January 1953, the *Chicago Tribune* placed the blame for the public's indifference on Truman's reluctance to declare the conflict in Korea a "war," which required a congressional declaration:

"The defense department concedes the justice of our observation the other day that Mr. Truman's Korean War is unpopular with the people. In order to offset what it terms public indifference to the conflict, it proposes that families with men in uniform revive the World War II custom of hanging service flags in their windows.

"We think it proper that men in the service of their country receive any acknowledgement or honor that is pleasing to them or their family. If service flags or lapel buttons will make absence and sacrifice more tolerable, there can be no objection.

"But it is evident that the defense department is thinking less of the morale of the men and their families than of the morale of the departing Truman administration, which pushed young Americans into this senseless chopper in Korea. Mr. Truman, aware of his constitutional dilemma in ordering military action without a congressional declaration of war, has refused to call Korea a war. His defense department does not do so now, yet it is proceeding to authorize service flags which are never seen in the absence of war.

"The matter demonstrates how complicated things can become when politicians get snarled in their own contradictions."[2]

The issue of a declared war versus a military action had already been made painfully clear to the gold star mothers of the casualties in Korea. In July 1951, the *Chicago Tribune* reported on the efforts of two gold star mothers to receive the government's next-of-kin pin for gold star family members:

"Membership in the Gold Star Mothers organization has been denied two Tucson mothers whose sons, both Marines, were killed in the Korean War. The commandant of marines in Washington informed them that 'only widows and mothers whose sons were killed during World War II may be issued official Gold Star buttons.'

In a July 1951 letter to President Truman, Mrs. William P. Lindsey requested a gold star pin in honor of her son, Pfc. John R. Lindsey, who was killed in Korea in November 1950. The reply, signed by General Vaughn, advised that while lapel pins were currently restricted to parents of deceased veterans of World War II, proposed legislation was expected to expand that right to include those who died in the "Korean emergency."[3] On August 21, 1951, legislation was amended to include deaths from the "enemy conflict of the Korean situation" as eligible for the next-of-kin pin (commonly referred to by the public as the "gold star mother's pin").[4]

AGSM Calls for an Honorable and Just Peace

Media representatives at the sixteenth national AGSM convention in Chicago reported on the organization's hopes for an imminent peace in Korea:

"Mrs. Auge W. Nielsen of Chicago, president, read a resolution prepared by the executive board, which stated, "We mothers, members of American Gold Star Mothers, Inc.... do hereby resolve that the imminent peace will be an honorable and just peace, and will perpetuate these principles.'

Delegates among the 1,200 persons registered for the convention voted unanimous approval of the resolution. What the organization would consider an 'honorable and just' peace will be clarified at subsequent sessions of the convention, Mrs. Nielsen said."[5]

The 1953 convention was held in early June 1953. The Korean Armistice was signed July 27, 1953.

AGSM Leaders of the 1950s

Eleanor Boyd [Fig.8-2]
National President, 1950–1952
As the 1950s got underway, Eleanor Boyd was halfway through her unprecedented third term as AGSM's national president. While some members felt that her star had begun to tarnish due to the Memorial National Home controversies and her punitive reaction to those

Fig. 6-8: The 1956 installation of officers for the East Los Angeles-Montebello Chapter.
(AGSM Collection)

Fig. 8-2: Eleanor Boyd, AGSM National President 1946–1947; 1948–1952
(AGSM Collection)

Fig. 8-3: Elsie C. Nielsen, AGSM National President 1952–1955
(AGSM Collection)

Fig. 8-4: Ruth Singer, AGSM National President 1955–1957
(AGSM Collection)

Fig. 8-5: Maude E. Fry, AGSM National President 1957–1958
(AGSM Collection)

who questioned her methods, the vast majority of members were still enthralled by her apparent selflessness, presence, style, and energy.

Mrs. Boyd often spoke as a solicitous guardian who wanted to shield her wards—the organization's membership—from anything unpleasant or difficult.

Since first becoming national president in 1946, Mrs. Boyd had adamantly insisted that all ritual and ceremonial functions of the organization adhere strictly to the written guidelines. It was her decision in 1950, seconded by the national executive board, that members or officers who had been sworn in with a ceremo-

ny that deviated from the established ritual were not legally installed and must be reinstalled using the approved protocols.

Mrs. Boyd continued to challenge the membership to aspire to the highest standards of behavior and to always serve as a shining example of American motherhood:

"One does not gain prestige through publicity. Prestige comes by setting an example of fine citizenship. One is not loved and remembered, if a member of a destructive force. To gain trust, love and respect, one just radiates it from the heart. There must be real warmth and sincerity."[6]

Fig. 8-6: AGSM national president Ruth Singer (in dark dress at center) is shown with members of the East Los Angeles-Montebello Chapter in 1956.
(AGSM Collection)

Although Mrs. Boyd claimed to hold no hatred for any person or group, she was very clear in her contempt for one organization when she spoke in January 1952 before a civic gathering in Spokane, Washington:

"I've been to Europe, behind the iron curtain. I hate communists. I hate them, not only because they still hold the sacred ground in the Russian sector of Berlin where some of our sons still lie, but because they don't believe in God and have no sense of decency or dignity."[7]

Despite Mrs. Boyd's admonitions to members to maintain the highest standards, and her frequent references to her own selfless and ladylike behavior, Eleanor proved a frightening adversary to those who challenged or inadvertently crossed her.

As Eleanor Boyd served her five terms as national president and then continued to strongly influence the national executive board in two terms as national parliamentarian, she increasingly epitomized the infamous "iron fist in the velvet glove." Her self-righteousness, influence, and contempt for the wishes of the membership caused the AGSM to experience the most difficult, contentious, and costly decade in its history.

Elsie C. Nielsen [Fig. 8-3]
National President, 1952–1955

A native of Chicago, Elsie Nielsen was the wife of A. W. Nielsen. Parents of two sons, their eldest, Capt. Robert C. Nielsen, an officer of the 393rd Infantry, was killed in Belgium during the Battle of the Bulge in December 1944.

Mrs. Nielsen was one of the organizing members of the Chicago chapter of the American Gold Star Mothers. Prior to joining, she had long been active in other veteran-connected organizations. She served for two years as the Chicago chapter's first vice president and for three years as chapter president. At the time of her election as national president, she had served as national historian for two years.

She was clear in her goals for the organization, both under her leadership as national president and into the future:

"As an organization, I would like to see us grow but NOT with future-made Gold Star Mothers. There are thousands of Mothers in the country who have lost sons and whom we make welcome to our organization, but I repeat there should NOT be any more Gold Star Mothers than there are now!... We need all the Mothers who have lost sons—and they need us."[8]

Fig. 8-7 : Mabel C. Troy, AGSM National President 1958–1959
(AGSM Collection)

Fig. 8-8 : Lorraine I. Desser, AGSM National President 1959–1960
(AGSM Collection)

Elsie's quiet ways did not prevent her from making her mark on the organization and moving it forward through difficult times, as reported by the *Chicago Tribune*:

"Petite, modest mannered, quiet voiced is Mrs. Aage W. Nielsen of Constance Avenue, but the American Gold Star Mothers have reason to know their national president moves on her mission from one end of the country to the other as if shod with seven league boots. When next week's annual convention in Miami Beach, Florida, brings Mrs. Nielsen's three year administration to a close, it will end a tenure which has seen a rapid advance in expansion, solidification and prestige of the organization."[9]

Ruth Singer [Fig. 8-4]
National President, 1955–1957

The mother of four sons, Ruth Singer became a gold star mother when her son, Murray, a twenty-four-year-old Army private, was killed in World War II in the African Campaign.[10] He was posthumously awarded the Purple Heart and the Bronze Star.

During her terms as national president, Ruth had unusual opportunities to represent the gold star membership. In 1956 she led the Pledge of Allegiance at the meeting of the Board of Supervisors, City of Los Angeles. This was a "signal honor" as Mrs. Singer was the first woman ever to enjoy this privilege.[11] In 1957, she attended the Inauguration of President Eisenhower and Vice President Nixon and the Inaugural Ball.[12]

Ruth was integrally involved on behalf of the AGSM in the Memorial National Home Foundation lawsuit and worked closely with the AGSM attorneys on every aspect of the case. Via *The Gold Star Mother,* she reported the case's milestones, decisions and setbacks to the membership over the period of several years it took for the case to be resolved through the courts and subsequent appeals by the Home Foundation.

Maude E. Fry [Fig. 8-5]
National President, 1957–1958

A member of Michigan's Grand Rapids chapter, Maude Fry was born in 1899. She joined American Gold Star Mothers, Inc., in December 1944 following the death of her son, Emerson Bice Brown, in World War II. Emerson was serving in the Navy when his ship was torpedoed in June 1943.[13]

At the convention where she was elected national president, Mrs. Fry emphasized her wish that AGSM have a chapter in every city where there was a VA hospital or a national cemetery. She stressed that an active chapter near a national cemetery made her feel that the graves of "soldier-heroes" were in tender and understanding hands.[14]

Maude's wonderful sense of humor and kindness came through in everything she did. In a 1957 letter to President Eisenhower requesting a statement related to Gold Star Mother's Day, she wrote that she wasn't sure of the proper way to make her request so she was just going to be "straightforward" about it. She added a postscript, however, advising the president that he could check with Representative Gerald Ford Jr. and Senator Potter to assure that she wasn't a "crackpot."[15] In 1957, serving as first national vice president, she had been delighted when, attending a banquet in her honor put on by the Department of Georgia, she had been named Mrs. Georgia Peach in a resolution signed by Georgia's governor.[16]

At the Department of Michigan convention in June 1959, Maude spoke modestly of her talents, and encouraged the mothers to embrace their gold star sisters for only they could offer the special comfort needed to those who had lost loved ones in war:

"I have stated many times that I am a very simple person. I have no great talent, but the one gift which God was so good in giving me I use—I love people. I see good in all people; I suffer with them; I rejoice in their happiness. To me, American Gold Star Mothers, Inc. is just people, the finest of all women. To me, AGSM is THE organization for a gold star mother to belong to, to work in, to serve. Even without the huge amount of volunteer hospital service and community service which is done by our members, you do something else no one else can do. Just by loving, visiting with, and understanding our fellow members, that is a wonderful gift to mankind.

"A gold star mother is a casualty of war. Have you any idea how many of our members lost their only child? Do you realize that by just smiling during our meetings, listening to a mother, telephoning them once in a while, how much good you are doing?"

Asked to speak at the Chapel of the Four Chaplains in April 1958, Mrs. Fry spoke movingly of the honor associated with being a gold star mother:

"You and I didn't ask to be a gold star mother—we certainly didn't want to be a gold star mother. We watched our sons and daughters grow, encouraging them to think for themselves, proud of their clean minds and bodies. Yes, and after we had taught them to THINK for themselves, we didn't like it when they said, 'Ma, I just have to help.' They had a sense of responsibility; we were afraid, and all we could do was pray. No, we didn't want to be a gold star mother—but we are one. We have the HONOR and privilege of being the mothers of sons and daughters who were co-workers with God, helping to stop men of evil from conquering the world and making slaves of mankind."[17]

Mabel C. Troy [Fig. 8-7]
National President, 1958–1959

If Mabel C. Troy had a trademark other than her terrific sense of humor, it was her hats. In almost every photograph during her time in office, she is seen wearing a hat—sometimes a chapeau with a sweeping brim, sometimes a close-fitting cloche, some adorned with flowers, others with bows—indoors or out, her outfit was never complete without a hat. An accomplished musician, Mrs. Troy often played the piano at AGSM events, sang as a soloist, and led the group in singing.[18]

Originally a member of the Paterson, New Jersey, chapter, Mrs. Troy was the widow of James J. Troy, chief of the Paterson Fire Department and a disabled World War I veteran. She was the mother of five sons, four of whom served in World War II:

"It is a privilege, a very high honor to be your National President, and with all privileges there are obligations. It isn't even a privilege I have earned for myself—my seventeen-year-old son, my first born, who enlisted in the United States Navy the week he graduated from high school—and God gave me this honor.

Each of us has had this high honor bestowed upon us. That is why the membership of AGSM Inc. is the finest group of women in the world."[19]

Mrs. Troy worked diligently to help heal the organization from the turmoil it had experienced in the previous years, and the harm it had caused to relationships among the mothers:

"As long as we work with the Construction Crew, and not with the Wrecking Crew, we will build an organization of love, tolerance, forgiveness, charity and understanding which no one can tear down. Look for something good in everyone and you will find it.[20]

Her messages to the membership about getting the organization back on track were plain and simple, but softened by humor:

"You know, I once read that every organization is composed of three sets of bones: the Wish-bones, the Jaw-bones and the Back-bones. The Wish-bone group is always wishing something would be done; the Jaw-bone crowd is never satisfied unless they are criticizing everything that has been done; but the Back-bones are those who make the organization what it is by doing the work that the other two groups should have done in the first place."[21]

Mrs. Troy lamented about the personal toll that traveling took following a cross-country road trip in which she met with gold star chapters and departments:

"First thing on the agenda [in California] was an interview with the press and a picture taken. Believe me when I say THIS one would have been better if it had not been taken. I don't profess to being photogenic, but on this one, I looked like something the cat had dragged in… [Over the border in Mexico] we had our picture taken on one of the donkey carts. I told one of our mothers it would be hard to tell which was the donkey, only he had stripes."[22]

Perhaps Mrs. Troy's sense of humor was hereditary, for following her election as national president, her sons sent her the following telegram:

> GRAY HAIR WE MAY HAVE GIVEN
> OUR MOTHER WITH A HEART OF GOLD,
> WE ARE THE PROUDEST FAMILY EVER
> FOR THE HONOR YOU NOW HOLD.
> SIGNED, THE BOYS[23]

At the 1958 Gold Star Mother's Day observances at Arlington National Cemetery, Mrs. Troy spoke of the gold star mothers' resolve:

Fig. 8-9: A sketch of AGSM's Headquarters building from their 1957 Christmas card. *(AGSM Collection)*

"The Gold Star Mothers of our beloved country bow their heads in reverence of their sons' and daughters' heroism, but instead of shedding tears in remembrance, they are ready in all humility to rededicate their lives to courage, strength, understanding and tolerance that the simple truths of mankind, which will benefit all humanity, be preserved. To the world they are lifting their faces with a smile of determination to see that a just and honorable peace and a free world will come forth, that their sons and daughters will not have died in vain."[24]

Lorraine I. Desser [Fig. 8-8]
National President, 1959–1960
Lorraine Desser took the AGSM into a new decade—a decade in which the nation would become involved in yet another war. In this case, although the war was fought overseas, the repercussions on the home front tore the fabric of the nation as no conflict had done since the Civil War.

Mrs. Desser was born in 1902 of Swiss and American parentage. She spent her entire life in Bridgeport, Connecticut. At eighteen, she married Harold Norman Wallace; at twenty, she was a widow with a one-year-old son. Mrs. Dessler was aided by her mother who devoted the rest of her life to helping care for the child. Mrs. Dessler went to school to learn linotyping and was employed by a local newspaper for the next decade. In 1930, she married Samuel Desser and they had one son. In World War II, her older son served in the South Pacific in the Troop Carrier Command as a glider pilot and was killed on a mission in Manila Bay in July 1945.

In 1948, Mrs. Desser joined AGSM. Not having been affiliated with any organization before, she quickly became interested and involved in AGSM work. She served as the Veterans Administration Volunteer Services (VAVS) representative to the West Haven V.A. hospital for five years. For two of those years, she drove five volunteers to the hospital one day every week.[25]

Headquarters Purchase

One of the most exciting and far-sighted events of the 1950s was the purchase of a property to serve as the national headquarters of American Gold Star Mothers, Inc. Such a step would have been financially impossible in previous decades, but the post-war growth of the organization had contributed to a bright future and financial stability previously unknown to the group. For many years, the organization had worked out of donated spaces and tiny rented offices. Now, more space was desperately needed due to membership increases and the resulting administrative burden. A decision was made to move the publication office of *The Gold Star Mother* from California to Washington, D.C.

National president Elise C. Nielsen was the impetus behind the purchase. She began to look at available properties in Washington, D.C., early in 1954 after polling the national executive board for approval. One of the first five properties she viewed seemed well matched to the organization's needs: [Fig. 8-9]

"The one house I thought would be practical is located four or five blocks from DuPont Circle, one block from Connecticut Avenue. It is referred to as a Town House, one of a row. This would be an advantage as there is no lawn or shrubbery that would require maintenance and heating would be at a minimum as it is not isolated or exposed. It is an old house, 7 rooms, two baths with another room and toilet in rear at ground level which is part of the basement. Oil heat. With a little cleaning and decorating, it could be used 'as is' and we can have possession on settlement. Property is owned by the Episcopal Church and their Clergyman is living there now.

"Price asked was $26,500, reduced to $25,000. Cash required $7,500, balance of $17,500 in monthly payments of $152, which includes interest, payment on principal, and prorated taxes. The Church pays no taxes and maybe we shouldn't either. They amount to about $250 per year. Maintenance, over and above monthly payment, would be the fuel bill of about $200.00 per year, electric light, and fire and liability insurance."[26]

Mrs. Nielsen offered to make the down payment on the property as a gift to the organization:

"As I stated to the Board, I was willing to make the down payment and sign a note for the balance with the understanding, of course, that the Organization would assume this obligation… We will have to have $1,500 to accompany the signed contract and balance of $6,000 cash. If the Finance Committee feels they can advance the $1,500, well and good. If not, and the property sounds good to you, I will advance the entire amount of $7,500 cash needed. By the way, Grace [McClellan, national treasurer] reports a balance of $14,000 on hand with all bills paid to date. If, in a few years, we can afford something better and larger, we can always sell this or turn it in. Personally, I am willing to take the chance."[27]

The decision to move forward with the purchase was not unanimous. Ruth Singer expressed concerns about the propriety of the national executive board making such a momentous decision rather than bringing it before a national convention for a vote by the membership, stating "So important a change should be discussed by our members at the National Convention. I do not feel that 25 members should make any final decision for 20,000 or more members."[28]

Mrs. Nielsen forwarded Mrs. Singer's letter to the finance committee with a note attached:

"We are paying $1,800 rent [$150 per month for a small apartment that served as a national office] which would more than pay interest and maintenance on a house… Therefore it is up to the Finance Committee and that is why I polled the Board, asking for their consent to leave the decision with the Finance Committee. Score: Yes—13; No—1; Doubtful—1."[29]

Careful to consider all aspects of the potential purchase, Mrs. Nielsen reminded the board that there would be some additional initial expenses associated with the property if purchased:

"If the deal goes through, there will be an additional expense at this time of necessary cleaning and decorating, insurance policies for fire and liability, title guarantee policy, and a few other incidentals, totaling together about $700—an expense we would not have next year."[30]

With permission from more than two thirds of the board to go ahead, an offer was made for the property in the name of American Gold Star Mothers, Inc. On March 20, 1954 their offer was accepted. Thirty days later, the townhouse located at 2128 Leroy Place NW, Washington, D.C., became the national headquarters of American Gold Star Mothers, Inc. This same property still serves as the national AGSM headquarters today.

Sharing HQ With The Membership

As soon as the mothers took possession of the property, they began working diligently to make it comfortable and practical. As national custodian of records, Maude Fry moved into the building as the on-site representative, hostess, and building manager—a job that soon morphed into decorator, painter, repair person, cook, and gardener, much to Maude's delight.

She began to write a column for *The Gold Star Mother* newsletter called "Coffee Time" but often referred to as the "Headquarters' Party-line." In a warm, personal, and chatty manner, Maude told readers of the day-to-day activities at the new headquarters, the visitors who dropped by, the gatherings that were held, and other interesting bits of information. Members from distant states who would never have an opportunity to visit the headquarters soon felt that they knew the headquarters and its environs as well as they did their own homes and neighborhoods:

June 1955: "Guess what? New neighbors! Our good friends, the American War Mothers. They bought at 2124 Leroy for their national headquarters."

September 1955: "Did you know we have a kitten in Headquarters? I named her Dirty Face. Loves to help me type."

October 1955: "My kitten ran away. No one to help me type and I need help too… My good friend… gave the office… a Parker 51 desk set. So if I can't type very well, I should be able to write with such a nice pen.

"We have a new cover for our daybed, which is in the office. Now, doesn't that sound as if I am a 'little lazy,' but I am not really. Grace McClellan gave the

money to buy the cover… and I just found the time to buy it."

Maude continued the "Coffee Time" column through May 1956 when it was seamlessly taken over by her successor as custodian of records and HQ hostess, Harriet Massincupp:

September 1956: "Last Sunday afternoon one of my longtime friends and I explored the streets just west of Headquarters. Almost hidden in beautiful gardens with huge trees shading them, are the prettiest, coolest-looking houses and we just know the most interesting people must live in them. We saw the embassies of Ecuador, Iceland and Finland—a part of Washington I had never seen before. On Leroy Place, we have the Libyan Chancery directly across the street, the Greek Military Mission right next door, the Brazilian Chancery a few doors up the street and the Columbian and Italian down towards Connecticut Avenue. Have two families from India on this street, the women wearing the most beautiful and cool-looking saris."

October 1956: "Forgot to mention that my little nine-year-old granddaughter has signed the guest book several times. She lives in Rockville, Maryland, and comes down frequently so next time I'll be sure to hide the guest book or there will be a Marilyn Masincupp on every page.

"300 [guests were] entertained at Headquarters following Gold Star Mother ceremonies on Gold Star Mothers Day."

March 1957: "[We] braved the cold weather here in Washington, but a water pipe that went out to the front froze and broke… Leroy Place hasn't changed much since last May—still as busy as ever except on Saturday and Sunday when the Embassies' offices are closed. I am trying to locate 'Dirty Face,' she would be a big cat by now, but haven't seen her."

April 1957: "Had a nice visit and I gave her a cup of coffee with some of Maude Fry's famous chocolate cookies. Maude made the dough but I baked them—so I CAN make cookies!"

November 1957: "I have been mailing so many of the new Constitution and By-laws! The other day I really had more than I could manage at one time and as I went past the Columbian Embassy, the liveried chauffeur decided I had too many packages so he took over some of them and walked me down to the Post Office. Pennsylvania's large package really got mailed in style!"

Furnishing HQ

As Elsie Nielsen reminded the board when purchasing the headquarters building, "we are starting from scratch with no furniture, except a few pieces in the apartment." But that empty feeling didn't last long. Chapters, departments, and individuals soon began generously donating furniture, dishware, linens, artwork, and other items to the new building. The donations were gratefully acknowledged in the "Coffee Time" column, first by Maude Fry, then by Harriet Massincupp:

October 1955: "Mrs. Sidney Smith, a member of the Cedar Rapids, Iowa chapter… brought a beautiful 4-yard linen tablecloth for Headquarters. It was a cloth given to Mrs. Smith to be a present to her son when he was married. The son did not return and so Mrs. Smith gave us the cloth, feeling he would want her to."

June 1956: "Spring is really here in Washington, wisteria blooming on the house at the corner and headquarters looks so very nice with the lovely new drapes given by the Department of New York and the very beautifully landscaped yard given by the Department of Illinois.It looks so beautiful and green and is growing beautifully."

February 1957: "We had the most wonderful surprise last week. Caton Chapter, Catonsville, Maryland must be mind readers because they sent us 24 place settings of the prettiest dishes and now the Board and their guests can actually have matching dishes and SAUCERS to put under the cups. One of the Board members, I won't tell you which one from New England, actually forgot she had a saucer at one of our swank restaurants here and set her cup back on the table. Now we can have enough of everything for everyone so the Board won't acquire any bad habits, thanks to the Caton Chapter."

In January 1958, the Hollywood, California chapter donated a beautiful crystal chandelier to be installed at headquarters. It was installed in the national executive board's meeting room but that room required some work before it was ready to host the new chandelier:

"Before placing the chandelier, the ceiling was freshly painted white, woodwork painted off-white, new taupe venetian blinds installed and a plain textured taupe paper hung. The meeting room for the National Executive Board really has a 'new look' now."[31]

However, not all their decorating attempts went quite so smoothly:

"Philadelphia Chapter presented the National President with a check… in November so they will be pleased to know that the second and third floor halls have been papered with a light, geometric-figured paper and the dark woodwork has been painted an off-white shade. It looks just beautiful. While we were papering, it was decided to paper the ceiling in the second floor bedroom (over the old paper) and about three nights later—what a noise about four o'clock in the morning! The new paper had pulled the old paper down with it and big streamers came down, one after the other. It has all been taken care of again and looks just fine now, but it was one big mess."[32]

Gifts from the membership continued to arrive at 2128 Leroy Place NW. Every item, large and small, and every donation was mentioned in the "Coffee Time" column:

February 1958: "We have two beautiful oil paintings in the meeting room painted and given by two members of the Seibold Chapter, Washington, D.C., Johanna Trondson and Louise Tansing, in memory of their sons, and are so inscribed on the backs of the pictures."

October 1958: "Alice L. Daggers, a World War One mother and member of Broome County Chapter [New York], sent a handmade novelty quilt to Headquarters. It is made in the wedding ring design, and in the center of each design is an embroidered motif. There are 1,768 pieces in the quilt. The letter she sent with the quilt speaks of her love for the Gold Star Mothers."

August 1959: "A beautiful gold star quilt was presented as a gift by the Department of Indiana in June 1959 at the Dallas convention. Each Indiana chapter shared in the expense. Many long hours were spent by the committee appointed in purchasing materials, designing, sewing, embroidering and quilting this unusual Gold Star quilt."

Whenever possible, the mothers at headquarters did the necessary repair work themselves:

August 1959: "Our new Custodian of Records, Bernice Shepard, has been working like a beaver making some of our furniture and draperies look like new ones. She painted the lower kitchen furniture and refinished two dressers in the dormitory bedroom. Washed and pressed the drapes in the meeting room and the president's suite, 'a labor of love' she told me, but I know it took a lot of energy and strength to do these.

"We also bought covering for the first floor kitchen, and your national president and custodian of records laid it. You should have seen us maneuvering the refrigerator around that little space, but we made it and it looks very nice. We saved quite a little expense by doing it ourselves."

All the mothers took pride in the new headquarters and it didn't take much for a social gathering to turn into a housekeeping event. According to Elsie Neilsen, even the gold star dads were not immune to the need to shine and polish the new building:

"Several of the national officers stopped over in Washington en route home from the convention and inspected the new national headquarters. All were most enthusiastic, but being homemakers primarily, with pride in their surroundings, they found several things that needed attention. For instance, Grace McClellan, our revered national treasurer, insisted that the marble around the fireplace was not clean and we could not convince her to the contrary. It happens to be white marble with a mottled effect and we told her it was the natural color. But closer inspection proved she was right and Maude Jones and Laura Cosper accepted the challenge. They had put in long hours at the convention, but you should have seen them down on their hands and knees scouring and polishing that hearth until even Grace was satisfied.

"And we had guests for luncheon. Gertrude Williams, Department President of Michigan, and her good husband, dropped in on their way home to Kalamazoo, Michigan, and they were invited to break bread with us. As we sat around the table, someone, unidentified, called attention to the lovely crystal chandelier. Immediately all eyes were lifted to the ceiling and again those good housekeepers yearned for soap and water. But it's an old house with eleven and a half foot ceilings and the Finance Committee questioned the advisability of allowing any mother to climb to that dizzy height and the possibility of filing a claim on our new liability insurance.

"No one seems to be very clear on what happened next except that Daddy Williams mounted the stepladder and made each crystal sparkle until all those meticulous housekeepers were satisfied. What would we do without our gold star dads?"[33]

The Furnace Fund

If there was one problem with the new headquarters building, it was the furnace. From the beginning, the mothers realized that the furnace was living on borrowed time: "the old furnace is chugging away, but it is very old and very temperamental so it won't be long before it really gives up."[34] The furnace became the particular bane of Harriet Massincup who claimed at the 1957 convention that "it is the oldest one in Washington. We use water in the boiler and it has to be put in every night. You have to tend it like a baby." Now and then the furnace would go out in cold weather, allowing pipes to freeze and break, which resulted in a flooded basement. The only up-side to these events was that HQ's basement often had the "cleanest floor" in Washington.[35]

Donations of money soon began to come to headquarters identified specifically for the furnace fund. Each donation was duly and appreciatively noted in the "Coffee Time" columns. At the 1957 convention, national president Ruth Singer reported a total of $465 in the furnace fund, still less than half the cost of a replacement.

Paying Back the HQ Loan

At the September 1955 board meeting, the national executive board authorized the repayment of the $6,000 advanced in 1954 by Elsie Nielson for the purchase of the national headquarters building. The board stated that "the organization is deeply grateful to Mrs. Nielsen for having made available a sum which enabled us to acquire our present headquarters."[36]

Conventions

Thirteenth National Convention—1950
Detroit, Michigan
The thirteenth AGSM national convention, notably also the first national convention of the new decade, was held in Detroit, Michigan, at the Book-Cadillac Hotel in June 1950. Edgar A. Guest, poet, writer, radio star, and Poet Laureate of Michigan (and a close personal friend of Eleanor Boyd), served as toastmaster for the main banquet, alternately charming and entertaining the attendees with stories, poems, and jokes.

Several amendments to the by-laws concerning the Memorial National Home were adopted by unanimous consent of the delegation. Only one proposed resolution was not approved by the membership. That resolution would have changed the requirement for AGSM membership from "natural mother" to "natural mothers or mothers established by law, or step-mothers, having assumed full responsibility of son or daughter since childhood."[37]

The national custodian of records reported that in the twelve months since the last convention, 2,169 new memberships had been approved and fifty-three charters had been granted to form new chapters. Mrs. Boyd reported that despite unexpected legal fees the organization was in fine financial form.

Eleanor Boyd was re-elected national president for her fourth term.

Fourteenth National Convention—1951
Washington, D.C.

The nation's capital was the site of the fourteenth national convention held at the Statler Hotel over the Memorial Day weekend from May 29 to June 3, 1951. Newspapers reported that more than a thousand delegates, members and visitors took part in the event. One special guest was a much-loved representative of the organization's early years, George Seibold, husband of founder Grace Seibold.

In addition to the scheduled banquets and meetings, the extended length of the convention allowed delegates to participate in a variety of scheduled events:

- A Senate and House of Representatives tour
- Visit Mt. Vernon and participate in a memorial ceremony at the tomb of George Washington
- A National Cathedral tour
- Attend Memorial Day services at Arlington National Cemetery
- Attend a reception for senators, congressmen and other distinguished guests
- Take an historic tour of Washington, D.C.
- Attend a national memorial service for organization founder, Grace Darling Seibold

A resolution approved at the convention called for the flag of the United Nations to be used and displayed only during official functions of the UN. Convention delegates disapproved strongly with the display of the UN flag on an equal basis with the flag of the United States. Eleanor Boyd explained the reasoning behind the resolution, explaining "We are perfectly willing that the United Nations flag fly over the United Nations building and on United Nations Day. But we feel that over our public buildings only the United States flag should fly."[38]

An amendment to recognize stepmothers and adoptive mothers as eligible for membership in AGSM "lost heavily" in the voting by delegates. The loss meant that the policy continued of only birth mothers being eligible for membership. Delegates also mandated that AGSM would publish an official publication in the interest of the organization and its members, and that publication would be *The Gold Star Mother*.

The *New York Times'* coverage of the convention reported on June 6 that the "Gold Star Mothers Oppose Deferments":

"More than 1,000 delegates... voted unanimously today against any educational or other special deferments under the draft or universal military training ... 'Certainly we need scientists,' said Mrs. Eleanor D. Boyd of Long Beach, California, president, as she presented the resolution. 'But they can lead in the uniform of our country and not be exempted.'"[39]

Not immune to the Red scare gripping the nation, whipped to a frenzy by Senator Joe McCarthy, one controversial aspect of the convention was the requirement that every convention participant sign a loyalty oath. A *Chicago Tribune* article about the loyalty oaths quoted Mrs. Boyd's concerns about "subversives" within the organization:

"Delegates to the national convention of American Gold Star Mothers are being required for the first time to sign a pledge of loyalty to the government. Mrs. Eleanor D. Boyd... said at a news conference the pledge is being invoked 'in an effort to combat subversive influences which have tried to get control.'

"'You might think an organization of mothers who lost their sons in war would be the last to succumb to the communistic influences, but that is not necessarily so," Mrs. Boyd said. 'The line of subversive attack is to say, "You poor dear, you sacrificed your son and what did your government do for you?" That argument is bound to find some acceptance.'

"Mrs. Boyd said every delegate, as she registers, swears to support and defend the Constitution and also swears she does not advocate nor does she belong to a political group that advocates the overthrow of the government by violence."[40]

The *New York Times* also covered the story:

"Gold Star Mothers, at the rate of 100 an hour, signed today a pledge of loyalty to the United States Government as part of the registration for their fourteenth annual convention held here the rest of this week... Eleanor D. Boyd ... said that this action, taken for the first time this year, was in keeping with a resolution adopted earlier this week by the executive board. More than 1,500 delegates, alternates and Gold Star Dads... signed pledges at the registration table."[41]

The national chaplain reported that 102 gold star mothers and two associate members, gold star fathers, had died since the last convention.[42]

Eleanor Boyd was again elected national president, her fifth term in that office.

Fifteenth National Convention—1952
Long Beach, CA

The fifteenth AGSM national convention was held in Long Beach, California, which had also been the site of the 1947 convention. The event was held at the Long Beach Municipal Auditorium, the only building in Long Beach capable of housing the more than 2,000 participants representing thirty-three states. The theme of the convention was "Fiesta!" to celebrate California's historical roots.

California Governor Goodwin Knight gave the welcoming address. One of the entertainers at the convention was Marion Darlington, a concert bird singer whose unique repertoire of bird calls was often utilized by the movie industry. Miss Darlington had entertained at the 1947 convention as well.[43]

In addition to the business, entertainment and memorial events planned for the convention, the mothers were offered tours as well. One was a two-hour bus ride to Toyon Ranch, the Memorial National Home Foundation property in Ojai, where the mothers would have an opportunity to tour the existing Manor House and property to get an idea of what was planned for the Memorial Home. Before they got there, they were treated to an experience that only the television and movie center of the nation could have offered:

"Enroute to Ojai, the Mothers were guests of the nationally broadcast and locally televised popular program 'Queen for a Day!' They enjoyed it all the more when one of their number, Mrs. Laura Newby, of Wichita, Kansas ... was chosen 'Queen for a Day.' When asked what she wanted as a reward for winning the honor, Mrs. Newby asked for a big Gold Star Flag for her Chapter and a matching American flag and also 12 American flags for the Boy Scouts in Wichita. They will get them."[44]

In her address to the convention, national president Eleanor D. Boyd spoke of the work she saw before the membership, which now consisted largely of World War II mothers:

"The challenge has come to the World War II Mothers... [of] protecting the work of the World War I Mothers, progressing with the needs following World War II, and extending the hand of fellowship to the Korean conflict Mothers whose sons invested their lives in Korea."[45]

Those challenges, however, would not be met under the leadership of Eleanor Boyd:

"After Mrs. Eleanor D. Boyd, who has headed the organization for the last five years, declined to let her name be submitted for re-election, the delegates chose Mrs. Elsie C. Nielsen of Chicago as the 1952–1953 President."[46]

Sixteenth National Convention—1953
Chicago, Illinois

On the first day of their sixteenth national convention, held at the Sherman Hotel in Chicago, the gold star mothers called unanimously for "an honorable and just peace" in Korea. More than 1,200 delegates, members and guests attended the convention.

One reporter spoke with gold star mothers who had children currently serving in the military:

"Twelve hundred women are saying minute-by-minute prayers in the Hotel Sherman that Korean peace will come within the next two days.

"Hoping for an armistice in Korea, the delegates earlier passed a resolution asking that it be 'an honorable and just peace.'

"Two Gold Star Mothers, both of whom still have sons in service, clarified their stand further.

"'Even with the sacrifice we have already made, we don't want a half-peace,' said Mrs. Joseph J. Riddle. 'Our sons did not die for something temporary—or unjust.'

"Mrs. Riddle had three sons in service during World War II. Her second eldest was killed in New Guinea in 1942. A second son is now stationed with the Navy air corps in North Africa and her youngest son is registered for the draft.

"Mrs. J. J. Peddle... has sent five sons to service, with her youngest leaving for the Army on June 15. Her oldest, an infantry lieutenant, was killed June 15, 1944. Another son is now in Korea.

"'I have lived with war for the last 10 years,' Mrs.

Fig. 8-10: Gold star mothers attended the unveiling and dedication of the statue "Mother's Joy" at Forest Lawn Memorial Park in Burbank, California on Mother's Day 1955 (May 8). The statue was sculpted by Dante Zoi. Past national president Mae Cushman unveiled the statue. *(AGSM Collection)*

Peddle said. 'But unless it means a just and honorable peace, I am determined not to give up.'

"Like the other delegates, Mrs. Riddle and Mrs. Peddle said they would 'sink to their knees' if peace in Korea could be announced at this Gold Star Mothers convention.

"'It would be like a direct answer to our prayers,' said Mrs. Riddle. 'It would be like the word was sent to us.'"[47]

Among the decisions approved by the attendees was one to "organize the club's 500 chapters into a system of departments having the same boundaries as states."[48] This decision would have significant influence upon the organization as the membership continued to grow. Departments had been part of the organizational hierarchy since the late 1940s but their establishment changed from a suggestion to a requirement with this resolution.

Elsie C. Nielsen was re-elected national president.

Seventeenth National Convention—1954
Boston, Massachusetts

The seventeenth national convention was held in Boston, Massachusetts. Headquarters for the convention was the Sheraton Plaza Hotel. Attendees were delighted to find that entertainer Jimmy Durante was also staying at the hotel and he graciously posed for photographs with many of the mothers.

Taking action on the resolution approved at the prior convention, the organization had been busy forming itself into departments by states. In the past year, twenty-seven departments had been formed and forty-three new chapters had been chartered.[49] The national chaplain reported that in the year since the last convention 314 mothers and 230 fathers had died.

Among the resolutions passed at the Boston convention was a protest against sending arms to any country that might send them to Russia or Red China;

a requirement that one must serve as a chapter president before becoming a department president; and a directive that department conventions must be held at least three months prior to a national convention.[50] Elsie C. Neilsen was elected national president for a third term.

Eighteenth National Convention—1955
Miami Beach, Florida

The eighteenth national convention was held in Miami Beach, Florida at the Hotel di Lido. In keeping with the tropical location, a load of coconuts was delivered to the hotel lobby each day to be taken as souvenirs by the attendees. The theme for the convention was Forward with Faith, Confidence and Unity.

Much of the discussion period was devoted to detailed questions about the appropriate interpretation of rituals, reporting requirements for treasurers, how to fill out organizational forms and protocols for wearing the uniform. Ruth Singer and Maude Fry responded to the questions:

"Jewelry: When we carry the flag we do not wear earrings or bracelets or a necklace; you must not carry a handbag on your arm or any kind of a purse. And we only wear our capes outdoors... When we are sitting in our position, we do not cross our legs, we must keep them on the floor.

"AGSM Hats: If a Mother conducts herself with dignity and reverence while she is wearing that cap, I don't think we should lay down any specific rules as to where it should be worn... If you wear ... the American Gold Star mother hat, do not tilt it; wear it straight. Wear it straight, not with a lot of bobby pins in it; wear it straight.

"[One national officer reported receiving] a 10 page letter from a Chapter where they were complaining that the color guards were going to a memorial service ... and wore their caps in the automobile in which they were being transported to the services; and some of the members of that chapter were criticizing the color guards very severely for that. They said they should have kept them out of sight or something until they got there. I think you know that at a convention some years ago some mothers wore their caps in night clubs, etc. So I just always say that if a mother conducts herself with dignity and reverence while wearing that cap, then it is all right.

"Opening the Bible at meetings: I notice that our National Chaplain opens the Bible to start the meeting with one hand. In our Chapter we open it very slowly and close it the same way, but with both hands. Is that optional? Elsie Nielsen responded: I should think it is."[51]

National officers provided delegates with a demonstration of how to drape the charter appropriately in the event of a death among the membership.

A total of 645 attendees were registered by convention officials: 481 delegates; 49 alternates; 47 members; 24 guests; and 44 associate members (dads).[52] It was noted that two-thirds of the organization's 535 chapters were located east of the Mississippi River and three-fourths of the balance were concentrated along the Pacific Coast or adjacent to it.[53] Since the decision at the 1953 convention to organize states into departments, the total number of departments had grown from eight to thirty.

The national treasurer reported that there were now 541 chapters, 20 of which were new since the last convention. In the last year, there had been 1,102 new applications for membership and 870 new members admitted. Transfers had been approved for 97 members. The total membership was 19,215 gold star mothers.[54]

To spotlight the tenth anniversary of the United Nations, Lt. Colonel Frank Montgomery Dunbaugh, Ret., Florida Chairman of the American Association of the United Nations, told the mothers, "You hold the key. You can let the world know that you, the American Gold Star Mothers, are heart and soul in favor of our country solving our problems with other nations with peaceful talks around a table instead of mowing each other down with bombs."[55]

Twenty resolutions were adopted by the delegates. The first was "we support our President [Dwight D. Eisenhower] and government in their efforts to achieve the aims of the United Nations." Other resolutions included action relating to hospital volunteer representatives; a petition to Congress for a pilgrimage of gold star mothers to the overseas military cemeteries of WWII and Korea; and a request to Congress to pass a current House of Representatives bill (H.R. 619) to authorize a "Pray for Peace" stamp.

Following the Florida convention, attendees had an opportunity to join a weekend cruise to Havana, Cuba. In July, Maude Fry wrote an article about the trip titled "A Tour of Havana with Chino" for *The Gold Star Mother*:

"Friday afternoon saw a delegation of one hundred and eighty mothers and dads, and not to forget the children, leave beautiful Miami Beach, Florida for a cruise to Havana, Cuba. After the hustle and bustle of embarking on the S.S. Florida, we settled down to enjoy with happy anticipation the next four days…

"Here could be heard the many noises of busy city life, the hum of motors, the husky honk of the auto horns, the shrill whistle of the steamers in the harbor, the voices of the newsboys and fragments of music strummed on guitars. Most every time the car stopped the serenaders were there… Chino introduced us to a new treat in refreshments: cocoanut ice cream frozen in the half shell. All I can say is 'Delightful and refreshing.'"[56]

Maude also mentioned that part of their tour of old Cuba included a cockfight, which was a first for most of the travelers.

Ruth Singer was elected national president.

Nineteenth National Convention—1956
Tulsa, Oklahoma

The Mayo Hotel in Tulsa, Oklahoma, was the site of the nineteenth AGSM national convention. [Fig. 8-11]

Ruth Singer, national president, highlighted organizational accomplishments during the past year for the 490 conference attendees, starting with the announcement, "I am Ruth K. Singer and I am president of 536 Chapters!"[57] She advised the audience that at least 125 chapters were represented at the convention, and the organization now had nearly 20,000 members. Eleven new chapters had been added in the past year in addition to three new departments. The California, Nevada, and Arizona Department was the largest with 60 chapters; the New York Department and the Pennsylvania Department were next in line with 52 chapters in each. New report forms had been developed so chapters could report more quickly and accurately to the department level.[58]

President Singer commented on the growth of the organization and its response to changes made by other patriotic organizations:

"We should never lose sight of the fact that our organization was founded by World War I mothers. Let us not try to keep changing it to be like other veteran organizations. We are an organization of all gold star mothers and dads; an organization that is non-political, but one that is respected by every other organization. We are a patriotic organization, and we should stand for God and Country, for our American gold star mothers, and for the hospitalized veterans and their families who cannot serve themselves."[59]

An unexpected highlight of the convention was the arrival of a stranger dressed in full Native American tribal regalia who offered a traditional blessing to the convention attendees:

"I am Chief Shunatonam, an Otto Indian… my father was Chief of the Ottos. Being the eldest son in our family, when he passed away quite a few years ago, I inherited the title. Through this authority it gives me great pleasure to cordially welcome … all these lovely mothers to Oklahoma, the land of the Red Man… And before I leave, to all these wonderful gracious Mothers: 'May the Great Spirit send down His choicest gifts to you. May the Sun Father and the Moon Mother shed their softest beams on you. May the Four Winds of Heaven blow gently on you and all with whom you share your hearts and your wigwams.'"[60]

Drama unfolded as nominations were made for the position of national president. Prior to the convention, a group of members had asked Ruth Singer to run for a second term. She had initially agreed but, having given it further thought, she declined the nomination when her name was called:

"Ruth Singer: Nominations are now open from the floor. My name has been brought in for National President. At the time, I did say I would accept. I have had such a wonderful year, and you have all been wonderful, but I must say I decline.

"Voices from attendees: No, no, no.

"Marie Hula: I move that we draft our President, Ruth K. Singer of California, as your National President nominee.

"Mrs. Helsing: May I second that motion?

"Ruth Singer: I still decline. I am sorry."

The delegates continued to pressure Mrs. Singer to accept the nomination. She repeatedly stated that she had made the decision to not run again for national president. Finally, she agreed to accept the nomination, stating that she didn't know if she would be elected, but that she would allow her name to be put forward. She was elected national president for a second term by a margin of more than 150 votes. Following the voting she spoke of her mixed pride and chagrin at the way the voting had gone:

"I don't know whether I need congratulations or condolences for your having elected me as your president. I wanted to quit while I was ahead, but I do thank you from the bottom of my heart for your confidence in me, for your loyalty and your cooperation, for your

Fig. 8-11: Banquet guests at the 1956 national convention at the Mayo Hotel in Tulsa, Oklahoma. *(AGSM Collection)*

love and your understanding and your prayers. That is the only reason I reconsidered and permitted my name to be brought up from the floor again. Still, I did want to retire. I think one year is enough. I think if you have a good year and you have done everything you can, you should pass it along."[61]

National treasurer Grace McClellan reported that the net value of the AGSM treasury was $58,265.02 as of May 1956. Her report initiated an open discussion about whether national officers received compensation and/or expense reimbursements, and if so, how much.

Once again, as in past conventions, attendees expressed concerns about proprieties when participating in chapter meetings or representing the organization in public:

"Earrings: The only rules we have about wearing jewelry when presenting Colors apply to our National Color Guards and they do not wear earrings when they are presenting our Colors... As to wearing earrings when not presenting colors, I said I thought some of our Mothers would catch cold if they didn't have earrings on. [There is] no national ruling—departments can do differently if they want to.

"Proper way to carry flags: We never tip our [American] flag. It is always carried straight. We dip our [gold star] banner when the Pledge of Allegiance is being said or sung and if a prayer is being offered but we never dip the American flag. It is always carried upright."[62]

And a correction was offered when asked about appropriate situations in which to wear the traditional white AGSM 'uniform' including the gold-lined cape and garrison cap: "We do not say uniform; we do not have a uniform."

Birch Mayo, another member of the hotel management, endeared himself to the mothers and earned a round of applause when he mentioned the beauty aid kits given out to attendees by the Mayo Hotel:

"I told them [mothers planning the convention] that I didn't think they needed them themselves, but if they could use them, they are welcome to them."[63]

Twentieth National Convention—1957
Cleveland, Ohio

The twentieth national convention was held in Cleveland, Ohio at the Hotel Cleveland. A total of 566 convention attendees were registered. A message from President Eisenhower was read during the opening business of the convention:

"Please give my greetings to the American Gold Star Mothers as they assemble for their Annual National Convention. Joined in the memory of sacrifice, and inspired by solemn pride, the Mothers who wear the Gold Star know the price of freedom. With God's help, let us continue our efforts to establish a just and enduring peace that will preserve our families from the consequences of war... I send best wishes for a memorable convention."[64]

Among the scheduled events for the mothers was a fashion show and luncheon sponsored by Higbee's Department Stores. As reported in the newsletter, "The luncheon and style show at Higbee's auditorium gave us all the last word on the Fall styles—all for slim people, however."[65]

Ralph Stone, Chief Benefits Director, U.S. Veterans Administration, spoke on the Survivor Benefits Act but also had kind words for the gold star mothers themselves:

"A couple of days from now you will be helping this great city of Cleveland celebrate Independence Day. I can't think of any delegation whose presence at such an occasion will be more appropriate. As American gold star mothers, you have a deeper concern with independence, and with freedom, than does the average citizen of America. For you have given your greatest possession, your children, that this nation might retain independence and freedom. More than most, you know freedom's cost.

"You are living reminders, if we need reminders, that freedom does not come easily and that the struggle for freedom is endless. The Fourth of July is not a holiday with echoes from the past alone. It commemorates the living, dynamic concepts of freedom and independence. By your great sacrifices, you have forever enriched those American traditions... I believe I can speak for all Americans, too, when I say that no group is more worthy of the nation's admiration and its deep gratitude... America is as great as she is because she always has been blessed with great-hearted women like yourselves, women of unconquerable valor."[66]

Among the resolutions adopted at the convention was one presented by the Department of Connecticut proposing that the current system of death notification in the Armed Forces (by telegram sent by a commanding officer) be changed so the Chaplain Corps had responsibility for those notifications.

Gladys Grubb, president of Monogalia Chapter in Morgantown, West Virginia, and a convention delegate, died following the first day's meeting. Her husband and several family members were with her at the hotel when she died. Ruth Singer made the announcement to convention attendees:

"I have very sad news and I knew it before we started this afternoon, but mothers, please, I implore you, I know the one of whom I speak would have wanted us to carry on the way we did. She was told not to come to this convention but she wanted to. She said if there wasn't anything else she did in this life, she wanted to attend a national convention, this national convention. God willed it that she did attend this convention and so when we close the meeting with prayer, please feel that it was God's will."

During an open session, a question was raised about the proper way to arrange and display the AGSM gold star pin, the government's next-of-kin gold star pin and other jewelry or adornments that a mother might be wearing:

"Usually we wear our corsages on the right side because we do not wear anything above our gold star pin. We always wear the gold star pin on the left side, right near our heart. We usually wear our official gold star pin above the government pin. We are not telling you that you have to do that but that is the way we wear it because the government pin is issued to mothers, fathers, sisters and brothers, step-fathers, step-mother... But the gold star pin, the organization pin, is the official pin showing that you are a member of our organization, the natural mother, as no one can wear that or buy it but a member of our organization."

Maude Fry of Grand Rapids, Michigan, was elected national president.

Twenty-first National Convention—1958
Denver, Colorado

Six-hundred and seven registered attendees took part in the national convention held at the Shirley-Savoy Hotel in Denver, Colorado. It was noted in the opening comments that AGSM currently had "around 560 chapters." Since the last convention, three chapters had relinquished their charters voluntarily and most of their members had joined other chapters. Five new chapters had been added and two more were "in the making." The national treasurer reported total assets of $52,854.31 as of May 1958.

A representative of Denver's mayor welcomed the group to the "climate capital of the nation" and tendered the mayor's apologies for not being able to appear as planned—he was out of the capital helping deal with a major influx of locusts that was destroying the state's agricultural crops. The mothers toured the Rocky Mountains and points of historic interest and were entertained by American Boy Scout Troop #22, also known as the Minnequea Indian Dancers, from Pueblo, Colorado. Following a daytime tour of the Red Rocks Amphitheatre, more than 200 delegates returned that night for a fried-chicken box dinner and an evening concert by Lawrence Welk and his orchestra.

National president Maude Fry read a telegram from President Eisenhower during the convention's opening ceremonies:

"Your heartfelt knowledge of the price of war is a

constant reminder of the cost of freedom. I know that all of you will do everything possible to help our beloved Nation in the noble work of building a world of peace and justice."

The issue of gold star dads vs. gold star fathers was discussed following a question from a delegate:

"In the event that the natural father is still living, would a fourth husband (laughter) of the gold star mother be considered a gold star dad and honored as such when deceased?

"Ruth Singer: The eligibility for a 'dad' is that he is the husband of the member... A mother may be married as many times as she can get a husband. (Laughter) The present husband with whom she is living and to whom she is married is considered the gold star dad.

"Voices: No.

"Singer: We did not say he was the gold star 'father.' We said he is a gold star 'dad.' As far as honoring him, he goes to the meetings—social meetings... As far as honoring him when he is deceased, if the Mother belongs to your chapter and you would like to honor him in any way, that is up to the chapter. (Applause)

"The question was whether this father could be honored as the gold star 'dad' when the father of the boy is still living. If the mother has remarried, he is the 'gold star dad.' The fathers do not belong to our organization unless they are living with the mothers who are members of our chapters.

"Maude Fry: I am sure that every chapter, every mother, would give honor to a gold star father and also respect the husband of a gold star mother."

An appeal by past national president Ruth Singer on behalf of the organization's remaining World War I members was met with applause from the delegates:

"Especially may I ask you, please take care of your World War I mothers. Many of them do not know a per capita tax from a screwdriver. The poor dears get confused and upset when someone calls them and says, 'We must have your dues.' Now I doubt if there is a chapter from Cape Cod to San Francisco or from the top of the United States to Florida which is going to feel that difference of one dollar and seventy-five cents or two dollars. If you have those World War I gold star mothers, please keep them as long as they live.

In Maude Fry's report on her year in office, she spoke to the delegates about the future of AGSM:

"All too often it is said, 'We are a dying organization.' Can you really feel that is true? We have a large potential eligible membership. We have the respect of every veteran and patriotic organization. Don't let anyone tell you we are a dying organization. As long as YOU honor your son or daughter by carrying out the principles for which this organization was founded thirty years ago this June, we will always have an organization which is 'alive,' doing for others and respected by all. We pray that there will never be more mothers made eligible through wars for membership in American Gold Star Mothers, Inc., but we all pray that as long as we live we shall have an active, respected organization."

Mabel Troy of New Jersey was elected as the next national president.

Twenty-second National Convention—1959
Dallas, Texas

Dallas' Baker Hotel was the site of the twenty-second national convention held June 26–July 1, 1959. The national custodian of records reported that, in the twelve months since the prior convention, 561 membership applications had been received, 8 charters for new chapters had been requested, and 77 requests for transfers had been processed.[68]

As part of the festivities, attendees were invited to "a Patio Party at the Dude Ranch of Dr. and Mrs. Frank Austin." Entertainment included a rifle and pistol shooting demonstration by "internationally known" Joan Ross and her seven-year-old son. The two were also Australian bullwhip experts and the show they put on was reported as "spectacular."[69]

Among the formal business accomplished at the convention, the board went on record to protest the manufacture of official United States flags by Japan or any other foreign country.

Following a discussion about establishing life memberships rather than yearly dues, it was stated that AGSM did not have and would not establish a life membership alternative for yearly dues. It was advised however that chapters could assume the cost of annual dues for their World War I mothers if so desired. After additional discussion, it was voted that annual dues would not be required for World War I mothers who were members as of 1960.

Attendees were also advised that legislative chairperson Mary Kelly had again presented an application to Congress to grant AGSM a Congressional charter.

A variety of awards were distributed to attendees. There was recognition of a three-star mother from

Rhode Island and eight two-star mothers. The oldest mother, eighty-six, was recognized, as was the youngest mother, forty-six. Recognition was given to:

- The mother with the most children —twelve
- The mother having the most grandchildren—thirty-eight
- The attendee from farthest away—Bellingham, Washington
- A mother who celebrated a birthday that day—her seventy-ninth (she had attended every department and national convention since she had joined fourteen years before)
- The youngest great-grandmother
- An attendee whose initials were GSM[70]

Gifts of white ceramic vases imprinted with a gold star were presented to the presidents of departments and chapters. They were made by hospitalized veterans at the Brockton, Massachusetts, VA Hospital.[71]

Lorraine I. Desser of Connecticut was elected as the next national president.

Organizational Growth

During the early 1950s, AGSM experienced rapid growth as World War II mothers continued to join and their numbers were supplemented by newer gold star mothers from the war in Korea. As the World War II mothers had done, the Korea gold star mothers joined existing chapters. This meant that in some chapters membership now included mothers from both World Wars and Korea. While the organizational growth meant that more gold star mothers were sharing in the healing camaraderie, and greater numbers of volunteers were available for service, it also led to confusion about protocols, difficulties in managing the administrative aspects of the growth, and new, sometimes controversial, ideas about how things should be done.

At the 1953 convention, it was reported that there were 508 chapters (including 20 new chapters instituted in the past year) and 19,937 members.[72] Three years later, twenty-eight new chapters had been added. AGSM received an average of 750 membership applications per year during the decade and this, in turn, resulted in rapid growth among the chapters. The Austin, Texas chapter, for example, increased its membership from fifty-six to ninety-eight in just one year.[73]

The nation's continental borders were no deterrent to growth. In 1959, the national executive board approved investigating the possibility of organizing chapters in Hawaii for the many gold star mothers living there.[74]

It was not only in numbers that American Gold Star Mothers expanded its influence in the 1950s. In May 1958, General William H. Wilbur, husband of Laura S. Wilbur, second vice president of the North Shore chapter, spoke at the Department of Illinois annual banquet. He was introduced as an "outstanding combat leader in World War II, the winner of our nation's highest award, the Congressional Medal of Honor, and a recognized authority on international, economic and political affairs". He told attendees that "American Gold Star Mothers is not only the most important leader group, it is the most honored, most respected and most worthy of any organization in our country… Your untiring services to veterans in hospitals is well known and a cause for much favorable comment."[75]

Due to the growing membership and the short period of time between World War II and the Korean War, there were some chapters in which membership was claimed by more than one generation of family members. In California, the Bakersfield chapter reported that a mother and daughter were both members of the chapter—World War II mother Letha Rigdon (mother) and Korean conflict mother Clara DeLisle (daughter and chapter president).[76] In New Jersey, three sisters were members of the same chapter:

"Mrs. Plewa, Mrs. Krzaczkowski, and Mrs. Wisz are sisters. They are also members of the South River Chapter, South River, New Jersey, for each sister lost one son in World War II. The women have a brother who lost a son in the last war. And Mrs. Wisz has a son now in Korea."[77]

Chapter Activities

In the 1950s, the rapid post-World War II growth of the membership and the large number of established chapters enabled the organization to accomplish more than ever before at the chapter level. While chapters with a veterans facility in the area spent much of their time volunteering at the hospital or domiciliary, they also required time to prepare for those visits and to earn money to support those activities.

The mothers were innovative and successful in their fundraising ideas. At the 1955 convention, it was reported that more than $35,500 had been earned and spent by the chapters in support of their volunteer and welfare activities. By 1956, more than $74,000 was re-

Fig. 8-12: Members of the East Los Angeles-Montebello Chapter visit a March of Dimes facility in the 1950s. The cart is full of games and puzzles donated to the children by the chapter. *(AGSM Collection)*

ported, and in 1958, the amount exceeded $75,000.[78]

In Ohio, the Dayton chapter raised funds "by sponsoring bazaars, rummage sales, baked food sales, lawn fetes and redeeming sales tax stamps." At their social meetings, the Dayton members sewed carpet rags for blind veterans to weave into rugs and also sewed items to be sold at fundraising bazaars.[79]

In California, the Bakersfield chapter established a birthday box into which each mother deposited a nickel on her birthday for "each of her years." On the chapter's anniversary each year the birthday box was opened and the accumulated funds were spent to help veterans' families.[80]

The Mahaska County chapter in Oskaloosa, Iowa, raised funds with a traveling apron:

"One member circulated an apron among all the members, and anyone else who cared to make a donation, by having them place their contributions under a patch that they whipped into place on the apron."[81]

At the 1956 convention, it was reported that chapters had earned money to support their activities by selling both commonplace and unique items: Christmas and greeting cards; nylon bags; homemade candy; recipe books with favorite recipes contributed by members; aprons; vanilla; shampoo; potted plants; hand-crocheted rugs; and fancy Easter eggs. An Illinois chapter collected 2,500 labels from dog food cans for a seeing-eye dog. Another chapter won a $50 prize at a table-setting contest and added their prize money to the chapter coffers. Rummage sales, dinners and card parties were also a source of funds.

In addition to their activities at veterans facilities, the mothers sponsored a variety of welfare activities, often related to the families of hospitalized veterans.

In September 1955, a touching article in the *Long Beach Press-Telegram* highlighted the activities of the Long Beach Friendship Chapter:

"Their common bond is rarely mentioned. The objective is not to mourn, but to find work for their hands as an outlet for the ache in their hearts... That is the motive behind the Gold Star Mothers' work, to help make life better and brighter for people of any race, creed or nationality. To this end, they have various projects to earn money to carry on their activities.

"Each month they send a small sum to the Veterans' Hospital to be used in an emergency, such as a telephone call or bus fare for a patient. They make layettes for servicemen's wives. They also give canned food to the Navy Chapel's Revolving Pantry.

"The first Saturday of every month finds some of them at the Armed Services YMCA at the Navy Landing, serving homemade cake and coffee in the facility's kitchen. Wearing aprons, they bring a bit of home and mother to the boys. The men in uniform express their appreciation by showing snapshots of home and family and sometimes volunteering to help wash dishes. The preference is for chocolate cake, but often some boy points to a certain cake and says, 'I'll have a piece of that cake. That's the kind my mom always makes.' A surge of pride and happiness sweeps through the baker. Both she and the boy get a lift.

"The Mothers of this small group vary in age from 50 to 84 years. Although some of their boys are resting beneath the blue Pacific—one in the battleship Arizona—these Mothers turn smiling, kindly faces toward the world."[82]

Other chapters sponsored worthy young students through gifts of scholarships to help with college tuition or the costs of other programs. And always the mothers did what they could for the troops overseas, at home and in transition. In Pasadena, California, the mothers saw to it that troops called to service had a memorable leave-taking:

"When Pasadena men are called to duty under the Selective Service Act, the Pasadena Chapter… gives them a royal sendoff. At a recent call, when 40 men were ordered to duty, the chapter staged a going-away party for 32—all who had responded to the invitation."[83]

In 1950, members of the Pittsburgh, Victory, South Hills, and Allegheny chapters (Pittsburgh, Pennsylvania area) were so touched by the courage of one young man at a local VA hospital that they "adopted" the soldier and his family as a special case. They combined their efforts to provide support beyond what could normally be offered to patients:

"While visiting Aspinwall Hospital for a ward party held by Pittsburgh American Gold Star Mothers, Inc., we observed a man who was in a wheel chair. He had both legs off and his right arm was amputated below the elbow. His left arm was to be amputated the following day.

"In the October issue of the *Reader's Digest,* there was an article [about] two 'basket cases' of World War

II. This Pennsylvania boy did not lose his limbs overseas as the veterans in the *Digest* article did. He lost his from Buerger's Disease, slowly, horribly, one at a time and with great pain and mental anguish, knowing after the first amputation that there would be others.

"Because of the nature of his handicap he cannot be fitted with artificial limbs as these other 'basket cases' have been. There is too much danger of infection for Harry Sminiski of Jennerstown, Pennsylvania. Harry is married and has three small daughters. His wife lost her brother in World War II. Although Harry's mother is dead, his mother-in-law is a Gold Star Mother.

"The Pittsburgh [gold star] mothers are interested in his case. They hope that a plan to make Harry self-supporting will be successful. At their December meeting, the Pittsburgh chapter, instead of exchanging gifts, took up a collection and sent Harry the check. The South Hills chapter collected a nice sum of money from seven of its members and mailed this in time for Thanksgiving for Harry. They made plans to send individual gifts to the children at Christmas.

"The Allegheny County chapter sponsored a bingo party and sent the family a check. The Victory chapter, instead of exchanging gifts at Christmas, brought wrapped gifts for the three little girls and these were taken to the Sminiski home.

"All who come in contact with this boy admire his courage, his ready smile, [and] his fine attitude toward his terrible handicap. Ordinarily, we do not choose individuals to help. We do our hospital work under our Veteran Administration representative and this work is coordinated with the Special Service program. But the folks at Aspinwall Hospital feel as we do - this is no ordinary case. We feel that he deserves our sympathy and our help. We will do our best for him here in Pennsylvania."[84]

Members often represented their chapters at civic and personal events. In Bakersfield, California, committees were appointed to "meet all dead veterans being returned and attend all funerals. Wreaths are sent to [funerals for those] boys whose mothers are members of the chapter."[85] In port towns where ships bearing the war dead docked, committees of gold star mothers from the local chapters made every attempt to meet each new arrival.

In the late 1950s, AGSM began to separately track the hours and funds expended by the mothers doing community service work versus the hours given to Veterans Administration Volunteer Services work at veterans facilities. Community service work included:

"Financial aid from Chapter treasury and volunteer hours given by chapter members to such projects as—all civic programs; all health programs; child welfare; Thanksgiving and Christmas baskets to needy; church programs; entertaining or giving aid to orphans or handicapped children; 4-H clubs; Campfire Girls; Scouting; civil defense; USO; radio or TV programs; Goodwill Industries; Salvation Army; entertainment for groups; baby-sitting; or any service for which you do not receive compensation."[86]

Organizations listed as community service recipients in 1959 included, in part: Bells for Peace; blood banks; charity nursing schools; the Crusade against Obscene Literature; old folks homes; Constellation Fund; Little Sisters of the Poor; soldiers homes; sky watching; vacation Bible schools; well-baby clinics; Community Chest; civil defense; clothing drives for needy children; and hearing-aid societies.[87]

In July 1958, *The Gold Star Mother* reported that 380 chapters had expended $27,839.14 in support of 65,049 hours of community service volunteering, exclusive of hospital time.[88]

Gold star mothers were often guests of honor in patriotic parades honoring Memorial Day, Veterans Day, Armistice Day, the Fourth of July, and other celebrations. In some cases they were chauffeured in a variety of cars but often they rode floats provided by local posts of the American Legion or Veterans of Foreign Wars (VFW).

From the viewpoint of the members of the more than 550 chapters, the decade of the 1950s was well described in 1955 by the president of the Beacon Chapter (Seattle, Washington) who shared her chapter's motto in *The Gold Star Mother*: "'Service' is our motto this year and 'Happiness is the flower we gather by the roadside of Service.'"[89]

The Gold Star Mother Newsletter

Although AGSM newsletters and bulletins had appeared in one form or another throughout the late 1940s, it was not until 1949 that such a publication became formalized. At the 1951 convention, it was decided that there would be one official AGSM publication and it would be called *The Gold Star Mother*. At that time, publication of the newsletter was done from Long Beach, California, under the direction of Eleanor

Boyd and her hand-picked staff. During her first term as national president in 1952, Elsie Neilsen managed to wrest control of the newsletter from Mrs. Boyd, moving the entire operation to Washington, D.C., where it was published from national headquarters.

In 1955, information about the newsletter was published for the membership:

Did You Know?
- That THE GOLD STAR MOTHER is our official national publication…
- That it has become a major enterprise of our organization.
- That approximately 22,000 copies are distributed each month.
- That it takes 49 mailbags to get the papers on their way to you.
- That it goes to 3,270 cities, towns and rural communities throughout the United States.
- That California leads with 452 post offices, Pennsylvania has 428, Ohio is third with 319, then New Jersey with 235 and New York has 212.
- That it goes to distant places like Alaska, Hawaii, the Canal Zone, South America and Canada.
- That it goes to the veteran hospitals and many public libraries.[90]

In July 1957, the newsletter began the practice of publishing names of members who were transferring from one chapter to another. Both the old and new chapters were named as part of the column.

While the majority of the newsletter was devoted each month to AGSM activities, there was always room for a bit of filler. These included factual tidbits, jokes, or inspirational quotations considered to be of general interest to readers. Sources for the quotations ranged from Socrates to evangelist Billy Sunday, and from Voltaire to Douglas MacArthur.

Poetry was extremely popular with the gold star mothers and most issues of the newsletter carried several poems. (See Appendix A for gold star poetry.) Many were written by the mothers themselves while others were borrowed from a variety of publications.

In 1959, a poetic speech given by a candidate for office in the past presidents club was printed in the newsletter:

Roses got thorns, doughnuts got holes,
Peaches got fuzz, gardens got moles.

Humans got problems, it's all in Life's plan,
We're all stuck with something! Enjoy what
you can.[91]

The National Gold Star Mothers

In the late 1940s, a small but vocal group of AGSM members charged that the Memorial National Home Foundation was being inappropriately managed by Eleanor Boyd and had been taken in a direction that was not in the best interests of AGSM. Dismissed out of hand by Mrs. Boyd, the group was unable to impede or halt the progress of the Home Foundation juggernaut. Due to Mrs. Boyd's tight management of publications and conventions, the group had no forum in which to bring the matter to the attention of the membership. At the 1949 convention they attempted to oust Mrs. Boyd by challenging her for the position of national president, nominating Evangeline Trenchard as their candidate. Mrs. Trenchard was defeated. Shortly thereafter, Mrs. Trenchard and her supporters resigned their AGSM memberships and formed a new organization —National Gold Star Mothers, Inc.

As recounted in a later lawsuit, Eleanor Boyd's reaction was immediate and damning. In the November 1949 issue, under the title "Loyalty Affirmed," Mrs. Boyd printed letters from worried AGSM members declaring that, although their names may have been mentioned in connection with the National Gold Star Mothers (NGSM), they were, in fact, not connected with the organization in any way.

Mrs. Boyd continued her campaign of vilification against National Gold Star Mothers and its membership at every opportunity.

At the Department meeting held in Boston in 1949, Mrs. Boyd stated: "They call themselves the National Gold Star Mothers. They could not be. It is against the law. They have circularized papers and applications. Are they just greedy or what? They are not honorable Americans and I will say it anywhere: in court, if necessary. We have women right in our own group willing to help the subversive element. In one case, there is money involved."

Even the national executive board was influenced as Mrs. Boyd continued to publicize her belief that subversives were infiltrating AGSM. At her urging in November 1949, at the national executive board meeting, it was ruled that any member of the American Gold Star Mothers who also belonged to some other gold star organization could not hold office at the chapter, department or national level in AGSM. Other gold star organizations included the American Legion Auxiliary, the VFW, American War Mothers, and local groups that had formed in some areas. This ruling greatly affected the membership since the majority of mothers was active in more than one gold star organization.[92]

The ruling created continuing confusion and hard feelings among the AGSM membership. When queried about the ratification of this ruling in convention, Mrs. Boyd consistently stated it had been ratified by the membership at the 1950 national convention in Detroit. However, the minutes of that convention were never released to the membership or national board; in subsequent years, no one in attendance ever verified that such an action had been taken. Without an official written record of the convention proceedings, however, there was no way to challenge Mrs. Boyd on the issue. As late as 1958, past national president Elsie C. Nielsen was still looking for proof, stating "Now, I don't know where the minutes of that convention are—maybe you do. I don't believe they are at Headquarters. I don't believe Mrs. Boyd ever turned them over to us. However, she told me subsequently that it was ratified by that convention."[93]

Many mothers withdrew from other gold star organizations in order to hold positions of increasing responsibility within AGSM. Others, however, refused to be influenced by the ruling:

"We have many Mothers in the Chicago Chapter who still belong to the Illinois group and will not withdraw. They say it is not an American procedure [and] that they can't be told what to do in that respect."[94]

It was still an issue of concern in 1958 when Maude Fry responded in response to a question from a convention delegate:

"There is nothing in the by-laws which states—and I have said this many, many times—that you cannot belong to another group and still be a member in good standing of American Gold Star Mothers. If you are a member in good standing of the American Gold Star Mothers, you can be elected to an office."[95]

As Mrs. Boyd continued to speak out against the National group in public, to the media, and within AGSM, she also turned to the courts for support, alleging that NGSM had intentionally created confusion between the two organizations and had fraudulently solicited memberships and monies from a confused public:

"The gist of the complaint is the charge that [the National Gold Star Mothers] has deliberately chosen a corporate name which is so much like [American Gold Star Mothers] that [National Gold Star Mothers] is able to benefit from a reputation and good will built by [American Gold Star Mothers] over a period of 22 years."[96]

The district court did not agree with AGSM's position and dismissed the complaint on the grounds that: (1) the law of the District of Columbia did not permit a charitable organization to prevent infringement of its name; and (2) "the names of the two organizations here involved are not so similar as to constitute one name an infringement of the other."[97]

Mrs. Boyd immediately initiated an appeal. In July 1951, a higher court reversed the ruling of the district court:

"American Gold Star Mothers, Inc. won a round today in its legal battle against National Gold Star Mothers, Inc. The United States Court of Appeals, in a 2-to-1 decision, reversed a District Court ruling throwing out a suit of American Gold Star Mothers for damages and an injunction against National Gold Star Mothers.

"American Gold Star Mothers, Inc. seeks to prevent the other organization from using the name National Gold Star Mothers, Inc., or any similar name. American Gold Star Mothers alleged the other organization deliberately chose its name so as to benefit from the reputation and good-will built by the older group."[98]

In August 1951, citing public confusion, the National Gold Star Mothers organization appealed to the editor of *The Gold Star,* a publication for gold star families, to publish a statement clarifying the aims and position of the NGSM organization. The statement was signed by Evangeline Trenchard, NGSM national president:

"The NATIONAL GOLD STAR MOTHERS, Inc. is an organization separate and distinct from any other Gold Star Mothers' organization.

"The NATIONAL GOLD STAR MOTHERS, Inc. is incorporated under the laws of Delaware and have their headquarters in Dover, Delaware.

"There are two national organizations of Gold Star Mothers and we do not intentionally want to mislead or confuse any prospective members. There is nothing in the by-laws of the NATIONAL GOLD STAR MOTHERS, Inc. nor in our course of administration that precludes any gold star mothers from belonging to more than one Gold Star Mothers' organization.

"The NATIONAL GOLD STAR MOTHERS, Inc. is the new organization and is growing throughout the United States. The NATIONAL GOLD STAR MOTHERS, INC., or any other Gold Star Mothers' organization, does not have a Congressional charter.

"The NATIONAL GOLD STAR MOTHERS, Inc. is a member of the Women's Patriotic Conference on National Defense, a patriotic organization composed of approximately forty women's patriotic organizations."[99]

Lawsuits and countersuits continued through the courts. Inexplicably, in early spring 1952, Mrs. Boyd approached the Friendship chapter of National Gold Star Mothers in Long Beach, California, which was comprised mainly of ex-AGSM members, and suggested that they rejoin the Long Beach Chapter of AGSM, the chapter from which they had withdrawn two years before. If they did so, all would be forgiven. However, when Mrs. Boyd advised AGSM's Long Beach Chapter (her home chapter) of her offer to the NGSM members, the chapter unexpectedly balked at her directive. They protested that "it was because of Mrs. Boyd that the members went out in the first place."[100]

It is difficult to know what prompted Mrs. Boyd's conciliatory offer to the NGSM chapter after having spent so much time, energy, and money trying to annihilate their organization. The Long Beach chapter had always been Eleanor's pet chapter, proud of the fact that she was a member and traditionally proving themselves willing to do anything she asked of them.

Perhaps Mrs. Boyd felt a need to consolidate her support base in the face of the Home Foundation legal challenges and hoped that by extending an olive branch to the exiled mothers, they would happily return to their original organization and be appropriately grateful for the opportunity she had given them. Facing a potentially huge lawsuit regarding the Home Foundation, perhaps she simply wanted to end the NGSM controversy; having made her point in the courts and the press she could gracefully offer an opportunity for reconciliation. Whatever her reason, the recalcitrance of the AGSM chapter members in this instance brought the issue to a swift conclusion despite Mrs. Boyd's anger with those responsible.

Following the election of a new national president and national executive board for the 1953–1954 term, AGSM soon took steps to withdraw all legal proceedings against the National Gold Star Mothers.[101] The National Gold Star Mothers, Inc., continued as an organization through the 1950s, never growing large or powerful enough to pose any sort of threat to American Gold Star Mothers, Inc.

Monuments and Memorials

As it had following World War I, the nation soon turned its mind toward honoring and memorializing the lives lost in World War II. By the 1950s, many World War II memorials had already been established or were being planned. The plans were as diverse as the people and organizations that conceived of them; some were personal, some were public—and gold star mothers were the impetus behind many of them.

National AGSM president Eleanor Boyd expressed her opinion in 1951 that the finest tribute that could be paid to the dead was to live an exemplary life:

"[There is] no better way of honoring the dead than by a living example which you and I can display to the world. We should be motherhood in its finest form with courage, love and understanding for all. If need be to preserve freedom, we can further sacrifice, even to our own personal lives."[102]

While not in disagreement with Mrs. Boyd, many gold star mothers across the nation chose more tangible forms for their memorials:

"In January 1950 in Glenoaks Park, now known as McCambridge Park, a site for a Memorial Garden was given by the City of Burbank [California] to the American Gold Star Mothers... Thirty Burbank Gold Star Mothers planted a rose bush in the first island in honor of their sons and daughters who gave their lives in World War II.

"Since that time the Mothers have filled five islands with rose bushes—and replaced all bushes that died or have not progressed as they should have. One island is planted entirely in gold roses. There are more than five hundred bushes in all the islands. This Memorial Rose Garden is maintained through the co-operation of the Burbank Park and Recreation Department and it is a source of great happiness to the mothers."[103]

The same chapter set up a Memorial Book Shelf in the Burbank Public Library. Gold star parents could place books on the shelf in honor of their child or children who gave their lives in World War I or II.[104] One of the first books to be placed on the shelf was The

History of Burbank from her Eventful Pioneer Days, signed by author Miss Carol Tuller and presented to gold star mother Adella Hinshaw, specifically for the Memorial Book Shelf.[105]

Caroline Berry, a member of the Lorain chapter in Ohio, was given an opportunity available to few when she christened the USS *Charles Berry* (DE-1035), named in memory of her son, Charles J. Berry. A Marine corporal, Charles had been posthumously awarded the Medal of Honor for "conspicuous gallantry and intrepidity at the risk of his life" on March 3, 1945, during the Battle of Iwo Jima:

"When infiltrating Japanese soldiers launched a surprise attack shortly after midnight in an attempt to overrun his position, he engaged in a pitched hand-grenade duel, returning the dangerous weapons with prompt and deadly accuracy until an enemy grenade landed in the foxhole. Determined to save his comrades, he unhesitatingly chose to sacrifice himself and immediately dived on the deadly missile, absorbing the shattering violence of the exploding charge in his own body and protecting the others from serious injury.[106]

Stella Halloran, first president of the Cuyahoga, Ohio, chapter, was also privileged to have a ship named after her son:

"Stella christened a destroyer escort ship, the USS *Halloran,* launched at Mare Island Naval Yard, California, January 14, 1944. Named in honor of her son, Ensign William I. Halloran who lost his life on the U.S.S. *Arizona* at Pearl Harbor."

On Memorial Day 1959, AGSM national president Mabel C. Troy presented a memorial plaque from AGSM for the Arlington National Cemetery's Trophy Room:

"As National President of the American Gold Star Mothers, Inc., with solemnity and deep reverence, I present, on behalf of the Sons and Daughters of our members, this memorial tribute to their comrades in arms, the Unknown American Heroes, World War I, World War II, and Korea."

The plaque was placed upon a velvet covered pedestal which stood before the sarcophagus (The Tomb of the Unknowns) for the remainder of the day after which it was taken to its place in the Trophy Room.[107]

The square plaque was made of wood with a beveled edge. A metal insignia containing a gold star and wreath read: "In Memory of the Unknown American Heroes." An engraved metal bar below the insignia reads: "American Gold Star Mothers, Inc., Presented May 30, 1959." Given a choice of two locations within the Trophy Room for permanent display, Mrs. Troy selected a spot in the center glass-and-bronze case on the second aisle to the left. The plaque would remain on display "as a permanent tribute to the sacrifices made and as a mute but elegant testimony to the heartfelt gratitude of our members."[108] The presentation of the plaque was noted in the *Congressional Record*.[109]

The Unknown Soldiers

As it had following World War I, the nation honored the unknown dead of World War II and the Korean War in 1958 by selecting and interring the remains of two unidentified soldiers, one from each war, at Arlington National Cemetery in the Tomb of the Unknown Soldier. AGSM national president Maude Fry was asked to witness the selection process for the World War II soldier aboard the USS *Canberra*. Thanks to Vice President Richard M. Nixon, AGSM received nineteen tickets to attend the reburial services at Arlington.[110]

A United Press International (UPI) dispatch painted a poignant word picture of a gold star mother mourning the unknown soldiers as the procession wound its way to Arlington:

"A white-haired mother gazed on the coffins of the nameless dead of World War II and Korea today and wept for her lost son. Mrs. Reginald Godfrey of Providence, R.I., flanked by two other gold star mothers, joined the silent parade of thousands who came to pay tribute to the unknown dead."[111]

Memorial Cemeteries Abroad Completed

In May 1957, *The Gold Star Mother* reported that the United States' $38 million construction program of memorial cemeteries to its overseas World War II dead would be completed by Memorial Day 1958. One year later, the newsletter reported comments by Senator Charles E. Potter of Michigan that indicated the work had been completed:

"The valiant dead of World War II have been laid to rest in fourteen cemeteries scattered throughout what were once the Atlantic and Pacific theatres of war... All told, 93,114 graves are contained in those cemeteries. Each cemetery also contains what is known as a 'Wall of the Missing' where the names of those 56,000 persons whose bodies were not recovered are inscribed for all to see."[113]

The "Gold Star Mothers' Hymn"

In 1953, gold star mother and AGSM member Yvonne M. Marsden of Pittsfield, Massachusetts wrote a song she titled, "The Gold Star Mothers' Hymn." The song was dedicated from "A Gold Star Mother for all Gold Star Mothers":

We're the GOLD STAR MOTHERS of America,
Whose sacrifice kept us free.
Our star is bright, with holy light,
The hope of immortality.
So we proudly wear our dear insignia,
Which radiates from sea to sea.
Untarnished we will hand it down,
With honor to posterity.
For our sons and daughters lit the beacon bright,
Still nourished by their crimson flame.
A glorious gift to patriots,
Their guerdon is eternal fame.
So we pledge our lives and all we hope to be
For the waiting world to see.
That we preserve for all mankind,
The lode-star of democracy.[114]

Mrs. Marsden copyrighted and self-published her song, including a brief history of AGSM on the back cover.

In February 1954, Mrs. Marsden received an official letter from Maude E. Fry written at the direction of the AGSM national executive board. The letter advised her that the Board "objects to the matter printed on the back of the song" which was a brief history of American Gold Star Mothers, Inc. Mrs. Marsden was told to provide letters from the printer and publisher of the song stating that they would no longer print the AGSM history on the sheet music.

Mrs. Marsden replied immediately stating that the board could be assured that no more copies of the song would be printed with the history as part of it and that she would "ink out" all the copies that she currently had. But while she complied with the Board's requirement, she did not agree with it:

"I am sorry that I cannot go along with your feelings on this matter, as I feel that there is nothing secret about our mission or preamble. We are not Masons or some such secret organization. We are the Gold Star Mothers who are banded together to help each other and our veterans and boys in hospitals. I cannot see any harm in proclaiming it to the world, and may I add that there are other mothers who feel as I do. However, please be assured that your wishes will be respected in this matter and there will be no more of the copies which you object to."[115]

Pilgrimages

Almost as soon as World War II ended, gold star parents began asking the government to sponsor pilgrimages, as it had done for World War I gold star mothers and widows, to the overseas cemeteries where the World War II dead now lay. Concerned with the aftermath of the war, the government made no promises, but the lack of response did not lessen the clamor for gold star pilgrimages. In February 1950, a group of Illinois gold star mothers wrote to President Truman asking "how long they will have to wait before they can be sent overseas to visit the graves of their dear ones?" The letter was referred to the Secretary of Defense for a response.[116]

Gold star parents who were able to afford trips to Europe or the Pacific to visit the graves of their children often shared their experiences with other gold star parents in articles published in *The Gold Star Mother*. Mrs. Dwight Dyar, past president of the Marietta, Ohio, chapter wrote:

"Mr. Dyar and myself have just returned from Normandy, France where we visited our son's grave. He is buried in the U.S. Military Cemetery overlooking Omaha Beach. The snow white marble crosses (that come to my shoulder) on a velvety green field of grass are the most beautiful sight I have ever seen. There are 9,963 of our sons buried in this cemetery. While standing near our son's grave, we could hear the water washing and splashing on the beach. The grass is always moist from the spray, so is soft and green the year around.

"At one end of the cemetery is a large Memorial building of tan marble and in the center of this Memorial is a large monument dedicated to the YOUTH of America. In front of this Memorial is a large reflecting pool and at the other end of the cemetery is the chapel. While at the Memorial you can see the chapel in the reflecting pool and while at the chapel you can see the Memorial in the same reflecting pool.

"We both feel proud that our son is in such a beautiful cemetery kept by our government that will remain that way as long as there is a United States of America."[117]

Mary R. Kelly, AGSM legislative chairwoman dur-

ing the 1950s, constantly monitored any legislation related to a pilgrimage and reported its status to the membership. She made this report in January 1956:

"At this time, there is no specific information available on the Pilgrimage. However, it is known that the National Commander of the Veterans of Foreign Wars, Mr. Timothy J. Murphy, is pushing this resolution through the Department of Defense and has requested that it be expedited so that the Gold Star Mothers will be able to visit the graves of their sons and daughters overseas."[118]

Throughout the decade, AGSM members were encouraged to write their legislators to initiate and support action on pilgrimage legislation. New York Representative John J. Rooney had presented pilgrimage legislation for several years; year after year, no action had been taken. In March 1956, his prompting resulted in a letter from Charles Vinson, Chairman of the House Committee on Armed Services, outlining the reasons that such a pilgrimage was impractical at the current time:

"You wrote to me on January 7 reiterating your keen interest in H.R. 478, a bill to enable the mothers and widows of deceased members of the armed services to make a pilgrimage to the overseas cemeteries where such persons were interred. On February 1st I requested the Army to state its current position on your bill and in response to that request I have today received the attached letter.

"I know that all of us have the most sympathetic feeling with the purposes of your bill. But some phases of this matter disturb me. As the Army states, I think it would be necessary to include the mothers and widows of the non-recoverables since the latters' names are to be inscribed on the battle monuments in overseas areas. Unfortunately, this would approximately double the estimated cost.

"In the next place, only six of the cemeteries are completed, the remaining ones being in various lesser states of completion. I simply do not know how we could arrange the pilgrimage to insure that mothers and widows would arrive at the cemeteries which are in a state of completion.

"If you have any suggestions, I would be happy to receive them but under current circumstances I am extremely doubtful that it would be appropriate to schedule this matter for hearing at this time."

The letter Mr. Vinson referred to was from C. J.

Hauck Jr., Brigadier General, GS, Chief of Legislative Liaison. In it, he outlined the many problems related to attempting to organize pilgrimages:

1. It was believed that the widows and mothers eligible for the pilgrimages would desire to see the cemeteries in their "state of maximum beautification." At least two more years would be required to complete the construction in all the cemeteries.
2. Approximately 6,674 persons participated in the pilgrimages following World War I, and three years were required for completion of the program. World War II pilgrimages would encompass a group nearly eight times that size. The five years proposed in the legislation was considered inadequate to complete the program.
3. It was estimated that the cost of the pilgrimages under the proposal's present provisions would be approximately $95,000,000. In the event the bill was amended to include widows and mothers of the missing whose names were inscribed in the cemeteries' chapels, the total cost of the pilgrimages would be approximately $170,000,000.
No such funding was available nor had it been proposed in any form.[119]

In May 1957, one AGSM department took action and organized a pilgrimage journey for its members:

"American Gold Star Mothers from Oregon, Washington and Idaho chapters boarded a Transocean airliner at Portland International airport... May 27 for an eight day visit in Hawaii. Headed by Mrs. Rose Decker, President of the Oregon Department, they will be honored guests at the Memorial Day services in the National Punchbowl cemetery. On that day, over 50,000 fragrant flower leis are distributed over the 15,000 graves and helicopters hover overhead dropping thousands of small vanda orchids. As ranking officer, Mrs. Decker has been invited to place a lei on the grave of the Unknown Soldier. Later that afternoon, the Hawaii chapter will host the mothers at tea and on the following day, the entire group will enjoy a cruise through Pearl Harbor as guests of the U.S. Navy. Some of the mothers have sons buried in Punchbowl cemetery and many of them lost their boys at sea. A special monument honoring these war dead will be dedicated this year."[120]

For gold star parents who dreamed of a pilgrimage but knew that the cost was far more than they could ever afford, a March 1953 article in *The Gold Star Mother* might have given them fresh hope. The article was reprinted from a local newspaper:

"Santa Claus came early to the home of Mr. and Mrs. Foster W. Stewart with a check for $364.65. Substituting for the busy old gent were the residents of Montecito, California, Stewart being their favorite and only mailman. It was just about the most welcome check anyone could get for it brought close to realization the Stewarts' dream of years to pay a visit to their son's grave in the United States military cemetery at Epinol, France.

"The Stewarts have been saving every dollar they could for a number of years to cover the expenses. Boosted by the donation from Santa Claus they now have been able to set the memorial journey for spring of 1953.

"Stewart has been carrying mail in the Montecito Park district for seven years. [Montecito Park was a Los Angeles suburb.] Being a man who makes friends readily, it wasn't long until he was receiving cheery greetings daily from those he met during the course of delivering letters, packages and papers. His quest for spare time jobs to add to the trip fund took him into such work as service station assistant, gardening and other occupations. It was only natural that the people on his route should learn, in the course of the years, that the Stewarts had subordinated everything they reasonably could to the aim of accumulating funds for their planned European voyage.

"Also, knowing the kindly nature of the Montecito Park people, it can surprise no one that they should want to help the Stewarts advance the day when they could pack their suitcases and start on their way.

"With the check to Stewart was this letter which is given word for word as it came to him:

OUR CHRISTMAS THOUGHT FOR YOU:
Dear Mr. Stewart: Down here in Montecito Park we believe in the old Biblical theory that "bread cast upon the waters will return after many days." And you, friend Stewart, have been casting bread upon the waters for years.

We are deeply interested in your planned pilgrimage to the shrine of your son's grave; we recognize and respect the sentiment that prompts it and, in our own way, we ask the privilege of sharing with you the problems involved.

The enclosed slip of paper [a check] is just a

token of our regard and appreciation of many courtesies. It comes with the thought that it may smooth some rough spot on your journey or give you greater leeway in its enjoyment. The enclosed list of names includes those of your friends in this vicinity whom we could readily reach and who ask your indulgence in this gesture of esteem and sympathy. One further thought—don't feel that we need any expression of thanks; the sacrifice is yours and we are privileged to be able to acknowledge it.

So—please just take it in stride, for it is our pleasure—not to be forgotten perhaps—but the thoughts that mean the most are often the hardest to voice.

Sincerely yours,
Your Montecito Park Friends

"Stewart was reticent about the gift today. 'They are wonderful people,' he remarked. 'We'll never forget them or their goodness, but it doesn't seem like something I can say much about. I'm not looking for publicity and I'm sure they aren't.'

"Efforts to obtain permission for use of the names of the donors or of the committee which headed the Christmas drive proved without results. Montecito Park residents said they would prefer being anonymous in the matter.

"The Stewarts have made their reservations for departure in April. They will be away from home an estimated 10 weeks. They intend to drive to New York and are due to sail from that port April 16. Their itinerary calls for 33 days in Europe. Originally they proposed a three week stay in Europe but found that it was impossible to obtain reservations for three weeks. It had to be either two weeks or approximately four weeks. So, with the help of Montecito Park, they made it the longer period.

"The grave they will visit is that of Sgt. Norman J. Stewart of the Eighth Air Force. He was a member of a bomber crew, based in England, which was on its way back from a run into Germany in World War II when the ship was hit and crashed. Sgt. Stewart bailed out but his chute failed to open, companions reported. After the war his grave was discovered in a German civilian cemetery in Rotherberg. The body was removed to St. Avold and then to Epinol. Sgt. Stewart was 19 years, 1 month old on the day of his death."[121]

Deaths Among the AGSM Membership

By the 1950s, the number of World War I members was rapidly diminishing. Each edition of the newsletter carried obituary notices for these mothers and fathers who had lost a child or children in a war many decades before. For many, their passing was mourned by a large multi-generational family group. For others, whose only child perished in the war, their passing was mourned solely by their sisters and brothers in AGSM. Sadly, the number of World War I mothers' deaths in the monthly newsletters of the 1950s was eclipsed by the death notices of gold star parents from World War II and Korea. Many of that generation of members died in their late fifties and early sixties although the average life span for Americans at that time was 68.2 years.[122] In July 1959, the national chaplain reported on the losses among members of AGSM in the last two years: in 1957–1958, 438 mothers and 369 dads died; in 1958–1959, 418 mothers and 451 dads. This represented nearly a 5 percent loss in membership each year.[123]

AGSM also lost a number of past officers and founding members during the 1950s, each of whom took part of the organizational memory with them in their passing. They had seen numerous organizational changes and growth following World War II, and had helped the organization find its way in earlier days. They included original charter members Kathryn Fagan, Mary Katherine Killeen, Isabel Adams, and past national president Elizabeth "Bess" Duncan Wells.

Another sorrowful loss during the 1950s came with the death of George Gordon Seibold, husband of AGSM founder Grace Darling Seibold, who died in his sleep at the age of ninety on May 30, 1955.

In July 1958, AGSM's long-time nemesis, Mathilda Burling, died of heart failure in a Queens Village, New York, nursing home. Newspaper obituaries named her the "founder of the Gold Star movement of mothers of service men killed in action." She was also identified as the primary force behind the gold star pilgrimages of the 1930s. Even her obituaries perpetuated the confusion with the *New York Times* obituary referring to Mrs. Burling's organization as "The New York State Gold Star Mothers." In November 1958, AGSM's national executive board found it necessary to make a statement in *The Gold Star Mother* to quell the confusion among members who had read of Mrs. Burling's death, explaining "A recent news item appeared in many local newspapers of the death of a Gold Star Mother in

New York, stating she was the founder of Gold Star Mothers. To clear up any confusion please note that the Founder of our organization was Mrs. Grace Darling Seibold."

Veterans Administration Volunteer Service (VAVS)

In 1946, a quiet revolution in care had begun at veterans hospitals and facilities across the nation. At the 1958 convention in Cleveland, James H. Parke, Chief of Volunteer Services for the Veterans Administration (VA), spoke to the attendees about what had been called "a miracle of common sense" by a long-time VA volunteer:

"Put very briefly and very badly, what happened was that in 1946 the Veterans Administration stopped trying to be nice and polite to the many outside groups of ladies who had been trying to help hospitalized veterans since World War II. All of a sudden, the VA took these under-foot ladies into its confidence and told them it would put them to work, which was what they had always wanted… the fancy handle for this new miracle of common sense was the Veterans Administration Volunteer Service, or VAVS."

American Gold Star Mothers, Inc. became a member of the National VAVS Committee in September 1948 while the VA was still working out the details of this new approach to community volunteer participation.

As Mr. Parke explained, volunteer service was nothing new at the VA facilities. People had been volunteering almost as long as there had been veterans hospitals:

"What was this new approach to service with and

ANGELS OF MERCY WEAR THE GOLD STAR BAND

Angels of Mercy with the Gold Star band
Are joined together through all the land
With courage and zeal, they labor and work
At tasks gigantic they do not shirk.

They visit the veteran on his bed of pain
And their soft spoken words are not in vain.
A welcoming smile and a touch of the hand
Greet the Angels of Mercy with the Gold
*   Star band.*

Though their hair is gray, and their steps
*   are slow*
The Gold Star Mothers are willing to go
To the VA hospitals throughout the land
As Angels of Mercy with the Gold Star band.

~Written January 19, 1954 by Ella F. Leven
as a tribute to the AGSM hospital workers.
The Gold Star Mother, June 1954, p8.

---

for our sick and disabled veterans? Please note those two prepositions—with and for… What we are interested in is you, what you bring in yourself, rather than things."[124]

What had changed was the perspective on what volunteers could provide, not in the material sense, but as one person to another. As the new VAVS program got underway following World War II, Mr. Parke said he had been told, "Oh, you will get support now when the bands are playing and the flags are waving, but wait a few years. You will see the volunteers falling by the wayside." But the pessimists were proven wrong—participation continued to grow by more than 36 percent in the first decade of the program. Even more importantly, the number of hours served jumped 47 percent.

In fact, the scope of the VAVS program was almost unimaginable by 1958. Mr. Parke reported that in 1957 an average of more than 90,000 volunteers came each month into the 173 VA hospitals and domiciliary homes on a regular basis. These volunteers assisted in twenty-five different hospital program areas, logging more than 5.5 million hours of volunteer service.

What was different? The volunteer workers were made part of the hospital team, just like the doctors and nurses:

"Our doctors and our nurses and our therapists are busy people. They could not afford to take the time to orient and supervise and train the volunteers unless the return on their investment of time and thinking and planning were worth this expenditure. Our medical staff has one basic responsibility—to give the patient the best possible medical care and treatment. They can't afford to spend their all too limited time on non-essentials.

"The professional staff of the Veterans Administration

hospitals is qualified to render superior medical service to every worthy veteran of your community. Yet, with all their advantages and training and equipment and with all the supplementation in the supporting staff, human services over and beyond technical and scientific skills is required for the resocialization of our hospitalized veterans.

"Let's take, for example, a veteran in the hospital with his arms in traction… You write a letter for him. [This] is a direct service that, in and of itself, is important. That letter would be written because a nurse or attendant or someone on the staff would write it, but it might not be written when the patient would like it written and, even when the nurse or attendant would find time from their professional duties to write this letter, they would be taking time from their professional duties. So you are making a direct contribution.

"Perhaps as important, sometimes I think even more important than writing the letter, is the indirect service that comes from the fact that you, as a member of the community, are there to remind that patient that a community is interested in him, that a community is anxious for him to return. [That] is the resocialization of the patient."[125]

The need for the socialization aspect of the volunteer work had become apparent very soon after the war. In 1950, just five years after the end of the war, the Veterans Administration reported that a survey conducted by their psychiatry and neurology division had disclosed that one third of the 52,000 mental patients in VA hospitals had not had one visitor in a year or more. In one hospital, only 219 of 785 patients had a visitor in the previous year. While in some instances visitors might be disturbing to a patient, visits were considered highly beneficial in the majority of cases. The survey also uncovered numerous cases of "forgotten veterans" whose families wanted to have nothing to do with them and who prolonged the patients' hospitalization because they refused to accept them back home when medical discharge was indicated. For these patients, and all those receiving care at a VA facility, visits from volunteers were crucial and often their only connection with the world outside the hospital. As Mr. Parke said:

"Volunteers in no way replace staff members. Instead they provide ingredients beyond the scope of a busy professional staff; a touch of home… a feeling of belonging… a bond with the outside world. Volunteers

do the HEART things, the HOME things… the therapy beyond the scope and time of a busy professional staff.[126]

"On this score, I am reminded of a volunteer at our tuberculosis hospital in Sunmount, New York who told me about a bawling out she got from a patient. She had been ill for a couple of weeks and unable to come to the hospital. On her return one of the patients greeted her with 'Hey, you goldbricker, where the devil have you been?' I was intrigued by the obvious pleasure with which the volunteer told me that story. For her, that patient 'bawling her out' meant that she was part of the outfit—an accepted member of the 'hospital team.'"[127]

What tasks did the gold star mothers perform in their volunteer activities at the VA facilities? At the 1956 convention in Tulsa, a portion of the program was devoted to VAVS activities, and a number of mothers from across the nation explained their responsibilities as part of the medical team at VA facilities in their areas:

Lou Doherty (American Lake VA Hospital; Tacoma, Washington): "We have a mental hospital. There are 972 patients in this one building. It is entirely devoted to women patients. Perhaps you wonder who the women patients are. They are the nurses, WAVEs and WACs who served during the three wars. We have some from the first world war, but most are from the second world war."

Laura Olson (Portland, Oregon): "I am assigned by a Social Service staff member to visit specified patients on a friendship therapy basis. Doctors have found that patients respond much more quickly to medication if there is someone to listen to their troubles."

Celia Everett (Sam Jackson VA Hospital; Portland, Oregon): "Ours is the unseen but necessary service. We see that linens and pajamas are mended and buttons sewed on for the patients' comfort. We also make laprobes and articles and mend clothing to donate to the veterans who need it.

Jewel Brown (Atlanta, Georgia): "I work through the Nursing Services Aide Program, which consists of assisting doctors with examinations, assisting the nurses with medication and preparing patients for operations, and giving information to the family of the patient, giving baths, feedings, taking temperatures, making beds, etc."

Natalie Hilgard (John Cochran VA Hospital; St. Louis, Missouri): "[As part of the] Volunteer Escort

Service we are on duty from 9 to 5 one or more days a week. Telephone calls to the volunteer room for errands come in from the wards constantly, in addition to the cases that are on the charts daily. In one day I average 50 errands. This means taking patients in wheelchairs or on litters to surgery, X-ray, or therapies (physical, corrective, occupational, X-ray and speech). We deliver blood to the wards from blood-banks, admit patients, clear patients, and take charts and X-ray files to wards and clinics."

Sonora Roe (Hines Veterans Hospital; Chicago, Illinois): "I go every Friday and make sketches of the patients which I give them the following week. I make about 12 sketches a day. [I am working now in the] psychopathic and neurotic closed wards with the mental patients, so if I act that way, you will understand."

Ruth Z. Kiernan (Albany, New York): "I work at the information desk. Every Wednesday evening I direct visitors to proper floors and wings of the hospital. I accept and sign for telegrams, letters, flowers and other packages for patients and deliver them to nurses' stations or to the patients. I answer the phone and give information and issue special passes for visitors to the psychiatric patients after getting permission by phone from the doctor in charge."

Mary Hiatt (VA Tuberculosis Hospital; Dayton, Ohio): "I am a volunteer for the Dietician. Menus are passed to each patient and each patient marks his own menu. It is returned to the dietician and given to me. I tabulate each menu so the chef will know how much food to prepare. Each menu is put with [the patient's] own card showing if he is a regular or diabetic. This is a daily program."

Eureta Wood (Albuquerque, New Mexico): "I show movies to TB patients unable to get out of their beds. I also render many other services but this ...is one many mothers do not like to do. There isn't any job to help my boys in the veterans hospital in Albuquerque that I won't do."[128]

The July 1957 issue of *The Gold Star Mother* stated that that during the past twelve months, with thirty-seven states reporting, 2,847 AGSM volunteers had accumulated 123,572 hours of hospital work at 110 VA hospitals, earning and expending $75,045.03 to support these activities.

By 1958, AGSM was represented in 119 of the 173 VA hospitals. These facilities included regular hospitals, mental institutions, tuberculosis hospitals, re-

habilitation workshops, and domiciliaries for patients who could never leave the site of their medical care. The work performed by the VAVS volunteers included escort services around the facilities, library work and distribution of reading material, nursing, occupational therapy, visiting with patients, helping feed a patient or helping one relearn life skills, such as talking. In short, the VAVS volunteers did anything that needed to be done.

Certificates of achievement were presented by the VAVS to volunteers who reached certain levels of volunteer hours. In 1956, three VAVS certificates were presented at the national convention:

- Beatrice Wallace (Providence chapter, Rhode Island)—more than 4,000 hours of service
- Eureta Wood (Albuquerque chapter, New Mexico)—more than 3,000 hours of service
- Elsie Pufahl (Milwaukee chapter, Wisconsin)— more than 2,000 hours of service, all performed in a clown costume! [130]

In May 1957, Edna Haug, VAVS representative in Pittsburgh, reported that nine mothers in that area had been recognized for more than 1,000 hours of VAVS service, including Anna Worden, seventy-seven years old, who worked one day each week in the Aspinwall VA Hospital and often gave another day to help with the ward games.[131]

While the VAVS volunteer work took much of the mothers' time and attention, it was by no means their only contribution to the welfare of hospitalized veterans. Often the chapters donated items they felt would improve the morale of those patients hospitalized for long periods of time. In 1951, the New Orleans chapter "presented the Veterans Hospital with skates for the patients who are learning to walk again."[132] In 1956, Louisiana's Alexandria chapter donated a television set for use by cardiac patients at the veterans hospital near Pineville.[133] Chapters in Ohio were particularly active in supporting the Chillicothe Veterans Hospital. One of the patients' favorite activities was a monthly dance:

"Nine carloads of Ohio Wesleyan coeds were in Chillicothe Thursday night for the monthly Ohio Wesleyan dance at the Chillicothe Veterans Hospital. The dance was sponsored by the Delaware County Gold Star Mothers who recruited the cars for transportation and served refreshments during intermissions. In this activity, the Gold Star Dads and friends were willing helpers."[134]

Realizing that coeds weren't always available, an official-sized pool table was presented to a ward as a gift from the combined chapters in Ohio in 1956. The chapters reported that the hospital's motto "is every activity is a new form of therapy," and the gift had been greatly enjoyed by the staff and patients.[135] In 1959, the Department of Ohio presented a popcorn machine to the Chillicothe veterans. It was reported that 150 bags a day were popped from September through April by "the patients who are able help in this project and the popcorn is served at the movies, sports events, recreation halls, etc."[136]

In June 1956, the Department of Illinois reported on an experimental treatment program that had been supported for several years by a number of Illinois chapters:

"During a VAVS meeting at Downey Hospital in September 1953, Paul Conte, a young therapist in the Catatonical Research Clinic at Downey, made a plea for some VA organization to sponsor a group of catatonics for 'off station' parties or picnics.

"During the fall and early winter the men were entertained at nearby farms, lakes and homes. On the farms, they were shown the barns and animals and our hosts were very kind and considerate, allowing us to roast hamburgers, etc. over the open fire. In the woods surrounding the small lakes they roamed about hunting hickory nuts which were used later at the hospital. In the homes they were seated at dining tables and the hostess treated them as she would any other guests.

"[Once, when seated at a luncheon,] Ray Florek, the therapist in charge for the day, asked Adolph [a patient] to say thanks. Adolph in turn asked Ray to have the men bow their heads. When his wishes had been complied with, he said, 'Thank you, God, for getting us away from the hospital even if it is only for one day.' Ray then asked another lad if he wished to add to Adolph's remarks and Jim replied, 'No, Mr. Ray, Adolph said just what we all wanted him to say.'

"During the cold weather, the Scout Executives turn the Boys Scout camp over to the group. The Boys enjoy the natural beauty of the campsite while the mothers prepare their lunch. Much of the food is from the hospital but the mothers always see to it that there are ample sweets as the men seem to crave this type of food. When funds are low the mothers donate the cakes, cookies and pies and, on occasion, baked beans and hamburgers."

For patients who were more mobile, small groups were sometimes able to leave the hospital grounds, accompanied by gold star mothers and fathers, to attend activities the hospitals could not provide. The Ice Follies of 1955 was a special treat for a group of Philadelphia patients:

"On the night of January 4, the Delaware County Chapter Mothers took a group from the ward to the spectacular Ice Follies of 1955. The seats were in the front row right next to the ice. All the beautiful girls skated right up to the row and even planted a friendly kiss on one fellow's forehead. The Mothers made it a slam bang affair by supplying the hot dogs and the traditional orange drinks. The boys were so enthused about the entertainment and wrote a very enthusiastic letter of thanks to the Chapter."[137]

For patients near Wodo, Wisconsin the big event of the year was the annual VAVS Carnival held at the Veterans Administration Center. More than forty volunteer service organizations, including AGSM, combined efforts to make this a special day for patients too disabled to attend public events:

"The 26 booths and concessions set up on the carnival grounds on the shore of Lake Wheeler are gaily decorated by the members of the various organizations. Each booth has a different type of game of chance such as bingo, fish pond, flying saucers, chuck-o-luck, ring toss, etc. and are operated by the volunteers. All the while that patients and members are playing the games a 40-piece band is playing all types of enjoyable music. We can conservatively say that at the peak of the carnival periods there are as many as 2,000 people on the grounds. Popcorn, Coca-Cola and ice cream are provided by the organizations for those patients and members who can indulge."[138]

What did these heroic efforts by the volunteers mean to the staff and patients at the VA facilities? In Maine, the Augusta, Lewiston, Auburn, and Portland chapters were honored guests at an elegant tea sponsored by the nurses and doctors at Togus Veterans Hospital in Maine in appreciation for their tireless work at the hospital. Staff members from other facilities wrote to express their own and the patients' thanks. Perhaps Dr. Leo D. Cady, physician manager of the Houston VA Hospital in Texas, said it best:

"The only way that we can keep up our payments on our debt to the Gold Star Mothers is through an all-out effort, every day in the year, to provide the very best medical care to all of our veteran patients."[139]

From the patients' perspective, the gold star mothers offered just what the VAVS program had hoped—a touch of home, a connection to the community, and the assurance that they had not been forgotten. All thirty-two patients in Women's Ward 85 at American Lake VA Hospital (a psychiatric facility in the Seattle/Tacoma area) signed the letter written by a fellow patient in appreciation of a silver coffee service set presented to the ward by the Department of Washington:

"Year after year the Gold Star Mothers have been coming to our ward bringing entertainment and refreshments (good things homemade from their own kitchens) and bringing themselves, trying to share with us this strange institutional experience. In the humble persistence of the Gold Star Mothers we read a firm determination: We who are cut off from home and friends through long years are not abandoned by our countrymen. That is the assurance their coming has brought us.

"Now these Mothers of veterans have done another typical thing in presenting this beautiful silver coffee service to the women patients of Ward No. 85. I say it is typical of them because the gift is precious, exceptional and beautiful. It tells us that the niceties and refinements of life were meant for us, too. Every time coffee is served from this lovely tray we will remember, Ladies, your persistent gallantry. Your beautiful gift, like a word 'fitly spoken' is as 'apples of gold in pitchers of silver.'"[140]

A poem printed in the November 1958 edition of *The Gold Star Mother* expressed another patient's appreciation:

Gold Star Mothers, we salute you,
Members of that noble band.
You who gave your sons in battle
In some far-off foreign land.
We who lie here in our illness,
Some in body, some in mind,
All love to see the Gold Star Mothers
For to us you are so kind.
Your hair has mostly turned to silver
But your hearts are solid gold.
All the veterans here adore you
May God keep you in his fold.
You have had your share of sorrows
In this world of grief and pain;
God is with you in your labors

When the veterans smile again.
You're the touch of home and mother
That we've sadly lacked for years.
For when we meet the Gold Star Mothers,
There are smiles, but never tears.

By Pat Hoover

Gold Star Mothers in the News

There was no shortage of press coverage for gold star mothers during the 1950s. Some humorous, some poignant, stories about gold star mothers were still of interest to the nation. Few events involving gold star mothers went unreported. There was an early start to the gold star media coverage in January 1950 when the story of a new gold star mothers' song was reported. The song had been introduced on stage in Texas by national president Eleanor Boyd's close friend—screen star, singer and famous sarong wearer, Dorothy Lamour:

"Nine Gold Star Mothers of Texas and the National President of the American Gold Star Mothers, Inc., Mrs. Walter H. Boyd of Long Beach, California, were honored Sunday, January 15, at The Shamrock in Houston, Texas where beautiful Dorothy Lamour introduced a song written especially for her Shamrock engagement, 'To the Gold Star Mother from the Lone Star State.'

"Like most entertainers who come to the hotel, Miss Lamour wanted a new idea for saluting Texas. While the usual tribute to Texans by the entertainers is teasing and frivolous, the glamour star found her subject for salute in a more serious vein. The mother of two young sons (she is Mrs. William Ross Howard III), she favored the brave women who lost their own sons in the war...

"From scattered cities in Texas, nine gold star mothers came to the Emerald Room to hear the touching tribute. As guests of Shamrock owner, Glenn McCarthy, the honorees were seated in the center of the room at a round table magnificently decorated with a gold star floral piece. During the vocal tribute, the spotlight was turned from the singer to the table where the gold star mothers sat and listened intently. More than 700 dinner club patrons rose to honor the brave mothers.

"Touching the hearts of all persons present, these words were dedicated to the 'Gold Star Mother from the Lone Star State:'

On the shores of Okinawa with the fighting
*   leathernecks*

There was one in every squadron and they called
  him "Tex."
The dream he cherished, we dedicate
To the Gold Star Mother from the Lone Star State.

Fifteen thousand sons of Texas lie beneath their
  crosses white
And the stars up in the heavens burn a vigil light.
But who knows better the endless wait
Than the Gold Star Mother from the Lone Star
  State.

Everywhere—everywhere—
On the land, the sea and in the air
Everywhere—everywhere—
You will find the flower of Texas planted there.
Oh, he rounded up the rustlers and he made the
  range so wide
That there's room for everybody in the world to
  ride
The dream he died for, we dedicate,
To the Gold Star Mother from the Lone Star State.[141]

In December 1951, two New Jersey gold star mothers offered to adopt a lonely young GI they heard speak on a television program. Private Matthew J. Stovall, twenty-eight, of West Point, New York, had been wounded in Korea, sent home for recuperation, and was now returning voluntarily to Korea because he has no close family ties. A contestant on a television broadcast, he told the audience that he wanted to go back to Korea "so somebody with a family can come home."

Alice V. Richie and Evelyn Jeffrey, each of whom lost a son in World War II, immediately contacted the television studio with offers to adopt the young soldier. They were both members of AGSM's Plainfield chapter. Assigned to Camp Kilmer and scheduled for reassignment, the soldier was unable to meet with his new "mothers" but they promised him letters and gifts as well as a huge homecoming celebration when his tour of duty was completed.

However, Private Stovall's story didn't end there. As a result of the adoption story in the *New York Times,* Matthew found out he wasn't alone in the world after all:

"Mrs. Elizabeth O'Connor… identified herself as the twin of Private Stovall. Mrs. O'Connor said she lost all trace of her family after she was adopted by a Brooklyn family when she was 9 years old. That was nineteen years ago.

"Only a week-end pass, on which Private Stovall

was away from Camp Kilmer, New Jersey, stood yesterday between the twins and immediate reunion. Camp officials said the soldier was due back by 6 a.m. today. Mrs. O'Connor, who said she would call the camp first thing in the morning, declared: "There's no reason for Matt to want to go back now. He's got a family now. I can't wait to see him."

"An Army spokesman said he doubted that the soldier would be sent back to Korea.

"The account in the *Times* gave West Point as Private Stovall's home town. That clinched his identity for Mrs. O'Connor. Her baptism papers showed West Point as her birthplace—June 7, 1923. Mrs. O'Connor said that when she and her brother were 9 years old, living then in Middletown, New York her mother offered her for adoption. She had no contact with the family after that.[142]

"After 19 years of separation, Matthew and Elizabeth met again on December 3.

"'I just said "hello" and then grabbed her,' he said later as he began plans to play Santa Claus for his 1-year old niece on 'the first good Christmas since I was a little kid.'

"Brother and sister agreed that their reunion was 'like a fairy tale,' said Mrs. O'Connor. 'You read these things about other people but you never think they'll happen to you.' She had been too excited to sleep at all the night before, she said, and "now that we're together to talk, it's been so long we don't know where to start.'"[143]

In 1952, to the delight of the local press, a gold star mother in Chicago was drafted for military service by the government:

"A Gold Star mother, classified 1-A by a draft board, asserted today that she was ready to go into military service if the Government continued its efforts to draft her. Mrs. Joe Willie Riley said that she had received frequent notices from a Chicago draft board. She had returned them marked 'no such person' or 'I am a mother' but they kept arriving. The latest one ordered her to report at 7 a.m. January 9 at an induction station. She said she would. The notices have been addressed to Joe Willie Riley.

"'My parents christened me Joe Willie after my grandmother, Joanna, and my aunt Willie,' Mrs. Riley said, adding, 'My efforts to find myself a job has failed because I'm more than 35. Yet the Government thinks I am good draft material. I've given both my sons to the service. What more do they want?'

"The draft board is investigating."[144]

By the next day, Joe Willie had been reclassified "strictly 4-F" by the State Selective Service board. Investigation determined that in 1949 Mrs. Riley's mailbox had been "plundered:"

"A check payable to Joe Willie Riley was among the loot. The thief could not cash the check without identification, so he strolled into the local draft board and registered in Mrs. Riley's name, Joe Willie Riley."[145]

Within a week of Mrs. Riley being declared "strictly 4-F," the FBI had captured the culprit:

"A man who registered 40 times with selective service—and thereby threatened a Gold Star mother with induction—was arrested yesterday... [He] confessed to registering under 40 names so he would have identification in cashing $7,400 in checks stolen from... letter boxes in the last two years. Among the checks was one for $60 issued by the Treasury Department—the monthly insurance benefit on the national service policy of [Mrs. Riley's] son killed in World War II."[146]

In 1953, gold star mother Marguerite Bezila sent this letter to the editor of a Johnstown, Pennsylvania, newspaper:

"You would be surprised at all the people who do not know what a Gold Star Mother is... The ordinary person has the impression that we are 'a sad and weepy lot' who meet to console each other in our grief. Nothing is further from the truth. We are a happy group of mothers. Knowing each has suffered, we do not talk about it. We have turned our backs on sorrow and, smiling bravely, we work cheerfully—for peace in the world.

"We are dedicated to the task of working unselfishly, tirelessly and ceaselessly for the boys in the veterans' hospitals. We lavish our love on the wounded and shattered hospitalized veterans who were our sons' comrades-in-arms.

"What is a Gold Star Mother? One who has given? No, rather one who has relinquished; her son gave. One who is willing to settle back into her own memories, expecting others to follow? No, rather one who has early learned that satisfaction lies in selfless thought of others. One upon whom a special brand of motherhood has been bestowed? No, hers were the same hopes and plans known to mothers everywhere, but the broadened scope of her understanding now includes other mothers' sons.

"What is a Gold Star Mother? She is one who

knows, beyond doubt, that she has an unalterable stake in the freedoms, blessings, opportunities, and obligations of our country."[147]

In honor of Memorial Day 1956, the *Chicago Tribune* published an in-depth article about mothers "for whom the nation's wars will never end":

"They are the Gold Star Mothers whose sons gave their lives in fighting for their country. The mothers have continued to give of themselves—in large and small ways—to help their communities.

"Typical of the thousands of Gold Star mothers in the state [Illinois] is Mrs. Frances Carey, 52, whose small gold star flag has hung in the window of her red brick bungalow since 1945. Her only son, Philip Pierce Cary, a Navy bomber pilot was killed in a crash shortly before he completed training in Corpus Christi, Texas, on September 20, 1943. It was two years before Mrs. Carey... had the courage to replace the blue star in her window with the gold one. Today, flying from a long pole outside the Carey home is the big American flag which draped Ensign Carey's coffin on his last trip home.

"While their thoughts are with the dead today, the mothers—working thru such organizations as the [Illinois Gold Star Mothers], the American Gold Star Mothers, Catholic War Veterans and... the American Legion Auxiliary—are very much concerned with the living.

"They visit at the bedsides of hospitalized veterans, plan parties for them, tag on Poppy Day, work with charity and health organizations, and serve their churches.

"Some who worked hard for others in the past, no longer are able to carry on volunteer work. Such a mother is Mrs. Mabel Swift, 76... whose loss occurred in France on August 11, 1918. Her son, Frank, a bugler with the 131st infantry, received the posthumous award of the Distinguished Service Cross. After two other runners had died, Swift volunteered to carry a message thru heavy fire when his company was in a perilous position. He was wounded but delivered the message, dying on his way to a dressing station.

"Like her son, Mrs. Swift was up front when volunteers were needed. She once ran a canteen in the city hall for returning doughboys. She helped organize the Illinois Gold Star Mothers in 1919 and was their first president.

"Last month she had to leave her Forest Park home

where a small, homemade cardboard gold star—set in a black square—had hung in her son's bedroom since 1918. The home was in the path of the Congress Street super-highway.

"Mothers with claims to two gold stars are Mrs. Clara Reiker, 58, who lost twin sons, and Mrs. Augusta Nenne, 63… who also lost two sons—on the same day.

"Mrs. Reiker's boys, Earl and Wilbert, are buried together in Italy. Earl, a field artilleryman, was killed February 26, 1944 in the Italian invasion at Anzio. His twin, an air force ground crewman, died January 1, 1954 in France when he went to the aid of a crew trapped in an exploding bomber. The soldier's medal for valor was presented posthumously.

"Unusual circumstances attended Mrs. Neene's double loss. Both sons were technical sergeants on air force bomber crews. On December 19, 1943 each flew on a mission to his death. John, the elder, was in a bomber shot down by an Italian plane. William's bomber, with its engine afire, led Jap planes away from the remainder of the squadron which was attacking a target in the Marshall Islands. He received the posthumous award of the Distinguished Flying Cross.

"After Mrs. Betty Luka's son, Marine Corp. Howard Svanberk, was killed on Okinawa, she found comfort in 'adopting' a young marine she discovered at Vaughn Hospital. He was paralyzed and without a family of his own to visit him. For three years, Mrs. Luka saw him every Sunday, sometimes arranging to have him brought to her home…

"'When he died,' she said, 'it broke my heart all over again.'

"A Gold Star mother who no longer can do hospital work because of her health is Mrs. Elizabeth King, 63. Mrs. King's only son, Pfc. James A. King, fighting with the engineers, was killed June 11, 1944 in France after taking part in the D-Day invasion. Formerly active with Gold Star and the World War II Mothers, Mrs. King now devotes her afternoons to her grandson, Paul Coombs Jr., 8, while her daughter works."[148]

In April 1958, Lorraine I. Desser, national sergeant at arms, submitted an article to *The Gold Star Mother* after convincing the subject, Carmen Raffin, that other gold star mothers would be fascinated by her story:

"Mrs. Carmen Raffin, President of Waterbury Chapter, Waterbury, Connecticut… worked for French saboteurs in World War II. A knock on the door of her home in the city of Clichy, a suburb of Paris, could be the ominous pounding of the Gestapo or the urgent rap of one of our own downed American fliers.

"Her life here in America is a placid one in contrast to those long years when France was under the iron boot of Hitler's Wehrmecht. During those years she executed some fifty orders relayed to her by the French underground headquarters. Discovery would mean death to her and probably her entire family.

"Mrs. Raffin said, 'When freedom is lost—a life is a small price to get it back.'"

"'Sometimes I was scared stiff,' admits Mrs. Raffin, showing a rolled parchment—an award from President Harry S. Truman and signed by Dwight D. Eisenhower, then General of the Army and commanding general of the United States Forces in the European Theater. The citation reads:

"'The President of the United States of America has directed me to express to Carmen Raffin the gratitude and appreciation of the American people for the gallant service in assisting the escape of Allied Soldiers from the enemy.'

"Who can tell, maybe our Mother Raffin helped one or more of our sons while doing her most important work?

"Mrs. Raffin, who came to Waterbury in…1948, lived in this country before for seventeen years. She was in New York City for two years, and later lived in Detroit for five years before returning to France. At the outbreak of war in Europe, Mrs. Raffin sent her two sons back to this country. They immediately enlisted in the American Air Force. One was shot down only ninety miles from where she lived in the village of Auber-Villiers. It was his first mission.

"In Mrs. Raffin's search for her son's grave she had some heartbreaking experiences. She searched every small town for news of the American whose body the Germans had tossed on a truck and toured the towns, shouting 'These are your liberators, look at them!' She finally found his grave at the side of a road.

"Mrs. Raffin's husband, Henri, an electronics engineer, worked independently of his wife during the Nazi occupation of France. He worked on slowing up Nazi production in the Societie Francaise Radio Electrique Plant in Paris. Mrs. Raffin and many heroic French people were constantly on the alert to help American and British fliers get back to friendly territory."[149]

Still Searching and Hoping

For many World War II mothers, the new decade had brought just one hope—that they would be able to learn more about the last moments of their sons' lives. Many mothers whose sons had been declared dead by the military, but whose bodies were never recovered, kept hope alive that their child might not be dead but unable to contact them due to illness, injury or mental breakdown. In the early 1950s, almost every issue of *The Gold Star Mother* carried one or more requests for information—any information—about specific soldiers and sailors who had never returned home. For these mothers and hundreds of others, an opportunity to speak or correspond with someone who had known their son would ease their grief a little. Others would continue to hope that somehow the official reports had been wrong, and that one day their sons would come home again.

Questions and Answers

It became the practice during the 1950s to occasionally publish short questions and answers in *The Gold Star Mother* to clarify what were identified as areas of concern among the membership. Some of the answers would change over time as social mores and organizational perspectives evolved:

Q: Is the Gold Star Organization strictly a religious organization?

A: American Gold Star Mothers, Inc. is non-partisan and interdenominational as far as politics and religion are concerned. We do have at our installations a rabbi, priest and Protestant minister, in that we are preserving the cornerstone of Americanism in preserving and maintaining the right to worship as one pleases which is a constitutional right of the American people. (January 1950)

Q: Is there any reason of character, religion, etc. that can keep any eligible Gold Star Mother from becoming a member?

A: There is no mother called ineligible because of her faith. Her eligibility is upon the government's decision of her son's death in the line of duty or combat. (January 1950)

Q: A sailor who was killed at his home during the war, on leave and in uniform, is his mother eligible to become a member?

A: We ask for Certificates of Death so as to have from the government's own office of eligibility the official document; from this document the mother's eligibility is decided. (January 1950)

Q: Can the president stand up and say disparaging things about the organization, stating she must tell the truth?

A: If the president feels she is presiding over mothers and holding office in an organization she does not personally feel is fine, she should resign her office and her membership. (October 1950)

Q: Do we salute each other and if no, when does a gold star mother salute?

A: The only salute that a Gold Star Mother makes is to the American Flag, when pledging allegiance or when it is passing within 50 feet, or when "The Star Spangled Banner" is being played in place of the Pledge of Allegiance to the flag. (January 1951)

Q: Are Negro mothers eligible to join American Gold Star Mothers?

A: Yes. We desire the Negro mothers to form Chapters whereby they will function the same as the white Chapters, having one delegate for each ten members being recognized at the national convention as delegates are from the other Chapters. Where there are only a few in the community, too small a group to form a Chapter, they may become members-at-large, which is the same as any white mother may do if she is in a community that is too small to form a Chapter. All members-at-large are eligible to attend the national conventions. (February 1952) [Note: In November 1954, *The Gold Star Mother* contained a photo of the officers of the newly instituted Victory Circle Chapter in Columbus, Ohio. All of the women were African-American gold star mothers, including several from World War 1.][150]

Q: Is it all right for us to belong to other Gold Star organizations?

A: No. It has been voted at national convention that our officers and members of American Gold Star Mothers, Inc., should belong to no other Gold Star organization. This does not mean American Legion, V.F.W. or D.A.V. Auxiliaries. There are several reasons. One is that few have money enough to belong to several Gold Star organizations. Few have strength enough, if they work as they should in American Gold Star Mothers, Inc., to work elsewhere. We, of American Gold Star Mothers, Inc. are without a doubt a good American organization. We do not want our members joining organizations of any type other than bona fide original veterans groups. (February 1952) [Note: This answer reflected national president Eleanor Boyd's position on the issue of belonging to more than one gold star organization. Shortly after her tenure ended, it was made clear that no amendments supporting such a position had ever been approved in convention, and AGSM members could belong to any organizations they chose.]

Q: What amount is charged now for new members?

A: On and after September 1st all applications must have $3 which includes initiation fee of $1 and $2 for national and state per capita which pays up to January 1955. Of course, each Chapter also collects the amount of their chapter dues. (September 1953)

Q: Is it permissible for members to wear caps and capes to restaurants after having worn them when attending a meeting?

A: American Gold Star Mothers caps and capes are never to be worn on the street or in any conspicuous place. Caps and capes may be worn at memorial services, at the funerals of our American Gold Star Mothers, and on the annual American Gold Star Mothers Day. It is optional, first, at funerals of returned veterans; second, at funerals of gold star fathers; third, color guards may wear caps and capes at chapter meetings and other appropriate meetings. (November 1955)

Q: Can chapters be named after individuals?

A: New chapters may be named for a World War I mother who has served as national president. (March 1958)

Q: What is the minimum number of members a chapter must have to continue?

A: It has been learned that some Chapters have fewer than ten active members, due to age, health, etc. The by-laws state only that there must be ten new members to form a chapter. (March 1958)

Q: Do we remove hats during the burial service at the funeral home or at the graveside service?

A: There is nothing in the constitution or by-laws that states a member should or should not remove hat or caps. Personally, I would keep my hat or cap on. I know that men take their hats off, but I have never seen a woman remove her hat during any service. (January 1959)

One issue that had bred confusion since the early years of the organization was the military status of members of the Merchant Marines. Mothers of Merchant Mariners who had died during war time had not been admitted to membership until 1946 when convention delegates approved a resolution to extend membership to the mothers of Merchant Mariners killed in the line of duty. In August 1952, *The Gold Star Mother* clarified the issue in an article entitled "Merchant Mariners Are Civilians, Says Congress":

"It was at the 1949 National Convention of American Gold Star Mothers, Inc. that the Gold Star Mothers found that Merchant Marine mothers were mothers of civilians, therefore they could not be members or hold office in American Gold Star Mothers, Inc., since the requirements for membership required… that the son or daughter had served and died honorably in the line of duty or combat or service-connected in the Armed Forces.

"This should complete for all Chapters the reason for the Merchant Marine mother not being accepted in American Gold Star Mother, Inc. membership—civilians are not eligible for GI benefits, therefore their mothers are not eligible for membership."[151]

Preparing for a New Decade

Despite the turmoil and discord of the 1950s, AGSM emerged stronger, more focused, and more capable than ever before. Their poise would soon be severely tested as the new decade brought another devastating war and new internal challenges as the role of women in the nation began to change.

Fig. 9-1: (Detail from panorama.) Attendees at the 15th National Convention in Long Beach, California had an opportunity to travel to the Memorial National Home Foundation property in Ojai for the dedication of the first cottage on June 12, 1952. *(AGSM Collection)*

CHAPTER 9

The Memorial National Home Foundation

The record in this case discloses shocking breaches, abuses and abandonment of trusts by the Memorial National Home Foundation and its dominant and domineering figure, Eleanor D. Boyd, which made a mockery of the ethical and moral standards imposed upon a charitable trust.
—BRIEF OF RESPONDENT AGSM. DISTRICT COURT OF APPEAL, 2nd Appellate Dist. State of CA, Div. Two, 2nd Civil No. 22766, p3

DESPITE A YEAR OF STELLAR accomplishments as AGSM national president, Eleanor Boyd made it clear at the 1947 national convention that she was ready to turn over the presidential gavel to her elected successor. Mrs. Boyd had already cast herself in a new role for the coming year and she needed only the approval of the delegates to turn her plan into action. Mrs. Boyd's dream of a national home for needy gold star mothers would be the bane of the organization for the next ten years—and the long-term salvation of AGSM in the decades to come. The national home controversy polarized the membership, and the decade of bitterness, threats, slander, and lawsuits took a terrible toll on the organization.

Gaining Support For Her Vision
On the second day of the 1947 convention, Mrs. Boyd spoke to the delegates about her vision of a home where gold star mothers could live and be cared for during their final years:

"While working in the hospitals and generally looking for ways to solve the needs of our returned veterans, your national president found, among the American Gold Star Mothers, many who were forced to live on a meager subsistence level. Some did not have adequate shoes or clothes to wear on the street. Some were existing—not living—in basements without windows. Many badly needed what they were not getting. Someone who really cares for them in every sense of the word is a necessity. These are mothers whose sons died for their country but today are forgotten except for too few dollars received monthly.

"I feel we should keep faith with our sons and daughters by forming a foundation within our present organization for a national memorial home for these forgotten mothers. This can be done under the direction of the American Gold Star Mothers, Inc. which is a non-profit organization. It will demand a lot of work with the satisfaction of a job well done as our only pay. It is now needed by many of our World War I mothers. Many of our World War II mothers are in need of aid. Their numbers will grow with the years.

"This is a project that lies close to my heart and I am sure you too would feel as I do, had you seen some of the really pitiful cases of neglect that have come to my attention in the last year. To carry this to a successful conclusion could well be the most important concern of all of us in this coming year.

"As American Gold Star Mothers, Inc., we have a duty to those who carried the flag—and fell. We must pick it up. We must go forward. We must espouse those things which we know they would want us to. We may face enemy action as they did, but also as they did we must go forward until we are victorious for the right, and let us pray, God, we can be so powerful in our efforts that there may be no future swelling of our ranks."[1]

A resolution was proposed to give Mrs. Boyd the

authority to move forward on this project on behalf of AGSM:

"I would like to speak a few words about a subject which our National President spoke of in her opening address this morning, about a Memorial National Home for Gold Star Mothers. This I know is something that our President is very much interested in, and I feel that her travels from coast-to-coast as she has served us as National President have enabled her to come in contact with more of the mothers and their needs than any of us have been able to do. And due to the fact that she has given so much of herself and her time to the organization, and has accomplished so many things, not only in the name of Gold Star Mothers, but in the name of Eleanor D. Boyd, that I would like at this time to present a resolution to the convention.

"Resolved that President Eleanor D. Boyd be hereby authorized and directed to proceed with the formation and establishment of a national home for needy members of Gold Star Mothers, which home shall at all times be under the auspices of the American Gold Star Mothers, Inc.

"Resolved further that President Eleanor D. Boyd be hereby directed to make a full report as soon as possible showing the action which she has taken with respect to the formation of the memorial national home."[2]

Mrs. Boyd immediately turned the podium over to the first vice president so she could answer questions about the proposed home outside her duties as national president and chairperson of the convention:

"If you want to ask questions, I will be glad to answer them. Every chapter will participate on an equal basis. It can be done so that the World War II mothers can benefit from this too. I had calls and letters from mothers saying, 'I am all alone; my husband is dead; my son died on the battlefield, and I can work another five years. Then what is going to happen to me? I haven't enough to take care of myself after all that time.'

"We have some [architectural] plans to present to you... We are not voting on the plans. You are voting on the Home and you should know how interested the architect was, not because he is going to get a dollar, but because he is going to contribute his skill to the mothers of sons and daughters who didn't come back... If we do it in California, it should be very 'Californian.'"[3]

Delegate Mollie Kadner (Cleveland, Ohio) then asked, "Where would this home be located? I suggest that it could be more centrally located."

Mrs. Boyd responded:

"Let us think, if you will, of where the mothers can get out... Then, we have got to think of the expense, the upkeep of that home. Remember that if you have them outside the greater part of the year, it is important. You can stay one month; one week; six years; twenty years. There will be no one as Director that will be allowed one cent of salary. We will be doing for our mothers who cannot do for themselves."[4]

Alice Scalfonte (Akron, Ohio) expressed concern that the chapters would be required to pay annual assessments in order to support such a property. Mrs. Boyd reassured the delegates saying:

"Not all of it will come from the Chapters. We will have to get it other ways. Many gifts have been promised, but I wouldn't take them because I wanted to 'OK' it first. We will need special nurses—the foundation will get money outside the chapters, because you couldn't finance it yourselves. If we find that a lot of mothers need it, we will make it large enough right at the start; if not, there will be wings added from time to time. It will be the condition we will work on. We don't want a big structure. We don't need it right now. We will build it as we need it."[5]

Expressing concern for gold star couples, Anna Larkin (Salem, Oregon) asked, "If we have this home, if there is a mother and father both living, and they are neither one able to work, would it be possible that they both would have a home there?"

Mrs. Boyd explained that the main beneficiaries of the Home would be gold star mothers but the fathers would be "protected":

"Our incorporation... will not mention the fathers, because most of [the needy]... are widows, without relatives of any kind. We will protect the fathers ... [and] build a cottage for a few of them where it is necessary. We will meet the problem when we come to it."[6]

Anna Page (Detroit, Michigan) asked how destitute a mother had to be to qualify for residency, "If the mother is a widow, does she have to be without any other child to help her?" Mrs. Boyd responded that the "rule would be flexible."[7]

With no further discussion, the delegates enthusiastically endorsed the proposal to form a foundation to establish a home for gold star mothers in need or without means. To celebrate the resolution, a total of $441 in one-dollar bills was collected from the delegates as seed money for funding the new home.

Mrs. Boyd had planned her campaign well. The fact that she had preliminary architectural drawings to show might have warned the membership that steps toward this goal had already been taken and the approval they were now asked to provide was, at best, a token endorsement. As she made her selfless appeal to the convention audience, it would have been obvious to all that Mrs. Boyd, a stylish, wealthy socialite, was not going to end up as a destitute elderly mother. However, many convention delegates who did not share Mrs. Boyd's social and financial position could easily imagine such a scenario for themselves and those they knew. Harsh memories of the Depression were still vivid for these women, and the possibility of being in a position of need in years to come would have been frightening. And, since Mrs. Boyd had already announced that she would not be a candidate for re-election to the organization's presidency for the next year, delegates may have seen approval of her resolution as a way of thanking her for her year of hard work on AGSM's behalf.

Having orchestrated the response she wanted from the membership, when the convention ended, Mrs. Boyd had a mandate, freedom from other organizational duties and the power to carry out her plan. She had proven herself a great strategist and, bolstered by legal support she had already contracted from the most prestigious law firms in Los Angeles, she wasted little time.

Establishing a Memorial National Home Foundation

The Articles of Incorporation for the Memorial National Home Foundation (Home) had already been drafted when the project was presented to the AGSM convention in June. Finalized and filed in July, less than a month after the convention, a charitable non-profit corporation was created under California law:

"The original articles… adopted the name 'American Gold Star Mothers, Incorporated, Memorial National Home Foundation.' Its purposes as therein stated are to acquire, manage and maintain homes, rest homes, etc. for distressed and needy members in good standing of American Gold Star Mothers, Incorporated in any State or Territory; and to receive funds and other property to be used for the protection, health, welfare and relief of sick, destitute, distressed and needy members in good standing of American Gold Star Mothers, Inc."[8]

The Articles established a board of five directors and prescribed that "[a] majority thereof shall be members in good standing of American Gold Star Mothers, Incorporated." Mrs. Boyd personally selected the board members from the AGSM membership. One, Marion C. Harr of Cleveland, a former assistant AGSM treasurer, would later testify that "she signed the original Articles of Incorporation in Dr. Boyd's office under Mrs. Boyd's instruction to 'Hurry up and put your name there, Harr,' without being given an opportunity to read the Articles and without knowing she was thereby becoming a Director of the Foundation." Mrs. Harr never attended a Home board meeting and later stated that she always believed the Home Foundation to be part of AGSM. "I had so much faith in Mrs. Boyd, I thought she could do no wrong," Mrs. Harr later explained. "You don't lose faith in a person overnight. It is a cumulative thing."[9]

As the head of the Home Foundation, Mrs. Boyd began corresponding directly with the AGSM membership in bulletins separate from the AGSM newsletter. Usually, activities reported as needing to occur or having just occurred were, in fact, long since completed. In July 1947, in the first Home bulletin, she informed readers that the Foundation had to be set up separately from AGSM for "tax exemption purposes." This step had, in fact, already been taken, although the bulletin implied that the Foundation had only recently been informed of the requirement.

This separation from the main organization was the final straw for many concerned AGSM members who already feared the project was too costly for AGSM to pursue. AGSM's national executive board took immediate action. The following notice was sent "to all chapters and members of American Gold Star Mothers Incorporated" by national president Anna G. Hagerty:

"This is a full and complete copy of the articles of Incorporation for the National Memorial Home. This Corporation AS SET UP WAS REJECTED, in full, by the National Executive Board of the American Gold Star Mothers, Inc. This action was taken at the meeting of the National Executive Board…

"Please be advised that the National Home Foundation is NOW under the control of the American Gold Star Mothers, Inc. National Executive Board and all future contributions for the Home Foundation should be made payable to American Gold Star Mothers, Inc. National Home Fund and forwarded to me."[10]

Confronted by the board's declaration, Mrs. Boyd

maintained that her mandate had been approved by the membership at a national convention and could be revoked only through a resolution from the membership at a future convention. Contentious exchanges continued between Mrs. Boyd and the national board even as she began negotiating for the property she had already selected as the site of the future Home. She kept the membership advised of her position on these matters through monthly Home bulletins.

Aware of the managerial and financial concerns of the AGSM national board, in *Memorial National Home Bulletin* No. III (December 1947) Mrs. Boyd focused again on the validity of her mandate for establishing the Home, specifically justifying the reasons behind the decisions that had been made thus far:

"Some question has been raised as to the authority of this Foundation to proceed with its work.

"Some two years before I was elected your National President in Philadelphia, I had been talking before Chapters, stating that we must establish 'care' for our mothers so that there would be no stigma attached to the "care" as it would be free from any institutional taint. Having this in mind, when given the authority to organize the Memorial National Home Foundation, I chose counsel familiar with such matters, whose services are donated. Counsel advised that there are numerous reasons why the corporation should be a separate unit from the parent body, i.e. American Gold Star Mothers, Inc., but that a majority of the directors should be members of the American Gold Star Mothers, Inc.

"It was deemed advisable to have as directors a businessman and a lawyer for a number of reasons, which would be too numerous to list, but perhaps two of the most important should be mentioned:

"That large gifts usually have 'strings' on them or involve tax and business problems. There are also investment problems, property management problems, etc. that will arise. It is, therefore, obvious that an experienced businessman and an experienced lawyer must be a part of the directors and must be in California so that a majority of the directors can always be present for a meeting.

"It must be recognized that the Gold Star Mothers as a group will become older and older so that their ability to keep in touch with business problems and manage the Home Foundation would become a problem. Experiences of the Grand Army of the Republic, Spanish American War Veterans and others have shown the advisability of the plan we have adopted.

"Incidentally, the articles of incorporation of the Memorial National Home Foundation prevent any of the directors [from] receiving any benefit at any time. An essential in the raising of money for charitable purposes is that the donor of such monies as well as the recipients be assured that money raised shall be used for only one purpose, in this case, the benefit of the gold star mothers. That could not be done under the constitution of the American Gold Star Mothers, Inc. Therefore, acting under California laws and by virtue of the authority given me by the enclosed resolution, a non-profit corporation was established.

"The resolution also stated that the Home shall at all times be under the auspices of the American Gold Star Mothers, Inc. For that reason, the Corporation was named The American Gold Star Mothers, Inc. Memorial National Home Foundation, and bylaws provided that a majority of the directors should be members of the American Gold Star Mothers, Inc.

"The enclosed resolution further provides that I 'make a full report as soon as possible, showing the action which she has taken with respect to the formation of the National Home.' This I have done through two previous bulletins."[11]

As she continued, the true effect of the separation between the Home Foundation and the AGSM national board was finally made clear to her readers. Mrs. Boyd considered herself accountable only to the AGSM membership when gathered in a sanctioned convention setting:

"I am now in receipt of a letter from the National President of the American Gold Star Mothers, Inc., demanding that the National Board have complete control of the Memorial National Home Foundation, that I surrender all monies to her [national president Anna G. Hagerty] and that I cease sending bulletins to the Chapters. A bulletin has also been issued on her letterhead, which states the Corporation [meaning the Home Foundation as a separate entity] has been rejected by the National Board.

"The [Home Foundation] is still a legal and functioning corporation. It will remain so until action taken by legal delegates in a legally called annual National Convention of the AGSM, Inc. decrees otherwise. The National Officers of the American Gold Star Mothers, Inc., are separate and distinct from the Directors of the Memorial National Home Foundation, and rightly so. The Officers of the American Gold Star Mothers, Inc. owe their obligation wholly to the organization they represent. The Directors of the Memorial National Home Foundation have a dual obligation. Their responsibility lies not only in providing a National Home for distressed and needy members of American Gold Star Mothers, Inc., but they must conduct their affairs in such a way that no donor to the Memorial National Home Foundation shall ever question the singleness of purpose for which the funds they gave are applied.

"The National President and National Board of American Gold Star Mothers, Inc. have plenty to do to establish new Chapters and carry on other work of the parent organization. It is impossible to determine the damage that has been done to the establishment of the Home Foundation by the action of certain National Officers, but rest assured, I will continue my efforts in your behalf and I will be happy when I can state in a future bulletin [that] your Memorial National Home is an actuality.

"I told you in Convention, June 1947, that the National President of the American Gold Star Mothers, Inc. and the President of the Memorial National Home Foundation should not be the same person. I believe the present situation proves the wisdom of the statement made at Convention. Please read this to all members in the Chapter. They should know what is happening. It is important for each individual's welfare.

"We need your cooperation if we are to benefit the gold star mothers. You are free at all times to write and ask questions or to give suggestions, which will be presented to the directors. It is our wish to make this Foundation so fine that it will be truly a Memorial."[12]

Attempting to stop the Home Foundation from moving even further forward, in December 1947 national president Anna G. Hagerty again wrote to Mrs. Boyd on behalf of the national board. Her letter expressed both the frustration and anger resulting from their repeated but unsuccessful attempts to halt Mrs. Boyd's relentless Home activity:

"You and the other people connected with your California set-up have received innumerable requests to stop all action regarding a home foundation for our organization and [to stop] using our name. You, and they, have received our objections, our protests, and an expression of our desire to handle the home foundation program ourselves. I say to you again:

"1. Do not send out any more bulletins, letters, etc. to any of our Chapters or Members. Stop using our Mailing List. It is our property and no one else's to use. Your Bulletin No. 3 was an audacious thing to mail in view of all the letters sent to you since November 11. Do not send out any Bulletin No. 4 or anything else.
2. Stop using the name American Gold Star Mothers, Inc.
3. Give consideration to the letters forwarded to Mr. Faries and Mr. Ferguson by our Counsel and the National Officers of our Organization.
4. Who are the three Gold Star Mothers on your Board?

"We do not care for nor want Mr. Faries' counsel or interpretation of facts. [Mr. Faries, a prominent Los Angeles jurist, was a close personal friend of the Boyds and a Memorial National Home Foundation board member.] As for his request, as you say, for a certified copy of any resolutions of the Board, he has received sufficient information regarding its action to put all of you on notice that all of you people are acting without approval of the [AGSM] Board. The matter of our disapproval of your actions will have considerable weight in the future and it is recommended that you adhere to our protests and objections."[13]

Acquiring the Home Property

As soon as the 1947 convention had approved her proposal, Mrs. Boyd had entered into negotiations to acquire the property she desired for the memorial home. She had long considered the government's Truman Boyd Manor property in Long Beach, California to be an ideal location for the establishment of the Home. Named for her youngest son, who had died in World War II, the Truman Boyd Manor had been constructed in 1941 by the government as a temporary wartime housing project for defense workers and armed forces personnel. More than 1,000 housing units (built to lower-than-normal construction standards in accordance with wartime temporary housing codes), an infirmary and various other buildings covered the ninety-one acres associated with the project.[14]

Thousands of soldiers and sailors who shipped out of the Port of Long Beach during the war had promised themselves that they would return one day to the place where the sun seemed always to shine and winter was just a state of mind. They kept that promise and, following the war, a huge influx of young families moved to the Southern California area, creating a desperate housing shortage and record unemployment. To ease the situation, the government made a few wartime housing projects available as temporary rental properties for ex-military personnel.

At the Truman Boyd Manor, the growing families living in the more than 1,000 bungalow-style apartments formed a city within the city. In addition to active military tenants and ex-military renters, Japanese internees, unable to purchase housing due to deed restrictions against minorities that had been enacted during the war, were also housed at the Truman Boyd Manor following their return from government relocation camps in 1945.

In August 1947, following the convention, Mrs. Boyd began her campaign to encourage the U.S. government and the City of Long Beach to relinquish the Truman Boyd Manor housing project to the Memorial National Home Foundation under the Lanham Act. Following the war, the government had begun divesting itself of properties that were no longer considered critical to the national defense. Municipalities and universities had the first option to acquire those properties. Laying the groundwork early for a future gold star home, Mrs. Boyd had already influenced legislators to include the phrase "and organizations that have as their purpose the benefit of members in good standing of American Gold Star Mothers, Inc." in the legislation to expand the institutions that could benefit from the Lanham Act.[16] Housing and properties transferred under the Lanham Act were sold at the original cost of the land with no additional cost assigned for improvements. This was a tremendous financial opportunity for cities and universities, and became a boon for gold star mothers as well.

Mrs. Boyd was well positioned to realize her dream of a national home for gold star mothers. As the head of the Home Foundation, supported by handpicked board members who were unwilling to question her actions, she had complete freedom to direct the Foundation as she chose. As a gold star mother of two sons and past national president of AGSM, she was virtually an icon —an icon who wielded enormous political, financial, and emotional power. Proactively working with legislators and agencies, she had cleverly positioned the law to support the Foundation's acquisition of the property she had wanted for the Home. The sanction of the AGSM membership for the Home project added to her political clout.

It was at this time that Mrs. Boyd's actions began to take on a confusing duality. Although the Home Foundation was now legally separate from AGSM, that relationship was seldom clear to those with whom she dealt. She later claimed she always represented only the Foundation in her dealings, yet those with whom she bargained believed that she was representing American Gold Star Mothers, Inc., as well:

"It was documented repeatedly in testimony by legislators and other decision-makers that, during the legislation and property acquisition negotiations, she repeatedly established and reinforced her 'credentials' with those in authority. Those credentials included the fact that she was a gold star mother of two sons and a past president of AGSM. She used AGSM stationery for correspondence, signing herself as president of that organization (although she no longer held that office) and chairman of the board of the Memorial Home Foundation. Congressman Clyde Doyle of Long Beach later stated that 'he participated with Mrs. Boyd in the Congressional and Navy Department discussions at the time… and it was assumed on all sides that this was a charitable project of the AGSM.'"[17]

Mrs. Boyd had no hesitation about using her gold star status to achieve her personal goals for a memorial home.

Under continuing pressure from Mrs. Boyd, the City of Long Beach relinquished its option to purchase the Truman Boyd Manor in December 1948, clearing the way for the Home Foundation to buy it. A newspaper report on the transaction offered Mrs. Boyd an opportunity to comment on the Home Foundation's plans for the property:

"The City's first option to purchase Truman Boyd Manor, a 90 acre federal housing project… was relinquished this morning to the American Gold Star Mothers, Inc., to be used as a national American Gold Star Mothers home. Mrs. Walter H. Boyd, president of the Memorial National Home Foundation, said the project would continue on its present status, with the foundation using it for needy Gold Star Mothers as vacancies arise.

"The Federal Housing Authority has approved the plan, subject to the city's action."[18]

Before the transaction could be finalized, however, the government placed a freeze on all such relinquishments.

Severing the Home Foundation from AGSM

Mrs. Boyd was not stymied by a temporary delay in acquiring the Truman Boyd Manor. She used the time to again amend the Foundation's charter. In January 1948, a significant change to the charter was ratified by the Home Foundation's directors without advising the AGSM national board. In essence, the change removed all mention of American Gold Star Mothers, Inc. as either sponsor or beneficiary of the Home. With this change, Mrs. Boyd effectively severed the relationship between the Home Foundation and AGSM:

"The name was changed to 'Memorial National Home Foundation' thus dropping the words 'American Gold Star Mothers, Incorporated.' The provision that a majority of directors must be members of Gold Star [AGSM] was changed to read: A majority thereof shall be Gold Star Mothers (mothers whose children were killed in service of the United States of America).

"The purpose clause of the articles was amended to eliminate reference to members of Gold Star and to say, for the 'welfare and relief of sick, destitute, distressed and needy Gold Star Mothers (mothers whose children were killed in service of the United States of America).'

"This was done without the knowledge or consent of Gold Star, its officers or National Executive Board. It was a plain attempt to change the scope of a charitable trust by mere amendment of the trustees' charter."[19]

The result of these changes was that the Memorial National Home would now benefit all gold star mothers, not just those who were members of AGSM, and AGSM would no longer be directly connected to the Home.

Mrs. Boyd's rancorous relationship with the AGSM national board continued. In *Memorial National Home Bulletin IV* (March 1948) she explained why some of the planned organizational developments had not occurred on time:

"It has taken some time to get things in order after some of the National Officers saw fit to interfere. Therefore, we were unable to get our Advisory Committee and others things established that we had intended to provide in the setting up of the committees for the foundation."[20]

She also alleged that donations to the Home were being diverted by the AGSM national board:

"[Unless you have] received an official receipt properly numbered and signed by me, with a thank you letter from the Memorial National Home Foundation directors, the money or contribution has not gotten through to me. Monies sent anywhere else have not been forwarded to the Memorial National Home Foundation. This in itself proves how necessary it is to have the finances of the Memorial National Home Foundation separate and distinct from any business transaction of the National Board or officers of the National Board of the American Gold Star Mothers, Inc."[21]

The announcement of the separation of AGSM and the Home produced "an indignant reaction from the National Executive Board."

Although Mrs. Boyd was well aware that the changes to the Foundation's articles had severed the relationship between the Foundation and American Gold Star Mothers, Inc., she continually pressured the AGSM membership for both personal and organizational donations to the Home. Encouraging competition between AGSM chapters, Mrs. Boyd suggested fundraising efforts that included bazaars, raffles, sales of plaques, donations in honor of her birthday, etc.[22]

During the late 1940s and early 1950s, *The Gold Star Mother*, the official AGSM organizational publication, contained a "constantly and continually increasing series of reports regarding... the Memorial National Home Foundation, numerous appeals for funds by Mrs. Boyd, and innumerable chapter projects and individual and chapter contributions by the [chapters] for the Home... Every issue of the newspaper contained instructions on how to make out checks to the Memorial National Home Foundation."[23] Mrs. Boyd still served as the editor of *The Gold Star Mother* and was entirely responsible for the content of the publication. Working out of Mrs. Boyd's home, the newsletter team answered only to Mrs. Boyd.

Mrs. Boyd Elected AGSM President for Another Term

After a year of energetically courting the membership on behalf of the Home Foundation while adroitly blocking or ignoring every effort of the national executive board to end her stewardship of the project, Mrs. Boyd ran for a second term as AGSM national president at the 1948 convention. Always spinning the facts about the Home Foundation to the delegates, Mrs. Boyd continued to deny the truth to the membership about the Home's management and progress. At the convention she "offered an ambiguous report on the activities of the Foundation."

Ever popular with the rank-and-file membership,

Fig. 9-2: Attendees at the 15th National Convention in Long Beach, California had an opportunity to travel to the Memorial National Home Foundation property in Ojai for the dedication of the first cottage on June 12, 1952. *(AGSM Collection)*

Mrs. Boyd was again elected national president of AGSM, Inc., despite the year's Home-related controversy and animosity. She was subsequently re-elected to the presidency each year until 1952, a series of terms in office that has never been matched in the organization. Despite her popular election at the 1948 convention, delegates did adopt a clarifying resolution in an attempt to assure AGSM's control of the Home Foundation:

"We, the members of American Gold Star Mothers, Inc.... desire that the Memorial National Home Foundation be an integral part of our organization under the supervision and management of our duly elected and appointed officers and committees."[25]

The membership in convention rejected a resolution proposed by Mrs. Boyd's supporters that read:

"We, the delegates, desire that the present directors of the Memorial National Home Foundation, American Gold Star Mothers, Inc. be kept and the Foundation [continue] under present management."

Although the rejection of the Boyd-supporters' resolution indicated continuing concern over the management of the Home Foundation, its defeat did not hinder Mrs. Boyd, who simply ignored the adopted resolution in her subsequent communications and Home

Foundation activities. In fact, Mrs. Boyd was now part of the "duly elected and appointed officers" in her position as national president, so the resolution passed by the membership was essentially rendered moot. The majority of the membership fell dutifully and quietly into line behind their new president who had done so much for the organization during her prior tenure in office.

While the purchase of the Truman Boyd Manor property remained in governmental limbo for several years due to the Korean Conflict, questions and challenges regarding the Home Foundation were not welcomed by Mrs. Boyd. At the 1951 convention, she responded threateningly to a question from a delegate and explained why details were being withheld from the membership:

"Every time we have told you the full particulars, somebody has written a smarty, vicious letter to some official, Congressman, or even to the City officials, and held up our work for us... You will be surprised at the filthy letters that have gone out there to officials. And I can assure you now... that every one of them has been sent to me by the officials. So I know exactly who signed them."[26]

An Alternate Property Purchased

As the 1951 convention neared, Mrs. Boyd became concerned that she would be challenged about the fact that there was still no actual Home property to show for all

INSPECTION OF MEMORIAL NATIONAL HOME FOUNDATION AND DEDICATION OF THE FIRST COTTAGE AT OJAI CALIF JUNE 12, 1952 · AMERICAN GOLD STAR MOTHERS · FIFTEENTH NATIONAL CONVENTION

of the funding and energy that had been expended. The result was the purchase of the Toyon Ranch property in Ojai, California, a small, upscale artists' community and spa resort in the foothills near Santa Barbara. The eight-acre ranch was purchased for $55,330 in May 1951, a month before the national convention. AGSM's national executive board was neither consulted nor advised about the acquisition.

The Ojai purchase was hurried and proved to be a bad investment. Zoned only for single-family residences, the only building on the property was a single residence with servants' quarters. Later studies revealed that only six of the eight acres could actually be used due to zoning requirements, easements, and power lines. Records showed that the Home Foundation spent $20,212 on improvements, mainly for the construction of a model home for needy mothers. All of the Home Foundation's cash at that time, with the exception of $1,097, was invested in the Ojai property:

"The inference is inescapable… that no consideration was given to the feasibility of the property for a home and that no serious effort to make the existing facilities into a home was ever contemplated. There [was] much talk and showing of plans, and dedications… [but] nothing beyond construction of one brick cottage (never occupied) had been done, nor could anything be done to make a home there… The property stood idle and vacant, at a loss of thousands of dollars each year, and its sole utility appeared to be as an overnight and weekend retreat for a favored few…

"Once acquired, it was discovered that existing zoning would not permit execution of plans. Mrs. Boyd then sought to change the zoning restrictions to allow two-family units, but at a meeting before the Planning Commissioner…property owners appeared and strong opposition was expressed to any change in zoning on the grounds that there was an extreme water shortage in the area. The effort to break the zoning restrictions at Ojai resulted in failure. [Mrs. Boyd] expressed… 'amazement at the opposition of local people to this worthwhile project.'"[27]

Despite having been thwarted in its efforts to develop the Toyon Ranch property, the Home Foundation subsequently acquired an option to purchase an adjoining thirty-two acre tract for further development. Mrs. Boyd attempted to solicit funds from the AGSM membership for the purchase on an emergency basis. Each chapter was asked to donate $200 to the purchase, but there was little response and no purchase was made. The Ojai property operated at a loss during the entire time it was held by the Home Foundation.[28]

Whistleblowers Within AGSM: Duncan and Hadra

While many members of AGSM expressed their dissatisfaction about the Home Foundation and the manner in which Mrs. Boyd was managing it, few had the courage to directly charge Mrs. Boyd with wrongdoing. But two mothers, Stella Duncan in New York and Erna

Hadra in Los Angeles, refused to be silenced despite threats from Mrs. Boyd. As a result, both mothers' AGSM memberships were challenged and eventually rescinded at Mrs. Boyd's direction.

Stella G. Duncan was an energetic World War II gold star mother from New York. An eager and able committee-woman, she rose rapidly within her own chapter and moved quickly into the presidency of the New York State Department. In 1946, she was elected national third vice president in Eleanor Boyd's new administration. Mrs. Duncan's relationship with Mrs. Boyd soured early when she questioned several decisions made by Mrs. Boyd.

Mrs. Duncan claimed that the idea for a gold star mothers' home had originated with her in 1945. Funds in support of that project had been collected from the New York membership and placed in a bank account to be used as seed money. This claim, which Mrs. Duncan put forward frequently in writing to and speaking with AGSM members, must have infuriated Mrs. Boyd, who had always stated that the idea for a home was the result of her first year in office as national president during which she became aware of the poor conditions in which many elderly gold star mothers lived.

At the 1948 convention, when Mrs. Boyd was re-elected as national president, a clarifying resolution was approved that placed the management and responsibility for the Home into the hands of the national board. One week later, Mrs. Duncan wrote to Mrs. Boyd:

"Now, to the matter of the National Home Foundation Fund which must be taken care of immediately. That idea is nearest and dearest to my heart, as I am the one who started the ball rolling, not through any desire to head the Board of Directors, but to have a place where lonely Gold Star Mothers can spend their declining years in peaceful living. I never dreamed it would become as distorted as it was, nor that it would be used as a springboard for ambition. It has been a disgrace to all concerned, and I am glad that the delegates disposed of the matter at convention [by passing a resolution putting the Home Foundation under the direction of AGSM's national executive board]. It would be far better to have no Welfare Project than to have a repetition of this degrading situation...

"Am quite sure that this matter will be cleared up promptly, as you surely know that you cannot serve as President of our organization and President of the National Home Foundation at one and the same time...

"Along this line, may I say that your language to me at the joint Board Meeting, namely 'Sit down, Duncan' has had its repercussions. Please, Mrs. Boyd, do not ever speak thus again. I believe I understand you, hence passed over it at the time. Am sorry now that I did so. However, may I say here and now, that I shall never do anything to hinder the smooth development of the organization and shall concur with any of your plans that are constructive, provided they are presented in the proper manner, not forced upon us. I also state that I will fight to my last breath any plan that will work a hardship on our members or bring unrest or unhappiness to them."

One month later, Mrs. Duncan again wrote to Mrs. Boyd:

"You do not seem to realize the seriousness of the position in which you have placed yourself by your statements and actions. Your utter disregard for the dignity of our organization and the constitutional rights of its officers and members must cease...

"Only a very vicious or a very ignorant woman could fail to see the damage that is being done by such methods as you are employing. Since you do not fall into either category, you will, I am sure, adjust yourself to the situation as it stands before it is too late."[29]

In her response, Mrs. Boyd's outrage was clear:

"In regard to the dignity of the Organization, I can assure as long as I am its National President, there will be dignity and integrity at all times. I am glad that you recognize that those of us who were part of this very fine Organization before you were privileged to become a member, did a conscientious worthwhile job. May I state that those of us who were giving of our services before you were a part of our Organization, whether in a Chapter or any other place, did so because we believed in our Nation and were keeping faith with the men and women who gave their lives. None of us have the time for pettiness and misrepresentation and vindictiveness. We have been busy over these years giving Service...

"If I can help you get your feet on the ground and your viewpoint kind and impartial, I shall be glad to do so. I am at your service under these conditions. Otherwise, I shall spend my energies on the Mothers who sincerely wish to have constructive work and advancement encouraged for the good of all."[30]

In September 1948, Mrs. Duncan again wrote to

Mrs. Boyd expressing both her fury and her frustration with the actions being taken by Mrs. Boyd regarding the Home. She also took exception to the changes that the newly re-elected Mrs. Boyd was putting in place on AGSM's national executive board. Mrs. Duncan felt the changes contradicted the organization's constitution and by-laws. By adding new national officers, such as an aide to the president, a national pianist, and a national music director, and giving them the right to vote on executive board issues, Mrs. Boyd was expanding her cadre of supporters to the point that the original, duly elected members of the board were now in the minority.

At the 1949 convention, Mrs. Duncan, unable to attend due to pending surgery, sent a report of her activities as third vice president for the past year. Although her chapter president had offered to read the report to the membership on her behalf, Mrs. Boyd refused to allow the report to be read to the convention attendees. In her report's cover letter, Mrs. Duncan declared that she could handle the gossip and rumors directed at her but when her dead son's military service was called into question, she could no longer allow the calumny to continue without challenge:

"It is also well known that I have fearlessly stood for RIGHT, and have consistently fought to enforce our Constitution and By-Laws, for only in this way can we hope to keep our organization Democratic.

"It is generally known that there are some among us who constantly overstep the limitations of their office and resent any curbing of their supposed 'power.' These members have waged a Gossip Campaign against all members who dare to stand for the RIGHT instead of MIGHT. This in itself is deplorable, but when this campaign reaches the state where our dead sons are involved, then action is necessary.

"All abuse that has been heaped on me, personally, has been treated with pity and contempt for the members involved in its circulation, for the outpourings of such women are unworthy of consideration. However, when the venom sinks so deep into the hearts of a few members that, in an effort to hurt me, they stoop to defile my dear, dead son, then I must ACT."[31]

Frustrated in her attempts to discredit Mrs. Duncan with the membership, and unable to force Mrs. Duncan to rescind her relentless efforts to keep the membership advised of the facts as she saw them, Mrs. Boyd took a risky step at the 1951 convention in Washington, D.C.

She directed the convention membership committee to deny Mrs. Duncan a delegate card, an action that made Mrs. Duncan no more than a guest at the proceedings, unable to take the floor to comment or to question the actions taken by convention delegates. Mrs. Duncan immediately challenged that treatment in the courts.

Disregarding the court's suggestion to find a respectful and amiable solution to the situation, Mrs. Boyd turned to the national board to enforce her wishes. Just two weeks after the convention, the national secretary wrote to Mrs. Duncan "advising her of her expulsion from the organization and giving her thirty days in which to make a demand for a hearing." Mrs. Duncan immediately demanded a hearing, asking for a more detailed statement of the charges against her. The legality of that hearing was later brought into question by Mrs. Duncan's legal team:

"It is quite apparent that the hearing left a great deal to be desired. Lasting from mid-afternoon on one day until approximately five o'clock a.m. the next morning, it was a terrible physical and mental strain, not only on Mrs. Duncan and her counsel, but on the members of the Board as well; and it is our conviction that there was no atmosphere of calm and impartial deliberation, such as we hoped for and such as, we are sure, you would expect. The hearing was not only an ordeal because of its length, but it was marked by clashes of personality between Mrs. Boyd who presided and us as we attempted to represent Mrs. Duncan."[32]

On November 13, 1951, following the hearing before the national board, Mrs. Duncan was expelled from the membership of American Gold Star Mothers, Inc.:

"Mrs. Duncan had seven specific charges made against her in connection with her expulsion, and that by secret ballot of the National Executive Board, all of the charges save one were voted as unanimously sustained. Charge No. 7 concerning ineligibility by reason of her son's lack of line of duty status was sustained by a vote of eighteen members for sustention, one contra and one abstention. The Chairman of the Board, Mrs. Boyd, refrained from voting. The hearing complied in every respect with the By-laws of our organization for the expulsion of members and with all principals of due process of law.

"Mrs. Duncan was represented at the hearing by two attorneys, and had every opportunity and, in fact, did present her side of the case by way of introducing documents, cross-examining witnesses, testifying on her own behalf, offering witnesses on her own behalf, and otherwise giving herself and her attorneys full opportunity to be heard. Despite the fact that all charges were sustained, and any one of such charges would have been a sufficient basis for the expulsion or suspension, the Board did advise Mrs. Duncan that in the event the line of duty status of her son was changed by the official action of the Government as required by the eligibility requirements of our organization, her application for reinstatement would be considered, provided her conduct and deportment from that time forward merited consideration of reinstatement."

Despite loyal support from Mrs. Duncan's home chapter, Manhattan No. 9, and their frequent requests for Mrs. Duncan to be reinstated, no further action was taken by the national board. When Mrs. Boyd's stranglehold on the organization was finally broken with the election of Elsie Nielsen as national president in 1952, Mrs. Duncan again sought reinstatement through her attorneys. One of their key points was that history had proven Mrs. Duncan correct in her charges against Mrs. Boyd and that she deserved to be vindicated as a result. When the chapter threatened to reinstate Mrs. Duncan as a member of their chapter, if not a member of the national organization, the board finally responded. In April 1954, national president Elsie Nielsen met with the members of Manhattan Chapter No. 9 regarding Mrs. Duncan and the action that had been taken. The chapter's membership was advised that the reason Mrs. Duncan had given for her expulsion, namely that her son's death was not in the line of duty, was just one of seven charges leveled against Mrs. Duncan. (No record of the other charges has been found.) It was also explained that the chapter did not have the power or the prerogative to reinstate Mrs. Duncan as a member of either their chapter or AGSM. Following this meeting, the chapter withdrew its efforts to support Mrs. Duncan's reinstatement.

Erna L. (Liz) Hadra was a West Coast gold star mother who refused to be intimidated or suppressed by Eleanor Boyd. Mrs. Hadra was the mother of Jay Donald Hadra, a 2nd Lieutenant in the U.S. Army Air Corps who died at the age of twenty in a 1945 plane crash "in the interior of China."[33] Mrs. Hadra joined AGSM in 1949. While she missed the initial discussions of the Home Foundation at the 1947 and 1948 conventions, she began to have doubts about the Home from her first exposure to it at the 1950 convention and from reading *The Gold Star Mother* newsletters. Unwilling to accept Mrs. Boyd's assurances for how things stood between AGSM and the Home Foundation, Mrs. Hadra went to the Los Angeles County Registrar's office where she saw firsthand the Articles of Incorporation for the Memorial National Home Foundation; she also read what she referred to as "the Amendments and the Amended Amendments" that had been made without AGSM's knowledge or approval.

In May 1952, Mrs. Hadra sent a letter to every chapter, asking that it be read to the membership. In her correspondence she delineated what she had found in her investigations and issued a call for the membership to take control of the Home Foundation and demand an accounting from Mrs. Boyd and the Home's board of directors. In addition to calling the attention of the AGSM membership to what she considered malfeasance in a position of trust by Mrs. Boyd, she also accused Mrs. Boyd and the Home Foundation of postal fraud, a Federal offense:

"In the office of the Postal Inspector this representative group of members… told the Inspector that they, personally, as well as their Chapters had sent money through the U.S. Mails to our National President in response to the urgent appeals constantly appearing in the 'GOLD STAR MOTHER' for the 'HOME.' They stated that they believed, from what they read in our paper that the 'HOME' was PART OF, BELONGING TO and for the BENEFIT of members in good standing of the American Gold Star Mothers, Inc. They added that they had never been informed of the complete change of PURPOSE and MANAGEMENT which has been effected by the AMENDMENTS and AMENDED AMENDMENTS. They were horrified to discover that the PURPOSE OF THE ORIGINAL 'HOME'—to minister to the SICK, needy, distressed and destitute members-in-good-standing of the American Gold Star Mothers, Inc., has been eliminated. That, although the NAME of the 'HOME' recently has been spoken and printed SEPARATED from the name of our ORDER, the constant solicitation of donations in our paper has continued. And, at NO time has the paper mentioned or explained the VITAL changes in the USES and MANAGEMENT of the 'HOME.' This omission left the uncounted thousands of members all over the United States to continue to believe the ORIGINAL USE and PURPOSE of the 'Home' had not been changed…

"At the Washington, D.C. Convention, we TRIED to tell you—THE MEMORIAL NATIONAL HOME FOUNDATION, Inc. does NOT belong to A.G.S.M.,

Inc. Our newspaper, *The Gold Star Mother,* is published from the residence of our National President WHO IS ALSO the LIFE-TIME HEAD of the 'HOME,' [and] is the main means of collecting funds for the 'HOME.' It goes through the U.S. MAILS and unknown THOUSANDS (estimated a year ago at $75,000.00) go through the U.S. MAILS to the home of our National President."[34]

She delineated the changes to the Home Foundation amendments that she believed had been made without the knowledge or approval of AGSM membership. They included:

- Changing the original name from American Gold Star Mothers, Inc., Memorial National Home Foundation to Memorial National Home Foundation, Inc.
- Originally incorporated "for the sick, destitute, distressed and needy members in good standing of AGSM," the word "sick" had been eliminated. Mrs. Hadra noted, "How many of us are WELL? (Average age over 60!)"
- Intended originally for the relief of gold star mothers who were members of American Gold Star Mothers, an amendment had been changed to benefit "gold star mothers" in general, regardless of whether they were members of AGSM.
- Intended beneficiaries changed from members of American Gold Star Mothers, Inc. to "parents of persons who served in the armed forces during World War II and who died of service-connected illness or injury." This meant that gold star mothers from World War I, Mrs. Boyd's particular focus when she asked for permission to pursue a Home Foundation, were no longer eligible to live at the Home. It also changed the focus from gold star mothers to gold star parents.
- Original Home Foundation articles stated that "a majority of the [five] board members" would be members of AGSM; amended articles required only that the "majority thereof would be gold star mothers" and not necessarily members of AGSM.

Although Elsie Neilsen was elected as national president at the 1952 convention, Mrs. Boyd continued to pull strings at the national level as national parliamentarian, a position she created for herself. Mrs.

Hadra was one of the first mothers to experience her machinations from behind the scenes.

Following the 1952 convention, at the next meeting of the Santa Monica chapter (Mrs. Hadra's home chapter), she was advised by the chapter president that she "was not in good standing with the 'The National'" and was refused an opportunity to speak at the chapter meeting. Assuming that she was being suppressed at the direction of Mrs. Boyd, Mrs. Hadra told the chapter members that "they had just witnessed a preview of a Dictator State. This obviously was done by order of the persons who still believe they can continue to have the Mothers believe that the 'Home' has some connection with our Order."

In a continuing barrage of correspondence to the chapters, paid for by Mrs. Hadra and a few supporters, Mrs. Hadra persisted in her demand that she have an opportunity to present her findings to the national executive board and that a complete and lawful accounting be required of Home Foundation.

In September 1952, Mrs. Hadra was informed that "acting upon charges filed by the Santa Monica Chapter... the national executive board voted to expel you as a member of the American Gold Star Mothers, Inc." A number of Mrs. Hadra's supporters in the Santa Monica chapter immediately wrote to the national executive board decrying the action and supporting Mrs. Hadra. The women stated that, contrary to organizational protocol, they had not been advised nor made aware of any meeting at which Mrs. Hadra's membership status was to be discussed.

Mrs. Hadra's response to her expulsion was outrage:

"To even suggest that I should be expelled from AGSM for ANY reason is not only craven and contrary to the precepts of honorable and righteous living; it's plain IMPUDENT. To fasten the 'charges' on the decent uninformed Members of my Chapter is even lower than impudent. It smells just like Dictator-tactics. In fact, the whole history of the terror, expulsions, illegal re-writing of the 'Constitution and By-laws,' the EDICTS—all trumped up to KEEP UP THE ILLUSION of 'sweetness and light' by PURGING intelligent Mothers who have only the WELFARE of ALL honorable Gold Star Mothers in mind—it's YOUR DUTY to really clean house...

"By 'expelling' me, you do not in the slightest degree injure the fine record of my family's service to the U.S.A.

"By 'expelling' me, you brand YOURSELVES as

cowardly, TERRORIZED and unworthy of your Sons… And, may God have mercy on all the little, frightened SMELLY souls and consciences."

Despite being expelled from the organization, Mrs. Hadra continued her efforts to inform the AGSM membership about the Home Foundation. She stated "I WOULD NOT DARE GIVE YOU ANYTHING BUT FACTS BASED ON DOCUMENTS OR I WOULD HAVE BEEN SUED LONG AGO."[35]

While on the surface it seemed that the national board was taking little action under new president Elsie Neilsen, Mrs. Hadra did report progress that she attributed to her having sounded the alarm. In a handwritten note to the membership she reported:

"Every chapter of AGSM must demand that the National Executive Board tell the whole truth to all Chapters.
1. EB [Eleanor Boyd] did not "resign" from the paper. Mrs. Neilsen took it away from her.
2. Long Beach Chapter, California, voted to expel EB [Eleanor Boyd] and is now waiting for the National Executive Board to act.

Meanwhile, EB should be suspended until her record is cleared and every Chapter should be told of this. Chapters hereabouts were told by National Officers not to send any more money to the "Home." Yet a Philadelphia Gold Star Mother visiting here reports that her Chapter recently sent $200 to E.B. Did you notice? Not a word about the "Home" in recent *Gold Star Mother*. The Board is weak and terrified—I am NOT. Wake up ALL AGSM.

Love to all of you, E. L. Hadra"[36]

In an October 10, 1953, letter to specific members of AGSM, Mrs. Hadra reported that Mrs. Boyd's ulterior motives had come to fruition with the acquisition of the Truman Boyd Manor for the Memorial National Home Foundation. The most important part of her letter, however, was a listing of the entities and individuals to whom she had presented her evidence:

"We have informed the office of the Republican National Committee.

"Senator Knowland's Secretaries, Mr. George F. Wilson and Mr. William P. Jaeger, EXAMINED ORIGINAL DOCUMENTS when I presented them in Senator Knowland's office in Washington, D.C. in mid-November 1952, just after election…

"I have visited the office of the California Attorney General in San Francisco TWICE and in Los Angeles also, showing them documents re California Inc. #91095, now known as the 'Memorial National Home Foundation, Inc.'"[37]

Mrs. Hadra's visits to the California Attorney General's offices would soon bear fruit; as a direct result, AGSM soon became involved in a civil lawsuit initiated by the State of California that would consume the attention and resources of AGSM for the next five years and determine the future of the Memorial National Home Foundation.

Mrs. Hadra's continued anger over her expulsion became clear when she initiated a lawsuit on her own behalf against "six members of the Santa Monica Chapter, AGSM, Elsie Nielsen, Ruth Singer, Eva Hines, Grace McClellan, and Eleanor D. Boyd." Mrs. Hadra claimed she had been "expelled from the national organization… on groundless and baseless charges."[38] She further contended that the expulsion had been done in a manner designed to "harass and humiliate her" so she would halt her inquiry into the finances and operation of the Memorial National Home Foundation.

In addition to reinstatement as a member in good standing of AGSM, Mrs. Hadra's suit asked for $100,000, plus $1,500 for travel expenses and $300 for medical expenses.

In November 1955, Mrs. Hadra's lawsuit against Mrs. Boyd and the American Gold Star Mothers, Inc. was decided. Despite her claims of harassment, humiliation, and unlawful expulsion from the organization, the Court found in favor of Mrs. Boyd and AGSM.

In the late 1950s, hoping to mitigate the hard feelings created during the Boyd administration, the national executive board offered an opportunity to those mothers who had been expelled during that time to rejoin the organization as members in good standing if they so chose. Mrs. Hadra was one such mother who was given a choice to let bygones be bygones in recognition of the common loss shared by all gold star mothers.

But Mrs. Hadra was never willing to let bygones be bygones. Mrs. Hadra was never reinstated as a member of AGSM. Stella Duncan, however, did take advantage of the offer of reinstatement and was a valued member of her chapter for many years to come.

Taking Control of the Manor

In May 1953, the Truman Boyd Manor was finally relinquished by the government to the Memorial National Home Foundation for $138,404.63. This amount included $133,182.49 for the original cost of the land, exclusive of improvements, although the land itself had been appraised at $900,000. Other components included a payment in lieu of taxes of $4,227.48 and the sum of $944.66 for accounts receivable. A down payment of $944.66 was paid with a personal check written by Dr. Boyd. The remainder was to be paid over five years.

At this time, the Manor property had a gross annual income of approximately $500,000 from the rent for the bungalows. Although improvements to the property—a thousand bungalows, a meeting hall, swimming pool, etc.—were appraised at nearly $2.7 million, under the Lanham Act the Home Foundation was required only to pay for the original unimproved cost of the land.[39] By any method of evaluation, the Truman Boyd Manor property was an incredible bargain for the Home Foundation and promised to be a lucrative investment.

AGSM Takes Action

While Mrs. Boyd and the Home Foundation celebrated the culmination of a long acquisition campaign, news of the purchase and Mrs. Boyd's repudiation of an AGSM link galvanized the gold star mothers into action. Their reaction was described as "a revolution in the ranks" by the Long Beach Press-Telegram.[40]

By June 1, 1953, just three days after news of the Truman Boyd Manor purchase had appeared in the newspaper, three new resolutions had been forwarded to the AGSM convention planners. The resolutions proposed that the American Gold Star Mothers, Inc. take the following action at the June convention in Chicago:

- Unseat Mrs. Boyd from her position as a member of the AGSM national executive board
- Bring the Memorial National Home Foundation back under control of AGSM
- Dissolve the Memorial National Home Foundation

In addition to Mrs. Boyd's stunning denial of a relationship between AGSM and the Home Foundation, one of the primary concerns was AGSM's ability to finance such a project. As Mrs. Margaret Winter, president of the Long Beach chapter, told a reporter,

"Gold Star Mothers is not a wealthy organization and it would take a wealthy organization to handle such a large deal."[41]

By June 1953, a total of $73,577.12 had been contributed to the Foundation, largely as donations from AGSM chapters and individual members.[42] More than $55,000 had already been spent to purchase the Ojai property and another $20,000 had been committed there for improvements. When the Truman Boyd Manor purchase was announced, the Home Foundation was essentially penniless.

The national convention in Chicago began on June 7, 1953, and the main topic of discussion was the status and activities of the Home Foundation. The delegates went on record as having voted to "do all things ... necessary to regain control of the Memorial National Home Foundation":

"The Convention adopted a resolution, which criticized the Foundation for changing the original purpose of permitting only members of American Gold Star Mothers, Inc. to use a home or homes to be acquired by [the Home Foundation].

"In case the American Gold Star Mothers, Inc. does not succeed in regaining control of the [Home Foundation], the resolution adopted by the Convention demands that any money collected from Chapters or members of AGSM be returned to a trust agency to be established by American Gold Star Mothers, Inc."[43]

The national executive board of AGSM was empowered by the delegation to hire counsel and take any necessary steps to carry out the resolutions of the national convention.

Mrs. Boyd was present at the convention and, upon her return to Long Beach, she issued a statement that gave the matter her own personal interpretation:

"It is difficult to understand that American Gold Star Mothers, Inc. wants to 'regain' control of the Foundation when at all times the Foundation has been an independent nonprofit corporation in no way subject to the jurisdiction of American Gold Star Mothers, Inc. Apparently, American Gold Star Mothers, Inc. wants to have the housing at Truman Boyd Manor limited to just its own members."[44]

Mrs. Boyd's subsequent actions, however, indicated that she was feeling some pressure following the convention. Upon her return, the Home Foundation hurriedly placed a plaque on a bedroom door at the Ojai Manor House that read "The American Gold Star

Mothers, Inc." It was later contended in litigation that the total property owned by the AGSM and devoted exclusively to its needy members was "one bedroom at Ojai of 187 square feet in area, together with the right to use jointly with other occupants a service area of 2,407 square feet, not counting 8.14 acres of land."[45] The value of that particular room was based upon the amount of contributions made by AGSM members ($2,170.08) prior to the January 1948 amendment of the Home Foundation's articles in which the words "American Gold Star Mothers, Inc." were eliminated. In simple terms, Mrs. Boyd was willing to acknowledge that in six years of dedicated fundraising, AGSM members had contributed enough money to buy one room at the Ojai Manor House.

Mrs. Boyd and her cadre of legal advisors moved quickly to take control of the situation following the convention. On August 1, 1953, the Home Foundation filed suit in Los Angeles Superior Court. As a proactive measure, they requested legal determination of the Foundation's relationship with AGSM. The suit asked that the court determine "rights and duties of the two organizations in regard to each other, the cost of the suit and other relief the court may see fit to give."[46] The complaint contended that the two organizations had always been separate.

Compared to the legal and financial resources available to the Home Foundation, which could now draw on large monthly rental revenues from the Truman Boyd Manor project, AGSM had limited cash reserves from which to draw funds for legal services. AGSM contacted a California attorney who directed them to George Wise, a young attorney in Long Beach. A close and caring relationship was formed between Mr. Wise and the gold star mothers that has lasted more than fifty-five years.

When Mr. Wise entered the controversy in 1953 on behalf of the AGSM national executive board, there were literally no funds available to pay him. He charged the gold star mothers $10 per hour, although his going rate was much more. It was agreed that if the court decided to order an additional fee, he would not ask his gold star mother clients to pay more than $10 per hour. Working with his partner, Robert J. Kilpatrick, he took on the case of the American Gold Star Mothers, Inc.

Brown vs. Memorial National

Home Foundation

In June 1954, California State Attorney General Edmund G. "Pat" Brown placed the Foundation/AGSM controversy in the hands of the courts. As Attorney General, Brown had responsibility for the state's charitable trusts. He indicated that his office "had been unable to determine the precise nature of the charitable trust and for that reason wanted the court to determine the issue."[47] To achieve that, Brown filed a declaratory relief suit: *Brown vs. Memorial National Home Foundation.* This action acknowledged that two organizations were claiming the properties of the single trust and left it up to the courts to decide.

This step did not please Mrs. Boyd and the Home's attorneys. Speaking on behalf of the Home Foundation, attorney Trent G. Anderson Jr. indicated that "we don't believe that the Attorney General should have taken any action in this case. Under provisions of the state Corporation Code dealing with non-profit corporations, he can step in only when something is found wrong. The Attorney General's office approved the Foundation audit last June and we have had no adverse report since."[48] The suit moved forward despite the Home Foundation's disapproval.

On June 24, 1954, headlines in the *Long Beach Press-Telegram* reported that Mrs. Boyd had been "charged with deceit." One of the first salvos from the AGSM side was a cross-complaint filed in the Attorney General's suit. In it they charged that Mrs. Boyd had used her office to "deceive and mislead" public housing officials in the sale of assets estimated at more than $1,000,000 (the Truman Boyd Manor). In addition, they accused Mrs. Boyd of seizing control of the Home Foundation while soliciting more than $75,000 from the gold star chapters on the representation that the Home Foundation was an agent of the parent group.

It was also charged that the "purpose of this conduct by Mrs. Boyd was in furtherance of a scheme and design on her part of power, domination and self-aggrandizement and was against the best interest of the Gold Star Mothers and the public at large."[49] George Wise later heard that the charge of self-aggrandizement had infuriated Mrs. Boyd more than any other allegation made during the case.

On July 1, Mrs. Boyd's response to the court action, a demurrer, was filed. In it, Mrs. Boyd's intentions for the Home were finally clarified in print:

"Memorial National Home Foundation is a

California non-profit corporation organized for charitable purposes and with the primary purpose of establishing a home or homes for Gold Star parents. There are more than 500,000 Gold Star parents in this country, including the members of American Gold Star Mothers, Inc.

"It is our purpose to help Gold Star parents who need such housing, including the members of American Gold Star Mothers, Inc.

"American Gold Star Mothers, Inc., which is a Washington, D.C. corporation organized for the benefit of its members, claims to have 20,000 members. The cross-complaint filed by American Gold Star Mothers, Inc. appears to be an attempt to take Truman Boyd Manor away from Gold Star parents generally for the benefit of these approximately 20,000 members."[50]

After the demurrer was filed, coverage of the case died down in the press and the public's attention focused on other issues.

AGSM Conflict at the Chapter Level

While the legal case continued its slow journey through the courts, there was unrest within AGSM over the issue of Mrs. Boyd's status as a member of the organization. The transcript of a May 23, 1955, hearing before a subcommittee of the AGSM national executive board tells a sad and confusing tale of conflict within Mrs. Boyd's own Long Beach Chapter.[51]

Mothers who supported Mrs. Boyd and those who sought to have her expelled from the chapter's membership had been unable to reach a compromise. In protest over Mrs. Boyd's perceived manipulation of the chapter, twenty-nine Long Beach chapter mothers resigned their membership in AGSM and joined the National Gold Star Mothers group. Some members of the chapter felt that Mrs. Boyd had applied continuing and excessive pressure on the chapter for donations to the Home Foundation. She repeatedly challenged the chapter to set a standard for contributions from chapters across the nation and shamed them when contributions fell short of her expectations.

Many of the Long Beach chapter mothers felt that their questions about the Home Foundation were not satisfactorily answered. Meetings became contentious as Mrs. Boyd, a past president of the chapter, attempted to override Mrs. Margaret Winter, the current chapter president. At least six members of the Chapter continued to support Mrs. Boyd. They believed that she epitomized the ideal gold star mother, setting a standard toward which all could aspire.

The six mothers claimed to have been ostracized by some of the other chapter members for taking a position in support of Mrs. Boyd. As a result, they ceased to take part in or support chapter activities that they believed were designed to harm Mrs. Boyd's status in the organization. For some, this meant a refusal to participate in their duties as elected officers. They also began to express their concerns by writing directly to the national executive board, a move that infuriated Mrs. Winter.

The Long Beach chapter initiated expulsion proceedings in 1953 in which the six mothers were accused of insubordination and disloyalty. The six mothers refused to participate individually in the hearings required by the AGSM articles, and the chapter refused to meet with them as a group. The six mothers soon indicated that they had an attorney, Trent G. Anderson Jr., to advise and represent them. Interestingly, Mr. Anderson also handled Foundation affairs on behalf of Mrs. Boyd. Testimony indicated that only one mother had actually agreed to be represented by the attorney, but the others went along with his suggestions, including Mrs. Edwards, who, with her husband, was employed by the Home Foundation at the Ojai property as caretakers. None of the six mothers could explain how Mr. Anderson was going to be paid for his services.

The Long Beach chapter was thwarted in its efforts to expel Mrs. Boyd from the organization. When it had become apparent that the chapter would vote to expel her, Mrs. Boyd had quietly requested and received member-at-large status by mail from the AGSM national custodian of records. This membership category was usually assigned on an interim basis when a mother moved from one chapter to another. Members-at-large were not affiliated with a particular chapter until they chose to join one. As a member-at-large, Mrs. Boyd was no longer under the jurisdiction of the Long Beach chapter and she could not be expelled from the organization at the chapter level. The national custodian of records, Mary Etta Woods, was a member of the Long Beach chapter. She indicated that she had been unable to attend chapter meetings after assuming her custodial duties and was unaware of the chapter's intent and efforts to expel Mrs. Boyd.[52]

Available records do not indicate the outcome of the expulsion hearings for the six mothers. Although Mrs. Boyd was no longer a member of the Long Beach chapter, she had generated a legacy of turmoil within her own chapter. Her influence would long be felt both by those who had supported her and those who had disagreed with her.

Keeping the AGSM Membership Informed

Even as the court proceedings progressed, Mrs. Boyd continued to write bulletins to the AGSM membership. In March 1955, members' confusion about the Home Foundation's status prompted national president Elsie Nielsen to write in *The Gold Star Mother:*

"Numerous letters have been received at National Headquarters from Chapter members inquiring about literature being sent to our members by Mrs. Boyd concerning the Memorial National Home Foundation. As you may know, American Gold Star Mothers, Inc., is now involved in a lawsuit, filed by the California Attorney General in the U.S. Federal Court at Los Angeles, California, in which we are seeking to have returned to us, as trustee, the properties of the Memorial National Home Foundation on the basis that the properties now held by the Memorial National Home foundation were originally intended to be for the benefit of American Gold Star Mothers, Inc. We hope and expect that we will soon be in a position to administer our Home as has always been intended.

"The feelings of the National Executive Board are that Mrs. Boyd and the Memorial National Home Foundation should not be controlling funds or dispensing the same and the pending lawsuit, if successful, will establish that, and we can then make the Home a reality.

"Meantime, no 'Home' as such where mothers can or are being taken care of is in existence. The Memorial National Home Foundation does own property, at Ojai, California and a large WWII federal housing project at Long Beach, California, which produces a large income to Memorial National Home Foundation, but neither is in any sense an operating Home for our members or others. Our information is that the charity being accomplished by the Memorial National Home Foundation consists of small gifts, e.g. $25.00–$100.00 to some persons claiming need.

"We cannot, nor do we desire to prevent the application by any member in need to Memorial National Home Foundation or any other organization in a position to dispense aid. We do want to make it clear, however, that Mrs. Boyd and the Memorial National Home Foundation, by verified pleadings in court, have taken the position that our organization has no rights or voice whatsoever with respect to the Home Foundation, although it was originally formed under the auspices of this organization as a Home for needy members and we hope that the Federal Court will soon recognize our rights so that a Home may be established."[53]

The trial proceeded slowly. Knowing the membership was concerned about the case, the national executive board kept the mothers apprised of the case's status through *The Gold Star Mother* and other communication opportunities, such as national conventions.

An Initial Victory for AGSM

On October 11, 1956, after nearly four months of testimony and hearings, the trial ended. Judge Lloyd S. Nix advised that he was going to delay his decision in order to study the evidence. On October 25, 1956, Judge Nix announced his ruling in favor of the American Gold Star Mothers, Inc.:

"Judge Nix issued a four-page order in which he decreed that the property and funds of the Foundation be held in trust for the Gold Star Mothers. He said there was hostility, strife and antagonism under the previous set-up. Under the order, the Foundation and its officers were restrained from using the assets of the trust other than for the normal operation of the Truman Boyd Manor and an eight-acre tract in Ojai. A new trustee for the Foundation's assets is to be designated by the Court at a later date."[54]

Judge Nix's decision specifically ordered that the Home Foundation be taken out of the hands of Mrs. Boyd and the current Home board:

"The Court further finds that the defendant and cross-defendant corporation, Memorial National Home Foundation, and its Board of Directors are under the dominant control of Eleanor D. Boyd, and that while the Court does not question the honesty and integrity of Eleanor D. Boyd, it feels that she lacks experience to operate either of the two trusts as herein set forth and is unduly influenced by passion and prejudice emanating from personal differences with members of the National Executive Board and members of the Chapters of American Gold Star Mothers, Inc.; that certain other members of the Board of Directors, while having experience and ability, wholly lack the time necessary to devote to the affairs of these trusts; that certain other members of the Board of Directors were chosen by Eleanor D. Boyd for her personal reasons and are mere figureheads on the Board of Directors; and that all of the members of the Board of Directors delegate their authority to Eleanor D. Boyd and permit Eleanor D. Boyd to dominate and control the actions of the Board of Directors.[55]

"The Court further finds that the defendant and cross-defendant, Memorial National Home Foundation, has abused and abandoned its trusts and new trustees should be appointed to carry out the trusts."[56]

Finally, in the December 1956 issue of *The Gold Star Mother,* the national board had good news to share under the headline "Court Decides Home Foundation Suit in Favor of American Gold Star Mothers; Order Removes Memorial National Home Foundation as Trustees." Judge Nix's concern for the organization went far beyond rendering a favorable court decision. When the new corporation was formed, Judge Nix attended every board meeting for many years to ensure everything went properly. At Nix's request, the new corporation's original Articles of Incorporation required that the board members be appointed only with the approval of the Presiding Judge of Los Angeles County—Judge Nix's own position at the time. He saw the provision as one way of ensuring that no single individual would ever again be able to unduly influence the organization.

In January 1957, readers of *The Gold Star Mother* were advised that the judge had signed a provisional judgment and placed a receiver in charge of the assets of the Home Foundation to protect them until a new trustee corporation could be named to act as successor. Not unexpectedly, there was also news about Mrs. Boyd and her legal team:

"Memorial National Home Foundation and Mrs. Eleanor D. Boyd have filed a notice of appeal on the Judgment seeking to reverse the orders of the trial court. It may therefore be many months before the proceedings are concluded."[57]

In the next issue, readers were advised that it could take up to a year before the appeal would be resolved.[58]

In May 1957, *The Gold Star Mother* contained a "complete report on the American Gold Star Home." Readers were advised that the Memorial National Home Foundation had been removed as trustee and the assets under its control were transferred to two local businessmen appointed by the court to act as receivers who would hold and manage the trust assets temporarily under the direct supervision of the court. Judge Nix had been very clear about his vision of who would be selected as trustees for the new corporation:

"During the trial… the Judge expressed his thoughts that a trustee corporation should be composed of competent, experienced business persons equipped to deal with problems of the magnitude here involved and further expressed that while American Gold Star Mothers, Inc., should have representation on the Board, the trustee corporation should not be under the control of the American Gold Star Mother, Inc., but that maximum advantage should be taken of business experience in the naming of Board Members."[59]

The national board advised the membership that it agreed with Judge Nix that a new corporation should be formed to manage the assets of the old Home Foundation. Despite unanimous approval by the national executive board, the matter still had to be ratified by the membership either in convention or by voting in the chapters. Although the court had rendered its judgment, there were still decisions to be made.

The American Gold Star Home Replaces the Memorial National Home Foundation

The Articles of Incorporation of the new corporation were filed on January 24, 1957. The name of the new foundation was "The American Gold Star Home." The Articles of Incorporation provided for a board of seven trustees appointed by the court and two additional trustees who would be members of AGSM's national executive board. The nine trustees would be responsible for more than $3.5 million in corporate assets.

National president Ruth K. Singer and national corresponding secretary Lennie Johnson, both California residents, were the first two national executive board members to be appointed by AGSM. The other seven members of the Board of Trustees were California residents actively engaged in business or the professions, welfare work or activities, government work, or veterans' work.

Endorsing the American Gold Star Home

The 1957 national convention held in Cleveland, Ohio devoted the majority of its open discussion to the issue of the American Gold Star Home. Before the convention, president Ruth Singer's message in *The Gold Star Mother* advised the membership that there would be an opportunity for all questions to be answered. Attorney George Wise took the convention podium to provide a case history, answer questions and provide his perspective on what AGSM could reasonably hope to accomplish in attempting to withhold approval and negotiate with Judge Nix.

Rose Decker, president of the dissenting Oregon Department, immediately challenged Mr. Wise when the discussion was opened for questions:

"We feel that among the 17,000 to 20,000 members in the American Gold Star organization there must surely be some who are capable. We know that we have businessmen, brilliant businessmen in our organization… Don't you think the Gold Star Mothers should have a majority—that we shouldn't be confined to seven men of whom we know nothing about and in whose choosing we had no voice? You stated in the beginning that we had finally crystallized our idea of a Home. Do you think giving our property over to seven men of whom we know nothing, that that is our dream of owning a Home, of having a Home?"

Questions from the floor were directed in a flood to Mr. Wise and the emotional temperature of the discussion increased rapidly. Several mothers called for a time out to shut down personal accusations that were passing between members.

A resolution was proposed from the floor that the convention act to approve and ratify the successor trustee, the American Gold Star Home, as appointed by the court with a board of nine trustees, seven of whom were prominent businessmen and two of whom would be members of the national executive board of American Gold Star Mothers, Inc. Rose Decker immediately took the floor:

"I would like to make an amendment to your resolution to read as follows: I would like to amend it to strike out 'two members of American Gold Star Mothers, Inc., shall be members of the trusteeship' and change it to read, and shall read, 'The majority members of this trusteeship shall be American Gold Star Mothers, Inc.'"[60]

Speaking over the applause that followed Mrs. Decker's proposed amendment, national president

Ruth Singer responded:

"May I say we are not making the rules. The Judge, and the Attorney General, has made that ruling in his decision and we cannot tell the Judge what we want."[61]

Mrs. Decker responded that most of the mothers didn't understand what they would be giving up if they approved this resolution:

"Mothers, we don't have to vote on a resolution that takes your property and might take it out of your hands. You have much to lose by doing so, and nothing to gain. Have a conference with the court, do something before you vote your property and your future security away, which is what will happen. I predict it will."[62]

Her comments were again met with applause from many delegates. Mary Hiatt of Ohio asked that the delegates ratify the successor trustee because under the articles of the new corporation, AGSM had more control and influence in the Home than it had for the past ten years:

"We have never had anyone on the board. Wouldn't it be better to have two from our organization than none at all? We must surely trust in these people and do not judge. Let's stop this arguing and work together and not go through this every year. We have done this for 10 years and we are tired of it. Let's stop arguing."[63]

Her comments drew applause from the delegates. First national vice president Maude Fry added:

"In these incorporation papers, it states that two directors shall be members of the National Executive Board but to all directors and trustees, the books are open. Our two members are responsible to the National Executive Board.

"When we had five members on the Memorial National Home Foundation and one of them asked for a financial statement, they were told it was none of their business.

"I very sincerely believe if we vote 'no' we are taking a tremendous chance on not knowing what becomes of the property at all."[64]

Rose Decker's proposed amendment to require majority representation by AGSM on the new board was voted upon and lost. Proving that emotions ran high over this issue, in the first round of voting on the American Gold Star Home as the successor trustee, thirty-three more ballots were cast than there were registered voting delegates.[65] In subsequent voting, the proposed successor trust was approved with a vote of 360 for and 115 against.[66]

An Extended Appeal Process

In the next issue of *The Gold Star Mother,* readers were advised of the membership's approval of the successor trustee at the convention but were cautioned that the battle was not yet won. It could take another year or more to resolve the appeal of Judge Nix's ruling by the Memorial National Home Foundation. Until that appeal was resolved, the new American Gold Star Home corporation could not take over the management of the Home Foundation.[67]   While the two court-appointed receivers managed the business of the American Gold Star Home, both sides of the suit waited anxiously for the decision on the appeal by Mrs. Boyd and the Memorial National Home Foundation. More than a year later, on August 1, 1958, the California District Court of Appeal unanimously upheld Judge Nix's judgment in favor of American Gold Star Mothers, Inc. The Appeal Court approved the removal of Memorial National Home Foundation and Mrs. Boyd as trustees and held that all the assets were subject to a trust for the benefit of needy members of American Gold Star Mothers, Inc.:[68]

"The story is long, but the result seems clear—that the Foundation did acquire property (cash and other donations and grants) to be held in trust for Gold Star and having done so diverted them to uses divergent from and partially destructive of those of Gold Star and also excluded Gold Star from any voice in administration of the trust."[69]

Mrs. Boyd's attorneys immediately filed an appeal for a hearing with the California Supreme Court. Thirteen more months passed before that court denied the Memorial Home's petition for a hearing. In October 1958, *The Gold Star Mother's* readers were told that Judge Nix's decision would stand "as the final decision in the case."[70] That elation proved premature, however, for in the next issue it was reported that:

"The final conclusion of the Memorial National Home Foundation lawsuit has been delayed because of steps taken by the Memorial National Home Foundation to attempt to gain a hearing of the matter in the Supreme Court of the United States. A temporary stay has been obtained by the Foundation preventing any further action on the matter until the United States Supreme Court decides whether or not to take the matter over. Meanwhile steps are being taken by our attorneys to oppose the action in the United States Supreme Court."[71]

Unwilling to concede defeat, the Home Foundation had filed a petition for certiorari, which called for a writ from the higher court to the lower one requesting a transcript of the proceedings of the case for review. The case was fully briefed in the Supreme Court and the petition was rejected, thereby again affirming Judge Nix's ruling. There was no further recourse through the courts for the Foundation. After years of effort, the American Gold Star Mothers, Inc., had finally won their battle. Assets of the Memorial National Home Foundation were turned over to the American Gold Star Home, the new trustee, on November 1, 1959.[72]

Preparing the Home for Gold Star Parents

More than 300 applications from gold star mothers interested in living at the American Gold Star Home had been received by the time the final court appeals were resolved. Carrying out Judge Nix's orders, the court-appointed receivers embarked upon a program to landscape and rehabilitate 208 housing units at Truman Boyd Manor (now the American Gold Star Home) for immediate use as a home for members of AGSM. Additional units were scheduled for rehabilitation as they became available. The goal was to have "1000 single units each equipped with Rock Maple Furniture, a General Electric Refrigerator, stainless steel sinks, individual heating units and when the remodeling was

Fig. 9-3: The interior of a newly refurbished two-bedroom apartment at the American Gold Star Home in the early 1960s.
(Fenelon Collection)

Fig. 9-4: A rose-covered bungalow-style apartment building at the American Gold Star Home in the 1960s.
(Postcard: Jasper Nutter Photography, Long Beach, CA— Image #66297: Fenelon Collection)

Fig. 9-5: A two-story apartment building at the American Gold Star Home in the 1960s.
(Postcard: Jasper Nutter Photography, Long Beach, CA— Image #66295: Fenelon Collection)

done, they would all have their own flower beds and individual patios."[73] In addition to refurbishing the apartment units, there were plans for landscaping and construction of patios, shuffleboard courts and sprinkling systems.[74] [Figs. 9-3, 9-4, 9-5]

In November 1959, national president Lorraine Desser reported on her visit to the new Home:

"One quarter of this project is now being redecorated, the three and four room apartments that were being made ready for our members, occupancy con- sisted of a living room, one or two bedrooms, kitchen and bath. Each apartment will be furnished with new and refinished furniture, new bedspreads, curtains and draperies. The kitchens too have been redecorated, sinks rebuilt and trimmed in stainless steel, new refrigerators and new ranges. The floors have been refinished, the living room in the model apartment is very cozy, with studio couch and easy chairs. A new television will be in every apartment. Aluminum doors and awnings are being installed, everything has been thought of to insure comfort and security for our members."[75]

Past national officer Katherine M. Kelley also reported on what she had noticed while visiting the Home:

"There are about 30 Gold Star Mothers living on the premises at the present time, and one in particular was pointed out to us. She was outside, taking care of her lovely plants and flowers which were beautiful. On the premises there is also an employee who does all the maintenance work, cleaning the streets, raking the lawns and clearing away all debris. There is a Medical Center situated near the office, which will be used to care for those mothers who do become ill and need medical care… We then walked to the Maintenance shop, where Gold Star Dads were employed stripping and refinishing furniture, making shelves and doing all kinds of carpenter work, getting ready for the fall renovation."[76]

By February 1960, at a cost of $256,000, 212 of the original 1,000 Truman Boyd Manor units had been refurbished and furnished for use by gold star mothers and fathers. Boasting all new furnishings, the sparkling three- and four-room apartments rented for $39 a month, including utilities. Thirty gold star couples were in residence and the American Gold Star Home community was beginning to establish itself.[77]

The relationship between AGSM and the American Gold Star Home has remained strong through subsequent decades. Two representatives of the AGSM national executive board continue to hold positions on the Home's nine-person board of trustees. Thousands of gold star parents have lived at the Home over the years, and found it to be a haven of companionship and support.

Fig. 10-1: A quiet moment at the Vietnam Veterans Memorial. *(AGSM Collection)*

CHAPTER 10 ★

The Vietnam Decades: 1960–1979

Unlike World War II, the war in Vietnam has cost us dearly in our self-confidence and our pride. We are now a nation given to moments of shame and self-doubt. We sometimes question our motives, our past achievements and even the ideals for which we fought with so much determination just 25 years ago.
—REMARKS OF HONORABLE WILLIAM S. BROOMFIELD, Member U.S. Congress (October 1970)

AS THE GOLD STAR MOTHERS of AGSM moved into the new decade of the 1960s, it appeared that their years of unending controversy were left behind. The legal battle with the Memorial National Home Foundation was finished, the American Gold Star Home was operational with World War II gold star mothers rapidly filling the apartments, and the mothers of World Wars I and II, and Korea, had formed a harmonious coalition whose efforts at VA hospitals and in their home communities was inspirational.

In the early 1960s, for the mothers and for the nation at large, Vietnam was just a name among many on a map of Southeast Asia. Few anticipated or could have estimated the effect that the struggle against communism in that small nation would ultimately have on the United States in terms of human life, the level of trust between the American public and its government, and a generation of young Americans.

The War in Vietnam

Nearly four decades after the last American soldier withdrew from the rice fields and jungles of Vietnam, the memory of the war fought there still polarizes our nation and continues to haunt many of the Americans who served there. Although few Americans were aware of it at the time, the United States' interest and commitment in South Vietnam dated back to the early 1950s. Adherents of the Domino Theory believed that when a nation fell to communism, surrounding nations would soon fall as well. Hoping to prevent the fall of Vietnam and its neighboring countries to communism, Presidents Harry S. Truman, Dwight D. Eisenhower and John F. Kennedy provided U.S. military aid and military advisers, first to the French as they struggled to maintain their colonial foothold in Vietnam and then to South Vietnam when the nation was divided by the Geneva Accords in 1956. By 1963, 16,300 American military advisers were in South Vietnam training and supporting the South Vietnamese military; the nation also received hundreds of millions of dollars in U.S. aid every year.[1]

After a reported attack against the USS *Maddox* by North Vietnamese patrol boats in August 1964, the U.S. Congress passed the Gulf of Tonkin Resolution, which empowered President Lyndon B. Johnson to "take all necessary steps, including the use of armed force" to prevent further attacks against the U.S. forces. Only two senators voted against the resolution; one was Senator Ernest Gruening of Alaska who said "all Vietnam is not worth the life of a single American boy."[2] But opinion polls showed that 85 percent of Americans supported President Johnson's retaliatory bombing raids and many newspapers supported the resolution.[3]

In March 1965, 3,500 Marines, the first American combat troops, arrived in Vietnam, joining the 23,000 military advisers already there. At a press conference in July, President Johnson told the public that he would be increasing U.S. troops on the ground in Vietnam to 125,000 men. He promised to meet the requirements of the military so that there would be a victory, stating, "We will stand in Vietnam." He also spoke of the difficulty of the decision:

"I do not find it easy to send the flower of our youth, our finest young men, into battle. I have spoken to you today of the divisions and the forces and the battalions and the units, but I know them all, every one. I have seen them in a thousand streets, in a hundred towns, in every state in this union working and laughing and building, and filled with hope and life. I think I know, too, how their mothers weep and how their families sorrow."[4]

At the end of 1965, U.S. troop levels in Vietnam reached 184,300. And more than 1,800 young Americans had died there.

A year later, troop levels had more than doubled with more than 5,000 deaths and 30,000 wounded. An October 1967 poll found that 46 percent of Americans felt that U.S. involvement in Vietnam was a "mistake" but most believed that America should "win or get out" of Vietnam. By the end of 1967, 463,000 troops were in place with 16,000 combat deaths recorded; more than one million American soldiers had already served in Vietnam.[5]

Despite news broadcasts direct from the battlefield, most Americans, accustomed to more traditional warfare, didn't understand the realities of the combat that young American soldiers were facing in Vietnam. Marine Brigadier General Oscar F. Peatross, speaking to gold star mothers in 1968, described the Viet Cong as "one of the most vicious enemies Americans have ever faced. Today's enemy is one who blends into an often terrified population – an enemy who strikes from the shadows of the night and the jungles."[6]

The number of U.S. troop levels in Vietnam peaked in April 1969 at 543,400. At this point, 33,641 Americans had died in Vietnam, more than had died in the Korean Conflict. Following his election in 1968, President Nixon periodically withdrew American troops from Vietnam; by early 1972, only 135,000 American troops remained and those were largely involved with helping the South Vietnamese Army become self reliant, a program President Nixon called "Vietnamization." In late 1972, the United States started large-scale bombings of North Vietnam after peace talks again failed.[7] Finally, in January 1973, a cease-fire agreement was brokered between the U.S., South Vietnam, North Vietnam, and the Viet Cong. In April 1975, with the fall of Saigon, South Vietnam was taken over by the North Vietnamese army.

The United States' longest war and, in the opinion of some, its first defeat, had cost more than 58,000 American lives and left more than 150,000 soldiers seriously wounded. But the nation, having decided that the war was morally wrong, had little time or compassion for the soldiers who returned from Vietnam, especially those who were apparently unharmed. It did not take long to realize, however, that many of these soldiers had emotional and psychological wounds from their military service that virtually crippled them and made their return to civilian life impossible. The damage done to a generation of young Americans by the Vietnam War would haunt the nation for decades to come.

During the Vietnam War, for the first time since World War I, blue star flags seldom appeared in the windows of American homes where someone was serving in the military. There were many reasons. The time elapsed since the Korean Conflict had allowed the memory of blue and gold star flags to fade from the collective public mind. War protests and the rising wave of public discontent with the war made some families fearful of retaliation if they made public the fact that a family member was serving in the military. Despite a *Chicago Tribune* correspondent who felt that displaying a service flag would "have a most salutary effect on those who think it groovy to be unpatriotic— the draft card burners, student protesters, et al," most families chose not to display a service flag.[8] For those families that did choose to display one, a non-traditional version of the banners became available. Called a Vietnam bannerette, the banner had the traditional colors, shape and stars of a service flag, but included a large V in the lower half for Vietnam.

AGSM Leaders, Conventions and Resolutions of the 1960s

At the peak of their membership in the early 1960s, AGSM entered a two-decade period in which, for the first time, a new national president was elected each year. With few controversial issues facing the organization to create a need for long-term, consistent leadership, a one-year term became the norm. Some mothers believed that this was an appropriate way to reward the many World War II mothers who had been part of the organizational chain of leadership for nearly two decades. Others, however, felt that a one-year term as national president didn't give the women elected enough time to realize their goals or initiate new activities that might require more than a year to set in motion.

Each side of the discussion had merit. By the time a mother achieved the organization's highest office, she may have spent as many as two decades holding chapter, department, and national offices, sometimes filling a position for several years. There was only one national president's position and there were many more women in line for it than would ever achieve it. On the other side, once a national president took office, much of her term was already dedicated to established activities in which she was required to take the lead. Usually within a few weeks of the national convention, the national president and first vice president would spend a week or longer in California as a guest of the American Gold Star Home where they attended a board meeting, met the other trustees, and engaged in a week of activities with the residents of the Home. When possible, they would extend their visits to spend time with chapters in California, Oregon, and Washington while on the west coast. Gold Star Mother's Day and the weekend of related activities at the end of September required significant organization and planning and each national president wanted to put her own personal stamp on the events. The national president was also invited to AGSM installations and investitures across the nation, activities that could fill up every week of her term with travel. (Louise Desser, national president in 1959 and 1960, reported traveling more than 22,000 miles during her year in office.[9]) And planning the next national convention required travel and detailed coordination throughout the president's entire year in office. Despite the pressures, vast responsibilities, and the short time frame in which to accomplish their tasks, the national presidents of the 1960s and 1970s fulfilled their duties with grace and style.

The conventions themselves, although held in various locations across the country, took on a cookie-cutter sameness of presentations and speakers. Almost inevitably, a high-level speaker from the Veterans Administration would discuss recent changes and trends in the Veterans Administration Voluntary Service (VAVS) programs at the VA hospitals and reinforce the importance of the gold star mothers' efforts there. The American Gold Star Home was almost always represented by the Home director who discussed plans for remodeling and re-designs, encouraged the gold star mothers to consider moving to the Home, and shared stories and photographs of activities in which the residents of the Home participated.

The conventions ended with the investiture of the most recent past national president into the Old Gray Mares, a group made up of past national presidents and officers. Lead by Queenie (the group's elected leader) and Lady Scratch (the group's secretary), the past national president was usually given an outlandish equine-themed bonnet to wear and was then required to lead a conga-line of the other "old gray mares" out of the convention meeting room, which ended the convention amid laughter and fun.

Lorraine I. Desser, 1959–1960

Lorraine I. Desser led AGSM as national president in the transition year between the 1950s and the 1960s. She held her end-of-term convention in New York City in 1960. To open the convention, she read a letter from President Dwight D. Eisenhower congratulating the mothers on their convention and telling them:

"Yours is the deep personal knowledge of the cost of war. Yours also is the pride that comes from the realization of supreme service to country. Your fellow citizens, united in the building of a just and honorable peace, find strength in your spirit."[10]

An unusual aspect of the New York convention was that the City of New York donated $5,000 to the convention to help defray costs. This allowed AGSM to lower the costs on all planned events (e.g., banquets, trips, receptions) so more of the 741 registrants could participate. In addition to a trip to the national cemetery at Framingdale in Long Island, New York, attendees were entertained by the Seoul Chorale, a group of Korean students studying in the United States who "wanted to show their gratitude to the American people" and particularly the gold star mothers by providing a program of beautiful music. AGSM had given nearly $2,000 in 1955–1956 to the American-Korean Foundation to help support Korean orphans and war widows following the Korean War.[11]

Several important resolutions were passed at the 1960 convention. One allowed the gold star mothers living at the American Gold Star Home in Long Beach, California to establish an AGSM chapter solely for residents of the Home. Prior to this, mothers in residence at the Home had kept their membership in the chapter they had moved from or joined a chapter near the Home, even though transportation often proved difficult. Following this resolution, the Home Chapter of AGSM was established in September 1960 with Velda Steele elected as the first chapter president. The Home Chapter quickly became one of the largest and most active chapters in the organization.

The issue of adoptive mothers' eligibility for membership was raised once again. Always controversial, this topic ignited discussion among the delegates. The major concern was that allowing adoptive mothers to be members might result in two "mothers" of the same child joining the organization—the adoptive mother and the birth mother. Another aspect of concern was defining the difference between an adoptive mother and a stepmother, which some people might unknowingly interpret to be the same thing. After much discussion, the resolution passed with the result that eligibility was changed to include mothers who adopted a child prior to its fifth birthday. Legal proof of adoption was required to differentiate between adoptive mothers and stepmothers who took over the care of a child through marriage but without a legal adoption process.[12]

The delegates also approved a resolution that all past national presidents, by virtue of that service, would be granted individual votes at national conventions. This was a step toward simplifying the always confusing issue of voting strength at conventions for chapters, departments and past national officers.[13]

A resolution that was not passed proved to be very controversial. The resolution proposed that eligibility for membership be changed to include "all mothers whose son or daughter was serving their country in the line of duty at the time of their death after January 31, 1959..." Referring to the small but growing conflict in Vietnam, many mothers felt that allowing membership for the mothers of soldiers killed there when no war had been declared would detract from the purpose of AGSM, which they stated was "banding together of mothers who lost their sons in war-time."[14]

Frances High, first national vice president, stated that AGSM had always taken the position that if the soldier was serving in the military, whether in training, a transport accident or combat, and died during that service, they were considered to be killed in the defense of the country and their mother was eligible for membership if all other requirements were met, e.g. citizenship, etc.

Other mothers offered their opinions on the issue of "on duty" vs. "during wartime." Mothers mentioned the fact that the war in Korea had never been a declared war, yet gold star mothers of the Korean Conflict had been admitted to membership. Frances High again offered historical perspective, commenting:

"As far as the eligibility dates are concerned, our eligibility for World War II starts in 1938. We were not at war in 1938... It would help erase a very deep hurt that many mothers have who have lost their sons by getting shot down by accidents when they happened to come over a piece of Russian territory, or even in training, if they were flying a plane and were killed while they were in training. These mothers feel that they have given their sons. That is the point of the resolution."

Nelle Krieger of Florida spoke of the common bond that connected the mothers of children killed in military service, regardless of the situation:

"I think we lose sight of the fact that we have been in a cold war for a long time, and these mothers who lose their sons in this cold war feel just as bad as we did when we lost our sons and we never know what minute or what hours this is going to turn into a hot war, and I think we should consider these mothers. They have feelings just like we do."[15]

Despite emotional appeals for its passage, the motion was not approved.

Frances High
National President, 1960–1961

Frances High of Houston, Texas was fifty-nine years old when she was elected national president in 1960 at the national convention in New York City. A World War II gold star mother, she took over the organization at a time when there were more than 20,000 members nationally. A charter member and first president of the Houston chapter, she had been instrumental in organizing the Department of Texas where she had served two terms as president.[16]

Her end-of-term convention was held at the Statler-Hilton Hotel in Los Angeles. Opening the event, she read a telegram from President John F. Kennedy:

"I am pleased to greet the American Gold Star Mothers on the occasion of your 24th Annual Convention. In my inaugural address I requested my fellow Americans to 'ask not what your country can do for you, ask what you can do for your country.' By the sacrifice you have made, by your continuing activities in behalf of our veterans, particularly your participation in the Veterans Administration Voluntary Service program in which you unstintingly lend your understanding help with the rehabilitation of hospitalized veterans, and by countless other actions, you now and in the past truly make these words of actions by your deeds.

"May you, victims of inhumanity, continue to express through your solicitude for veterans and your work for a peaceful world the human values we all cherish."[17]

Many activities were planned for the 24th national convention, including a visit to the American Gold Star Home in nearby Long Beach. With 842 in attendance, it was a simple matter to fill ten buses with gold star mothers, guests and family members to share lunch with the residents and the Home's board of trustees. Goodwin J. Knight, former governor of California, was the principal speaker at the convention's banquet; Frank Gard Jameson, director of the Valley Forge Freedom's Foundation, gave "a most inspiring and enlightening talk about our Polaris fleet ballistic missile system." A highlight of the first afternoon session was the burning of the mortgage for the national headquarters building.[18]

Dorothy N. Baxter
National President, 1961–1962

Elected national president at the 1961 convention in Los Angeles, Dorothy N. (Fairbanks) Baxter was born in 1897 in West Medway, Massachusetts. Her two children, George and Mary, were both deceased at the time of her election. George had died in 1945 during the battle of Iwo Jima.[19]

Mrs. Baxter had a special interest in the VAVS activities of the organization as she explained in an issue of *The Gold Star Mother*:

"Most of you know of my deep interest in the VA Hospitals, and especially the one in Rutland Heights, Massachusetts, where my husband has been confined so long. As a registered volunteer, I know what it means to give service and from him, I've learned how much the patients appreciate it."[20]

Her end-of-term convention was held in Boston.

Mary R. Kelly
National President, 1962–1963

Mary R. Kelly was well known to the readers of *The Gold Star Mother* for she had served as the editor of the newsletter for four years. A resident of Washington, D.C., she was the first gold star mother of the Korean Conflict to serve as national president. She was born in 1902 in Scranton, Pennsylvania. She and husband Peter T. Kelly had two sons, Paul and John. A veteran of World War II, John had served eight years on active duty in the U.S. Air Force at the time of his death in Korea.[21]

Her end-of-term convention was held Washington, D.C. Little detail about the convention could be found other than there were approximately 600 attendees. The delegates were given a tour of the White House Rose Garden with Special Assistant to the President, Brooks Hays.

Mary F. Neiman
National President, 1963–1964

Born in Hallstead, Pennsylvania, Mary had married Albert P. Neiman in 1917 and they had three children. Their only son, Albert Jr., enlisted in the 18th Infantry of the First Division on his eighteenth birthday, just two weeks before Pearl Harbor. He served in the African and Sicilian campaigns and died in Sicily in August 1943. Mrs. Neiman had joined AGSM in 1947 and had held all of the offices in her chapter as well as serving as department and national treasurer. While Mrs. Neiman served as national president, AGSM had, for the first time, an unofficial mascot—a red dachshund named Analiese that Mrs. Neiman said "goes everywhere with me except to church."[22]

In an interview in 1963, Mrs. Neiman said that while most organizations are "looking to increase their membership, the gold star mothers are on a steady decline." She hoped there would never be another war where more men would be killed, thereby adding to AGSM's membership. When asked if she felt her son had died in vain because of conflict now going on in the world, she answered, "No, I do not feel as though he died in vain. I feel as though the country has made great strides and that appeasement should continue with other countries of the world if it will stop a shooting war."[23]

Approximately 400 delegates attended Mrs. Neiman's end-of-term convention in Asheville, North Carolina.

Mildred A. Lee
National President, 1964–1965

Mildred A. Lee had been a member of the Denver Chapter since 1948. The Fourth of July timing of her end-of-term convention presented the attendees with an opportunity to attend a Salute to America given at the Denver University Stadium. An attendee reported that it was "a magnificent affair ending with the most outstanding fireworks saluting Gold Star Mothers."[24]

A resolution that had been held over for further consideration from the 1963 national convention was proposed once again at the 1964 convention. The resolution concerned changes in the eligibility requirements that would allow stepmothers to become members. This time it was very specific about the circumstances in which such membership would be allowed:

"Whereas, a Stepmother who reared a child from babyhood, loved and cherished it, had the same void in her heart when he or she gave his life for this country;

"Be it resolved, that provided documentary proof is given that the natural mother of the child is deceased; also proof that the marriage of the stepmother to the father of the child occurred prior to the time the child reached the age of 5 years, and she reared the child from that time who later served and died in line of duty... such stepmothers will be eligible for membership."[25]

The resolution was not approved by the convention delegates.

Emma C. Eunick
National President, 1965–1966

The mother of SSGT Charles Thomas Eunick, Jr., Mrs. Eunick became a gold star mother following the death of her son in an aircraft accident in England in January 1952. Mrs. Eunick's end-of-term convention was held in New Orleans, Louisiana. More than 375 delegates attended this convention, AGSM's twenty-ninth national convention.

Recognizing that attendance at national conventions was decreasing, delegates approved a resolution to establish that a quorum at a national convention would be 125 registered delegates, a reduction from the prior requirement of 200. This ensured that business could be officially conducted at future national conventions.[26]

Rose F. Decker
National President, 1966–1967

Rose Decker was born in Milwaukee, Wisconsin in 1895. She moved to Portland, Oregon, in 1918 where she worked as a secretary for many years. Her only child, Eugene Forsgren, Jr., joined the Marines when war broke out in Korea and was killed in action there. She became a member of the Honor Chapter in Portland and held many chapter offices including that of chapter president. In 1963, she and her husband moved from Portland to the American Gold Star Home in Long Beach, California.

She was elected national president at the 1966 national convention in New Orleans. In her acceptance speech, she was one of the first national presidents to speak publicly about the war in Vietnam:

"In these troubled times our country is facing a serious challenge in Vietnam—a challenge of tyranny over freedom—the freedom and the preservation of human dignity for all peoples for which our sons gave their lives —it is important that we express even greater loyalty to our country, and faith that freedom will prevail...

"There is another matter which should be our concern. I feel that we, as gold star mothers, have a responsibility individually and as a group to the mothers who are now losing their sons in the cause of freedom. Let us make sure that these mothers never feel that they are alone in their grief. To this end I would like to ask that whenever you learn of a mother who has lost a son in Vietnam that you call on her so that she will know that her sacrifice is appreciated and honored ... It is not a matter of whether or not this mother joins our organization, but rather of fulfilling our obligation of giving her sympathetic understanding at a time when it is most needed."[27]

In early 1967, speaking at the Department of Michigan convention, she mentioned her concerns about the Vietnam War once again, stating "we are all deeply concerned over the war in Vietnam, for it is a fighting war and we are losing our fine young men—we more than anyone else know the sorrow and heartache of war."[28]

Mrs. Decker's end-of-term convention was held in Milwaukee, Wisconsin, her home town. More than 450 attended the convention where Governor Knowles of Wisconsin was the principal speaker.

As a cost-saving measure, a motion was approved

by the delegates that the minutes of this and future national conventions would no longer be printed and sold. Demand had been low for copies from prior conventions and they were expensive to produce. It was agreed that a report on future conventions would be printed in the August and September issues of *The Gold Star Mother*.[29]

In response to a telegram of support sent to President Johnson by delegates, he wrote back to president Decker stating:

"I was gratified and encouraged by the generous confidence expressed in the recent resolution of the Thirtieth National Convention of AGSM. Women of your high ideas and principles helped make America great. And in the ranks of organization such as yours that greatness is preserved for generations yet unborn. You have understood the true meaning of freedom—and the price it sometimes unhappily places on those who share it. I appreciate your comforting words and I assure you that we are daily working for a peace with honor—a peace that will prove your confidence well placed."[30]

Marie Hart
National President, 1967–1968

Marie Hart was sixty-two years old when she was elected as AGSM's national president. She had lived her entire life near Cleveland, Ohio. A World War I war bride, she married William Hart in 1917 while he was serving with the 37th Division. They had two daughters and three sons; their sons served in the Army, Air Corps and Navy during WWII. In 1945, one of their sons was killed in the line of duty. With nineteen grandchildren at the time of her election as national president, Marie was used to being busy, a skill that served her well during her year in office.[31]

The site of the thirty-first annual convention was Portland, Oregon. Among the issues that were brought to the 464 delegates for consideration was once again the question of admitting stepmothers to membership in AGSM. This issue had not been approved at the past two conventions. There was a long discussion of the issue before it was brought to a vote. This time, the delegates approved the change to the eligibility requirements, based on specific parameters:

"Stepmothers who are citizens of the United States … who assume the responsibility of a son or daughter under the age of five years and reared this son or daughter who served and died in the line of duty… are eligible for membership in AGSM when documentary proof has been established that the natural mother is deceased."[32]

Speaking on behalf of Oregon Governor McCall at the national convention, General Anderson brought touching greetings to the convention attendees:

"The American Gold Star Mothers have an abiding claim on our esteem and affection. On the field of battle their Sons made the supreme sacrifice to defend the Freedoms we enjoy today. For that alone we are eternally in their debt. There are additional reasons for doing honor to our Gold Star Mothers. They have helped to maintain the ideals and aspirations for which their sons fought and died. Every year they donate thousands of hours as volunteers in veterans hospitals throughout the country, comforting the sick and cheering the lonely servicemen.

"The State of Oregon is proud to salute these courageous Gold Star Mothers who have stood fearlessly to meet every crisis, to face every challenge and to offer up their Sons in times of peril and national emergency."[33]

Mamie P. Simmons
National President, 1968–1969

Mamie Pearl Forbis was born in Lincoln County, Oklahoma (known then as Indian Territory) on August 23, 1902. She and her husband, Claude B. Simmons, had three sons and a daughter before his death in 1936. Then a single mother with young children to raise, Mrs. Simmons moved to Joplin, Missouri, where she attended business school. Her two older sons, Claude and Clyde, enlisted in the Air Corps during World War II and became pilots. Claude served in the South Pacific; Clyde was serving in England when he died. Following the war, Mrs. Simmons moved to Tulsa where she joined American Gold Star Mothers, Inc.

At the Arlington National Cemetery ceremony for Gold Star Mothers Sunday in 1968, Mrs. Simmons spoke of the doubt that sometimes assailed gold star mothers:

"I know, being a Gold Star Mother, we often wonder if the sacrifice was all in vain, but we must continue to carry on our work for their ideals, and now more than ever for the many Vietnam Mothers who are suffering from the same heartache. We must do our part to preserve Liberty, and our own way of life.

"Freedom is not free, and we, the Mothers, join

whole-heartedly in carrying to every corner of our Land in clear and understanding words the message that 'Freedom is not Free.'"[34]

Mrs. Simmons' end-of-term national convention was held in Tulsa, Oklahoma, and was kicked off with a proclamation of support by Tulsa Mayor J. M. Hewgley asking that "the citizens of Tulsa show their concern by flying or displaying 'OLD GLORY' for the duration of the convention."[35] A total of 320 delegates attended the convention and seven past national presidents were in attendance.

Special events were planned for the gold star dads that included a tour of the Sunray DX refinery, a baseball game between the Tulsa Oilers and an Indianapolis club, and "a trip to the 'World's Most Famous Gun Collection' in Claremore, Oklahoma, returning by the Catoosa Canal."[36] In the September 1969 issue of *The Gold Star Mother*, national custodian of records Elva P. Newman shared a story about one of the dads at the convention:

"I have a little story to tell you about one of our enterprising Dads. At our convention in Tulsa, all our dads received a coffee mug as a registration gift. One of our dads was sitting in the lobby with the mug in his hand and someone came along and dropped in a few pennies. Immediately an idea was conceived and this dad carried that mug at all times, gathering a few pennies, nickels, or dimes and sometimes even quarters and at the close of the convention he presented me with $12.00 to be used for something at Headquarters. This dad was none other than our Norris Calkins from the Gold Star Home. My sincere thanks to Norris for his wonderful idea. It sure paid off."[37]

Helen T. Willour
National President, 1969–1970
Born Helen Theresa Pendergast in Boston in 1899, she married Mark Lewis Willour in 1923. They had two sons. Vincent Edward joined the Army Air Corps in 1942 and was killed in action in June 1944 at the age of nineteen. She was a charter member of the Brookline, Massachusetts chapter that formed in July 1949, and she held multiple offices at the chapter, department, and national levels.[38] In her August 1969 President's Message, Mrs. Willour told the membership that "my affection is not only for our organization as a whole, but for each member individually as each person has something special of her own to contribute."[39]

In May 1970, president Willour appeared on the *Today* show where she was interviewed about AGSM by host Hugh Downs, who she described as "a very kind and gracious gentleman." She reported to the AGSM membership that she also had an opportunity to meet Barbara Walters and Art Linkletter in the studio.[40]

Mrs. Willour's end-of-term convention was held in Miami Beach, Florida. The 420 delegates in attendance greeted with applause the news that 1,009 new members had joined AGSM and seven new chapters had been added in the last year.[41]

An unusual resolution was brought before the membership at this convention. On Christmas Eve 1968, Apollo 8 astronauts circling the moon had read, in a public broadcast, the first ten lines of the Book of Genesis in the Old Testament of the Bible, which describes the Creation. Flamboyant atheist Madelyn Murray O'Hair, who had already taken prayer out of the schools, subsequently filed a lawsuit against NASA to block what she called "proselytizing" by the government's space program. Although her lawsuit was ultimately dismissed, AGSM's Department of California, Arizona, and Nevada took exception to her action and asked AGSM to pass a resolution supporting personal prayer in any location or situation as a basic American freedom. Their resolution read, in part:

> WHEREAS: The United States of America is a free country and all peoples have a right to their own privilege of worship; and
>
> WHEREAS: A space traveler should have the privilege of praying in his own personal belief;
>
> THEREFORE: Be it resolved that the Department... go on record as opposing any ban on the personal observance of Prayer or Religion, by any person, whosoever, no matter where on earth or in space he may be stationed.[42]

The resolution was approved.

AGSM Leaders, Conventions and Resolutions of the 1970s

Myrtle E. Foster,
National President, 1970–1971
New national president Myrtle E. Foster was clear on what the focus of her term in office would be. In November 1970, she told readers of *The Gold Star*

Mother that "two big projects of my year as president will be to stress new membership and [to celebrate] the 25th anniversary of the V.A. Voluntary Service."[43]

As she opened her end-of-term convention, she read a message from President Richard Nixon:

"The American Gold Star Mothers have earned their nation's deepest admiration and respect. The courageous way in which you have endured the greatest personal sacrifices, only to be strengthened in your love of country and of its heritage, gives each of us something to think about.

"Your sons, whose unfinished work you have so willingly accepted as your own, would be intensely proud of you, just as the nation is proud of you.

"No words, however eloquent, could fully capture the qualities of heart that characterize the purpose of your organization and so advance the cause of peace and freedom in the world."[44]

The convention was held in Philadelphia where an evening gathering was scheduled just for gold star mothers of the Vietnam War. Mary Teator reported:

"We got together… the Vietnam mothers, and we had a lovely meeting… all mothers like to brag about their children so we thought it would be nice to get together and discuss where the boys were, and we had many mothers break down, which is good for the soul, and we were all there to console, …and we cried on each others' shoulders and we have had a marvelous time. It's amazing that some of the mothers got together and discovered that some of their boys served with another boy and this brought them closer together. And our meeting, I would say, lasted about two hours and we all felt very close unity. Thanks to you older mothers, we have learned this from you."[45]

There were forty-one Vietnam-era gold star mothers in attendance at the Philadelphia convention and twenty-seven Korean Conflict mothers. It was also announced that there were still twenty-three World War I members of AGSM.

A question from a delegate initiated a discussion of the war in Vietnam and how it differed from past conflicts. Asking who determined eligibility for AGSM—AGSM or the government—the answer was that AGSM determines eligibility. The delegate explained the concern:

"We had a case this year of a mother who applied, whose son was a suicide victim in Vietnam, and yet she was denied, and the mothers in our organization felt that Vietnam being the kind of war it is, this individual was probably driven to his suicide and was a victim of the war just as surely as those who were killed."

The response was that the application would be returned by the Department of Defense indicating that the death had "not occurred in the line of duty." Based on AGSM requirements, the mother of that soldier would not be eligible for membership.[46]

Another concern was raised about changes to the law that specified who was eligible to receive the government's next-of-kin gold star pin. An unidentified delegate stated that AGSM had been responsible in part for the government not changing the requirement that the death had to occur in a combat zone, rather than in the line of duty:

"In 1958, a law was passed that said [only] those who were killed in the combat zone… were entitled to the Gold Star pin. This is not fair by any means. We have lost two planeloads of boys on their way to Vietnam, we have lost one planeload on their way back. There were veterans who have been in Vietnam and went to Hawaii for rest and recuperation and died in a forest fire. We have had over 30,000 servicemen killed since the inception of the Vietnam so-called war—30,000 who have been killed outside the United States.

"This law was brought before… Congress and passed unanimously, endorsed 100 per cent by the Department of Defense. And yet last December, when it got to the Senate Armed Forces Committee, I am sad to report to you that they scrapped it because our National Organization had never sent in a recommendation … Congressman Hanley, who is the sponsor of this bill, made this statement at our convention. He felt that since he had never heard from [AGSM]… that the Gold Star Mothers Organization was not in favor. I told Congressman Hanley that this had to be a mistake, since these mothers are eligible and we do have many of them in our chapter."

Mrs. Kittredge, a delegate, responded that if the law was changed then "you would be giving everybody a lapel pin and it wouldn't mean anything … if you give everyone a button you lose the value of the button. This is actual combat. Now my son was actually killed in service [after] five battles, so I feel I am a member of this organization. If he were not, we would not accept him."

The unnamed delegate then asked, "But don't you feel that these mothers whose sons were on their way to Vietnam…" She was interrupted by Mrs. Kittredge who said, "No. They aren't actually fighting, not in conflict."[47]

Examples were shared of other women who had been denied a gold star pin and membership in AGSM:

"There were two mothers that did not receive their pins… their sons were being sent over to Vietnam, they were killed in that plane crash with 64 other boys going over. They cannot get a lapel pin because they were not killed in action. Another mother… her son was in Vietnam, he was taking a message from one officer to another officer in a jeep and the jeep hit a mine and he was blown up, but he was not in action."[48]

A past national officer reminded the national president that "in World War II, some of our mothers' sons never left the United States, some of them were drowned falling off a ship in dry dock and they received those pins."

Anne C. Richards
National President, 1971–1972

President Richards held her end-of-term convention in Dallas, Texas. Little information was provided about the thirty-fifth national convention. One poignant moment was reported when Mrs. Evelyn Barker of Mount Clemens, Michigan, a member of Macomb County Chapter, met a soldier who was wounded in action near the Naktong River in South Korea on September 1, 1950, the same action in which her son John Gerald Barker lost his life. After twenty-one years of exchanging letters with the soldier, the two finally had an opportunity to meet in person.[49] The caption that accompanied the photo of their meeting read in part, "This was a very happy occasion for her as is shown by the picture."

Regina Coughlin
National President, 1972–1973

When Regina Coughlin was elected national president, she announced that the theme for her time in office was "let there be peace and let it begin with me."[50] In September 1972, she told readers of *The Gold Star Mother* that she had been elected to serve on the board of governors of the organization Star:

"This is an organization formed to create a wholesome image [of the United States] to the peoples of other countries other than that which they now have: such

as deserters, hippies and aimless groups of Americans. This will be done by sponsoring high school bands and television coverage, etc."[51]

Mrs. Coughlin held her end-of-term convention in Detroit, Michigan.

Helen S. White
National President, 1973–1974

A resident of the American Gold Star Home in Long Beach, California, Mrs. White joined AGSM in 1946 and had held positions at the national level for six years. Her national convention, AGSM's thirty-seventh, was held in San Francisco, California.

Josephay Fleming
National President, 1974–1975

Mrs. Fleming held her end-of-term convention, the thirty-eighth national convention, in Atlanta, Georgia. Among the activities planned for the delegates were a Grand Tour of Atlanta, lunch at Stone Mountain, and a day spent exploring the national park. The all-day tour of the national park, including lunch, cost $10.75.[52]

Among the resolutions approved at the convention was one delegates hoped would re-energize patriotism through a visible display of the American flag by members of AGSM:

"Whereas, our Nation is now at a low tide where patriotism is concerned, and

"Whereas, American Gold Star Mothers are dedicated to 'Maintain true allegiance to the United States', it is our hope to inculcate lessons of patriotism and love of country, to inspire respect for the Stars and Stripes in the youth and to promote peace and good will for the United States and all other nations.

"Therefore be it resolved that it is our desire to have all members of the AGSM display a flag in their own homes or on their property. By our actions we hope this will encourage the public to re-establish a stronger feeling of allegiance to America."[53]

Josephine J. Holmes
National President, 1975–1976

Mrs. Holmes joined AGSM in 1945 following the death of her son, Arthur J. Holmes, in September 1944. Arthur, a Marine, was killed on Palau Island in the South Pacific. Very active in church, school, and civic affairs in her community, Mrs. Holmes had already been recognized by the VA for having served more than 12,650 hours volunteering at the VA Hospital in New

York City; in May 1976, she was given a Special Honor Award of a gold medallion for 15,000 hours as a volunteer.[54]

Mrs. Holmes' national convention, the 39th, was held in Atlantic City, New Jersey. To open the convention, Mrs. Holmes read a message from President Gerald R. Ford:

"No organization in the United States has a greater personal knowledge of the cost of protecting our freedom and the principles we cherish than the Gold Star Mothers. No group has given more in the defense of our priceless heritage. During our Bicentennial year, I especially welcome the opportunity to thank you on behalf of a grateful nation for your inspiring perseverance and continuing sense of civic responsibility."[55]

Mary E. King
National President, 1976–1977

Mrs. King joined AGSM's Wampanoag Chapter in East Providence, Rhode Island, in 1948. Her son, John Edward MacLane, a member of the 8th Fleet Naval Reserves while still in high school, was called to active service shortly after Pearl Harbor. The recipient of the Purple Heart and the Navy-Marine Corps Medal, John lost his life while serving on the USS *Franklin* in the Asiatic Sea in March 1945. Mrs. King's six surviving children had presented her with twenty-nine grandchildren and twenty great grandchildren at the time of her election.

Mrs. King's end-of-term convention, AGSM's fortieth convention, was in Salt Lake City, Utah. A resolution passed at the convention requested that an unknown soldier of the Vietnam War be laid to rest among his fellows at the Tomb of the Unknowns at Arlington National Cemetery. The resolution was unanimously passed by the delegates:

"Whereas, the hostilities ceased in Vietnam January 27, 1973;

"Whereas, because of the conflicts of the United States of America's involvement in Vietnam, no national recognition or honors have been bestowed for the men who fought and died in Vietnam,…

"Therefore be it resolved that the American Gold Star Mothers, Inc., petition… to inter the remains of a Vietnam Unknown Soldier in the Tomb of the Unknowns in Arlington National Cemetery, therefore Vietnam combatants will receive the same tributes as the Soldiers from other wars."[56]

Another resolution empowered the national executive board to petition the government for a number of privileges that they felt had been long withheld. This was a departure from the normal course of business for the mothers and may have indicated an end to their patience with waiting for these privileges to be granted. Their position was that veterans are granted similar privileges without having sacrificed anything and that the mothers were only receiving what their sons and daughters would have been eligible for had they survived their military duty:

"Whereas, we Gold Star Mothers have given our sons and daughters in the defense of our liberty, and they were willing to sacrifice the ultimate, their lives; and

"Whereas, the Gold Star Mothers serve in aiding the living veterans, especially those who are ill or disabled in veterans hospitals throughout the United States; and

"Whereas, others receiving privileges have not sacrificed anything;

"Therefore we, the American Gold Star Mothers will petition Congress… to grant to all Gold Star Mothers:

- A pension for life;
- Commissary and Post Exchange privileges;
- Honorary membership to all Officer and Enlisted Mens Clubs;
- Right to a single son's GI Schooling benefits which would have been entitled to him;
- Assistance officers to contact and assist her once a month concerning her welfare, well-being and whereabouts;
- Freedom from paying taxes on Gold Star Mothers Headquarters and donations received or purchases made; and
- Ensure a parking place by the Gold Star Mothers Headquarters for mothers who drive to Headquarters."[57]

It is interesting that the list did not include medical and hospital benefits through the VA system, a benefit that the organization had pursued at various times over several decades.

Regina Wilk
National President, 1977–1978

A gold star mother from Silver Springs, Maryland, Mrs. Wilk's end-of-term convention was held in Washington, D.C., and coincided with the fiftieth anniversary of the founding of AGSM. Theodosia D. Seibold Nelson, daughter of founder Grace Darling Seibold, spoke at the convention, stating that "My hope for each of you individually is that you will carry home from this convention: hope for the future; the will to do what we believe is right; joy in the accomplishment of what we attempt; and my love and appreciation for each member of the organization."[58]

A resolution approved at the convention amended the term of existence for AGSM, stated as sixty years in the original 1929 articles of incorporation, to "perpetual."[59]

Emogene M. Cupp
National President, 1978–1979

Born in Daviess County, Kentucky, Emogene M. Cupp (Mrs. James R. Cupp) was the mother of Robert William Cupp. Drafted into the Army in August 1967, he arrived in Vietnam on March 2, 1968; on June 6, he stepped on a mine and was killed instantly. He was buried in a family plot in Alexandria, Virginia on his twenty-fifth birthday. Mrs. Cupp promptly joined the AGSM. She was already familiar with the term "gold star mother" for in World War II, her grandmother had lost one son and her aunt had lost two sons.

Like many mothers of the Vietnam era, Mrs. Cupp held a full-time job. Since 1951, she worked for the Army and Air Force Exchange Service where she was a Merchandising Specialist (a buyer of drugs and cosmetics). She quickly became involved in the Alexandria, Virginia, chapter's activities, serving as chapter chaplain for three years and president for four years. In her acceptance speech as the new national president, she told the delegates that she had never missed a chapter meeting since joining AGSM.[60]

The second Vietnam-era mother to serve as national president, Mrs. Cupp attributed her success in part to her World War II predecessors, "I got my training from the World War II mothers, which was good." The theme for her year as national president was 'Teamwork with Love.'[61]

As soon as she took office, Mrs. Cupp was faced with a financial situation that required immediate ac-

tion. The organization, faced with a declining membership, had no financial reserve:

"Knowing I had to come up with a fundraiser or we would be no more, I met with a representative from Brick Mill Studios to start a card program. I signed a five year contract and recruited my Corresponding Secretary to assist me with getting the necessary info together so we could get started. The treasurer had a lot of added work but was very happy to do it because it got us on track with some money to operate. The card program saved us from financial disaster."[62]

The program consisted of a boxed collection of cards that was sent to every member of AGSM. Each member was asked to send back five dollars for the cards. It was up to the member whether she kept the cards herself, sold them to someone else or donated them to a hospital or church. After one year, a profit of nearly $3,000 had been realized from the card sales program and the treasury, for the moment at least, was out of peril.

A lack of cooperation among the sponsoring chapters turned Mrs. Cupp's end-of-term convention into a homemade affair:

"The 42nd national convention was held... at the Arlington Hotel in Hot Springs National Park, Arkansas... The [Arkansas] mothers had a disagreement and decided not to raise the funds to support the convention. It ended up that Alma Nutt of Arkansas, a gold star mother, was the only one to help me ... As it turned out, we all had a good time. With Alma's assistance, she got some country musicians she knew to come to play and we had a Hee Haw. It was fun."[63]

The Arkansas National Guard Band and Arkansas Air National Guard provided the colors and the color guards for the opening ceremonies. The son of Mrs. Cupp's close friend was the convention dinner speaker; he had known Emogene's son and had himself lost an eye while serving in Vietnam. Mrs. Cupp's granddaughters danced at the banquet as one evening's entertainment and her daughter Sue made the table favors. Mrs. Cupp later said "since we didn't have money in the treasury, everyone had to pitch in and donate their time and ability."[64]

Betty Bryce
National President, 1979–1980

Mrs. Bryce was the mother of one son, David Dalton, who applied for immediate induction after gradua-

Fig. 10-2: Francis E. "Duke" Cortor, Jr., son of AGSM member Francis Turley, died in Vietnam in 1969.
(Image provided by the Turley family.)

Fig. 10-3: Richard Davis, son of AGSM member Theresa Davis, was a member of the Special Forces in Vietnam. He was awarded a Silver Star for his actions related to the ambush in which he died at age nineteen in June 1968.
(Image provided by the Davis family.)

tion from high school. He entered the Army in June 1944 where he served as a medic; he died in Germany in March 1945 at the age of eighteen. A Mt. Pleasant, Michigan gold star mother, Mrs. Bryce selected 'Love with the Human Touch' as her theme for her term in office.[65] Her end-of-term convention, AGSM's forty-third, was held San Diego, California. The delegates voted to support the Vietnam Veterans Memorial Fund efforts to build a national memorial to the veterans of the Vietnam War.

Gold Star Mothers of the Vietnam Era

As the casualties began to rise in Vietnam, the members of AGSM realized that the organization could help the gold star mothers of this new war in ways no other group could. In 1966, for the first time in any American war, the office of the Assistant Secretary of Defense began to send the names of the Vietnam casualties directly to AGSM Headquarters on a weekly basis. The names were then forwarded to the department chaplains so contact could be made in the hope that "the expression of sympathy will lend strength to the bereaved families."[66] In past wars, the gold star mothers of AGSM had found out about casualties from local newspapers and through word of mouth; delays often meant that they were not available to help the families of the dead at a critical time. And too often, opportunities to be of assistance were missed entirely due to lack of information. In 1968, national president Mamie Simmons wrote:

"These are days of conflict and strife and our Country once more faces serious challenge, and we must express even greater loyalty to promote a just and lasting Peace, and give assistance to all Gold Star Mothers, now including many Vietnam Mothers. May they never feel that they are alone in their grief and may they realize that they need the organization."[67]

The mothers soon realized that just contacting the families of the war dead was not enough. They had to explain to many of this new generation of mourners exactly what a gold star mother is. In Lucas County (Ohio), the local AGSM chapter sent the following note to every family that lost a child in Vietnam as soon as they were advised of the death:

Dear Friend, In many homes in Lucas County, since the outbreak of hostilities in Viet Nam, "blue stars" have turned to "gold." You have no doubt received cards signed "A Gold Star Mother." The sender wanted you to know they too had lost a son in the service of his Country and were [sic] extending to you sympathy and understanding. For some this tragic loss has been but a short time; for others it has been years, but it is never forgotten.

To this end, we dedicate ourselves as we offer to you the hand of fellowship and invite you into our membership. We fully realize there are mothers who at this time do not wish to become members of any group or organization. We respect their wishes and will not put pressure on them for membership, but we hope someday they will accept our invitation and become members of our chapter.[68]

The chapters soon found out that recruiting the gold star mothers of the Vietnam War was not as simple as they had expected. These young mothers were truly of a different generation than the long-time members of AGSM. Young, often employed full-time, frequently divorced and still raising younger children, many simply did not have the time to give to the organization, much less to devote to volunteer work.

Faced with a great need for the membership of the Vietnam-era mothers and knowing the solace that other gold star mothers could provide, the chapters became more creative about educating the new gold star mothers about the organization and encouraging them to join. National president Anne C. Richards wrote in 1972 that "many of our chapters are having afternoon teas, bingo parties and inviting the new young Gold Star Mothers to be their guests and getting them in-

terested in our organization.[69] Other chapters hosted gatherings that included both the new gold star mothers and dads.

Slowly, gold star mothers of the Vietnam War began to join the organization. Items began to appear regularly in *The Gold Star Mother* about the energy that the new mothers brought to the chapters and how quickly they took on responsibilities:

Nelle Twele (1968): "In my chapter alone we have 14 Vietnam Mothers. They are the most terrific girls. They get out, they work, they are interested and in turn they bring their friends and their neighbors in and we are getting volunteers in our hospital through them.[70] [Volunteers who were not gold star mothers could dedicate their volunteer hours to an AGSM chapter.]

Lake County Chapter (Illinois) (1969): "Elected Vietnam gold star mother Grace Patterson as chapter president. Vietnam mothers Elizabeth Smrtnik and Mary Leslie were elected as Custodian of Records and Historian, respectively.[71]

Illinois Department Convention Report (1970): "We had a fine delegation of Vietnam Mothers attending and a lovelier group of young Mothers would be hard to find. They were so eager to know and understand more about our organization and its history. I feel they can contribute so very much, not only to our organization but most of all to our Nation and to the world for everlasting Peace."[72]

San Diego Chapter #3 (1971): "The new president of our chapter is a Vietnam mother as was our outgoing president."[73]

Campbell County Chapter (Kentucky) (1971): "Installed four Mothers who have lost sons in Vietnam as their new officers. We now have 23 Vietnam Mothers and 25 WWII Mothers in our chapter."[74]

Santa Ana Chapter (1977): "[We are] fortunate to have seven Vietnam mothers as officers this year and after the election in October there will be six who will continue as officers, along with twelve mothers from WWII. Newly elected president Bette Freeman will be the sixth Vietnam mother to be president since 1970... The Santa Ana Chapter has benefited enormously from these younger mothers who have given enthusiastically their talent, ability and devotion to missions."[75]

The mothers of World War II had challenged the World War I membership. In the same way, the mothers of the Korean Conflict questioned the World War

II mothers about the hows and whys of the organization. Similarly, the Vietnam-era mothers did not easily accept every aspect of the AGSM traditions. In 1975, national president Josephay Fleming acknowledged the challenges presented by the new mothers and told the membership that she found them to be beneficial to the organization:

"I am always so pleased to see the enthusiasm of the younger Mothers. They are eager to learn and look to us for help. We must be understanding and willing to give them chairmanships and offices in our organization and listen to their suggestions and ideas. We do have guidelines in our Constitution and By-laws and Ritual. We must all follow those rules, but we do not have to follow some of the old customs. We are living in a changing world and we must change if we are to survive. Over fifty thousand American boys gave their lives in the South Vietnam conflict. Most of those boys have Mothers, and we need them and I believe they need us. I know many are working. I also worked for twelve years. I had a sick husband and a son in school, but when I quit work I needed the American Gold Star Mothers organization and I believe that will be true of the Vietnam mothers."[76]

Even with new members, AGSM was facing a bleak future. They continued to lose members far faster than new members were joining. At the 1975 convention, Mrs. Fleming stated the problem bluntly:

"Once again and for the last time, I will close with a warning about the future of our organization. Without substantial increase in membership we are in serious trouble. With the constant decrease - 506 Mothers lost by death this year and new membership only 186, need I say more? Our government tells us we have 56,000 Vietnam Gold Star Mothers. We must all work to find them and get them to join us."[77]

While the majority of the new gold star mothers were encouraged and appreciated, not all of them felt welcome. Some of the mothers recall hearing quiet comments about how the children of the World War II mothers had died in a "war" rather than a "conflict"— as if that provided greater status for their loss. These types of comments were something that the Korean mothers had occasionally been subjected to as well. Thankfully, the Vietnam-era gold star mothers moved past the occasional unkind comments and committed themselves to the organization. In 1978, perhaps in response to comments of this sort, the following was printed in *The Gold Star Mother* under the title of "An Appropriate Analogy":

"All ages are needed in the American Gold Star Mothers organization. The work of the older Mothers must be balanced with that of the younger mothers or one day we will be without leaders. The old and young are like hands on a clock. The young, the minute-hand moving quickly, and the old, the hour-hand moving slowly; it takes both to tell the time. We are in trouble if either group thinks the other is not needed."[78]

Many of AGSM's gold star mothers of World War II and Korea found that, sadly, their prior losses could not prevent them from losing family members in the nation's most recent war. In Hartford, Connecticut, Elizabeth Foy, a Korea gold star mother "was informed that she had lost another son in Vietnam—news came during a chapter meeting. The tragedy and heartache felt were manifest in the very silence among those present."[79] Campbell County Chapter in Kentucky reported in 1970 that they had the only known "mother-daughter" gold star mother combination in that part of the country—Martha Miller, sixty-seven, of Newport, and Ruth Adamson, forty-four, of Dayton. Mrs. Miller's son (Ruth's brother) died in April 1944 in the Pacific and Mrs. Adamson's son was the first Campbell County loss in Vietnam.[80] Vietnam casualty Sgt. Bobby G. Callison, the son of Fred and Pearl Callison, was the third member of his family to die in service. All Marines, one Callison brother had died in Saipan during World War II and another was killed in Korea.[81] And when the Paterson Chapter of New Jersey held its twenty-forth installation of officers in 1972, the installing officer, past chapter president Elsa Tacelt, had the "honor and distinction of installing her daughter, Ann Biber, a Vietnam mother, as chapter president."[82]

Membership Growth

The membership of AGSM had been remarkably stable during the 1950s with gold star mothers of World War II and Korea continuing to join long after the wars that had made them gold star mothers had ended. Although it could not match the post-World War II membership of nearly 21,000, the 1960 membership was reported to be more than 20,000 in "nearly 600" chapters. In 1961, AGSM was represented in every state in the continental United States by 552 chapters. California and Pennsylvania had the largest share of chapters with fifty-three and fifty, respectively, followed by New York with forty-seven and Ohio with forty-six. The District of Columbia and six states (Delaware, Idaho, Mississippi, South Dakota, Tennessee, and Wyoming) each had one chapter.[83]

However, in the early 1960s, the large number of deaths among the aging membership began to take a toll. The loss of hundreds of gold star mothers each year created a void that was not being filled by new members. In 1965, national president Mildred A. Lee reported on a trip to Grand Junction, Colorado, where she had instituted a new chapter:

"Mildred Williams, a past president of Denver Chapter, deserves a great deal of credit for this new chapter. I wish there were more. The fields are fertile, but the workers are few."[84]

As the fighting in Vietnam worsened in the late 1960s, a small new membership surge occurred, but by 1970, despite more than 500 new Vietnam gold star mothers having joined, total membership had dropped to fewer than 18,000.[85]

Looking forward, the American Gold Star Home hired a consultant in 1971 to determine what the future population of gold star mothers would be who might elect to live at the Home. The consultant determined that the total membership in the AGSM in January 1972 was 16,500. World War II members represented 72 percent of the membership; Korean Conflict mothers 13 percent and mothers of the Vietnam War 15 percent. Amazingly, there were still two World War I members. The consultant indicated that only active and successful recruitment of thousands of new members for AGSM could mitigate the vacancy problem that would threaten the Home in future years. At that time, more than 98,000 American lives had been lost in Korea and Vietnam, but according to the consultant, AGSM was doing little to reach out and attract the thousands of gold star mothers created by these losses, a situation that would create future problems for both AGSM and the American Gold Star Home.[86]

In her 1977 report on the Women's Forum gathering, Regina Wilk told the membership that she had been surprised to find that other organizations were also suffering from a decline in membership:

"Our organization is not the only organization whose membership is decreasing. It seems that all organizations are having difficulty obtaining new members. There are a few organizations that have memberships

below 5,000 which was quite shocking especially when you know the names of the organizations. So we all seem to be struggling for membership. It is all the more reason why we must all try to get at least one new member per chapter which would considerably increase our membership or at least keep it stable for the year."[87]

By 1979, membership had dropped to 8,166, less than half what it had been ten years earlier. The decline in membership would continue, severely compromising the organization in terms of effectiveness, financial health and the ability to pursue its agenda of veterans advocacy.

Chapter Activities

The gold star mothers of the Vietnam era carried on with activities that had been handed down from their sisters in prior decades—volunteering in their communities and at veterans facilities, caring for gold star mothers in need, working as advocates for veterans and their families, and preserving patriotic traditions. But the chapters were facing new, difficult problems and sometimes found there were simply no solutions. The membership of the organization continued to decrease as the gold star mothers of earlier conflicts died or found themselves unable to continue with their activities. The Irvington Chapter in New Jersey found itself facing this problem in 1970 when of their total membership of ninety, only twenty-nine were active.[88] Some chapters found that there were not enough members to continue effectively as a discrete chapter and it became necessary to disband. When possible, the mothers who could still participate would transfer their membership to another chapter as in 1973 when the Irvington Chapter accepted eleven members from a disbanded chapter in Newark, New Jersey. Too often, though, there were no other chapters close enough for the mothers to attend.[89]

Despite the difficulties they faced individually and organizationally, many of the mothers simply "soldiered" on, doing what they could to serve the veterans and their communities. The steady quiet work of World War II gold star mother Susan Neikus, an eighty-two-year-old member of the Grand Rapids Chapter, was highlighted in 1960 in an article titled "Smiles and Word of Thanks are Her Pay":

"Say, Mother, can you sew on a button for me?"

Familiar words in any home but no mother

Fig. 10-4: Campaigning for the presidency, John F. Kennedy met with gold star mothers at the Newport, Kentucky home of Ethel R. Steil on October 6, 1960. Other gold star mothers at the meeting included Stella Wagner and Mary Shay. *(Fenelon Collection)*

could have as many requests as Mrs. Bernard G. Neikus, fondly called "Mother" or Susie by her "boys" who live in the Michigan Veterans Facility.

Susie Neikus… has been sewing for the men, and for the women too, at the Facility for the past four years. She turns shirt collars that are worn, patches trousers, mends sheets and pillow cases and does a hundred and one other sewing tasks. And every bit of her time is volunteered. She counts her pay in words of thanks or friendly smiles.

She averages about 1,200 hours of volunteer work a year, mostly sewing but occasionally arranging parties and teas or other entertainment at the Facility. She has been volunteering her services for about 20 years… She's usually on the job six hours a day.[90]

The chapters tried to maintain gold star traditions. In Lansing, Michigan, gold star mothers continued to meet the young men called by the draft and bid them farewell as they boarded early morning buses to go to their induction centers.[91] Mothers of the Medford Chapter in Oregon helped cut up 1,600 pounds of watermelon in August 1972 for the annual Watermelon Bust at the VA's White City, Oregon, Domiciliary. In New York, tall patients at the local VA hospital experienced new comfort when Buffalo Chapter No. 26 presented a seven-foot-long bed to the facility. Mobile Azalea Chapter (Alabama) mothers were honored guests at a Veterans Day parade that traveled through

three counties; they reported that they had been "in the lead car in the parade, just behind our chapter colors. The parade route was 26 miles long with about 25 cars parading." [92]

A new chapter in South Carolina—Palmetto Chapter in Greenville—wasted little time in becoming involved in gold star mother work:

"The twenty very busy and determined mothers of our very young chapter have made their city and most of the state aware of what the American Gold Star Mothers, Inc., are. In the short nine months they have six hundred hours community service, sent hundreds of cards and letters, and many packages have been sent to our boys in Vietnam. They have made three trips of two hundred and forty miles each to Fort Jackson Military Hospital and entertained, served refreshments and given candy, cigarettes and magazines to over 200 patients there … They have very good coverage from their radio and television stations. They make their own wreaths with the Gold Star which is carried to each family that has lost a son in Greenville County. Their many bake sales, rummage sales, hot dog and hamburger suppers and bingo parties provide the finances for this Chapter."[93]

The Bay Bridge Chapter was responsible for erecting an Amputee Shelter in 1964 at Kezar Stadium in San Francisco. This easily accessible haven for amputee and paraplegic combat veterans was said to be the only shelter of its kind in the world. Dedicated on October 24, 1964, the 31,695 football fans in attendance shared a minute of silence in memory of those lost in the nation's wars. Through the generosity of a California state senator, the gold star mothers served lunch to the veterans in the newly dedicated shelter.[94]

The Lorain Chapter in Lorain, Ohio, illustrated their sympathy for victims of war by financing a home for a Korean family of eight. The project was adopted after the mothers read the story of an impoverished Korean family in *The Gold Star Mother*. The article described the primitive living conditions among Korean war victims and told how their circumstances could be helped through the American-Korean Foundation, Inc., a non-profit, non-sectarian organization that offered a home-building kit that enabled poor families to build a permanent, safe home for themselves. For a donation of $149.35, a Korean family received an earth brick-making machine, eighteen bags of cement, windows and doors, lumber, nails and roof tiles, along with plans and instructions on how to build a trim, secure cottage. The chapter received photographs of their adopted family standing in front of their original paper and tin shack and, smiling broadly, before their new home.[95]

At Christmas in 1965, Camden County Chapter (New Jersey) mothers sent out 75 Christmas cards to servicemen stationed in Vietnam and asked a question—was there anything the Camden County gold star mothers could do for them? In response to that question they received the following reply:

"I could not resist answering your query for our need. The Battalion is engaged in the support of a small Christian orphanage for blind Vietnamese boys. We are starting from scratch and these poor blind children need everything from vitamins to clothing. Christ said, 'That which ye do to the least of mine, ye also do unto me.' Signed, Commanding Officer, 1st Lt. John D. Shepard of the 71st Military Police, Battalion "A" in Saigon, Vietnam."

In reply, the chapter gathered a large package of clothing, vitamins, candles, soaps, valentines and other useful articles for 1st Lt. Shepard. He responded as soon as the box arrived, telling the mothers that the orphanage would be able to use everything that was sent and thanking them for their thoughtfulness.[96]

In 1966, Camden County Chapter secretary Irene Fox again wrote to sixty-one servicemen from the area who were serving in Vietnam. At the chapter meetings she read the answers received from the men in Vietnam, including this thoughtful response from Captain Dick Noble, 1st Air Commandos, serving in Bien Hoa, South Vietnam:

"I was overwhelmed by the thoughtfulness of your organization at Christmas time. Christmas in my family, and I'm sure in all of yours, is a time when friends exchange good wishes. I am sincerely pleased that this year you number me among your friends. You, better than most, know that in a war, happiness is a full mailbox and I appreciate your interest in my happiness. Most of us are too busy doing our jobs to worry about the Vietniks [anti-war protesters], but I am concerned about the amount of publicity they get compared to patriotic and knowledgeable groups like yours. I firmly believe that the only way to leave [Vietnam] would be to quit like the French people did ten years ago. That would be a tragic waste of lives, past and future, because Communism would not stop its aggression after here anymore than they did in Korea. I'd be proud to know that there are few if any quitters in my home town and that a group of fine ladies, who know what this is all about, are behind us. Please don't get discouraged if you have an opportunity to repeat this kindness again next year for some other South Jersey boy. We still have a big job to do.

"Please pray for me and my family (who as you know also makes great sacrifices at a time like this). Pray first that I do my job well and second that I will return with honor.[97]

Tacoma Chapter in Washington paid their annual visit to the McNeill Island Honor Farm in 1971, a tradition they had started fifteen years before. The residents at the Honor Farm were prisoners from McNeill Island Penitentiary who had earned special privileges through their good behavior, and the Farm served as a halfway house for many men who were getting ready to be released. Most of the men there belonged to the Self Improvement Group that had been started by the Tacoma Chapter in 1956 as an educational project. The program had been copied by many prisons across the nation. The inmate study program was supported by educators from town who went to the facility to conduct classes.

Each Mother's Day, the Honor Farm residents issued an invitation for the Tacoma Chapter mothers to attend a special day planned just for them. As one mother reported:

"They have a [musical] program prepared, [provide] corsages and we eat with them the regular prison fare. They are a group of some very intelligent men and have their various trades and many are now prepared to take positions outside. Their courtesies and playing for us make the day worthwhile. They take us over on a boat and often on a tour of the Island, then take us back on the boat.[98]

In *The Gold Star Mother* the Tacoma Chapter shared the following letter written by one of the Honor Farm prisoners:

"Were it not for your chapter of the Gold Star Mothers, Mother's Day at McNeill Island would be a sad day indeed. Embodied within you is the personification of each man's mother, on whom, on this of all days, each man's thoughts dwell. As you share this special day with us, let us forget where we are and think rather of the person this day ennobles, whose name is legion and sacred in each heart – our Mother. May this day be as pleasant and meaningful for you as it is for us."[99]

Far too often, some of the plans put forward by the chapters had to be dropped for lack of funds. As they had in decades past, gold star mothers kept coming up with creative new ideas to earn the funds necessary to implement their plans. The Decatur, Illinois, chapter made some local young people very happy and added funds to their activity account by sponsoring a 1966 New Year's Eve party. Knowing the youth of Decatur had few options for an appropriate New Year's celebration, the gold star mothers took over the National Guard Armory and hired a popular local rock 'n' roll band to entertain. A group of gold star mothers chaperoned the dance and served soft drinks in the kitchen of the armory. Mrs. Irene Finley, second vice president of the Decatur Chapter, said, "They come in droves when they know a rock 'n' roll group will be playing."[100]

In 1969, the gold star mothers of the Plattsburgh, New York, chapter decided that a monument in a local park was needed to honor soldiers from the town who had died in Vietnam. They considered how they could raise the $3,500 needed for the project and came up with an unusual and successful fundraising event:

"Four servicemen in Plattsburgh gave a lesson in heroism, courage and plain, dogged endurance during September when they marched 100 miles to raise money to assist the local Gold Star Mothers to erect a monument in Trinity Park to the Vietnam dead... They challenged Plattsburgh and Clinton County merchants to bid competitively on the number of miles they could walk.

"Their trek started at 8 a.m. on Wednesday, September 11, in pouring rain and wind. Rouses Point, which is on the Canadian border, treated them to steak dinner... and they spent the night free at the Champlain Hotel. They left at 5 a.m. on Thursday for Mooers, New York. Air Force man George Provencher interrupted his march with a stomach ache. Then, within a half mile of Mooers, Army man Gary Flaherty's knee locked and he was taken to the Plattsburgh Air Force Base Hospital. The remaining recruiters continued marching to Ellenburg Depot, spending the night in the Lakeside Hotel.

"At 5:30 a.m. on Friday, Flaherty reappeared on crutches and continued marching over Danemora Mountain. On leaving Saranac at 5pm, Navy man Phillips had a high fever and was hospitalized at the Base Hospital. This was three casualties since the trip had started.

"At Cadyville, Provencher and Phillips rejoined the marches, walking non-stop the rest of the way. They all arrived at Trinity Park in Plattsburgh at 11:30 a.m. where they were greeted by the Mayor and gold star mothers. A throng of Plattsburgh citizens joined them as they marched through Plattsburg and many pressed donations into their hands. A shoeshine boy gave his earnings and three youngsters gave their collection from a house-to-house canvass of their neighborhood...

"Flaherty's knee trouble stemmed from injury he suffered several years ago. It is believed he walked a world's record on crutches—a total of 57 miles... By October 8, contributions had climbed to $5,300."[101]

In 1970, the *Los Angeles Times* told the story of a gold star mother who believed that an event planned by her chapter hadn't received the attention from the government that she thought appropriate:

"The chaplain of the Gold Star Mothers local chapter was upset because no high-ranking officials would agree to attend Memorial Day ceremonies. So she wrote a letter of complaint to President Nixon. Because of Mrs. Ethel McDonald's letter the White House is sending a Marine Corps general to today's ceremony.

"The military and government officials were invited to the dedication of a $50,000 carillon, the third largest in the world, at the Veteran's Administration national cemetery north of Houston. Mrs. McDonald sent a telegram direct to Mr. Nixon saying 'it is most disappointing' that no high official could come.

"She got action. Mrs. Ginger Sevell, a White House

secretary, called Mrs. McDonald saying the president had seen the telegram personally and had demanded that something be done. Major General Dewain Faw, judge advocate of the Marine Corps, would be there to represent the President and the armed services, Mrs. Sevell said. She also said the president was excited about the 330-bell carillon for which the Gold Star mothers had campaigned so long. Mrs. Sevell said the President had not realized that the cemetery, with its 175,000 gravesites, was the nation's second largest national cemetery.

"'She said the President wanted to be represented here,'" Mrs. McDonald said."[102]

Finances

In 1954, AGSM had been able to purchase property for a national headquarters and then pay off the mortgage in six years. However, as the 1960s unfolded, finances became a significant problem for the mothers. Increasing costs for publications and conventions, significantly declining membership and the associated loss of revenue, and continuing upkeep on the headquarters property quickly reduced the organization's comfortable nest egg that had been established during the 1950s.

By 1969, publication of *The Gold Star Mother* had come under close scrutiny. In June, more than 16,700 copies of the newsletter were published each month at a cost of more than $8,000 per year. Initially, efforts were made to lower the printing and publication costs and eliminate non-active addresses from the mailings (there was a cost associated with the return of each undelivered newsletter). By February 1974, the national executive board voted unanimously to publish the newsletter every other month beginning with the April issue. This action, they explained, "is necessitated by the skyrocketing cost of postage and the increase in the cost of printing. For the past two years every possible means for continuing the paper on a monthly basis have been explored. Our organization is the last Patriotic and Veteran Auxiliary publication to revert to six issues a year."[103]

Late in 1975, all chapters and departments received a letter from the national executive board asking for financial assistance to "help sustain our national Headquarters up-keep, our Gold Star mother newspaper and operating expenses." No set amount or schedule was established, but departments and chapters were asked to send what they could to assist with the un-

avoidable costs accrued at the national level.[104]

Finally, as costs continued to increase, AGSM took a step in 1978 that the organization had tried to avoid in every way possible. Annual per capita dues were raised to "$4.00 of which 70 cents will be retained by the department with the balance to go to the national. Applications for membership [will also] increase from $4 to $5."[105] Although this was an increase of only one dollar per member per year for national dues, the national executive board had postponed such a move for fear that even this modest increase might be more than some gold star mothers could afford and might result in their withdrawal from the organization.

When Emogene Cupp took office in 1978, the fifty-year anniversary of AGSM, she realized that immediate fundraising action was required or the organization might not survive. Over the objections of some officers and members, she initiated a five-year program of selling boxed greeting cards with the income going to the national organization. In the first year, a profit of nearly $3,000 saved the organization from bankruptcy and provided time for financial stability to be established, albeit on a shoestring budget.[106]

Not wanting the membership to think that the national board was not doing its part to manage expenses, president Cupp reported on a national board meeting that had been held in February 1979. Due to the depleted treasury, for the first time in AGSM history, each officer was required to pay her own transportation to the national board meeting. As they usually did, all officers contributed to a food fund for their meetings, and delicious meals were prepared at headquarters by Elva Newman, Custodian of Records. Headquarters became a boarding house to spare the officers any lodging costs:

"The National Executive Board always has a board meeting in February to make plans for the national convention. Since we had no money, all the board members had to pay their own expenses. If they couldn't afford it, they were excused. With 15 members of the board, sleeping conditions were a bit crowded. But everyone loved it, snoring and all."[107]

Deaths

In the 1960s and 1970s, AGSM experienced such a high rate of death among its membership that many feared it could not survive—even as new gold star mothers of the Vietnam era found their way to the organization.

During the 1960s, an average of more than 830 gold star mothers and dads died each year. In the 1970s, the death rate slowed somewhat to an average of just under 600 per year. The deaths included the very elderly—World War I–era mothers such as Oregon's Carrie Nash, who died in April 1969 at the age of 105, and Lizzie Johnson, the nation's oldest gold star mother at the time, who died at 105 in 1972. But the young were not immune, such as Ohio gold star mother Jonnie Mae Atkinson who died in 1969 at the age of fifty-one.[108]

The passing of many past national AGSM presidents during this period rocked the organization. With each death, more of the organizational memory was irredeemably lost and the link to the rituals and traditions became weaker:

• Dr. Emma L. Balcom, a World War I mother who served as national president from 1941–1942, died June 14, 1960 in Clearwater, Florida. Although she had not joined AGSM until 1936, she was already involved in gold star mother activities in New York, her home state, and was soon named state organizer. She was responsible for organizing several chapters as well as one of the first state departments. In her later years, she had moved to Florida, organizing a chapter there that was named the Emma Balcom Chapter in her honor. One of the last official acts of Mrs. Balcom's term as national president was opening AGSM membership to World War II gold star mothers.[109]

• In July 1960, the death of Ruth Singer at age sixty-four was announced in *The Gold Star Mother*. Mrs. Singer, who served as national president from 1955–1957, was well known to the membership for her tireless efforts during the long-running court battle over the Memorial National Home Foundation. The organization's first Jewish national president and chaplain, Mrs. Singer was named Ayshet Chayil ("a woman of Valor") by the rabbi at her memorial service, a "woman who is able to transform sorrow into service… transcending personal suffering by service to humanity." George Wise, AGSM's attorney for the Memorial National Home Foundation lawsuit, had worked closely with Mrs. Singer for many years and referred to her as "a person of grace, a person of tact and… a fighter." In 1957, he told the delegates at the national convention that "Ruth… gave [her] heart and her health to the cause."[110]

• Frances High, national president from 1960–1961, died in January 1964. A World War II gold star mother, Mrs. High was sixty-two when she died in Houston, Texas.[111]

• Mabel C. Troy died on January 30, 1965. She was remembered for her many hats and her love of music. National president from 1958–1959, four of her five sons served in World War II.

• Mae M. Cushman died on September 3, 1968 at the age of ninety-one. She was the last surviving World War I–era national president and was one of the most beloved to hold that office. National president from 1940–1941, Mrs. Cushman had been committed to keeping the nation out of another war unless there was an attack on American soil. When elected in 1940, she said, "We're going to talk peace until the last breath."[112]

• Mary F. Neiman, national president from 1963–1964, died December 27, 1976. She was a member of the Broome County Chapter in Binghamton, New York.[113]

• Anne C. Richards of New Jersey died April 29, 1977. She held the office of national president from 1971–1972.[114]

• Anna G. Hagerty of New Jersey died June 12, 1977. A World War II gold star mother, she was a member of the Atlantic County Chapter and served as national president from 1947–1948. Her mother, Elizabeth I. Millard, a gold star mother of World War I, had served as the second national president of AGSM.[115]

• Mary R. Kelly, national president from 1962–1963, died November 9, 1979. She was a member of the Grace Darling Seibold Chapter in Washington, D.C.[116]

It was not only the loss of past national officers that saddened the membership. Members who had long been part of the organization's history were also mourned:

• Grace Kitt, a feisty World War I gold star mother, died at the age of ninety-two in April 1960. For many decades she had taken special care of the blind patients she called her "boys" at the Sawtelle Veterans Hospital in Los Angeles.

She was often seen on the local freeways, her car full of blind veterans, driving them to dances and other events where they could mingle outside the hospital.[117]

• Stella Duncan, whose AGSM membership had been revoked when she challenged national president Eleanor Boyd on the issue of the Memorial National Home Foundation, died in December 1965. Her death at the age of 81 was announced by her home chapter, Manhattan Chapter #9, and they referred to her as their "beloved Mother Duncan." Mrs. Duncan, active at the local, department and national levels in the late 1940s and early 1950s before losing her membership, rejoined the organization in the late 1950s when the national board offered "an opportunity to forgive and forget" to those mothers whose membership had been revoked during those turbulent years.[118]

• Broome County Chapter No. 3 in Binghamton, New York announced the death of Mother Alice Daggers at the age of ninety-seven in January 1967. A World War I gold star mother, Mrs. Daggers had organized the Broome County Chapter and many others following the war. She had become an unofficial member emeritus through her thoughtful and caring correspondence shared in *The Gold Star Mother* and her frequent gifts to headquarters of quilts and lacework she made to keep busy after being confined to a wheelchair.[119]

• Margaret E. Loveless, one of the last survivors of the Mother Chapter who signed the original organizational charter in 1928, died in February 1968 at the age of 100. She had lived her entire life in Washington, D.C., raising seven children after the death of her husband in 1923. Norman, her eldest, died in France in World War I.[120]

• Gunda P. Borstrom, the Utah mother who lost four sons in World War II, died on March 20, 1971. An immigrant from Norway, Gunda and her husband Albon (who died in 1956) settled in Utah where they raised nine children. Five of their sons served in World War II and, within a five-month period in 1944, four of the young men were killed in action. By presidential order, the fifth son was released from military duty with the Marines and returned home.[121]

• World War I gold star mother Harriet L. (Hattie Lee) Hurley, died in August 1972 at the age of 101. She was the last surviving charter member of the Grace Darling Seibold Chapter in Washington, D.C. Born in Chantilly, Virginia, she was remembered for her "tireless devotion in the service of humanity."[122]

• Three-star gold star mother Katie Nemeth of Coplay, Pennsylvania, a member of Allentown Chapter, died in April 1973. Controversy had arisen following World War II when her lack of citizenship resulted in her application for AGSM membership being denied. Many felt that the loss of three sons was far more important than her citizenship status. In 1954, Mrs. Nemeth became a citizen and was immediately admitted to AGSM membership. The mother of thirteen, she was visiting another gold star mother at the time of her death, two days after her seventy-seventh birthday.[123]

• Joe Willie Riley, the gold star mother called up for induction into the military during the Korean Conflict, died in Chicago in December 1976. In her obituary, it was reported that "Mrs. Riley has lived thru [sic] two hotel fires, two train wrecks, a shipwreck, a tornado, an auto plunge from a bridge, a bus wreck and five major operations." When she was unable to convince her draft board that a mistake had been made, she told reporters she was ready to go since she was finding it difficult as a middle-aged woman to find employment, and she thought going into the military might solve the problem.[124]

• Carmen Raffin, the gold star mother whose sons served in the American military while she assisted the French Resistance in France during World War II, died in June 1979. She was a member of the Waterbury Chapter in Connecticut since her return to the United States following the war.[125]

The passing of one of AGSM's most controversial and powerful past national presidents occurred without organizational notice. Eleanor Boyd, who served five terms as national president, died in Long Beach, California on January 10, 1975, just one week prior to her seventy-seventh birthday.

Fig. 10-5: Anti-war protestors picketing the White House in January 1968.
(U.S. News & World Report Magazine Photograph Collection (Library of Congress);
Ref. LC-DIG-ppmsca-24360)

Protests, Prisoners of War, and Amnesty

As the war in Vietnam became increasingly unpopular and the number of Americans killed there continued to rise, many Americans, particularly the young, took to the streets to demand that the war end. As the demonstrations continued, the protesters became more organized, greater numbers joined the marches, and the protests spread around the world. In April 1967, more than 200,000 people marched in San Francisco and New York; four days of anti-war protests in New York resulted in nearly 600 arrests, including world-famous pediatrician Dr. Benjamin Spock. More than 200,000 students boycotted classes in New York in April 1968 and 10,000 anti-war protesters disrupted the Democratic national convention in August 1968. Soon the protesters took their demonstrations to the next level, citing the American tradition of civil disobedience to justify taking over university buildings and occupying them, usually peacefully, for days.

In May 1970, Ohio National Guardsmen were called in to keep the peace at an anti-war protest at Kent State University. They fired into the crowd of students, killing four and wounding more than a dozen. The response across the nation was immediate and more than 400 colleges and universities across America closed in protest of the violence. In Washington, nearly 100,000 protesters surrounded various government buildings, including the White House and historical monuments. Mass protests were held on a monthly basis, drawing larger and larger crowds.

The Vietnam Veterans Against War organization planned a peaceful anti-war protest in April 1971 that included gold star mothers. As part of a four-day protest and meetings with legislators, more than a thousand Vietnam veterans, led by gold star mothers, marched to the Arlington National Cemetery gate near the Tomb of the Unknowns. When they arrived, the gates of the cemetery had been locked in anticipation of their arrival. The protesters were denied entry; the wreaths they carried to place on the graves were left outside the gate as they peacefully returned to the capital. The march and the refusal to allow them to stand among the graves of their fellow soldiers were captured by news cameras and seen by millions of viewers around the world.[126]

As it had since its beginnings, AGSM did not take a position about the war. Instead, it supported the government and the troops. AGSM national president Mamie P. Simmons shared her hopes for the soldiers in her first message for 1969:

"I will close my message as this is my prayer for the New Year. It is with hearts of deep concern that we remember our Service Men who are engaged in battle in Vietnam, and on duty around the World. They are in danger zones in our behalf; for some of them, the first time away from home, some are coming home, others are going to take their places and some have gone to their eternal Home. It is not through choice but duty; not through pleasure but service; not through ease, but labor; and not through evasion but dedication that these servicemen respond to the call of their Country. As we pray tonight, ask God for these men's safety and also pray that this will soon be over, and our world can live in peace and service to the common needs of all men everywhere."[127]

The mothers' deep and constant concern for the soldiers did not mean, however, that they felt a need to let the actions of the anti-war protesters go unremarked. In a newspaper article about Gold Star Mothers Day activities in 1969, several gold star mothers expressed their pain and unhappiness with the nation's young protesters:

"Sixty-six Phoenix mothers whose sons have died on battlefields stretching from Iwo Jima to Pork Chop Hill, today denounced demonstrators who demand that the U.S. get out of Vietnam.

"'My son would be very hurt if he knew how shameful these young Americans are acting,' said Mrs. Iva Morisette, president of the Phoenix Chapter in Arizona. Mrs. Morisette's son was killed on Iwo Jima during World War II. He had been a fighting Marine in the 5th Division, 28th Regiment—the Ira Hayes Division.

"'I think it's terrible when college students hold such demonstrations,' said Mrs. Ethel B. Twitchell. 'Our sons gave up their lives for freedom.'

"Other gold star mothers, their faces creased by years of worry and hands gnarled by working to help others, echoed her statement. The Gold Star Mothers are a unique group of women. They have carried scars that will never quite heal. And despite the fact that they are 'organized' into a working club, they are, in reality, alone."[128]

At the 1967 national convention, a resolution was approved to send a letter of support to President Lyndon B. Johnson on behalf of AGSM:

"Whereas, the members of the American Gold Star Mothers, Inc., are alarmed by the increasing demonstrations against the government of the United States, the desecration of our American flag, and the burning of draft cards in protest of our participation in the Vietnam War;...

"Whereas we, as a patriotic organization, vigorously resent the attitudes displayed by such demonstrators who are privileged to live in a Country which owes its freedom to the brave men and women who gave their lives in the pursuit of such freedom since the days of the American Revolution,...

"[We herewith] send a message to President Lyndon B. Johnson expressing our confidence in his policy in the Vietnam War and also, commending him for his vigorous and untiring efforts in behalf of peace."[129]

The Moratorium to End the War in Vietnam held on October 15, 1969 was a huge event with millions of protestors participating around the world. It was followed a month later by a moratorium march held in Washington, D.C., in which more than half a million protesters took part. Many of the protestors carried signs on which were written the names of the nation's Vietnam War dead. One group of protesters started their march at Arlington National Cemetery where each picked up a sign on which was printed the name of an American soldier who had died in Vietnam. Wearing their signs, they walked silently in single file to the White House. There, each protestor ascended to a stage, shouted the name of the soldier on their sign and deposited the sign in an open coffin that stood nearby. That was more than some members of AGSM were willing to allow:

"A large group of Vietnam Mothers protested their Sons' names being carried on posters by the anti-Vietnam war demonstrators. It became quite a thing with Attorney James Phelan Jr. serving the Mothers without pay. He got an injunction ... which forbad the desecration of their dead Sons' names being carried in a demonstration which included Viet Cong flags, with American Flags trampled upon. The mothers went to Washington on Veterans Day to continue the fight for the honor of their Sons' names.

"President Nixon wrote a beautiful letter to Mrs. Rita Secrest, one of the mothers who sparked the protest against the demonstrators: 'You and the other Philadelphia Gold Star Mothers have paid your sons the highest tribute in expressing your desire that their names not be among those read at protest rallies.' Mrs. Secrest, who is chaplain of the Philadelphia Chapter, AGSM, said she received the letter Wednesday morning. Her son, Army Sgt. Edward W. Secrest, 20, was shot fatally in Vietnam when he attempted to rescue two other soldiers who had been injured...

"Mr. Nixon said he was sure the sons of mothers who blocked use of their names in the anti-war demonstrations would be very proud of their stand. 'When the peace for which all of us pray comes in Vietnam there will be a special place in the hearts of free men throughout the world for your sons, for each of you, and for all the others who have sacrificed so much to bring freedom into this suffering land.'"[130]

An unattributed newspaper clipping in an AGSM scrapbook tells the story of another group of gold star mothers who stood up against the use of their childrens' names in the protests. It is probable that this was the very active Alexandria, Virginia chapter of AGSM:

"A small group of 'Gold Star Mothers'—those who have lost a son in a war—yesterday protested the use of their sons' names in last week's 'March against Death' here and signed a 'Faithogram' supporting President Nixon's Vietnam policies. Five women, accompanied by a Gold Star dad and two girls, said they objected to the use of the names in the march because the marchers 'weren't fighting for the same things our sons were.'"[131]

POWs/MIAs

The issue of the prisoners of war held by the North Vietnamese and the American soldiers who were missing in action was an important one for AGSM. As early as July 1970, the organization stated that it was "deeply concerned over Hanoi's refusal to give names of the missing in action and prisoners of War, and to protect the safety and security of our people."[132] The Redlands Chapter in California set up tables at civic events where the public could sign petitions on behalf of the prisoners of war. The petitions were directed to the government of North Vietnam, asking for "the release of names, addresses and state of health of the prisoners; repatriating or moving to a neutral country all those who are sick or wounded; permitting the Red Cross or

some other international humanitarian organization to help monitor the prison camps and help minister to the needs of the captives; and allowing prisoners to send and receive mail, including shipments of food, clothing, medical supplies, and educational and recreation materials."[133]

At a February 1971 national board meeting, a resolution was approved encouraging the membership to become involved by writing to Hanoi:

"Whereas, There are 1600 men missing in the Asian Conflict who are called "America's Forgotten Men"—339 have been listed, but only 15 have been photographed, and

Whereas, The prisoners of war are suffering barbaric, inhuman and illegal treatment by their captors in North Vietnam, and

Whereas, The wives, children and parents of these prisoners are suffering untold grief and worry over their loved ones being held captive,

Therefore, be it resolved that the American Gold Star Mothers, Inc. become involved and urge our members to continue writing Hanoi demanding that the 1959 Geneva Conference rules be observed."[134]

In May 1971, *The Gold Star Mother* contained an article about the 500 known prisoners of war and the 1,000 other Americans who were missing in action, stating that more than 200 of the POWs had already spent more than five years in captivity and one Navy flyer was in his seventh year of incarceration, longer than any American prisoner of war in any prior conflict:

"Out of the 1100 listed as Missing in Action, only Hanoi and its allies know their fate. The men in the prison camps have been subjected to torture, abuse, malnutrition and disease. They have been humiliated and subjected to public degradation. ... Many others have been kept in isolation for years. Some were so badly wounded that they are unable to care for themselves. Their families have been left alone for years wondering if they are relatives or mourners. They, too, are victims of Hanoi's torture."[135]

The article concluded with a call for action by the American public: "Every voice is needed because every example of silence only proves to Hanoi that we don't care and that's what they rely on, us not caring about our men and international law."[136]

After the signing of the Paris Peace Accords in

January 1973, nearly 600 POWs returned home during Operation Homecoming, which lasted from February through April 1973. Despite President Nixon's assertion that all POWs had been returned home, concern grew about those missing in action who had not been accounted for. Following a resolution at the New York Department convention in 1975, department president Mary E. Wheeler wrote to President Ford concerning the missing:

"As mothers of sons who gave their lives for our great country we feel our involvement in Vietnam is not over until every man is accounted for, whether he be a prisoner of war or gave his life. Mr. President, you owe this to the parents of these men who are now feeling that we have forgotten them."[137]

Amnesty

Even before the war in Vietnam officially ended, the question of amnesty was raised for those who had fled the country rather than serve in the military. AGSM, along with other prominent political and veteran organizations such as the American Legion, came out clearly against amnesty or clemency at any level. At the 1972 AGSM convention in Dallas, the delegates unanimously passed a resolution against amnesty that stated:

"Whereas, Many boys have answered their Country's call to serve in time of war or in the protection of other Countries from invaders, and

Whereas, many boys were willing to go, others unwilling, but went in simple obedience to duty as they knew it, many giving their lives,

Therefore be it resolved that: The American Gold Star Mothers, Inc. petition the government of the United States to refuse amnesty to those who evaded the draft or deserted until they fulfill their obligation to the Country in which they have enjoyed our American Way of Life."[138]

Just one month later, AGSM reported that the American Legion's strong stand against amnesty was already imperiled:

"The first crack in the American Legion's stand against amnesty for draft evaders occurred last week when the Maryland Department [of the American Legion] in convention passed a resolution proposing amnesty on a selected basis... Evasion and not desertion is the basic issue of the Maryland resolution. The

Legion and other major veterans' groups have stood out against any let-down in the law on desertion and evasion until the Vietnam War is concluded."[139]

In September 1974, gold star mother Lupe P. Rodriguez of the East Los Angeles—Montebello Chapter wrote to Congressman Chet Holifield explaining plainly how she felt about any proposed amnesty program:

"It is very hard for any mother to accept amnesty when her oldest son came home partly disabled and another son gave his life for his country and the people. He loved life just like the cowards that fled... They say they have suffered enough, that they want to come home. What the ***** do these so-called men know about suffering? They should go see our men in the hospitals, and take a good look at them and then they should go to a little dark corner and search their minds and hearts... I feel if amnesty is given, whether full or part pardon, then our country is weakening."[140]

In answer to an October 1976 letter from AGSM reconfirming its position and objections to amnesty, Milton E. Mitler, Deputy Special Assistant to President Ford, expressed the president's disappointment in the response to an earlier clemency program that had been offered to draft dodgers and deserters, which required a period of public service:

"As you know, in September of 1974, a clemency program was instituted until January 1975 and was then extended for another two months. This program permitted those individuals who fell within either of the above categories the right to return to this country by accepting an obligation for some service other than military. While the President hoped all would take advantage of this move, unfortunately, only about 21,500 did see the opportunity. At the present time, there are no plans to reinstate the Clemency Board or to take any other action."[141]

Many AGSM members spoke out individually against amnesty. Katherine Mannion, who would later become national president of AGSM, expressed her opinions in a letter to the *Baltimore New Post*:

"Amnesty? No! There are questions I would like to ask those who fled our country when needed: How did they know they would be called into the service of their country? How did they know they would be accepted? Could they pass the mental or physical tests? How did they know they would be sent to Vietnam? How did they know they would go into combat?

"All the government asked was a two-year draft. Those who ran away didn't care then, so why should we care now? Had they been accepted into the Armed Services they could have voiced their objections as conscientious objectors, etc. But they didn't even give it a try; they fled.

"I have been to Canada and also to Switzerland and have met and talked with American draft dodgers. Leave them where they are. They deserve it."[142]

In May 1974, AGSM member Mrs. Bernard Gorski appeared on national television to respond to a CBS-station editorial calling for conditional amnesty. She stated:

"Now that the Vietnam War is over, all of a sudden many of these boys [draft-evaders] are homesick. Are we to feel sorry for them because they left the country to beat the draft? I say let them stay in the country of their choice. It would not be right to restore their privileges when we might be involved in another war. Who's to say they wouldn't run away again? What good did it do, then, for our boys who lost their lives for our country?

"Those boys who evaded the draft may be homesick, but we parents are heart-sick. They may be deprived of their country and family, but we have been deprived of a precious life of a boy who had not yet begun to live. I firmly believe granting amnesty in any form would be a mockery of the sacrifices of those men who did their duty and assumed their responsibilities in time of conflict."[143]

AGSM felt itself challenged by the well publicized efforts of a gold star mother who became a national figure supporting unconditional amnesty. Louise Ransom's son, Robert Crawford "Mike" Ransom, Jr., was the oldest of six brothers from a New York suburb. After attending Officer Candidate School, he was commissioned a second lieutenant and received orders for Vietnam, arriving there on March 7, 1968:

"On May 3, 1968, Company A was moving into a night ambush position near Landing Zone Sue when a mine detonated. Mike Ransom was hit. Despite severe wounds, he urged his men to remain calm, organizing them into a tight defensive perimeter until they could receive assistance. He refused medical attention until other injured men had been treated. Subsequently, he was evacuated to a field hospital where his condition deteriorated. He died on Mother's Day, May 11, 1968, his death officially attributed to pneumonia and peritonitis resulting from his wounds."[144]

Louise Ransom later published her son's letters in a book titled *Letters from Vietnam*. She, her husband and her other sons became active in anti-war protests and demonstrations and she became the affiliate director of Americans for Amnesty. In 1974, she told a reporter:

"'We must make something good come out of [the Vietnam War]. My son's life and 57,000 others will have been wasted if there is no visible gain for our country for their loss… The kind of country that can grant universal and unconditional amnesty would be a country my son was proud to serve. It would demonstrate that we are compassionate, that we care about human beings, that we are honestly devoted to the kind of principles we say we are—social justice, freedom of dissent, freedom of conscience. If we can reach the point of granting amnesty, then something good would come out of Vietnam for this country. It would be a reaffirmation of the things for which the nation was founded'

"Mrs. Ransom … disagrees sharply with President Nixon's view that amnesty would dishonor those who served in Vietnam.

"'Nothing we say here or do here can dishonor what they did,' she said flatly. 'Those who served had courage, but that does not preclude war resisters having another kind of courage or patriotism.'

"Mrs. Ransom explained that universal amnesty means amnesty for draft resisters, deserters and servicemen who received less than honorable discharges—a total of nearly 535,000 Americans.

"'Unconditional amnesty means no alternative service, no punitive measures and no case-by-case judgments,' Mrs. Ransom said. 'That's another point. Amnesty means forgetting—it comes from the same Greek word as "amnesia." It is not forgiving. Forgiving implies wrongdoing and wrongdoing requires punishment.'"[145]

The organizational and public confusion surrounding Mrs. Ransom and her possible link as a gold star mother to AGSM finally necessitated a clarifying statement by national president Helen S. White in 1974:

"It has been brought to my attention that there are two women, Mrs. Louise Ransom, of Bronxville, NY, and Mrs. Patricia Simon of Boston, Massachusetts, both Gold Star Mothers, so the articles state, who are touring our Country, urging amnesty for men who deserted or fled our Country to avoid serving in any branch of the services of the United States during the Vietnam conflict. These women are, no doubt, Gold Star mothers, but they are absolutely NOT members of American Gold Star Mothers, Inc. We have actual proof of this. Because they are NOT, we have no jurisdiction over their activities. To put articles against their activities in any public newspaper would make our Organization open to a libel suit brought by them, against us."[146]

AGSM responded with outrage when it discovered that the Vietnam Era Reconciliation Act had been passed without fanfare by a House committee and had started on its road to becoming law. The national executive board called upon the membership to contact their legislators to vote against the passage of the bill:

"It has been brought to our attention... that Bill 9596 (Vietnam Era Reconciliation Act)... that grants unconditional amnesty to Vietnam-era draft dodgers and deserters has been quietly approved by a House Judiciary subcommittee. The bill now goes to... the full Judiciary Committee where passage is expected. The bill was drafted with the help of the American Civil Liberties Union and would grant amnesty to all those submitting a certificate... saying they dodged the draft, went A.W.O.L. or refused lawful orders because of their disapproval of the United States' military involvement in Indochina. Additionally... the bill would give citizenship back to those who renounced their Country because of the war... restore all rights and full citizenship to those war resisters who fled to Canada, Sweden or elsewhere; and grant 'certificates of unconditional reconciliation' for those granted amnesty under the act. Such certificates would supersede any dishonorable discharges; release all people now performing alternate service under President Ford's Clemency Program; and expunge the records of all draft resisters and deserters who have been convicted of crimes and already served jail terms.

"The American Legion states: Passage of this bill would be a gross miscarriage of our judicial system, to the sacrifices made by those who served and are still serving, their families, prisoners-of-war, missing-in-action and to the American People"[147]

Just a few months later, at the 1976 national convention, the delegates went on record as strenuously opposing the Vietnam Era Reconciliation Act by unanimously approving the following resolution:

Whereas, Bill HR 9596, commonly called the "Vietnam Era Reconciliation Act"... would grant unconditional amnesty to Vietnam Era draft dodgers and deserters and return full citizenship to those, who by their actions, renounced their Country.

Whereas, this is called an Act of Reconciliation and would in essence nullify the sacrifices made by loyal servicemen and women and their loved ones.

Be it Resolved: The American Gold Star Mothers, Inc.... go on record as unanimously and unalterably opposing Bill 9596 and a copy of this resolution be sent to President Gerald R. Ford, etc....[148]

National president Mary E. King reassured the membership that letters had been mailed to President Ford and Jimmy Carter before he became president and after he was inaugurated stating that AGSM was on record as opposing amnesty for deserters. "Let them remain in Canada and elsewhere," she stated.[149]

Nonetheless, just a day after his inauguration in 1977, President Jimmy Carter made good his campaign promise to grant a full presidential pardon to those who had avoided the draft during the Vietnam War by not registering or by moving abroad. By doing so, the government gave up the right to "prosecute what the administration said were hundreds of thousands of draft-dodgers."[150] The pardon did not extend to deserters or soldiers who had received less than honorable discharges.

Headquarters

One of the most exciting events relating to AGSM Headquarters during this period was announced in December 1960 in *The Gold Star Mother*:

"The national executive board proudly announces that the entire mortgage on our national headquarters... has been paid. Our headquarters is now completely free of debt. Over $2,000 has been spent in refinishing the interior and laying a new floor in the basement. We are very proud of the appearance of our Headquarters. One more project, storm windows for the office and the downstairs is yet to be complete. We are planning a 'Burning of the Mortgage' at the National Convention."[151]

The turn-of-the-century headquarters building was purchased in 1954 for $25,000 with a starter loan from a past national president. That loan was paid back within the first year and now, within six years, the orga-

Fig. 10-6: AGSM headquarters in the early 1970s. *(AGSM Collection)*

nization was debt free and owned, outright, a valuable piece of Washington, D.C., real estate. As announced, there was a ceremonial "burning of the mortgage" at the 1961 national convention, a moment of drama and laughter involving a wastebasket, a match and far too much smoke.

Although it had been anticipated that there would be annual upkeep costs when the building was purchased, the mothers were often surprised at how many things could go wrong in an older building. Interior and exterior painting, roof repairs, plumbing problems, safety upgrades, and weather-related problems plagued the two mothers who lived at headquarters year-round. In 1960, convention attendees were told of a problem that had a relatively simple solution:

"We have had a very distressing problem with pigeons and that has been taken care of. We have strung up chicken wire from our building to the next so that at night Mary and Dorothy can sleep without lots of cooing every time they turn on the light."[152]

In 1962, it was necessary to install a new bathroom on the second floor.[153] Serious problems with the heater and water pipes continued to occur. In March 1971, Elva Newman, national custodian of records, reported on the results of a January cold spell:

"A broken water pipe caused a flooded basement and one week later the furnace went on the blink and we had no heat for several days. Fortunately... Mary Kelly had invited us for lunch on one of those days when we had no heat and we really took advantage of that invitation and spent the entire day. She insisted we bring her electric blanket home with us, but we managed to keep warm by staying in the kitchen with the gas oven burning.[154]

Gifts and furnishings arrived often at headquarters, sent by members and friends. The Butte County Chapter in Oroville, California, sent a gold star quilt (gold stars on a white background) in 1960 that was handmade by the chapter's mothers.[155] Clara Rose Myers sent a "lovely ceramic eagle" made by "patients at the Veterans Hospital" where she volunteered. It was given a place of honor on the mantel in the reception room. In 1978, Al Price of Oklahoma City, Oklahoma, sent a "beautiful star with a base." The star and its base were "designed and carved from a single piece of walnut wood. It was presented to our National President and is the only star of this nature in existence and shall be the only one ever carved by Mr. Price. It will be displayed at National Headquarters."[156]

To help with the burgeoning upkeep costs of headquarters, national president Helen Willour created a Memorial Book in 1970. A custom-made album with a white vinyl cover inscribed "Memorials" was presented to headquarters. Inside, the pages were divided into two columns: "Remembered By" on the left side and "In Memory Of" on the right side. Members, their families and others had their memorial donations recorded in the book and all memorial gifts were used exclusively for the maintenance of headquarters. Each issue of the *The Gold Star Mother* listed memorial gift donors and the names in which those gifts had been made. Often it was in memory of a son or daughter who had died, a past national officer, gold star mothers and dads, and sometimes, when the gift was given by a chapter, it was simply in memory of "our children."[157]

During the 1960s, the national board became aware that many of their sister organizations, due to their non-profit status, were not paying taxes on their

Washington, D.C., properties. A committee was established to look into this discrepancy and to hire an attorney, if necessary, to pursue the issue with the appropriate District of Columbia commissions. They were still fighting the tax issue as the 1960s became the 1970s. On other fronts, however, they had more luck.

In 1978, Regina Wilk and Elva Newman approached the Transportation Division and asked that the two-hour parking sign in front of headquarters be removed. Parking on Leroy Place, a short and very narrow street, was always a problem and having a two-hour parking restriction created headaches for visitors and officers at headquarters. Elated by their victory, Regina Wilk told the membership in *The Gold Star Mother* that the next step would be to "try to get a reserved parking space just for visitors at Headquarters."[158]

When talking with members, headquarters has always been referred to as "your Headquarters" and members were invited to visit if they were going to be in Washington, D. C. Apparently the membership had been enjoying this privilege a little too much, for in March 1970 the following "Directive from the National Board" appeared in *The Gold Star Mother*:

"Members of American Gold Star Mothers, Inc., exclusive of national officers, are permitted to come to National Headquarters for an overnight stay, but not for extended visits. Such guests are expected to reimburse the national Custodian of Records $1.50 for laundry. No more than two guests can be accommodated at one time."[159]

Memorials

As it had in past conflicts, the nation looked for ways to memorialize those who had died in the war in Vietnam so their names and sacrifices would not be forgotten. Gold star mothers worked tirelessly alone and with other organizations to create monuments to the fallen, even as the domestic conflict about the war continued. But there was still some unfinished work from the past wars. In November 1960, members of the Wampanoag Chapter in Providence, Rhode Island attended a dedication of twelve bridges that spanned the new Route 95 highway in East Providence. Each bridge was named in honor of a son of a Wampanoag Chapter member. Those sons were casualties of World War II and the Korean Conflict.[160]

In the July 1962 issue of *The Gold Star Mother*, there was a photograph of National President Dorothy N. Baxter standing next to Elvis Presley. Mrs. Baxter was on her way to the USS *Arizona* Memorial Dedication at Pearl Harbor where she had been asked to represent Mr. Presley as well as AGSM. Mr. Presley had raised $67,000 toward the completion of the memorial but his film work prevented him from attending the dedication.[161]

The memorials of this era were not only to the soldiers who had died. In 1965, Maine State Representative George Carroll authored legislation that designated the Maine Turnpike as the Gold Star Memorial Highway. Known as "Mr. Transportation of Maine," Carroll had written the bill after meeting with a group of World War II gold star mothers and sensing that they felt forgotten by their state and country. In November 2001, the Maine Turnpike Commission rededicated the highway to honor the Maine gold star mothers of all wars. Carroll, then eighty, was the guest speaker at the rededication.[162]

In Southbridge, Massachusetts a granite memorial inscribed with the words "Perpetuating the noble principles for which their sons fought and died" was dedicated as the Gold Star Mothers Memorial. It was placed at the Gold Star Circle on May 30, 1965, by the town of Southbridge.[163] A chiding article in a Southbridge newspaper a few months before may have been the impetus behind the memorial. The article was titled "Gold Star Mothers—20 Years Later":

"A pitifully small representation of veteran organizations and their auxiliaries attended the annual Memorial Gold Star Mothers Mass last Sunday at Notre Dame Church. Rev. Raymond Page... spoke eloquently about the great sorrow of these mothers who gave their sons in the defense of our liberty. He spoke, too, of the benefits we have today because of the supreme sacrifice made by these hero sons. Many attending shed tears, and our hearts beat a bit faster when the organ sounded Taps and then went into the National Anthem.

"Twenty years ago, when our country was at war and hundreds of our Southbridge boys were called to fight and sometimes die, a Gold Star in the window brought to its household a sense of awe and reverence. It meant that this home had given a son in the defense of our country.

"Among the veterans organizations, the respectful affection for the Gold Star Mothers continues no different than 20 years ago. However, many others have forgotten what these women represented to us. Another generation does not know, and it does not appear interested. Our generation has chosen to forget, or it is too busy to remember. Anyway, what happened 20 years ago is ancient history, and it is not fashionable to be patriotic any more…

"My apology for saying the Gold Star Mothers have not been recognized. A few years ago the town did name the circle at the bottom of Main Street as the "Gold Star Circle." Certainly the Gold Star Mothers approached this each Memorial Day when the parade marches up and we join together to hold services on the well fertilized grass next to the telephone pole.

"A few years ago the Gold Star Mothers asked the town for $500 for a modest memorial for their Circle. Unfortunately the request was voted down. We had to put in a few new sewers that year. Last March, another request for a small memorial was presented, but now we are building "living memorials"—no special living memorial—any kind of living memorial. No sir, we are not buying stone slabs for anybody this year. Now we are in 1964. World War II ended 20 years ago. Korea is about 10 years in the forgotten past. How many more years will go by, dear Gold Star Mothers, before you get your small memorial on Gold Star Circle?

"You have appealed to the town, but you are just a handful now and you have no political pull, and we know that the few dollars you raise make possible your charity at veterans hospitals. Let's appeal to the citizens of Southbridge — no, to the conscience of the citizens of Southbridge. If this doesn't work, then we can remember your sons in our prayers, and I can thank God every day that my family never had to show a gold star in the window."[164]

A memorial honoring gold star mothers was dedicated in Miami Beach, Florida on Memorial Day in 1970. Miami Beach chapter president Bessie Roop placed a floral gold star at the base of the monument, which had an inscription by Nettie Parks Hutchings:

TO THE TRULY BRAVE—THE MOTHERS
Do you ask for a song of courage
In this day of bloodshed and woe,
When all about us are heroes
And brave men wherever we go?
To crown all of these, could there be yet another
Who's ahead in each contest, how and where
It is fought?
Indeed, yes, there is! Her name?
It's just "Mother"
With courage that can never be bought.
        —Dedicated Memorial Day 1970
        to the American Gold Star Mothers[165]

The story of a Peace Chapel near Angel Fire, New Mexico was reported in the July 1971 issue of *The Gold Star Mother*:

"A grieving father dedicated a Vietnam Veterans Peace Chapel, which took him three years to build and is situated on a lonely hill in northern New Mexico, to the memory of his soldier son as 'a gift to mankind which has no strings attached.'

"'My son was killed three years ago this day, and the chapel speaks for itself and it speaks eloquently,' said Dad Westphall, whose son, Marine Lt. Victor D. Westphall III, was killed with 13 comrades on May 22, 1968, in a Viet Cong ambush while he led a reconnaissance patrol. Part of the cost of the Chapel was paid by his service insurance…

"Inside the building, still in need of a coat of stucco, a small eternal flame burned beside a 13-foot high cross. There were no benches or chairs for the crowd which streamed into the building. At the rear of the wedge-shaped Chapel, a non-denominational structure, hung pictures of the 13 marines who died along with Dad Westphall's son on the patrol.[166]

"At the suggestion of the young soldier's mother, Jeanne Westphall, the family decided to use the money from David's life insurance policies to create the 'Vietnam Veterans Peace and Brotherhood Chapel' even as the nation was still experiencing unrest and anger over the war. Building a memorial to honor Vietnam veterans was not popular during this time; the country was still involved in an increasingly unpopular war in Vietnam. However, the Westphall family persevered, relying primarily on its own financial resources… It was the first major memorial created to honor the veterans

Fig. 10-7: Vietnam Veterans Peace Chapel in Angel Fire, New Mexico. *(Fenelon Collection)*

of the Vietnam War, and inspired the establishment of the Vietnam Veterans Memorial in Washington D.C....

"Victor 'Doc' Westphall dedicated his life to the Memorial. He lived in an apartment on site, and his entire purpose was honoring his son and the more than 58,000 others who died in Vietnam. He reached out to the families that had lost their loved ones, and welcomed home the "maimed in body and spirit."[167]

In the July 1977 issue of the *American Disabled Veterans' Magazine,* it was reported that "many visitors say that the Vietnam Veterans Peace and Brotherhood Chapel qualifies as one of the most beautiful and inspiring buildings in the world." In that article, Dr. Westphall expressed his hope for what would become the legacy of his son and all the other soldiers who died in Vietnam: "If those who died can, in any measure, become a symbol that will arouse all mankind and bring about a rejection of the principles which defile, debase and destroy the youth of the world, perhaps they will not have died in vain."[168]

El Paso, Texas, chapter president Magdalena Barnes probably didn't really expect to be successful when she invited President Gerald R. Ford to attend the dedication of a plaque that listed the names of El Paso's Vietnam dead. It was, after all, the nation's bicentennial year and planners for every commemorative event hoped to have the president attend. But President Ford did accept the El Paso chapter's invitation and both he and Mrs. Ford attended the April 10, 1976 dedication at the War Memorial Plaza. Mrs. Barnes expressed her appreciation to the president in a note written the day of the event:

"We, the members of the El Paso Chapter of the American Gold Star Mothers, wish to express our deep gratitude to you for being so kind as to participate in our dedication.

"This was a once in a lifetime opportunity for us. We feel honored more than any words can express. Again we would like to say thank you, Mr. President, for taking a few moments of your valuable time in order to make our dedication a day that will be long remembered by all of us."[169]

In his response, President Ford called the dedication "a very inspiring ceremony for everyone present" and commended Mrs. Barnes for her efforts and interest in the commemorative program.[170]

Among the most memorable and heartfelt symbols of the Vietnam era were the prisoner of war bracelets. A simple curved metal strip, each was engraved with the name of an American prisoner of war (POW) held by the North Vietnamese and the date of his capture. Millions of the bracelets were sold. The original plan was that when the POWs returned home, the bracelets would be given to them. But several thousand of the bracelets served another purpose in 1973:

"A most unusual memorial has just been completed in Spokane, Washington and it was made from 6,000 Prisoners of War bracelets. Every prisoner of war is represented in the memorial which was sculpted by Harold B. Balazas, Jr. and it is said to be the most beautiful thing which the Spokane Foundry has ever made."[171]

The permanent home of the POW memorial was to be the Freedoms Foundation in Valley Forge, Pennsylvania.

Often the major supporters of memorials to those lost in Vietnam were the gold star mothers of the specific town or county. In Greater Johnstown, Pennsylvania, two gold star mothers eventually became the only supporters of a proposed memorial, but their efforts over several years finally resulted in a beautiful and unusual memorial to the Vietnam veterans who did not return home:

"Members of Greater Johnstown Chapter are proud of the memorial which has been erected in memory of the service men and women who gave their lives in defense of their Country but it has been a long time in arriving and it has taken months, that stretched into years, of hard work.

"A beautiful sculpture of a life-size soldier in full jungle attire holding a Vietnamese child, stands high on a hill. It is a breathtaking sight.

"Margaret Siegrist, a Vietnam mother, started the idea and contacted a veteran organization to solicit their aid but they did not become very active. She finally organized a committee and, within a year, from small projects and sales, they had raised $2,000 but the committee members became discouraged and dropped out as active members, leaving only Margaret Siegrist and Louise Gavin, another member of the chapter to carry on.

"Undaunted, these two determined women kept working for three years. They sold farm produce ... anywhere they could find space. Louise Gavin made beautiful quilts and sat in shopping centers to sell tickets for chances on them and other items which were given away at three spring calendar parties...

"At last the sum of $12,000 was in the fund for the

Fig. 10-8: Gold star mothers of many conflicts gather at the Vietnam Veterans Memorial.
(AGSM Collection)

memorial and it has been completed and the dedication is expected to take place this spring."[172]

In 1979, *The Gold Star Mother* printed the words spoken by General Melvin Zais, U.S. Army Retired, at the dedication of the 101st Airborne Division Memorial at Arlington National Cemetery. The editor of the newspaper believed that "his words aptly apply to all Vietnam men and women veterans and to the memory of those who died in combat":

> *To men who saw their duty and simply
>   performed it;*
> *To men who surely were aware of a way out,
>   but preferred to stay in;*
> *To men who witnessed the weakness of others,
>   who heard the cries of discouragement and
>   despair and who rejected the safe for the
>   honorable;*
> *To men who, proudly wearing the patch of the
>   screaming eagles, were aware of the heritage
>   of soldiering and the sacrifice reflected therein;*
> *To men who knew fear and overcame it, who
>   knew fatigue and ignored it;*
> *To those men who served themselves, their
>   country and their God with lasting glory,
>   I present this monument for dedication.*[173]

The Vietnam Veterans Memorial

More than 58,000 young Americans died fighting in Vietnam. Many of those who returned from their military service were wounded in body and soul, returning home with a sense of displacement that did not diminish. Unlike soldiers of past wars, these veterans didn't return home to march in parades with their fellow soldiers, surrounded by celebrating citizens. Instead, they came home individually, traveling as civilians, often with no one to mark their return except family members. Many found that only other Vietnam veterans could understand their fears, regrets and feelings of no longer belonging in their hometowns.

In May 1979, the United States Conference of Mayors discussed the problems of the Vietnam vets during their gathering and succinctly summed up the situation in a problem statement:

"This statement describes the myriad of problems that confront many of the nation's 2,800,000 Vietnam veterans and almost 9,000,000 persons who served during the Vietnam era. There has never been an overall plan by the federal government to ensure that they are: employed (and many are not); receive adequate educational assistance and psychiatric care (and many do not); are relieved of unjust disabilities as a result of service experiences (and many are not); and that they received a decent thank you for their service (and most did not)."[174]

In April 1979, a group of Vietnam veterans established the Vietnam Veterans Memorial Fund, Inc.:

"Our success—building a memorial to American war casualties and veterans through private contributions—will be a historical first. Yet there is something here of perhaps greater significance to our society as a whole. The Vietnam era was the most turbulent and divisive in recent American history. Thus far there has been nothing associated with the war that has been able to achieve a sense of reconciliation among those who favored and who opposed the U.S. involvement in Indochina. We have created the Vietnam Veterans Memorial Fund to provide a project that can perhaps provide a focal point for the reconciliation and reunification of the country still needed after the divisive Vietnam Conflict...

"Through the success of the Vietnam Veterans Memorial Fund, the generations that follow us shall have a permanent reminder of how much the people of America care for its sons."[175]

The three Vietnam veterans behind the plan were Jan C. Scruggs, a wounded and decorated infantryman, Robert Doubek, an attorney and former Air Force officer and Jack Wheeler, a graduate of West Point, Yale Law School and Harvard business school. Their plan was twofold: build a perpetual memorial to Vietnam War Veterans and complete the Vietnam Peace and Brotherhood Chapel in Angel Fire, New Mexico.[176] Their initial plan for the Vietnam Memorial called for "a suitable piece of land close to the White House... for the memorial which will be in the form of a carillon with the names of the Vietnam veterans on it."

The funds to build the memorial would all come through public donations. It was hoped that the government would provide a site on the national mall where the memorial could be built. In 1979, Jan Scruggs met with AGSM's national executive board, described the plans and asked if the mothers could provide space at AGSM Headquarters as a place for the Memorial Fund group to establish an office and central location for their volunteers to work. The national executive board asked for time to consider the request and, although they supported the memorial wholeheartedly, they decided that it would be "impossible" to have the memorial fund work be carried on at AGSM Headquarters.

In *The Gold Star Mother,* Jan Scruggs described the plan for the memorial and told the membership what they hoped the mothers could provide:

"Nothing can replace the sons that many of you lost in this unpopular war. Yet this memorial will assure that our country will always remember them. Each name will be displayed in our nation's capital eternally. We DO NOT want the Gold Star Mothers to contribute any money to this planned memorial; you have already sacrificed too much. We would, however, like to ask for your support in this endeavor by writing to your representative in Congress for his or her endorsement of our goals and requesting their support."[177]

Early support for the memorial came from Charles Mathias, Jr., and John W. Warner, Republican Senators from Maryland and Virginia, respectively. Senator Mathias introduced legislation in November 1979 to authorize the use of national park land for the memorial. Senator Warner and his wife, actress Elizabeth Taylor, launched a fundraising campaign that resulted in working funds for the memorial organization.

As they entered the 1980s, the Vietnam Memorial Fund launched a huge public donation program to raise the funds to build the Vietnam memorial and began to consider the question of who should design it.

VAVS

The challenges of an aging membership made little difference in AGSM's support of the Veterans Administration Voluntary Service (VAVS) program. Gold star mothers and dads simply became more creative at ways to aid patients and staff at the VA facilities. One AGSM member assigned to social work in the hospital learned that a long-term hospitalized patient had never had a visit from his wife due to the distance from their home in another state and his wife's physical limitations. She arranged sponsorships by gold star mothers who paid the wife's expenses. Then the volunteer arranged for the wife to be assisted in boarding a bus in her home town, met her at the end of her trip, and escorted her to the hospital where her husband was "overwhelmed to see her." After the visit, the representative took the wife to dinner and saw to it that she was aboard the bus in time for her journey back home. The patient died two weeks later.

At the 1971 national convention, gold star father Harold Nelson was recognized for having given more than 15,000 hours of service to his local VA hospital. In addition to helping at the hospital, Mr. Nelson also logged time going "to the post office [where] he picks up... undeliverable magazines and articles... and makes three trips a week to the VA hospital" to deliver the materials, which were eagerly awaited by the patients. Helen Rettig, an eighty-two-year-old World War II member of Butler Chapter in Butler, Pennsylvania, helped with hospital parties every month and visited the wards every holiday, but her efforts to help finance the parties and other patient activities seemed to never cease. She organized and helped with flea markets, rummage sales, the selling of donated jewelry, card parties, and still found time to make lap robes for the patients at Butler Veterans Hospital. In 1975, she reported having made sixty-five lap robes that she donated, figuring that it took about six hours to make each one.[178]

From 1960–1979, members of American Gold Star Mothers, Inc. gave over 1.5 million hours of volunteer service to VA hospitals and facilities. During that time they also earned nearly $1 million dollars to support their hospital activities and as donations to VA facilities. While an organizational goal was to have gold star mothers volunteering at every veterans facility, they were unable to meet that mark. At their peak in 1970, AGSM mothers were represented at 120 of the 166 VA locations. In 1969, the busiest year reported during the period, 3,111 volunteer gold star mothers were either routinely scheduled or occasional volunteers. The numbers reported each year by the National Hospital Chairman were always conservative, for not all the departments provided reports on the work of their chapters. In 1966, the work of only 195 of the 541 chapters was reported and in 1972, only twenty-eight of the thirty-five departments turned in a VAVS report.

Many AGSM gold star mothers and fathers were recognized by the VAVS for their continued devotion to the veterans. In 1973, Martha Gilman was recognized for having given 30,871 hours of volunteer service at the Manchester, New Hampshire, VA Hospital over twenty-three years of volunteering. In many cases, the facilities also feted their own volunteers for their work, as did the East Orange Veterans Hospital in New Jersey in 1960 when they recognized fourteen gold star mother volunteers who together had given more than 19,000 hours of time since 1952 when the hospital opened.[179]

Many of the events that the gold star mothers helped with had long been traditions at the hospitals and domiciliaries: cookouts, bingo nights, birthday parties, holiday shows and parties, carnivals, sing-a-longs, Christmas gift shops, trips to major league baseball games and many others. The money they earned funded both these events as well as more quiet activities appreciated by some of the patients such as books, magazine subscriptions, puzzles, radios, televisions, and movies.[180] In 1963, more than 960 gold star sponsored parties were reported by the hospital representatives.[181]

As new treatment protocols were put in place at the hospitals, many chapters became involved with their implementation. In 1965, Newark Chapter in New Jersey reported on its sixth annual Operation Cinderella event held in July for thirty men from the Lyons VA Hospital:

"This is a psychiatric hospital and the patients have little contact with the outside world. However, as a therapeutic endeavor, a privileged few are given a week's vacation during the summer months. They are entertained by various veterans organizations that are affiliated with the VAVS program and a different group of 30 are taken out every day for a week. Some are entertained at picnics, some are taken to ball games, some are taken on fishing and swimming parties and still others to shore dinners. Newark Chapter always gives them a shore dinner at one of the resorts."[182]

The chapter reported that in addition to the shore dinner, games, candy, fruits and gifts (including a new pair of sunglasses for each patient) were part of their Operation Cinderella efforts.

New challenges presented themselves as the wounded soldiers from the Vietnam War began to fill the veterans hospitals. In 1971, Peter Miller, Chief Director of the VAVS program in Washington, D.C., spoke candidly to the attendees at the thirty-fourth national AGSM convention:

"The Vietnam veterans have presented the VA with a complex challenge. Approximately 300,000 have been admitted to our hospitals to date and about a third of them have had psychiatric problems. About 15 per cent of our hospital patients today are Vietnam veterans. As you know, they are more severely wounded and many of them have multiple amputations; a large number of them have spinal cord injuries, and many are drug addicted...

"We owe them, the Vietnam veterans, the honest recognition that many of our VA programs, conducted primarily by employees much older than they are, are not attuned to their needs, their lifestyle and their problems."[183]

As the number of wounded Vietnam veterans grew in the VA hospitals, so did the number of new gold star mothers from that conflict. Knowing that this generation of gold star mothers would be critical in keeping the organization viable, AGSM worked hard to interest younger mothers in the work at VA facilities. Many of the Vietnam-era mothers were surprised by the satisfaction they found in volunteering. North Shore Chapter (Highland Park, Illinois) chapter secretary Adris Krimston "who lost a son in Vietnam, and is the Hospital Chairman, gives seven hours every Tuesday at the VA Hospital teaching swimming and is elated over her work as it is so fulfilling for her." Another mother found she was able to "do something good for the injured war survivors as her own son was in a coma for five years from injuries sustained in Vietnam. All she could do for her son was sit by his bed and watch him die, but I can help these boys, she said."[184]

At the 1969 national convention, Marilyn Berdget, director of volunteers for the Oklahoma City Veterans Hospital, challenged the delegates to consider another focus and outcome for their volunteer work—providing inspiration for the restless and unhappy young people of the nation who were challenging the "establishment":

"The American public should ask no more of you, our Gold Star Mothers, than your most tragic sacrifice of your sons and daughters—but we must. It is organizations such as yours, founded on patriotism and love of country, which must speak to our worried world. The question you must answer for us is: What has made it possible for you to turn your sorrow into service? Your gold star, brightly shined by your tears, has something to say—but are you really letting it speak? All around us young people are being taught and professing the belief that you must destroy and build from the ashes what they think will be a better world.

"That's funny—this concept is so against the nature of the gold star mother, she cannot even believe it is happening to America.

"When those 25 mothers met in June of 1928, it was to organize for mutual comfort and service—not to destroy the 'establishment' that had taken their beloved son or daughter. Instead you became a patriotic organization which would perpetuate in service the memory of those brave young men and women. They are gone, but the strength and vigor of their youth is alive in your hearts forever.

"You have all lost children. Here is an opportunity to regain your loss in the inspired use and teaching of young people. 'Escapism' is the name of the game for young people today and yet 'reality' is the world we live in. You can teach them how to live with sorrow, not with bitterness but in service."[185]

If there was ever any doubt in the minds of the gold star mothers and fathers that their efforts were appreciated by the patients at the VA facilities, a letter of appreciation signed by sixty-two veterans at the Mount Sinai Satellite Clinic in New York would have calmed their concerns. The letter expressed the gratitude the patients felt for five gold star parents who planned, prepared, and paid for a monthly home-style dinner that they shared with the patients. Their letter of appreciation spoke of those "who have unfailingly given of themselves, their time and economic resources to make

our lot as disabled veterans... a more satisfied and fulfilled one... We are their sons by proxy and are indeed fortunate to be regarded as such."[186]

Community Service

As the gold star mothers grew older, their commitment to community service grew. VA facilities were often hours away from the towns where the chapters were located and as more mothers gave up driving or dealt with illnesses that made travel difficult, they turned their willing hands and hearts to the needy who were closer to their own homes.

Reports on the hours and dollars committed to community service projects are difficult to compare from year to year. Although the reporting format was standardized, the number of departments reporting sometimes fell to as few as nineteen of thirty-five, meaning that nearly half of the community service may have gone unreported. For example, in 1975, the contribution of only 154 of the more than 500 chapters was reported.

Nonetheless, the mothers were busy. In 1971, 103,882 volunteer hours were reported and $34,723 were earned and spent in support of the community service work. By 1979, the total hours had dropped to 54,782 with $27,560 spent. In addition to the many more well known charitable organizations that the mothers supported, such as the United Fund, Community Chest, USO, Boys' Town, Leukemia Society, March of Dimes, Cancer Drive, and the Heart Fund, they also gave to other, lesser known organizations that touched their hearts in some way, including leper colonies, the Mississippi-Louisiana Flood Fund, Toys for Children in Vietnam, Working Home for the Blind, and senior citizen organizations.

They also turned their energies to efforts at the neighborhood level, preparing Christmas and Thanksgiving food baskets and collecting clothing and furniture for the needy. They helped at religious and state orphanages, visited the sick and transported them and the elderly to church, hospitals, doctors, and shopping, and worked with "the sick, blind and those less fortunate than ourselves." Sewing, crocheting, knitting, and cancer dressing preparation resulted in lap robes, pillows and various other items useful to the veterans and others who were ill.

The American Gold Star Home

By the beginning of the 1960s, the American Gold Star Home in Long Beach, California was running smoothly and providing a safe, affordable haven for the gold star mothers of World War II. In December, 1960, the one-hundredth gold star mother took up residence at the home. She was Sarah Bedell who, with her husband George, had moved from Ann Arbor, Michigan. Just five years later, the five-hundredth gold star mother, Vera G. Ashton of Franklin County, Vermont, moved to the home. Each issue of *The Gold Star Mother* listed the members moving to the home; in December 1960 and January 1961, thirty-nine mothers from across the nation transferred to the home. Their states of origin included Alabama, Arizona, California, Florida, Illinois, Michigan, New York, Washington, and Wisconsin.[187]

The rent for an apartment at the home was $39 per month or one quarter of the mother's income, whichever was less. That included all utilities except for a telephone; a new television was provided for each apartment. From the beginning, the home management tried to do everything possible for the gold star parents who lived at the home. In 1959, each mother received a turkey for Thanksgiving.[188] As the years passed, a Dads' Workshop was established; a community garden plot was made available to anyone wishing to grow flowers or edible plants; a large recreation hall was built so all residents could gather to participate in activities; a professional greenhouse was added for the orchid growers; and an electric bus was purchased, driven by gold star volunteers, that made regular stops around the home property so residents could get from one place to another easily. And, with the permission of the home management, the dads set up a nine-hole golf course on some unused land that belonged to the home.

The residents of the home quickly bonded with each other and shared many activities. One gold star father set up a fix-it service for the residents; they would bring broken appliances and other items to him and he would repair them for just the cost of any parts that were required. Velda Steele, a resident and registered nurse, set up a health check service for residents, traveling from one apartment to another with a basket of "band-aids, aspirins and good cheer."[189] Clubs of all sorts sprang up quickly—a garden club, an orchid club, various card playing groups, and exercise groups. College classes were offered on-site by local professors and college credit could be earned. Gold star parents with automobiles drove those without to markets, appointments,

and events of interest. An enthusiastic article about the various activities at the home appeared in each issue of *The Gold Star Mother* along with information on how to apply for an apartment in the facility.

When the home was established by the court, based on the parameters of its predecessor, the Memorial National Home Foundation, the home could only accept gold star mothers from World War II. In 1962, a resolution was passed at the AGSM national convention "requesting that the trustees of American Gold Star Home apply to the Superior Court... for a modification of the charitable trust" to include gold star mothers of other wars.[190] In October 1962, members were advised that "the Superior Court has ruled that World War I and Korean Mothers now have the same status as World War II Mothers at the American Gold Star Home in Long Beach, California."[191] This wonderful news to many of the gold star mothers of World War I who were now elderly and often without income of any kind. During this period, more than one World War I mother moved to the Home where, based on her income, she paid no rent and her food and medicines were provided by management. It had truly become the home that had originally been envisioned for needy gold star mothers.

In 1957, management of the Home during the court proceedings had been put in the hands of two court-appointed receivers, George D. Lyon and R.E. Allen. George D. Lyon stayed on as executive director of the home until his retirement in July 1968. His replacement was Jesse T. Berger who managed the home until his death in 1975. Edward F. Leonard was appointed executive director of the home in July 1975 and served in that position until 1991. A former Commanding Officer of the Long Beach Naval Station with twenty-eight years of military service, Captain Leonard had been a stockbroker before coming to the home.[192]

From 1959 to 1972, 1,057 gold star mothers and dads lived at the home. In 1972, the 602 gold star parents in residence at the home represented World Wars I and II, the Korean Conflict and Vietnam. More than 90 per cent of the residents were gold star mothers of World War II.

The Truman Boyd Manor had originally been constructed under war-time building codes which allowed short cuts to be taken. Part of the agreement when the government had sold the property was that the original structures would be removed by a certain date. Having successfully lobbied for postponement of that requirement more than once, the American Gold Star Home management had remained under continuing pressure from the City of Long Beach to upgrade, demolish, or rebuild the structures. After years of planning and construction, the new facility was ready for its dedication. On January 21, 1976, more than a thousand residents, guests, and supporters gathered at the dedication ceremony. George Wise, who had represented AGSM so successfully through the long years of litigation, was the guest speaker.

A $6 million housing project, the new facility, now called the American Gold Star Home and Manor, consisted of 348 individual apartments in ten apartment buildings. The dedication audience watched as a time capsule containing a complete history of events in the development of American Gold Star Mothers, Inc., the American Gold Star Home and the new American Gold Star Manor was put in place at the base of the home's flagpole. Sealed beneath a bronze plaque, the time capsule would be opened on August 1, 2015, the day the final payment of the Home mortgage was scheduled to be paid.[193]

The final stage of the home's remodeling was the rededication of the Memorial Park. The newly landscaped area contained an expansive lawn, a rose garden, concrete walkways, a lighted fountain, and a flagpole array surrounded by a mass of colorful flowering plants and stately trees. The gold star memorial that had been dedicated in 1963 was part of the new Memorial Park and was rededicated on June 2, 1977. The words on the memorial were paraphrased from Ralph Waldo Emerson's "Concord Hymn" written in 1836:

> Spirit that made those heroes dare to die
>   to leave their children free
> Bid time and nature gently spare this memorial
>   to them and thee.
>   —In memory of the sons and daughters
>   of American Gold Star Mothers Inc.
>   Dedicated May 26, 1963
>   Rededicated June 2, 1977

Regina Wilk, AGSM national president, was the keynote speaker for the Memorial Garden dedication. She told the audience that the Memorial Park was a place for pride, not sadness:

"As you sit in our Memorial Park, don't feel sad for the loss of your loved one. Think of the many beautiful memories he or she gave you. Remember, it was God who chose us to be Gold Star Mothers. We were made Gold Star Mothers not by our choosing… God has a reason for everything. If it weren't for patriots who were willing to sacrifice the ultimate—their lives—people would not be free in this wonderful land of ours…God chose our sons and daughters, the cream of the crop, to be his vanguards."[194]

Freedoms Foundation

As it had since the creation of the Freedoms Foundation in 1949, AGSM continued it close relationship with the non-profit organization throughout the Vietnam era. Freedoms Foundation at Valley Forge, Pennsylvania was a national organization that worked "on a year-round basis at the vital task of stimulating a better appreciation and understanding of America's Constitutional Republic." Each year, the AGSM national president served as a member of a panel charged with selecting the winner of a national essay contest in which thousands of high school students participated.[195]

In October 1961, AGSM set a new challenge for itself when it committed to be responsible for building the flagpole, base, and surrounding patio (referred to as the flagpole promenade) at the new Freedoms Center that was scheduled for construction. Five thousand dollars were needed for the project. The response was tremendous and, in less than a year, the entire $5,000 had been raised. In July 1962, it was reported that "to date, 17 departments, 214 chapters, 12 individuals and the national organization have contributed the $5,000 necessary to complete this part of the installation."[196]

The flag promenade became a point of pride for the gold star mothers and every gold star trip to the Freedoms Foundation included a stop to see what the mothers' gift had built. In 1975, it was reported that "the American Gold Star Mothers' flagpole can be seen from all areas of the grounds. Freedoms Foundation has many flagpoles. Ours has the elite location. The highest and the only one that flies the flag twenty four hours a day."[197]

That same year, it was reported by national president Josephay Fleming that the wind and weather took a serious toll on the flags displayed on the mothers' flagpole and at least four flags were required each year. Since AGSM had taken responsibility for building the flag promenade, it was felt that the organization should also take responsibility for the flags that flew from it. The national executive board announced that "this should be the responsibility of the departments" and encouraged the establishment of a flag fund.[198]

Twice during the Vietnam era, the Freedoms Foundation selected AGSM's official publication, *The Gold Star Mother,* as the recipient of their Honor Certificate Award for non-profit publications. In 1962, the Award was given to the publication and its editor; in 1975, it was awarded to the publication.[199]

Pilgrimages

The thought of traveling to where their sons' or daughters' last moments had been spent continued to be a dream of many gold star parents. Although the U.S. government had not sponsored pilgrimages since those in the 1930s for gold star mothers of World War I, the desire remained strong with gold star parents of later wars. Following World War II, many petitioned the U.S. government to send them, as they had World War I mothers, to where their children had died. Finally the government was forced to make it clear that no such pilgrimages would be sponsored due to the sheer magnitude and cost of such an endeavor. Similarly, the mothers of the soldiers lost in Korea were never offered a pilgrimage opportunity by the U.S. government.

In 1962, a remarkable offer was made to certain gold star mothers of World War II by the Netherlands War Graves Committee. It was an opportunity for the World War II mothers of American servicemen who were buried in the Netherlands, Belgium and Luxembourg to travel to those cemeteries for only the cost of their airfare, which was offered at a greatly reduced price through the efforts of Pan American Airways. The travelers would stay for nine days as the guests of the Dutch families who had gratefully adopted the graves of their American liberators following the war and had passed that responsibility down to subsequent generations.

The first such Pilgrimage to Margraten took place in September 1962. The cost of the ten-day trip was $217, the cost of the airfare from New York. The Netherlands War Graves Committee explained the background of the pilgrimage and what the people of the Netherlands hoped to show the gold star mothers of America:

"Seventeen years ago, this May 8th, peace came to Europe and the Free World, thank God. There was much to restore and rebuild and the work began. Everyone was so busy that some things were overlooked. But time makes one cognizant of this neglect.

"As the beautiful cemeteries for our valiant ones were created, many, many heartfelt, warm and meaningful ceremonies and words were offered because of their sacrifice. This was tribute and as it should have been, but again time soon faded many things to many people. Except those to whom total peace never came.

"It is long past the time when this should have been accomplished. To Gold Star Mothers who have sons that never returned, a final reunion must be provided. Many have the knowledge that the graves of their sons are in hallowed peaceful havens and that families in the areas have adopted their sons. They are reassured by authorities and governments that no more fitting meeting place with God could have been provided. But yet there can be no substitute for visible and personal contact.

"Many people in our nation are aware of the debt of gratitude owed to the Gold Star Mothers of America. Through their efforts and with the cooperation of Pan American Airways and the officials and citizens of the Netherlands, the first step toward providing this ultimate reunion has been taken. It is predicted than many more will follow.

"On September 14, 1962 a plane carrying the first group of Gold Star Mothers will begin a 10-day Pilgrimage to Margraten Cemetery in Holland. While in Holland, the Mothers will stay with and be hosted by Dutch Families in private and as near identical surroundings as can be arranged. While in Holland they will meet the families who have adopted their son's grave and with whom most have been communicating...

"In addition to the opportunity for quiet and reverent reunion, the Mothers will see first-hand a Nation that also commiserates with them in a deep and humble way. They will find grateful people very much like themselves who are tremendously desirous of expressing personally their true gratitude. In this way, it is believed that when this Pilgrimage returns to America … that final peace will be in the heart of each Gold Star Mother."

AGSM worked with the War Graves Commission to register the travelers for the trip. In June 1962, *The Gold Star Mother* reported:

"It is deeply gratifying to hear from the Mothers who are overwhelmed at the thought of having a dream come true, in being able to visit their Sons' graves in Margraten. Even if the body was temporarily interred in Margraten before being returned to the U.S., the mother is eligible for the trip."

Mothers did not have to be members of AGSM to

participate and their husbands and dependent children were eligible to go with them. The first trip had eighty openings for travelers; the first gold star mother to sign up for the pilgrimage was AGSM national president Mary R. Kelly, whose son was buried at Margarten.[200] Mrs. Kelly provided a detailed account of her travels in the October and November 1962 issues of *The Gold Star Mother*.

Similar pilgrimages were scheduled in 1965, 1970, 1971 and 1972. More than one-hundred gold star family members took part in the 1970 pilgrimage. One of the travelers, the son of AGSM member Emma Karn Hall, described his fellow travelers for a report in *The Gold Star Mother*:

"Among them was an 86-year-old mother visiting her son's grave for the first time; another mother, partially blind, whose one wish to see her son's grave before becoming totally blind was fulfilled; an Air Force Sergeant stationed in Alaska visiting his brother's grave; a young man visiting the grave of his father who he could not remember in life; an 83-year-old father (who celebrated his birthday on the trip) visiting his son's grave; and other mothers, fathers, widows, sisters and brothers of boys who are buried so far from home.[201]

An unexpected invitation in 1975 by the government of Korea gave gold star mothers of the Korean Conflict an opportunity to visit Korea as guests of that nation on an all-expenses-paid trip. A large group from the American Gold Star Home and Manor in Long Beach, California, including past national president Rose Decker, made the trip.[202]

The Gold Star Lily

The tradition of the gold star lily, a story that started during the battle on Okinawa in World War II, came to an end in 1964. As San Clemente Chapter president Adella Hinshaw wrote for *The Gold Star Mother*:

"It was on the battlefield of Okinawa at Easter time. Fighting had been waging for days and nights. To George Walker, Chief Carpenter's Mate, it was grim. He was a Navy Commando and had hit the beach as a Control Officer. He was dismayed by the hatefulness of it all. He felt there was nothing worthwhile fighting for in the whole world anymore, even though he had lived through Pearl Harbor… and other actions.

"Then he saw it. While he and his comrades were rushing about through the heat and smoke of exploding shells, there at his feet he saw a delicate flower, a pink lily with a white cross in its center. He marveled, how did this tiny plant survive in this devastated spot?… Impulsively he grasped the flower and pulled it up, bulb and all, and thrust it into the pocket of his battle jacket.[203]

"When the battle ended, George examined the flower more closely and discovered that the markings appeared to be a cross and a gold star.

"When George returned home from the war, he remembered the lily bulb and pulled it out from among his belongings. Although it was 'wrinkled and deadlooking,' he planted it in his garden:

"He nurtured it carefully and just one year after he had found it on Easter, it bloomed again. George Walker's faith was restored. He was convinced that nothing ever dies. The lily meant more to him now. It was a symbol. The pink petals represented young men and women who had given their youth, their lives. The white cross signified a hope for Eternal Life. The gold stamens, Mothers who lost a loved one in our country's wars.[204]

"One day he heard a mother say, 'I wish I had something from Okinawa where my son was killed, a stick or a stone even.' Then came an inspiration. He would give each gold star mother who requested one, a lily bulb. That is when he named it "Gold Star Lily— The Lily of Remembrance."[205]

Word spread quickly and George was inundated with requests for gold star lily bulbs. The first years he asked each mother to send him a bulb after theirs had bloomed to help build up his supply. Many did, so he was able to send bulbs to others. He sent more than 4,000 bulbs to gold star mothers all over the world:

"When one of the mothers asked George how much the bulb cost, he replied, 'There is no price tag, for they belong to you mothers. I am always glad to see one go home. It's a gift beyond material things. There was no price tag on your son in the war.' That's why the lily, which mothers call priceless, is never sold. It goes through the mails as a gift."[206]

In 1964, nearly twenty years after World War II ended, the task had grown too large for George to handle alone. With eighty bulbs still promised, he turned to gold star mothers who already had their own lilies growing and they provided bulbs to those who were waiting. AGSM's San Clemente Chapter gave bulbs to a nursery in southern California where they were to be nurtured until there were enough to start a gold star memory garden. At the 1965 national AGSM convention, the delegates passed a resolution commending and thanking Mr. Walker for his years of dedication and service to the nation's gold star mothers.

An Alabama gold star mother who lost her son in Vietnam found solace in a gift of a gold star lily bulb in 1966. Pfc. Jimmie Williams, son of Mrs. Johnnie Williams of Wetumpka, Alabama was denied a burial place in their local cemetery "because he was a Negro." When Adella Hinshaw heard of the situation, she sent Mrs. Walker a lily bulb, a copy of the story of the gold star lily and a color photograph of the blooming plant. Mrs. Williams wrote back, "Your kind deed will never be forgotten. Pray that I'll live long enough to see the pretty flower bloom. Thank you ever so much. I'm forever grateful."[207]

Questions and Answers

As it had in past decades, the "Question and Answer" section in *The Gold Star Mother* and question and answer opportunities in other venues such as conventions allowed confusing issues to be dealt with simply, clearly, and publicly, not to mention humorously in some situations. The questions often covered issues that for some reason could not be (or had not been) clarified in other settings such as chapter or department meetings. Protocol, membership guidelines, attire and traditions were just a few of the issues that were clarified through question and answer opportunities:

Q: Where should gold star mothers be placed in a parade on Memorial Day if riding in cars?

A: Gold star mothers never march in a parade. When riding in cars the parade master will usually place them first, immediately behind the colors.[208] (1960)

Q: If a representative of a gold star mothers' chapter or department is seated with other representatives of patriotic organizations at a head table, is there a proper seating for the gold star mother?

A: A mother always sits where the chairman of the affair places her.[209] (1960)

Q: When a national or departmental president is attending a chapter function such as a memorial service or the placing of a wreath, where is her place? Doesn't she approach with the chapter president?

A: Honey, you ain't got no place. (Laughter) Your place is where the chapter president has the courtesy to

ask you to be. In our organization there is no prescribed form for such things. (Answered by national president Frances High at the 1961 national convention.)[210]

Q: Do we have a standard uniform?

A: No. Caps and capes are available, but the purchase of them is not obligatory.[211] (1969)

Q: What is the official use of our white caps and when should we wear them?

A: The caps are usually worn in parades and memorial services. Use your own judgment and common sense in this matter.[212] (1969)

Q: If a member severed her membership in the organization and later joins as a new member, should she be given the honors she had in the chapter before she left?

A: No.[213] (1960)

Q: If a delinquent charter member decides to make application as a new member, instead of paying all back dues, would she still be a charter member?

A: No. When a member becomes delinquent and decides to apply as a new member, she is just that — a new member. She forfeits all honors that she had before dropping her membership.[214] (1960)

Q: Does AGSM have an "honorary" membership status?

A: There are no honorary AGSM memberships, only active and associate (gold star dads).[215] (1961)

Q: If a member is considered troublesome in any way, can a chapter refuse to accept her dues?

A: Positively not! If the member is in good standing and she is considered troublesome, the chapter treasurer or any other chapter officer has no authority to refuse her dues. Charges must be brought to the department and if the problem cannot be solved there, then the national board should be advised. [216] (1962)

Q: Should new members, including the Vietnam gold star mothers, be included in all chapter meetings, social and patriotic functions, etc?

A: Yes.[217] (1969)

Q: What is [considered] an active member?

A: One who attends 75% of all chapter meetings in one year.[218] (1970)

Q: Who approves our new membership?

A: The Department of Defense certifies if the son or daughter was killed in the line of duty and the organization approves it.[219] (1971)

Q: Can a chapter pay a member's dues for a good reason?

A: Yes, and do it quietly.[220] (1970)

Q: Is it correct to use the American flag as part of a bouquet or table decoration?

A: No.[221] (1962)

Q: When the [American] flag is carried, should it ever be dipped?

A: The flag should never be dipped to any person or thing, with one exception: Navy vessels, upon receiving a salute of this type from a vessel registered by a nation formally recognized by the United States, must return the compliment.[222] (1970)

Q: Has the Gold Star Mothers ever been a secret organization?

A: American Gold Star Mothers has never, to my knowledge, been a secret organization. All of the ritual is written, all of the constitution and bylaws are written.[223] (1961)

Q: What is the meaning of the five points of our star?

A: The five points represent commemoration, service, light, hope and peace.[224] (1964)

Q: If a mother passes away and the dad is [at the American Gold Star Home], would he have to leave?

A: Not as long as he stays a widower or if he should happen to marry one of the widows out there. (Laughter) He can't go courting outside the home. He can't bring a new bride into the home.[225] (1961)

Q: What has happened to Ojai? [The property bought in 1951 to be developed as a home for gold star mothers.]

A: That property has been sold and eventually, when the court decides that this home is to be for mothers and dads of World War I and the Korean Conflict, the money derived from that sale will be turned over to the foundation in order to provide the necessary outlay for these members.[226]

Gold Star Mothers in the News

During the Vietnam era, news coverage about gold star mothers and their activities declined greatly from the levels during and following World War II and the Korean Conflict. Whereas newspapers in the past had reported on gold star meetings, gatherings, and issues, and always identified gold star mothers as such in news stories, the media during this era seemed focused on other issues. But they were not completely forgotten as shown in this 1962 editorial that appeared in *The Retrospect:*

"Few nationally organized groups have more right to be considered true Americans, and to pray for peace, than the Gold Star Mothers. We read one of their paper issues several days ago which gives a good cross-section at a national level of all they are doing, hope to do and believe in: 'Perpetuating the Noble Principles for Which They (our servicemen) Fought and Died.'

"Of all the organizations of men, as well as women, formed to commemorate the sacrifice which war takes as its toll, none is so likely to survive as those who paid with the lives of their children. It remains as a bitter and sad experience so long as such parents live.

"There is no glory of war—no emotional jag when a band plays—no pageantry—just the memory of a kid who was once in diapers—who cried and took his first steps—a kid who caught the measles—who once went to kindergarten. A son who stepped forth on commencement night to receive his high school diploma. He died somewhere on a battlefield or a sea of war. Even the most idealistic cannot at times, help wondering WHY?"[227]

In 1965, a Memorial Day tribute to gold star mothers sponsored by a local car dealership appeared in the *Mattoon Daily Journal-Gazette* in Mattoon, Illinois:

"Behind that little gold star that hangs in a cottage window is a mourning mother who will never forget. Her son gave his all in Okinawa, over Dusseldorf, in some concentration camp... or on the high seas. That was HER boy, the little, curly-head lad who once climbed on her knee and knew nothing of men's greed and lust for conquest. It is fitting that we pause a moment in thought and prayer with those many mothers whose sons willingly made the supreme sacrifice. They are carrying on without tears or hatred, these mothers. Let us revere them too for the sacrifices THEY have made that we, the living, may still be free!"[228]

On July 4, 1978, a reporter on *Good Morning America*, a nationally syndicated television program, told program host Hugh Downs of the government's apparent lack of regard for the American Gold Star Mothers, Inc., organization and their struggles to bring attention to their issues of concern:

"Today, the fourth of July orators will pay homage to the men and women who have died for their country. There might even be a stirring word about the gold star mothers who have lost sons and daughters in past wars. But lip service doesn't seem to be worth much in Washington. The gold star mothers will gather in Washington today to commemorate their fiftieth Anniversary. Their president, Regina Wilk, says many of the mothers have been saving for years to pay for the trip.

"Seven months ago, they wrote to President Carter requesting a brief meeting while they are in Washington. Their request was refused. One gold star mother, recalling a recent White House party, said sadly: 'It's too bad we're not a jazz band.'

"Mothers have also applied for tax exempt status for their small national organization. Larger organizations with political clout—such as the Daughters of the American Revolution and the Colonial Dames of America—have been granted a tax exemption. But the gold star mothers were refused.

"Three years ago, the mothers requested a postage stamp to commemorate their fiftieth anniversary. The request was refused. They also asked for commissary privileges for mothers of soldiers killed in action. The commissaries are open to foreign diplomats in Washington. But the gold star mothers were refused.

"In 1940, President Roosevelt declared that the last Sunday in September—I'm quoting—shall hereafter be known as 'Gold Star Mothers Day." He said "It shall be the duty of the president to request its observance." Every year, the Mothers have asked the president to issue such a proclamation. Every year their request has been refused. The Gold Star Mothers are so upset over their treatment that some of them wanted to picket the White House. But the proposal was rejected. You see, the majority didn't want to cause the president any embarrassment.

"Meanwhile, they will continue to dedicate their lives to helping the veterans who, unlike their own sons, have survived. The Gold Star Mothers, since they were organized in 1928, have given over two million hours of voluntary service in Veteran's Hospitals."[229]

In 1965, a *Chicago Tribune* correspondent self-identified as a gold star mother, chided the public for a lack of patriotism in a letter to the editor:

"Today, at the American Legion parade, I saw the old men marching, so proud of the flag and their country. The few Legionnaires on the sidelines saluted as the flag passed, but I was surprised at the large number of other spectators who didn't bother to salute or show any other regard for the flag.

"Once, as the flag passed, I looked out over the crowd near me. There must have been at least 50 people. I didn't see one show any respect for the flag. What has happened to Americans?

"Weren't they ever taught love of their country and their flag? Didn't they ever serve their country? If these people had half the experience of the men marching, I know it would have meant something to them. As a Legion auxiliary member, I stood with my hand over my heart. It really swelled with pride. Wake up, America. Stand up, salute and cheer as our flag passes by."[230]

A Kentucky gold star mother found support from her community when a poignant souvenir of her son's loss was stolen:

"'Please return my flag.'

"That plea, spoken by Mrs. Helen Martin and echoed by *The Kentucky Post* and Congressman Gene Snyder, has been answered.

"Around midnight, the thieves, perhaps stricken with guilty consciences, returned the flag that had hung for 24 years in memory of Mrs. Martin's son, Harold, who was killed in the Pacific during World War II. The Navy Memorial flag had been draped across her son's bier and was later presented to her by Navy Officials. She had displayed it every Memorial Day and on other occasions.

"But last Memorial weekend the 5-by-11 foot flag was stolen from Mrs. Martin's porch. And, as if to add to her grief, it was her birthday.

"But her flag is back, and Mrs. Martin is happy.

"'It means so much to me, and no one else would have a use for it. I'm just glad it's back,' she sighed.

"Mrs. Martin found the flag wrapped in brown paper with a newspaper clipping of the stolen flag taped to the front.

"'I guess they felt sorry for me when they read the article in the paper,' she said. 'I'm thankful—my prayers have been answered.'"[231]

A gold star mother living at the American Gold Star Home in Long Beach was granted what she called "my life's miracle" when the body of her son was discovered in a wrecked B-24 plane in the wilds of New Guinea in 1979, thirty-four years after he was declared missing. Helen Challenor said she "never gave up hope. Somehow in my mind I just knew he would be found. I was stunned and relieved that my long wait was finally over. You cannot just write someone off as dead unless you know for sure." Helen Challenor flew to Arlington National Cemetery for the burial of her son,

Cpl. George Challenor, the tail-gunner on the bomber, who was twenty-one when he died in 1945. The bodies of the seven other crew-members were also found on board the plane.[232]

Australian mother Rose Manson was in the news again when she made her fifth trip to the United States to visit with gold star mothers she had been unable to reach on her previous trips. Mrs. Manson was the Australian mother who had grown to know many of the young Americans serving in Australia during World War II and had corresponded throughout the war with the mothers of those soldiers who were buried in a cemetery near her home.

Not all of the news concerning gold star mothers was good. In 1963, the *Chicago Tribune* reported on the court conviction of a World War II gold star mother in Rapid City, South Dakota:

"Mrs. Lavange Michael, 67, South Dakota's former 'gold star mother of the year,' today began a three-year suspended sentence on a charge of performing abortions for more than three decades.

Mrs. Michael was chosen as the '1962 Gold Star Mother of the Year' by South Dakota veterans organizations. She admitted she had been performing abortions since the late 1920s. She said her clients came from every section of the country.

"Circuit Judge Leslie Hersrud said he was giving the woman a suspended sentence because of her physical condition. She is blind in one eye and going blind in the other. She also has a broken arm. Police said Mrs. Michael charged as little as $150 and as much as $1500 for her operations."[233]

In 1964, a World War I gold star mother who was a member of AGSM was found murdered in Massachusetts:

"An elderly couple was found dead at home [in] Roxbury, Massachusetts with a cardboard sign reading 'Help' hanging from the front door. Police said it was an apparent murder and suicide. The bodies of Rudolph F. Gerlach, 81, and his wife of 10 months, Eva, 88, were discovered by Gerlach's daughter, Constance Scribner… Mrs. Scribner, who visited her father and stepmother regularly, found the hand-painted sign on the outside door knob. The body of Mrs. Gerlach, honored last year as the oldest gold star mother in Massachusetts, lay on a bed with a wound to her head."[234]

In 1972, *The Gold Star Mother* reported on a startling event that had occurred to an AGSM member in Atlanta, Georgia:

"Mrs. Lee Fenster… has had a most unfortunate tragedy strike again in her life. Her son, Martin Fenster, dean of students at John Marshall University, was shot and killed March 6, by a masked intruder in his mother's home as she and his brother sat bound and helpless in chairs a few feet away… He died of a single gunshot wound in the back of his head.[235]

In 1964, the St. John family of Schenectady, New York, published a song dedicated to all gold star mothers and fathers. The song, "There are Extra Stars Up in the Heavens Tonight," was written by Mary E. St. John, Stephen St. John, Sr., and Stephen St. John, Jr. The sheet music's cover showed a gold star mother in the traditional AGSM hat and cape looking skyward toward an American flag:

I can't write to everyone whose loved one's gone to the land of tomorrow so I will sing this song.
There are extra stars up in the heavens tonight to guide us and brighten our way
And each single one stands for some mother's son who died in a land faraway.
Fought for you and me, tried to make the world free, my eyes fill with tears as I say.
There are extra stars up in the heavens tonight to guide us and brighten our way.[236]

Surviving Vietnam

The psychological, cultural and emotional repercussions of the war in Vietnam continued to affect the nation in the decades that followed. The Vietnam era left American Gold Star Mothers, Inc. struggling to remain viable with a membership that was sixty per cent smaller than it had been twenty years before. Despite the new energy brought to AGSM by gold star mothers of the Vietnam War, every aspect of the organization's existence was greatly compromised by the loss of membership. AGSM's focus and energy now required redefinition as the mothers struggled to remain effective as an advocate and resource for veterans, maintain the organization's financial viability and continue as a national service presence in VA hospitals and local communities.

Fig. 11-1: Korean War gold star mother Molly Snyder at the Korean War Veterans Memorial in Washington, D.C.
(AGSM Collection)

CHAPTER 11

AGSM Challenged: 1980–1999

To say that Gold Star Mothers have given much to this country is an understatement. You have taught the country the true meaning of fidelity, dignity and love.

—TOGO D. WEST JR.,
Veterans Affairs Secretary (1998)[1]

AS THE COUNTRY REDEFINED ITSELF nationally and internationally following the Vietnam era, AGSM faced a daily struggle as its membership continued a precipitous decline. In 1980, the membership was more than 7,300; within ten years, membership had dropped by more than 60 percent and numbered fewer than 3,000. And by the year 2000, it had declined again by more than half, with a total membership of less than 1,300. Finding ways to remain viable and effectively continue the work of AGSM as the membership declined and aged was the all-consuming and challenging focus of the organization during these decades.

Called by some the "world's policemen," the United States was involved in a number of military actions during the 1980s and 1990s although none remotely approached the scope of Vietnam. Peacekeeping activities (sometimes alone and sometimes as part of an international coalition), protection and rescue of American citizens abroad, terrorism (domestic and international), and tragic military accidents contributed to the gold star losses of this era. Major incidents included:

Iran hostage crisis (November 4, 1979 to January 20, 1981): Following the takeover of the American embassy by Islamist students and militants, fifty-three Americans were held hostage for 444 days. After negotiations failed, a military rescue, Operation Eagle Claw, was attempted on April 24, 1980. The effort failed and resulted in the death of eight American servicemen. Despite economic and diplomatic sanctions, the hostages were not released until President Jimmy Carter's term in office ended. Just minutes after Ronald Reagan was sworn in as president, the terrorists announced that the hostages were free to return home.

Beirut, Lebanon (1983): *The Gold Star Mother* reported that "just before dawn broke on October 23, 1983, a truck carrying explosives leveled the Aviation Safety Building at the edge of Beirut International Airport, the temporary headquarters of the 24th Marine Amphibious Unit—the Peacekeepers. More than 241 Marines, sailors and soldiers were instantly killed. They came in peace during 1982–1983."[2] Nearly 300 went home in flag-draped coffins.

Grenada (1983): Two days after the attack in Lebanon, a mixed force of approximately 1,200 U.S. soldiers invaded the British Commonwealth nation of Grenada on October 25, 1983. Their mission was to ensure the safety of approximately a thousand Americans there, mainly students, following a Marxist coup in the country. In less than two months, all U.S. troops were withdrawn with nineteen lost in the action.[3]

Gander, Newfoundland (1985): On December 12, 1985, a chartered aircraft carrying U.S. servicemen stateside from a six-month assignment in a Sinai peacekeeping force crashed in Gander, Newfoundland. Everyone aboard the plane (256 passengers and crew) died in the crash. All but twelve were members of the 101st Airborne Division. Official Canadian and U.S. government reports blamed the crash on weather conditions, although an Islamic extremist group immediately claimed responsibility.

Operation Just Cause (December 1989): As reported in *The Gold Star Mother*, "in the wake of anti-American actions led by General Manuel Noriega, over 27,000 troops entered Panama to ensure the continued operation of the canal and protect the 35,000 U.S. citizens in the area." The United States lost 23 servicemen in Operation Just Cause.[4]

Desert Storm (August 1990–February 1991): Also called the Gulf War, Desert Storm was the military effort initiated by a U.N.-authorized coalition force against Iraq after it invaded, occupied and annexed Kuwait in August 1990. Concerned with Iraq's ability to move quickly and easily into Saudi Arabia after taking over Kuwait, the U.S. immediately responded to Saudi Arabia's call for military assistance with Operation Desert Shield, sending troops to Kuwait for defensive purposes. A U.N. resolution authorized the use of force if Iraq did not withdraw from Kuwait by January 15, 1991; on the morning of January 16, the coalition launched full military operations. After punishing bombing and ground assaults, Iraqi troops retreated from Kuwait on February 26, leaving a trail of burning oil wells behind them. On February 27, 1991, President Bush called for a cease-fire and declared that Kuwait had been liberated. There were more than 300 U.S. battle deaths in the Desert Storm operation.

Bosnia and Zaire (1997): In November 1996, President Clinton announced that the United States would send 8,500 U.S. soldiers to Bosnia early in 1997 as part of a NATO force and send as many as 4,000 troops to Central Africa as part of an international humanitarian relief force.

Presidents, Conventions, and Resolutions of the 1980s

As it had in the past two decades, AGSM continued to elect a new national president every year with none serving more than a single term. The mothers of the Vietnam era were now AGSM's most active group as many World War II and Korean Conflict mothers found it necessary to curtail their activities due to age and health issues. In many cases, the length of time that the elected mothers had been part of the organization was significantly reduced from past decades when as many as two decades or longer of organizational service were accrued before election to the highest office.

Katherine Mannion
National President, 1980-1981

Mrs. Mannion's son, Todd, died in Vietnam in December 1966 when he volunteered to accompany a truck convoy to Pleiku and the convoy was ambushed; nineteen of the thirty-five men on the mission died. A much decorated hero and athlete, Todd had been offered contracts by several major league baseball teams before entering the service. A week before Todd's twenty-first birthday, a young Army sergeant brought the news of Todd's death to the Mannions. Mrs. Mannion later said, "He just stood there. I didn't know whether I should comfort him or he should comfort me. It turned out that it was the first time he had ever had to tell a parent that a son had been killed in action." Mrs. Mannion joined AGSM in May 1967.[5]

At the 1980 convention in San Diego, California, an important resolution was passed. Effective immediately, only five members would be required to start a chapter, reduced from the requirement of ten members that had been in place since the organization's inception.[6] Delegates also approved a two fold resolution, condemning the militants who were holding the American hostages in Iran and supporting any action that the U.S. government chose to take to resolve the situation:

> Whereas, 50 Americans have been held hostage by Iranian Militants since November 1979 in blatant and outrageous disregard of all customs and procedures of diplomacy and international law, and
>
> Whereas, terrorism and lawlessness threatens the rights and freedoms of all people, no matter what rationale for their actions are offered by the perpetrators, and
>
> Whereas, American Gold Star mothers...
> share with the families and friends of the hostages, their anguish and heart-break,
>
> Now, therefore be it resolved... that we condemn the Iranian Militants for their actions taken against American Citizens, and also condemn the Iranian Government which has ultimate responsibility for the actions of those holding Americans hostages, and
>
> Be it further resolved, that the American Gold Star Mothers support those actions taken by our Government which are intended to pressure Iran into a swift and safe resolution of the hostage crisis.[7]

Pressed by financial concerns, a motion was passed at Mrs. Mannion's 1981 end-of-term convention in Spokane, Washington to establish a committee to investigate the feasibility of selling AGSM's headquarters building as a cost-cutting measure. Headquarters represented the organization's most valuable asset and was also the source of its most crippling expenses, according to those who supported the sale of the building.[8]

Continuing to look for ways to streamline the operations and expenses of AGSM, the national board presented several resolutions pertaining to the tasks of AGSM officers. In the interest of economy, the office of assistant treasurer was eliminated and those duties were transferred to the Custodian of Records. Rather than electing a national historian, the national president would now select an existing member of the national board to serve as historian. These two resolutions, which eliminated two board positions, were approved by the delegates in convention. Delegates also approved a resolution that allowed gold star mothers living in insular and territorial possessions (Hawaii, Alaska, Virgin Islands, Guam, Puerto Rico) to be eligible for membership at large with their dues paid to the national organization rather than a chapter.[9]

Mary Teater,
National President, 1981–1982

Mrs. Teater's son, Wayne, was the recipient of three Purple Hearts and seventeen other medals following his death in April 1965, the most citations ever awarded to a soldier at that time. A member of the 57th Helicopter Ambulance Corps, his helicopter ambulance was evacuating fifteen wounded men in Operation Dust Off when he died. Mrs. Teater joined AGSM in 1968.[10]

Helen Stuber
National President, 1982–1983

Helen Stuber was the mother of two children—a son and a daughter. Her daughter, Judy, was stricken with sleeping sickness at age nine, sleeping for thirteen months before waking. She remained an invalid until her death at age twenty-eight. Mrs. Stuber's son, Dan, joined the Marines in August 1966. Based on the USS *Okinawa* with the 3rd Division, "C" Company, Special Helicopter Landing Team, he died in October 1967 near the demilitarized zone north of Da Nang. Dan was married with a four-month old son when he died at the age of twenty-three. At the encouragement of her

mother, Helen Stuber attended her first AGSM meeting just ten days after her son's funeral.

June Everett
National President, 1983–1984

June Everett was the mother of two sons, Stanley and Kenneth. Stanley joined the Marines in May 1968 and died in June 1969 in Vietnam "from wounds taken in a hostile explosion."[11] During Mrs. Everett's year as national president, AGSM received the long sought Congressional Charter from Congress. It was also during Mrs. Everett's term that AGSM began the tradition of placing an American flag on each panel of the Vietnam Veterans Memorial on Gold Star Mothers' Day.[12]

June Everett's end-of-term convention in Houston, Texas, presented the national board with a problem—for the first time in the organization's history, there were not enough delegates to constitute a quorum. Rather than the one-hundred registered delegates required, there were only eighty-six in attendance. Technically, without a quorum, no resolutions could be decided and no elections could be held. The delegates in attendance approved a decision to omit the quorum requirement for the 1984 convention so that decisions could be made and organizational business be conducted. Realizing that with falling convention attendance they could not guarantee a quorum for future conventions, a motion from floor was approved to reduce the number required for a quorum to twenty-five.[13] The delegates also approved a motion to raise per capita dues to $6 per year.[14]

Lois Freeman
National President, 1984–1985

Sixty years old when she took office in 1984, Mrs. Freeman was a registered nurse and had served in the Army Nurse Corp in World War II. Her son, Marine Lance Cpl. Joseph L. Freeman Jr., died in Vietnam in March 1969 at the age of twenty-one.

The dinner speaker for the 1985 convention held in Atlanta, Georgia was former Secretary of State Dean Rusk. His topic was about concerns for the youth of America.[15]

Nora J. Golsh
National President, 1985–1986

Nora Golsh was born in Southern California and lived there all her life. She and her husband, Paul, a former Navy pilot who retired with the rank of Commander, had two children: Stephen and Paula. Stephen died in Vietnam in 1970 while serving with the 101st Airborne. Mrs. Golsh joined the Glendale (California) Chapter in 1972.[16]

At the 1986 national convention in Costa Mesa, California, a resolution was passed that clarified decades of questions about an official AGSM "uniform":

> "Whereas; the American Gold Star Mothers, Inc. has never had an official dress code; and
> Whereas; some members are wearing white overseas caps with our Gold Star Insignia as our official head piece; and
> Whereas; we should all be uniformly dressed;
> Therefore Be It resolved; that white be designated as the official dress code of The American Gold Star Mothers, Inc., to be worn at the opening of the National Conventions, Department Conventions, funerals and all functions appropriately designated by National, Department or Chapter."[17]

In full Native American regalia, Iron Eyes Cody of the popular "Keep America Beautiful" ad campaign presented a Peace and Friendship medal to convention speaker General Turnage, Administrator of Veterans Affairs.[18] Renowned poet Bruce Joseph Seevers read several poems from his book *An American in Love with America* and received many standing ovations from the delegates.[19] The framed Congressional Charter was displayed at the convention, the only time it would be taken from its place of honor in the foyer of the headquarters building.[20]

Opal L. Johnson
National President, 1986–1987

Born in 1919 in Bolivar, Ohio, Opal Johnson was a graduate of Ohio's Aultman Hospital School of Nursing in 1941. She entered the U.S. Army Air Corps in May 1942 as a 2nd Lt. and was assigned to Station Hospital in Miami Beach, Florida, as a nurse in the Medical Branch of the Army Air Corps. It was there that she met her future husband, William O. Johnson. Parents of one son and two daughters, they moved to Houston, Texas where Bill worked for the FBI and Opal worked as a surgical nurse during the school year and as a summer camp nurse for the Girl Scouts. Their son Robert entered the service in 1963 and became a medic in the Green Berets. He was killed in action in May 1967. Opal joined AGSM in 1972.[21]

The delegates at the fiftieth national convention in Seattle, Washington (June 1987) approved a resolution honoring the oldest gold star mothers of the organization. It was agreed that members over ninety years of age would henceforth be exempt from paying dues. While honoring the oldest mothers, it also added to the financial woes of the organization for there were 175 members (about 5 percent of the total membership) who qualified for this dues exemption.[22]

In January 1986, while serving as national first vice president, Opal Johnson wrote to President Ronald Reagan concerning the loss of the Challenger crew:

> "The Space Shuttle Challenger disaster brought back into my mind the devastating loss of a loved one. The grief of a mother for her son or daughter, whether they be killed on the field of battle or in the exploration of space is limited to no national boundary, no racial or ethnic background and no religious belief… Sometimes I think of what would happen if we mothers were to unite in country after country. What if we in America had a counterpart in Soviet Russia, in Iran, in Iraq, in Afghanistan, in Ireland, in El Salvador, in Nicaragua, in Cuba, in North Korea, in South Korea, in Vietnam and every other country in this world which is torn with conflict and strife. What if mothers the world wide were to demand that old men would no longer start wars in which young men and women would be maimed or killed. What if mothers demanded that the perspective of nations be redirected from conflict and confrontation and be focused instead on peace. Just the thought of such a movement boggles the mind. Just think of the hungry children who could be fed, the disease and suffering that could be eliminated if the time, effort, brain power and money the world now expends on warfare and its implements could be diverted to food, medicine and education."[23]

Shirley Jones Delanoy
National President, 1987–1988

Born in 1923 in Ilion, New York, Mrs. Delanoy worked for the New York Telephone Company and Rhodes General Hospital, a temporary Army hospital, following high school. The mother of two boys and one girl, her son Tom died in May 1967 in Vietnam. She was a charter member of the Utica, New York chapter formed in 1969. She retired from New York Telephone in 1984.[24]

At the 1988 national convention in Buffalo, New York, a largely ceremonial resolution was passed by the delegates. It established that all past national presidents would be part of an advisory council for the current national president. The advisory council members would have no votes, no policy-making powers, and none of their expenses would be paid. This resolution merely formalized the role that the past national presidents had always played as advisors to the sitting national board.

Margaret Vinyard
National President, 1988–1989

Born in March 1924 in Kansas City, Missouri, Mrs. Vinyard worked for many years as an administrator at the Westminster, California, police department. The mother of two boys and one girl, her youngest son, John, enlisted in the Army in 1967. A member of the 25th Infantry Division, Lightning Brigade, he died at age nineteen in June 1968 of a gunshot wound.[25]

Anna Biber
National President, 1989–1990

Born February 1922 in Haledon, New Jersey, Mrs. Biber was the mother of five children—three sons and two girls—and the daughter of a World War II gold star mother. Mrs. Biber's son Joseph was drafted; after serving for a year in the Marines, he volunteered to go back to Vietnam for another tour of duty. He died there in September 1968. Anna joined AGSM in 1969.[26]

During Mrs. Biber's term in office, a $5 million lawsuit was filed against the National Headquarters of AGSM, Inc. The lawsuit was the result of injury suffered by a person attending a chapter's fundraising activity. Although resolved in AGSM's favor, expenses of more than $3,000 were incurred. Mrs. Biber told members that "we cannot afford this expense. Our Liability Insurance also tripled in cost as a result."[27]

Presidents, Conventions, and Resolutions of the 1990s

Gladys Jewett
National President, 1990–1991

Robert Elvis Stallings died in Vietnam. His mother, Gladys Jewett, joined AGSM in 1967 and served seven years on the national executive board before being elected national president. Her second husband, his son, and grandson were lost in a boating accident at sea.

As the national board continued to look for ways to streamline operations for efficiency and cost, resolutions were proposed at the 1991 Long Beach, California, convention. However, for the first time, the national board experienced some push-back. Proposals to combine the offices of first and second vice president into a single vice president position, and to combine the positions of corresponding secretary and recording secretary into a single secretary position were defeated. Approved proposals included eliminating the position of national historian; changing the title of the national custodian of records to national service officer; raising the per capita to $10 per year ($9 to national; $1 to Department); and, requiring that a candidate be a member of a chapter, have served as chapter president and department president, and served two terms on the national board before being eligible to be elected national president, first vice president or second vice president.[28]

The 1991 convention was held at the American Gold Star Home in Long Beach, California. It was reported as the "best convention ever with the least expense to the individual members." Attendees stayed with residents of the Home and the Home Foundation paid for all meals except the banquet. A sightseeing trip to Catalina Island was planned and a poolside luau (muu-muus required for the mothers) was a long remembered event.[29]

One important resolution decided in Long Beach eliminated the member-at-large membership status. Current members-at-large were given an amnesty period to transfer their membership to the closest chapter without paying a transfer fee.[30]

Winona L. Tucker
National President, 1991–1992

Mrs. Tucker was the mother of three daughters and one son; when she took office in 1991, she had thirteen great grandchildren. Her son, Arthur Leslie, died in 1968 at the age of nineteen in Vietnam.[31]

The 1992 convention was held in Washington, D.C., at the Vista Hotel.

Violet C. Long
National President, 1992–1993

Violet Catherine Long was the mother of three sons and one daughter. Starting as a clerk-typist, she advanced to the position of Executive Director and Chairperson of the Commonwealth of Pennsylvania's Historical and Museum Commission.[32] Her son, SP4 Charles Elbert

Long (U.S. Army, 26th Infantry, 1st Infantry Division), died in September 1969 in Vietnam after just eight months of deployment. Her husband of fifty-one years died a few months before she took office in 1992.

During Mrs. Long's term in office, the "Gold Star Banner" stamp was issued by the United States Postal Service. First issued on May 31, 1993, the flag showed a service flag with a gold star in a window and the words "Gold Stars Mark World War II losses." The 29-cent, first-class stamp was part of the World War II 50th Anniversary series. [Fig. 11-2]

Jeanne Penfold
National President, 1993–1994

A native of New York, Mrs. Penfold earned her RN certification in 1944. Working in New York, she married Allan Thomas Penfold in 1946 and they had six children. Their oldest child, Peter Allen, died in Vietnam at the age of twenty while serving with the Third Marines.[33]

At the 1994 national convention in Harrisburg, Pennsylvania, a resolution was passed that, for the first time, gave gold star dads an official position within AGSM. It was agreed that dads could be appointed as deputies to the AGSM Representative at the VA Medical Centers. This resolution acknowledged that many dads had to drive the mothers who were hospital representatives to their VAVS meetings and so gave the dads an official status within AGSM. [34]

Delegates also endorsed the efforts of the American Gold Star Home and Manor to look into establishing a gold star home in the eastern United States.[35] Many gold star mothers reported that they were interested in living in a facility like the Home, but that moving away from their families and friends in the eastern part of the nation was just too much to ask.

Carol L. Tabor
National President, 1994–1995

Born in Portland, Oregon, Mrs. Tabor was the mother of six children. Her oldest son, Richard, a Spec.4, died in January 1971 in Vietnam while serving with the 173rd Airborne Division.[36]

Valerie May
National President, 1995–1996

Daughter of a World War II gold star mother, Mrs. May was born in 1931 in Kalamazoo, Michigan. Mrs. May was the mother of eight children. Her son, Rollie

Northouse, died in Vietnam.[37]

The 1996 national convention delegates in Saginaw, Michigan passed a resolution that amended a 1987 resolution that made members over the age of ninety exempt from paying AGSM dues. The new resolution required that the mother must have had a five-year membership history to be eligible for the dues exemption. At this point, the organization had 204 members who were ninety or older, more than 10 percent of the total membership of 1,755.

Frances J. Turley
National President, 1996–1997

Mrs. Turley's oldest son, Francis E. Cortor, Jr.(known as Duke), served one tour in Vietnam with the Army. He was killed in October 1969, four months into his second tour. Frances was a nurse for twenty years at the VA Medical Center, Jefferson Barracks Hospital in St. Louis, Missouri.[38]

Theresa Davis
National President, 1997–1998

Born in Hanover, Massachusetts, Mrs. Davis was a gold star sister, having lost a brother serving in the Canadian Army Engineers in World War I. She and her husband, Richard, had five children. Their oldest, Richard, earned his Green Beret in the Army's Special Forces; he died in Vietnam in June 1968.[39]

In her acceptance speech as national president, she said:

"Our country has given us freedom, a chance to succeed, open spaces to raise our families with love, laughter and joy. In turn—we each gave up one of our children to America's Call. The price was high and not paid willingly; for our sons and daughters paid the highest price—they gave their lives. In our efforts to make sure they are not forgotten—let us not forget that every soldier, every veteran, is someone's child."[40]

The 1998 national convention held in Boston, Massachusetts was significant in one way—for the first time, there were no resolutions brought before the delegates for consideration.

Bette A. Freeman
National President, 1998–1999

Bette Freeman had been a member of AGSM for twenty-six years when she was elected national president. Born in Berlin, New Hampshire, she had six children.

Her son, Marine Lance Cpl. Gregory C. Davis, died in December 1971 at the age of twenty-two in a helicopter crash in the Bay of Bengal. He had been evacuating Americans out of Pakistan when the crash occurred.[41]

Mrs. Freeman's year in office was fraught with sorrow. In October 1998, her youngest son, Garry, died suddenly and unexpectedly. Thanking the membership for their support, she wrote in the November/December 1998 issue of *The Gold Star Mother:*

"It was such a shock to all of us. We were talking with him one minute and he was gone the next... Now that I have lost three sons, 1971, 1995 and 1998, I am praying that the Lord let's [sic] me keep what I have left —two boys and a girl."

But on New Year's Day 1999, another of Mrs. Freeman's sons died. She wrote to the membership:

"This is probably the hardest year of my life, having lost another son, Geoffrey, on New Year's Day. I am so thankful for the condolences received from so many of the mothers who were aware of the tragedy. ...Life shouldn't be this way, but only the Lord above makes those decisions... I now have lost four sons. I wish it were only a bad dream, not a reality. Thank goodness, I still have a son and a daughter to lean on."[42]

In her final report as national president, she wrote:

"This year has brought joys and sadness. It has brought passings and beginnings. It has brought sorrow and comfort. It has brought out the strength of love and friendship. Thank you, Mothers, for your compassion and support."[43]

Mary Elizabeth Wheeler
National President, 1999–2000
Born in 1926, Mary thought she would follow her grandparents with a career as a Salvation Army Officer. But "a handsome young soldier stole her heart" and she married Charles R. Wheeler. They had five children, sadly losing two of them shortly after birth. Their son, PFC Joseph Keith Wheeler, USMC, died in March 1968 at Khe Sanh in Vietnam. Mrs. Wheeler joined the Utica, New York, chapter in 1969. The first female supervisor at the General Electric plant in Utica, she retired in 1986 after thirty-seven years of service. While raising her family, she continued teaching, consulting and organizing youth activities for the Salvation Army.[44]

VAVS and Community Service

As the aging organization continued to lose members, those who remained made every attempt to continue their volunteer activities with the VA and in their own communities for as long as possible. But it was unrealistic to hope that their lessened presence in the hospitals could accomplish as much as before. During the 1980s, an average of 750 AGSM volunteers worked on a regular schedule or occasionally in VA facilities. This was a significant decrease from the decade before when there were more than 3,000 AGSM volunteers working in VA hospitals. In the 1990s, the average dropped to just over 400 volunteers and by the end of the decade, the number of volunteers dropped below 300.

The contributions made to community service work decreased as well. In 1971, 103,882 volunteer hours were reported and $34,723 was earned and spent in support of community service work. Ten years later, the 1981 total (45,343 hours) was less than half of that. By 1998, as the decade neared its end, just 19,419 hours of community service were reported.

As always, there were flaws and inconsistencies in AGSM's calculations for VAVS and community service work. There was never a year when every chapter's work was included and in some years there was no public report made. Yet, even with the decreasing number of volunteers and the aging of many of those who continued to work, the hours donated across the nation by AGSM volunteers was still a stunning contribution. In the 1980s, well over half a million hours of volunteer time were given by AGSM; in the 1990s, nearly 400,000 hours were recorded. The service legacy of the organization was still intact and providing the nation with a true gift of commitment and caring.

Deaths

Fifteen past national presidents died between 1980 and 1999. The death of each of these women represented a serious loss of history and guidance for the current members:

Myrtle Foster (national president 1970–1971) died July 1980[45]

Maude Fry Barnett (national president 1957–1958) died September 1983

Elsie Nielsen (national president from 1952–1955) died December 1984[46]

Rose Decker (national president 1966–1967) died October 1985[47]

Fig. 11-2: A May 31, 1993 first day of issue cachet for the stamp series memorializing World War II honors the five Sullivan brothers who died in 1942.
(First day of issue Collection, Fleetwood No. 93-3: Fenelon Collection)

Regina M. Coughlin (national president 1972–1973) died April 1987[48]

Marie Hart (national president 1967–1968) died February 1988

Josephay Fleming (national president 1975–1976) died August 1988[49]

Dorothy Baxter (national president 1961–1962) died January 1989[50]

Lorraine I. Desser (national president 1959–1960) died October 1990; Mrs. Desser's son, Phillip, performed the AGSM ritual and reading at her funeral in Bridgeport, Connecticut because there were no other AGSM members left to do so in the area[51]

Helen S. White (national president 1973–1974) died November 1990[52]

Mary King (national president 1976–1977) died May 1992[53]

Mildred Lee Edelen (national president 1964–1965) died July 1995; in her acceptance speech as national president, she had said, "The real joy of life begins when we give to the world more than we take from it."[54]

Betty Bryce (national president 1979–1980) died February 1997; a woman of many interests, Mrs. Bryce said that "the American Gold Star Mothers were always first [in her mind] because they were the ones who helped her through those trying years and to whom she would always be grateful." [55]

Mamie Pearl Simmons (national president 1968–1969) died December 1997[57]

Emma Eunick (national president 1965 – 1966) died February 1998[58]

Helen T. Willhour (national president 1969–1970) died March 1999[59]

Violet Catherine Long (national president 1992–1993) died March 1999[56]

The deaths of others who had not served as national officers were also mourned by the organization:

Judge Lloyd S. Nix, presiding judge of the Los Angeles Superior Court, died February 21, 1986. Judge Nix had been the judge for the Memorial National Home Foundation lawsuit and his abiding love for the gold star mothers had made him a loyal friend who was actively involved in the management of the Home until his death.

Theodosia Darling Seibold Nelson, the daughter

of AGSM founder Grace Seibold, died in December 1992 at the age of ninety-seven. The mother of two daughters, Mrs. Nelson had served as the Assistant to the Deputy Commissioner of the IRS during World War I; instituted the women's basketball program at George Washington University in Washington, D.C. (her alma mater); and had been the Eastern Division Women's singles tennis champion in 1919.[60]

Rose Fitzgerald Kennedy, although not a member of AGSM, had been an inspiration to many gold star mothers over the years. She died on January 25, 1995 at the age of 104. Her oldest son, Joseph, died in World War II and she later lost sons John and Robert by assassination. She once told an interviewer, "I've learned to be brave and put my faith in the will of God." President Kennedy called her "the glue that held the family together."[61]

Congressional Charter

Probably the most significant event of the 1980s for AGSM was the acquisition of a Congressional Charter. Sporadic efforts over five decades had proven unsuccessful, but in March 1984, legislation introduced by the Honorable Albert Gore, Jr. as Bill HR3811 won the mothers their charter. As Mr. Gore said:

"It is apparent that after 55 years of public service this organization is a resource truly deserving our recognition. I strongly believe that granting a national charter would be the appropriate action for us to take to acknowledge and assist them in their continued work ... I don't think in my eight years in the Congress I have ever felt more privileged to introduce a particular piece of legislation than this. These women are so courageous; indeed, it is moving to be with them."[62]

June Everett, national president of AGSM, spoke before the Senate subcommittee about what a Congressional Charter would represent to the mothers of AGSM:

"By being granted the Federal charter, we would feel we are being given the highest recognition for the loss of our loved ones. A Federal charter would enhance our ability to recruit new membership and further the goals of our organization. Vietnam mothers have been reluctant to join for the reason we do not have a Federal charter. They, at present, are our only available source of membership."[63]

There was wide bipartisan support for the charter and it passed easily. Mrs. Everett reported than many of the Congressmen she spoke with were surprised at the proposal for they believed that AGSM had been granted a Congressional Charter decades earlier.

At the 1984 convention, Mrs. Everett outlined the benefits associated with a charter for the organization:

"We are at last... Congressionally recognized as an organization. Hopefully we will be tax exempt as far as taxes on Headquarters, something many have worked on for several years... Already, as a result of the charter, I was invited to participate in the Memorial Services for the Vietnam Unknown. We were seated according to the year we received a charter. In the past, national presidents have never been asked to participate at various functions in D.C. Hopefully more awareness of our organization will come about. This could enhance more membership."[64]

The Vietnam Veterans Memorial

The Vietnam Veterans Memorial Fund, Inc., that had been established in April 1979 continued its effort to achieve national reconciliation by establishing a tangible, non-political symbol of recognition and respect for the men and women who had fought in Vietnam. On July 1, 1980, Congress authorized a site near the Lincoln Memorial for the Vietnam Veterans Memorial. It was then announced that the design of the memorial would be selected through a national competition open to any American citizen age eighteen or older. Eight internationally known artists and designers served as the design review jury. Out of 1,421 entries, the jury unanimously selected the design of a twenty-one-year-old Yale University student— Maya Lin.

Ms. Lin's design was described as "a park within a park—a quiet protected place unto itself, yet harmonious with the site."[65] Carved into the black granite walls of the memorial are the names of the 58,191 American men and women who lost their lives in Vietnam, inscribed in chronological order by the dates of their deaths. In this way, said Ms. Lin, "the names would become the memorial."[66] It was later decided to add a flagstaff and a more traditional statue of the soldiers of the Vietnam War to the memorial site. Washington sculptor Frederick Hart was selected to design the sculpture. [Fig.11-4]

Fig. 11-3: Visitors to the Vietnam Veterans Memorial leave behind personal mementoes to honor the memory of those whose names are carved on the black granite walls of the Memorial. *(Memorial Day 2006; Carol M. Highsmith Archive (Library of Congress); Ref. LC-DIG-highsm-04895)*

Fig. 11-4: Standing near the Vietnam Veterans Memorial, this sculpture of American soldiers serving in Vietnam was created by sculptor Frederick Hart. *(Carol M. Highsmith Archive (Library of Congress); Ref. LC-DIG-highsm-04696)*

The memorial was dedicated on November 13, 1982; the life-size sculpture of three American fighting men, described as "a mute but everlasting tribute to those who made the supreme sacrifice," was installed in late 1984.[67] On November 11, 1984, the memorial was accepted as a gift to the nation by President Ronald Reagan. The entire $7 million cost of the memorial had been raised through public and private contributions.

AGSM was part of the effort and a staunch supporter of the Vietnam Veterans Memorial from its earliest days. In 1980, Jan Scruggs told the organization:

"Your sons are not forgotten by those of us who served with them in that terrible war. Their memory is alive in our hearts and minds. We shall make certain that the people of this nation never forget that your son was taken from you in the conflict."[68]

The mothers instinctively understood from the very beginning what the memorial could accomplish for the nation and for the individuals who fought in Vietnam. Their May 1981 report on status of "The Wall" and the selection of Ms. Lin's design included these words:

"Nowadays, though, patriotism is a complicated matter. Ideas about heroism, or art, for that matter, are no longer what they were before Vietnam. And there is certainly no consensus yet about what cause might have been served by the Vietnam War.

"But perhaps that is why the V-shaped, black granite lines merging gently with the sloping earth make the winning design seem a lasting and appropriate image of dignity and sadness. It conveys the only point about the war on which people may agree; that those who died should be remembered."[69]

A television commentator said the following about the dedication of the Vietnam Veterans Memorial:

"It's been a strange week. Not so much because of the event, but because of the feelings. Suddenly, there's a welcome feeling that every American is a member of one family, the United States, and that some of the members of that family were in danger for a long time, and now most of them are home and safe again, and for a while, we just wanted to look at them. But then you do have to ask, why only now and not before? Why are we so emotional and patriotic over their return, when we virtually ignored and even worse than ignored the heroes who served, or were captured, or were wounded or were killed in Vietnam, Laos, Cambodia, and those that were captured on the Pueblo? I think we know why. It's probably because for a brief period of our history; and it was brief, but still it was much too long; we weren't a family. It wasn't that an American wasn't an American. It was that one kind of American was politically different than another kind and it made a difference. If it was a family at all, it was a family divided, and a family divided can't give much of a homecoming … Though the time for saying it is late, we could finally say what they still deserve to hear: Welcome Home; and Thanks."[70]

The Vietnam-era gold star mothers of AGSM immediately became an integral living part of the Vietnam Memorial. Wearing their traditional white outfits that made them immediately identifiable, they served as unofficial docents at "The Wall," helping people find the names they were searching for, talking with family members and Vietnam veterans, and embracing those—and there were many—who found the memorial to be a difficult but cathartic experience.

A letter addressed to "all Gold Star Mothers everywhere" was published in the September/October 1995 issue of *The Gold Star Mother*. Written by Dennis L. Mitchell, a retired U.S. Army officer, the letter describes the effect that "The Wall" continues to have on its visitors, particularly those who had served in Vietnam, even decades after the war had ended:

"My name is Dennis Mitchell. I am a 47-year-old Vietnam veteran and I am only recently coming home. I'm sure you all know what I mean. I had heard of Gold Star Mothers but had no real appreciation for what you do and the impact you have on the lives you touch. In my ignorance, I guess I only imagined you to be a group of mothers who had lost sons or daughters in Vietnam and who had organized to provide comfort to each other; a national support group if you will, and nothing more. Then God led me to Opal and Bill Johnson through my church.

"Although I had already been through individual and group therapy with other Vietnam veterans, thanks to the Veterans Administration, there was still a huge painful void in my heart over the homecoming experience. So much of my pain inside centered around the loneliness and the overwhelming darkness of feeling that no one understood what I was going through. I resigned myself to the truth of what I had been told by a fellow veteran. He leaned across the desk at me and shouted, "NO, people who weren't there DON'T understand and they NEVER will. Quit beating your head against the wall trying to MAKE them understand. Only your brothers who were there will ever understand our pain." I found this to be true until I met Opal and Bill.

"I had been to The Wall once before, right after it was built. I was on a tour bus that was touring the major monuments in Washington. When the bus pulled up in front of The Wall, I began trembling. It was like I was facing a firing squad or one of those many, many rocket attacks in Vietnam. I absolutely could NOT get off the bus and face that pain. I just wasn't ready to deal with it.

Fig. 11-5: Korean War gold star mother Molly Snyder at the Korean War Veterans Memorial in Washington, D.C. *(AGSM Collection)*

"Shortly after meeting Opal, she invited me to go with her to the Memorial Day ceremony at The Wall in 1994. I never told Opal this, but I was scared; I was scared to death. But with her loving kindness, she urged me to go with her. This wasn't your typical urging. There was a deep urgency about it that seemed to say, "Trust me, I love you." Well, I went. I'm sure you have all seen the emotions that surface out of veterans at The Wall. I was no different, I guess. My male, macho, bubba-ego pride kept it in as long as it could, but when I broke, I broke. I finally allowed myself to cry. I cried for myself. I cried for my brothers on The Wall. I cried for my brothers in the tree line on the hill opposite The Wall who STILL can't come down. In Opal's arms, I cried for her and her son. I suddenly found myself surrounded by other Gold Star Mothers, mothers who had every right to be permanently crippled by their own pain over their own loss, but who have chosen to come out of the darkness into the light and help others in need. More healing took place in those moments in front of The Wall than had happened through months and months of therapy. And I owe it all to Opal and your fine organization.

"Your gold stars are more than an object on a wall in Washington. They are beacons of shining light to those of us whose ships have yet to come home. Never let them stop shining. God is working through you in ways you will never fully understand. I share your pain. I share your pride in your sons and daughters, and now, thank God, I share the joy you have brought into my life again through your healing love. God BLESS you, each and every one."[71]

Other Memorials

Other memorials took shape during this period. On the ninety-fifth birthday of Rose Kennedy in 1985, the City of Boston dedicated a Memorial Rose Garden to her and all gold star mothers. The one-acre garden features a granite fountain surrounded by fifty Japanese ornamental cherry trees and hundreds of tea roses. AGSM was represented at the dedication.[72]

A memorial program in Hawaii called "A Million Trees for Aloha" invited guests representing government, patriotic, and other organizations to plant memorial trees at the National Cemetery of the Pacific at Punchbowl near Honolulu. Punchbowl is the burial place for soldiers of World War II, Korea and Vietnam. On June 16, 1985, Ann Y. Sherman, a member of the Alexandria, Virginia chapter living in Hawaii, planted tree number ninety-two of one-hundred on behalf of American Gold Star Mothers, Inc. calling it "a living gift of love."[73]

In June 1986, the City of Chicago sponsored a three-day celebration of Vietnam vets, calling it a "knee-deep ticker-tape parade and welcome home party." Led by General William Westmoreland and two paraplegic veterans, the three-mile parade was the longest in Chicago's history, taking "nearly four hours to pass at any given point." Veterans participated from across the United States and were joined by Vietnam veterans from Australia and Canada. Many wives and children marched with the vets. Alongside the Governor of Illinois and the Mayor of Chicago, AGSM was represented in the reviewing stand by department and chapter members.[74] The Moving Wall, a half-sized replica of the Vietnam Veterans Memorial, was set up in Grant Park.

The gold star mothers themselves were the recipients of a memorial in Arlington National Cemetery in 1993. A Blue Atlas Cedar tree was planted and a bronze plaque dedicated "in honor of all Gold Star Mothers" in Section 2 of the cemetery, near the John F. Kennedy gravesite. The plaque shows AGSM's star logo and the words "Organized 1928." Members of AGSM participated in the tree planting and dedication on April 3, 1993.[75]

The veterans of America's "forgotten war" were honored in July 1995 with the dedication of the Korean War Veterans Memorial in Washington, D.C. A 164-foot-long reflective wall made of polished granite, nineteen larger-than-life statues of combat soldiers and a reflecting pool of still water in a grove of trees create a haunting tribute to the more than 36,000 U.S. soldiers who died in Korea.[76] [Fig,11-5]

To honor the twenty-seven Florida soldiers among the 241 American peacekeepers who died in the terrorist attack in Beirut, Lebanon, the Beirut Memorial was dedicated in May 1996 in North Miami Beach, Florida. The black granite monument reads: "They came in peace. Dedicated to the men of Florida who gave their lives in Beirut, 23 October 1983. Marines." On the back of the monument are inscribed the words "Beirut, Lebanon" "23 October 1983" and a large gold star. Members of AGSM from the Miami chapter participated in the dedication of the monument.[77]

Gold Star Home

The American Gold Star Home and Manor entered a difficult period in the 1980s when, for the first time, the organization had to go outside the ranks of gold star mothers to fill their vacancies. By 1987, only fifty gold star couples, mothers, and widowers were in residence at the home. That left nearly 300 apartments without gold star tenants and there was no waiting list for admittance as there had been in years past. It became necessary to open the home to "qualified tenants whose loss, backgrounds or interests are similar to the patriotic and service-connected interests of gold star mothers."[78] That included gold star fathers who were widowers, widows and widowers of war dead, and female veterans. Gold star mothers who subsequently applied for an apartment were given preference over the non-gold star tenants, but there was little interest from gold star mothers at this time. In 1992, the *Los Angeles Times* reported that just 71 of the 348 apartments were rented to gold star mothers.[79]

Numerous possibilities were cited for the lack of interest in the Gold Star Home among gold star mothers. Some blamed AGSM at the national level for not getting the word out to eligible gold star mothers, although members of AGSM were well aware of the

home and the organization had no method for contacting gold star mothers who did not join the group. Catherine Poteet, a Vietnam gold star mother who lived at the Home with her husband Ben, felt the complex might not be appealing to the gold star mothers of the Vietnam era because of their feelings about the war:

"Most of the Vietnam mothers I have talked to are still bitter, so upset because of the war that they don't want to be reminded of it by coming to a place like this. I've tried to explain to many mothers who are widows and lost sons in Vietnam that they could have a much better life if they moved here. We've had open houses, but Vietnam mothers did not come. Especially now with the recession, you would think they would want to move here, particularly if they were in need.[80]

AGSM and the Vietnam Veterans

Since the Vietnam War, the relationship between AGSM and Vietnam veterans has remained especially close. Veterans, both individually and in groups, have seemingly adopted the mothers and do everything they can to support them and their efforts (large and small):

"[In 1990,] two Vietnam veterans from Illinois… flew into D.C. bringing with them the young son of their buddy who had been missing in action since the helicopter he and three other service men were passengers on disappeared over Vietnam 22 years ago. Now the bodies of their buddy and his friends have been recovered from the crash site and returned to the United States for burial in Arlington Cemetery with full military honors. These Vietnam veterans and the son of their buddy were among those present for the burial … While at Headquarters they gave a donation of money, a beautiful plaque and not only that, they put three of our new air conditioners back into the windows after storage for winter in our basement. We thank them so much."[81]

In 1994, the VIETNOW organization donated a fax machine and computer to the national headquarters, a much appreciated gift for the mothers who were just beginning to enter the computer age.[82] In 1980, the mothers reported an unexpected benefit to having attended a VIETNOW dinner/dance, explaining "They asked for a donation of $10 to dance with a Gold Star Mother and $5 to cut in. They raised almost $1,000 for us."[83]

AGSM returned the favors whenever it could, working diligently on behalf of the Vietnam veterans. In 1989, the national executive board received a $15,000 grant from the Vietnam Veterans Aid Foundation to furnish Vietnam veteran-related material to all VA centers, including a video tape about the Vietnam Veterans Memorial. Finding that there was no appropriate video of "The Wall," in 1990 a video program called "Come to The Wall with the Gold Star Mothers" was developed and distributed. In 1991, they received a $7,500 grant to provide additional materials to all VA centers and to federal prisons where there were incarcerated Vietnam veterans.[84]

Sale of Headquarters

At the 1981 national convention, a resolution was approved to form a committee to look into the feasibility of selling AGSM's headquarters building as a cost-saving measure. In the November/December 1981 issue of *The Gold Star Mother,* the National Treasurer's Report and the Interim Report on Selling AGSM National Headquarters appeared side-by-side, representing opposing views of the necessity for such a sale.

National Treasurer Elizabeth F. Barber came down firmly on the side of selling the building. Her reasons included the continuing poor financial health of the organization; the apparently never-ending and always escalating costs of maintaining the more than eighty-year-old building; increasing property taxes; safety concerns such as no fire escape; infrequent use of the facility other than providing a home for the two national officers (national custodian of records and the director of publications) who lived at HQ to take care of day-to-day business; and no proven need or benefit to maintaining a headquarters property in the incredibly expensive District of Columbia. National president Mary Teater referred to the treasurer's report as "grim" but did not indicate that she felt it was inaccurate.[85]

Past national president Regina Wilk headed the committee charged with exploring the pros and cons of selling the property. In her report, she admitted that, for a period of time, finances had been difficult but AGSM was currently in good financial shape and was, in fact, investing in money market certificates which would provide a reserve should times again become difficult. Arguing that it did not make sense to sell the headquarters building, she cited the fact that although the building was more than eighty years old, it was still solid and well built; it was paid for entirely and taxes had recently been reduced. She also outlined the extremely high costs associated with holding events at a hotel or hall versus the small cost of opening Leroy Place for such events. She called headquarters a focal point for the organization and emphasized the importance of retaining what past members of the organization had worked so hard to provide. She refuted Mrs. Barber's claim that the building was not safe, stating that her son, a Washington D.C., fireman, would certainly not let her sleep in a building that was not safe.

The organization's constitution stated that the national headquarters could not be "encumbered, transferred, sold or otherwise disposed of without the consent of a two-thirds vote of delegates... at a national convention." In June 1982, just before the convention at which the sale of headquarters would be discussed, a letter was received from the Grace Seibold Chapter in Washington, D.C., protesting the potential sale and stating that the organization needed to stay where it was originally founded and where all branches of government could be found. The chapter had been using headquarters as their meeting location since it was purchased.

After much discussion of the potential sale at the 1982 national convention in St. Louis, Missouri, there was a motion for a written ballot on the issue. The resolution to sell AGSM's headquarters building was not passed.[86]

A Different Type of Pilgrimage

Robert Hammer is a southern California investment banker, a Marine, a Vietnam veteran and a man who keeps his promises. He promised his injured and dying buddies in Vietnam that he would see their mothers when he returned to the U.S. But when he met the gold star mothers of many of his combat brothers, he wasn't happy with what he saw. It seemed to him that the women received far too little recognition for the sacrifices they had made. And when he found that

very few had been able to travel to Washington, D.C., to visit the memorials to their sons, he decided to do something about it.

He started asking friends and organizations for contributions. He donated generously from his own funds. Finally, he had enough money to take a group of gold star mothers to the nation's capital where they could stand before the war memorials erected to honor their sons, the soldiers who died fighting for the nation. Only women who had never been able to make the trip were eligible to participate. To help keep costs down, the traveling mothers stayed at AGSM headquarters. At least four groups of mothers took this memorial pilgrimage during the late 1990s. As gold star mother Martha Arnold said, "It's so impressive to go back there and see your son or daughter's name on 'The Wall.' To see the veterans and have them call you 'mom' and to actually touch 'The Wall,' it's something every mother should do."[87]

Facing the Challenges

The final two decades of the twentieth century presented problems and challenges to AGSM that mothers of earlier decades could not have imagined. With the responsibility of leadership passing to the gold star mothers of an unpopular war, a war that for many reasons did not draw its gold star mothers in great numbers into AGSM fellowship as past wars had, there was still much to do but fewer resources with which to accomplish the work. Looking forward, the mothers realized that there were decisions and compromises to be made if the organization was to remain viable. What would become of the priorities if all of the traditional work of the organization could not continue? How would they maintain a cohesive organization as more chapters closed, making it difficult for the members who remained active to stay involved? As the century ended, these were the issues facing the members and leaders of American Gold Star Mothers, Inc.

Fig. 12-1: AGSM members gather at The Wall for a ceremony honoring those who fought and died in Operation Iraqi Freedom and Enduring Freedom.
(AGSM Collection)

CHAPTER 12

2000 and Beyond: New Wars and an Evolving Organization

I realized I was one in a long line of mothers from the American Revolution to the present… mothers who have watched their sons and daughters go into harm's way to protect our freedom. Along with the little gold pin I now wear, I have inherited a community of mothers and a lifetime of sharing their grief.

—RUTH STONESIFER,
AGSM National President[1]

A NEW YEAR, A NEW century, and a new millennium—Americans celebrated these new beginnings with hope and optimism. But on October 17, 2000, a terrorist attack by suicide bombers against the USS *Cole* killed seventeen Americans and injured dozens of others in a Yemen port that was thought to be safe. Terrorism had moved a step closer to home, although it was still possible to dismiss terrorism as something that happened in other lands. Less than a year later, that sense of safety ended.

On September 11, 2001, the nation learned that terrorism has no borders. Americans experienced a new emotion in addition to grief and horror, an emotion that had never before been part of our culture—vulnerability. Suddenly, Americans were part of the world in a terrifying new way.

Soon the nation was at war again, this time with an elusive enemy who viewed its efforts as a religious mission in which death would be rewarded. AGSM national president Judith C. Young described them as "a faceless enemy with deep anger and hatred for what America represents" and offered a frightening perspective on what the future would hold when she said "the war on terrorism, I believe, will never have a time frame."[2] As the War on Terrorism unfolded, many young Americans volunteered for the armed services to fight this new enemy and keep their nation safe. And, once again, the membership of American Gold Star Mothers, Inc., began to grow.

In addition to war, this first decade of the new century brought serious challenges to AGSM. Public challenges to organizational traditions, a seldom supportive press, new technology, and the controversial activities of gold star mothers who were not part of AGSM seemed to besiege the organization at every turn.

Presidents, Conventions, and Resolutions

Iris Walden
National President, 2000–2001
Born 1932 in Tennessee, Iris Fox Walden fell in love with a "young, handsome 82nd Airborne Paratrooper, Marion Frank Walden" and they married in 1950. The parents of five children, their son, PFC Marion Frank Walden Jr., died at nineteen years of age in Vietnam in December 1968, having served less than a year. Mrs. Walden was unaware of AGSM until 1982 when she and her husband traveled to the dedication of Vietnam Veterans Memorial where she met AGSM representatives. Returning home, she helped organize a new AGSM chapter, the Volunteer Chapter in Knoxville, Tennessee, in April 1983.[3]

It was during Mrs. Walden's term in office that the AGSM began to embrace the new communication technology. In the fall of 2000, a note in *The Gold Star Mother* stated that several mothers had forwarded their email addresses for communicating with the national organization.[4]

Georgianna Carter-Krell
National President, 2001–2002; 2008–2009

Mrs. Carter-Krell was born in August 1931 in Bennington, Vermont. Her son, Marine Pfc. Bruce Wayne Carter, died in Vietnam in 1969 at the age of nineteen. In 1972, he was posthumously awarded the Congressional Medal of Honor, the nation's highest award for valor in action against an enemy force, for "gallantry and intrepidity at the risk of his life above and beyond the call of duty" at Quang Tri Province on August 7, 1969:

"Pfc. Carter's unit was maneuvering against the enemy during Operation Idaho Canyon and came under a heavy volume of fire from a numerically superior hostile force. The lead element soon became separated from the main body of the squad by a brush fire. Pfc. Carter and his fellow marines were pinned down by vicious crossfire when, with complete disregard for his safety, he stood in full view of the North Vietnamese Army soldiers to deliver a devastating volume of fire at their positions. The accuracy and aggressiveness of his attack caused several enemy casualties and forced the remainder of the soldiers to retreat from the immediate area.

"Shouting directions to the marines around him, Pfc. Carter then commenced leading them from the path of the rapidly approaching brush fire when he observed a hostile grenade land between him and his companions. Fully aware of the probable consequences of his action but determined to protect the men following him, he unhesitatingly threw himself over the grenade, absorbing the full effects of its detonation with his body. Pfc. Carter's indomitable courage, inspiring initiative, and selfless devotion to duty upheld the highest traditions of the Marine Corps and the U.S. Naval Service. He gallantly gave his life in the service of his country."[5]

In 2008, the VA hospital in Miami was renamed as the Bruce W. Carter Department of Veterans Affairs Medical Center.

Mrs. Carter-Krell joined AGSM in 1976. A force to be reckoned with in her volunteer work, she had already been recognized for giving more than 5,500 hours of volunteer service over ten years in Florida. A friend and admirer wrote of Georgie:

"It is the quality of your caring that most impresses me. You totally listen to the person you are with. You take care of our veterans as if each one were Bruce. You plunk on a Santa hat and pass out candy at Christmas. You know the Easter Bunny. You are tireless in your committees and organization. You zip someone around in a wheelchair at top speed. You spread cheer to anyone who is sick. You share your time and energy with others, along with kind words, a sense of humor and sometimes a few cuss words."[6]

Georgie brought that same energy and strength to AGSM as she led the organization in the days following the attacks on September 11, 2001. Just two weeks after the attacks, she led the traditional Gold Star Mother's Day wreath-laying ceremony at Arlington National Cemetery. But her comments were non-traditional and heartfelt:

"Each year the Gold Star Mothers come here to Arlington National Cemetery to honor our sons and daughters. Usually we honor the service members who gave their lives for our great country. This year, however, the nation's fallen includes ever so many more. This afternoon, along with our military veterans, we honor the nearly 6,500 men, women and children who died on September 11. On that day, an enemy breached our homeland—and as many have said—our lives will never be the same.

"In a way, I am glad my son was not here to see those horrible, horrible scenes at the World Trade Center and Pentagon. My Bruce—a Marine through and through—he'd want to take on those terrorists with his bare hands. Heck, come to think of it, so would I! But, it's not up to an old woman from Miami. It's up to our Armed Forces to defend America and they will."[7]

Mrs. Carter-Krell was re-elected as national president for the 2008–2009 term. It was the first time in fifty years that an AGSM national president had been elected to serve more than a single term.

Dorothy Oxendine
National President, 2002–2003

Born in Middle Village, Long Island, New York, Dorothy married Willie Oxendine, a friend of her brother, in 1945. They had three children. Their son, Willie French Oxendine III (Frenchy), followed his father into the Marine Corps. A paratrooper, Frenchy died in May 1968 while on a reconnaissance patrol, just two months after arriving in Vietnam. Hoping to keep her mind busy after Frenchy's death, Mrs. Oxendine taught medical assisting at night as well as working full-time. For twenty-eight years she worked as a medical assistant, most of the time as an office manager. She also attended a school of theology and became a Eucharistic Minister, subsequently receiving the Bishop's Medal, the highest honor afforded a lay person, for her work.

Mrs. Oxendine joined AGSM in 1969 and her love of the organization "gave her the healing she was searching for."[8] In 2003, she spoke of the comfort that she experienced when visiting the Vietnam Veterans Memorial:

"No matter what the occasion, nor how many times I visit 'The Wall,' it is always a healing experience. The peace and solitude let me renew my faith; the companionship of those who have suffered the same loss helps ease the burden; the compassion of so many veterans and their families comfort me."[9]

Ann Y. Sherman Wolcott
National President, 2003–2004

Mrs. Wolcott's son, Cpl. Rex M. Sherman, died in November 1969 at the age eighteen. He was an Airborne Ranger with the 75th Infantry Regiment, Charlie Company. The Rangers' motto was "Rangers Lead the Way" and Mrs. Wolcott borrowed that phrase for the theme of her year in office—'Leading the Way.'[10]

Mrs. Wolcott's end-of-term convention was held in Norfolk, Virginia. Although the membership had been slowly growing as gold star mothers of the Iraq and Afghanistan wars joined, for reasons unknown attendance at the convention was the smallest ever reported —just thirty-eight registered delegates. In her final speech as national president, she described her year in office as "very difficult and emotional," citing the loss of more than 800 servicemen and women in Iraq and Afghanistan.[11] She also noted:

"My trip to Vietnam was the highlight of my year… That trip brought everything together for me. I do not believe in 'closure' but I can see more clearly now. I have reconciled my thoughts about the war in Vietnam and my son dying there. I have finally accepted that it happened. I can move forward and devote my life to his mission, which was Peace, Country and caring for others, as I have always done."[12]

Ann Herd
National President, 2004–2005

Born in 1927 in Sulphur Springs, Texas, Ann married Buster Herd following high school. They had four children; their son, Ronnie, died in August 1970 in Vietnam.

Mrs. Herd didn't become aware of AGSM until 1997. In her parting speech at the national convention in Dallas, Texas, she expressed her thanks to a group that had offered AGSM support for many decades:

"I want to thank the veterans for the many ways they have supported the gold star mothers. All the good times they have made possible for us; just being with us was enough. We have told them many times that they are our other sons and how much their hugs mean to us."[13]

Judith C. Young
National President, 2005–2006

With the terrorist attack on the Marine barracks in Beirut, Lebanon in 1983, Judith C. Young became a gold star mother. She and her husband, Jack Young, were the parents of two sons. Marine Sgt. Jeffery Dennis Young died October 23, 1983, in the attack against the Peacekeepers in Beirut. Their other son also served in the Marines from 1984–1988. In 1984, she began the *Beirut Connection,* a newsletter for the families and veterans of Beirut attack.

Mrs. Young came into office at a time when AGSM was under attack from the public, lawmakers, and gold star mothers over the requirement of American citizenship to become a member of AGSM. The issue had developed with wildfire speed in the media and careless comments made by some members of AGSM fanned the flames, compromising the organization's ability to deal quickly with the issue. In her acceptance speech as national president, Mrs. Young spoke of the damage that had been done to the organization:

"We have our work cut out for us this year. A lot of fences need to be mended. Our organization is under close scrutiny for everything it does in the next few months. Some people have set out to destroy all the good works that thousands of moms have done all these years and we cannot let their sacrifices be tarnished. A good many people have never heard of the American Gold Star Mothers and therefore are ill informed, but that did not stop them from passing judgment."[14]

Just a month into Mrs. Young's term as national president, another controversy shook the organization. Cindy Sheehan, an anguished mother who lost a son in Iraq, demanded that President George W. Bush meet with her to discuss the war and the loss of her son. A gold star mother by her loss, but not a member of AGSM, she made headlines that brought the wrath of the uninformed public down on AGSM in the belief that the organization had a connection with Mrs. Sheehan and therefore supported her vitriolic commentary.

Mrs. Young's business background in banking led to an overhaul of the traditional AGSM record-keeping systems, using computer-based programs that simplified the processes while making additional detail available. She told the membership that "we should embrace the technology that's available to us to keep up with change."[15]

Betty Pulliam
National President, 2006–2007
A Kansas farm girl, Betty married in 1942, a marriage that lasted fifty-six years. An Army veteran, her husband had survived five major World War II battles including the Battle of the Bulge and the landing at Normandy. They had four children. The oldest, Stan, served in the Marine Corps for three years before his death in Vietnam.

At the urging of her granddaughter, Mrs. Pulliam took up competitive running at age sixty-five and competed successfully in many races.

Mary Jane Kiepe
National President, 2007–2008
Born in Lawrencetown, Missouri, Mrs. Keipe took up secretarial work after finishing high school. She met her husband, Glenn, when he returned from four years in the Air Force. They had five children. Her son, Lt. Kent Michael Keipe, was a Naval aviator who flew a FA/18 Hornet. He served in Operation Desert Shield, then lost his life at age twenty-nine in a Navy air crash while serving at Point Mugu Naval Air Weapons Station in California. When her youngest child entered school, Mrs. Keipe went to school as well and became a licensed practical nurse. She worked for twenty years as a physical therapy assistant before retiring.

Ruth Stonesifer
National President, 2009–2010
Ruth's son, Kristofor, was deployed as an Army Ranger following the September 11, 2001 attacks on U.S. soil. Specialist Stonesifer died in the crash of a Black Hawk helicopter on October 19, 2001, the first night of Operation Enduring Freedom. In addition to being a proud gold star mother, Ruth is the mother of retired Army Chief Warrant Officer Frederic Stonesifer and has three very active grandchildren.

Originally from Middletown, Delaware, Ruth re-

ceived her Bachelor's of Science in Home Economics from the University of Delaware. She now lives in southeastern Pennsylvania. A potter, a wearable art craftsman, and now a long-arm quilter, she teaches quilting classes and runs a Quilts of Valor program that makes presentation quilts for the wounded soldiers at Walter Reed Medical Center.

Following her son's death, Ruth quickly became involved in AGSM. She later recalled with humor how she suddenly became a member of the national executive board:

"In June of 2005, just as I was about to make a clean get-away from my second AGSM convention experience, I was asked by Judith, the incoming national president, to become the Director of Communications and Corresponding Secretary. Oh, yes, the job description was a little vague, and I quote: 'You'll just have a few letters to write.'"[16]

Molly Morel
National President, 2010–2011
Molly Morel was elected national president at the 73rd National Convention which was held in Plymouth Meeting, Pennsylvania. She and husband Mike had two children—Brent and Marcy. Her son, Marine Captain Brent L. Morel, died April 7, 2004, just three weeks after being deployed to Iraq. A Recon Marine, he was leading security for a convoy when his lead Humvee was attacked by rocket-propelled grenades.

Two events that occurred during Molly's time in office stand out in her memory:

"The most special was our fundraising campaign for Fisher House. [Fisher Houses provide lodging for military families to be near a loved one during hospitalization for an illness, disease or injury.] As we kicked off the campaign, Fisher House staff contacted me to ask if we would be interested in choosing a house to support that was about to break ground at Dover AFB.

"With Dover being the central mortuary for the military, and my own son having come to Dover on his final flight, I knew that I would do my best to convince the national executive board that we should select it as our project. Everyone, of course, felt the same emotions that I did. The Fisher House project was my idea, and I wanted to go full force. The staff at Fisher House suggested that we choose a goal that set the bar high without being unreasonable. After convincing the board that we should start at no less than $50,000, we set that as our goal. In fairly short order, we had passed the $50,000 mark and raised the bar to $60,000. We ended the campaign at just over $80,000! There were so many naysayers in our group; we had never done a national campaign like this before.

"It began late in Ruth Stonesifer's term and we were invited to Dover AFB for the ground-breaking ceremony. As AGSM's national president, Ruth was asked to break ground with other dignitaries. I was so proud to be there. At the dedication, I was asked to help cut the ribbon with two other ladies. It will always be first in my mind as the best thing that I did. When Brent was killed in 2004, families were not allowed to go to Dover. The Dover Fisher House is now available to families like ours and for the escort officers who were perform such an important job.

"The other huge event that was extremely meaningful to me was participating in the Wreaths across America convoy from Maine to Arlington National Cemetery. We stopped at numerous schools and events along the way, educating about WAA's program of 'Remember, Honor & Teach'. Placing wreaths on graves in Section 60 meant a lot to me."

Norma Luther
National President, 2011–2012
Norma Luther was elected as national president in June 2011 at the convention in Nashville, Tennessee. Born in West Virginia, she and her husband Jim raised three children. Her oldest son, Captain Glen P. Adams, Jr., was a West Point graduate. He died in a helicopter crash on a foggy mountain pass in Germany on April 5, 1988 at the age of 27.

Norma read about AGSM in a book she checked out of the library on grief. She contacted Emogene Cupp's chapter in Virginia. Norma credits Emogene, a Vietnam-era gold star mother and past national president of AGSM, with showing her that life can go on and be worth living if you become involved in doing something for others. Working with veterans and the homeless, Norma found, as so

many gold star mothers before her had discovered, that working for others helps the griever move forward and grow.

Norma's goal during her year as national president is to double AGSM's membership by reaching out to the mothers of non-combat casualties (accidents, training accidents and other incidents related to military service) as well as combat moms. "There are thousands of gold star mothers out there who don't know they are eligible for membership or have never heard of us. I want to fix that," she says.

A Decade of Public Controversy

During this decade, AGSM was repeatedly been in the public eye, often in situations that they would not have chosen, had there been a choice. AGSM's public image was tarnished unfairly by these crises and the organization has worked hard to establish the public respect that they had always enjoyed.

AGSM came face-to-face with the power of the Internet early in 2001 when a false and misleading story about the organization appeared and flashed across cyberspace at light speed.

As originally reported by *www.newsmax.com* on May 26, 2001, a delegation of New York gold star mothers visiting the Capitol in February was able to meet with every one of their elected representatives except one—Hillary Clinton. Senator Clinton's detractors immediately jumped on the story, gleefully claiming that she had refused repeated requests to meet with the gold star mothers and had snubbed them on the day of their visit.

As quickly as possible, AGSM posted a statement on their website about the false report, stating that they "deeply regret the misunderstanding about Senator Hillary Clinton" and they "would appreciate it if the emails and negative comments about Senator Clinton would cease." They reported the facts of the incident in the statement. The two gold star mothers visiting that day did not have an ap-

Fig. 12-2: Senator Hillary Clinton and a group of gold star mothers. *(AGSM Collection)*

pointment and were not an official AGSM delegation. Their visit was spontaneous and no meeting had been requested in advance. Even more to the point, Senator Clinton wasn't even in her office that day.

AGSM learned a bitter lesson about the Internet with this debacle. Anyone can post a news item or e-rumor, whether factual, flawed or false, but it is almost impossible to correct or stop a story once it has hit the Web. Three months later, despite extensive efforts to clarify and stop the story, the *Albany Times-Union* reported that, based on comments from a former New York Republican Congressman, the Tri-County Council of Vietnam Veterans had revived the rumor and "reprinted [an] Internet-published column... lambasting Clinton for 'snubbing' the ladies during a visit to Washington."[17]

One of the mothers involved later admitted that the story had been "blown out of proportion, in a way" and the situation had been, in part, the result of wounded pride:

"[The mothers] were disappointed when they stopped by Clinton's office to lobby for legislation to provide annuities for Gold Star parents and weren't even given a few moments with a staff member. She said Clinton's receptionist seemed oblivious to Gold Star Mothers, the Vietnam War and the losses American families suffered because of it."[18]

Senator Clinton apologized about the mothers' reception, citing that the temporary basement office she was assigned in the first few months of her term was understaffed and the skeleton staff she did have was undertrained. Her staff had subsequently reached out to communicate with the gold star mothers about the legislation and many other issues. A spokesman said, "Senator Clinton, who is the daughter of a veteran herself, has enormous respect for Gold Star Mothers and the heroism and tremendous sacrifice of their children."[19] A cordial relationship between AGSM and Senator Clinton subsequently developed.

Four years later, AGSM reported that Headquarters was still receiving weekly inquiries about the Hillary Clinton–gold star mothers rumor. Referring to it as an urban legend, readers were advised that the facts appeared on *www.snopes.com,* a website devoted to determining the truth about stories appearing on the Web. With wry pride, it was announced that "we made it to the Top 10 list of urban legends!"[20] In 2010, a clarifying statement about the story still appeared on the American Gold Star Mothers, Inc., website under "Frequently Asked Questions."

Since 1928, when AGSM was founded, one membership requirement had not changed—a gold star mother must be an American citizen to be eligible to join AGSM. Some World War I applicants had proudly reported that, after having spent decades in the United States, they had become an American citizen in order to apply for AGSM membership. In World War II, mothers who were not citizens were disappointed to find they were not eligible for membership and there was some limited commentary about the issue in the press. However, those mothers also became citizens in order to belong to the organization; in fact, one mother was sworn in as a member of AGSM in the courtroom immediately following the ceremony at which she became an American citizen. In 2005, AGSM's membership requirement for citizenship was again challenged—by design and very publically.

A group of Veterans of Foreign Wars (VFW) members in Yonkers, New York, had become aware of AGSM's citizenship requirement and decided that it should be changed, even though, ironically, the VFW itself required its members to be American citizens. Ben Spadaro, a past senior commander of a New York VFW post who spoke for the small group of activists, said, "I don't want to hurt anyone. We're just a bunch of old men who want to see a wrong righted."[21] But in order to launch their crusade, they needed a gold star mother who was not a citizen to submit an application for AGSM membership. Spadaro said, "We decided to tell the absolute truth on the application. We put down 'not an American citizen.' It was a ploy to get them to reject her and then we said they should change the rules... The only way we were going to straighten this thing out is by exposing the fact that they discriminate against other gold star mothers."[22]

The group found their gold star mother in Yonkers. Ligaya Lagman was the mother of Anthony Lagman, an Army staff sergeant who died in a 2004 firefight in Afghanistan at the age of twenty-six. Anthony Lagman was a United States citizen; his mother, Filipino by birth, was a permanent resident who had lived in the United States for more than twenty years. Anthony's death made Mrs. Lagman a gold star mother in the eyes of the United States government and the public—eligible for her son's military insurance benefits if so assigned and eligible for the government's gold star lapel button commonly referred to as the gold star pin or the gold star mothers pin. The VFW group told Mrs. Lagman about AGSM and when she expressed interest, they filled out the application for her, knowing that it would be rejected because of citizenship.

The application was sent to AGSM headquarters in Washington, D.C. When received, it was forwarded without review to the treasurer of the New York State Department for handling, in accordance with organizational policy. According to AGSM, when it was reviewed by the Department treasurer, it was found to be incomplete:

"It was not completed or signed by the applicant, nor did it have the required copy of the death certificate and the payment of the first year's dues. There were several inaccuracies on the application as to the dates required. A certified letter was mailed to Mrs. Lagman requesting the application be completed in full and returned for approval."[23]

Mr. Spadaro disputed that, stating "a completed application was sent to the organization's headquarters … and he watched Lagman sign it."[24] He also reported that, prompted by inquiries from the VFW group, AGSM's national executive board had previously met to discuss the citizenship issue but "voted against the change."[25]

When Mrs. Lagman received the correspondence from AGSM, the VFW group went public. AGSM was blindsided by an explosion of media coverage and furious public commentary that included "threats, malicious accusations and disturbing emails, phone calls and faxes."[26] First vice president Judith Young reported that they received more than 18,000 emails and phone calls in just a few days, almost all of them demanding a change.

Posting a statement on their website, AGSM attempted to clarify the facts: the application had been incomplete when received and could not be processed without additional information; the board had voted at a prior meeting not to make changes to the constitution and by-laws without proper investigation but no vote had been taken regarding the citizenship requirement; and the national board had been unaware of Mrs. Lagman's application when that meeting had taken place and no vote regarding membership had been taken.[27]

AGSM asked for time to deal with the issue in accordance with their organizational constitution and by-laws, which required approval of changes by the mem-

bership meeting in convention. Shocked and heartsick over the vitriolic communications they were receiving, they also clarified their mission:

"This organization of moms joined together to support each other and also support the veterans who are fortunate to [have] come home. They have spent the last 77 years devoting their time and energy in service to the Veterans Administration, volunteering in VA hospitals and nursing homes, accruing millions of hours helping those who honorably served their country."[28]

It quickly became apparent that there was internal discord in AGSM about the issue. National president Ann Herd appeared to take a hard line on the issue when she wrote "my heart goes out to her, but we have rules we have to go by":

"To remove the word 'American' from the title of the organization, and to change the by-laws would require demolishing the entire organization and building a new one. I am sure you understand this is not feasible. We [do not] discriminate nor do we want to turn away any mothers who have suffered the pain of a loss such as ours; however, the organization was founded as such and the repercussions of changing it at this point are devastatingly many."[29]

Dorothy Oxendine, a past national AGSM president, took a different position:

"I don't care if she's a citizen or not, she still has the same grief, and her family is going through the same thing that I'm going through or any other gold star mother is going through. How could you discriminate?"[30]

Judith Young, national first vice president and in line to be elected national president at the AGSM national convention to be held in less than a month, acknowledged that the issue required investigation, but cautioned that changes required approval by AGSM membership:

"The charter was written 77 years ago and we're in the next generation, I realize that. Things have changed, times have changed, people have changed… [but] it's not something you just Wite-Out or change."[31]

Worried about her hospitalized husband and "shaken up" by the public response and the attention she was receiving, Mrs. Lagman dropped her bid to become a member.[32] Her son, Chris Lagman, who remained a voice of calm and reason during the uproar, asked the media to spare his mother so she could care for her very ill husband. "All she wants is recognition as the mother of this fallen soldier," he said. He later commented that "the family does not want to break apart the organization or form a new one, but to 'correct the mistake' that bars non-Americans from joining."[33]

The Florida chapter of AGSM adopted a resolution calling for the national organization to let non-citizens join. Past national president Georgianna Carter-Krell told the press that the chapter would push for a rule change at the upcoming annual convention. Referring to the earlier national executive board discussion about citizenship that had ended with agreement that further examination of the issue would be needed, she said:

"That... was because we had a couple of hard-noses on there, and we just didn't fight them. But we're not going to put up with that now. Right now, we are forcing it and it's going to go through... We've been piddling with this for awhile. Years ago, we wanted everyone to become an American citizen. This goes back to 1928, let's face it. It hasn't been brought up in awhile ... so it... just got left behind."[34]

A day later, Mrs. Carter-Krell admitted that she expected a fight over the issue:

"That doesn't mean the convention is going to approve it. We're going to have a couple of hard-noses there that are going to filibuster, and it might take days. It's really going to be a mess. There's going to be tears and hair-pulling. Really."[35]

There was still one impediment before the issue could be brought before the membership at the convention. Resolutions had to be filed at least thirty days before the convention in order to be eligible for consideration and the Florida resolution had not met that deadline. But the national executive board had the authority to grant exceptions and thereby allow the proposal to be brought before the delegates.

At the convention, one reporter found that despite the anticipation of "arguments and hair pulling ... the animosity seems to have settled down."[36] Even those who had originally taken a hard line on the issue had softened their stance, recognizing that tremendous harm was being done to the organization by the controversy and it had to be dealt with. Many members had threatened to resign if the policy continued. The majority of the members appeared to agree with past national president Ann Wolcott who said:

"The world isn't like it was in 1928 [noting there were 30,000 non-citizens serving in the U.S. armed forces at the present time]. Times have changed, people have changed and it's time for organizations to change. I don't care where the mothers are from. They gave their blood, they gave their children to this country's military service."[37]

At the convention when it was proposed to suspend the rule requiring thirty days notice for resolutions, the delegates voted unanimously to suspend it. This opened the way for the resolution to be brought forward. A discussion followed on the "very serious problem" of continuing to require citizenship as a membership requirement. Letters from legislators, the military and the public were read. When it was proposed to add the words "or Legal Resident" to the membership and eligibility section of the constitution and by-laws, one vote was taken and the resolution was passed with just three "no" votes. Membership in AGSM would henceforth be open to gold star mothers who were "citizens or legal residents" of the United States.

New national president Judith Young later commented that "this change to our constitution was the right thing to do, but we had to make the change the right way" and that AGSM would "continue to be evolutionary, not reactionary."[38] Mrs. Lagman and two other gold star mothers who were legal residents soon joined the organization.

Before the dust had settled from the 2005 convention, another controversy overtook AGSM. Although the organization was only a bystander in this case and Mrs. Sheehan was not a member of AGSM, the nation's confusion about gold star mothers and AGSM drew the organization deeply into the fray.

Army Specialist Casey Austin Sheehan was a twenty-four-year-old Humvee mechanic who served with the 1st Battalion, 82nd Field Artillery Regiment, 1st Cavalry Division out of Fort Hood, Texas. He enlisted in 2000; after completing his tour of duty, he re-enlisted in order to stay with his unit although he knew they would be sent to Iraq. Casey died on April 4, 2004, at the age of twenty-four when his unit was attacked in a fire-fight outside Baghdad. He had volunteered for the mission in which he died and was one of seven American soldiers who died in that battle. Casey was posthumously awarded the Purple Heart and Bronze Star with V for Valor.

On November 4, 2004, Casey's mother, Cindy Sheehan, wrote a scathing public letter to President George W. Bush, filled with the heartbreak that every gold star mother knows. In it, she laid the responsibility for her son's death on the president and his policies:

"George, it has been seven months today since your reckless and wanton foreign policies killed my son, my big boy, my hero, my best-friend: Casey. It has been seven months since your ignorant and arrogant lack of planning for… peace murdered my oldest child."

Referring to a public comment the president had made about working hard, Mrs. Sheehan gave him a gold star mother's perspective on hard work:

"Hard work is seeing your oldest son, your brave and honorable man-child go off to a war that had, and still has, no basis in reality. Hard work is worrying yourself gray and not being able to sleep for two weeks because you don't know if your child is safe.

"Hard work is seeing your son's murder on CNN one Sunday evening while you're enjoying the last supper you'll ever truly enjoy again.

"Hard work is having three military officers come to your house a few hours later to confirm the aforementioned murder of your son… your first born… your kind and gentle sweet baby.

"Hard work is burying your child 46 days before his 25th birthday. Hard work is holding your other three children as they lower the body of their big 'baba' into the ground. Hard work is not jumping in the grave with him and having the earth cover you both.

"But, Dear George, do you know what the hardest work of all is? Trying to digest the fact that the leader of the country that your family has fought for and died for, for generations, lied to you and betrayed your dear boy's sense of honor and exploited his courage and exploited his loyalty to his buddies. Hard work is having your country abandon you after they killed your son. Hard work is coming to the realization that your son had his future robbed from him and that you have had your son's future and future grand-children stolen from you. Hard work is knowing that there are so many people in this world that have prospered handsomely from your son's death."

Unable to meet or speak with President Bush, Cindy Sheehan and a group of followers camped out at the edge of President Bush's ranch property in Crawford, Texas, vowing to stay there until the president agreed to meet with her. Despite the summer heat and arid surroundings, Camp Casey grew to include hundreds of protesters, some staying there full-time and others coming and going. Her vigil attracted international attention and support. Mrs. Sheehan and others formed a

Fig. 12-3: A sketch of AGSM Headquarters in 2000. (*AGSM Collection*)

group—American Gold Star Families for Peace—to further their efforts to end the wars in the Middle East.

The coverage of Mrs. Sheehan's activities soon brought unwanted attention to AGSM. Mistaking Mrs. Sheehan's group for AGSM, thousands of hate-filled emails and telephone messages bombarded AGSM headquarters. AGSM national president Judith Young reported, "I had someone call me at our Washington headquarters, call me a bitch, and hang up. We were slimeballs, low-lifes. Another caller threatened to kick me in the butt, and someone else was going to slap me in the face."[39]

AGSM was not the only national military family group that was under attack. Several groups issued a joint statement on August 23, 2005, seeking to distance themselves from the Sheehan group:

"The American Gold Star Mothers, Inc., Gold Star Wives of America, Inc., Sons and Daughters in Touch and American WWII Orphans Network object to 'American Gold Star Families for Peace' misusing the term 'Gold Star' in its political demonstrations.

Fig. 12-4: The Gold Star Mother Memorial at Kent, New York by sculptor Andrew L. Chernak was dedicated on July 2, 2006. *(AGSM Collection)*

"These four organizations—representing the mothers, wives and children of U.S. service personnel killed in WWII, Korea, Vietnam, Iraq, Afghanistan and other U.S. military conflicts—are nonpolitical and do not take a position on the merits of the political demonstration being carried out by the group calling themselves 'American Gold Star Families for Peace.'

"Our loved ones gave their lives to protect the freedom to protest, and we know all too well the pain that these families are now suffering. However, the Gold Star symbol—authorized by Congress to honor a family's loss in service to our nation—must not be tarnished by partisan political demonstrations."[40]

Fig. 12-5: Sculptor Andrew L. Chernak and gold star mothers at the dedication of the Gold Star Mother Memorial. *(AGSM Collection)*

On August 25, 2005 AGSM posted a statement on their website clarifying that there was no connection between AGSM and the Sheehan group:

"Cindy Sheehan is currently in the news. She and her organization have no connection whatever with American Gold Star Mothers, Inc. We... do not engage in political activities. We do support our troops. They are, after all, our children."[41]

Cindy Sheehan eventually turned her anti-war efforts to other forums and as the publicity subsided, so did the pressure on AGSM. But as late as 2010, the statement above still remained on the AGSM website's list of frequently asked questions.

Deaths

The first decade of the new century was marked by the loss of many of AGSM's past national presidents. They included:

> Katherine M. Mannion (national president 1980–1981) died in June 2002
> Anna Biber (national president 1989–1990) died in December 2002
> Jeanne Penfold (national president 1993–1994) died in January 2005
> Opal Johnson (national president 1986–1987) died in December 2004
> Regina Wilk (national president 1977–1978) died in November 2004

Nora J. Golsh (national president 1985–1986) died in December 2007

In 2003, gold star father Dr. Victor Westphall died. Dr. Westphall had built the Vietnam Veterans Peace and Brotherhood Chapel at Angel Fire, New Mexico, as a tribute to his son and all those who died in Vietnam, hoping it would become a symbol of peace for future generations.

Membership

In 2001, AGSM reported a membership of 1,089 individuals including associate members (dads and siblings); 64 of the members were over ninety years of age. As the membership declined and the mothers aged, chapter after chapter had closed, leaving some states without a single active AGSM chapter. In 2003, the *Seattle Times* reported that "in Washington, once-flourishing chapters in Seattle and Tacoma have closed, leaving only the Spokane chapter, one of a few remaining in the nation."[42] In 2004, the Department of Washington, Oregon, and Idaho closed, leaving no active chapters in that corner of the nation.[43] National president Judith Young reported in 2006:

"Thirty years ago when our veteran Vietnam moms were joining, many states had dozens of chapters and they had somewhere to belong. Using New Jersey as an example, there were 27 chapters and now there are six with none having had meetings in years."[44]

AGSM was caught in a delicate balancing act and needed time. There were new gold star mothers out there. According to a spokesman for the American Legion, "sales of blue star banners have exploded since our forces landed in Iraq."[45] The gold star mothers of AGSM knew only too well that when there were blue star banners, many of those stars would sadly turn to gold. As in decades past, the organization needed to make itself known to this generation of gold star mothers from these new conflicts and offer them sympathy, support, and a place to belong. Past national president Emogene Cupp, a Vietnam-era gold star mother, observed in 2004 that:

"The mothers of this war's casualties seem more willing to join than those from other more recent conflicts, including the Gulf War. The Vietnam mothers didn't join as readily as in other wars because it was to them like it was to the boys. It wasn't welcome. Everybody seems to have more sympathy for the mothers now than they did for us. There seems to be more

patriotism, for sure."[46]

Nonetheless, by 2005, membership rolls reflected only 935 members.

In early 2007, the *Los Angeles Times* reported that AGSM currently had 145 chapters, down from a post-World War II high of more than 550. Some of the remaining chapters had only one member. And while a few new chapters were forming—the Azalea Chapter in North Carolina, the Scenic Chapter in Georgia—seemingly nothing could be done to stop the closing of the older chapters:

"Just when a new chapter of Iraq moms popped up in Tennessee, the Toledo group fell apart as its five remaining mothers moved into nursing homes. There are no Nevada chapters anymore; those mothers have had to join what's left in California. And one 85-year old woman is single-handedly representing the entire state of Delaware."[47]

During this time, out of necessity, a change came about in how AGSM business was conducted. In the past, the focus of the members had been at their chapter level. The mothers communicated with their chapter officers; the chapter officers communicated with the department officers; and the department officers communicated with the national board. It had been an efficient process and, given the size of the organization in past decades, it had enabled the organization to interact smoothly at all levels.

Now, however, with members in locations where there were no chapters to join, a change occurred. Aided by technology that enabled them to reach out instantly across the United States, like email, Internet, and cell phones, the individual members, in essence, became the chapters. Where a dozen gold star mothers might have attended a serviceman's funeral, now a single gold star mother might represent the organization. Where twenty-five mothers might have volunteered at a VA hospital, now just one gold star mother and friends she recruited might represent the organization. The Internet enabled the gold star mothers of a specific war to bond together, creating virtual chapters that shared a common bond although the members might be thousands of miles apart. Individual members could reach out instantly to the officers at the national level for support and advice. The profile of AGSM had changed—it had been leveled in such a way that there was a closer bond between the members and the national organization and more independence at the member level.

Technology also made it easier for gold star mothers to access information about AGSM. In the past, a gold star mother might have had to rely on word-of-mouth information or a random newspaper article to learn about AGSM. Even if the mother has never heard of AGSM, a simple Internet search now connects her with the AGSM website (www.goldstarmoms.com) where she can read about the history and purpose of the organization, learn what the membership requirements are, see a report on recent activities and get news about upcoming events.

Late in the decade, membership again began to rise. The gold star mothers of Iraq and Afghanistan became more aware of AGSM and what it stood for. Their worst grief was perhaps behind them. As it had to their sisters of earlier conflict, AGSM offered the solace of shared loss and a community of shared purpose. In 2008, a membership turning point was reached where essentially half the membership was from the Vietnam era and the other half was post-Vietnam membership. Forty new members joined in January/February of 2008; forty-nine new members joined in September/October of 2008; and in November/December of 2009, sixty-two new members joined. By January 2010, AGSM had 1,800 members with new members joining every month. A new generation of gold star mothers would be ready to carry on.

Memorials

Although the public law authorizing the construction of a World War II memorial was signed in 1993, it took eleven years for the memorial to come to fruition. Situated between the Lincoln Memorial and the Washington Monument, the site was dedicated in 1995. Funded largely by private contributions, nearly $200 million dollars was collected to complete the Memorial. Groundbreaking was held on Veterans Day 2000, although there was still controversy over the location and design of the memorial. Actor Tom Hanks joined President William Clinton, World War II veteran and former senator Bob Dole and a crowd of 7,000 at the groundbreaking ceremony. But the highlight of the event was Winifred Lancy, a World War II gold star mother and member of AGSM for more than fifty-five years. At 101, she was the nation's oldest surviving World War II gold star mother.[48] A delegation of AGSM members were part of the groundbreaking cer-

emony. The memorial was opened to the public in April 2004 and officially dedicated one month later.[49]

America's first gold star mother statue was dedicated in Putnam County, New York, in July 2006. [Fig. 12-3] A bronze life-sized statue of a grief-stricken World War II woman holding a crumpled telegram illustrates the grief of a gold star mother at the moment she learns that her child has been killed in the military. Sculptor Andrew Chernak's design was chosen by AGSM national president Dorothy Oxendine for its expression of the "the dignity and strength that co-existed with the grief and sorrow."[50] The statue was unveiled before a crowd of gold star mothers from several states and many dignitaries:

"The customary applause did not happen at the moment of unveiling. Three minutes of silence was broken by staggered sobs and sighs. The smiles on the tear streaked faces of the Gold Star Mothers gave testimony that the project was worth the four years of effort on the part of so many."[51]

AGSM is now putting together support to have a similar statue be placed in a park in Washington, D.C.

A new form of tribute came about during this decade—gold star license plates. By 2010, forty-five of the fifty states had either already distributed or authorized official gold star license plates to be developed. In some states, only gold star mothers are eligible to purchase the plates; in others, extended gold star family members are eligible. Each state has designed its own gold star plates and AGSM members have been a vital force in getting approval for the plates in various states.

The American Gold Star Home and Manor

In April 2008 Rear Admiral John Higginson (USN Ret.), president and chief executive officer of the American Gold Star Home and Manor, retired after fifteen years of managing the Home and caring for its residents. Businessman and past Home trustee, Terry Geiling, was elected to take over the helm of the Home. John Higginson died in January 2010 following a long illness.

Pilgrimages

As it had in earlier wars, the desire to visit the place where their son or daughter had died continued to be universal among many gold star mothers. A Vietnam veteran, hearing a Vietnam-era gold star mother express such a wish while visiting the Vietnam Veterans Memorial, decided to do something about it. The National Dusters-Quads-Searchlights Association, a group of Vietnam veterans, began to raise funds that would enable them to escort gold star mothers to Vietnam and show them the places that had been known to their children. In early 2000, a notice appeared in *The Gold Star Mother* announcing that an opportunity was available to travel to Vietnam and several trips were planned. It also cautioned that "top physical condition" was required as well as "a release from your doctor."[52]

The first trip to Vietnam under Operation Gold Star was conducted from July 16–28, 2000. Past national presidents Mary Wheeler, Theresa Davis, and Valerie May, accompanied by past national officer Irene Tschan, were the first mothers to travel. The trip proved arduous but the mothers agreed that they would remain eternally grateful for the opportunity to have walked where their children had spent their last days.[53] The National Dusters-Quads-Searchlights Association sponsored several more pilgrimages to Vietnam during the early years of the decade, eventually ending the program as the mothers and veterans found the travel to be increasingly difficult.

Moving Forward

As AGSM looks forward to the next decade, there are mixed emotions of sadness and pride among the members. Each generation of gold star mothers has hoped and prayed that the conflict that cost their child's life had been "the war that would end wars"; they hoped for a future in which there would be no new gold star mothers. Sadly the world continues to find it easier to wage war than to keep the peace. But there is pride as well among the gold star mothers of AGSM, for they have an incredible history of service to America's veterans and the nation to look back on; they have truly "perpetuated the memory of those whose lives were sacrificed in our wars" through decades of dedicated service to those who survived. As the American Gold Star Mothers, Inc., continues to evolve, there will always be a place for those women whose children have made the ultimate sacrifice for their nation to find comfort, understanding and shared purpose.

> As long as we live, your sons shall be loved.
> As long as we live, your sons shall
>   be remembered.
> As long as we live, your sons shall live.[54]

Appendix A:

Presidents and Conventions 1928-2012

Appendix A: Presidents and Conventions, 1928-2012

TERM	PRESIDENT (HUSBAND)	FROM	THEME	CVN #	LOCATION	DATES	# THERE
1928 – 1932	Grace Darling Seibold (George Gordon Seibold)	Washington, DC		1	Hotel Hamilton Washington, D.C.	Nov. 9 – 10	
1932 – 1934	Elizabeth I. Millard	Rochester, NY		2	The Gold Room, Hotel Hamilton Washington, D.C.	May 28 – 30	47
1934 – 1936	Mary J. Bates (William Bates)	Jackson, MI		3	Book – Cadillac Hotel Detroit, MI	June 9 – 12	100
1936 – 1938	Della Towne Blake (Horace B. Blake)	Philadelphia, PA	Let there be peace – and fewer Gold Star Mothers.	4	Hotel Walton Philadelphia, PA	May 10 – 13	119
1938 – 1939	Bess Duncan Wells (Thomas Emerson Wells)	Portland, OR		5	Portland Hotel Portland, OR	June 6 – 10	
1939 – 1940	M. Jennie Williams (Gerlynn Walter Williams)	New Bedford, MA		6	Parker House Boston, MA	June 4 – 7	
1940 – 1941	Maretta Mae Cushman (Jesse Willard Cushman)	Hollywood, CA		7	Biltmore Hotel Los Angeles, CA	June 10 – 13	
1941 – 1942	Emma Balcom (William H. Balcom)	Bronx, NY		8	Hotel New Yorker New York, NY	June 9 – 12	
1942 – 1946	Mary Frances Hill (David Franklin Hill)	Philadelphia, PA			No convention due to wartime restrictions		
1946 – 1946	Emily M. Cunningham (John S. Cunningham)	Milton, MA		9	Hotel Philadelphia Philadelphia, PA	June 3 – 5	
1946 – 1947	Eleanor D. Boyd (Walter H. Boyd, M.D.)	Long Beach, CA		10	Municipal Auditorium Long Beach, CA	June 4 – 6	
1947 – 1948	Anne G. Hagerty (O. E. Hagerty)	Atlantic City, NJ		11	Chelsea Hotel Atlantic City, NJ	June 1 – 6	
1948 – 1949	Eleanor D. Boyd (Walter H. Boyd, M.D.)	Long Beach, CA		12	Hotel Sherman Chicago, IL	June 4 – 9	
1949 – 1950	Eleanor D. Boyd	Long Beach, CA		13	Book – Cadillac Hotel		1,500+
1950 – 1951	Eleanor D. Boyd (Walter H. Boyd, M.D.)	Long Beach, CA		14	Statler Hotel Washington, DC	May 29 – June 3	1,000+
1951 – 1952	Eleanor D. Boyd (Walter H. Boyd, M.D.)	Long Beach, CA		15	Long Beach Municip'l Auditor'm Long Beach, CA	June 8 – 13	2,000+
1952 – 1953	Elsie C. Nielsen (Aage W. Nielsen)	Chicago, IL		16	Sherman Hotel Chicago, IL	June 7 – 12	1,200
1953 – 1954	Elsie C. Nielsen (Aage W. Nielsen)	Chicago, IL		17	Sheraton Plaza Hotel Boston, MA	June 6 – 11	
1954 – 1955	Elsie C. Nielsen (Aage W. Nielsen)	Chicago, IL		18	Hotel Del Lido Miami Beach, FL	June 19 – 22	645
1955 – 1956	Ruth K. Singer	Los Angeles, CA		19	Mayo Hotel Tulsa, OK	June 18 – 22	490
1956 – 1957	Ruth K. Singer	Los Angeles, CA		20	The Hotel Cleveland Cleveland, OH	June 30 – July 5	566
1957 – 1958	Maude Fry	Detroit, MI		21	Shirley-Savoy Hotel Denver, CO	June 15 – 20	
1958 – 1959	Mabel Troy (James J. Troy)	Paterson, NJ		22	Baker Hotel Dallas, TX	June 26 – July 1	
1959 – 1960	Lorraine I. Desser (Samuel Desser)	Bridgeport, CT		23	Henry Hudson Hotel New York, NY	June 21 – 23	
1960 – 1961	Frances High	Houston, TX		24	Statler Hilton Hotel Los Angeles, CA	June 19 – 21	
1961 – 1962	Dorothy N. Baxter	Worcester, MA		25	Bradford Hotel Boston, MA		
1962 – 1963	Mary P. Kelly (Peter T. Kelly)	Washington, DC		26	Mayflower Hotel Washington, DC		
1963 – 1964	Mary F. Nieman (Albert P. Nieman)	Binghamton, NY		27	Battery Park & George Vanderbilt Hotels; Ashville, NC	June 28 – July 1	
1964 – 1965	Mildred A. Lee	Denver, CO	For God So Loved the World	28	Hilton Hotel Denver, CO	July 4 – 7	
1965 – 1966	Emma C. Eunick (Charles Thomas Eunick)	Westminster, MD		29	Jung Hotel New Orleans, LA	July 3 – 7	
1966 – 1967	Rose F. Decker	Long Beach, CA	Troubled times, yes, but blessings too	30	Sheraton-Schroeder Hotel Milwaukee, WI		
1967 – 1968	Marie Hart (William Hart)	Cleveland, OH		31	Hilton Hotel Portland, OR	July 22 – 24	

1968 – 1969	Mamie P. Simmons	Tulsa, OK		32	Mayo Hotel Tulsa, OK	June 22 – 25	
1969 – 1970	Helen T. Willour (Mark Lewis Willour)	Brookline, MA		33	Deauville Hotel Miami Beach, FL	July 12 - 15	420
1970 – 1971	Myrtle E. Foster	Milwaukee, WI		34			
1971 – 1972	Anna C. Richards	Jersey City, NJ		35	Philadelphia Sheraton Philadelphia, PA	June 27 – 30	385
1972 – 1973	Regina Coughlin	Philadelphia, PA	Let there be Peace and let it start with me.	36	Baker Hotel Dallas, TX	June 25 – 28	296
1973 – 1974	Helen White	Long Beach, CA		37	Sheraton-Cadillac Hotel Detroit, MI	June 24 – 27	257
1974 – 1975	Josephay Fleming	Portland, OR		38	Sheraton Palace San Francisco, CA	June 30 – July 3	
1975 – 1976	Josephine J. Holmes	New York, NY		39	Sheraton Biltmore Atlanta, GA	July 13 – 16	263
1976 – 1977	Mary E. King	Providence, RI		40	Chalfonte-Haddon Hotel Atlantic City, NJ	June 27 – 30	221
1977 – 1978	Regina Wilk (Anthony Wilk)	Silver Springs, MD	Love One Another	41	Washington, D.C.	June 26 – 29	231
1978 – 1979	Emogene M. Cupp (James Cupp)	Alexandria, VA	Teamwork with Love	42	Arlington Hotel Hot Springs, AK	July 8 – 11	187
1979 – 1980	Betty Bryce (Harold Bryce)	Mt. Pleasant, MI	Love with the Human Touch	43	Holiday Inn Embarcadero San Diego, CA	June 22 – 25	193
1980 – 1981	Katherine Mannion (August Mannion)	Baltimore, MD	Love and Reach Out	44	Ridpath Hotel and Motor Inn Spokane, WA	June 21 – 24	151
1981 – 1982	Mary Teater (McClellan Teater)	Albuquerque, NM	We are a family.	45	Regent of Albuquerque Hotel Albuquerque, NM	July 4 – 7	194
1982 – 1983	Helen Stuber (William Stuber)	Fountain Valley, CA	Friends in Harmony	46	Radisson Hotel St. Louis, MO	June 26 – 29	177
1983 – 1984	June Everett (Jack Everett)	Otis Orchards, WA	Caring and Sharing	47	Radisson Hotel, Houston, TX	June 24 – 27	
1984 – 1985	Lois Freeman (Joseph Lloyd Freeman)	Greenville, SC	Service with Love	48	Sheraton – Atlanta Hotel Atlanta, GA	June 23 – 26	129
1985 – 1986	Nora J. Golsh (Paul Golsh)	La Crescenta, CA	Dedicated with Purpose	49	Westin South Coast Plaza Hotel Costa Mesa, CA	June 29 – July 2	143
1986 – 1987	Opal Johnson (William O. Johnson)	Houston, TX	Take One Day at a Time, with Love	50	Stouffer-Madison Hotel Seattle, WA	June 28 – July 1	110
1987 – 1988	Shirley Jones Delanoy (Roy Delanoy)	Howes Cave, NY	Peace and Patriotism	51	Buffalo Hilton, Buffalo, NY	June 26 – 29	159
1988 – 1989	Margaret Vinyard (Thurman Vinyard)	Marshfield, MO	United with Love	52	Amway Grand Plaza Hotel Grand Rapids, MI	June 25 – 28	92
1989 – 1990	Anna Biber	Branchville, NJ	Be A Friend	53	Headquarters Plaza Hotel Morristown, NJ	July 1 – 4	58
1990 – 1991	Gladys Jewett (Harry M. Jewett)	Spokane, WA	Love and Peace	54	American Gold Star Manor Long Beach, CA	June 23 – 26	128
1991 – 1992	Winona L. Tucker	Jerseyville, IL	For Their Sake	55	Washington Vista Hotel Washington, DC	July 12 – 15	118
1992 – 1993	Violet C. Long (Elbert (Sam) Long)	Lemoyne, PA	Because We Care	56	Ramada Inn Overland Park, KS	June 27 – 30	97
1993 – 1994	Jeanne K. Penfold (Allen Thomas Penfold)	Oceanside, NY	Keep in Touch	57	Harrisburg Hilton & Towers Harrisburg, Pennsylvania	June 26 – 29	98
1994 – 1995	Carol L. Tabor	Cheyenne, WY	Always Be There	58	Crowne Plaza Miami Miami, Florida	June 25 – 28	76
1995 – 1996	Valerie May	Midland, MI	Love one another and SHOW it	59	Four Points Sheraton Inn Saginaw, MI	June 23 – 26	71
1996 – 1997	Frances J. Turley (Homer Turley)	DeSoto, MO	In Service & Sacrifice	60	Holiday Inn Select St. Louis, MO	June 22 – 25	79
1997 – 1998	Theresa O. Davis (Richard Davis)	Holbrook, MA	Reach Out	61	Radisson Hotel Boston, MA	June 14 – 17	146
1998 – 1999	Bette A. Freeman (Russell Freeman)	Anaheim, CA	Freedom & Patriotism	62	Buena Park Hotel Buena Park, CA	June 20 – 23	78
1999 – 2000	Mary E. Wheeler (Charles R. Wheeler)	Utica, NY	Friendship & Peace	63	Crowne Plaza Albany Hotel Albany, NY	June 25 – 28	88
2000 – 2001	Iris Walden (Frank Walden)	Lenoir City, TN	Love & Friendship	64	Hilton Hotel Knoxville, TN	June 23 – 38	78
2001 – 2002	Georgianna Carter-Krell (Frank Krell)	Virginia Gardens, FL	Above & Beyond	65	Marco Polo Beach Resort North Miami Beach, FL	June 1519	72
2002 – 2003	Dorothy M. Oxendine (Willie Oxendine)	Farmingdale, NY	Happiness is Helping Others	66	Executive Inn Evansville, IN	July 6 – 9	83
2003 – 2004	Ann Y. Sherman Wolcott	York, PA	Rangers Lead the Way	67	Sheraton Norfolk Waterside Norfolk, VA	July 4 – 7	38

2004 – 2005	**Ann Herd** (Buster Herd)	Dallas, TX	Freedom & Peace	68	Crowne Plaza Dallas Addison/Dallas, TX	June 25 – 29	60
2005 – 2006	**Judith C. Young** (John F. (Jack) Young)	Moorestown, NJ	You'll Never Walk Alone	69	Doubletree Guest Suites Mount Laurel, New Jersey	July 7 – 11	
2006 – 2007	**Betty Jean Pulliam**	Haysville,KS	Love, Peace & Unity	70	Hyatt Regency Hotel Wichita, Kansas	June 28 – 27	56
2007 – 2008	**Mary Jane Kiepe** (Glen Kiepe)	Festus, MO	Keeping Pride and Patriotism Alive	71	Lodge of the Ozarks Branson, MO	June 28 – 29	49
2008 – 2009	**Georgianna C. Krell** (Frank Krell)	Virginia Gardens, FL	Above & Beyond	72	Marco Polo Beach Resort Sunny Isles Beach, FL	June 19 – 22	77
2009 – 2010	**Ruth Stonesifer**	Kintnersville, PA	Be Inspired, Then Make It Happen!	73	Doubletree Guest Suites Plymouth Meeting, PA	June 25 – 27	
2010 – 2011	**Molly Morel** (Mike Morel)	**Martin, TN**		74	**Radisson Hotel at Opryland Nashville, TN**	**June 24 – 26**	
2011 – 2012	**Norma Luther** (Jim Luther)	**Wilmington, NC**	**Reach Out!**	75	**Holiday Inn National Airport Hotel Arlington, VA**	**June 22 – 25**	

Appendix B:

National Presidents
1928-2012

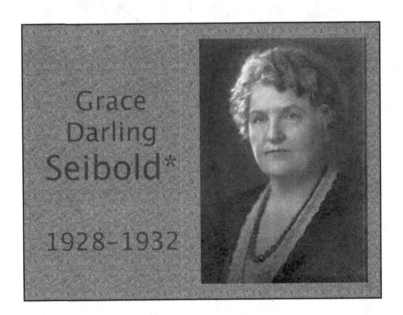

Grace
Darling
Seibold*

1928–1932

★ = Deceased

Elizabeth Millard*

1932 – 1934

Mary J. Bates*

1934 – 1936

Della Towne Blake*

1936 – 1938

Bess Duncan Wells*

1938 – 1939

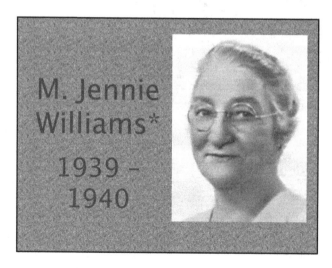

M. Jennie Williams*

1939 – 1940

Maretta Mae Cushman*

1940–1941

Appendix B: National Presidents

Emma Balcom*

1941 – 1942

Mary F. Hill*

1942 – January 1946

Emily M. Cunningham *

January 1946 – June 1946

Eleanor D. Boyd*

1946 – 1947

Anna G. Hagerty*

1947 – 1948

Eleanor D. Boyd*

1948 – 1952

Elsie Nielsen*

1952–1955

Ruth Singer*
1955–1957

Maude Fry*

1957–1958

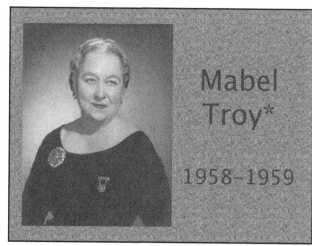
Mabel Troy*

1958–1959

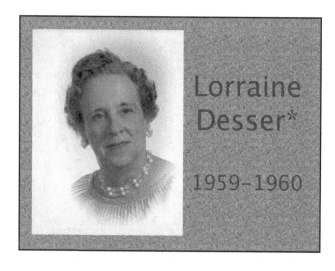
Lorraine Desser*

1959–1960

Frances High*

1960–1961

Dorothy
N. Baxter*

1961–1962

Mary P.
Kelly*

1962–1963

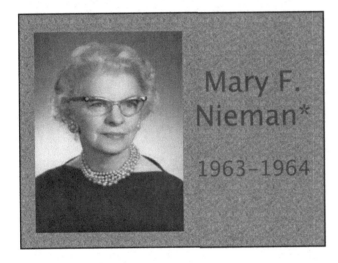

Mary F.
Nieman*

1963–1964

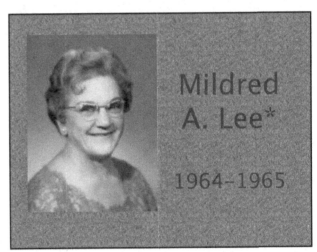

Mildred
A. Lee*

1964–1965

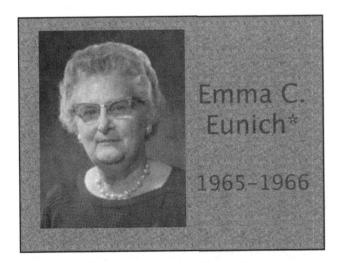

Emma C.
Eunich*

1965–1966

Rose F.
Decker*

1966–1967

Marie Hart*

1967–1968

Mamie P. Simmons *

1968–1969

Helen T. Willour*

1969–1970

Myrtle E. Foster*

1970–1971

Anna C. Richards*

1971–1972

Regina Coughlin *

1972–1973

Appendix B: National Presidents

Helen White*

1973–1974

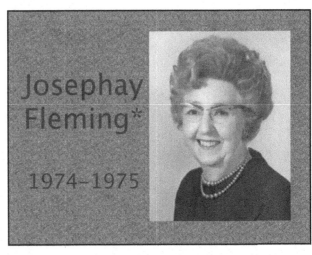

Josephay Fleming*

1974–1975

Josephine J. Holmes*

1975–1976

Mary E. King*

1976–1977

Regina Wilk*

1977–1978

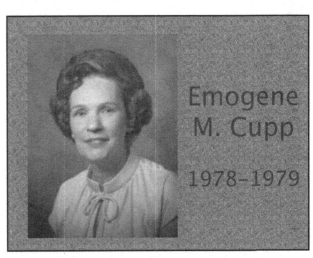

Emogene M. Cupp

1978–1979

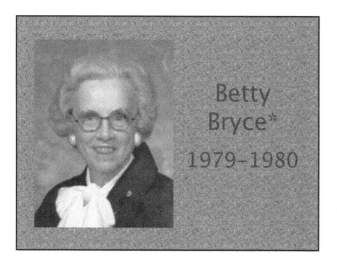

Betty Bryce*
1979–1980

Katherine Mannion*
1980–1981

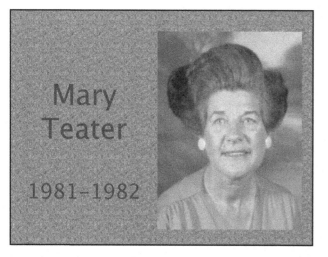

Mary Teater
1981–1982

Helen V. Stuber*
1982–1983

June Everett*
1983–1984

Lois Freeman
1984–1985

Nora J. Golsh*

1985–1986

Opal L. Johnson*

1986–1987

Shirley Delanoy Jones

1987–1988

Margaret Vinyard Golden

1988–1989

Anna Biber*
1989–1990

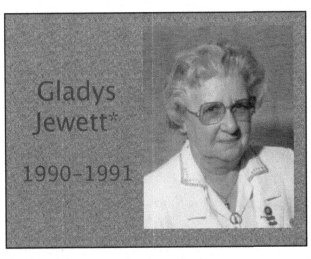

Gladys Jewett*

1990–1991

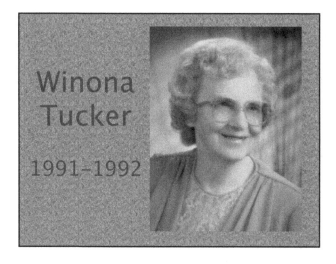

Winona Tucker
1991–1992

Violet C. Long*
1992–1993

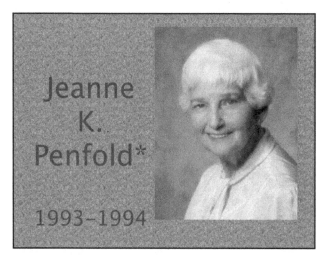

Jeanne K. Penfold*
1993–1994

Carol Tabor
1994–1995

Valerie May
1995–1996

Frances J. Turley
1996–1997

Theresa O. Davis

1997–1998

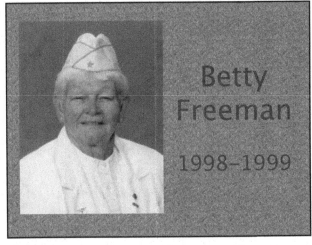

Betty Freeman

1998–1999

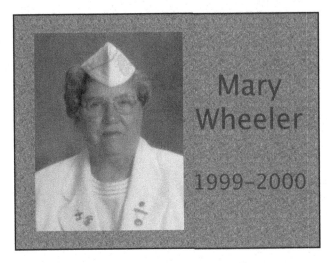

Mary Wheeler

1999–2000

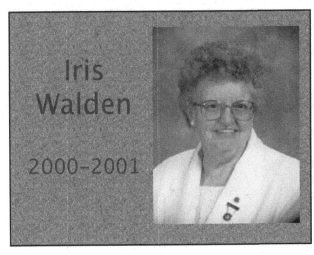

Iris Walden

2000–2001

Georgianna C. Krell

2001–2002

Dorothy M. Oxendine

2002–2003

Ann Y. Sherman Wolcott

2003–2004

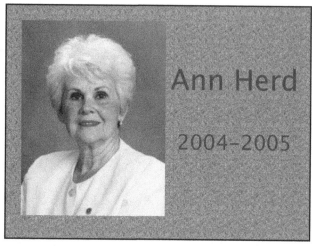

Ann Herd

2004–2005

Judith C. Young

2005–2006

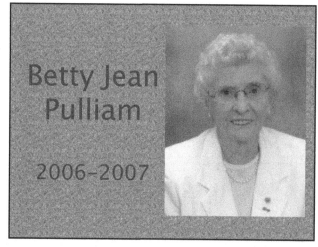

Betty Jean Pulliam

2006–2007

Mary Jane Kiepe

2007–2008

Georgianna C. Krell

2008–2009

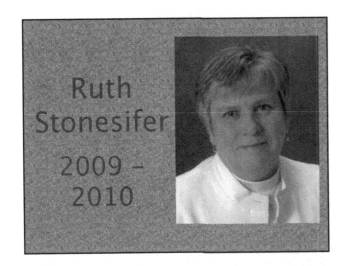

Appendix C:

Gold Star Poetry and Clippings

To A Gold Star Mother (1919)

My chum, he's lying there asleep,
So still, so calm, so dignified,
That even in his sleep he seems to dwarf
US, for whom he gallantly and gladly died.

That simple cross above him, with his name
In plain black lettering. How much it means to you,
To you whose loss no words can measure and to US, who fought beside your boy.
We love him too.

John C. Gabourel <u>Soldiers and Sailors Magazine</u> July 1919, Volume 1, page 35

Untitled

To the Mother whose son through lasting night
Lies under a cross of gleaming white;
Who bears in her heart a pain age-old —
The Mother who wears the heart of gold.

Mary Graniss Haight (undated)

Untitled (1930s)

Envisioning the trenches and the Flanders Fields afar
I see through hot and burning tears
A wee, gold star ---
And it doesn't seem to matter
About the lesser things
When I think of what they did for us
Those heroes who were Kings.

Time, hope and solace bring,
Taking away the anguish
That was made by Death's deep sting.
And though in Flanders' fields there sleeps
the only Son I had,
In spite of the bitterness and pain,
I cannot but be glad
Glad for his life – his patriot soul
That saw where duty lay,
That held the torch of courage high,
Tho steep and rough the way.

These are the things that oft come to us
But shall I not lift my head
And greet his Spirit shining through?

He lives—HE IS NOT DEAD.
There is no Love like a Mother's
Tis the sun that shineth forth.
There is no Truth like a Mother's
Tis a Star that points the north.

There is no Hope like Mother's
Tis the April in the clod.
There is no Trust like a Mother's
Tis the Charity of God.
The Love and Truth, The Hope and Trust

That makes the Mortal more than dust.

Found in AGSM Scrapbook #3 (No date/author)

A Gold Star Mother Speaks (1930)

My little lad of other days sleeps there.
He bore the brunt of battle;
I must bear the agonizing loneliness of years.
He played his part. Shall I give way to tears?

He loved tall fragrant lilies, and they grew
In our old fashioned garden, bright with dew.
I'm taking these; their beauty shields my loss.
They'll guard his grave, and bloom about his cross.

Virginia A. Nelson Evening Star, Washington, D. C. May 19, 1930 Found in AGSM Scrapbook #3.

Untitled (1937)

I wear a poppy on my breast
Where once a boyish head found rest
And often when the day is done
I see again my soldier son.

He comes to me in such a way
That I can almost hear him say,
"Do not worry, Mother dear,
I am coming home some day."

And when the tears unbidden start
I place a hand above my heart
To there caress a tousled head
But only find a poppy red.

Found in AGSM Scrapbook

Gold Star Mothers of the USA (1939)

God bless our Gold Star Mothers,
And keep them free from care,
May their lives be happy
Every minute, everywhere.

May they keep in the ranks of faith and courage,
Always proud to say,
I am a Gold Star Mother of a Soldier
Of the good old U.S.A.

Kathleen V. Clarkin (Gold Star Mother) Brooklyn, New York

A Gold Star Pin (1939)

There are pins of all descriptions,
Round and square and oblong too.
But you'll find no pin like this one,
Though you search the whole world through.

There are pins for all occasions,
Made in colors bright and gay.
But this pin outshines all the others,
That you see from day to day.

Just a tiny golden emblem
Nestled on a field of white
There it rests in sacred memory
Symbol of a gallant fight.

Just a pin, a tiny emblem,
Just a tiny golden star
Representing someone's laddie
Who has crossed the Celestial Bar.

There are pins of all description
And for all occasions too.
But the tiny sacred gold star
Tells a story frank and true.

Fenna Downey (Read on September 18, 1939
at the installation of gold star mothers in Detroit.)

Gold Stars

They rest upon a Mother's breast
    These tiny Stars of gold,
And great and many are the deeds,
    The tiny emblems hold.
A symbol of that sacrifice
    From where none e'er return
So undisturbed the soldier sleeps
    While memory's candles burn.
And passing time cannot erase
    The symbol of that tiny star.
It represents a Mother's lad
    Who crossed the fair Celestial Bar.

Fenna Downey

Greetings, Gold Star Mothers (1939)

We greet you, Gold Star Mothers,
Specially on Mother's Day.
May sunny days and happy hours,
Be scattered on your way.

And when the day is over,
Gone beyond recall,
May golden memories fill your heart
As twilight shadows fall.

And may our Heavenly Father,
"From whom all blessings flow,"
His love and understanding
And peace on you bestow.

From the Gold Star Sisters By Feena Downey, Detroit, Michigan

The Unknown Soldier (1940)
Reminiscences of a Gold Star Mother at his Tomb—Dedicated to the Gold Star Mothers of America

How beautiful and peaceful is this place,
With such a monument, so full of grace,
This tomb of marble for a soldier boy,
That elements or time will not destroy.

"THE UNKNOWN SOLDIER"—wonder, who he is,
And if he could have known, this grave of his
Would be the place, where Gold Star Mothers find
A solace in their sorrow, peace of mind,

When memories of war would make them yield
To horrid pictures of the battlefield;
Yes, vivid fantasies of living hell,
Where sons of theirs are facing shot and shell,
Where man kills man with gas and liquid fire,
Where boys hang bleeding on the barbed wire;
Of blackened fields where dying soldiers lie
With sightless eyes staring at the sky,
Where parts of human bodies lie around,
here men are blown to bits – and never found.

Why bring back those memories of old;
So few would understand me, if I told
Them of each day of fear, each sleepless night,
When dreadful visions filled my heart with frights,
The anguish I went through, when he was gone.

This precious gift of God – my only son.
The thought, that somewhere out in "no man's land"
My boy might wounded be, I couldn't stand.
So hard was this uncertainty and dread,
I found relief, when learning he was dead.

A letter came, that dressed my world in black,
It said they missed him after an attack.
My friends were telling me I must be brave,
But how? My son was dead – without a grave.
They never found him.
Still there is a chance
It was my boy they chose to send from France
With military splendor to be laid
Among the nation's great, heroic dead.

And that it's him, I make myself believe,
It helps me, when my mother-heart will grieve,
It gives me hope, when tears my eyes will dim,
It comforts me – the thought it might be him.
I tell myself to banish ev'ry fear,
And that it is my boy, who's resting here.

Somehow it fills the space within my heart,
That felt so empty, since we had to part.
Why shouldn't I take comfort from the thought
It is my soldier boy, whom here they brought.
Here, where a grateful nation bows its head
In silent tribute to its soldier dead.
"THE UNKNOWN SOLDIER," nameless though he be,
Is my beloved son – at least to me.

By Einar C. K. Arnild, Minneapolis MN, August 1940

The War Mothers

For the boys who died on the field of glory,
No words will be left unsaid.
That can illumine their wondrous story,
Ere they join our heroic dead.

But what of the poignant suffering,
Of the mothers of these boys,
As they put away the balls and bats,
The trinkets and the toys.

Forever her little boy shall sleep,
Close to her mothering breast.
As in memory she rocks his cradle,
When the sand-man brought him rest.

She will hear again his little feet
As they toddle along the floor,
She will see again his golden smile
Filling the open door.

She will be going her soft and gentle way,
Thinking of her boy,
Helping other stricken souls,
Trying to bring them joy.

As she passes, we feel the stir of wings,
The presence of one divine,
A separation from earthly things,
That is difficult to define.

In the sight of God, she has become a saint,
Let us bow in veneration,
For in our hearts she has become,
The Mother of our Nation.

John P. Fahey (undated)

The Young Dead Soldiers Do Not Speak (1943)

Nevertheless they are heard in the still houses; who has not heard them?

They have a silence that speaks for them at night and when the clock counts.

They say, We were young. We have died. Remember us.

They say, We have done what we could but until it is finished it is not done.

They say, We have given our lives but until it is finished no one can know what our lives gave.

They say, Our deaths are not ours; they are yours. They will mean what you make them.

They say, Whether our lives and our deaths were for peace and a new hope or for nothing
   we cannot say; it is you who must say this.

They say, We leave you our deaths. Give them their meaning. Give them an end to the war and
   a true peace. Give them a victory that ends the war and a peace afterwards. Give them
   their meaning.

We were young, they say. We have died. Remember us.

Archibald McLeish, Heroes' Day, September 16, 1943

Untitled (1945)

"We regret to inform you," the telegram said,
And all that I know is, my son is dead.
My boy is dead, and my life goes on,
My son, my son, are you really gone?

This wire I hold in my trembling hand
Tells me you died in a foreign land,
Tells me you died as a soldier should –
You'd want it that way, I know you would.

I should be brave and shouldn't cry,
But, my boy, you were too young to die;
And somewhere out there, wherever you've gone,
Perhaps you'll be happy if I carry on.

Poem printed on a first day of issue envelope postmarked July 18, 1945

Gold Star Mother's Prayer (1950)

God, help me to be worthy of the son I bore
Who, by his sacrifice in the white-hot hell of war,
Paid the price of freedom;
Help me pray for peace;
That men may find wisdom and that wars shall cease.

God, help me to be humble when homage is shown
To me, his mother;
This honor is not mine alone.
In his name I am proud to accept it posthumously;
That honor alone is enough for me.

God, keep me ever true with courage so strong
That, through the bitter struggle for peace be long,
My faith in the principles he died to uphold
May make me worthy to wear the star of gold.

Alice Conner Harness Batavia, Iowa

The Gold Star (1950)

There is a gold star in our window
It has been there, oh, so long.
And has taken the place of a blue star,
And our loved one is gone.

Gold stars are in many windows,
Which will cause your heart to weep;
Yes, God, our star is really gold,
And all we have to keep.

I used to think gold was pretty,
And of course I still do,
But it has a different meaning
Than the star that was blue.

Gold, somehow, seems false,
The other brave and true.
Dear God, why must our star be gold?
Why couldn't it have stayed blue?

*By Coy Burrell, "in loving memory of his big brother, Hershel Samuel Burrell,
who was killed in action June 16, 1944." The Gold Star Mother. January 1950.*

Untitled (1951)

When you were young you ran to me,
Thrilled in childish ecstasy,
And said, "The teacher says I are
So good that I deserve a star!"
I shall never forget that phrase –
It haunts me in these barren days
For now the star is mine to keep
While you lie sleeping in the deep.

Dolores Bromley The Gold Star Mother. 1951

Gold Star Mother (1955)

She gave him birth and watched him grow
And dressed him up from top to toe
She taught him how to smile and walk
To eat and drink and how to talk
She made his lunch for school each day
And showed him how to work and play
She urged him on and helped him choose
And nursed each cut and bump and bruise
She guided him from wrong to right
She told him when and how to fight
But almost of all, right from the start,
She gave her boy her loving heart.
While he in turn, was more than glad
To give up all he ever had
That you and I and other sons
Might never meet the blazing guns
So let us pay our deep respect
And solemnly let us reflect
Upon the grave she gave that we
Might carry on to victory.

By James J. Metcalfe The Gold Star Mother. May 1955

Gold Star Mothers Ritual (1956)

One small gold star is ours to keep
Against the hours of wakeful sleep;
Against our longing through the years,
The disbelief, the unshed tears,
When eyes no longer dare to weep.

Still bonds of faith will surely hold,
While seasons pass, and the years are told.

We toil through tears and scarlet rain,
Praying for peace in a ceaseless refrain;
We mothers of stars of gold.

Louise Preston Greene The Gold Star Mother. October 1956

To Gold Star Mothers (1956)

The Gold Star is a symbol
Which everyone respects
It rests upon a broken heart
Which in our eyes – reflects.
We do not wear it willingly
But we accept it – now
We know that in God's Wisdom
He will explain – somehow.

We wear it very proudly
It represents so much
For stars and stripes and freedom's ring
He gave his life for such.

When stars of blue were turned to gold
We failed to understand
Just why it had to be our sons
Who lost their earthly stand.

We shut our eyes and barred our hearts
And failed to see beyond –
Another Mother, whose own Dear Son
Was severed from her bond.

But now – as years go marching by
And worldly values dim –
We know our sons go hand in hand
In lasting Peace – with Him.

Emma M. Kiernan Warren Co. Chapter, PA The Gold Star Mother. September 1956

Tribute to Gold Star Mothers (1956)

We are paying a tribute to Mothers
Of boys who went "over there"
To fight a terrible battle
On land, on sea and in air.

These Mothers who waited for letters
From their boys far over the sea,

Letters saying "Mom, do not worry,
We will bring you Victory."

Then came that terrible message
With tears and heart-aches they read,
"Your boy has been killed in action
His blood for his Country is shed."

The sacrifice has been very bitter,
Your army of Women is strong,
Tho fighting the battle of heartaches,
With courage you carry on.

You are wearing the Gold Star Emblem,
Which tells every passerby,
"I'm a Gold Star Mother,
My boy for his country did die."

And up in that beautiful region
Where heroes meet one another,
Your boys will be one of those heroes,
Who prays for his "Gold Star Mother."

Mrs. Lillian Morel, Adjutant Navy Mothers Club, No 369, New Orleans, LA
The Gold Star Mother. September 1956

Open the Door (1957)

God opened a door and my son went through.
He opened another and your son went too.
You made a mistake, you closed your door
I made a mistake and closed mine too.
And we sat alone as Time went by
Two selfish mothers – you and I.

And then one night we saw stars in the sky
And they talked to us and they seemed to say
Throw open your door, there is work to be done,
Work for the ones less fortunate than your son.
There are those who are crippled, some cannot see.
There are some like babies who will never be free.

As we listened we knew that our sons were so safe
And other mothers' sons needed care and relief.
And we knelt in prayer, both you and I,
And asked forgiveness for our closed doors.

We went to the hospitals and worked for the Boys
And brought comfort to them and to us we brought joys.

We gave of ourselves, your son and my son now look down
And with wide boyish grins add more stars to our crowns.

Cecile Easingwood, The Gold Star Mother 1957

From Blue to Gold (1958)

She remembers so well …all a mother can tell
Ere the blue in his star turned to gold.
She relinquished her son that a war might be won
And the glory to freedom be told.
She remembers each phase of his babyhood days.
She remembers him going to school
She remembers his pranks, his rewards and his spanks
They reflect in her memory pool.

She remembers the day he traveled away
She remembers the heartache and tears
When the word was received – that she hardly believed -
Making fact of the worst of her fears.

And our hearts wouldn't err, in remembering her
Who was loosed of her heaven-sent hold
Who was forced to stand by 'neath a war-blackened sky
While the blue in his star turned to gold.

Margaret Rourke The Gold Star Mother July 1958

The Unknown Soldier (1958)

You think I've slept for years, but you are wrong.
For every Spring I hear the robin's song,
I see the flowers bloom and fade away
And feel the tears of Mothers as they pray.

I have an Irish mother, who believes
That I'm the warrior son for whom she grieves,

A Jewish mother names me in her prayers—
A million mothers think of me as theirs.

I like to feel that I belong to all,
For I was a waif, abandoned in a hall,
I never knew a mother – think what joy
Is mine when over me they cry, "My boy!"

And thus, in death, from pulsing life I steal
That which it stole from me, when life was real;

A mother's love, so tender and profound,
And tears… that keep me warm… the year around.

N.K., The Gold Star Mother , June 1958

The Silent Tears (1958)

Oh, Gold Star Mother you know well,
The million silent tears that fell
From eyes that pierced into the night
To glimpse a once familiar sight.

How often did you wake from sleep
Expecting to see him at your feet.
Sitting with some favorite toy
He often played with as a boy.

Remember how fast your heart would beat
At a certain sound of moving feet
Because you thought it might be he
Returning unexpectedly.

It took some time, before you learned
To say, my son will not return,
But you soon found out, that hearts can take –
The cruelest pains and yet, not break.

But I believe that, if we could see
A glimpse of Heaven there would be
For Mother a crown of crystals clear
God made with all those silent tears.

Helen K. Lambert, The Gold Star Mother, November 1958

The Gold Star Mother (1958)

She kneels before the hallowed cross
That marks a hero's grave.
She knows a deep and bitter loss,
But still her soul is brave.
White crosses stand in endless rows,
With that which guards her own,
And through her sorrowing she knows
She weeps there not alone.

Her only son, who marched away, with colors streaming proud,
Beneath the poppies sleeps today
With glory for his shroud.

In glory's name, he fought and died,
Although, throughout the years,
No crown of glory ever dried a grieving mother's tears.

She seems to see him by her side,
With boyish hopes on high,
Resplendent in his youthful pride,
The day he said goodbye.
She seems to feel the loving grasp
Within his warm embrace;
But all her hungry arms may clasp
Is cold and empty space.
Her thoughts go back to cradle days,
And long to linger there,
As softly down those distant ways
She hears a baby's prayer.
A flood of wistful visions bring
To her, from far apart,
The touch of tiny hands that cling
Around her aching heart.

No lonely path was his that led
Upon that final quest;
A might host of honored dead
Lies there with him at rest.
The world shall miss those martyred sons,
But time bedims regret,
And mothers are the only ones
Who never can forget.

In mother's love, he never dies,
For she shall ever see
The best he meant in mother's eyes
And all he hoped to be.
Her life its full and precious store
Of memories may hold
But where her Heaven shone before
Now shines one star of gold.

B.C. Bridges, Alameda, CA The Gold Star Mother November 1958

Survival of the Fittest (1958)

We come again to the end of the year
That's been pleasant with toil
But never a tear.
For the love that binds us all together
Is the deep-seated love of a Gold Star Mother.

Sometimes we forget the pledge we have said,
The self and ambition are way out ahead
When we stop to consider and balance the score
The work of the Chapter is worth much more.
Be happy instead you are able to do
The tasks that are demanded of the tried and the true
For all are not fitted to carry on
The load that is heavy for the brave and strong.

We should be content with what we can do
It is just as important as the morning dew
The strong and the weak, the quick and the slow
All work together to make it so.

Now let's try to do everything we can
To help our unfortunate and fallen man
And be more considerate – one for the other –
Of all Gold Star Mothers and our veteran brothers.

Ella F. Leven Miami Chapter No 1, The Gold Star Mother, December 1958

This Man I Knew (1959)

Days will pass,
The seasons too,
And smiles must follow tears;
Still this man I knew
Will live for me.
Long through the hallowed years.

Mark him well this man I knew
For courage and for duty,
Oh, mark him well, dear God above,
For a heart distilled with beauty.

He held the line,
He fought the foe,
In a land begot with madness:
And in moments rare
With thoughts to spare,
He dreamt of home and gladness.

Mark him well, this man I knew,
No selfish whim or faction,
Oh, mark him best of all dear Lord,
For a hero killed in action.

The Gold Star Mother, **March 1959**

Our Gold Star Family (1968?)

One night our star was turned to gold,
Two officers came and the story told.

"We regret to inform you your son is lost."
Thus, a "Gold Star" into our night was tossed.

It was so cold and bleak and grey,
We wondered if such could turn to day.

But as nights come and go, our hearts seem lighter;
The glittering symbol makes our hopes grow brighter.

Soon our entire sky will turn to gold,
To blossom forth a million-fold.

Julitta Poe Wells (A Vietnam War gold star mother)
Soul Eruptions of a Gold Star Mother, Circa 1968

A Mother's Star (1969)

The Star in my window is not gold
It's very faded, tattered and old
I've kept it there for a path back home
Knowing Eddie would never roam.

No one can see my Star but me
It's just a dream, not reality
As I secure my home for the night
I touch my Star – it shines so bright.

Then I lay down and pray to God
Let me dream of my son where his feet have trod
I see him standing by my bed
So strong and tall
He's not the young son who went away at all.

He holds out his hands
To help me on my feet
But I keep reaching out,
Our hands will never meet
I heard his voice from my dreams
Saying you grieved long enough it seems

Smile, Mother, while you're here on earth

You've done good things since my birth.
Change your old Star to a new
And I'll wait at heaven's gate for you.

Gold Star Mother Mary Benton, Chaplain, Scenic Area Chapter, Tennessee. Mother of John Austin Benton, L.C. USMC, KIA 1967 China Sea; written for Mary Kennett when her son was killed, Charles Edward Smith, Army Ranger, 1969, Vietnam, <u>The Gold Star Mother</u>, March/April 2000, p3

Mothers Day in Korea—1954

If I could be a boy once more
With wisdom of a child,
I could express my love for you
In phrases sweet and mild.

I'd pull upon your dress,
Look up to see you smile,
Babble forth my love for you
Then linger for awhile.

A gift of love I'd give to you
On very special days,
By words of love from little lips
My Mother I would praise.

I'd cause you many worries
Indoors and out of sight;
I'd cause you wakeful moments
With illness through the night.

But through your trials and troubles
You'd smile and comfort me,
Then brush away a falling tear
For fear that I would see.

Now comes the sad awakening:
I'm not a little boy—
The years are now behind me
To fill your life with joy.

But, on this special day of days
I want to let you know –
The glow remains within my heart,
The flame is never low.

Lt. Cdr. J. T. (Jimmy) Davis, USN <u>The Gold Star Mother.</u> May 1970, p5

Gold Star Mother (1960)

She smiles a while, she even sings,
For in her heart sweet solace brings,
The knowledge that the lad who's gone,
Gave up his life to speed along
The torch of freedom on its way,
That Peace for us might still hold sway.

Her Mother's heart well knows he's blest
In Heaven above, in peace at rest.
She smiles and sings because she knows
That as along life's path she goes
Each newborn day brings still more near
The day she'll meet that boy so dear.

And furtive tears give way to Peace
To know that when for her may cease
The earthly cares of daily life,
She'll find that land beyond all strife
The land that's filled with Love and Joy
And there with God she'll find "Her Boy."

Elaine Loomis Ensworth, <u>*The Gold Star Mother*</u> *, October 1960, p5*

Gold Star Mother (1962)

Many years have gone by since the letter was sent,
 The first thing she saw was the words "we regret."
The flash of that message pierced deep through her heart
 'Twill stay till the day her last breath does depart!
The loved son's relieved of his suffering and pain,
 But the Mother's deep grief comes again and again.
The sweethearts, the brides of the boys who are gone
 Forget, wed again, and new lives they lived on;
But the Mothers must carry her grief all alone
 And try hard to hide a heart heavy as stone.
She may join in life's actions; appear gay and bright.
 But her loss will recur to her night after night!
She will chill at the newscasts or rumors of war
 For she knows all too well what has happened before!
The hurt was so deep, and so great was the pain,
 She says, "Nothing on earth will e'er hurt me again!"
But great God above chose to claim her fond boy,
 And strengthen her faith in another world's joy.
She's grown older now and her thoughts wander back
 To the days of the childhood of her Joe or her Jack.
Had he lived, he'd have wed; she'd have grandchildren now

To soften the wrinkles on her furrowed brow!
Let her daydream in comfort; no scorn should she find!
Let her talk to herself; she's not losing her mind!
Her heartbreak she'll carry till her final breath;
Then gladly she'll welcome the Angel of Death!

The world should hold these fond Mothers in praise;
Their Gold Star they'll take to the end of their days!

Maureen J. Duffy Point Pleasant, NJ, The Gold Star Mother, November 1962, p8

Father's Day (1963)

Today we honor dear old Dad
In homes both near and far;
So give a special thought to him
Who wears the golden star.

He, too, has suffered cruelly
So Freedom might be won;
He, too, has given all he could,
His daughter or his son.

Look deep into his heart today
And read his secret pain;
Give him your understanding love
So he may smile again.

Too often he is overlooked
In all Life's scramble mad
So give a special thought today
To him, a Gold Star Dad.

Stella Duncan, The Gold Star Mother, June 1963, p3

Gold Star Mothers (1970)

A mother sat a dreaming …
When a letter came, one day…
Informing her … her boy
in line of duty … passed away.
He made the supreme sacrifice
Defending liberty …
With tear-dimmed eyes … I heard
This anguished mother bravely say.

"I'm proud to be the mother of a hero…
Proud my boy was glad to do his share…

'Tho my heart is filled with grief,
I'll be brave ... in my belief
That we two shall meet again ...
Sometime ... somewhere.
The little star ... that's shining in
  My window...
Is a symbol of a life ... I gave ...
  It's dear...
But I know 'twas not in vain...
And ... until we meet again ...
God bless Gold Star Mothers everywhere.

Jo Francis Weber, <u>The Gold Star Mother</u>, May 1970, p5

To Our Gold Star Mothers (1970)

Dry your tears, brave Gold Star Mothers,
Wherever you are.
How shall we console you, who wear forever a Golden Star?
Your son gave his life for the land we love
His courage will always remain in every mother's heart.

You have given flesh and blood and sacrifices and your greatest dreams,
In public you try to smile, though your heart is breaking apart.
Pray for him daily, Mothers, and he will be your guiding star, near and far.

It's a land where birds are always singing and the sky is always blue,
On the other side of the rainbow, where your soldier boy waits for you.
Safe at last from the sins and malices of mankind and the horrors of war,
In this beautiful heaven among the angels, is this boy that you adore.

In his eyes are the stars that shine above, on his face the same loved smile.
In God's city there are no tears, sorrows, suffering nor cares.
He is just waiting with open arms that some day he will great you there.

America is proud of you for the sacrifice and love you gave to save us,
And for the crown you won, May God himself reward you,
Who gave to the world His Only Son!

Mary Singer Goudemant, World War II GSM, <u>The Gold Star Mother</u>, July 1970, p8

What is Charity? (1972)

It's silence when your words would hurt.
It's patience when your neighbor's curt.
It's deftness when a scandal flows.
It's thoughtfulness for others' woes.
It's promptness when stern duty calls.
It's courage when misfortune falls.

Anonymous *The Gold Star Mother.* *March 1972, p8*

Star of Gold (1972)

It seems strange that there are those
Who do not know it was God who chose
You mothers to wear this golden pin;
That it wasn't merely a social whim.

They do not know this golden star
Shows you lost a son in war.
And that your mission is to try
To help his buddies who did not die.

A mother's courage, a mother's love.
Faith in your country and God above;
All these things are simply told
By your emblem — a star of gold.

Shine brightly, little star of gold,
'Til all the world has been told
What you mean, and what you are—
A son replaced by a golden star.

Edgar L. Smith *The Gold Star Mother* *December 1972, p2*
The above poem was written by the son of Ethel Smith, a member of Dallas, TX
chapter and past departmental president of Texas. He wrote it after hearing so
many people ask the question, "What is a Gold Star Mother?"

A Gold Star Mother (1973)

What is a Gold Star Mother?
        A Mother whose grieving heart
Reaches out to comfort another
        Whose world seems falling-apart.
A mother who feels compassion
        When casualty lists are read.
A mother who suffered the heartache
        Of hearing her son was dead.
A mother whose dreams were shattered

On a battlefield afar.
A mother who has the privilege
    Of wearing the little Gold Star.
A mother who walks so bravely
    To a fallen hero's grave.
A mother who loves the Nation
    Her son gave his life to save.
This is a Gold Star Mother.
    A mother with courage and pride
Whose son went forth to battle
    And in the line of duty, died.

Margaret H. Rutherford, Central Florida Chapter, The Gold Star Mother, May 1973, p7

Untitled (1974)

A group of mothers I was honored to meet.
I watched them working and planning side by side.
May I help you? Would you help me?
Of course, came a reply.
The elderly, the young, they all had something to share.
For there were grief, sorrow and memories to bear.
Every last one of them has the title, "Mom"
Fighting for our Country, they had lost a son.
Their aim is to help, to work, to lend a hand.
To the veterans, to their parents, to each other if they can.
What is life if we can't help one another?
I am so proud to have met these Gold Star Mothers.

Mildred Jones, a guest at a gold star installation for the New Bedford, Massachusetts chapter, presented this poem to the department president in 1974 The Gold Star Mother. February 1974, p5

How would my boy look today? (1975)

How do you think my Boy would look today?
He was so young when he went away.
Would his hair thin out?
It was so thick with curls.
Would his shoulders stoop with problems?
He was so straight and proud.
I can't picture him growing old
He was so young when he went away,
I wonder, do others wonder
How would their Boys look today?

Helen Kalletta, Bellerose, NY The Gold Star Mother. May/June 1975, p2

My Shining Star (1975)

There's a gold star in my window
    In memory of you
It lights my darkest hours
    And turns grey skies to blue
There's a new star in the Heavens
    That I search for every night
For it stands for faith and courage
    And a cause you thought was right
You tried once to explain to me,
    My precious brave young son
Just why we had to fight this war
    And help get justice done.

There's a gold star in my window
    That will guide me through the years
Even though the road ahead
    Is dark and wet with tears
So sleep on, my gallant hero,
    For even though you lost, you won
The heart of a grateful nation
    You're second best to none.

Virginia Dabonka , The Gold Star Mother, January/February 1975, p5

Gold Star Mothers (1975)

A most exclusive order, is the band
    Whose emblem is a gleaming golden star.
Their entrance fee, no coinage of the land;
    It's bought by grief — a higher price by far.

These mothers, joining hands with ardor true,
    Find strength to forge ahead, and ever try
To keep the faith their sons and daughters knew,
    Each lifts the fallen torch and holds it high.

They teach true brotherhood for all mankind,
    Respect for law, and honor to the flag.
They strive for lasting peace with heart and mind.

Good deeds and noble purposes shine far
    When mothers hold aloft their golden star.

Mary L. Lisher, The Gold Star Mother, January/February 1975, p7

Untitled (1976)

When day's at an end—dusk finds me alone—
I lie in my bed—in my silent home.
I try hard to erase unpleasant memories of time—
For mine was a happy life with those boys of mine.

They grew to be men —so straight and tall—
Then Vietnam loomed in the news—about to fall—
With determined faces and tear-dimmed eyes—
They left on the planes—bid us all goodbye.

Who would think two sons so brave—
Would return within two years—to lie in their grave?
Who am I to question why they died—
I know they upheld U.S. standards with pride.

Then I jerk awake and think what a coward I've been—
Lying here brooding is certainly a sin.
When God lent those babies for me to attend—
He never promised there'd be joys without end.

I can't help but wish I could have saved them their fate—
But with my head high I can proclaim they were great.
And I know I wouldn't give back one single moment with them—
So I won't fret—but thank God—for those happy years spent.

*In loving memory of PFC Edward A. McWright, USMC, and PFC Dale S. McWright, USMC—
and all GOLD STAR MOTHERS, The Gold Star Mother, November/December 1976, p2*

Gold Star Mother (1977)

Hear me, Gold Star Mother,
Whoever, wherever you are
Your loved one's up here waiting
And watching from afar.

Chin up there, Gold Star Mother,
Don't let him see you cry
Let him know you're happy
As you gaze up to the sky.

Be proud there, Gold Star Mother,
You were the lucky one
To be chosen as the mother
Of that gallant, noble son.

Be brave, dear Gold Star Mother,
As he was on that day
When in the course of battle
God took him home to stay.

I'm sure there, Gold Star Mother,
If you listen hard, one day
That voice now stilled, will speak once more
And you will hear him say.

Don't cry, my Gold Star Mother,
I'm happy in God's care
But my love and deep devotion
I send to you down there.

Virginia Dabonka (A Gold Star Mother), <u>The Gold Star Mother</u>, July/ August 1977, p2

My Son (1979)

I knelt in prayer at the grave of my son
Who lost his life in Vietnam,
My heart full of sorrow, my thoughts in turmoil
He gave his life to defend foreign soil.

Crying out in anger and despair
Nothing in this world is fair,
Shunned by many, honored by few,
America has forgotten you.

Then I heard his voice
Coming deep within the ground
To hear the answer to my anguish I found
"No, mom, I did not die in vain
From Hawaii to Alaska
From California to Maine
This is still the home of the brave and free
Because of the sacrifices made by others and me.
So build me a Memorial!
By standing up there proud and tall
And tell the world about this land
Whose Constitution on Liberty and Justice stand
Where man can still fulfill his dreams
Because your son served in the U.S. Marines.

Ruth Nadeau, National Corresponding Secretary <u>The Gold Star Mother.</u> January/February 1979, p2

Gold Star Mother (1980)

They gave me the flag
that draped your remains -
They sent a lone escort
Along on the train,
And filled the white chapel
As the young soloist sang.

They scattered the flowers
Admired, amidst dust of the lane –
They slowly tread – muted drums.
Eight guns, volley and flame-
They lowly bow heads
as the heaven weeps rain.

They softly utter … "Amen."
A prayer by the chaplain –
A bugler sounds taps
With an echo refrain
As in silence, I offer
To God — "Your Name."

Ralph A. Fisher Sr. (Gold Star Dad), <u>The Gold Star Mother</u>, January/February 1980, p3

A Tear Fell (1980)

Over a little barren desert mound
Of hot baked sand,
Where her tear fell, it fell on Navajo land.

We called him papoose
But she called him son.
Where her tear fell,
It fell scorched by the sun.

Then on the morrow
A wildflower in ecstasy
Shared the mound.
For where her tear fell
It fell upon hallowed ground.

Ralph A. Fisher Sr. (Gold Star Dad), <u>The Gold Star Mother</u>, May/June 1980, p8

Soldier Going Home (1980)

When your time has come
And the Master calls you home
Would you give this message to my soldier boy
Just tell him who it's from
Mom, dad, sister, brothers, relatives and friends galore
You're very much a part of us, each day we miss you more
We have wonderful memories of the short time we had with you
Keep on smiling, son, the years are just a few
Just remember, son, we love you very dear
You haven't been forgotten, son,
It seems like you're still here.

Berniece Farris <u>*The Gold Star Mother*</u>*. September/October 1980, p2*

Gold Star (1986)

Gold Star, I'll wear you upon my chest
You show the world my son's at rest.
He was my first born, my pride and joy,
He died for his country, my soldier boy.
Gold Star, do you hear my heart skip a beat?
Or hear the roar of a football crowd,
Rooting their team on with cheers long and loud.
Gold Star, do you see the tears I hide
When I come face to face with his intended bride?
She's wed to another, as well she should,
She's a picture of beauty, so kind and so good.
Gold Star, do you feel the terrible ache
Of the place in my heart that no one can take
The place that's reserved for him alone,
Filled only with memories, now that he's gone.
Gold Star, I'll cherish you, much more than a toy,
For you were the last gift of my darling boy.
He paid the highest price he could pay,
And I'll wear you gladly, day after day.
Gold Star, will you go with me to my resting place?
We will meet all our boys in that vast space.
And when I meet God with you on my chest
He'll know I'm the Mother of one of America's best.

In loving memory of my son, Pfc. Larry J. Martin
Patsy Civero <u>*The Gold Star Mother*</u>*. January/February 1986, p6*

Beside the Purple Heart It Lies (1989)

On the shelf beside the Purple Heart it lies,
In a private shrine of loving memory
Of one who died in a far land,
The Gold Star tended by my hand
That rocked the cradle in the nursery.
My hand that tends the thought that never dies.

Now near my aching heart I wear my gold –
The gold that I would gladly give away
If I could see my son returned
As he was then, as I have yearned
To see him as the youth he was that day,
When we were all so young, who now are old.

Those were the times our young men did their part
In two world wars, Korea, Vietnam;
For some their part was bitter death;
And I, as long as I have breath
Will wear my gold in memory. I am
A Gold Star Mother with a broken heart.

Gene Jannuzi , The Gold Star Mother, January/February 1989, p6

When the Blue Star Turns to Gold (1992)

He went one day with a cheery wave,
    A gay farewell, and a smile he gave,
And he went—with a purpose true.
    In a window was hung a star of blue
He did the task that was given him,
    To help rid the world of greed and sin
He fought a good fight—so the message told
    But the star of blue has turned to gold.
Dear Father, be near those homes, we pray,
    Where the message has come, or will some day
Comfort each heart with Thy love so true
    Where a gold star hangs in place of blue.

Roselyn C. Steere, The Gold Star Mother. July/August 1992, p3

A Gold Star Mother's Prayer (1992)

A purple heart, a folded flag,
    A blue star turned to gold;
Tangible objects unyielding
    Are hers to have and hold.
She gazes on a photograph
    Alone this Veterans Day;
She clasps her tired hands and
    God hears a Gold Star Mother pray:
I thank thee for this victory,
    Enduring may it be;
May peace now stand memorial
    For the son I gave to Thee.

Waunita Williams, <u>The Gold Star Mother</u>, November/December 1992, p2

The Mother on the Sidewalk

The mother on the sidewalk as the troops are marching by
Is the mother of Old Glory that is waving in the sky.
Men have fought to keep it splendid, men have died to keep it bright.
But the flag was born of woman and her sufferings day and night.
'Tis her sacrifice has made it, and once more we ought to pray
For the brave and loyal mother of the boy that goes away.

There are days of grief before her, there are hours that she will weep;
She has heard her country calling and has risen to the test,
And has placed upon the altar of the Nation's need, her best.
No man shall ever suffer in the turmoil of the fray
The anguish of the Mother of the boy who went away.

You may boast men's deeds of glory, you may tell their courage great,
But to die is easier service that alone to sit and wait.
And I hail the little mother, with the tearstained face and grave
Who has given the Flag a soldier – she's the bravest of the brave.
And that banner we are proud of, with its red, blue and white,
Is a lasting tribute holy to all mother's love or right.

Edgar A. Guest 1991 National Convention Program

The Promotion (1994)

In the Heavenly ranks
Up in the sky,
You went from Private First Class to Angel,
In the twinkling of an eye.

You didn't need to study,
Or take a final test —
Your reward was Heaven,
For being your very best.

And while God's gain
Is my loss,
I cannot hold your soul.
But oh, my son, I miss you
More than you'll ever know.

Sandra Van Orman, (Poem from Persian Gulf War) Membership Report.
The Gold Star Mother, May/June 1994, p2

Reflections (1995)

It's in an older part of town, kind of small – a bit run down
    But it seemed to me a mansion when I was young
And what I wouldn't give it I could only live
    in the corner house where the Gold Star hung.

I asked my Daddy who lived there, Clark Gable, Maybe Fred Astaire?
    A star like that would surely mean celebrity
I saw my Dad grow misty-eyed as he knelt down by my side
    and I still recall the words he said to me.

"Years ago the whole world was at war, and we all knew then what we were fighting for
    so we sent our young across the oceans wide.
They bravely fought in others' wars to keep the battles from our shores
    I'm sad to say that many of them died.

In honor of their memory each and every family
    received a Gold Star for all the world to see
A star to be displayed with pride to show a loved one here who died
    to keep our country free for you and me."

Now each time I pass that way I bow my head a bit and say
    "Thank you for my freedom whoever you are."
And I never will forget that I owe a grateful debt
    to that corner House still wearing the Gold Star.

Gloria W. Palmer, Lilburn, GA, The Gold Star Mother, May/June 1995, p5

Memories Mingled with the Taps (1995)

Each time I hear the taps, I scarce can take it in.
The memories come rushing back, as I touch my Gold Star Pin.
Our sons and husbands seemed so strong, as they march off to war,
But as we listen to the taps, we know they are no more.
Our loved ones didn't die in vain, 'cause they fought to keep us free;
So let's be faithful to our land, as we honor their memory.

Phyllis Olson Aubin, Stillwater, Minnesota , The Gold Star Mother, May/June 1995, p5

When the Blue Star Turns to Gold (1995)

A service flag hung in the window
With a star of heavenly blue.
Telling a boy had left the home
To serve his country true.
He went bravely into the service
The story so of't has been told
But ere long you could see in passing
The blue star had turned to gold.
It is as old as the centuries
Causing such grief untold
Such loneliness, such heartache
When a blue star turns to gold.
Heartaches and tears are mingled
In this wide, wide world today.
Our boys are fighting and dying
While mothers at home weep and pray.
Oh, God, be with each brave heart
And Care for each precious soul.
Keep them in the hollow of Thy hand
While the blue star turns to gold.

Submitted by Marguerite Bezila (Johnstown, PA)
The Gold Star Mother, September/October 1995, p2

Over There (1997)

I stood upon a crowded street,
And watched the soldiers come;
I could hear the bugle sounding,
And the rolling of a drum.
I could see their flags a-waving,
Then I heard the band's gay blare

As they struck up the same old tune
That took them "OVER THERE."
But I stood beside a mother,
And I couldn't cheer a note,
As I looked into her tear-dimmed eyes,
A lump rose in my throat,
For she told me in a soft sweet voice
About her son so fair –
That this was his company passing,
But – they'd left him 'OVER THERE.'

"I know I ought to smile," she said,
"And cheer these brave boys on.
But it's hard to watch them passing
And to know my own is gone;
Why it seems 'twas only yesterday
The he marched down past this square,
And called, "I'll be back , Mother,"
But - he's lying 'OVER THERE.'

"I smiled to hide my tears then
Though he knew my heart was sad;
Then I asked the Lord to spare him
For my boy was ALL I had.
There were so many thousand, and
I felt he'd hear my prayer
And return my boy safe to me –
But, He called him 'OVER THERE.'

That is just one mother's story
Of the sacrifice she made,
But it made me think of others
Who were watching that parade;
Though the shouts and cheering lingered,
Some were missing for their share,
But we know God will reward them
For their brave deeds 'OVER THERE.'

From the 60th National Convention Program, June 22–25, 1997, no author listed.

•

A Gold Star Mom (undated)

My life is rolling along,
     challenging but good, full and happy.

Until that fateful night …
     a knock on my door
A Marine in dress blues
     with those words that struck fear in my heart
     " …we regret to inform you …"

With those five words, my life is changed forever,
My heart – shattered in a million pieces.
Is this hole in my heart ever going to heal?
How do I pick up the pieces and go on?

Then into my life comes my sisters in white
Hearts open-arms outstretched
     to embrace me in my hour of need.

They have been there.
They have walked in my footsteps.
They know my pain.

At the Tomb of the Unknown Soldier
     they weep— as taps are played—
     and relive the pain just like the
     first time they heard it.

At the Wall
     They are also there for me as they show me
     where their sons' names have been
     etched in granite.

And as we weep together—sharing each
     other's pain, I realize the experience
     is forever burned in my heart.

I also come to the realization that my load
     Is a little lighter—
     That my burden has been shared by these
     Dear, sweet, compassionate ministering angels.

To THE LADIES IN WHITE—THE GOLD STAR MOMS
Diane Deanne, Persian Gulf Gold Star Mom

Ladies of Gold (1999)

They are stars that shine so bright
But they don't shine just at night
For they are mothers — from near and far
Who have lost a son, in a war.

They shine as does a loving smile
And as does the glint of a tear
For they gave the gift
Of one they held so dear.

Their dearest treasure was snatched away
So that, in liberty, others might live today
The pain in their hearts; it does ache
They are proud of the stand their sons did take.

To fight for freedom
And to dash tyranny
They did this for you
They did this for me.

I, for one, stand ready to do my part
And take each mother into my heart
And let her know, that it is a lie
For not in vain, did her son die.

And these ladies
Be they young or old
Are truly worth
Their weight in gold.

I'll take them in my arms, their tears on my chest
I'll tell them, he was America's best
My hope, if I may be so bold,
Is for the light from their eyes, to shine like gold.

A Gold Star Mother
They'll always be
We owe them plenty
Everyone … you, you and me.

Ed Allen October 1999, National Dusters-Quads-Searchlights Association

Untitled (2001)

Yes, we grieve.
In the stillness of the night
Echoes the silent primal howl
Of rage and refusal to believe.

In private moments of the day-to-day,
We weep our silent tears;
Sorrow does not lessen with the
Passage of the years.

Oh, yes, we weep and hide
Our desolation with words
Like duty, gallantry and pride.

Still we cry.

For the bright, sweet child who was,
We cry.
For the valiant man he became,
We cry.
For the man he would have been,
We cry.

We grieve.
With dry and stinging eyes,
We weep tears than can't relieve.

For his loneliness, his fear, his pain,
Knowing our aching, empty arms
Cannot hold him close again,
We cry.

But for the solace that it gives,
In the love he left us in our care
And in his memory we'll forever share –
Still he lives — Eternity his legacy.

E.E. Moreno (Newton Chapter #24, Massachusetts) 2001
The Gold Star Mother, January/February 2004, p6

A Mother's Heart (2002)

I got a phone call the other day,
Lady said, Sir my mother passed away,
'And I was wondering if you would come and speak.
I said, I'm sorry, but I believe you have a wrong number
I don't believe I knew your mother

And I'm sure I'm not the one you seek.

She said I know that you entertain folks
With funny stories, songs and jokes.
But in her voice I could hear a quiet despair.
No, Sir, you didn't know my mom.
Or my brother who died in Nam,
But we asked you, because you were over there.

I know, sir, the excuses you could use,
And you have every right to refuse,
And maybe you wouldn't even know where to start
See Jimmy was hit by a rocket, Tet of sixty eight
So all we had to bury was an empty crate
So Mom's most prized possession was his Purple Heart.

So I went to speak at her final service,
And discover that I wasn't even nervous
As I stepped up behind the speakers stand.
The lines I had prepared now seemed all wrong
The rehearsed phrases were suddenly gone
As my eyes found the medal clutched in her hand.

For in this little piece of metal and purple cloth
Were all the memories of a son she'd lost.
Skinned knees, climbed trees and his screams of "MOM"
First grade, first date, the prom, were in each thread
From the first cry in delivery to the telegram that read,
"We regret to inform you, your son was killed in Vietnam."

They handed her a flag and his Purple Heart
And even in death she still won't part
With these symbols of the son that she had lost,
He'd served his country, his buddies and the Corps
Things he thought were worth fighting for
And she, like he, had paid the cost.

If there is heaven, surely she got in,
To see her son, once again.
Her baby, the Marine, the Vietnam Vet,
In my mind there plays a story,
Of her with him, beneath Old Glory,
As she pins that Purple Heart on her Son's chest.

Gary Lyn Harp, Disabled Vietnam Vet
The Gold Star Mother, March/April 2002, p1

Gold Star Mother (2003)

There's a gold star mother somewhere
Thinking of her son today.
She remembers how he left her,
As he proudly marched away,
Just a gold star mother somewhere,
Who recalls the days gone by
When her son was just a youngster
Fun and laughter in his eye.

"But he heard the bugle calling
With the rest he stepped in file
Turned his back on home and loved ones—
Left them with a parting smile.
Went across and did his duty
Did it right up to the end—
And I am very glad I knew him
As a comrade and a friend.

Heard the call and met his Maker
Like the soldier that I knew—
Never fearing for an instant
As he passed his last review.
May this gold star mother somewhere
As she thinks of him today
Just remember as a soldier
How proudly he marched away.
Just remember him as happy

Glad to be in with the rest
Never shirked a single duty
Always stood up with the best
May she know that all his comrades
Scattered through the countryside
Never will forget their buddy—
Who has crossed the great divide.

B.E. Lincoln, The Gold Star Mother, May/June 2003, p6

In the Garden (2006)

If **ENTHUSIASM** was contagious, we could have an **EPIDEMIC.**

It is too late for spring planting but we can still **REAP A GOOD HARVEST**
If we **PLANT A GARDEN NOW – THE GARDEN OF OUR ORGANIZATION.**

First plant five rows of peas:
> **PRESENCE,**
> **PERSUASION,**
> **PROMPTNESS,**
> **PREPARATION,**
> **PERSEVERANCE.**

Next to these, plant three rows of squash:
> **SQUASH GOSSIP,**
> **INDIFFERENCE** and
> **UNWARRANTED CRITICISM.**

Then plant six rows of lettuce:
> Let us actively **RECRUIT NEW MEMBERS**
> Let us respect **RULES AND REGULATIONS**
> Let us be **TRUE** to our **OBLIGATION**
> Let us be **FAITHFUL to DUTY**
> Let us be **LOYAL** and **UNSELFISH**
> Let us **LOVE ONE ANOTHER.**

No garden is complete without **TURNIPS:**
> Turn up for **MEETINGS**
> Turn up with a **SMILE**
> Turn up with **CONSTRUCTIVE IDEAS**
> Turn up with **DETERMINATION** to make everything count for something **GOOD**
> Turn up with the name of a **NEW MEMBER.**

BEWARE OF SHALLOW SEEDING lest the **WINDS OF DISSENTION BLOW AWAY THE SEEDS!**
MULCH WITH DEVOTION
WEATHER WITH ENTHUSIASM
AND WATCH OUR GARDEN GROW.

Price, Nan., The Gold Star Mother, May/June 2006, p8

Volunteers in Heaven (2006)

Many will be shocked to find, when the Day of Judgment nears,
that there's a special place in Heaven set aside for volunteers.

Furnished with big recliners, satin couches and footstools, there are no committee chairmen, no yard sales, no coffee to serve, no library duty or bulletin assembly. There will be nothing to print or staple, not one thing to fold or mail, and telephone lists will be outlawed. Just the snap of a finger will bring cool drinks and gourmet dinners with rare treats fit for a king.

You ask, "Who'll serve these privileged few and work for all they're worth?"
Why, all those who reaped the benefits and not once volunteered on Earth.

Anonymous, The Gold Star Mother, July/August 2006, p4

Gold Star Mom

The banner was small
But the star was large,
The color of a blue night sky.
She hung it in the window
With trembling fingers
And tried hard not to cry.
He was so young to go far away
As all soldiers have to do.
She knew that danger lurked everywhere,
As she touched the star of blue.
The weeks went by
The months rolled on
She knew he would not die.
Her faith in God held her head up high.
In her heart she sang a song.
But the battles raged,
The news was not good.
Why did so many have to die?
The thought made her cold
And she felt terribly old
As the day came that she faced
  With dread.
When a knock on the door
Shattered her life evermore,
And the blue star turned to gold.

Esther B. Campbell Gates, who lost her son Keith in Vietnam.
The Gold Star Mother, September/October 2006, p16

Gold Star Mother (2008)

I cried out in pain as I read the letter
My life from this day will never get better
The lines were blurred as I tried to see
The words that said my son died for country and me
The years go by, and I still call his name
The dreams I had will never be the same
The memories that were of the son I had
Are now nightmares when my days are bad
Part of me died when my son was killed
There is an emptiness that can never be filled
Night after night as I lay in my bed
I still can't believe my son is dead
But the love of a mother can never die
And I can't forget, and sometimes I cry
I keep on living, but I think of the past
The years go by ever so fast
When my life on this Earth is finally done
The emptiness will be gone for I'll be with my son
In my thoughts I can see him still
In my dream I call his name, Bill.

In memory of Catherine Niader and Pvt. William Niader,
KIA June 12, 1945, Kunishi Ridge, Okinawa *The Gold Star Mother,*
January/February 2008, p12

Untitled (2008)

Our sons and daughters gave all
Without any despair.
They answered the call,
And put themselves on the line
Fighting for our freedom
And a secure nation on their minds.
We know all too well
The deep heartache inside
Unbearable loss
For our loved ones that died.
We cannot change
These fatal events.
Just honor their memory
Shall be our intent.
It is now our job
To remind everyone.
Just how brave they were,
Our daughters and sons.

We stand proud for them now
And we do what we can.
To support their comrades
Until this war comes to an end.
And when we die,
Don't be sad for us then.
As we will be in the arms
Of our sons and daughters again.

By Cathy Hicks (a gold star mother)
The Gold Star Mother, November/December 2008, p8

Appendix D:

Gold Star Mothers Stamp Cachets

On the day that a new commemorative postage stamp is issued, envelopes, postcards and other postal materials bearing the new stamp are specially postmarked by the post office where the stamp is introduced. Prized by many stamp collectors, the "first day covers" are marked with a special cancellation stamp indicating that it was issued on the first day the stamp became available. Often, the envelope or other postal item displays a postal cachet, which is artwork related to the stamp's subject.

These cachets are from first day of issue envelopes honoring the Gold Star Mothers stamp which was issued September 21, 1948 (Commemorative Stamp #969). The stamps were first issued in Waterloo, Iowa, the home of the Sullivan family.

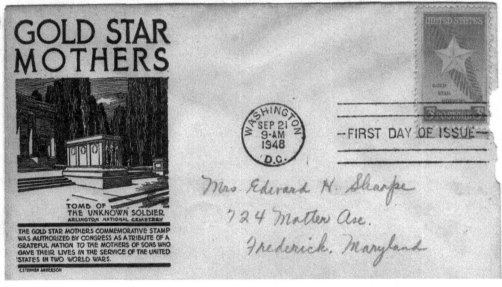

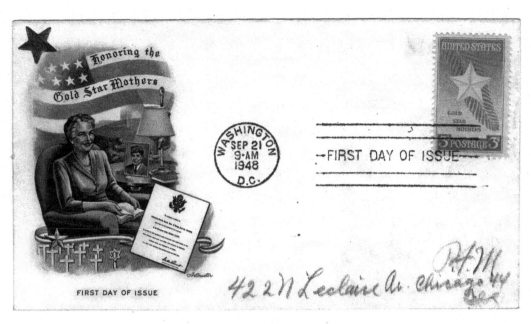

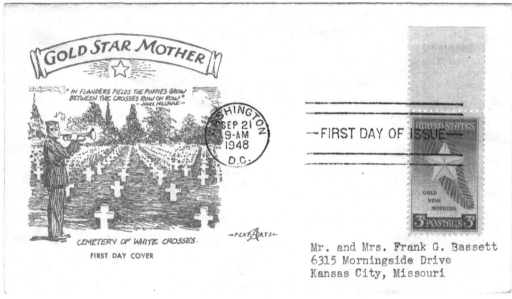

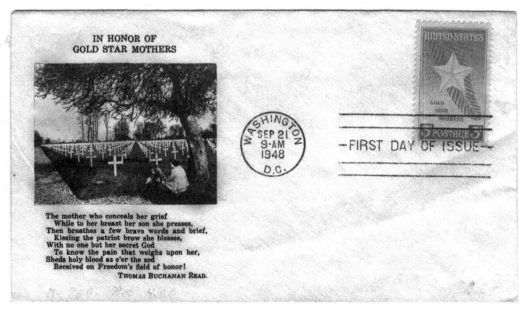

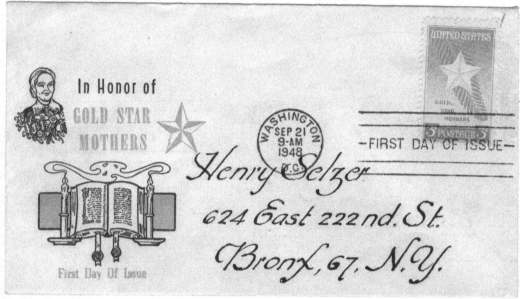

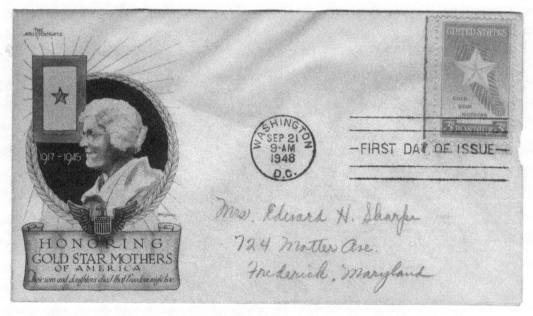

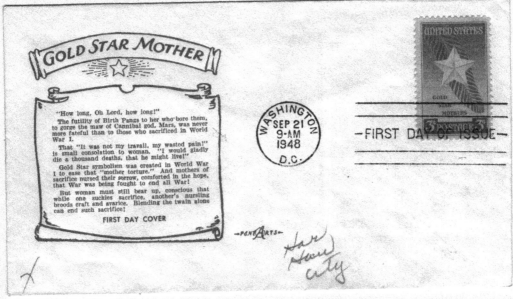

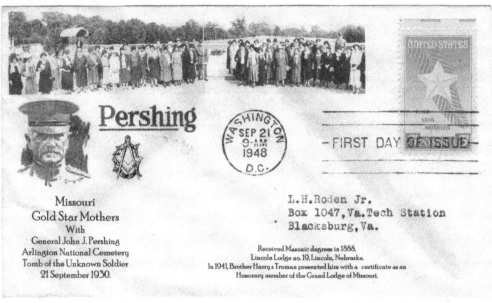

Pershing

Missouri
Gold Star Mothers
With
General John J. Pershing
Arlington National Cemetery
Tomb of the Unknown Soldier
21 September 1930.

WASHINGTON
SEP 21
9-AM
1948
D.C.

— FIRST DAY OF ISSUE —

L.H.Roden Jr.
Box 1047,Va.Tech Station
Blacksburg, Va.

Received Masonic degrees in 1888,
Lincoln Lodge no. 19, Lincoln, Nebraska.
In 1941, Brother Harry s Truman presented him with a certificate as an
Honorary member of the Grand Lodge of Missouri.

IN TRIBUTE TO
GOLD STAR MOTHERS

WASHINGTON
SEP 21
9-AM
1948
D.C.

— FIRST DAY OF ISSUE —

Mrs. Oscar N. Wooley
626 Chestnut Street
St. Louis 1, Missouri.

1917-18   1941-45
IN HONOR OF THE
GOLD STAR
MOTHERS

CACHETCRAFT   L.W. STAEHLE

WASHINGTON
SEP 21
9-AM
1948
D.C.

FIRST DAY OF ISSUE

George P. Gersib
1620 Capitol
Des Moines 16, Iowa

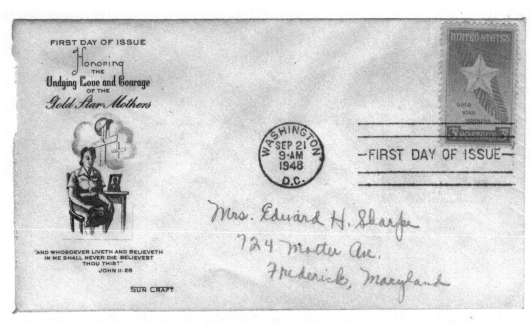

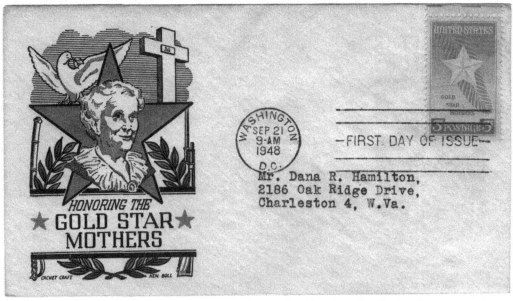

Gold Star Mothers Stamp Cachets | 383

Endnotes: Chapters 1–12

Chapter 1
The World War and the Gold Star

1. Van Trump, Harold (Editor). *Fulton County in the World War.* No publisher/date, p9.

2. "Service Flags—Who May Display—Meaning of Stars": *1919 World Almanac* p637.

3. Ibid.

4. Ibid.

5. Ibid.

6. Ibid.

7. Ibid.

8. Sterba, Christopher M. "More Than Ever, We Feel Proud to be Italians. World War I and the New Haven Colonia, 1917–1918." *Journal of the American Ethnic History,* Winter 2001, Volume 20, Issue 2.

9. "Hobo Army, 30,000 Strong, Will Raise Service Flag." *Chicago Daily Tribune.* October 20, 1918, p1.

10. "Comeback of Blue Star Flags?" *Fredricksburg Free Lance-Star.*

11. *Ladies Home Journal.* April 1919, p34

12. Herschell, William & St. Clair, Floyd. *The Service Flag.* Sam Fox Publishing Co. 1918.

13. Armstrong, Paul B. & Klickman, F. Henri. "There's A Little Blue Star in the Window and It Means All The World to Me." Frank K. Root & Company, 1918.

14. "That Service Flag." *Cleveland Advocate.* January 19, 1918.

15. Service Flags. *Chicago Daily Tribune.* October 10, 1917, p8.

16. Peattie, Elia W. Service Flags. *Chicago Daily Tribune.* December 2, 1917, pD5.

17. Grossman, Bernard & De Costa, Harry. *The Little Grey Mother Who Waits All Alone.* M. Witmark & Sons, 1915.

18. *Mother's Day 1918.* YMCA publication

19. Mott, John R. (General Secretary of the National War Work Council of the YMCA; United War Work Campaign) "The Tradition of the American Mother: A Message to the Fathers and Mothers Who Live in the Homes with Service Flags." November 11–18, 1918.

20. Rinehart, Mary Roberts. *The Altar of Freedom— An Appeal to the Mothers of America.* Houghton Mifflin Company. April 1917, p3.

21. Tally & Mayo; Gaskill, Clarence. "That's A Mother's Liberty Loan." M. Witmark & Sons, 1917; Sterling, Andrew B. America, He's For You! Joe Morris Music Co.; 1918; Egan, Raymond; Kahn, Gus; Van Alstyne, Egbert. So Long, Mother (Al Jolson's Mother Song). Jerome H. Remick & Company; 1917; Sterling, Andrew B. & Lange, Arthur. America, Here's My Boy. Joe Morris Music Co. 1917; Frost, Jack. When A Boy Says Goodbye to His Mother and She Gives Him to Uncle Sam. McKinley Music Company, 1918.

22. Sterling, Andrew B. & Lange, Arthur. A Mother's Prayer for Her Boy Out There. Joe Morris Music Co.; 1918; Sweet, Al. & Baskette, Billie. Each Stitch a Thought of You, Dear. Leo Fiest, Inc. 1918; Rodgers, Howard E. & Kay, Jerome E. There's A Battlefield In Every Mother's Heart. Waterson, Berlin & Snyder Co., 1918; Sporn, Edward. There's a Grey-Haired Mother Waiting. Royal Music Company, 1918 (Collection of Robert J. Arner); Grossman, Bernie & Marr, Alex. Say A Prayer for the Boys Out There. Joe Morris Music Co., 1917;

23. Potter, Clinton J. & Whitmore, F. E. In the Gloaming, Mother Darling, When the Message Comes To You. Whitmore Publishing, 1918. (Collection of Robert J. Arner); Caddigan, Jack &

Story, Chic. Mother—I'm Dreaming of You. Jack Mendelsohn Music Co.,1918; Dempsey, J.E. & Burke & Joseph E. A Soldier's Rosary. A. J. Stasney Music Co. 1918; Boyden, George. If I'm Not at the Roll Call, Kiss Mother Good-bye for Me. Leo. Feist Inc., 1918; Harris, Charles K. Break The News to Mother. Charles K. Harris Publishers, 1897.

24. Pottle, Emory. *Saturday Evening Post* (undated clipping—Fenelon Collection)

25. Cronson, Joe & Freeman, Harold B. There's A Little Gold Star in the Service Flag. Harold Freeman Music Co., 1918.

26. Letter from Caroline Seaman Read to Woodrow Wilson, May 3, 1918. The Papers of Woodrow Wilson, Volume 48, p28-29.

27. A Gold Star as the National Symbol of Mourning. Union Progress. (Union, South Carolina) May 7, 1918. Special thanks to Sharon Rupp, Community Service Librarian, and the Union County Carnegie Library Collection (Union, South Carolina)

28. Letter from Woodrow Wilson to Anna Howard Shaw. May 16, 1918. *The Papers of Woodrow Wilson,* Vol. 48, p27.

29. Letter from Anna Howard Shaw to Woodrow Wilson; May 21, 1918. *The Papers of Woodrow Wilson,* Vol. 48, p111.

30. Letter from Woodrow Wilson to Anna Howard Shaw, May 22, 1918. *The Papers of Woodrow Wilson,* Vol. 48, p117.

31. Tucker, Spencer C. *The Great War 1914–1918.* Indiana University Press, Bloomington, IN 1998, p176.

Chapter 2
The Post-War Period:
Shaping the Memory of the War

1. Rumer, Thomas A. *The American Legion—An Official History—1919–1989.* M. Evans & Company, New York. p 25-26.

2. *American War Mothers History.* No publisher information, 1966(?), p4.

3. Ibid. p5.

4. Ibid. p6.

5. Foreman, Edward R. (editor). *World War Service Record—Rochester and Monroe County, New York.* The Du Bois Press; Rochester, New York; Published by the City of Rochester—1924. p641–643

6. Ibid.

7. America's 77,000 Overseas Dead. *The American Legion Weekly.* November 11, 1921, p 10.

8. Lest We Forget. *The Outlook.* February 18, 1920.

p231

9. Fiske, Charles H. Fallen on the Field of Honor. The Outlook. February 25, 1920. p277

10. Let Them Rest. *The Outlook.* February 25, 1920. p272

11. Gordon, Mrs. O. L. A Plea from a Mother. *Chicago Daily Tribune.* January 20, 1920. p8

12. America's 77,000 Overseas Dead. The American Legion Weekly. November 11, 1921, p 10.

13. The Day of the Gold Star Hosts. *The American Legion Weekly* May 30,1924, p17.

14. The Voice of the Legion: A Casket and a Civilian. *The American Legion Weekly.* October 7, 1921, p 13.

15. White, Windsor T. How Shall We Commemorate Their Victory? *The Outlook,* November 17, 1919.

16. University of Tennessee Collection: Papers of Mrs. Frank DeGarmo: Box 3, Folder 23 (Special thanks to Holly Adams, Librarian, University of Tennessee)

17. Ibid.Note: Not a stranger to the public eye, Mrs. DeGarmo was well known long before her formation of this group. Dedicated to improving the health care of children in America, she had organized and promoted the first "Better Babies" event in 1908 at the Louisiana State Fair to promote interest in improving the physical health and intelligence of children from six months to three years of age. Programs based on her prototype rapidly spread across the nation.

18. DeGarmo: Box 5, Folder 43

19. DeGarmo: Box 4, Folder 4

20. DeGarmo: Box 2, Folder 26

21. DeGarmo: Box 11, Folder 11

22. Ibid.

23. Ibid.

24. DeGarmo: Box 4, Folder 7

25. http://www.thinker.org/legion (3-14-2006)

26. *The American Legion Weekly.* May 30, 1924, p3.

27. Ibid. February 1934, p62.

28. Pershing, John J. Forever America. *American Legion Monthly* May 1927, p14.

29. Ibid.

30. *Annual Report of the American Battle Monuments Commission to the President of the United States (Fiscal Year 1925).* Government Printing Office, Washington, p5.

31. Address of Major General James G. Harbord, U.S. Army—Dedication of "Belleau Wood" July 22, 1923.

32. McNutt, William Slavens. The Soldier Comes Home. *The American Legion Weekly,* November

11, 1921, p6

33. Worthington, R. C. Homecoming. *The American Legion Magazine.* November 1938, p3.

34. Pershing, John J. Dear War Mothers: McCalls. November, 1927, p5, 13.

Chapter 3
Creating the American Gold Star Mothers, Inc.

1. Obituary: Mrs. Seibold , 78, Dies; First Head of Gold Star Mothers. *Washington Star,* Washington, D.C. June 13, 1947.

2. Obituary: George G. Seibold, 90, Dies; Star Printer Retired at 81. *Washington Star,* Washington, D.C. May 28, 1955.

3. Obituary: Mrs. Seibold , 78, Dies; First Head of Gold Star Mothers. *Washington Star,* Washington, D.C. June 13, 1947.

4. Obituary: Lieut. G. V. Seibold Killed in Action. *Washington Star,* Washington D.C. December 15, 1918.

5. Ibid.

6. Sloan, James J., Jr. *Wings of Honor: American Airmen in World War I. Schiffer Military/Aviation History,* Atglen, NY 1994 p195.

7. Obituary: Lieut. G. V. Seibold Killed in Action. *Washington Star,* Washington D.C. December 15, 1918.

8. Ibid.

9. Ibid. Sloan, p203

10. Nelson, Theodosia D. Seibold. Early History of American Gold Star Mothers, Inc. Presentation to 1978 AGSM National Convention.

11. Ibid.

12. Obituary: Lieut. G. V. Seibold Killed in Action. *Washington Star,* Washington D.C. December 15, 1918.

13. Ibid. Sloan, p203.

14. Nelson, Theodosia D. Seibold. Early History of American Gold Star Mothers, Inc. Presentation to 1978 AGSM National Convention.

15. Ibid.

16. AGSM Petition for Incorporation—1931; p3

17. Speech by Mrs. G. G. Seibold at 1st National AGSM Convention, November 9, 1932.

18. Gold Star Mothers Hold Monthly Meeting September 18. *The Leatherneck.* November 1928, p19.

19. Gold Star Mothers. *The Leatherneck.* February 1929, p19.

Chapter 4
The Gold Star Mothers of the Great War

1. *American Legion Monthly Magazine.* March 1930, p 69.

2. Kolata, Gina. *Flu—The Story of the Great Influenza Pandemic of 1918 and the Search for the Virus that Caused It.* Farrar, Straus & Giroux, New York. 1999, page IX.

3. Ibid. p5

Chapter 5
The Gold Star Pilgrimage

1. A St. Louis Gold Star Mother's Tour of France, 1925. The Papers of Mrs. Frank DeGarmo, Special Collections Library, Hoskins Library, University of Tennessee, Knoxville. Special thanks to Holly Adams, Special Collections Librarian.

2. Ibid. Private Leland Reynolds is buried in Plot A, Row 1, Grave 29 at the Aisne-Marne American Cemetery (Belleau Wood). He served with the 5th Regiment of the US Marine Corp, 2nd Division, and was killed on June 24, 1918. Thanks to Christopher Sims, Flanders Field American Cemetery, Belgium for providing this information.

3. Transcript of testimony before the House of Representatives Committee on Military Affairs, held hearings on H. R. Bill 4019. February 1924

4. Ibid. p12.

5. Ibid. p20.

6. Minutes of the Hearing before the Committee of Military Affairs, House of Representatives, 70th Congress, 1st Session. January 27, 1928, p3.

7. Elaborate Preparations Lie behind the Gold Star Pilgrimage Success. *Kansas City Times.* June 24, 1931.

8. Du Puy, William A. Pilgrimage of Mothers to Europe's War Graves. *The New York Times.* February 23, 1930.

9. List of Mothers and Widows of American Soldiers, Sailors and Marines Entitled to Make a Pilgrimage to the War Cemeteries in Europe. House Document 104. December 1929, p3

10. Other Uses for $5,000,000. *The New York Times.* (Letters to the Editor) February 7, 1930.

11. Papers of President Herbert C Hoover. Letter to President Hoover from Mrs. C. D. DuBois dated March 17, 1930.

12. Address by General DeWitt to the Officers of the Gold Star Mothers and Widows Pilgrimage. Hotel

Pennsylvania, New York City. April 15, 1930.

13. Ibid.

14. Ibid.

15. Papers of President Herbert C Hoover. Telegram to President Hoover from Catherine B. Daniels dated May 31, 1930.

16. Papers of President Herbert C Hoover. Telegram to George Akerson from Tom Canty dated May 3, 1930.

17. The Nation. July 23, 1930.

18. Ibid.

19. 60 Negro Gold Star Mothers Sail Abroad on Segregated Ship. *The Chicago Daily Tribune*. July 13, 1930, p6.

20. Races: "We are Insulted." *Time Magazine*. June 1930.

21. Gold Star Mothers in France. *The New York Amsterdam News*. August 13, 1930.

22. Du Puy, William A. Pilgrimage of Mothers to Europe's War Graves. *The New York Times*. February 23, 1930.

23. Wilson, Major Louis C. Q.M.C. The War Mother Goes "Over There." *Quartermaster Review*. May-June 1930.

24. Ibid.

25. Ibid.

26. Seibold, Grace D. Pilgrimage experience report. AGSM Collection, Library of Congress.

27. Pilgrimage Journal of Mrs. Belle M. Harner. William Dienna Collection. Our special thanks to Bill Dienna for sharing his wonderful collection of Pilgrimage materials.

28. Pilgrimage Journal of Nora G. Weld. Fenelon Collection

29. Ginsburgh, Captain Robert. This, Too, Is America. *The American Legion Monthly*. November 1933. p16

30. Ibid.

31. Ibid.

32. Ibid.

33. Ibid.

34. Ibid.

35. Ibid.

36. Laubach, Lt. Col. James H., Q.M.C. A Sacred Duty Ends. The *Quartermaster Review*. September-October 1933, p22.

37. Army Cuts Red Tape for Mother to Visit Grave of Son in France. *Washington Star*. May 19, 1930.

38. Report on Pilgrimages of Mothers and Widows to Cemeteries in Europe. Major General B. F.

Cheatham, Ret'd to the Quartermaster General. July 7, 1930. Source: Lisa M. Budreau, "The Construction of American Memory Abroad" (Ph.D. dissertation., Oxford University, 2004)

39. An Appreciation. *Quartermaster Review*. September–October 1931. Letter written by Mrs. Edith A. McCormick, Brooklyn, New York.

40. Ibid. Ginsburgh. p16.

Chapter 6
The 1930s: Remembrance, Respect, and Recognition

1. August 5, 1936. Transcript of radio interview: Radio Station WIXBS—Waterbury, CT.

2. Ibid.

3. Ibid.

4. Ibid.

5. Ibid.

6. "Vets Mourn Passing of "Mother Millard." & "Veterans Hold Rites for Gold Star Mother." AGSM Scrapbook #1 clipping—undated, unattributed.

7. Cutlip, Lillian. "Red Propaganda Amazes Gold Star Mothers' Head" AGSM Scrapbook #1 clipping—undated, unattributed.

8. Ossining Gold Star Mothers Unit Inducted into National Group. AGSM Scrapbook #1—undated, unattributed.

9. President's Letter. *The Gold Star Bulletin*. June 1937, p1.

10. Letter from G.D. Seibold read on her behalf the 1932 Convention.

11. AGSM Scrapbook #3 : Unattributed February 3, 1933 clipping.

12. FDR Presidential Papers (File 461)

13. Meeting minutes of 2nd National Convention

14. Ibid.

15. Ibid.

16. Silvery Haired War Mothers Convene for Annual Session. Detroit News June 12, 1936. AGSM Scrapbook #1

17. Opening statement at national convention. Convention minutes May 12, 1938

18. Ibid.

19. Ibid.

20. GOLD STARS IN VAIN! Mothers Meet, See War Clouds. AGSM Scrapbook #1: May 11, 1938, unattributed.

21. Letter to Mrs. Dillard from FDR. May 31, 1939. FDR Presidential Papers (1534)

22. AGSM Scrapbook #3 clipping—undated, unattributed.

23. Mothers' Groups Unite. AGSM Scrapbook #4 Clipping—undated, unattributed.

24. AGSM Bulletin. June 1937, p1.

25. AGSM National Board Meeting Minutes. June 1934.

26. AGSM National Board Meeting Minutes. September 24, 1938

27. Mother's Day at Arlington. *American War Mothers Magazine.* June 1930, p7.

28. Gardiner, Alexander. Known but to God. *American Legion Monthly.* January 1933, p18.

29. Report from Mrs. L. Landwehr. AGSM Scrapbook #3, undated.

30. Gold Star Mothers, Five Blind Veterans Enjoy Sunday Here. AGSM Scrapbook #3 clipping—undated, unattributed.

31. AGSM Scrapbook #3 clipping—undated, unattributed.

32. Handwritten report from Alice DeMay Williams. AGSM Scrapbook #3 clipping: November 11, 1933, unattributed.

33. 73rd Congress, 1st Session, H. R. 5178 in the House of Representatives April 22, 1933; which was referred to the Committee on Naval Affairs.

34. Letter to Mrs. Taylor, AGSM Long Beach Chapter 2, from E. M. H. Guedry. May 5, 1933

35. Annual Report of Long Beach Chapter No. 2, AGSM (1933).

36. AGSM Scrapbook #3 clipping - undated, unattributed.

37. AGSM Scrapbook #4 clipping—undated, unattributed.

38. Knight Ridder/Tribune Information Services 2005. http://www.mcclatchydc.com/reports/veterans/story/13136.html (12-15-2008)

39. In Re: Bill S. 459 and H.R. 9. AGSM Scrapbook #3 clipping—undated, unattributed.

40. Petition for Congressional Charter—1931. page 3

41. Gold Star Mothers Helped Bonus Army. AGSM Scrapbook #3—undated, unattributed.

42. Transcript of Congressional Testimony: March 9, 1937: H.R. 1538, H.R. 1539 and H.R. 2005 to amend certain laws and veterans' regulations affecting world war veterans and their dependents.

43. Aid for Mothers May Be Granted. AGSM Scrapbook #1 clipping —March 9, 1937, unattributed.

44. 1938 Report of Activities of the National President. May 1938.

45. 1938 Report of Activities of the National President. May 1938

46. Ibid.

47. Presidential Report of Activities 1936-1938.

48. FDR Presidential Papers (461)

49. Gardner, Alexander. Known But To God. American Legion Monthly. January 1933, p188.

50. May 18, 1933 interoffice memo in FDR Presidential Papers (461).

51. Wallace, Rich. Old Gold Star Bridge Held Many Memories. Traveling through Time with the Shelby County (Ohio) Historical Society. http//www.shelby-county history.org (October 1999)

52. All American. *American Legion Monthly,* January 1933, p37; Gold Star Mother's Newsletter. April 1960.

53. Dickson, Paul and Allen, Thomas B. Marching on History. Smithsonian Magazine. February 2003; p85.

54. Steinberg, Neil. If at All Possible, Involve a Cow. http://home.att.net/~Storytellers/nsteinb.html (January 23, 2006)

55. AGSM Scrapbook #1 clipping—Long Beach Press Telegram. May 13, 1937.

56. Letter to Mrs Gudery from Mrs. Seibold. January 26, 1939.

57. AGSM Executive Board Meeting Minutes—December 1, 1931.

58. Letter to Colonel Kenyon from Ella Guedry. December 26, 1932. Library of Congress—AGSM Holdings

59. FDR Presidential Papers (File 461)

60. 1938 letter—unsigned and unattributable. Library of Congress—AGSM Holdings.

61. Letter from Colonel Kenyon to Mrs. Guedry. January 6, 1933. Library of Congress—AGSM Holdings.

62. Arrest Gold Star Mother for Rum Sale. *Chicago Daily Tribune.* April 15, 1930, p1.

63. Friends Rally to Gold Star Mother Facing Rum Charge. *Chicago Daily Tribune.* June 1, 1930, p18.

64. Ferryboats get Feminine Names. AGSM Scrapbook #1 clipping—undated, unattributed.

Chapter 7
The 1940s: Growth, Recognition, and Discord

1. Gold Star Mothers Unalterably Opposed to Fighting on Alien Soil, Declares New Leader. *Los Angeles Times*. July 1, 1940, p6.

2. Shallet, Sidney. 4-Day Weekend Lifts Fair's Hopes. *New York Times*, May 28, 1940, p25.

3. More Mothers Join War Bill Fight. *Chicago Tribune*. February 26, 1941, p3.

4. Ibid.

5. "The Pearl Harbor Attack." (April 8, 2007) http://www.history.navy.mil/faqs/faq66-1.html

6. United Veterans Emblem Agency of Los Angeles sales brochure, copyrighted 1942.

7. Crocheted Service Flag. *Chicago Tribune*. August 29, 1943, p13.

8. '17–'18 Mothers Fret About New Lads Over There. *Chicago Tribune*. November 12, 1942, p14.

9. Lost First Son in Other War; 2d Now Fights. *Chicago Tribune*. May 10, 1942, p SW1.

10. October 17, 1942 newspaper clipping; Newspaper unknown. Courtesy of Liberty Memorial Museum Collection, Kansas City, MO.

11. Ibid.

12. Obituary: Mrs. Mary McCoy, Gold Star Mother. *New York Times*. May 22, 1943.

13. Common Grief Unites Mothers of Two Wars. *Chicago Tribune*. November 3,1945, p13.

14. Army Airmen's Mothers Share Joy and Grief. *Chicago Tribune*. August 29, 1944, p11.

15. Mother Loses Three Sons at Pearl Harbor. *Chicago Tribune*. May 5, 1942, p1.

16. http://www.history.navy.mil (April 8, 2007)

17. Letter from FDR to Aleta Sullivan. February 2, 1943 Navy Department Press Release.

18. Most Courageous Mother in America. *Los Angeles Times*. May 6,1943, p11.

19. Pastor Mourns Five Sons; Four were Chaplains. *Chicago Tribune*. August 19, 1945, pS2.

20. Seek Discharge of 5th Hero Son. *Chicago Tribune*. October 4, 1944, p1.

21. Handbook: "Mothers of World War No. 2. A National Organization." Copyrighted 1943. p 21.

22. Williams, Rudi. Blue Star Mothers Offer Constant Care. American Forces Press Service. March 28, 2000.

23. Gold Star Mother's Legion Scrapbook, Missouri Valley Special Collections, Kansas City Public Library, Kansas City, Missouri. http://www.kclibrary.org/localhistory/collections.cfm?collID=46 (April 2, 2007)

24. Gold Star Mother Vies with Draft "Mourners." *New York Times*. August 29, 1940.

25. Mrs. Mary F. Hill Dies at Age of 75. February 10, 1946. Uncredited clipping from AGSM scrapbook.

26. 1946 AGSM national convention minutes.

27. Long Beach, California Community Book: 1944.

28. *Long Beach Press—Telegram*. June 3, 1943.

29. *Long Beach Press—Telegram*. June 6, 1946.

30. *Long Beach Press—Telegram*. February 2, 1943.

31. *Long Beach Press—Telegram*. June 3, 1943.

32. AGSM Bulletin No. 1 (June 30, 1946)

33. Ibid.

34. *Long Beach Press—Telegram*. May 25, 1947.

35. *American Gold Star Mothers Bulletin*—Volume 1, No. 2, p4. February 1949.

36. "Truman orders loyalty checks of federal employees." http://www.history.com/tdih.do? action=tdihArticleCategory&id=2614. (March 30, 2007)

37. Rep. Chester E. Holifield (D–California). Speech on Truman Loyalty Program. June 27, 1947. www.teachingamerican history.org/library March 29, 2007

38. *American Gold Star Mothers Bulletin* No. 1. July 8, 1947.

39. Letter from Stella Duncan, Department President, to New York state members. September 17, 1947.

40. California Woman Head of Gold Star Mothers. *Chicago Tribune*. August 4, 1940, pE2.

41. The 29 chapters were: Akron, Battle Creek, Bronx, Broome County, Detroit, Golden Gate #2, Grand Rapids, Jackson, Kalamazoo, Long Beach, Los Angeles, Middlesex, Muskegon, New Bedford, Norfolk, Ossining, Philadelphia, Portland, Rochester, Saginaw, San Diego, San Francisco #1, Santa Ana, Scranton, Seattle, Grace Darling Seibold, Suffolk, Tacoma, and Worcester.

42. Letter from Marie Koeneke to President Franklin D. Roosevelt. May 21, 1942. FDR Presidential Library Collections.

43. Letter from President Roosevelt to Marie Koeneke. May 29, 1942. FDR Presidential Library Collection.

44. States represented were California, Oregon, Ohio, Iowa, Wisconsin, Michigan, Missouri, Delaware, New Jersey, Massachusetts, Pennsylvania, Illinois, New York, West Virginia, Utah, Oklahoma plus the District of Columbia.

45. *Long Beach Press-Telegram*. June 6, 1947.

46. Ibid.

47. Favor Military Drill. *New York Times*. June 2, 1948.

48. Minutes of 1947 AGSM National Convention. p77.

49. Ibid. p3.

50. Youth Training Urged by Gold Star Leader. *Los Angeles Times*. June 5, 1947, p2.

51. Urges More Aid for Veterans. *New York Times*. June 6, 1948.

52. Wins Member Suit. New York Times. December 11, 1949.

53. *Long Beach Press-Telegram*. August 23, 1944.

54. Ibid.

55. For Aid to Women Vets. *New York Times*. October 16, 1945.

56. Gold Star Mothers Ask Aid." *New York Times*. October 4, 1947.

57. *American Gold Star Mother Bulletin* No. 3. October 20, 1947.

58. Mother of Trio Who Died in War to get U.S. Citizenship. *Chicago Tribune*. December 21, 1947, p8.

59. American Gold Star Mothers, Inc. Meeting Minutes—January 17, 1948.

60. *American Gold Star Mothers Bulletin* No. 2. August 22, 1947, p2.

61. Hearings before the Committee on World War Veterans' Legislation. House of Representatives, 76th Congress 1940, p 49.

62. Mothers Assail Plan for Tours to Sons' Graves—Gold Star Group Recalls Previous Fiasco. *Chicago Tribune*. September 24, 1944, p23.

63. Gold Star's Voice Raised to Halt Ax. *Los Angeles Times*. February 20, 1949, pC10.

64. Presidential Proclamation dated September 14, 1940. FDR Presidential Library Collection.

65. Letter from Caroline Seaman Read to Woodrow Wilson, dated May 3, 1918. The Papers of Woodrow Wilson. Volume 48, p28–29. Library of Congress Collection.

66. May 20, 1945 letter from Hazel I. Curry to President Truman. Truman Presidential Library Collection.

67. June 9, 1945 correspondence between John E. Kerrigan, Mayor of Boston, MA and William Hassett, Secretary to President Truman. Truman Presidential Library Collection.

68. 32 CFR (Code of Federal Regulations—Title 32—National Defense) Part 578.25 Accolade and Gold Star lapel button.

69. Ibid.

70. Stiles, Kent B. The World of Stamps. New York Times. August 22, 1948.

71. http://www.history.navy.mil

72. "Ranks of Gold Star Mothers Fade." www.new.math.uiuc.edu/~tfrancis/dailyRecord/gold-star.html

73. December 16, 1945 letter to President Truman from Julia McAuley, Englewood, N.J,; handed to Major Heitzeber on December 28, 1945. Truman Presidential Library Collection.

74. Mrs. Seibold, 78, First National Head of Gold Star Mothers. *Washington Post*. June 12, 1947.

75. Gold Star Mothers' Aide Dies. *New York Times*. March 22, 1949.

76. *Gold Star Mother*. April / May, 1949.

77. Gold Star Mothers Sue Group's Founder. *New York Times*. February 5, 1948.

78. Gold Star Mother Meets Court Order, Is Freed From Jail. *Chicago Daily Tribune*. August 14, 1949., p26.

79. Jailed Gold Star Mother Crochets as Row Boils. *Los Angeles Times*. August 11, 1949, p11.

80. Mother of Dead GI Takes Jail to Avoid 'Unjust' Court Order. *Chicago Daily Tribune*. August 5, 1949., p2.

81. Gold Star President Flies to Aid of Mother Jailed in GI Insurance Row. *Los Angeles Times*. August 7, 1949, p1.

82. Jailed Gold Star Mother Crochets as Row Boils. *Los Angeles Times*. August 11, 1949, p11.

83. Gold Star Mother Meets Court Order, Is Freed From Jail. *Chicago Daily Tribune*. August 14, 1949., p26.

84. Gold Star Mother Convicted of Murdering Husband. *Chicago Tribune*. August 4, 1948, p 1; Gold Star Mother Convicted of Murder to Seek New Trial. *Chicago Tribune*. August 5, 1948, pB7; Gold Star Mother Calm as She Hears Sentence for Murder. *Chicago Tribune*. August 11, 1948, p20.

85. Ibid.

86. Gold Star Mother Helps Capture Parolee in Her Home. Chicago Tribune. February 21, 1949, p1.

87. U.S. Insists Mother Wrong on Identity of Son's Body. *Los Angeles Times*. September 7, 1947, p1.

88. Gold Star' Mother Rewarded for Patience as 'Dead' Son is Found. *Stars and Stripes—Pacific Edition*. June 15, 1947, p2.

89. Blind Gold Star Mother, Family to Live Rent-free. *New York Times*. May 1, 1947.

90. Gold Star Mother Ask Return of Son's Picture. *New York Times*. November 13, 1945.

91. Christian Behavior. *Chicago Tribune*. January 20, 1946, p18.

92. Reporting Atrocities. *Chicago Tribune*. June 7, 1948, p22.

93. Gold Star Mothers. *Chicago Tribune*. August 14, 1947, p16.

94. They Lost Their Son. *Chicago Tribune*. August 22, 1947, p16.

95. Gaskill, Robert (Lansdale, PA) *Reminisce Magazine*. 1993, p158.

96. Anders, Dr. Steven. *Quartermaster Professional Bulletin*. Autumn/Winter 1994.

97. 600 Mourn War Dead at Army Base Here. *New York Times*. November 27, 1947.

98. Cromie, Robert. Field of Living Pays Honor to GIs Who Died. *Chicago Tribune*. October 20, 1947, p1.

99. *American Gold Star Mothers Bulletin* No. 3. October 20, 1947.

100. Hughes, Carol. Mother to Silent Heroes. *Coronet Magazine*. April 1949, p65.

101. http://www.ipswich.qld.gov.au/residents/cemeteries/manson_park/ (April 3, 2008)

102. Hughes, Carol. Mother to Silent Heroes. *Coronet Magazine*. April 1949, p65.

103. http://www.ipswich.qld.gov.au/residents/cemeteries/manson_park/ (April 3, 2008) letter dated August 30, 1944

104. Hughes, Carol. Mother to Silent Heroes. *Coronet Magazine*. April 1949, p66-68

105. Ibid. p66.

106. Ibid.

107. Ibid

108. http://www.ipswich.qld.gov.au/residents/cemeteries/manson_park/ (April 3, 2008)

109. Hughes, Carol. Mother to Silent Heroes. *Coronet Magazine*. April 1949, p66.

110. Ibid.

111. Ibid. p67.

Chapter 8, The 1950s
Dissension and Challenges

1. Gen. William H. Wilbur Speaks. *Gold Star Mother*. June 1958, p6.

2. Norman, Lloyd. U.S. Tries to End Indifference to Korea War. *Chicago Daily Tribune*. January 15, 1953, pC2.

3. Letter to President Truman from Mrs. William P. Lindsey dated July 24, 1951. Truman Presidential Library Collection.

4. The *Gold Star Mother*. August 1952, p6.

5. Doyle, Sally. War Mothers Cry for Just Peace Terms. *Chicago Daily Tribune*. June 9, 1953, pA3.

6. Mrs. Boyd Installs; Chapter Tells Pride. The *Gold Star Mother*. February 1950, p3.

7. Understanding Key to Peace, She Declares. The *Gold Star Mother*. January 1952, p5.

8. A Message for 1953 from your National President. The *Gold Star Mother*. January 1953, p1.

9. Convention Set by Gold Star Group. *Chicago Daily Tribune*. June 12, 1955.

10. Mrs. Ruth Singer. *New York Times*. July 1, 1960.

11. Past National President's Report. The *Gold Star Mother*. August/September 1957, p4.

12. Los Angeles Mothers Participate at Sports Arena Dedication. The *Gold Star Mother*. August 1959, p1.

13. National President's Message. The *Gold Star Mother*. January 1958, p1.

14. Newly Elected President. The *Gold Star Mother*. July 1957, p1.

15. Letter from Maude E. Fry to President Eisenhower dated August 20, 1957. Eisenhower Presidential Library Collection.

16. Happenings in Departments and Chapters. The *Gold Star Mother*. June 1957, p5.

17. Remarks by National President Maude E. Fry at the Chapel of the Four Chaplains. The *Gold Star Mother*. April 1958, p4.

18. Happenings in Departments and Chapters: District of Columbia. The *Gold Star Mother*. December 1957, p5.

19. Newly Elected President. The *Gold Star Mother*. July 1958, p1.

20. President's Message. The *Gold Star Mother*. August 1958, p6.

21. President's Message. The *Gold Star Mother*. February 1959, p3.

22. President's Message. The *Gold Star Mother*. June 1959, p4.

23. Minutes of the 1958 AGSM national convention, p70.

24. President's Message at Amphitheater. The *Gold Star Mother*. October 1958, p5.

25. Your First National Vice President. The *Gold Star Mother*. June 1959, p3.

26. Undated letter to members of the AGSM finance committee from Elsie C. Nielsen.

27. Ibid.

28. Letter To Elsie C. Nielsen from Ruth Singer dated March 1, 1954.

29. Undated letter to members of the AGSM finance committee from Elsie C. Nielsen.

30. Letter from Elsie C. Nielson to fellow board members dated March 14, 1954.

31. Coffee Time. The *Gold Star Mother*. January 1958, p3.

32. Ibid.

33. President's Message. The *Gold Star Mother*. July 1954, p1.

34. Coffee Time. The *Gold Star Mother*. February 1957, p2.

35. Coffee Time. The *Gold Star Mother*. March 1957, p6.

36. National President's Report. The *Gold Star Mother*. July 1956, p5.

37. Delegates Discuss National Convention. Newsletter. The *Gold Star Mother*. July 1950, p8.

38. National Convention Story. The *Gold Star Mother*. July 1951, p6

39. Gold Star Mothers Oppose Deferments. *New York Times*. June 1, 1951.

40. Gold Star Mother Delegates Asked to Pledge Loyalty. *Chicago Daily Tribune*. May 29, 1951, p1.

41. Gold Star Parents Take Loyalty Oath. *New York Times*. May 30, 1951.

42. Chaplain's Report. The *Gold Star Mother*. August 1951, p8.

43. Delegates from 33 States Come to National Meeting. The *Gold Star Mother*. July 1952, p4.

44. Ibid.

45. Ibid. p3.

46. Ibid.

47. Chicago Papers Discuss Convention Delegates. The *Gold Star Mother*. July 1953, p8.

48. Gold Star Mothers. *Chicago Daily Tribune*. June 12, 1953, page 4.

49. National President's Report as Given at National Convention. The *Gold Star Mother*. September 1954, p1.

50. Resolutions Passed at Convention, Boston, 1954. The *Gold Star Mother*. December 1954, p3.

51. Minutes of 1955 AGSM national convention, p64.

52. National Assistant Custodian of Records Report. The *Gold Star Mother*. July 1955, p5.

53. Report of Stewardship. The *Gold Star Mother*. July 1955, p6.

54. National Treasurer's Report 1954–1955. The *Gold Star Mother*. August 1955, p1.

55. Dunbaugh, Frank M. The Brotherhood of Man. The *Gold Star Mother*. July 1955, p4.

56. Jones, Maude. A Tour of Havana with Chino. The *Gold Star Mother*. July 1955, p1.

57. Minutes of 1956 AGSM national convention, p25.

58. Ibid. p10, 25.

59. Ibid. p9.

60. Ibid. p37.

61. Ibid. p83.

62. Ibid. p89-90.

63. Ibid. p69.

64. Minutes of the 1957 AGSM national convention, p4.

65. Convention Highlights. The *Gold Star Mother*. July 1957, p3.

66. Stone, Ralph—Chief Benefits Director, U.S. Veterans Administration. Text of Remarks Made by Chief Benefits Director. The *Gold Star Mother*. July 1957, p4.

67. Minutes of the 1957 AGSM national convention, p90.

68. National Custodian of Records Report. The *Gold Star Mother*. September 1959, p2.

69. 22nd Annual National Convention Report. The *Gold Star Mother*. August 1959, p6.

70. Ibid.

71. Ibid.

72. Financial Report. The *Gold Star Mother*. June 1953, p7.

73. Report of the National Custodian of Records. The *Gold Star Mother*. September 1956, p8.

74. President's Report. The *Gold Star Mother*. November 1959, p3.

75. Gen. William H. Wilbur Speaks. The *Gold Star Mother*. June 1958, p6.

76. Chapter Activities. The *Gold Star Mother*. June 1958, p5.

77. 3 Sisters Lost Sons in War II. The *Gold Star Mother*. February 1951, p1.

78. Minutes of the 1958 AGSM national convention, p36.

79. Chapter Busy with Varied Activities. The *Gold Star Mother*. February 1950, p4.

80. Chapter Has First Anniversary Event. The *Gold Star Mother*. January 1950, p6.

81. Oskaloosa Sews Money on Apron. The *Gold Star Mother*. January 1952, p5.

82. Long Beach Press-Telegram. September 25, 1955.

83. Ready to Go. The *Gold Star Mother*. November 1952, p1.

84. Sad Case Being Helped by Chapter. The *Gold Star

Mother. January 1950, p7.

85. Chapter Has First Anniversary Event. *The Gold Star Mother.* January 1950, p6.

86. Lee, Mildred A., National Community Service Chairman. A Reminder From Your Community Service Chairman. *The Gold Star Mother.* February 1959, p6

87. Community Service. *The Gold Star Mother.* July 1959, p7.

88. National Community Service Report. *The Gold Star Mother.* July 1958, p4.

89. Happenings in Departments and Chapters. *The Gold Star Mother.* February 1955, p3.

90. Did you know? *The Gold Star Mother.* October 1955, p4.

91. President's Message. *The Gold Star Mother.* June 1959, p1.

92. Minutes of the 1958 National Convention, p25.

93. Ibid.

94. Ibid.

95. Minutes of the 1958 AGSM national, p25.

96. United States Court of Appeals for the District of Columbia Circuit, No. 10897: American Gold Star Mothers, Inc., appellant v. The National Gold Star Mothers, Inc., et al, appellees, p2.

97. Ibid.

98. Mothers Group Decision. New York Times. July 13, 1951

99. Letter to the Editor. *The Gold Star* magazine. August 1951, p7.

100. Brief of Respondent—American Gold Star Mothers; District Court of Appeal, Second Appellate District, State of California, Division Two, 2nd Civil, No. 22766, p113.

101. Brief of Respondent—American Gold Star Mothers; District Court of Appeal, Second Appellate District, State of California, Division Two, 2nd Civil, No. 22766, p116.

102. President's Message. *The Gold Star Mother.* August 1951, p1.

103. Happenings in Departments and Chapters: California. *The Gold Star Mother.* August 1958, p7.

104. Memorial Book Shelf Placed in City's Public Library. *The Gold Star Mother.* January 1951, p3.

105. Burbank, California Presents Books. *The Gold Star Mother.* November 1954, p6.

106. Medal of Honor citation of Corporal Charles J. Berry, USMC (as printed in the official publication "Medal of Honor, 1861–1949, The Navy", page 157.)

107. Plaque Presented on Memorial Day. *The Gold*

Star Mother. June 1959, p1.

108. Ibid.

109. Placing of Trophy in Memorial Amphitheatre at Arlington National Cemetery. Congressional Record —Appendix. June 1, 1951, pA4610.

110. Letter from Treasure A. Porter, AGSM national custodian of records, to Vice President Richard M. Nixon dated June 3, 1958.

111. A Gold Star Mother Weeps for Unknown. *New York Times.* May 30, 1958.

112. Overseas Memorials. *The Gold Star Mother.* May 1957, p12.

113. Senator Potter Speaks at Memorial Dinner. *The Gold Star Mother.* June 1958, p1

114. Marsden, Yvonne M. The Gold Star Mothers' Hymn. Copyright 1953, self-published.

115. Letter from Yvonne M. Marsden to members of the AGSM national executive board, dated February 8, 1954.

116. Letter from Mrs. George B. Modela on behalf of gold star mothers of Illinois to President Truman, dated February 25, 1950. Truman Presidential Library Collection.

117. A Letter to You. *The Gold Star Mother.* January 1955, p5.

118. G.S.M. Pilgrimage. *The Gold Star Mother.* January 1956, p8.

119. Undated letter from C. J. Hauck Jr., Brigadier General, GS, Chief of Legislative Liaison, to Carl Vinson, Chairman, Committee on Armed Services, House of Representatives. *The Gold Star Mother.* June 1956, p12.

120. Hawaiian Trip. *The Gold Star Mother.* June 1957, p3.

121. Mailman Realizes Dream through "Santa Claus" *The Gold Star Mother.* March 1953, p11.

122. http://ebtx.com/dead/mortable.htm April 22, 2008

123. Chaplains Report. *The Gold Star Mother.* July 1959, p8.

124. A Decade of Devotion and Service. *The Gold Star Mother.* June 1956, p10.

125. A Miracle of Common Sense. *The Gold Star Mother.* October 1957, p4.

126. Study Shows VA Mental Patients Lonely. *The Gold Star Mother.* January 1950, p5.

127. A Miracle of Common Sense. *The Gold Star Mother.* October 1957, p4.

128. The VA Program and the Volunteer. *The Gold Star Mother.* August 1959, p7.

129. Hospital Program at the Tulsa Convention. *The Gold Star Mother.* August/September 1956, p4.

130. At National Convention in Tulsa (photo caption) *The Gold Star Mother*. August 1956 p6.

131. Happenings in Departments and Chapters. *The Gold Star Mother*. May 1957, p10.

132. Skates are Given for Hospital Work. *The Gold Star Mother*. July 1951, p4.

133. Patients Get Television (photo caption). *The Gold Star Mother*. February 1956, p5.

134. Gold Star Mothers Sponsor Dance at Chillicothe Hospital. *The Gold Star Mother*. April 1953, p1.

135. Year Around Enjoyment. *The Gold Star Mother*. August 1956, p5.

136. Chillicothe, Ohio (photo caption). *The Gold Star Mother*. December 1959, p7.

137. Vets Entertained at Ice Follies. *The Gold Star Mother*. May 1955, p5.

138. Hospital Program at Tulsa Convention. *The Gold Star Mother*. September 1956, p5.

139. Undated letter from Leo D. Cady, M.D., Manager, Houston, Texas VA Hospital to Ruth Singer. *The Gold Star Mother*. October 1956, p2.

140. Department of Washington Presents. *The Gold Star Mother*. September 1956, p3.

141. Actress Sings New Number for Mothers. *The Gold Star Mother*. January 1950, p1.

142. News Story Discovers Twin Sister for G.I. Who Said He Had No Kin. *New York Times*. December 3, 1951.

143. Johnston, Laurie. Reunion with Long-Lost Sister 'Like Fairy Tale' to Korea G.I. *New York Times*. December 4, 1951.

144. Gold Star Mother Gets Draft Call in Chicago. *New York Times*. January 2, 1952.

145. Gold Star Mother Reclassified 'Strictly 4-F' After a False Registration as Strictly 1-A. *New York Times*. January 3, 1952.

146. FBI Nabs Check Thief Who Got Woman into 1-A. Chicago Tribune. January 10, 1952, p10.

147. Thanks to World War II gold star mother Marguerite Bezila (Johnstown, PA) for providing this 1953 Letter to the Editor.

148. Gold Stars Spell Sorrow, but Inspire Good Deeds. *Chicago Daily Tribune*, May 30, 1956, p1.

149. Desser, Lorraine I. Connecticut Proud of Mrs. Carmen Raffin. *The Gold Star Mother*. April 1958 p7.

150. Untitled photo caption. *The Gold Star Mother*. November 1954, p4.

151. Merchant Mariners Are Civilians, Says Congress. *The Gold Star Mother*. August 1952, p6.

Chapter 9
The Memorial National Home Foundation

1. 1947 AGSM National Convention Transcript. p3

2. Ibid. p19

3. Ibid. p20

4. Ibid.

5. Ibid. p21

6. Ibid.

7. Ibid.

8. Opinion: Brown vs. Memorial National Home Foundation, Ruling by District Court of Appeal, 2nd District, Division 2, California, September 24, 1958, p122

9. Opinion: p123

10. Opinion: p145

11. Opinion: p166

12. Memorial National Home Foundation Bulletin No. 2, October 10, 1947

13. Ibid.

14. Letter from Anne G. Hagerty to Eleanor Boyd dated December 17, 1947

15. The Gold Star Mother. Findings of Facts #XII, January 1957, p5

16. Telephone interview with George Wise, March 9, 1999

17. Opinion: p126

18. Long Beach Press-Telegram. December 24, 1948

19. Opinion: page 124

20. Memorial National Home Foundation Bulletin No. 4, March 1948

21. Ibid.

22. P 178 Hadra testimony

23. Opinion: p46

24. Opinion: p125

25. Ibid.

26. 1951 AGSM National Convention Transcript. p61

27. p151: Court Proceedings

28. Opinion: p128

29. Letter from Stella Duncan to Eleanor Boyd dated July 22, 1948

30. Letter from Eleanor Boyd to Stella Duncan dated July 29, 1948

31. Letter from Stella Duncan to the National Convention, 1949 Returned by Boyd June 4, 1949

32. Letter from the Law Offices of Sachs and Jacobs, Washington, D.C. to Elsie Nielsen, AGSM national

president dated October 21, 1953

33. Erna L. Hadra's application for AGSM membership

34. Letter to members of AGSM from Erna L. Hadra dated May 12, 1952

35. Letter from Erna Hadra to "My Dear Mrs. T. K. (C----, PA Member, AGSM - AND many others writing me" dated October 10, 1953

36. Handwritten note from Erna Hadra - not dated but copy indicates it was postmarked April 4, 1953

37. Letter from Erna Hadra to specified members of AGSM dated October 10, 1953

38. Long Beach Press-Telegram, March 11, 1954

39. Long Beach Press-Telegram. May 29, 1953

40. Long Beach Press-Telegram. June 1, 1953

41. Ibid.

42. Opinion: p125

43. Long Beach Press-Telegram. June 15, 1953

44. Long Beach Press-Telegram. June 16, 1953

45. Opinion: p128

46. Long Beach Press-Telegram. August 7, 1953

47. Long Beach Press-Telegram. June 9, 1954

48. Long Beach Press-Telegram. June 24, 1954

49. Long Beach Press-Telegram. June 29, 1954

50. Long Beach Press-Telegram. July 1, 1954

51. Reporter's Transcript of Proceedings: Hearing before the Subcommittee of the National Executive Board of AGSM, Inc. - Monday, May 23, 1955, pX

52. Ibid. p248

53. Regarding Memorial National Home Foundation. The Gold Star Mother. April 1955, p1

54. Long Beach Press-Telegram. October 26, 1956

55. The Findings of Fact and Conclusions of Law filed by the Superior Court on December 10, 1956 - Finding XIX. The Gold Star Mother. January 1957, p5

56. Ibid. Findings

57. Court Makes Findings in Memorial National Home Foundation. The Gold Star Mother. January 1957, p1

58. National President Reports - Home for GoldStar Mothers. The Gold Star Mother. February 1, 1957, p1

59. Report on Brown v. Memorial National Home Foundation. The Gold Star Mother. May 1957, p1

60. 1957 Convention Minutes. p12, 23

61. Ibid.

62. Ibid

63. Ibid. p62

64. Ibid.

65. Ibid. p62

66. Ibid. p72

67. Convention Delegates Endorse the American Gold Star Home as Successor to Memorial National Home Foundation. The Gold Star Mother. July 1957, p1

68. Appellate Court Upholds American Gold Star Mothers in the Memorial National Home Foundation Suit. The Gold Star Mother. August 1958 p1

69. Opinion: p121

70. FLASH! The Gold Star Mother. October 1958, p1

71. Memorial Home Foundation Law Suit Delayed. The Gold Star Mother. November

72. Report on the American Gold Star Home. The Gold Star Mother. November 1959, p1

73. Report on the American Gold Star Home. The Gold Star Mother. August 1959, p4

74. Kelley, Katherine M. My Personal Visit to the American Gold Star Home. The Gold Star Mother. November 1959, p4

75. Report by Lorraine Desser. The Gold Star Mother. December 1959, p4

76. Kelley, Katherine M. My Personal Visit to the American Gold Star Home. The Gold Star Mother. November 1959, p4

77. Long Beach Press-Telegram, Feb. 13, 1960

Chapter 10
The Vietnam Decades: 1960–1979

1 http://www.historyplace.com/unitedstates/vietnam/bw-index-1961.html

2 Ibid.

3 Ibid.

4 Ibid.

5 Ibid.

6 Comments at Arlington by Brigadier General Oscar F. Peatross, USMC, on Gold Star Mother's Day. The Gold Star Mother. October 1968, p3

7 http://www.olive-drab.com/od_history_vietnam_nixon.php 01-10-2010

8 Mueller, G.A. Service Flags. Chicago Tribune. November 15, 1967, p18

9 National President's Report. The Gold Star Mother. July 1960, p1

10 Letter from Dwight D. Eisenhower to Lorraine I.

Desser, AGSM national president. April 29, 1960

11 23rd National Convention Minutes. (1960). p30, 59.

12 Ibid. (1960) p85

13 bid. (1960) p73

14 Ibid. (1960), p73.

15 Resolutions Passed at the 1960 National Convention. *The Gold Star Mother.* July1960, p3.

16 Gold Star Mothers Elect. *New York Times.* June 24, 1960; Frances High. *The Gold Star Mother.* April 1960, p3.

17 24th National Convention Minutes (1961), p13.

18 Convention Report. *The Gold Star Mother.* July 1961, p1.

19 Newly Elected President. *The Gold Star Mother.* July 1961 p1; National Officer. *The Gold Star Mother.* March 1960, p5.

20 The National Hospital Chairman. *The Gold Star Mother.* August 1963, p3.

21 Mary R. Kelly. *The Gold Star Mother.* July 1962, p1.

22 Mary F. Nieman. *The Gold Star Mother.* June 1963, p3.

23 Departments and Chapters. *The Gold Star Mother.* October 1963, p5.

24 Convention Report. *The Gold Star Mother.* August 1965, p1.

25 For Vote of Delegates at National Convention. *The Gold Star Mother.* May 1965, p3.

26 1966 National Convention Minutes. p27.

27 National President's Acceptance Speech. *The Gold Star Mother.* August 1966, p5.

28 National President Rose F. Decker's address at the Department of Michigan Convention. *The Gold Star Mother.* June 1967, p1.

29 Convention Report. *The Gold Star Mother.* August 1967, p1.

30 The Gold Star Mother September 1967, p5. The White House.

31 *The Gold Star Mother.* April 1960, p6.

32 1968 National Convention Minutes. p48.

33 Greetings from General Anderson. *The Gold Star Mother.* August 1968, p1.

34 Gold Star Mothers Day. *The Gold Star Mother.* October 1968, p1.

35 1969 National Convention Minutes. p5.

36 Entertainment for Dads at Convention (Tulsa). *The Gold Star Mother.* April 1969.

37 Coffee Time. *The Gold Star Mother.* September 1969, p5.

38 National President's Message. *The Gold Star Mother.* June 1970, p7.

39 National President's Message. The Gold Star Mother. August 1969, p1

40 National President's Message. *The Gold Star Mother.* June 1970, p7.

41 1970 National Convention Minutes. p3

42 Resolutions. *The Gold Star Mother.* March 1970, p3.

43 National President's Message. *The Gold Star Mother.* November 1970, p1.

44 AGSM 34th National Convention Proceedings: June 28–30, 1971, p3.

45 Ibid. p106.

46 Ibid. p56.

47 Ibid. p74.

48 Ibid. p78.

49 *The Gold Star Mother.* October 1972, p6.

50 *The Gold Star Mother.* January 1973.

51 National President's Report. *The Gold Star Mother.* September 1972, p7.

52 Call for the 38th Annual Convention. *The Gold Star Mother.* March/April 1975, p1.

53 Resolutions Passed at the National Convention. *The Gold Star Mother.* July/August 1975, p5.

54 Know your National President - Josephine J. Holmes. The Gold Star Mother. July/August 1975, p3; National President's Message. *The Gold Star Mother.* May/June 1976, p1.

55 Letter from President Gerald Ford to Josephine J. Holmes, National AGSM President, dated May 19, 1976. Gerald R. Ford Presidential Papers Collection.

56 National convention report. *The Gold Star Mother.* September/October 1977, p4.

57 Conv7. *The Gold Star Mother.* September/October 1977, p4.

58 Ibid.

59 From the President's Desk. *The Gold Star Mother.* November/December 1978, p1.

60 National President's Acceptance Speech. *The Gold Star Mother.* July/August 1978, p1.

61 Know your National President. The Gold Star Mother. July August 1978, p7; Acceptance Speech. *The Gold Star Mother.* July/August 1978, p7.

62 National President's Report for 1978–1979.

63 Ibid.

64 Ibid.

65 Convention Report. *The Gold Star Mother.* September/October 1979, p4.

66 Attention. *The Gold Star Mother.* January 1966,

p3.

67 National President's Message (Mamie P. Simmons). *The Gold Star Mother*. August 1968, p1.

68 *The Gold Star Mother*. July 1969, p8.

69 National President's Message. *The Gold Star Mother*. January 1972, p1.

70 Convention Minutes. *The Gold Star Mother*. September 1968, p4.

71 Departments and Chapters. *The Gold Star Mother*. January 1969, p4.

72 Departments and Chapters. *The Gold Star Mother*. June 1970, p5.

73 Departments and Chapter. *The Gold Star Mother*. February 1971, p8.

74 Departments and Chapter. *The Gold Star Mother*. February 1971, p8.

75 Annual Tea. *The Gold Star Mother*. January/February 1977, p7.

76 National President's Message—Josephay Fleming. *The Gold Star Mother*. May/June 1975, p1.

77 Hi-lites of the National Convention. *The Gold Star Mother*. September/October 1975, p4.

78 An Appropriate Analogy. *The Gold Star Mother*. May/June 1978, p3.

79 Departments and Chapters. *The Gold Star Mother*. April 1969, p4.

80 Departments and Chapter. *The Gold Star Mother*. September 1970, p8.

81 Camp Pendleton. *The Gold Star Mother*. October 1971, p5.

82 Installations of Chapter Officers—New Jersey. *The Gold Star Mother*. January 1973, p6.

83 Chapters in the United States. *The Gold Star Mother*. September 1961, p6.

84 Musings with Mildred. *The Gold Star Mother*. July 1965, p7.

85 Report of the Director of Publication. *The Gold Star Mother*. August 1969, p3.

86 Board of Trustees Meeting Minutes: January 14, 1972.

87 From the President's Desk. *The Gold Star Mother*. November/December 1977, p5.

88 Departments and Chapters. *The Gold Star Mother*. January 1970, p7.

89 Chapter Happenings. *The Gold Star Mother*. February 1973, p7.

90 Happenings. *The Gold Star Mother*. April 1960, p6.

91 Departments and Chapters. *The Gold Star Mother*. September 1969, p7.

92 White City Oregon Domiciliary. *The Gold Star Mother*. March 1972, p5; The Gold Star Mother. January 1961, p2; Departments and Chapters. *The Gold Star Mother*. December 1971, p6.

93 Departments and Chapters. *The Gold Star Mother*. October 1970, p4.

94 Veterans Amputee Shelter. *The Gold Star Mother*. January 1965, p8.

95 Warren, Doug. Lorainites Help Family in Korea. *The Gold Star Mother*. January 1966, p8.

96 *The Gold Star Mother*. April 1966, p8.

97 Departments and Chapters. *The Gold Star Mother*. February 1966, p6.

98 Departments and Chapters. *The Gold Star Mother*. July 1971.

99 Ibid.

100 Teen-age Dance. *The Gold Star Mother*. March 1966, p7.

101 Heroism & Endurance. *The Gold Star Mother*. March 1969, p6 The four local recruiters from four branches of the military service were (Marine) Gunnery Sergeant Thomas White, Army Staff Sergeant Gary Flaherty, Navy CPO John Phillips and Air Force Technical Sergeant George Provencher.

102 Gold Star Mother Wins Nixon's Aid. *Los Angeles Times*. May 30, 1970, p12.

103 Report of the Director of Publication—July 1968. *The Gold Star Mother*. August 1969, p3; Action of the National Executive Board. *The Gold Star Mother*. March 1974, p6.

104 National President's Message. The Gold Star Mother. November/December 1975, p1.

105 Notice. *The Gold Star Mother*. July/August 1978, p3.

106 National President's Report for 1978 -1979.

107 Ibid.

108 In Memoriam. *The Gold Star Mother*. April 1969, p8; Departments and Chapters—Florida. *The Gold Star Mother*. April 1972, p5; In Memoriam. *The Gold Star Mother*. January 1970 p2.

109 Mother Emma Balcom, PNP, Dies in Florida. *The Gold Star Mother*. October 1960, p2.

110 Mrs. Ruth Singer. *New York Times*. July 1, 1960; In Memoriam. *The Gold Star Mother*. July 1960, p2; Eulogy for Ruth Singer. *The Gold Star Mother*. August 1960, p2; 1957 National Convention Transcript, p17.

111 In Memoriam. *The Gold Star Mother*. March 1964, p2; Gold Star Mothers Elect. New York Times. June 24, 1960.

112 In Memoriam. *The Gold Star Mother*.

November 1968, p2; Gold Star Mothers Unalterably Opposed to Fighting on Alien Soil, Declares New Leader. *Los Angeles Times.* July 1, 1940, p6.

113   *The Gold Star Mother.* January/February 1977, p6.

114   In Memoriam. *The Gold Star Mother.* July/August 1977, p2.

115   In Memoriam. *The Gold Star Mother.* November/December 1977, p2.

116   *The Gold Star Mother.* November/December 1979, p5 (photo caption).

117   In Memoriam. *The Gold Star Mother.* April 1960, p2.

118   In Memoriam. *The Gold Star Mother.* February 1966, p2.

119   *The Gold Star Mother.* March 1967, p8.

120   Happy 100. *The Gold Star Mother.* February 1968, p3; The Gold Star Mother. November 1968, p3.

121   Utah Loses Four Star Mother. *The Gold Star Mother.* May, p4.

122   *The Gold Star Mother.* September 1972

123   A Three Star Mother. *The Gold Star Mother.* June 1973, p2.

124   In Memoriam. *The Gold Star Mother.* May/June 1977, p2; She Survives Disasters and Gets Security. *Chicago Tribune.* January 1962, p12.

125   In Memoriam. *The Gold Star Mother.* July/August 1979, p2.

126   http://www.vvaw.org/veteran/article/?id=295&hilite=dewey+canyon

127   National President's Message. *The Gold Star Mother.* January 1969, p6.

128   *The Gold Star Mother.* November 1965, p3; Gold Star Mothers Upset over Vietnam. *Phoenix American Paper.* September 26, 1969

129   *The Gold Star Mother.* August 1967, p1.

130   Departments and Chapters. *The Gold Star Mother.* February 1970 p6.

131   Gold Star Mothers Protest Use of Son's Names. Clipping—undated, unattributed.

132   At The Pentagon. *The Gold Star Mother.* July 1970, p1.

133   Departments and Chapters. *The Gold Star Mother.* January 1971, p4.

134   The Gold Star Mother. March 1971, p3; Regarding Resolutions. *The Gold Star Mother.* February 17, 1971.

135   P.O.W. Prisoners of War. *The Gold Star Mother.* May 1971, p7.

136   Ibid.

137   September 17, 1976 letter to Gerald R. Ford from AGSM Dept of NY president Mary E. Wheeler. Gerald R. Ford Presidential Papers.

138   Report on the 1972 National Convention. *The Gold Star Mother.* August 1972.

139   American Legion Stand Against Amnesty Review Board. *The Gold Star Mother.* August 1972, p5.

140   American Gold Star Mothers, Inc. against Amnesty. *The Gold Star Mother.* November/December 1974, p1.

141   October 13, 1976 letter from Milton E. Mitler, Deputy Special Assistant, to AGSM national president Josephine Holmes. Gerald R. Ford Presidential Papers Collection.

142   *The Gold Star Mother.* May 1975

143   *The Gold Star Mother.* June 1975

144   colby.edu/colby.mag/issues/fall00/vietnam (5/30/2010)

145   Vils, Ursula. Gold Star Mother Asks Amnesty for All. *Los Angeles Times.* May 3, 1974, pE1.

146   National President's Message. *The Gold Star Mother.* May/June 1974, p1.

147   Bill H.R. 9596 (Vietnam Era Reconciliation Act). *The Gold Star Mother.* January/February 1976, p4.

148   National Convention Report. *The Gold Star Mother.* September/October 1976, p6.

149   President's Message. *The Gold Star Mother.* March/April 1977, p4.

150   http://www.pbs.org/newshour/bb/asia/vietnam/vietnam_1-21-77.html

151   *The Gold Star Mother.* December 1960, p1.

152   1960 National Convention Minutes. p88.

153   National Headquarters Report. *The Gold Star Mother.* August 1962, p5.

154   Coffee Time. *The Gold Star Mother.* March 1971, p3.

155   *The Gold Star Mother.* December 1960, p3.

156   Convention Report. *The Gold Star Mother.* September/October 1978, p4.

157   Coffee Time. *The Gold Star Mother.* January 1970, p3.

158   From the President's Desk. *The Gold Star Mother.* January/February 1978, p2.

159   Directives from the National Executive Board. The Gold Star Mother. March 1970, p3.

160   Departments and Chapters. *The Gold Star Mother.* December 1960, p7.

161 *The Gold Star Mother.* July 1962, p5.

162 Nacelewicz, Tess. "Mr. Transportation of Maine" Mourned. *Portland Press Herald.* June 3, 2008.

163 Departments and Chapters. *The Gold Star Mother.* August 1965, p5.

164 Langevin, Albert J. Gold Star Mothers—20 Years Later. *The Gold Star Mother.* November 1964, p8.

165 1970 Convention Minutes. p3.

166 The Gold Star Mother. July 1971, p3.

167 http://www.angelfirememorial.com/ MemorialHistory.php 12-20-2009

168 Vietnam Veterans Peace and Brotherhood Chapel. *Disabled American Veterans Magazine.* July 1977.

169 May 3, 1976 letter from Magdalena E. Barnes, President, AGSM El Paso Chapter, to President Gerald. R. Ford. Gerald R. Ford Presidential Papers Collection.

170 April 19, 1976 letter from Gerald R. Ford to Magdalena E. Barnes. Gerald R. Ford Presidential Papers Collection.

171 Washington-Idaho. *The Gold Star Mother.* October 1973, p4.

172 Pennsylvania, Greater Johnstown Chapter. *The Gold Star Mother.* March 1974, p5.

173 A Tribute to the Vietnam Veteran. *The Gold Star Mother.* July/August 1979, p5.

174 The Facts on Vietnam Veterans. United States Conference of Mayors. May 10, 1979.

175 Undated letter from Vietnam Veterans Memorial Fund, Inc. (1979?)

176 Group Formed to Build Vietnam Veteran Memorial. *Army Times.* May 28, 1979, p25.

177 To All Gold Star Mothers. *The Gold Star Mother.* September/October 1979, p3.

178 Report of National Hospital Chairman National VAVS Representative. *The Gold Star Mother.* February 1968, p3; AGSM 34th National Convention Proceedings June 28–30, 1971, p42; Departments and Chapters. *The Gold Star Mother.* October 1972, p6; 82 Years Young. *The Gold Star Mother.* March/April 1975, p6.

179 1969 National Convention Report, p39; *The Gold Star Mother.* May 1960, p3; Certificates Awarded. *The Gold Star Mother.* March 1967, p5; *The Gold Star Mother.* March/April 1978, p5; *The Gold Star Mother.* May 1960, p3.

180 Report of National Hospital Chairman. *The Gold Star Mother.* August 1969, p6.

181 Report of National Hospital Chairman. *The Gold Star Mother.* August 1963, p7.

182 Operation Cinderella. *The Gold Star Mother.* August 1965, p4.

183 34th National AGSM Convention Proceedings (June 28–30, 1971), p16.

184 Gold Star Mothers Aid Vets. *The Gold Star Mother.* May/June 1977, p7; Departments and Chapters. *The Gold Star Mother.* January 1970, p4.

185 *The Gold Star Mother.* September 1969, p3.

186 Grateful Appreciation Eloquently Expressed. *The Gold Star Mother.* March /April 1978, p5.

187 *The Gold Star Mother.* December 1960, p7; The Five Hundredth Mother. *The Gold Star Mother.* February 1965, p1; Transfers. *The Gold Star Mother.* December 1960, p8; Transfers. *The Gold Star Mother.* January 1961, p8.

188 Gold Star Home. *The Gold Star Mother.* January 1961, p7.

189 Notes from Home. *The Gold Star Mother.* November 1960, p6.

190 Resolution. *The Gold Star Mother.* July 1962, p3.

191 *The Gold Star Mother.* October 1962, p1.

192 Trustees Honor George D. Lyon on Retirement. *The Gold Star Mother.* July 1968, p1; Edward F. Leonard Appointed Executive Vice President. *The Gold Star Mother.* July/August 1975. p3

193 Dedication of American Gold Star Manor. *The Gold Star Mother.* March/April 1976, p4; A Dream Come True. *The Gold Star Mother.* November/ December 1975, p5.

194 Memorial Park Dedication. *The Gold Star Mother.* July/ August 1977, p5; Gold Star Home Memorial Dedication. May 26, 1963. *The Gold Star Mother.* May 1963, p3.

195 Freedoms Foundation. *The Gold Star Mother.* November 1961, p1.

196 Report on Freedoms Foundation Flagpole Project. *The Gold Star Mother.* July 1962, p3.

197 President's Message. *The Gold Star Mother.* January/February 1975, p1.

198 President's Report. *The Gold Star Mother.* March/April 1975, p1.

199 *The Gold Star Mother.* July 1962, p1; President's Report. *The Gold Star Mother.* March/ April 1975, p1.

200 Pilgrimage to Margraten. *The Gold Star Mother.* June 1962, p3.

201 Pilgrimage to the Netherlands. *The Gold Star Mother.* December 1970, p7.

202 Rose Decker, Past National President. *The Gold*

Star Mother. November/December 1985, p1.

203 Hinshaw, Adella Burger. Final story of the Gold Star Lily. *The Gold Star Mother.* October 1965, p6.

204 Ibid.

205 Ibid.

206 Ibid.

207 Departments and Chapters. *The Gold Star Mother.* November 1966, p4.

208 Question Box. *The Gold Star Mother.* July 1960, p8.

209 Ibid.

210 1961 National Convention Minutes. p107.

211 Q & A. *The Gold Star Mother.* December 1969, p3.

212 Questions & Answers. *The Gold Star Mother.* November 1969, p7.

213 Action of the Board. *The Gold Star Mother.* November 1960, p6.

214 Questions & Answers. *The Gold Star Mother.* November 1960, p7.

215 1961 National Convention Minutes. p99.

216 Questions & Answers. *The Gold Star Mother.* November 1962, p3.

217 Questions & Answers. *The Gold Star Mother.* October 1969, p3

218 Questions & Answers. *The Gold Star Mother.* November 1970, p2.

219 President's Message. *The Gold Star Mother.* February 1971, p7.

220 Questions & Answers. *The Gold Star Mother.* February 1970, p7.

221 Questions & Answers. *The Gold Star Mother.* March 1962, p8.

222 Questions & Answers. *The Gold Star Mother.* August 1970, p2.

223 Questions & Answers. *The Gold Star Mother.* June 1961, p9

224 Questions & Answers. *The Gold Star Mother.* December 1964.

225 1961 National Convention Minutes. p110.

226 1969 National Convention Minutes. p22.

227 Here…There…Everywhere. *The Gold Star Mother.* January 1962, p7.

228 A Tribute … to Gold Star Mothers. *The Gold Star Mother.* June 1964, p5. Originally appeared in the *Mattoon Daily Journal-Gazette.*

229 Anderson, Jack. Transcript from "Good Morning, America: program. Aired July 4, 1978

230 Honor the Flag. *Chicago Tribune.* July 29, 1965, p12.

231 Prayers Answered… Thief Returns Flag. *The Gold Star Mother.* July 1970, p4.

232 Gold Star Mother Buries Her Son 23 years After Death. *The Gold Star Mother.* July/August 1979, p2.

233 Convict Gold Star Mother as Abortionist. *Chicago Tribune.* June 14, 1963, pA2.

234 *The Gold Star Mother.* December 1964, p2.

235 Tragedy Strikes. *The Gold Star Mother.* April 1972, p5.

236 St. John, Mary, Stephen Sr., and Stephen Jr. "There are Extra Stars Up in the Heavens Tonight." Stephen St. John Music Publishing Company, Schenectady, New York 1964.

Chapter 11
AGSM Challenged:
1980–1999

1 Cavaan, Azell Murphy. Mothers of War Dead Earn Their Gold Stars every Day. *Boston Herald.* June 18, 1998, p23.

2 *The Gold Star Mother.* September/October 1999, p2.

3 bid.

4 *The Gold Star Mother.* November/December 1989, p5.

5 Know Your President. *The Gold Star Mother.* July/August 1980, p7; Rasmussen, Frederick N. Katherine Mannion, 87, Gold Star Mothers Leader. Baltimore Sun. June 5, 2002.

6 National Convention Report. *The Gold Star Mother.* September/October 1980, p5.

7 Resolutions. *The Gold Star Mother.* September/October 1980, p5.

8 Committee on Sale of Headquarters. *The Gold Star Mother.* November/December 1981, p3.

9 Resolutions. *The Gold Star Mother.* September/October 1981, p5.

10 Know Your President. *The Gold Star Mother.* July/August 1981, p7.

11 Know Your President. *The Gold Star Mother.* July/August 1983, p3.

12 From our early files. *The Gold Star Mother.* September/October 1997, p4.

13 Convention Report. The Gold Star Mother. September/October 1984, p3.

14 *The Gold Star Mother.* July/August 1984, p4

15 AGSM National Convention—1985. *The Gold Star Mother.* July/August 1985, p3.

16 Nora J. Golsh. *The Veteran's Observer.* August/September 1985, p10.

17 AGSM National Convention. *The Gold Star Mother.* July/August 1986, p6.

18 National Convention. *The Gold Star Mother.* July/August 1986, p9.

19 AGSM National Convention. *The Gold Star Mother.* July/August 1986, p6.

20 National Convention. *The Gold Star Mother.* July/August 1986, p5.

21 Know Your President. *The Gold Star Mother.* July/August 1986, p9.

22 National Convention Report. *The Gold Star Mother.* July/August 1987, p5.

23 Letter to President Ronald Reagan dated January 30, 1986. Reagan Presidential Library Collection

24 Know Your President. *The Gold Star Mother.* July/August 1987, p9.

25 Know Your President. *The Gold Star Mother.* May/June 1988, p9.

26 Know Your President. *The Gold Star Mother.* July/August 1989, p7.

27 Special Notice to All Members. *The Gold Star Mother.* January/February 1990, p4.

28 Report of the Convention. *The Gold Star Mother.* July/August 1990, p3.

29 *The Gold Star Mother.* January/February 1991, p2.

30 Convention Report. *The Gold Star Mother.* July/August 1991, p6.

31 Know Your President. *The Gold Star Mother.* July/August 1991, p4.

32 Violet Catherine Long. *The Gold Star Mother.* May/June 1999, p3.

33 Know your president. *The Gold Star Mother.* September/October 1993, p3.

34 National Convention Report. *The Gold Star Mother.* July/August 1994, p12.

35 Carried National Convention Report. *The Gold Star Mother.* July/August 1994, p14.

36 Know Your President. The Gold Star Mother. September/October 1994, p2.

37 Know Your President. *The Gold Star Mother.* September/October 1995, p3.

38 Know Your President. *The Gold Star Mother.* September/October 1996, p3.

39 Know your president. *The Gold Star Mother.* September/October 1997, p3.

40 National President Theresa Davis. *The Gold Star Mother.* July/August 1997, p1.

41 Cano, Debra. Gold Star Chief on Mission to Help. *Los Angeles Times.* June 30, 1998, p3.

42 *The Gold Star Mother.* March/April 1999, p1.

43 From the desk of your president. *The Gold Star Mother.* May/June 1999, p1.

44 Know Your President. *The Gold Star Mother.* July/August 1999, p1.

45 *The Gold Star Mother.* September/October 1980, p2.

46 In Memoriam. *The Gold Star Mother.* March/April 1985, p2.

47 Rose Decker. *The Gold Star Mother.* November/December 1985, p1.

48 *The Gold Star Mother.* May/June 1987, p2

49 *The Gold Star Mother.* September/October 1988, p2.

50 *The Gold Star Mother.* March/April 1989, p4.

51 *The Gold Star Mother.* January/February 1991, p3.

52 Ibid.

53 Mary King. *The Gold Star Mother.* July/August 1992, p3.

54 *The Gold Star Mother.* September/October 1995, p4.

55 Mother Betty Bryce. *The Gold Star Mother.* May/June 1997, p3.

56 Violet Catherine Long. *The Gold Star Mother.* May/June 1999, p3.

57 Mamie P. Simmons. *The Gold Star Mother.* January/February 1998, p3.

58 Mrs. Emma Eunick. *The Gold Star Mother.* March/April 1998, p2.

59 Helen T. Willour. *The Gold Star Mother.* July/August 1999, p2.

60 *The Gold Star Mother.* January/February 1993, p1.

61 Remembering Rose. *The Gold Star Mother.* March/April 1996, p1.

62 Hearings Before the Subcommittee on Administrative Law and Government Relations of the Committee on the Judiciary, House of Representatives, 98th Congress, 2nd Session on H.R.3811, March 24, 1984, p9.

63 Ibid.

64 National Convention. *The Gold Star Mother.* July/August 1984, p3.

65 http://www.tourofdc.org/monuments/VVM/ February 1, 2010.

66 Ibid.

67 In Memorial. *The Gold Star Mother.* November/December 1984, p1.

68 Scruggs, Jan. Vietnam Memorial Drive Asks Gold Star Moms for Help. *The Gold Star Mother.* March/April 1980, p7.

69 Monument to the Forgotten. *The Gold Star Mother.* May/June 1981, p7.

70 Bruce Herschensohn Commentary, KABC-TV News, January 30, 1981.

71 *The Gold Star Mother.* September/October 1995, p6.

72 Rose Garden in Boston. *The Gold Star Mother.* September/October 1985, p3.

73 Hill of Sacrifice. *The Gold Star Mother.* September/October 1985, p2.

74 Illinois Welcomes Vietnam Veterans. *The Gold Star Mother.* September/October 1986, p4.

75 *The Gold Star Mother.* May/June 1993, p3.

76 Update on the Korean War Veterans Memorial Dedication. *The Gold Star Mother.* January/February 1995, p4.

77 *The Gold Star Mother.* July/August 1996, p11.

78 Gold Star Manor has Vacancies. *The Gold Star Mother.* November/December 1987, p2.

79 Hillinger, Charles. Rooms with a Few— Community for Gold Star Mothers has Many Vacancies. *Los Angeles Times.* April 2, 1992, p1.

80 Ibid.

81 At Rest in America—Our Home. *The Gold Star Mother.* May/June 1990, p4.

82 *The Gold Star Mother.* May/June 1994, p5.

83 From the Desk of Your President. *The Gold Star Mother.* January/February 1998, p1.

84 Extra! Extra! Extra! *The Gold Star Mother.* March/April 1989, p3; Report of the Convention. *The Gold Star Mother.* July/August/September 1990, p4; National Executive Board Receives Grant. *The Gold Star Mother.* May/June 1991, p3.

85 Committee on Sale of Headquarters. *The Gold Star Mother.* November/December 1981, p3.

86 Convention Report. *The Gold Star Mother.* September/October 1982, p3.

87 Mothers: Gold Star Had Special Message in World War I. Ventura Star. May 12, 1996, pB9.

Chapter 12
2000 and Beyond: New Wars and an Evolving Organization

1. What Does a Gold Star Pin Mean? *The Gold Star Mother.* September/October 2004, p4.

2. From the Desk of the National President. *The Gold Star Mother.* July/August 2005, p1.

3. Know Your President. *The Gold Star Mother.* September/October 2000, p1.

4. *The Gold Star Mother.* September/October 2000, p5

5. http://www.history.army.mil/html/moh/vietnam-a-l.html (2-8-2010)

6. Haworth, Candy. Above and Beyond. *The Gold Star Mother.* September/October 2001, p3.

7. Arlington National Cemetery. *The Gold Star Mother.* September/October 2001, p1.

8. Happiness is Helping Others. *The Gold Star Mother.* July/August 2002, p1.

9. Ibid.

10. From the Desk of the National President. *The Gold Star Mother.* July/August 2003, p1.

11. Parting is such sweet sorrow. *The Gold Star Mother.* July/August 2004, p2.

12. "Parting is such sweet sorrow." *The Gold Star Mother.* July/August 2004, p3.

13. *The Gold Star Mother.* July/August 2005, p2.

14. From the Desk of the National President. *The Gold Star Mother.* July/August 2005, p1.

15. *The Gold Star Mother.* July/August 2006, p2.

16. Looking with new eyes from a member with four years' experience. *The Gold Star Mother.* September/October 2006, p4.

17. Clinton Smooths Out Gold Star Flap. *Albany Times-Union.* August 3, 2001, Capital Region section, pB3.

18. Ibid.

19. Ibid.

20. From Gold Star Mothers' e-mail. *The Gold Star Mother.* May/June 2005, p5.

21. Becker, Maki. Gold Star G.I. Grief. *New York Daily News.* May 29, 2005.

22. Gold Star Moms open to citizens only. *The Denver Post.* May 30, 2005, 23A.

23. AGSM statement regarding national media attention concerning Ligaya Lagman and the "Denial of a Gold Star." May 27, 2005.

24. Ferrette, Candice; Corcoran, Terry; O'Connor, Timothy; and Foley, Catherine L. Gold Star May Change Rule. *The Journal News.* May 28, 2005

25. Cohen, Shawn. Deceased Soldier's Mother Denied Honor. *The Journal News.* May 26, 2005

26. AGSM statement regarding national media attention concerning Ligaya Lagman and the "Denial of a Gold Star." May 27, 2005

27. Ibid.

28. Ibid.

29. Editorial: Gold Star Mothers. *The Journal News.* May 27, 2005.

30. Cohen, Shawn. Deceased Soldier's Mother Denied Honor. *The Journal News.* May 26, 2005.

31. Fitzgerald, Jim (Associated Press). Gold star moms open to citizens only. *The Denver Post.* May 30, 2005, p23A.

32. Woman Drops Bid to Become Gold Star Mother. Associated Press. May 23, 2005.

33. Cohen, Shawn. Deceased Soldier's Mother Denied Honor. The Journal News. May 26, 2005; Matthews, Cara. Gold Star Debate Continues at Memorial Day Rites. *The Journal News.* May 31, 2005.

34. Cohen, Shawn. Gold star unit to call for a change. *The Journal News.* June 2, 2005.

35. Cohen, Shawn. Gold star expects a battle. *The Journal News.* June 3, 2005.

36. Cohen, Shawn. Gold star vote today on citizenship issue. *The Journal News.* June 27, 2005.

37. Cohen, Shawn. Gold star mothers prepare for Texas Showdown. *The Journal News.* June 28, 2005.

38. Cohen, Shawn. Gold star mothers accept noncitizens. *The Journal News.* June 28, 2005.

39. Colimore, Edward. Road gets rougher for gold star group leader. *The Philadelphia Inquirer.* August 25, 2005.

40. http://www.goldstarmoms.com/Home/PressRelease082305.htm (2-9-2010)

41. Wagner, Bill. Sheehan not a member of Gold Star Mothers. *The Times-Tribune.* August 25, 2005.

42. Bartley, Nancy. Mothers bound in sorrow and service. *Seattle Times.* March 2, 2003.

43. Convention Report. *The Gold Star Mother.* July/August 2004, p10.

44. From the Desk of the National President. *The Gold Star Mother.* March/April 2006, p1.

45. Batz Jr., Bob. Iraq conflict renews mission of Gold Star Mothers. *Post-Gazette* (Pittsburgh, PA). April 17, 2003.

46. Rozas, Angela. Heroes' Moms reach out to sisters in grief. *The Chicago Tribune.* January 4, 2004

47. Fiore, Faye. A club of grief, back in action. *Los Angeles Times.* March 13, 2007, p1.

48. McEntee, Marni. Groundbreaking for WWII Memorial This Weekend. *Stars and Stripes.* November 9, 2000.

49. Ibid.

50. www.goldstarmoms.com/Events/GSMMemorialDedicationKentNY/GSMMemorialDedicationKentNY. html (2-12-2010)

51. Ibid.

52. A Healing Journey. *The Gold Star Mother.* March/April 2000, p5.

53. Looking Back – Moving Forward. *The Gold Star Mother.* September/October 2000, p3.

54. Canadian Vietnam Veterans Memorial Inscription. *The Gold Star Mother.* May/June 2004, p7.

Index